MyEconLab® Provides the Power of Practice

Optimize your study time with **MyEconLab's** tutorial and assessment solution that personalizes the learning experience, giving students the practice and immediate feedback they need.

Study Plan

The Study Plan shows you the sections you should study next, gives easy access to practice problems, and provides you with an automatically generated quiz to prove mastery of the course material.

Unlimited Practice

As you work each exercise, instant feedback helps you understand and apply the concepts. Many Study Plan exercises contain algorithmically generated values to ensure that you get as much practice as you need.

Learning Resources

Study Plan problems link to learning resources that further reinforce concepts you need to master.

- **Help Me Solve This** learning aids help you break down a problem much the same way an instructor would do during office hours. Help Me Solve This is available for select problems.

- **eText links** are specific to the problem at hand so that related concepts are easy to review just when they are needed.

- A **graphing tool** enables you to build and manipulate graphs to better understand how concepts, numbers, and graphs connect.

MyEconLab®

Find out more at www.myeconlab.com

Real-Time Data Analysis Exercises

Up-to-date macro data is a great way to engage in and understand the usefulness of macro variables and their impact on the economy. Real-Time Data Analysis exercises communicate directly with the Federal Reserve Bank of St. Louis's FRED® site, so every time FRED posts new data, students see new data.

End-of-chapter exercises accompanied by the Real-Time Data Analysis icon include Real-Time Data versions in **MyEconLab**.

Select in-text exhibits labeled **MyEconLab** Real-Time Data update in the electronic version of the text using FRED data.

Current News Exercises

Posted weekly, we find the latest microeconomic and macroeconomic news stories, post them, and write auto-graded multi-part exercises that illustrate the economic way of thinking about the news.

Interactive Homework Exercises

Participate in a fun and engaging activity that helps promote active learning and mastery of important economic concepts.

Pearson's experiments program is flexible and easy for instructors and students to use. For a complete list of available experiments, visit *www.myeconlab.com*.

The Pearson Series in Economics

Abel/Bernanke/Croushore
Macroeconomics*

Acemoglu/Laibson/List
Economics*

Bade/Parkin
Foundations of Economics*

Berck/Helfand
The Economics of the Environment

Bierman/Fernandez
Game Theory with Economic Applications

Blanchard
Macroeconomics*

Blau/Ferber/Winkler
The Economics of Women, Men, and Work

Boardman/Greenberg/Vining/Weimer
Cost-Benefit Analysis

Boyer
Principles of Transportation Economics

Branson
Macroeconomic Theory and Policy

Bruce
Public Finance and the American Economy

Carlton/Perloff
Modern Industrial Organization

Case/Fair/Oster
Principles of Economics*

Chapman
Environmental Economics: Theory, Application, and Policy

Cooter/Ulen
Law & Economics

Daniels/VanHoose
International Monetary & Financial Economics

Downs
An Economic Theory of Democracy

Ehrenberg/Smith
Modern Labor Economics

Farnham
Economics for Managers

Folland/Goodman/Stano
The Economics of Health and Health Care

Fort
Sports Economics

Froyen
Macroeconomics

Fusfeld
The Age of the Economist

Gerber
International Economics*

González-Rivera
Forecasting for Economics and Business

Gordon
Macroeconomics*

Greene
Econometric Analysis

Gregory
Essentials of Economics

Gregory/Stuart
Russian and Soviet Economic Performance and Structure

Hartwick/Olewiler
The Economics of Natural Resource Use

Heilbroner/Milberg
The Making of the Economic Society

Heyne/Boettke/Prychitko
The Economic Way of Thinking

Holt
Markets, Games, and Strategic Behavior

Hubbard/O'Brien
Economics*

Money, Banking, and the Financial System*

Hubbard/O'Brien/Rafferty
Macroeconomics*

Hughes/Cain
American Economic History

Husted/Melvin
International Economics

Jehle/Reny
Advanced Microeconomic Theory

Johnson-Lans
A Health Economics Primer

Keat/Young/Erfle
Managerial Economics

Klein
Mathematical Methods for Economics

Krugman/Obstfeld/Melitz
International Economics: Theory & Policy*

Laidler
The Demand for Money

Leeds/von Allmen
The Economics of Sports

Leeds/von Allmen/Schiming
Economics*

Lynn
Economic Development: Theory and Practice for a Divided World

Miller
Economics Today*

Understanding Modern Economics

Miller/Benjamin
The Economics of Macro Issues

Miller/Benjamin/North
The Economics of Public Issues

Mills/Hamilton
Urban Economics

Mishkin
The Economics of Money, Banking, and Financial Markets*

The Economics of Money, Banking, and Financial Markets, Business School Edition*

Macroeconomics: Policy and Practice*

Murray
Econometrics: A Modern Introduction

O'Sullivan/Sheffrin/Perez
Economics: Principles, Applications and Tools*

Parkin
Economics*

Perloff
Microeconomics*

Microeconomics: Theory and Applications with Calculus*

Perloff/Brander
Managerial Economics and Strategy*

Phelps
Health Economics

Pindyck/Rubinfeld
Microeconomics*

Riddell/Shackelford/Stamos/Schneider
Economics: A Tool for Critically Understanding Society

Roberts
The Choice: A Fable of Free Trade and Protection

Rohlf
Introduction to Economic Reasoning

Roland
Development Economics

Scherer
Industry Structure, Strategy, and Public Policy

Schiller
The Economics of Poverty and Discrimination

Sherman
Market Regulation

Stock/Watson
Introduction to Econometrics

Studenmund
Using Econometrics: A Practical Guide

Tietenberg/Lewis
Environmental and Natural Resource Economics
Environmental Economics and Policy

Todaro/Smith
Economic Development

Waldman/Jensen
Industrial Organization: Theory and Practice

Walters/Walters/Appel/Callahan/Centanni/Maex/O'Neill
Econversations: Today's Students Discuss Today's Issues

Weil
Economic Growth

Williamson
Macroeconomics

*denotes MyEconLab titles   Visit www.myeconlab.com to learn more.

MACROECONOMICS

Daron Acemoglu
Massachusetts Institute of Technology

David Laibson
Harvard University

John A. List
University of Chicago

PEARSON

Boston Columbus Indianapolis New York San Francisco Hoboken
Amsterdam Cape Town Dubai London Madrid Milan Munich Paris Montréal Toronto
Delhi Mexico City São Paulo Sydney Hong Kong Seoul Singapore Taipei Tokyo

Vice President, Business Publishing: Donna Battista
Executive Acquisitions Editor: Adrienne D'Ambrosio
Executive Development Editor: Mary Clare McEwing
Editorial Assistant: Courtney Turcotte
Vice President, Product Marketing: Maggie Moylan
Director of Marketing, Digital Services and Products: Jeanette Koskinas
Senior Product Marketing Manager: Alison Haskins
Executive Field Marketing Manager: Lori DeShazo
Senior Strategic Marketing Manager: Erin Gardner
Product Testing and Learning Validation: Kathleen McLellan
Team Lead, Program Management: Ashley Santora
Program Manager: Nancy Freihofer
Team Lead, Project Management: Jeff Holcomb
Project Manager: Sarah Dumouchelle
Supplements Project Manager: Andra Skaalrud
Operations Specialist: Carol Melville

Creative Director: Blair Brown
Art Director: Jon Boylan
Vice President, Director of Digital Strategy and Assessment: Paul Gentile
Manager of Learning Applications: Paul DeLuca
Digital Editor: Denise Clinton
Director, Digital Studio: Sacha Laustsen
Digital Studio Manager: Diane Lombardo
Digital Studio Project Manager: Melissa Honig
Digital Content Team Lead: Noel Lotz
Digital Content Project Lead: Courtney Kamauf
Full-Service Project Management and Composition: Diane Kohnen, Ann Francis, S4Carlisle Publishing Services
Interior Designer: Jonathan Boylan
Cover Designer: Jonathan Boylan
Printer/Binder: Courier Kendallville
Cover Printer: Courier Kendallville

Library of Congress Cataloging-in-Publication Data

Acemoglu, Daron.
 Macroeconomics / Daron Acemoglu, David Laibson, John A. List. — First
Edition.
   pages cm
 Includes bibliographical references and index.
 ISBN-13: 78-0-321-38395-2
 ISBN-10: 0-321-38395-8
 1. Economics.   I. Laibson, David I.   II. List, John A.   III. Title.
 HB171.5.A276 2014
 330—dc23

                                        2013048486

V011
10 9 8 7 6 5 4 3 2

ISBN 10:   0-321-38395-8
ISBN 13: 978-0-321-38395-2

Dedication

With love for Asu, Nina, and Jennifer,
who inspire us every day.

About the Authors

Daron Acemoglu is Elizabeth and James Killian Professor of Economics in the Department of Economics at the Massachusetts Institute of Technology. He has received a B.A. in economics at the University of York, 1989; M.Sc. in mathematical economics and econometrics at the London School of Economics, 1990; and Ph.D. in economics at the London School of Economics in 1992.

He is an elected fellow of the National Academy of Sciences, the American Academy of Arts and Sciences, the Econometric Society, the European Economic Association, and the Society of Labor Economists. He has received numerous awards and fellowships, including the inaugural T. W. Shultz Prize from the University of Chicago in 2004, the inaugural Sherwin Rosen Award for outstanding contribution to labor economics in 2004, Distinguished Science Award from the Turkish Sciences Association in 2006, and the John von Neumann Award, Rajk College, Budapest in 2007.

He was also the recipient of the John Bates Clark Medal in 2005, awarded every two years to the best economist in the United States under the age of 40 by the American Economic Association, and the Erwin Plein Nemmers prize awarded every two years for work of lasting significance in economics. He holds Honorary Doctorates from the University of Utrecht and Bosporus University.

His research interests include political economy, economic development and growth, human capital theory, growth theory, innovation, search theory, network economics, and learning.

His books include *Economic Origins of Dictatorship and Democracy* (jointly with James A. Robinson), which was awarded the Woodrow Wilson and the William Riker prizes, *Introduction to Modern Economic Growth*, and *Why Nations Fail: The Origins of Power, Prosperity, and Poverty* (jointly with James A. Robinson), which has become a *New York Times* bestseller.

David Laibson is the Robert I. Goldman Professor of Economics at Harvard University. He is also a member of the National Bureau of Economic Research, where he is Research Associate in the Asset Pricing, Economic Fluctuations, and Aging Working Groups. His research focuses on the topic of behavioral economics, and he leads Harvard University's Foundations of Human Behavior Initiative. He serves on several editorial boards, as well as the boards of the Health and Retirement Study (National Institutes of Health) and the Pension Research Council (Wharton). He serves on Harvard's Pension Investment Committee and on the Academic Research Council of the Consumer Financial Protection Bureau. He is a recipient of a Marshall Scholarship and a Fellow of the Econometric Society and the American Academy of Arts and Sciences. He is also a recipient of the TIAA-CREF Paul A. Samuelson Award for Outstanding Scholarly Writing on Lifelong Financial Security. Laibson holds degrees from Harvard University (A.B. in Economics, Summa), the London School of Economics (M.Sc. in Econometrics and Mathematical Economics), and the Massachusetts Institute of Technology (Ph.D. in Economics). He received his Ph.D. in 1994 and has taught at Harvard since then. In recognition of his teaching, he has been awarded Harvard's Phi Beta Kappa Prize and a Harvard College Professorship.

John A. List is the Homer J. Livingston Professor in Economics at the University of Chicago, and Chairman of the Department of Economics. List received the Kenneth Galbraith Award, Agricultural and Applied Economics Association, 2010. He is a Member of the American Academy of Arts and Sciences, 2011; Editor, *Journal of Economic Perspectives*; Associate Editor, *American Economic Review*; and Associate Editor, *Journal of Economic Literature*. His research focuses on questions in microeconomics, with a particular emphasis on the use of experimental methods to address both positive and normative issues. Much of his time has been spent developing experimental methods in the field to explore economic aspects of environmental regulations, incentives, preferences, values, and institutions. Recently, he has focused on issues related to the economics of charity, exploring why people give, plus optimal incentive schemes for first-time as well as warm-list donors.

Brief Contents

Contents

CHAPTERS ON THE WEB

Web chapters are available on MyEconLab.

Preface

We love economics. We marvel at the way economic systems work. When we buy a smartphone, we think about the complex supply chain and the hundreds of thousands of people who played a role in producing an awe-inspiring piece of technology that was assembled from components manufactured across the globe.

The market's ability to do the world's work without anyone being in charge strikes us as a phenomenon no less profound than the existence of consciousness or life itself. We believe that the creation of the market system is one of the greatest achievements of humankind.

We wrote this book to highlight the simplicity of economic ideas and their extraordinary power to explain, predict, and improve what happens in the world. We want students to master the *essential* principles of economic analysis. With that goal in mind, we identify the three key ideas that lie at the heart of the economic approach to understanding human behavior: optimization, equilibrium, and empiricism. These abstract words represent three ideas that are actually highly intuitive.

Our Vision: Three Unifying Themes

The first key principle is that people try to choose the best available option: *optimization*. We don't assume that people always successfully optimize, but we do believe that people try to optimize and often do a relatively good job of it. Because most decision makers try to choose the alternative that offers the greatest net benefit, optimization is a useful tool for predicting human behavior. Optimization is also a useful prescriptive tool. By teaching people how to optimize, we improve their decisions and the quality of their lives. By the end of this course, every student should be a skilled optimizer—without using complicated mathematics, simply by using economic intuition.

The second key principle extends the first: economic systems operate in *equilibrium*, a state in which everybody is simultaneously trying to optimize. We want students to see that they're not the only ones maximizing their well-being. An economic system is in equilibrium when each person feels that he or she cannot do any better by picking another course of action. The principle of equilibrium highlights the connections among economic actors. For example, Apple stores stock millions of iPhones because millions of consumers are going to turn up to buy them. In turn, millions of consumers go to Apple stores because those stores are ready to sell those iPhones. In equilibrium, consumers and producers are simultaneously optimizing and their behaviors are intertwined.

Our first two principles—optimization and equilibrium—are conceptual. The third is methodological: *empiricism*. Economists use *data* to test economic theories, learn about the world, and speak to policymakers. Accordingly, data play a starring role in our book, though we keep the empirical analysis extremely simple. It is this emphasis on matching theories with real data that we think most distinguishes our book from others. We show students how economists use data to answer specific questions, which makes our chapters concrete, interesting, and fun. Modern students demand the evidence behind the theory, and our book supplies it.

For example, we begin every chapter with an empirical question and then answer that question using data. One chapter begins by asking:

Why are you so much more prosperous than your great-great-grandparents were?

Later in the chapter, we demonstrate the central role played by technology in explaining U.S. economic growth and why we are much better off than our relatives a few generations ago.

In our experience, students taking their first economics class often have the impression that economics is a series of theoretical assertions with little empirical basis. By using data, we explain how economists evaluate and improve our scientific insights. Data also make concepts more memorable. Using evidence helps students build intuition, because data move the conversation from abstract principles to concrete facts. Every chapter sheds light on how economists use data to answer questions that directly interest students. Every chapter demonstrates the key role that evidence plays in advancing the science of economics.

Features

All of our features showcase intuitive empirical questions.

- In **Evidence-Based Economics (EBE)**, we show how economists use data to answer the question we pose in the opening paragraph of the chapter. The EBE uses actual data that highlights some of the major concepts discussed within the chapter. This tie-in with the data gives students a substantive look at economics as it plays out in the world around them.

  The questions explored aren't just dry intellectual ideas; they spring to life the minute the student sets foot outside the classroom—*Is Facebook free? Is college worth it? Are tropical and semitropical areas condemned to poverty by their geographies? What caused the recession of 2007–2009? Are companies like Nike harming workers in Vietnam?*

Evidence-Based Economics

Q: Why are you so much more prosperous than your great-great-grandparents were?

The theoretical discussion in the previous section supports the central role of technology in explaining sustained growth. We will now see that empirical evidence also bolsters the conclusion that technology plays a key role.

To evaluate the sources of U.S. economic growth, we follow the same strategy as in the previous chapter. There, we used the aggregate production function and estimates of the physical capital stock and the efficiency units of labor across different countries to evaluate their contributions to cross-country differences in GDP. The only major difference here is that higher-quality U.S. data enable us to conduct the analysis for GDP per hour worked rather than GDP per worker, thus allowing us to measure the labor input more accurately. We start the analysis in 1950.

Exhibit 7.10 records average GDP per hour worked (in 2005 constant dollars), the average value of the physical capital stock per hour worked, and the most important component of the human capital of workers—the average years of schooling—for 10-year periods starting in 1950. (To remove the short-term effects of the last recession from our calculations on long-term growth, the last period is 2000–2007.) The exhibit shows the steady increase in GDP per hour worked, physical capital stock per hour worked, and educational attainment in the United States between 1950 and 2007.

We then use a methodology similar to that in the previous chapter to compute the contribution of physical capital, human capital (efficiency units of labor), and technology to the growth of GDP in the United States. The results are recorded in columns 4, 5, and 6 of the exhibit (in percentages). Column 7 then gives the annual growth rate of GDP per hour worked, which is the sum of the contributions of physical capital, human capital, and technology.

- **Letting the Data Speak** is another feature that analyzes an economic question by using real data as the foundation of the discussion. Among the many issues we explore are such topics as life expectancy and innovation, living in an interconnected world, and why Chinese authorities have historically kept the yuan undervalued.

Life Expectancy and Innovation

Life expectancy around the world was much lower 70 years ago than it is today.[4] In 1940, child and infant mortality rates were so high and adult diseases, such as pneumonia and tuberculosis, were so deadly (and without any cure) that life expectancy at birth in many nations stood at less than 40 years. For example, the life expectancy at birth of an average Indian was an incredibly low 30 years. In Venezuela, it was 33; in Indonesia, 34; in Brazil, 36. Life expectancy at birth in many Western nations was also low but still considerably higher than the corresponding numbers in the poorer nations. Consider that life expectancy at birth in the United States was 64 years.

In the course of the next three or four decades, this picture changed dramatically. As we saw in the previous chapter, while the gap in life expectancy between rich and poor nations still remains today, health conditions have improved significantly all over the world, particularly before the spread of the AIDS epidemic in sub-Saharan Africa starting in the 1980s. Life expectancy at birth in India in 1999 was 60 years. This was twice as large as the same number in 1940. It was also 50 percent higher than life expectancy at birth in Britain in 1820 (40 years), which had approximately the same GDP per capita as India in 1999. How did this tremendous improvement in health conditions in poor nations take place?

The answer lies in scientific breakthroughs and innovations that took place in the United States and Western Europe throughout the twentieth century. First, there was a wave of global drug innovation, most importantly the development of antibiotics, which produced many products that were highly effective against major killers in developing countries. Penicillin, which provided an effective treatment against a range of bacterial infections, became widely available by the early 1950s. Also important during the same period was the development of new vaccines, including ones against yellow fever and smallpox.

The second major factor was the discovery of DDT (Dichlorodiphenyl trichloroethylene). Although eventually the excess use of DDT as an agricultural pesticide would turn out to be an environmental hazard, its initial use in disease control was revolutionary. DDT allowed a breakthrough in attempts to control one of the major killers of children in relatively poor parts of the world—malaria. Finally, with the establishment and help of the World Health Organization (WHO), simple but effective medical and public health practices, such as oral rehydration and boiling water to prevent cholera, spread to poorer countries.

- In keeping with the optimization theme, from time to time we ask students to make a real economic decision or evaluate the consequences of past real decisions in a feature entitled **Choice & Consequence**. We explain how an economist might analyze the same decision. Among the choices investigated are such questions and concepts as the power of growth, foreign aid and corruption, and policies that address the problem of banks that are "too big to fail."

The Power of Growth

You have two choices. You can either start a job with a salary of $1,000 per month and a 6 percent increase in your salary every month. Or you can start with a salary of $2,000, but never get a raise. Which one of these two options do you prefer?

The answer might naturally vary from person to person. If you have an immediate need for money, you may be attracted by the prospect of a $2,000 paycheck. But before you rush to sign on the dotted line for the $2,000-per-month job, think of the implications of the 6 percent monthly increase. With a 6 percent-per-month increase, your monthly salary will already exceed $2,000 after only a year. After 4 years, it will be approximately $16,400 a month. So if you were thinking of staying in this job for more than a year, starting with a lower salary might be a much better idea.

The first option is attractive, at least for those of you intending to stay with it for a while, precisely because of exponential growth. The 6-percent-per-month increases

in salary do not apply to the base salary (if they did, this would have increased your salary by $60 every month). Rather, they compound, meaning that each 6 percent applies to the amount that has accumulated up to that point. Thus after 1 month, your salary will be $1,060. After 2 months, it is $1,060 × 1.06 = $1,123.60. After 3 months, it is $1,123.60 × 1.06 = $1,191.02, and so on. We will next see that exponential growth plays the same role in countries' growth trajectories as in your potential income in these two hypothetical jobs.

Organization

Part I Introduction to Economics lays the groundwork for understanding the economic way of thinking about the world. In *Chapter 1*, we show that the principle of *optimization* explains most of our choices. In other words, we make choices based on a consideration of benefits and costs, and to do this we need to consider trade-offs, budget constraints, and opportunity cost. We then explain that *equilibrium* is the situation in which everyone is simultaneously trying to individually optimize. In equilibrium, there isn't any perceived benefit to changing one's own behavior. We introduce the free-rider problem to show that individual optimization and social optimization do not necessarily coincide.

Because data plays such a central role in economics, we devote an entire chapter—*Chapter 2*—to economic models, the scientific method, empirical testing, and the critical distinction between correlation and causation. We show how economists use models and data to answer interesting questions about human behavior. For the students who want to brush up their graphical skills, there is an appendix on constructing and interpreting graphs, which is presented in the context of an actual experiment on incentive schemes.

Chapter 3 digs much more deeply into the concept of optimization, including an intuitive discussion of marginal analysis. We use a single running example of choosing an apartment, which confronts students with a trade-off between the cost of rent and the time spent commuting. We demonstrate two alternative approaches—optimization in levels and optimization in differences—and show why economists often use the latter (marginal) technique.

Chapter 4 introduces the demand and supply framework via a running example of the market for gasoline. We show how the price of gasoline affects the decisions of buyers, like commuters, and sellers, like ExxonMobil. As we develop the model, we explore how individual buyers are added together to produce a market demand curve and how individual sellers are added together to generate a market supply curve. We then show how buyers and sellers jointly determine the equilibrium market price and the equilibrium quantity of goods transacted in a perfectly competitive market. Finally, we show how markets break down when prices aren't allowed to adjust to equate the quantity demanded and the quantity supplied.

Part II Introduction to Macroeconomics provides an introduction to the field. In *Chapter 5* we explain the basic measurement tools. Here we explore the derivation of the aggregate output of the economy, or the gross domestic product (GDP), with the production, expenditure, and income methods, explaining why all these methods are equivalent and lead to the same level of total GDP. We also consider what *isn't* measured in GDP, such as production that takes place at home for one's family. Finally, we discuss the measurement of inflation and the concept of a price index.

In *Chapter 6* we show how income (GDP) per capita can be compared across countries using two similar techniques—an exchange rate method and a purchasing power method. We explain how the aggregate production function links a country's physical capital stock, labor resources (total labor hours and human capital per worker), and technology to its GDP and thus draw the link between income per capita and a country's physical capital stock per worker, human capital, and technology. We then use these tools to investigate the roles of physical capital, human capital, and technology in accounting for the great differences in prosperity across countries.

In **Part III, Long-Run Growth and Development**, we turn to a comprehensive treatment of growth and development. In *Chapter 7*, we show that economic growth has transformed many countries over the past 200 years. For example, in the United States today, GDP per capita is about 25 times higher than it was in 1820. In this discussion, we explain the "exponential" nature of economic growth, which results from the fact that new growth builds on past growth, and implies that small differences in growth rates can translate into huge differences in income per capita over several decades. We explain how sustained economic growth relies on advances in technology and why different countries have experienced different long-run growth paths. We also emphasize that economic growth does not benefit all citizens equally. For some citizens, poverty is the unintentional by-product of technological progress. For the instructors who want a more in-depth treatment of growth and the determinants of GDP, we present a simplified version of the Solow Model in an optional appendix to the chapter.

Why do some nations not invest enough in physical and human capital, adopt the best technologies, and organize their production efficiently? Put another way, why isn't the whole world economically developed? *Chapter 8* probes this question and considers the fundamental causes of prosperity. We discuss several potential fundamental causes, in particular, geography, culture, and institutions, and argue why the oft-emphasized geographic factors do not seem to account for much of the wide cross-country gaps in economic prosperity.

In **Part IV, Equilibrium in the Macroeconomy**, we discuss three key markets that play a central role in macroeconomic analysis: the labor market, the credit market, and the market for bank reserves. *Chapter 9* begins with the labor market—labor demand and labor supply. We first describe the standard competitive equilibrium, where the wage and the quantity of labor employed are pinned down by the intersection of the labor demand and labor supply curves. We then show how imperfectly flexible wages lead to unemployment. We then use this framework to discuss the many different factors that influence unemployment, including both frictional and structural sources.

Chapter 10 extends our analysis by incorporating the credit market. We explain how the modern financial system circulates funds from savers to borrowers. We describe the different types of shocks that can destabilize a financial system. We look at how banks and other financial intermediaries connect supply and demand in the credit market, and we use banks' balance sheets to explain the risks of taking on short-term liabilities and making long-term investments.

Chapter 11 introduces the monetary system. We begin by explaining the functions of money. The chapter then introduces the Federal Reserve Bank (the Fed) and lays out the basic plumbing of the monetary system, especially the role of supply and demand in the market for bank reserves. We explain in detail the Fed's role in controlling bank reserves and influencing interest rates, especially the interest rate on bank reserves (the federal funds rate). The chapter explains the causes of inflation and its social costs and benefits.

In **Part V, Short-Run Fluctuations and Macroeconomic Policy**, we use a modern framework to analyze and explain short-run fluctuations. Our analysis is inclusive and integrative, enabling us to combine the most relevant and useful insights from many different schools of economic thought. We believe that the labor market is the most informative lens through which first-year economics students can understand economic fluctuations. We therefore put the labor market and unemployment at the center of our analysis. In this part of the book, we also extend our discussion of the role of financial markets and financial crises. We present a balanced perspective that incorporates the diverse range of important insights that have emerged in the last century of theoretical and empirical research.

Chapter 12 lays the foundations of this approach, showing how a wide range of economic shocks cause short-run fluctuations and how these can be studied using the labor market. We trace out the impact of technological shocks, shocks to sentiments (including animal spirits), and monetary and financial shocks that work through their impact on the interest rate or by causing financial crises. In each case, we explain how multipliers amplify the impact of the initial shock. We also explain how wage rigidities affect the labor market response to these shocks. We apply our labor market model to both economic contractions and expansions and look at the problems that arise when the economy grows too slowly or too quickly.

Chapter 13 discusses the wide menu of monetary and fiscal policies that are used to partially offset aggregate fluctuations. We describe the most important strategies that have recently been adopted by central banks. We then discuss the role of fiscal policy and provide an analytic toolkit that students can use to estimate the impact of countercyclical expenditures and taxation.

In **Part VI, Macroeconomics in a Global Economy**, we provide a wide-angle view of the global economy and the relationships that interconnect national economies. In *Chapter 14* we show how international trade works, using the key concepts of specialization, comparative advantage, and opportunity cost. We study the optimal allocation of tasks inside a firm and show that firms should allocate their employees to tasks—and individuals should choose their occupations—according to comparative advantage. We then broaden the picture by focusing on the optimal allocation of tasks across countries and show that here, too, the same principles apply. We analyze international flows of goods and services and the financial consequences of trade deficits. We describe the accounting identities that enable economists to measure the rich patterns of globalized trade. We also discuss the critical role of technology transfer.

Chapter 15 studies the determinants of exchange rates—both nominal and real—between different currencies and how they impact the macroeconomy. We describe the different types of exchange rate regimes and the operation of the foreign exchange market. Finally, we study the impact of changes in the real exchange rate on net exports and GDP.

MyEconLab®

MyEconLab is an extraordinary online course management, homework, quizzing, testing, activity, and tutorial resource.

For Instructors

With comprehensive homework, quiz, test, activity, practice, and tutorial options, instructors can manage all their assessment and online activity needs in one place. MyEconLab saves time by automatically grading questions and activities and tracking results in an online gradebook.

Each chapter contains two preloaded homework exercise sets that can be used to build an individualized study plan for each student. These study plan exercises contain tutorial resources, including instant feedback, links to the appropriate chapter section in the eText, pop-up definitions from the text, and step-by-step guided solutions, where appropriate. Within its rich assignment library, instructors will find a vast array of assessments that ask the students to draw graph lines and shifts, plot equilibrium points, and highlight important graph areas, all with the benefit of instant, personalized feedback. This feedback culminates, when needed, with the correct graph output alongside the student's personal answer, creating a powerful learning moment.

After the initial setup of the MyEconLab course for Acemoglu/Laibson/List, there are two primary ways to begin using this rich online environment. The first path requires no further action by the instructor. Students, on their own, can use MyEconLab's adaptive Study Plan problems and tutorial resources to enhance their understanding of concepts. The online gradebook records each student's performance and time spent on the assessments, activities, and the study plan and generates reports by student or chapter.

Alternatively, instructors can fully customize MyEconLab to match their course exactly: reading assignments, homework assignments, video assignments, current news assignments, digital activities, experiments, quizzes, and tests. Assignable resources include:

- Preloaded exercise assignment sets for each chapter that include the student tutorial resources mentioned earlier
- Preloaded quizzes for each chapter
- *Interactive Reading Assignments* in MyEconLab enable educators to encourage core reading by providing an assessment incentive along the way. These short reading segments feature embedded exercises that prompt students to learn actively. These exercises are automatically graded, so educators can integrate assessment into reading assignments quickly and easily.
- Assignable and gradable exercises that are similar to the end-of-chapter questions and problems and numbered exactly as in the book to make assigning homework easier
- *Real-Time Data Analysis Exercises* allow students and instructors to use the very latest data from the Federal Reserve Bank of St. Louis's FRED site. By completing the exercises, students become familiar with a key data source, learn how to locate data, and develop skills in interpreting data.
- In the eText available in MyEconLab, select exhibits labeled MyEconLab Real-Time Data allow students to display a pop-up graph updated with real-time data from FRED.

- *Current News Exercises* provide a turnkey way to assign gradable news-based exercises in MyEconLab. Each week, Pearson scours the news, finds current economics articles, creates exercises around the news articles, and then automatically adds them to MyEconLab. Assigning and grading current news-based exercises that deal with the latest economics events and policy issues have never been more convenient.
- *Econ Exercise Builder* allows you to build customized exercises. Exercises include multiple-choice, graph drawing, and free-response items, many of which are generated algorithmically so that each time a student works them, a different variation is presented.
- Test Item File questions that allow you to assign quizzes or homework that will look just like your exams

MyEconLab grades every problem type (except essays), even problems with graphs. When working homework exercises, students receive immediate feedback, with links to additional learning tools.

- *Experiments in MyEconLab* are a fun and engaging way to promote active learning and mastery of important economic concepts. Pearson's Experiments program is flexible and easy for instructors and students to use.
  - Single-player experiments allow your students to play against virtual players from anywhere at any time as long as they have an Internet connection.
  - Multiplayer experiments allow you to assign and manage a real-time experiment with your class.

    Pre- and post-questions for each experiment are available for assignment in MyEconLab.

    For a complete list of available experiments, visit **www.myeconlab.com**.
- *Digital Interactives* immerse students in a fundamental economic principle, helping them to learn actively. They can be presented in class as a visually stimulating, highly engaging lecture tool, and can also be assigned with assessment questions for grading. Digital Interactives are designed for use in traditional, online, and hybrid courses, and many incorporate real-time data, as well as data display and analysis tools. To learn more, and for a complete list of digital interactives, visit **www.myeconlab.com**.

Learning Catalytics™ is a bring-your-own-device classroom engagement tool that allows instructors to ask students questions utilizing 18 different question types, allowing students to participate in real time during lectures. With Learning Catalytics you can:

- Engage students in real time, using open-ended tasks to probe student understanding.
- Promote student participation using any modern Web-enabled device they already have—laptop, smartphone, or tablet.
- Address misconceptions before students leave the classroom.
- Understand immediately where students are and adjust your lecture accordingly.
- Improve your students' critical-thinking skills.
- Engage with and record the participation of every student in your classroom.

Learning Catalytics gives you the flexibility to create your own questions to fit your course exactly or choose from a searchable question library Pearson has created.

For more information, visit **learningcatalytics.com**.

Customization and Communication MyEconLab in MyLab/Mastering provides additional optional customization and communication tools. Instructors who teach distance-learning courses or very large lecture sections find the MyLab/Mastering format useful because they can upload course documents and assignments, customize the order of chapters, and use communication features such as Document Sharing, Chat, ClassLive, and Discussion Board.

For Students

MyEconLab puts students in control of their learning through a collection of testing, practice, and study tools tied to the online, interactive version of the textbook and other media resources.

In MyEconLab's environment, students practice what they learn, test their understanding, and pursue a personalized and adaptive study plan generated from their performance on sample tests and from quizzes created by their instructor. In Homework or Study Plan mode, students have access to a wealth of tutorial features, including:

- Instant feedback on exercises that helps students understand and apply the concepts
- Links to the eText to promote reading of the text just when the student needs to revisit a concept or an explanation
- Animations of most of the textbook's exhibits provide step-by-step animation and audio to help students develop intuition in reading and interpreting graphs. The animations are accessible directly from the eText or from the Multimedia Library.
- Step-by-step guided solutions that force students to break down a problem in much the same way an instructor would do during office hours
- Pop-up key term definitions from the eText to help students master the vocabulary of economics
- A graphing tool that is integrated into the various exercises to enable students to build and manipulate graphs to better understand how concepts, numbers, and graphs connect

Additional MyEconLab Resources
- *Enhanced eText*—In addition to the portions of eText available as pop-ups or links, a fully searchable enhanced eText is available for students who wish to read and study in a fully electronic environment. The enhanced eText includes all of the animations and embedded links to all of the end-of-chapter questions and problems, enabling students to read, review, and immediately practice their understanding. The embedded exercises are auto-graded exercises and feed directly into MyEconLab's adaptive Study Plan.
- *Print upgrade*—For students who wish to complete assignments in MyEconLab but read in print, Pearson offers registered MyEconLab users a loose-leaf version of the print text at a significant discount.

MyEconLab and Adaptive Learning MyEconLab's Study Plan is now powered by a sophisticated adaptive learning engine that tailors learning material to meet the unique needs of each student. MyEconLab's new Adaptive Learning Study Plan monitors students' performance on homework, quizzes, and tests and continuously makes recommendations based on that performance.

If a student is struggling with a concept such as supply and demand or having trouble calculating a price elasticity of demand, the Study Plan provides customized remediation activities—a pathway based on personal proficiencies, number of attempts, or difficulty of questions—to get the student back on track. Students will also receive recommendations for additional practice in the form of rich multimedia learning aids such as an interactive eText, Help Me Solve This tutorials, and graphing tools.

The Study Plan can identify a student's potential trouble spots and provide learning material and practice to avoid pitfalls. In addition, students who are showing a high degree of success with the assessment material are offered a chance to work on future topics based on the professor's course coverage preferences. This personalized and adaptive feedback and support ensures that students are optimizing their current and future course work and mastering the concepts, rather than just memorizing and guessing answers. You can learn more about adaptive learning at **http://www.pearsonmylabandmastering .com/northamerica/myeconlab/educators/features/adaptive-learning**.

Dynamic Study Modules, which focus on key topic areas and are available from within MyEconLab, are an additional way for students to obtain tailored help. These modules work by continuously assessing student performance and activity on discrete topics and provide personalized content in real time to reinforce concepts that target each student's particular strengths and weaknesses.

Each Dynamic Study Module, accessed by computer, smartphone, or tablet, promotes fast learning and long-term retention. Because MyEconLab and Dynamic Study Modules help students stay on track and achieve a higher level of subject-matter mastery, more class time is available for interaction, discussion, collaboration, and exploring applications to current news and events. Instructors can register, create, and access all of their MyEconLab courses at **www.pearsonmylab.com**.

Instructor Resources

The **Instructor's Manual** for *Macroeconomics* was prepared by Rashid Al-Hmoud of Texas Tech University and includes:

- A chapter-by-chapter outline of the text
- Lecture notes highlighting the big ideas and concepts from each chapter
- Teaching Tips on how to motivate the lecture
- Common Mistakes or Misunderstandings students often make and how to correct them
- Short, real-world Alternative Teaching Examples, different from those in the text

Active Learning Exercises, included online and at the end of each Instructor's Manual chapter, were also prepared by Rashid Al-Hmoud and include:

- 3–5 Active Learning Exercises per chapter that are ideal for in-class discussions and group work

The **Solutions Manual**, prepared by Bruce Watson of Boston University, includes solutions to all end-of-chapter Questions and Problems in the text. It is available in print and downloadable PDFs.

Three flexible **PowerPoint Presentation** packages make it easy for instructors to design presentation slides that best suit their style and needs:

- Lecture notes with animations of key text exhibits, as well as alternative examples with original static exhibits.
- Exhibits from the text with step-by-step animation
- Static versions of all text exhibits

Each presentation maps to the chapter's structure and organization and uses terminology used in the text. Steven Yamarik of California State University, Long Beach created the Lecture PowerPoint presentation. Paul Graf of Indiana University, Bloomington prepared the step-by-step instructions for the animated exhibits.

The **Test Bank** for *Macroeconomics* was written by Anuradha Gupta and Julia Paul, and edited and reviewed by Todd Fitch of University of California, Berkeley; Gregory Gilpin of Montana State University; Grace O of Georgia State University; Nevin Cavusoglu of James Madison University; and Sang Lee of Southeastern Louisiana University. The Test Bank contains approximately 2,100 multiple-choice, numerical, short-answer, and essay questions. These have been edited and reviewed to ensure accuracy and clarity, and include terminology used in the book. Each question can be sorted by difficulty, book topic, concept covered, and AACSB learning standard to enhance ease of use. The Test Bank is available in Word, PDF, and TestGen formats.

The Test Bank is available in test generator software (TestGen with QuizMaster). TestGen's graphical interface enables instructors to view, edit, and add questions; transfer questions to tests; and print different forms of tests. Instructors also have the option to reformat tests with varying fonts and styles, margins, and headers and footers, as in any word-processing document. Search-and-sort features let the instructor quickly locate questions and arrange them in a preferred order. QuizMaster, working with your school's computer network, automatically grades the exams, stores the results on disk, and allows the instructor to view and print a variety of reports.

Instructor's Resource Center

Instructor resources are available online via our centralized supplements Web site, the Instructor Resource Center (**www.pearsonhighered.com/irc**). For access or more information, contact your local Pearson representative or request access online at the Instructor Resource Center.

Acknowledgments

As the three of us worked on this project, we taught each other a lot about economics, teaching, and writing. But we learned even more from the hundreds of other people who helped us along the way. For their guidance, we are thankful and deeply humbled. Their contributions turned out to be critical in ways that we never imagined when we started, and our own ideas were greatly improved by their insights and advice.

Our reviewers, focus group participants, and class testers showed us how to better formulate our ideas and helped us sharpen our writing. Through their frequently brilliant feedback, they corrected our economic misconceptions, improved our conceptual vision, and showed us how to write more clearly. Their contributions appear in almost every paragraph of this book. All of their names are listed below.

Our research assistants—Alec Brandon, Justin Holz, Josh Hurwitz, Xavier Jaravel, Angelina Liang, Daniel Norris , Yana Peysakhovich, and Jan Zilinsky—played a critical role at every phase of the project, from analyzing data to editing prose to generating deep insights about pedagogical principles that are woven throughout the book. These research assistants played many roles. We learned to trust their instincts on every element of the book, and quickly realized that their contributions were indispensable to the project's success. We are especially indebted to Josh, who has earned our eternal gratitude for many late work nights and for his brilliant editorial and economic insights.

We are grateful to Zick Rubin, who advised us as we started to organize the project and encouraged us as the book developed. We are also deeply thankful to the many inspiring economists who contributed major components of the project. Bruce Watson of Boston University, Anuradha Gupta, and Julia Paul contributed extensively to the development of the end-of-chapter questions and problems, which stand out as examples of inspiring pedagogy. Rashid Al-Hmoud of Texas Tech University wrote the innovative and intuitive Instructor's Manual and Active Learning Exercises. Steven Yamarik, California State University, Long Beach and Paul Graf, Indiana University, Bloomington created outstanding PowerPoint slides and animations that illuminate and distill the key lessons of the book. Anuradha Gupta and Julia Paul created the expansive test bank.

Most importantly, we acknowledge the myriad contributions of our editors and all of our amazing colleagues at Pearson. They have marched with us every step of the way. We wouldn't dare count the number of hours that they dedicated to this project–including evenings and weekends. Their commitment, vision, and editorial suggestions touched every sentence of this book. Most of the key decisions about the project were made with the help of our editors, and this collaborative spirit proved to be absolutely essential to our writing. Dozens of people at Pearson played key roles, but the most important contributions were made by Adrienne D'Ambrosio, Executive Acquisitions Editor, Mary Clare McEwing, Executive Development Editor, Nancy Freihofer, Production Manager, Sarah Dumouchelle, Andra Skaalrud, Diane Kohnen, and Ann Francis our Project Managers, Kathleen McLellan, Product Testing and Learner Validation Manager, Lori DeShazo, Executive Field Marketing Manager, Alison Haskins, Senior Product Marketing Manager, Noel Lotz, Digital Content Team Lead, Melissa Honig, Digital Studio Project Manager, and Margaret E. Monahan-Pashall.

We are particularly grateful to Adrienne who has been deeply committed to our project from the first day and has tirelessly worked with us at every key decision. We also wish to thank Denise Clinton, Digital Editor, who first got us started, and Donna Battista, Vice President Product Management, who championed the project along the way. All of these advisers transformed us as writers, teachers, and communicators. This book is a testimony to their perseverance, their dedication, and their brilliant eye for good (and often bad!) writing. Their commitment to this project has been extraordinary and inspirational. We are profoundly grateful for their guidance and collaboration.

Finally, we wish to thank our many other support networks. Our own professors, who first inspired us as economists and showed, through their example, the power of teaching and the joy that one can take from studying economics. Our parents, who nurtured us in so many ways and gave us the initial human capital that made our entire careers possible. Our kids—Annika, Aras, Arda, Eli, Greta, Mason, Max, and Noah—who sacrificed when our long hours on this book ate into family life. And, most profoundly, we thank our spouses, who have been supportive, understanding, and inspirational throughout the project.

This book is the product of many streams that have flowed together and so many people who have contributed their insights and their passion to this project. We are deeply grateful for these myriad collaborations.

Reviewers

The following reviewers, class test participants, and focus group participants provided invaluable insights.

Adel Abadeer, Calvin College

Ahmed Abou-Zaid, Eastern Illinois University

Temisan Agbeyegbe, City University of New York

Carlos Aguilar, El Paso Community College

Rashid Al-Hmoud, Texas Tech University

Sam Allgood, University of Nebraska, Lincoln

Neil Alper, Northeastern University

Farhad Ameen, Westchester Community College

Catalina Amuedo-Dorantes, San Diego State University

Lian An, University of North Florida

Samuel Andoh, Southern Connecticut State University

Brad Andrew, Juniata College

Len Anyanwu, Union County College

Robert Archibald, College of William and Mary

Ali Arshad, New Mexico Highlands University

Robert Baden, University of California, Santa Cruz

Mohsen Bahmani-Oskooee, University of Wisconsin, Milwaukee

Scott L. Baier, Clemson University

Rita Balaban, University of North Carolina

Mihajlo Balic, Harrisburg Area Community College

Sheryl Ball, Virginia Polytechnic Institute and State University

Spencer Banzhaf, Georgia State University

Jim Barbour, Elon University

Hamid Bastin, Shippensburg University

Clare Battista, California State Polytechnic University, San Luis Obispo

Jodi Beggs, Northeastern University

Eric Belasco, Montana State University

Susan Bell, Seminole State University

Valerie Bencivenga, University of Texas, Austin

Pedro Bento, West Virginia University

Derek Berry, Calhoun Community College

Prasun Bhattacharjee, East Tennessee State University

Benjamin Blair, Columbus State University

Douglas Blair, Rutgers University

John Bockino, Suffolk County Community College

Andrea Borchard, Hillsborough Community College

Luca Bossi, University of Pennsylvania

Gregory Brock, Georgia Southern University

Bruce Brown, California State Polytechnic University, Pomona

David Brown, Pennsylvania State University

Jaime Brown, Pennsylvania State University

Laura Bucila, Texas Christian University

Don Bumpass, Sam Houston State University

Chris Burkart, University of West Florida

Colleen Callahan, American University

Fred Campano, Fordham University

Douglas Campbell, University of Memphis

Cheryl Carleton, Villanova University

Scott Carrell, University of California, Davis

Kathleen Carroll, University of Maryland, Baltimore

Regina Cassady, Valencia College, East Campus

Shirley Cassing, University of Pittsburgh

Nevin Cavusoglu, James Madison University

Suparna Chakraborty, University of San Francisco

Catherine Chambers, University of Central Missouri

Chiuping Chen, American River College

Susan Christoffersen, Philadelphia University

Benjamin Andrew Chupp, Illinois State University

David L. Cleeton, Illinois State University

Cynthia Clement, University of Maryland

Marcelo Clerici-Arias, Stanford University

Rachel Connelly, Bowdoin College

William Conner, Tidewater Community College

Patrick Conway, University of North Carolina

Jay Corrigan, Kenyon College

Antoinette Criss, University of South Florida

Sean Crockett, City University of New York

Patrick Crowley, Texas A&M University, Corpus Christi

Kelley Cullen, Eastern Washington University

Scott Cunningham, Baylor University

Muhammed Dalgin, Kutztown University

David Davenport, McLennan Community College

Stephen Davis, Southwest Minnesota State University

John W. Dawson, Appalachian State University

Pierangelo De Pace, California State University, Pomona

David Denslow, University of Florida

Arthur Diamond, University of Nebraska, Omaha

Timothy Diette, Washington and Lee University

Isaac Dilanni, University of Illinois, Urbana-Champaign

Oguzhan Dincer, Illinois State University

Ethan Doetsch, Ohio State University

Murat Doral, Kennesaw State University

Tanya Downing, Cuesta College

Gary Dymski, University of California, Riverside

Kevin Egan, University of Toledo

Eric Eide, Brigham Young University, Provo

Harold Elder, University of Alabama, Tuscaloosa

Harry Ellis, University of North Texas

Noha Emara, Columbia University

Lucas Engelhardt, Kent State University, Stark

Hadi Esfahani, University of Illinois, Urbana-Champaign

Molly Espey, Clemson University

Jose Esteban, Palomar College

Hugo Eyzaguirre, Northern Michigan University

Jamie Falcon, University of Maryland, Baltimore

Liliana Fargo, DePaul University

Sasan Fayazmanesh, California State University, Fresno

Bichaka Fayissa, Middle Tennessee State University

Virginia Fierro-Renoy, Keiser University

Donna Fisher, Georgia Southern University

Paul Fisher, Henry Ford Community College

Todd Fitch, University of California, Berkeley

Mary Flannery, University of Notre Dame

Hisham Foad, San Diego State University

Mathew Forstater, University of Missouri, Kansas City

Irene Foster, George Mason University

Hamilton Fout, Kansas State University

Shelby Frost, Georgia State University

Timothy Fuerst, University of Notre Dame

Ken Gaines, East-West University

John Gallup, Portland State University

William Galose, Lamar University

Karen Gebhardt, Colorado State University

Gerbremeskel Gebremariam, Virginia Polytechnic Institute and State University

Lisa George, City University of New York

Gregory Gilpin, Montana State University

Seth Gitter, Towson University

Rajeev Goel, Illinois State University

Bill Goffe, State University of New York, Oswego

Julie Gonzalez, University of California, Santa Cruz

Paul Graf, Indiana University, Bloomington

Philip Graves, University of Colorado, Boulder

Lisa Grobar, California State University, Long Beach

Fatma Gunay Bendas, Washington and Lee University

Michael Hammock, Middle Tennessee State University

Michele Hampton, Cuyahoga Community College

Moonsu Han, North Shore Community College

F. Andrew Hanssen, Clemson University

David Harris, Benedictine College

Robert Harris, Indiana University-Purdue University Indianapolis

Julia Heath, University of Cincinnati

Jolien Helsel, Youngstown State University

Matthew Henry, Cleveland State University

Thomas Henry, Mississippi State University

David Hewitt, Whittier College

Wayne Hickenbottom, University of Texas, Austin

Michael Hilmer, San Diego State University

John Hilston, Brevard College

Naphtali Hoffman, Elmira College and Binghamton University

Kim Holder, University of West Georgia

Robert Holland, Purdue University

James A. Hornsten, Northwestern University

Gail Hoyt, University of Kentucky

Jim Hubert, Seattle Central Community College

Scott Hunt, Columbus State Community College

Kyle Hurst, University of Colorado, Denver

Ruben Jacob-Rubio, University of Georgia

Joyce Jacobsen, Wesleyan University

Kenneth Jameson, University of Utah

Andres Jauregui, Columbus State University

Sarah Jenyk, Youngstown State University

Robert Jerome, James Madison University

Deepak Joglekar, University of Connecticut

Paul Johnson, Columbus State University

Ted Joyce, City University of New York

David Kalist, Shippensburg University

Lilian Kamal, University of Hartford

Leonie Karkoviata, University of Houston, Downtown

Kathy Kelly, University of Texas, Arlington

Colin Knapp, University of Florida

Yilmaz Kocer, University of Southern California

Ebenezer Kolajo, University of West Georgia

Janet Koscianski, Shippensburg University

Robert Krol, California State University, Northridge

Daniel Kuester, Kansas State University

Patricia Kuzyk, Washington State University

Sumner La Croix, University of Hawaii

Rose LaMont, Modesto Community College

Carsten Lange, California State University, Pomona

Vicky Langston, Columbus State University

Susan Laury, Georgia State University

Myoung Lee, University of Missouri, Columbia

Sang Lee, Southeastern Louisiana University

Phillip K. Letting, Harrisburg Area Community College

John Levendis, Loyola University

Steven Levkoff, University of California, San Diego

Dennis P. Leyden, University of North Carolina, Greensboro

Gregory Lindeblom, Brevard College

Alan Lockard, Binghamton University

Joshua Long, Ivy Technical College

Linda Loubert, Morgan State University

Heather Luea, Kansas State University

Rita Madarassy, Santa Clara University

James Makokha, Collin County Community College

Liam C. Malloy, University of Rhode Island

Paula Manns, Atlantic Cape Community College

Vlad Manole, Rutgers University

Hardik Marfatia, Northeastern Illinois University

Lawrence Martin, Michigan State University

Norman Maynard, University of Oklahoma

Katherine McClain, University of Georgia

Scott McGann, Grossmont College

Kim Marie McGoldrick, University of Richmond

Shah Mehrabi, Montgomery Community College

Saul Mekies, Kirkwood Community College

Kimberly Mencken, Baylor University

Diego Mendez-Carbajo, Illinois Wesleyan University

Catherine Middleton, University of Tennessee, Chattanooga

Nara Mijid, Central Connecticut State University

Laurie A. Miller, University of Nebraska, Lincoln

Edward Millner, Virginia Commonwealth University

Ida Mirzaie, Ohio State University

David Mitchell, Missouri State University, Springfield

Michael Mogavero, University of Notre Dame

Robert Mohr, University of New Hampshire

Barbara Moore, University of Central Florida

Thaddeaus Mounkurai, Daytona State College

Usha Nair-Reichert, Emory University

Camille Nelson, Oregon State University

Michael Nelson, Oregon State University

John Neri, University of Maryland

Andre Neveu, James Madison University

Jinlan Ni, University of Nebraska, Omaha

Eric Nielsen, St. Louis Community College

Jaminka Ninkovic, Emory University

Chali Nondo, Albany State University

Richard P. Numrich, College of Southern
Nevada

Andrew Nutting, Hamilton College

Grace O, Georgia State University

Norman Obst, Michigan State University

Scott Ogawa, Northwestern University

Lee Ohanian, University of California,
Los Angeles

Paul Okello, Tarrant County College

Ifeakandu Okoye, Florida A&M University

Alan Osman, Ohio State University

Tomi Ovaska, Youngstown State University

Caroline Padgett, Francis Marion University

Peter Parcells, Whitman College

Cynthia Parker, Chaffey College

Mohammed Partapurwala, Monroe
Community College

Robert Pennington, University of Central
Florida

Kerk Phillips, Brigham Young University

Goncalo Pina, Santa Clara University

Michael Podgursky, University of Missouri

Greg Pratt, Mesa Community College

Guangjun Qu, Birmingham-Southern
College

Fernando Quijano, Dickinson State
University

Joseph Quinn, Boston College

Reza Ramazani, Saint Michael's College

Ranajoy Ray-Chaudhuri, Ohio State
University

Mitchell Redlo, Monroe Community
College

Javier Reyes, University of Arkansas

Teresa Riley, Youngstown State University

Nancy Roberts, Arizona State University

Malcolm Robinson, Thomas More College

Randall Rojas, University of California,
Los Angeles

Sudipta Roy, Kankakee Community College

Jared Rubin, Chapman University

Jason C. Rudbeck, University of Georgia

Melissa Rueterbusch, Mott Community
College

Mariano Runco, Auburn University at
Montgomery

Nicholas G. Rupp, East Carolina University

Steven Russell, Indiana University-Purdue
University-Indianapolis

Michael Ryan, Western Michigan University

Ravi Samitamana, Daytona State College

David Sanders, University of Missouri,
St. Louis

Michael Sattinger, State University
of New York, Albany

Anya Savikhin Samek, University of
Wisconsin, Madison

Peter Schuhmann, University of North
Carolina, Wilmington

Robert M. Schwab, University of Maryland

Jesse Schwartz, Kennesaw State University

James K. Self, Indiana University,
Bloomington

Mark Showalter, Brigham Young University,
Provo

Dorothy Siden, Salem State University

Mark V. Siegler, California State University,
Sacramento

Timothy Simpson, Central New Mexico
Community College

Michael Sinkey, University of West Georgia

John Z. Smith, Jr., United States Military
Academy, West Point

Thomas Snyder, University of Central
Arkansas

Joe Sobieralski, Southwestern Illinois
College

Sara Solnick, University of Vermont

Martha Starr, American University

Rebecca Stein, University of Pennsylvania

Liliana Stern, Auburn University

Adam Stevenson, University of Michigan

Cliff Stone, Ball State University

Mark C. Strazicich, Appalachian State
University

Chetan Subramanian, State University
of New York, Buffalo

AJ Sumell, Youngstown State University

Charles Swanson, Temple University

Tom Sweeney, Des Moines Area
Community College

James Swofford, University of South
Alabama

Vera Tabakova, East Carolina University

Emily Tang, University of California, San
Diego

Mark Tendall, Stanford University

Jennifer Thacher, University of New Mexico

Charles Thomas, Clemson University

Rebecca Thornton, University of Houston

Jill Trask, Tarrant County College,
Southeast

Steve Trost, Virginia Polytechnic Institute
and State University

Ty Turley, Brigham Young University

Nora Underwood, University of Central
Florida

Mike Urbancic, University of Oregon

Don Uy-Barreta, De Anza College

John Vahaly, University of Louisville

Ross Van Wassenhove, University of
Houston

Don Vandegrift, College of New Jersey

Nancy Virts, California State University,
Northridge

Cheryl Wachenheim, North Dakota State
College

Jeffrey Waddoups, University of Nevada,
Las Vegas

Donald Wargo, Temple University

Charles Wassell, Jr., Central Washington
University

Matthew Weinberg, Drexel University

Robert Whaples, Wake Forest University

Elizabeth Wheaton, Southern Methodist
University

Mark Wheeler, Western Michigan
University

Anne Williams, Gateway Community
College

Brock Williams, Metropolitan Community
College of Omaha

DeEdgra Williams, Florida A&M
University

Brooks Wilson, McLennan Community
College

Mark Witte, Northwestern University

Katherine Wolfe, University of Pittsburgh

William Wood, James Madison University

Steven Yamarik, California State University,
Long Beach

Bill Yang, Georgia Southern University

Young-Ro Yoon, Wayne State University

Madelyn Young, Converse College

Michael Youngblood, Rock Valley College

Jeffrey Zax, University of Colorado,
Boulder

Martin Zelder, Northwestern University

Erik Zemljic, Kent State University

Kevin Zhang, Illinois State University

Macroeconomics: Flexibility Chart

Core Approach	Emphasis on Long-Run Growth	Emphasis on International
Chapter 1: The Principles and Practice of Economics	**Chapter 1:** The Principles and Practice of Economics	**Chapter 1:** The Principles and Practice of Economics
Chapter 2: Economic Methods and Economic Questions (optional)	**Chapter 2:** Economic Methods and Economic Questions (optional)	**Chapter 2:** Economic Methods and Economic Questions (optional)
Chapter 3: Optimization: Doing the Best You Can (optional)	**Chapter 3:** Optimization: Doing the Best You Can (optional)	**Chapter 3:** Optimization: Doing the Best You Can (optional)
Chapter 4: Demand, Supply, and Equilibrium	**Chapter 4:** Demand, Supply, and Equilibrium	**Chapter 4:** Demand, Supply, and Equilibrium
Chapter 5: The Wealth of Nations: Defining and Measuring Macroeconomic Aggregates	**Chapter 5:** The Wealth of Nations: Defining and Measuring Macroeconomic Aggregates	**Chapter 5:** The Wealth of Nations: Defining and Measuring Macroeconomic Aggregates
Chapter 6: Aggregate Incomes	**Chapter 6:** Aggregate Incomes	**Chapter 6:** Aggregate Incomes
Chapter 7: Economic Growth	**Chapter 7:** Economic Growth	**Chapter 7:** Economic Growth
Chapter 8: Why Isn't the Whole World Developed? (optional)	**Chapter 8:** Why Isn't the Whole World Developed?	**Chapter 8:** Why Isn't the Whole World Developed? (optional)
Chapter 9: Employment and Unemployment	**Chapter 9:** Employment and Unemployment	**Chapter 9:** Employment and Unemployment
Chapter 10: Credit Markets	**Chapter 10:** Credit Markets	**Chapter 10:** Credit Markets
Chapter 11: The Monetary System	**Chapter 11:** The Monetary System	**Chapter 11:** The Monetary System
Chapter 12: Short-Run Fluctuations	**Chapter 12:** Short-Run Fluctuations	**Chapter 12:** Short-Run Fluctuations
Chapter 13: Countercyclical Macroeconomic Policy	**Chapter 13:** Countercyclical Macroeconomic Policy	**Chapter 13:** Countercyclical Macroeconomic Policy
Chapter 14: Macroeconomics and International Trade (optional)	**Chapter 14:** Macroeconomics and International Trade (optional)	**Chapter 14:** Macroeconomics and International Trade
Chapter 15: Open Economy Macroeconomics (optional)	**Chapter 15:** Open Economy Macroeconomics (optional)	**Chapter 15:** Open Economy Macroeconomics

1

The Principles and Practice of Economics

Is Facebook free?

Facebook doesn't charge you a penny, so it's tempting to say, "it's free."

Here's another way to think about it. What do you give up when you use Facebook? That's a different kind of question. Facebook doesn't take your money, but it does take your time. If you spend an hour each day on Facebook, you are giving up some alternative use of that time. You could spend that time playing soccer, watching Hulu videos, napping, daydreaming, or listening to music. There are many ways to use your time. For example, a typical U.S. college student employed 7 hours per week earns almost $4,000 in a year—enough to pay the annual lease on a sports car. A part-time job is just one alternative way to use the time that you spend on Facebook. In your view, what is the best alternative use of your Facebook time? That's the economic way of thinking about the cost of Facebook.

In this chapter, we introduce you to the economic way of thinking about the world. Economists study the choices that people make, especially the costs and benefits of those choices, even the costs and the benefits of Facebook.

CHAPTER OUTLINE

1.1	1.2	1.3	EBE	1.4	1.5	1.6
The Scope of Economics	Three Principles of Economics	The First Principle of Economics: Optimization	Is Facebook free?	The Second Principle of Economics: Equilibrium	The Third Principle of Economics: Empiricism	Is Economics Good for You?

⚙ Economics is the study of people's choices.

⚙ The first principle of economics is that people try to *optimize*: they try to choose the best available option.

⚙ The second principle of economics is that economic systems tend to be in *equilibrium*, a situation in which nobody would benefit by changing his or her own behavior.

⚙ The third principle of economics is *empiricism*—analysis that uses data. Economists use data to test theories and to determine what is causing things to happen in the world.

1.1 The Scope of Economics

Choice—not money—is the unifying feature of all the things that economists study.

Most people are surprised to learn how much ground economics covers. Economists study *all* human behavior, from a person's decision to lease a new sports car, to the speed the new driver chooses as she rounds a hairpin corner, to her decision not to wear a seat belt. These are all choices, and they are all fair game to economists. And they are not all directly related to money. Choice—not money—is the unifying feature of all the things that economists study.

In fact, economists think of almost all human behavior as the outcome of choices. For instance, imagine that Dad tells his teenage daughter that she *must* wash the family car. Though it may not be obvious, the daughter has several options: she can wash it, she can negotiate for an easier chore, she can refuse to wash it and suffer the consequences, or she can move out (admittedly, a drastic response, but still a choice). Obeying one's parents is a choice, though it may not always feel like one.

Economic Agents and Economic Resources

Saying that economics is all about choices is an easy way to remember what economics is. To give you a more precise definition, we first need to introduce two important concepts: *economic agents* and *resource allocation*.

An **economic agent** is an individual or a group that makes choices.

An **economic agent** is an individual or a group that makes choices. Let's start with a few types of individual economic agents. For example, a *consumer* chooses to eat bacon cheeseburgers *or* tofu burgers. A *parent* chooses to enroll her children in public school *or* private school. A *student* chooses to attend his classes *or* to skip them. A *citizen* chooses whether *or* not to vote, and if so, which candidate to support. A *worker* chooses to do her job *or* pretend to work while texting. A *criminal* chooses to hotwire cars *or* mug little old ladies. A *business leader* chooses to open a new factory in Chile *or* China. A *senator* chooses to vote for *or* against a bill. Of course, you are also an economic agent because you make an enormous number of choices every day.

Not all economic agents, however, are individuals. An economic agent can also be a group—a government, an army, a firm, a university, a political party, a labor union, a sports team, a street gang. Sometimes economists simplify their analysis by treating these groups as a single decision maker, without worrying about the details of how the different individuals in the group contributed to the decision. For example, an economist might say that Apple prices the iPhone to maximize its profits, glossing over the fact that hundreds of executives participated in the analysis that led to the choice of the price.

1.1

1.2

1.3

1.4

1.5

1.6

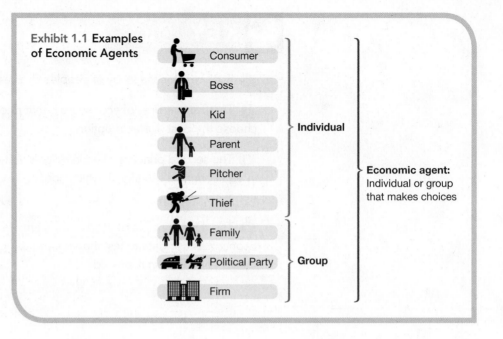

Exhibit 1.1 **Examples of Economic Agents**

Scarce resources are things that people want, where the quantity that people want exceeds the quantity that is available.

Scarcity is the situation of having unlimited wants in a world of limited resources.

The second important concept to understand is that economics studies the allocation of *scarce resources*. **Scarce resources** are things that people want, where the quantity that people want exceeds the quantity that is available. Gold wedding bands, Shiatsu massages, Coach handbags, California peaches, iPhones, triple-chocolate-fudge ice cream, and rooms with a view are all scarce resources. And so are most ordinary things, like toilet paper, subway seats, and clean drinking water. **Scarcity** exists because people have unlimited wants in a world of limited resources. The world does not have enough resources to give everyone *everything* they want. Consider sports cars. If sports cars were given away for free, there would not be enough of them to go around. Instead, sports cars are sold to the consumers who are willing to pay for them.

The existence of a marketplace for sports cars gives economic agents lots of choices. You have 24 hours to allocate each day—this is your daily budget of time. You choose how many of those 24 hours you will allocate to Facebook. You choose how many of those 24 hours you will allocate to other activities, including a job. If you have a job, you also choose whether to spend your hard-earned wages on a sports car. These kinds of decisions determine how scarce sports cars are allocated in a modern economy: to the consumers who are able and willing to pay for them.

Economists don't want to impose our tastes for sports cars, hybrids, electric vehicles, SUVs, or public transportation on you. We are interested in teaching you how to use economic reasoning so that *you* can compare the costs and benefits of the alternative options and make the choices that are best for you.

Definition of Economics

Economics is the study of how agents choose to allocate scarce resources and how those choices affect society.

We are now ready to define economics precisely. **Economics** is the study of how agents choose to allocate scarce resources and how those choices affect society.

As you might have expected, this definition emphasizes *choices*. The definition also takes into account how these choices affect society. For example, the sale of a new sports car doesn't just affect the person driving off the dealer's lot. The sale generates sales tax, which is collected by the government, which in turn funds projects like highways and hospitals. The purchase of the new car also generates some congestion—that's one more car in rush-hour gridlock. And it's another car that might grab the last parking spot on your street. If the new owner drives recklessly, the car may also generate risks to other drivers. The car will also be a source of pollution. Economists study the original choice and its multiple consequences for other people in the world.

Economics is the study of choice.

Positive economics is analysis that generates objective descriptions or predictions about the world that can be verified with data.

Normative economics is analysis that prescribes what an individual or society ought to do.

1.1

1.2

1.3

1.4

1.5

1.6

Positive Economics and Normative Economics

We now have an idea of what economics is about: people's choices. But what is the reason for studying choices? Part of the answer is that economists are just curious, but that's only a small part of the picture. Understanding people's choices is practically useful for two key reasons. Economic analysis:

1. Describes what people *actually* do (positive economics).
2. Recommends what people *ought* to do (normative economics).

The first application is descriptive and the second is advisory.

Positive Economics Describes What People Actually Do Descriptions of what people actually do are *objective* statements about the world. Such factual statements can be confirmed or tested with data. For instance, it is a fact that in 2010, 50 percent of U.S. households earned less than $52,000 per year. Describing what has happened or predicting what will happen is referred to as **positive economics** or positive economic analysis.

For instance, consider the prediction that in 2020 U.S. households will save about 5 percent of their income. This forecast can be compared to future data and either confirmed or disproven. Because a prediction is ultimately testable, it is part of positive economics.

Normative Economics Recommends What People Ought to Do **Normative economics**, the second of the two types of economic analysis, advises individuals and society on their choices. Normative economics is about what people ought to do. Normative economics is almost always dependent on *subjective* judgments, which means that normative analysis depends at least in part on personal feelings, tastes, or opinions. So whose subjective judgments do we try to use? Economists believe that the person being advised should determine the preferences to be used.

For example, if an economist were helping a worker to decide how much to save for retirement, the economist would first ask the worker about her own preferences. Suppose the worker expressed a high degree of patience—"I want to save enough so I can maintain my level of expenditure when I retire." In this case, the economist would recommend a saving rate that achieves the worker's desire for steady consumption throughout her life—about 10 to 15 percent of income for most middle-income families. Here the economist plays the role of engineer, finding the saving rate that will deliver the future level of retirement spending that the worker wants.

The economist does not tell the worker what degree of patience to have. Instead, the economist asks the worker about her preferences and then recommends a saving rate that is best for the worker given her preferences. In the mind of most economists, it is legitimate for the worker to choose any saving rate, as long as she understands the implications of that saving rate for expenditure after retirement.

Normative Analysis and Public Policy Normative analysis also generates advice to society in general. For example, economists are often asked to evaluate public policies, like taxes or regulations. When public policies have winners and losers, citizens tend to have opposing views about the desirability of the government program. One person's migratory bird sanctuary is another person's mosquito-infested swamp. Protecting a wetland with environmental regulations benefits bird-watchers but harms landowners who plan to develop that land.

When a government policy has winners and losers, economists will need to make some ethical judgments to conduct normative analysis. Economists must make ethical judgments whenever we evaluate policies that make one group worse off so another group can be made better off.

Ethical judgments are usually unavoidable when economists think about government policies, because there are very few policies that make everyone better off. Deciding whether the costs experienced by the losers are justified by the benefits experienced by the winners is partly an ethical judgment. Is it ethical to create environmental regulations that prevent a real estate developer from draining a swamp so he can build new homes? What if

1.1

1.2

1.3

1.4

1.5

1.6

Economic agents have divergent views on the future of this swamp. The owner of the property wants to build housing units. An environmentalist wants to preserve the wetland to protect the whooping crane, an endangered species. What should happen?

Microeconomics is the study of how individuals, households, firms, and governments make choices, and how those choices affect prices, the allocation of resources, and the well-being of other agents.

Macroeconomics is the study of the economy as a whole. Macroeconomists study economy-wide phenomena, like the growth rate of a country's total economic output, the inflation rate, or the unemployment rate.

Trying to choose the best feasible option, given the available information, is **optimization.**

those environmental regulations protect migratory birds that other people value? Are there other solutions to this seemingly unresolvable problem? Should the government try to buy the land from the real estate developer? And if land purchasing is the government's policy, how should society determine the price that the government offers the developer? Should the developer be forced to sell at that price? These public policy questions—which all ask what society *should* do—are normative economic questions.

Microeconomics and Macroeconomics

There is one other distinction that you need to know to understand the scope of economics. Economics can be divided into two broad fields of study, though many economists do a bit of both.

Microeconomics is the study of how individuals, households, firms, and governments make choices, and how those choices affect prices, the allocation of resources, and the well-being of other agents. For example, microeconomists design policies that reduce pollution. Because global warming is partially caused by carbon emissions from coal, oil, and other fossil fuels, microeconomists design policies to reduce the use of these fuels. For example, a "carbon tax" targets carbon emissions. Under a carbon tax, relatively carbon-intensive energy sources—like coal power plants—pay more tax per unit of energy produced than energy sources with lower carbon emissions—like wind farms. Microeconomists have the job of designing carbon taxes and determining how such taxes will affect the energy usage of households and firms. In general, microeconomists are called upon whenever we want to understand a small piece of the overall economy.

Macroeconomics is the study of the economy as a whole. Macroeconomists study economy-wide phenomena, like the growth rate of a country's total economic output, or the percentage increase in overall prices (the inflation rate), or the fraction of the labor force that is looking for work but cannot find a job (the unemployment rate). Macroeconomists design government policies that improve overall, or "aggregate," economic performance.

For example, macroeconomists try to identify the best policies for stimulating an economy that is experiencing a sustained period of negative growth—in other words, an economy in recession. During the 2007–2009 financial crisis, when housing prices were plummeting and banks were failing, macroeconomists had their hands full. It was their job to explain why the economy was contracting and to recommend policies that would bring it back to life.

1.2 | Three Principles of Economics

You now have a sense of what economics is about. But you might be wondering what distinguishes it from the other social sciences, including, anthropology, history, political science, psychology, and sociology. All of the social sciences study human behavior, so what sets economics apart?

Economists emphasize three key concepts.

1. Optimization: We have explained economics as the study of people's choices. The study of all human choices may initially seem like an impossibly huge topic. And at first glance, choosing a double-bacon cheeseburger at McDonalds does not appear to have much in common with a corporate executive's decision to build a $500 million laptop factory in China. Economists have identified some powerful concepts that unify the enormous range of choices that economic agents make. One such insight is that all choices are tied together by *optimization*: people decide what to do by consciously or unconsciously weighing all of the known pros and cons of the different available options and trying to pick the best feasible option. In other words, people make choices that are motivated by calculations of benefits and costs.

1.1

1.2

1.3

1.4

1.5

1.6

Optimization is the first principle of economics. Economists believe that optimization explains most of our choices, including minor decisions like accepting an invitation to see a movie, and major decisions like deciding whom to marry.

2. Equilibrium: The second principle of economics holds that economic systems tend to be in *equilibrium*, a situation in which no agent would benefit personally by changing his or her own behavior. The economic system is in equilibrium when each agent feels that he or she cannot do any better by picking another course of action. In other words, equilibrium is a situation in which everyone is simultaneously optimizing.

3. Empiricism: The third principle of economics is an emphasis on *empiricism*—analysis that uses data or analysis that is evidence-based. Economists use data to test theories and to determine what is causing things to happen in the world.

1.3 The First Principle of Economics: Optimization

Let's now consider our first principle in more detail. Economics is the study of choices, and economists have a theory about how choices are made. Economists believe that economic agents try to optimize, meaning that economic agents try to choose the best feasible option, given the information that they have. Feasible options are those that are available and affordable to an economic agent. If you have $10 in your wallet and no credit/debit/ATM cards, then a $5 Big Mac is a feasible lunch option, while a $50 filet mignon is not.

The concept of feasibility goes beyond the financial budget of the agent. There are many different constraints that determine what is feasible. For instance, it is not feasible to work more than 24 hours in a day. It is not feasible to attend meetings (in person) in New York and Beijing at the same time.

The definition of optimization also refers to the information available at the time of the choice. For example, if you choose to drive from San Diego to Los Angeles and your car is hit by a drunk driver, you are unlucky but you haven't necessarily failed to optimize. As long as you made your travel plans taking into account the realistic risk of a car crash, then you have optimized. Optimization means that we weigh the potential risks in a decision, not that we perfectly foresee the future. When someone chooses the best feasible option given the information that is available, economists say that the decision maker is being rational or, equivalently, he or she is exhibiting rationality. Rational action does not require a crystal ball, just a logical appraisal of the costs, benefits, and risks associated with each decision.

On the other hand, if you decide to let a friend drive you from San Diego to Los Angeles and you know that your friend has just had a few beers, this is probably a case in which you failed to optimize. It is important to note that the test of optimization is the quality of your decision, and not the outcome. If you arrive at your destination without a crash, that would still (probably) be a suboptimal choice, because you got lucky despite making a bad decision.

We devote much of this book to the analysis of optimization. We explain how to optimize, and we discuss lots of evidence that supports the theory that economic agents usually optimize. We also discuss important cases where behavior deviates from optimization. In the cases where agents fail to optimize, normative economic analysis can help them realize their mistakes and make better choices in the future.

Finally, it is important to note that *what* we optimize varies from person to person and group to group. Although most firms try to maximize profits, most economic agents are not trying to maximize only income. If that were our goal, we'd all work far more than 40 hours per week and we'd keep working well past retirement age. Most households are trying to optimize overall well-being, which requires income, leisure, health, and a host of other factors (like social networks and a sense of purpose in life). Most governments are trying to optimize a complex mix of policy goals. For most economic agents, optimization is not just about how much money we have.

Trade-offs and Budget Constraints

An economic agent faces a **trade-off** when the agent needs to give up one thing to get something else.

A **budget constraint** shows the bundles of goods or services that a consumer can choose given her limited budget.

To understand optimization, you need to understand trade-offs. **Trade-offs** arise when some benefits must be given up in order to gain others. Think about Facebook. If you spend an hour on Facebook, then you cannot spend that hour doing other things. For example, you cannot work at most part-time jobs at the same time you are editing your Facebook profile.

Economists use budget constraints to describe trade-offs. A **budget constraint** is the set of things that a person can choose to do (or buy) without breaking her budget.

Here's an illustration. Suppose that you can do only one of two activities with your free time: work at a part-time job or surf the Web. Suppose that you have 5 free hours in a day (once we take away necessities like sleeping, eating, bathing, attending classes, doing problem sets, and studying for exams). Think of these 5 free hours as your budget of free time. Then your budget constraint would be:

$$5 \text{ hours} = \boxed{\text{Hours surfing the Web}} + \boxed{\text{Hours working at part-time job.}}$$

This budget constraint equation implies that you face a trade-off. If you spend an extra hour surfing the Web, you need to spend one less hour working at a part-time job. Likewise, if you spend an extra hour working at the part-time job, you need to spend one less hour surfing the Web. More of one activity implies less of the other. We can see this in Exhibit 1.2, where we list all of the ways that you could allocate your 5 free hours.

Budget constraints are useful economic tools because they quantify trade-offs. When economists talk about the choice that an economic agent faces, the economist first specifies the budget constraint.

Opportunity Cost

We are now ready to introduce another critical tool in the optimization toolbox: opportunity cost. Our Web surfing example provides an illustration of the concept. The time that we spend on the Web is time that we could have spent in some other way: playing basketball, jogging, daydreaming, sleeping, calling a friend, catching up on e-mail, working on a problem set, working at a part-time job, and so on. You implicitly sacrifice time on these alternative activities when you spend time surfing the Web (unless you secretly use Facebook while you are being paid for a job—in this case, please keep your boss off your friend list).

Try generating your own list of alternative activities that are squeezed out when you surf the Web. Think about the best alternative to Web surfing, and put that at the top; then work down from there. Your list illustrates the concept of opportunity cost; you can either spend

Exhibit 1.2 Possible Allocations of 5 Free Hours (Round Numbers Only)

Each row reports a different way that a person could allocate 5 free hours, assuming that the time must be divided between surfing the Web and working at a part-time job. To keep things simple, the table only reports allocations in round numbers.

Budget	Hours Surfing the Web	Hours at Part-Time Job
5 hours	0 hours	5 hours
5 hours	1 hours	4 hours
5 hours	2 hours	3 hours
5 hours	3 hours	2 hours
5 hours	4 hours	1 hours
5 hours	5 hours	0 hours

a specific hour of your day surfing the Web or on some other activity. In most situations you can't simultaneously do both.

Evaluating trade-offs like this can be difficult because so many options are under consideration. Economists tend to focus on the best alternative activity. We refer to this best alternative activity as the **opportunity cost**. This is what an optimizer is effectively giving up when she surfs the Web.

The importance of opportunity cost is clear once we remember that resources are limited, or scarce. Whenever we do one thing, something else gets squeezed out. When you surf the Web for an hour, some other activity is reduced by an hour, though you may not think about it at the time. You can't write a term paper and update your Facebook page at the same time. Even if you only *postpone* the term paper, something else has got to give when that postponed time comes up. (Studying for the economics final?) Optimization requires that you take account of the opportunity cost of whatever you are doing. In essence, an optimizer always considers how else she could be using her limited resources.

Here's another example to drive home the concept. Assume that your family is taking a vacation over spring break. Your choices are a Caribbean cruise, a trip to Miami, or a trip to Los Angeles. (Assume that they all have the same monetary cost and use the same amount of time.) If your first choice is the cruise and your *second* choice is Miami, then your opportunity cost of taking the cruise is the Miami trip.

The concept of opportunity cost applies to all resources, not just your time budget of 24 hours each day. Suppose that a woodworker has a beautiful piece of maple that can be used to make a sculpture, or a bowl, or a picture frame. (Assume that they all use the same amount of wood and take the same amount of time.) If the woodworker's first choice is the sculpture and the *second* choice is the bowl, then the bowl is the opportunity cost of making the sculpture.

Assigning a Monetary Value to an Opportunity Cost Economists sometimes try to put a monetary value on opportunity cost. Translating benefits and costs into monetary units, like dollars or yen, makes everything easier to analyze. One way to estimate the monetary value of an hour of your time is to analyze the consequences of taking a part-time job or working additional hours at the part-time job you already have.

The opportunity cost of your time is at least the net benefit that you would receive from a job (assuming that you can find one that fits your schedule). Here's why. A part-time job is one item in the long list of alternatives to surfing the Web. If the part-time job is at the top of your list, then it's the best alternative, and the part-time job is your opportunity cost of surfing the Web. What if the part-time job is not at the top of your list, so it's not the best alternative? Then the best alternative is even better than the part-time job, so the best alternative is worth more than the part-time job. To sum up, your opportunity cost is either the net benefit of a part-time job or a value that is even greater than that.

To turn these insights into something quantitative, it helps to note that the median wage for U.S. workers between 16 and 24 years of age was $11.35 per hour in 2013—this data is from the U.S. Bureau of Labor Statistics. However, a job has many attributes *other* than the wage you are paid: unpleasant tasks (like being nice to obnoxious customers), on-the-job training, friendly or unfriendly coworkers, and resumé building, just to name a few.

If we ignore these non-wage attributes, the benefit of an hour of work is just the wage (minus taxes paid). On the other hand, if the positive and negative non-wage attributes don't cross each other out, the calculation is much harder. To keep things simple, we'll focus only on the after-tax wage in the analysis that follows—about $10 per hour for young workers—but we urge you to keep in mind all of the non-wage consequences that flow from a job.

Cost-Benefit Analysis

Let's use opportunity cost to solve an optimization problem. Specifically, we want to compare a set of feasible alternatives and pick the best one. Economists call this process *cost-benefit analysis*. **Cost-benefit analysis** is a calculation that adds up costs and benefits using a common unit of measurement, like dollars. It is used to identify the alternative that has the greatest net benefit, which is equivalent to benefits minus costs.

Opportunity cost is the best alternative use of a resource.

Cost-benefit analysis is a calculation that adds up costs and benefits using a common unit of measurement, like dollars.

To see these ideas in action, suppose that you and a friend are going to Miami Beach from Boston for spring break. The only question is whether you should drive or fly. Your friend argues that you should drive because splitting the cost of a rental car and gas "will only cost $200 each." He tries to seal the deal by pointing out "that's much better than a $300 plane ticket."

To analyze this problem using cost-benefit analysis, you need to list all of the costs and benefits of driving relative to the alternative of flying. You then need to translate those costs and benefits into a common unit of measurement.

From a benefit perspective, driving saves you $100—the difference between driving expenses of $200 and a plane ticket of $300. From a cost perspective, driving costs you an extra 40 hours of time—the difference between 50 hours of round-trip driving time and about 10 hours of round-trip airport/flying time. Spending 40 extra hours traveling is a cost of driving.

But we still don't know whether driving is a good idea or a bad idea, because we haven't yet expressed everything in common units. Suppose the opportunity cost of your time is $10 per hour (slightly below the median wage for U.S. workers between ages 16 and 24). This is the value of your time. Then the net benefit of driving relative to flying is

$$(\$100 \text{ Cost saving}) - (40 \text{ Hours of additional travel time}) \times (\$10/\text{hour})$$
$$= \$100 - \$400 = -\$300.$$

Hence, the net benefit of driving is overwhelmingly negative. An optimizer would choose to fly.

Your decision about travel to Miami is a simple example of cost-benefit analysis, which is a great tool for collapsing all sorts of things down to a net dollar benefit. This book will guide you in making such calculations. If you are making choices as to which house to buy, which job to take, or whether Medicare should pay for heart transplants, cost-benefit analysis can help. Economists are not popular for making some of these "cold-hearted" calculations, but it's nonetheless useful to be able to quantitatively analyze difficult decisions.

To an economist, cost-benefit analysis and optimization are the same thing. When you pick the option with the greatest net benefits—benefits minus costs—you are optimizing. So cost-benefit analysis is useful for *normative* economic analysis. It enables an economist to determine what an individual or a society should do. Cost-benefit analysis also yields many useful positive economic insights. In most cases, cost-benefit analysis correctly predicts the choices made by actual consumers.

Evidence-Based Economics

Q: Is Facebook free?

We can now turn to the question we posed at the beginning of the chapter. By now you know that Facebook has an opportunity cost—the best alternative use of your time. We will now estimate this cost. To do this, we're going to need some data. Whenever you see a section in this textbook titled "Evidence-Based Economics," you'll know that we are using data to analyze an economic question.

In 2013, Web users worldwide spent 250 million hours on Facebook each day. On a per person basis, each of the nearly 1 billion Facebook users allocated an average of 15 minutes per day to the site. College students used Facebook more intensively. The average college student spent about an hour per day on Facebook.

1.1

1.2

1.3

1.4

1.5

1.6

We estimate that the time spent worldwide on Facebook has an *average* opportunity cost of $5 per hour. We generated this estimate with a back-of-the-envelope—in other words, approximate—calculation that averages together every Facebook user's opportunity cost.

Here's how we did the calculation. First, we assume that users in the developed world—which represents wealthy countries such as France, Japan, and the United States—have an opportunity cost of $9 per hour, which is a typical minimum wage in a developed country. Employers are legally required to pay at least the minimum wage, and most workers in developed countries get paid much more than this. Even people who choose not to work still value their time, since it can be used for lots of good things like napping, texting, dating, studying, playing angry birds, and watching movies. It's reasonable to guess that these nonworkers—for instance, students—will also have an opportunity cost of at least the minimum wage.

Second, we assume that Facebook users in the developing world—which represents all countries, except the developed countries—have a relatively lower opportunity cost of time. We assume that Facebook users in the developing countries have an opportunity cost of $1 per hour—for instance, their employment opportunities are far less favorable than those in the developed world.

To evaluate the reasonableness of these estimates, ask yourself this question: "How much would someone need to pay *you* to take away an hour of your free time?" Does your answer correspond more closely to our estimate for the developed world ($9/hour) or the developing world ($1/hour)?

About half of Facebook users live in developed countries and half live in developing countries, so, given our assumptions, the average opportunity cost is $(1/2) \times \$9 + (1/2) \times \$1 = \$5$ per hour. Accordingly, the *total* opportunity cost of time spent on Facebook is calculated by multiplying the total number of hours spent on Facebook each day, by the average opportunity cost of time per hour:

$$\left(\frac{250 \text{ million hours}}{\text{day}} \right) \left(\frac{\$5}{\text{hour}} \right) = \left(\frac{\$1.25 \text{ billion}}{\text{day}} \right).$$

Multiplying this by 365 days per year yields an annualized opportunity cost of over $450 billion. This is an estimate of the cost of Facebook. As you have seen, this is only a crude approximation, since we can't directly observe the opportunity cost of each person's time.

We can also think about this calculation another way. If people had substituted their time on Facebook for work with average pay of $5 per hour, the world economy would have produced about $450 billion more measured output in 2013. This is more than the annual economic output of Austria.

Finally, we can also estimate the opportunity cost of a typical U.S. college student who spends 1 hour per day on Facebook. Assuming that this student's opportunity cost is equal to $10 per hour, the opportunity cost is $3,650 per year.

$$(\$10/\text{hour}) \times (365 \text{ hours/year}) = \$3,650 \text{ per year.}$$

We chose $10 per hour for the opportunity cost, since the median before-tax wage of 16- to 24-year-old U.S. workers was $11.35 per hour in 2013, and such low-income workers don't pay much in taxes.

So far, we have gone through a purely positive economic analysis, describing the frequency of Facebook usage and the trade-offs that this usage implies. None of this analysis, however, answers the related question: Are Facebook and other social networking sites worth it? We've seen that the time spent on sites like these is costly because it has valuable alternative uses. But Facebook users are deriving substantial benefits that may justify this allocation of time. For example, social networking sites keep us up-to-date

Exhibit 1.3 What Could You Buy with $3,650?

Everyone would choose to spend $3,650 in their own particular way. This list illustrates one feasible basket of goods and services. Note that this list includes just the monetary costs. A complete economic analysis would also include the opportunity cost of the time that you'll need to consume them.

	Cost per unit	Number of units	Total cost
Starbucks cappuccino	$4	52 cups	$208
iPhone	$400	1	$400
Roundtrip: NYC to Paris	$1,000	1	$1,000
Hotel in Paris	$250	4 nights	$1,000
Roundtrip: NYC to U.S. Virgin Islands	$300	1	$300
Hotel in Virgin Islands	$180	4 nights	$720
11 iPhone apps	$2	11	$22
Total			**$3,650**

on the activities of our friends and family. They facilitate the formation of new friendships and new connections. And Facebook and similar sites are entertaining.

Because we cannot easily quantify these benefits, we're going to leave that analysis to you. Economists won't tell you what to do, but we will help you identify the trade-offs that you are making in your decisions. Here is how an economist would summarize the normative question that is on the table:

> *Assuming a $10 per hour opportunity cost, the opportunity cost of using Facebook for an hour per day is $3,650 per year. Do you receive benefits from Facebook that exceed this opportunity cost?*

Economists don't want to impose their tastes on other people. In the view of an economist, people who get big benefits from intensive use of Facebook should stay the course. Economists don't want to dictate choices. Instead, we want economic agents to recognize the implicit trade-offs that are being made. Economists are interested in helping people make the best use of scarce resources like budgets of money and time. In many circumstances, people are already putting their resources to best use. Occasionally, however, economic reasoning can help people make better choices.

Question

Is Facebook free?

Answer

No. The opportunity cost of Facebook was $450 billion dollars in 2013.

Data

Facebook usage statistics provided by Facebook.

Caveat

We can only crudely estimate opportunity cost for Facebook's 1 billion worldwide users.

1.4 The Second Principle of Economics: Equilibrium

1.1

1.2

1.3

1.4

1.5

1.6

In most economic situations, you aren't the only one trying to optimize. Other people's behavior will influence what you decide to do. Economists think of the world as a group of economic agents who are interacting and influencing one another's efforts at optimization. Recall that *equilibrium* is the special situation in which everyone is optimizing, so nobody would benefit personally by changing his or her own behavior.

An important clarification needs to accompany this definition. When we say that nobody would benefit personally by changing his or her own behavior, we mean that nobody *believes* they would benefit from such a change. In equilibrium, all economic agents are making their best feasible choices taking into account all of the information they have, including their beliefs about the behavior of others. We could rewrite the definition by saying that in equilibrium, nobody *perceives* that they will benefit from changing their own behavior.

To build intuition—which means understanding—for the concept of equilibrium, consider the length of the regular checkout lines at your local supermarket (ignore the express lines). If any line has a shorter wait than the others, optimizers will choose that line. If any line has a longer wait than the others, optimizers will avoid that line. So the short lines will attract shoppers, and the long lines will drive them away. And it's not just the length of the lines that matters. You pick your line by estimating which line will move the fastest, which incorporates every-

In equilibrium

In equilibrium, everyone is simultaneously optimizing, so nobody would benefit by changing his or her own behavior.

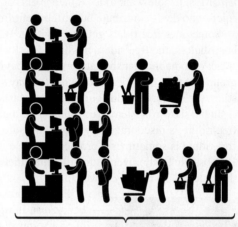

Out of equilibrium

thing that you can see, including the number of items in each person's shopping cart. Economists say that "in equilibrium" all of the checkout lines will have roughly the same wait time. When the wait times are expected to be the same, no shopper has an incentive to switch lines. In other words, nobody perceives that they will benefit by changing their behavior.

Here's another example. Suppose the market price of gasoline is $3/gallon and the gasoline market is in equilibrium. Three conditions will need to be satisfied.

1. The amount of gasoline produced by gasoline sellers—oil companies—will equal the amount of gasoline purchased by buyers.
2. Oil companies will only operate wells where they can extract oil and produce gasoline at a cost that is less than the market price of gasoline: $3/gallon.
3. The buyers of gasoline will only use it for activities that are worth at least $3/gallon—like driving to their best friend's wedding—and they won't use it for activities that are worth less than $3/gallon—like visiting their least favorite relatives. When gas prices go up, who in the family can't make it for Thanksgiving?

In equilibrium, both the sellers and the buyers of gasoline are optimizing, given the market price of gasoline. Nobody would benefit by changing his or her behavior.

In this book, we often study the behavior of groups of economic agents. A group could be 2 chess players; or 30 participants in an eBay auction; or millions of investors buying and selling shares on the New York Stock Exchange; or billions of households buying gasoline to fuel their tractors, trucks, mopeds, motorcycles, and cars. In all these cases, we study the equilibrium that emerges when all of these economic agents interact. In other words, we examine these environments using the assumption that everyone is constantly simultaneously optimizing—for instance, at every move in a chess game and during every trade on the New York Stock Exchange. Economists believe that this equilibrium analysis provides a good description of what actually happens when groups of people interact.

The Free-Rider Problem

Let's use the concept of equilibrium to analyze an economic problem that may interest you: roommates. Assume that five roommates live in a rented house. The roommates can spend some of their free time contributing to the general well-being of the group by throwing away used pizza boxes and soda cans and otherwise cleaning up after themselves. Or they can spend all their free time on activities that only benefit themselves—for instance, watching YouTube videos or listening to Pandora.

It would be beneficial to the group if everyone chipped in and did a little cleaning. But each of the five roommates has an incentive to leave that to others. If one roommate spends 30 minutes doing the dishes, all the other roommates benefit without having to lift a finger. Consequently, rentals with lots of roommates are often a mess.

Lazy roommates are an example of something that economists call the *free-rider problem*. Most people want to let someone else do the dirty work. We would like to be the free riders who don't contribute but still benefit from the investments that others make.

Sometimes free riders get away with it. When there are very few free riders and lots of contributors, the free riders might be overlooked. For example, a small number of people sneak onto public transportation without paying. These turnstile jumpers are such a small group that they don't jeopardize the subway system. But if everyone started jumping turnstiles, the subway would soon run out of cash.

In the subway system, free riding is discouraged by security patrols. In rooming groups, free riding is discouraged by social pressure. Even with these "punishment" techniques, free riding is sometimes a problem because it's not easy to catch the free rider in the act. It's possible to slip over a turnstile in a quiet subway station. It's easy to leave crumbs on the couch when nobody is watching.

A free rider in the New York subway system. Are *you* paying for him to ride the subway?

People's private benefits are often out of sync with the public interest. Jumping the subway turnstile is cheaper than paying for a subway ticket. Watching YouTube is more fun than sweeping up the remains of last night's party. Equilibrium analysis helps us predict the behavior of groups of people and understand why free riding occurs. People sometimes pursue their own private interests and don't contribute *voluntarily* to the public interest. Unfortunately, selfless acts—like those of a war hero—are exceptional, and selfish acts are more common. When people in a group act, each member of the group might do what's best for himself or herself instead of acting in a way that optimizes the well-being of the entire group.

Equilibrium analysis helps us design special institutions—like financial contracts—that reduce or even eliminate free riding. For example, what would happen in the rooming group if everyone agreed to pay $5 per week so the roommates could hire a cleaning service? It would be easier to enforce $5 weekly payments than to monitor compliance with the rule "clean up after yourself, even when nobody is here to watch you." Pizza crumbs don't have name tags. So equilibrium analysis explains why individuals often fail to serve the interest of the group and how the incentive structure can be redesigned to fix these problems.

1.5 The Third Principle of Economics: Empiricism

Economists test their ideas with data. We call such evidence-based analysis, empirical analysis or *empiricism*. Economists use data to determine whether our theories about human behavior—like optimization and equilibrium—match up with *actual* human behavior.

1.1

1.2

1.3

1.4

1.5

1.6

Of course, we want to know if our theories fail to explain what is happening in the world. In that case, we need to go back to the drawing board and come up with better theories. That is how economic science, and science in general, progresses.

Economists are also interested in understanding what is *causing* things to happen in the world. We can illustrate what causation is—and is not—via a simple example. Hot days and crowded beaches tend to occur at the same time of the year. What is the cause and what is the effect here? It is, of course, that hot days *cause* people to go swimming. It is *not* that swimming *causes* the outside air temperature to rise.

But there are other cases when cause and effect are hard to untangle. Does being relatively smart cause people to go to college? Or does going to college cause people to be relatively smart? Or do both directions of causation apply?

We'll come back to the topic of empiricism in general, and causality in particular, in great detail in Chapter 2. Sometimes causes are easy to determine but sometimes identifying cause and effect requires great ingenuity.

1.6 Is Economics Good for You?

Is taking this course good for you? Let's start by thinking about the costs. Though opportunity costs are often hard to see, they are still important. The key opportunity cost of this course is another course that you won't be able to take during the time spent as a student. What other course did economics crowd out? Japanese history? Biochemistry? Russian poetry? If you are taking the two-semester version of this course, then you need to consider the two other courses that economics is crowding out.

Now consider the benefits of an economics education. The benefits come in a few different forms, but the biggest benefit is the ability to apply economic reasoning in your daily life. Whether you are deciding how much to spend on a date, where to go on vacation, or how to keep an apartment with four other roommates clean, economic reasoning will improve the quality of your decisions. These benefits will continue throughout your life as you make important decisions, such as where to invest your retirement savings and how to secure the best mortgage.

> Learning to make good choices is the biggest benefit you'll realize from learning economics.

Most decisions are guided by the logic of costs and benefits. Accordingly, you can use positive economic analysis to predict other people's behavior. Economics illuminates and clarifies all human behavior.

We also want you to use economic principles when you give other people advice and when you make your own choices. This is normative economics. Learning how to make good choices is the biggest benefit you'll realize from learning economics. That's why we have built our book around the concept of decision making. Looking at the world through the economic lens puts you at an enormous advantage throughout your life.

We also think that economics is a lot of fun. Understanding people's motivations is fascinating, particularly because there are many surprising insights along the way.

To realize these payoffs, you'll need to connect the ideas in this textbook to the economic activities around you. To make those connections, keep a few tips in mind:

- You can apply economic tools such as trade-offs and cost-benefit analysis to any economic decision. Learn to use them in your own daily decisions. This will help you master the tools and also appreciate their limitations.
- Even if you are not in the midst of making a decision, you will learn a lot of economics by keeping your eyes open when you walk through any environment in which people are using or exchanging resources. Think like an economist the next time you find yourself in a supermarket, a used car dealership, a soccer match, or a poker game.
- The easiest way to encounter economic ideas is to keep up with what's happening in the world. Go online and read a national newspaper like the *New York Times* or the *Wall Street Journal*. News magazines will also do the job. There's even a newsmagazine called *The Economist*, which is required reading for prime ministers

and presidents. Almost every page of any magazine—including *People*, *Sports Illustrated*, and *Vogue*—describes events driven by economic factors. Identifying and understanding these forces will be a challenge. But over time, you'll find that it gets very easy to recognize and interpret the economic story behind every headline.

Once you realize that you are constantly making economic choices, you'll understand that this course is only a first step. You'll discover the most important applications *outside* class and *after* the final exam. The tools of economics will improve your performance in all kinds of situations—making you a better businessperson, a better consumer, and a better citizen. Keep your eyes open and remember that every choice is economics in action.

Summary

✺ Economics is the study of how agents choose to allocate scarce resources and how those choices affect society. Economics can be divided into two kinds of analysis: positive economic analysis (what people actually do) and normative economic analysis (what people ought to do). There are two key topics within economics: microeconomics (individual decisions and individual markets) and macroeconomics (the total economy).

✺ Economics is based on three key principles: optimization, equilibrium, and empiricism.

✺ Choosing the best feasible option, given the available information, is optimization. To optimize, an economic agent needs to consider many issues, including trade-offs, budget constraints, opportunity costs, and cost-benefit analysis.

✺ Equilibrium is a situation in which nobody would benefit personally by changing his or her own behavior.

✺ Economists test their ideas with data. We call such evidence-based analysis empirical analysis or empiricism. Economists use data to determine whether our theories about human behavior—like optimization and equilibrium—match actual human behavior. Economists also use data to determine what is causing things to happen in the world.

Key Terms

economic agent *p. 3*
scarce resources *p. 4*
scarcity *p. 4*
economics *p. 4*
positive economics *p. 5*

normative economics *p. 5*
microeconomics *p. 6*
macroeconomics *p. 6*
optimization *p. 6*
equilibrium *p. 7*

empiricism *p. 7*
trade-off *p. 8*
budget constraint *p. 8*
opportunity cost *p. 9*
cost-benefit analysis *p. 9*

Questions

All questions are available in MyEconLab for practice and instructor assignment.

1. Why do we have to pay a price for most of the goods we consume?

2. Many people believe that the study of economics is focused on money and financial markets. Based on your reading of the chapter, how would you define economics?

3. Examine the following statements and determine if they are normative or positive in nature. Explain your answer.

   a. The U.S. automotive industry registered its highest growth rate in 5 years in 2012; U.S. auto sales increased by 13% compared to those in 2011.

   b. The U.S. government should increase carbon taxes to reduce carbon emissions that cause global warming.

4. How does microeconomics differ from macroeconomics? Would the supply of iPhones in the United States be studied under microeconomics or macroeconomics? What about the growth rate of total economic output in the national economy?

5. What does a budget constraint represent? How do budget constraints explain the trade-offs that consumers face?

6. This chapter introduced the idea of opportunity cost.

   a. What is meant by opportunity cost? How are the opportunity costs of various choices compared?

   b. What is the opportunity cost of taking a year after graduating from high school and backpacking across Europe? Are people who do so being irrational?

7. Suppose your New Year's resolution is to get back in shape. You are considering various ways of doing this: you can sign up for a gym membership, walk to work, take the stairs instead of the elevator, or watch your diet. How would you evaluate these options and choose an optimal one?

8. Suppose the market price of corn is $5.50 per bushel. What are the three conditions that will need to be satisfied for the corn market to be in equilibrium at this price?

9. Economists are often concerned with the free-rider problem.

   a. What is meant by free riding? Explain with an example.

   b. Are public parks subject to the free-rider problem? What about keeping city streets clean? Explain your answer.

10. Explain the concept of causation with the help of a simple real-life example.

11. Identify cause and effect in the following examples:

    a. Lower infant mortality and an improvement in nutrition

    b. A surge in cocoa prices and a pest attack on the cocoa crop that year

Problems

All problems are available in MyEconLab for practice and instructor assignment.

1. In an episode of the sitcom *Seinfeld,* Jerry and his friends Elaine and George are waiting to be seated at a Chinese restaurant. Tired of waiting, Elaine convinces the others that they should bribe the *maître d'* to get a table.

   a. What factors should they consider when they are deciding how high to make their bribe?

   b. Jerry, Elaine, and George had tickets for a movie after dinner. How would this have affected the amount that they were willing to pay as a bribe?

   c. The amount that they finally decide to pay is higher than the value of the meal that they would have had. Does this mean that they are being irrational?

   Adapted from: http://yadayadayadaecon.com/clip/10/

2. You are thinking about buying a house. You find one you like that costs $200,000. You learn that your bank will give you a mortgage for $160,000 and that you will have to use all of your savings to make the down payment of $40,000. You calculate that the mortgage payments, property taxes, insurance, maintenance, and utilities would total $950 per month. Is $950 the cost of owning the house?

   What important factor(s) have you left out of your calculation of the cost of ownership?

3. You have 40,000 frequent flier miles. You could exchange your miles for a round-trip ticket to Bermuda over spring break. Does that mean your flight to Bermuda would be free? Explain your reasoning.

4. You have decided that you are going to consume 600 calories of beer and snacks at a party Saturday night. A beer has 150 calories and a snack has 75 calories.

   a. Create a table that shows the various combinations of beer and snacks you can consume. To keep things simple, use only round numbers (e.g., you could choose 1 or 2 beers but not 1.5 beers).

   b. What is the opportunity cost of a beer?

5. There is an old saying that "The proof of the pudding is in the eating," which means that by definition good decisions work out well and poor decisions work out badly. The following scenarios ask you to consider the wisdom of this saying.

   a. Your friends live in a city where it often rains in May. Nonetheless, they plan a May outdoor wedding and have no backup plan if it does rain. The weather turns out to be lovely on their wedding day. Do you think your friends were being rational when they made their wedding plans? Explain.

b. You usually have to see a doctor several times each year. You decided to buy health insurance at the start of last year. It turns out you were never sick last year and never had to go the doctor. Do you think you were being rational when you decided to buy health insurance? Explain.

c. Given your answers to the first two parts of this question, do you agree or disagree that "The proof of the pudding is in the eating?" Explain.

6. Consider the following three statements:

i. You can either stand during a college football game or you can sit. You believe that you will see the game very well if you stand and others sit but that you will not be able to see at all if you sit and others stand. You therefore decide to stand.

ii. Your friend tells you that he expects many people to stand at football games.

iii. An economist studies photos of many college football games and estimates that 75 percent of all fans stand and 25 percent sit.

Which of these statements deals with optimization, which deals with equilibrium, and which deals with empiricism? Explain.

7. The costs of many environmental regulations can be calculated in dollars, but the benefits often are in terms of lives saved (mortality) or decreases in the incidence of a particular disease (morbidity). What does this imply about the cost-benefit analysis of environmental regulations? There is an old saying "You can't put a price on a human life." Do you agree or disagree? Explain.

8. This chapter discussed the free-rider problem. Consider the following two situations in relation to the free-rider concept.

a. The Taft-Hartley Act (1947) allows workers to be employed at a firm without joining the union at their workplace or paying membership fees to the union. This arrangement is known as an open shop. Considering that unions negotiate terms of employment and wages on behalf of all the workers at a firm, why do you think that most unions are opposed to open shops?

b. For your business communication class, you are supposed to work on a group assignment in a team of six. You soon realize that a few of your team members do not contribute to the assignment but get the same grade as the rest of the team. If you were the professor, how would you redesign the incentive structure here to fix this problem?

2 Economic Methods and Economic Questions

Is college worth it?

If you are reading this book, there is a good chance that you are either in college or thinking about taking the plunge. As you know, college is a big investment. Tuition averages almost $2,500 per year at community colleges, almost $5,000 per year at public colleges, and almost $25,000 per year at private colleges. And that's not the only cost. Your time, as we have seen, is worth $10 or more per hour—this time value adds at least $20,000 per year to the opportunity cost of a college education.

As with any other investment, you'd like to know how a college education is going to pay you back. What are the "returns to education," and how would you measure them? In this chapter you'll see that you can answer such questions with models and data.

CHAPTER **OUTLINE**

2.1	EBE	2.2	EBE	2.3
The Scientific Method	**How much more do workers with a college education earn?**	**Causation and Correlation**	**How much do wages increase when an individual is compelled by law to get an extra year of schooling?**	**Economic Questions and Answers**

KEY IDEAS

⚙ A model is a simplified description of reality.

⚙ Economists use data to evaluate the accuracy of models and understand how the world works.

⚙ Correlation does not imply causality.

⚙ Experiments help economists measure cause and effect.

⚙ Economic research focuses on questions that are important to society and can be answered with models and data.

2.1 The Scientific Method

The **scientific method** is the name for the ongoing process that economists and other scientists use to (1) develop models of the world and (2) test those models with data.

Recall that empiricism—using data to analyze the world—is the third key principle of economics. We explored the first two principles—optimization and equilibrium—in the previous chapter. Empiricism is the focus of this chapter.

Empiricism is at the heart of all scientific analysis. The **scientific method** is the name for the ongoing process that economists, other social scientists, and natural scientists use to:

1. Develop models of the world
2. Test those models with data—evaluating the match between the models and the data

Economists do not expect this process to reveal the "true" model of the world, since the world is vastly complex. However, economists do expect to identify models that are useful in understanding the world. Testing with data enables economists to separate the good models—those that approximately match the data—from the bad models. When a model is overwhelmingly inconsistent with the data, economists try to fix the model or replace it altogether. We believe that this process enables us to find more useful models that help to explain the past and to predict the future with some confidence. In this section, we explain what a model is and how a model can be tested with data.

Models and Data

A **model** is a simplified description, or representation, of the world. Sometimes, economists will refer to a model as a *theory*. These terms are often used interchangeably.

Everyone once believed that the earth was flat. We now know that it is more like a beach ball than a Frisbee. Yet the flat-earth model is still actively used. Go into a gas station and you'll find only flat road maps for sale. Consult your GPS receiver and you'll also see flat maps. Nobody keeps a globe in the glove compartment.

Flat maps and spherical globes are both models of the surface of the earth. A **model** is a simplified description, or representation, of the world. Because models are simplified, they are not perfect replicas of reality. Obviously, flat maps are not perfectly accurate models of the surface of the earth—they distort the curvature. If you are flying from New York to Tokyo, the curvature matters. But if you are touring around New York City, you don't need to worry about the fact that the earth is shaped like a sphere.

> **All scientific models make predictions that can be checked with data.**

Scientists—and commuters—use the model that is best suited to analyze the problem at hand. Even if a model/map is based on assumptions that are known to be false, like flatness of the earth, the model may still help us to make good predictions and good plans for the

Exhibit 2.1 Flying from New York to Tokyo Requires More Than a Flat Map

This flat map is a model of part of the earth's surface. It treats the world as perfectly flat, which leads the map maker to exaggerate distances in the northern latitudes. It is useful for certain purposes—for instance, learning geography. But you wouldn't want to use it to find the best air route across the Pacific Ocean. For example, the shortest flight path from New York to Tokyo is not a straight line through San Francisco. Instead, the shortest path goes through Northern Alaska! The flat-earth model is well suited for some tasks (geography lessons) and ill-suited for others (intercontinental flight navigation).

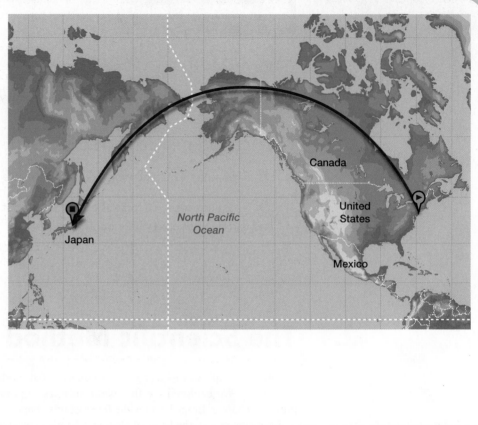

Exhibit 2.2 New York City Subway Map

This is a model of the subway system in New York City. It is highly simplified—for example, it treats New York City as a perfectly flat surface and it also distorts the shape of the city—but it is nevertheless very useful for commuters and tourists.

future. It is more important for a model to be simple and useful than it is for a model to be precisely accurate.

All scientific models make predictions that can be checked with **data**—facts, measurements, or statistics that describe the world. Recall from Chapter 1 that economists often describe themselves as empiricists, or say that we practice empiricism, because we use data

Data are facts, measurements, or statistics that describe the world.

Empirical evidence is a set of facts established by observation and measurement.

Hypotheses are predictions (typically generated by a model) that can be tested with data.

to create **empirical evidence**. These terms all boil down to the same basic idea: using data to answer questions about the world and using data to test models. For example, we could test the New York City subway map by actually riding the subway and checking the map's accuracy.

When conducting empirical analysis, economists refer to a model's predictions as **hypotheses**. Whenever such hypotheses are contradicted by the available data, economists return to the drawing board and try to come up with a better model that yields new hypotheses.

An Economic Model

Let's consider an example of an economic model. We're going to study an extremely simple model to get the ball rolling. But even economic models that are far more complicated than this example are also highly simplified descriptions of reality.

All economic models begin with assumptions. Consider the following assumption about the returns to education: *Investing in one extra year of education increases your future wages by 10 percent.* Let's put the assumption to work to generate a model that relates a person's level of education to her wages.

Increasing a wage by 10 percent is the same as multiplying the wage by $1 + 0.10 = 1.10$. The returns-to-education assumption implies that someone with an extra year of education earns 1.10 times as much as she would have earned without the extra year of education. For example, if someone would earn $15 per hour with 13 years of education, then a 14th year of education will cause her hourly wage to rise to $1.10 \times \$15$, or $16.50.

Economists use assumptions to derive other implications. For example, the returns-to-education assumption implies that *two* additional years of education will increase earnings by 10 percent twice over—once for each extra year of education—producing a 21 percent total increase.

$$1.10 \times 1.10 = 1.21.$$

Consider another example. *Four* additional years of education will increase earnings by 10 percent four times over, implying a 46 percent total increase.

$$1.10 \times 1.10 \times 1.10 \times 1.10 = (1.10)^4 = 1.46.$$

This implies that going to college would increase a college graduate's income by 46 percent compared to what she would have been paid if she had ended her education after finishing high school. In other words, a prediction—or hypothesis—of the model is that college graduates will earn 46 percent more than high school graduates.

In principle, we can apply this analysis to *any* number of years of education. We therefore have a general model that relates people's educational attainment to their income. The model that we have derived is referred to as the returns-to-education model. It describes the economic payoff of more education—in other words, the "return" on your educational investment. Most economic models are much, much more complex than this. In most economic models, it takes pages of mathematical analysis to derive the implications of the assumptions. Nevertheless, this simple model is a good starting point for our discussion. It illustrates two important properties of all models.

First, *a model is an approximation*. The model does not predict that *everyone* would increase their future wages by *exactly* 10 percent if they obtained an extra year of education. The predicted relationship between education and future wages is an average relationship— it is an approximation for what is predicted to happen for most people in most circumstances. The model overlooks lots of special considerations. For example, the final year of college probably does much more to increase your wages than the second-to-last year of college, because that final year earns you the official degree, which is a key item on your resumé. Likewise, your college major importantly impacts how much you will earn after college. Those who major in economics, for example, tend to earn more than graduates in most other majors. Our simple model overlooks many such subtleties. Just as a flat subway map is only an approximation of the features of a city, the returns-to-education model is only an approximation of the mapping from years of education to wages.

Second, *a model makes predictions that can be tested with data*—in this case, data on people's education and earnings. We are now ready to use some data to actually evaluate the predictions of the returns-to-education model.

Evidence-Based Economics

Q: How much more do workers with a college education earn?

To put the model to the test we need data, which we obtain from the Current Population Survey (CPS), a government data source. This survey collects data on wages, education, and many other characteristics of the general population and is available to anyone who wants to use it. When data are available to the general public, they are called "public-use data."

Exhibit 2.3 summarizes the average annual earnings for our test. The returns-to-education model does not match the data perfectly. The exhibit shows that for 30-year-old U.S. workers with 12 years of education, which is equivalent to a high school diploma, the average yearly salary is $32,941. For 30-year-old U.S. workers with 16 years of education, which is equivalent to graduation from a four-year college, the average salary is $51,780.

If we simply divide these two average wages—college wage over high school wage—the ratio is 1.57.

$$\frac{\text{average salary of 30-year-olds with 16 years of education}}{\text{average salary of 30-year-olds with 12 years of education}} = \frac{\$51,780}{\$32,941} = 1.57.$$

Recall that the returns-to-education model says that each additional year of education raises the wage by 10 percent, so four extra years of education should raise the wage by a factor of $(1.10)^4 = 1.46$.

We can see that the model does not *exactly* match the data. Going from 12 years of education to 16 years is associated with a 57 percent increase in income. However, the model is not far off—the model predicted a 46 percent increase.

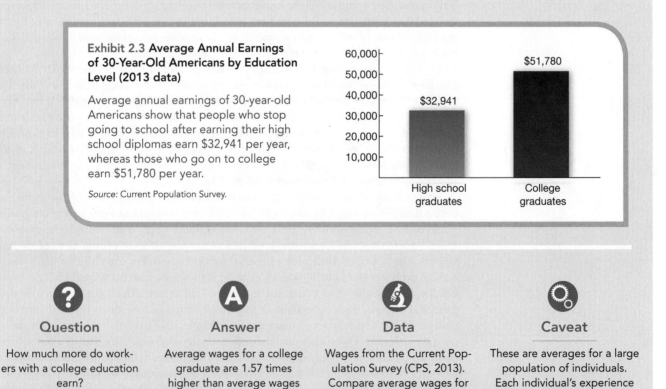

Exhibit 2.3 Average Annual Earnings of 30-Year-Old Americans by Education Level (2013 data)

Average annual earnings of 30-year-old Americans show that people who stop going to school after earning their high school diplomas earn $32,941 per year, whereas those who go on to college earn $51,780 per year.

Source: Current Population Survey.

? Question

How much more do workers with a college education earn?

A Answer

Average wages for a college graduate are 1.57 times higher than average wages for a high school graduate.

Data

Wages from the Current Population Survey (CPS, 2013). Compare average wages for 30-year-old workers with different levels of education.

Caveat

These are averages for a large population of individuals. Each individual's experience will differ.

Means

2.1

You may wonder how the data from the CPS can be used to calculate the wages reported above. We used the concept of the *mean*, or *average*. The **mean** (or **average**) is the sum of all the different values divided by the number of values and is a commonly used technique for summarizing data. Statisticians and other scientists use the terms *mean* and *average* interchangeably.

The **mean**, or **average**, is the sum of all the different values divided by the number of values.

We can quickly show how the mean works in a small example. Say that there are five people: Mr. Kwon, Ms. Littleton, Mr. Locke, Ms. Reye, and Mr. Shephard, each with a different hourly wage:

$$Kwon = \$26 \text{ per hour},$$
$$Littleton = \$24 \text{ per hour},$$
$$Locke = \$8 \text{ per hour},$$
$$Reye = \$35 \text{ per hour},$$
$$Shephard = \$57 \text{ per hour}.$$

If we add the five wages together and divide by 5, we calculate a mean wage of $30 per hour.

$$\frac{\$26 + \$24 + \$8 + \$35 + \$57}{5} = \$30.$$

This analysis of a small sample illustrates the idea of calculating a mean, but convincing data analysis in economics relies on using a large sample. For example, a typical economic research paper uses data gathered from thousands of individuals. So a key strength of economic analysis is the *amount* of data used. Earlier we didn't rely on a handful of observations to argue that education raises earnings. Instead, we used data from more than thousands of surveyed 30-year-olds. Using lots of data—economists call them *observations*—strengthens the force of an empirical argument because the researcher can make more precise statements.

To show you how to make convincing empirical arguments, this course uses lots of real data from large groups of people. Credible empirical arguments, based on many observations, are a key component of the scientific method.

Argument by Anecdote

Education is not destiny. There are some people with lots of education who earn very little. There are some people with little education who earn a lot. When we wrote this book, Bill Gates, a *Harvard dropout* who founded Microsoft, was the richest man in the world. Mark Zuckerberg, the Facebook CEO, also dropped out of Harvard.

With these two examples in mind, it is tempting to conclude that dropping out of college is a great path to success. However, it is a mistake to use two anecdotes, or any small sample of people, to try to judge a statistical relationship.

Here's another example of how the amount of data can make a big difference. Exhibit 2.4 plots data from just two people. They are both 30-years-old. As you can see, the exhibit does not reproduce the positive relationship between education and earnings that is plotted in Exhibit 2.3. Instead, it looks as though rising education is associated with *falling* earnings. But the pattern in Exhibit 2.4 is far from shocking given that it plots only two people. Indeed, if you study two randomly chosen 30-year-olds, there is a 25 percent chance that the person with only a high school diploma has higher earnings than the person with a four-year college degree. This fact highlights that there is much more than education that determines your earnings, although getting a college degree will usually help make you money.

When you look at only a small amount of data, it is easy to jump to the wrong conclusion. Keep this warning in mind the next time a newspaper columnist tries to convince you of something by using a few anecdotes. If the columnist backs up her story with data reflecting the experiences of thousands of people, then she has done her job and may deserve to win the argument. But if she rests her case after sharing a handful of anecdotes, remain skeptical. Be doubly skeptical if you suspect that the anecdotes have been carefully

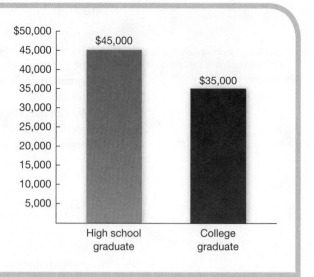

Exhibit 2.4 Annual Earnings for Two 30-Year-Old Americans by Education

Even though Exhibit 2.3 taught us that the average annual earnings of college graduates is 57 percent higher than those of high school graduates, it is not difficult to find specific examples where a high school graduate is actually earning more than a college graduate. Here we learn of one such example: the high school graduate earns $45,000 per year, whereas the college graduate earns $35,000.

selected to prove the columnist's point. Argument by anecdote should not be taken too seriously.

There is one exception to this rule. Argument by example is appropriate when you are contradicting a *blanket* statement. For example, if someone asserts that *every* National Basketball Association (NBA) player has to be tall, just one counterexample is enough to prove this statement wrong. In this case, your proof would be Tyrone Bogues, a 5-foot 3-inch dynamo who played in the NBA for 14 years.

2.2 Causation and Correlation

Using our large data set on wages and years of education, we've seen that on average wages rise roughly 10 percent for every year of additional education. Does this mean that if we could encourage a student to stay in school one extra year, that would *cause* that individual's future wages to rise 10 percent? Not necessarily. Let's think about why this is not always the case with an example.

The Red Ad Campaign Blues

Assume that Walmart has hired you as a consultant. You have developed a hypothesis about ad campaigns: you believe that campaigns using the color red are good at catching people's attention. To test your hypothesis, you assemble empirical evidence from historical ad campaigns, including the color of the ad campaign and how revenue at Walmart changed during the campaign.

Your empirical research confirms your hypothesis! Sales go up 25 percent during campaigns with lots of red images. Sales go up only 5 percent during campaigns with lots of blue images. You race to the chief executive officer (CEO) to report this remarkable result. You are a genius! Unfortunately, the CEO instantly fires you.

What did the CEO notice that you missed?

The red-themed campaigns were mostly concentrated during the Christmas season. The blue-themed campaigns were mostly spread out over the rest of the year. In the CEO's words,

The red colors in our advertising don't cause an increase in our revenue. Christmas causes an increase in our revenue. Christmas also causes an increase in the use of red in our ads. If we ran blue ads in December our holiday season revenue would still rise by about 25 percent.

Does jogging cause people to be healthy? Does good health cause people to jog? In fact both kinds of causation are simultaneously true.

Unfortunately, this is actually a true story, though we've changed the details—including the name of the firm—to protect our friends. We return, in the appendix, to a related story where the CEO was not as sharp as the CEO in this story.

Causation versus Correlation

> **Think of causation as the path from cause to effect.**

Causation occurs when one thing directly affects another through a cause-and-effect relationship.

A **correlation** means that there is a mutual relationship between two things.

People often mistake *causation* for *correlation*. **Causation** occurs when one thing directly affects another. You can think of it as the path from cause to effect: putting a snowball in a hot oven *causes* it to melt.

Correlation means that there is a mutual relationship between two things—as one thing changes, the other changes as well. There is some kind of connection. It *might* be cause and effect, but correlation can also arise when causation is not present. For example, as it turns out students who take music courses in high school score better on their SATs than students who do not take music courses in high school. Some educators have argued that this relationship is causal: more music courses cause higher SAT scores.

Yet, before you buy a clarinet for your younger sibling, you should know that researchers have shown that students who already would have scored high on their SATs are more likely to also have enrolled in music classes. There is something else—being a good student—that causes high SAT scores and enrollment in music. SAT scores and taking music courses are only correlated; if a trombone player's arm were broken and she had to drop out of music class, this would not cause her future SAT scores to fall. When two things are correlated, it suggests that causation may be possible and that further investigation is warranted—it's only the beginning of the story, not the end.

A **variable** is a factor that is likely to change or vary.

Positive correlation implies that two variables tend to move in the same direction.

Negative correlation implies that two variables tend to move in opposite directions. When the variables have movements that are not related, we say that the variables have **zero correlation**.

Correlations are divided into three categories: *positive correlation*, *negative correlation*, and *zero correlation*. Economists refer to some factor, like a household's income, as a **variable**. **Positive correlation** implies that two variables tend to move in the same direction—for example, surveys reveal that people who have a relatively high income are more likely to be married than people who have a relatively low income. In this situation we say that the variables of income and marital status are positively correlated. **Negative correlation** implies that the two variables tend to move in opposite directions—for example, people with a high level of education are less likely to be unemployed. In this situation we say that the variables of education and unemployment are negatively correlated. When two variables are not related, we say that they have a **zero correlation**. The number of friends you have likely has no relation to whether your address is on the odd or even side of the street.

When Correlation Does Not Imply Causality   There are two reasons why we should *not* jump to the conclusion that a correlation between two variables implies a particular causal relationship:

1. Omitted variables
2. Reverse causality

An **omitted variable** is something that has been left out of a study that, if included, would explain why two variables that are in the study are correlated.

An **omitted variable** is something that has been left out of a study that, if included, would explain why two variables are correlated. Recall that the amount of red content in Walmart's ads is positively correlated with the growth rate of Walmart's sales. However, the red color does not necessarily cause Walmart's sales to rise. The arrival of the Christmas season causes Walmart's ads to be red and the Christmas season also causes Walmart's month-over-month sales revenue to rise. The Christmas season is an omitted variable that explains why red ads tend to occur at around the time that sales tend to rise. (See Exhibit 2.5.)

Is there also an omitted variable that explains why education and income are positively correlated? One possible factor might be an individual's tendency to work hard. What if workaholics tend to thrive in college more than others? Perhaps pulling all-nighters to write term papers allows them to do well in their courses. Workaholics *also* tend to earn more money than others because workaholics tend to stay late on the job and work on weekends. Does workaholism cause you to earn more and, incidentally, to graduate from college rather than drop out? Or does staying in college cause you to earn those higher wages? What is cause and what is effect?

Reverse causality occurs when we mix up the direction of cause and effect.

Reverse causality is another problem that plagues our efforts to distinguish correlation and causation. Reverse causality is the situation in which we mix up the

Exhibit 2.5 An Example of an Omitted Variable

The amount of red content in Walmart's ads is positively correlated with the growth of Walmart's revenue. In other words, when ads are red-themed, Walmart's month-over-month sales revenue tends to grow the fastest. However, the redness does not cause Walmart's revenue to rise. The Christmas season causes Walmart's ads to be red and the Christmas season also causes Walmart's sales revenue to rise. The Christmas season is the omitted variable that explains the positive correlation between red ads and revenue growth.

Cause: Christmas

(Omitted variable)

Effect: red ads

Effect: rising revenue

direction of cause and effect. For example, consider the fact that relatively wealthy people tend to be relatively healthy too. This has led some social scientists to conclude that greater wealth causes better health—for instance, wealthy people can afford better healthcare. On the other hand, there may be reverse causality: better health may cause greater wealth. For example, healthy people can work harder and have fewer healthcare expenditures than less healthy people. It turns out that both causal channels seem to exist: greater wealth causes better health and better health causes greater wealth!

In our analysis of the returns to education, could it be that reverse causality is at play: higher wages at age 30 cause you to get more education at age 20? We can logically rule this out. Assuming that you don't have a time machine, it is unlikely that your wage as a 30-year-old causes you to obtain more education in your 20s. So in the returns-to-education example, reverse causality is probably not a problem. But in many other analyses—for example, the wealth-health relationship—reverse causality is a key consideration.

Economists have developed a rich set of tools to determine what is causation and what is only correlation. We turn to some of these tools next.

Experimental Economics and Natural Experiments

An **experiment** is a controlled method of investigating causal relationships among variables.

One method of determining cause and effect is to run an **experiment**—a controlled method of investigating causal relationships among variables. Though you may not read much about economic experiments in the newspaper, headlines for experiments in the field of medicine are common. For example, the Food and Drug Administration (FDA) requires pharmaceutical companies to run carefully designed experiments to provide evidence that new drugs work before they are approved for general public use.

To run an experiment, researchers usually create a treatment (test) group and a control group. Participants are assigned randomly to participate either as a member of the treatment group or as a member of the control group—a process called *randomization*. **Randomization** is the assignment of subjects by chance, rather than by choice, to a treatment group or to a control group. The treatment group and the control group are treated identically, except along a single dimension that is intentionally varied across the two groups. The impact of this variation is the focus of the experiment.

Randomization is the assignment of subjects by chance, rather than by choice, to a treatment group or control group.

If we want to know whether a promising new medicine helps patients with diabetes, we could take 1,000 patients with diabetes and *randomly* place 500 of them into a treatment group—those who receive the new medicine. The other 500 patients would be in the control group and receive the *standard* diabetes medications that are already widely used. Then, we would follow all of the patients and see how their health changes over the next few years. This experiment would test the causal hypothesis that the new drug is better than the old drug.

Now, consider an economics experiment. Suppose that we want to know what difference a college degree makes. We could take 1,000 high school students who cannot afford college, but who want to attend college, and randomly place 500 of them into a treatment group where they had all of their college expenses paid. The other 500 students would be placed in the control group. Then, we would keep track of *all* of the original 1,000 students—including the 500 control group students who weren't able to go to college because they couldn't afford it. We would use periodic surveys during their adult lives to see how the wages in the group that got a college education compare with the wages of the group that did not attend college. This experiment would test the hypothesis that a college education causes wages to rise.

One problem with experimentation is that experiments can sometimes be very costly to conduct. For instance, the college-attendance experiment that we just described would cost tens of millions of dollars, because the researchers would need to pay the college fees for 500 students. Another problem is that experiments do not provide immediate answers to some important questions. For example, learning about how one more year of education affects wages over the entire working life would take many decades if we ran an experiment on high school students today.

Another problem is that experiments are sometimes run poorly. For example, if medical researchers do not truly randomize the assignment of patients to medical treatments, then the experiment may not teach us anything at all. For instance, if patients who go to cutting-edge research hospitals tend to be the ones who get prescribed the newest kind of diabetes medication, then we don't know whether the new medication caused those patients to get better or whether it was some other thing that their fancy hospitals did that actually caused the patients' health to improve. In a well-designed experiment, randomization alone would determine who got the new medicine and who got the old medicine.

When research is badly designed, economists tend to be very skeptical of its conclusions. We say "garbage in, garbage out" to capture the idea that bad research methods invalidate a study's conclusions.

If we don't have the budget or time to run an experiment, how else can we identify cause and effect? One approach is to study historical data that has been generated by a "natural" experiment. A **natural experiment** is an empirical study in which some process—out of the control of the experimenter—has assigned subjects to control and treatment groups in a random or nearly random way.

A **natural experiment** is an empirical study in which some process—out of the control of the experimenter—has assigned subjects to control and treatment groups in a random or nearly random way.

Economists have found and exploited natural experiments to answer numerous major questions. This methodology can be very useful in providing a more definitive answer to our question at hand: What are you getting from your education?

Evidence-Based Economics

Q: How much do wages increase when an individual is compelled by law to get an extra year of schooling?

Many decades ago, compulsory schooling laws were much more permissive, allowing teenagers to drop out well before they graduated from high school. Philip Oreopoulos studied a natural experiment that was created by a change in these compulsory schooling laws.[1] Oreopoulos looked at an educational reform in the United Kingdom in 1947, which increased the minimum school leaving age from 14 to 15. As a result of this change, the fraction of children dropping out of school by age 14 fell by 50 percentage points between 1946 and 1948.

In this way, those kids reaching age 14 before 1947 are a "control group" for those reaching age 14 after 1947. Oreopoulos found that the students who turned 14 in 1948 and were therefore compelled to stay in school one extra year earned 10 percent more on average than the students who turned 14 in 1946.

Natural experiments are a very useful source of data in empirical economics. In many problems, they help us separate correlation from causation. Applied to the returns to education, they suggest that the correlation between years of education and higher income is not due to some omitted variable, but reflects the causal influence of education.

Evidence-Based Economics *(Continued)*

The returns-to-education model thus obtains strong confirmation from the data. Does a 10 percent return to each additional year of education increase your appetite for more years of schooling?

Question	**Answer**	**Data**	**Caveat**
How much do wages increase when an individual is compelled by law to get an extra year of schooling?	On average, wages rise by 10 percent when kids are compelled to stay in school an extra year.	United Kingdom General Household Survey. Compare kids in the United Kingdom who were allowed to drop out of school at age 14 with others who were compelled to stay in school an extra year due to changes in compulsory schooling laws.	Factors other than the change in the compulsory schooling laws might explain why the kids who were compelled to stay in school eventually earned more in the workforce (this is an example of an omitted variable).

2.3 Economic Questions and Answers

Economists like to think about our research as a process in which we pose and answer questions. We've already seen a couple of these questions. For example, in the current chapter, we asked, "How much do wages increase when an individual is compelled by law to get an extra year of schooling?" and in Chapter 1, we asked, "What is the opportunity cost of your time?"

Good questions come in many different forms. But the most exciting economic questions share two properties.

1. ***Good questions address topics that are important to individual economic agents and/or to our society.*** Economists tend to think about economic research as something that contributes to society's welfare. We try to pursue research that has general implications for human behavior or economic performance. For example, understanding the returns to education is important because individuals invest a lot of resources obtaining an education. The United States spends nearly a tenth of its economic output on education—$1.5 trillion per year. It is useful to quantify the payoffs from all this investment. If the returns to education are very high, society may want to encourage even more educational investment. If the returns to education are low, we should share this important fact with students who are deciding whether or not to stay in school. Knowing the returns to education will help individuals and governments decide how much of their scarce resources to allocate to educational investment.

2. ***Good economic questions can be answered.*** In some other disciplines, posing a good question is enough. For example, philosophers believe that some of the most important questions don't have answers. In contrast, economists are primarily interested in questions that can be answered with enough hard work and careful reasoning.

Here are some of the economic questions that we discuss in this book. As you look over the set, you will see that these are big questions with significant implications for you and for society as a whole. The rest of this book sets out to discover answers to these questions. We believe the journey will be exhilarating—so let's get started!

Chapter	Questions
1	Is Facebook free?
2	Is college worth it?
3	How does location affect the rental cost of housing?
4	How much more gasoline would people buy if its price were lower?
5	In the United States, what is the total market value of annual economic production?
6	Why is the average American so much richer than the average Indian?
7	Why are you so much more prosperous than your great-great-grandparents were?
8	Are tropical and semitropical areas condemned to poverty by their geographies?
9	What happens to employment and unemployment if local employers go out of business?
10	How often do banks fail?
11	What caused the German hyperinflation of 1922–1923?
12	What caused the recession of 2007–2009?
13	How much does government spending stimulate GDP?
14	Are companies like Nike harming workers in Vietnam?
15	How did George Soros make $1 billion?
Web Chapter 1	Do investors chase historical returns?
Web Chapter 2	What is the value of a human life?
Web Chapter 3	Do governments and politicians follow their citizens' and constituencies' wishes?

Summary

✹ The scientific method is the name for the ongoing process that economists and other scientists use to (a) develop mathematical models of the world and (b) test those models with data.

✹ Empirical evidence is a set of facts established by observation and measurement, which are used to evaluate a model.

✹ Economists try to uncover causal relationships among variables.

✹ One method to determine causality is to run an experiment—a controlled method of investigating causal relationships among variables. Economists now actively pursue experiments both in the laboratory and in the field. Economists also study historical data that have been generated by a natural experiment to infer causality.

Key Terms

scientific method *p. 21*
model *p. 21*
data *p. 22*
empirical evidence *p. 23*
hypotheses *p. 23*
mean (average) *p. 25*

causation *p. 27*
correlation *p. 27*
variable *p. 27*
positive correlation *p. 27*
negative correlation *p. 27*
zero correlation *p. 27*

omitted variable *p. 27*
reverse causality *p. 27*
experiment *p. 28*
randomization *p. 28*
natural experiment *p. 29*

Questions

All questions are available in MyEconLab for practice and instructor assignment.

1. What does it mean to say that economists use the scientific method? How do economists distinguish between models that work and those that don't?

2. What is meant by empiricism? How do empiricists use hypotheses?

3. What are two important properties of economic models? Models are often simplified descriptions of a real-world phenomenon. Does this mean that they are unrealistic?

4. How is the mean calculated from a series of observations? Suppose 5,000 people bought popsicles on a hot summer day. If the mean of the average number of popsicles bought is 2, how many popsicles were sold that day?

5. How does the sample size affect the validity of an empirical argument? When is it acceptable to use only one example to disprove a statement?

6. Explain why correlation does not always imply causation. Does causation always imply *positive* correlation? Explain your answer.

7. Give an example of a pair of variables that have a positive correlation, a pair of variables that have a negative correlation, and a pair of variables that have zero correlation.

8. What is meant by randomization? How does randomization affect the results of an experiment?

9. This chapter discussed natural and randomized experiments. How does a natural experiment differ from a randomized one? Which one is likely to yield more accurate results?

10. Suppose you had to find the effect of seatbelt rules on road accident fatalities. Would you choose to run a randomized experiment or would it make sense to use natural experiments here? Explain.

Problems

All problems are available in MyEconLab for practice and instructor assignment.

1. This chapter talks about means. The median is a closely related concept. The median is the numerical value separating the higher half of your data from the lower half. You can find the median by arranging all of the observations from lowest value to highest value and picking the middle value (assuming you have an odd number of observations). Although the mean and median are closely related, the difference between the mean and the median is sometimes of interest.

   a. Suppose country A has five families. Their incomes are $10,000, $20,000, $30,000, $40,000, and $50,000. What is the median family income in A? What is the mean income?

   b. Country B also has five families. Their incomes are $10,000, $20,000, $30,000, $40,000, and $150,000. What is the median family income in B? What is the mean income?

   c. In which country is income inequality greater, A or B?

   d. Suppose you thought income inequality in the US had increased over time. Based on your answers to this question, would you expect that the ratio of the mean income in the US to the median income has risen or fallen? Explain.

2. Consider the following situation: your math professor tells your class that the mean score on the final exam is 43. The exam was scored on a total of 100 points. Does this imply that you, too, scored poorly on the exam? Explain.

3. This chapter stressed the importance of using appropriate samples for empirical studies. Consider the following two problems in that light.

   a. You are given a class assignment to find out if people's political leanings affect the newspaper or magazine that they choose to read. You survey two students taking a political science class and five people at a coffee shop. Almost all the people you have spoken to tell you that their political affiliations do not affect what they read. Based on the results of your study, you conclude that there is no relationship between political inclinations and the choice of a newspaper. Is this a valid conclusion? Why or why not?

   b. Your uncle tells you that the newspaper or magazine that people buy will depend on their age. He says that he believes this because, at home, his wife and his teenage children read different papers. Do you think his conclusion is justified?

4. Some studies have found that people who owned guns were more likely to be killed with a gun. Do you think this study is strong evidence in favor of stricter gun control laws? Explain.

5. As the text explains, it can sometimes be very difficult to sort out the direction of causality.

   a. Why might you think that more police officers would lead to lower crime rates? Why might you think that higher crime rates would lead to more police officers?

   b. In 2012, the *New England Journal of Medicine* published research that showed a strong correlation between the consumption of chocolate in a country and the number of Nobel Prize winners in that country. Do you think countries that want to encourage their citizens to win Nobel Prizes should increase their consumption of chocolate?

6. The chapter shows that in general people with more education earn higher salaries. Economists have offered two explanations of this relationship. The human capital argument says that high schools and colleges teach people valuable skills, and employers are willing to pay higher salaries to attract people with those skills. The signaling argument says that college graduates earn more because a college degree is a signal to employers that a job applicant is diligent, intelligent, and persevering. How might you use data on people with two, three, and four years of college education to shed light on this controversy?

7. Maimonides, a twelfth-century scholar, said, "Twenty-five children may be put in the charge of one teacher. If the number in the class exceeds twenty-five but is not more than forty, he should have an assistant to help with the instruction. If there are more than forty, two teachers must be appointed." Israel follows Maimonides's rule in determining the number of teachers for each class. How could you use Maimonides's rule as a natural experiment to study the effect of teacher-student ratios on student achievement?

8. Oregon expanded its Medicaid coverage in 2008. Roughly 90,000 people applied but the state had funds to cover only an additional 30,000 people (who were randomly chosen from the total applicant pool of 90,000). How could you use the Oregon experience to estimate the impact of increased access to healthcare on health outcomes?

9. A simple economic model predicts that a fall in the price of bus tickets means that more people will take the bus. However, you observe that some people still do not take the bus even after the price of a ticket fell.

   a. Is the model incorrect?

   b. How would you test this model?

Appendix

Constructing and Interpreting Graphs

> A well-designed graph summarizes information with a simple visual display—the old adage "a picture is worth a thousand words" might help you understand the popularity of visual images.

As you start to learn economics, it's important that you have a good grasp of how to make sense of data and how to present data clearly in visible form. Graphs are everywhere—on TV, on the Web, in newspapers and magazines, in economics textbooks. Why are graphs so popular?

A well-designed graph summarizes information with a simple visual display—the old adage "a picture is worth a thousand words" might help you understand the popularity of visual images. In this textbook, you will find many graphs, and you will see that they provide a way to supplement the verbal description of economic concepts.

To illustrate how we construct and interpret graphs, we will walk you through a recent study that we have conducted, presenting some data summaries along the way.

A Study About Incentives

Would you study harder for this economics class if we paid you $50 for earning an A? What if we raised the stakes to $500? Your first impulse might be to think "Well, sure . . . why not? That money could buy a new Kindle and maybe a ticket to a Beyoncé concert."

But as we have learned in Chapter 1, there are opportunity costs of studying more, such as attending fewer rock concerts or spending less time at your favorite coffee house chatting with friends. Such opportunity costs must be weighed against the benefits of earning an A in this course. You might conclude that because this question is hypothetical, anyway, there's no need to think harder about how you would behave.

But it might not be as imaginary as you first thought.

Over the past few years, thousands of students around the United States have actually been confronted with such an offer. In fact, Sally Sadoff, Steven Levitt, and John List carried out an experiment at two high schools in the suburbs of Chicago over the past several years in which they used incentives to change students' behavior. Such an experiment allows us to think about the relationship between two *variables*, such as how an increase in a financial reward affects student test scores. And it naturally leads to a discussion of cause and effect, which we have just studied in this chapter: we'll compare causal relationships between variables and consider simple correlations between variables. Both causation and correlation are powerful concepts in gaining an understanding of the world around us.

Experimental Design

There are two high schools in Chicago Heights, and both have a problem with student dropouts. In terms of dropouts, it is not uncommon for more than 50 percent of incoming ninth-graders to drop out before receiving a high school diploma. There are clearly problems in this school district, but they are not unique to Chicago Heights; many urban school districts face a similar problem.

How can economists help? Some economists, including one of the coauthors of this book, have devised incentive schemes to lower the dropout rates and increase academic achievement in schools. In this instance, students were *paid* for improved academic performance.[2]

Let's first consider the experiment to lower the dropout rate. Each student was randomly placed into one of the following three groups:

Control Group: No students received financial compensation for meeting special standards established by experimenters (which are explained below).

Treatment Group with Student Incentives: Students would receive $50 for each month the standards were met.

Treatment Group with Parent Incentives: Students' parents would receive $50 for each month the standards were met.

A student was deemed to have met the monthly standards if he or she:

1. did not have a D or F in any classes during that month,
2. had no more than one unexcused absence during that month,
3. had no suspensions during that month.

Describing Variables

Before we discover how much money these students actually made, let's consider more carefully the variables that we might be interested in knowing. As its name suggests, a variable is a factor that is likely to vary or change; that is, it can take different values in different situations. In this section, we show you how to use three different techniques to help graphically describe variables:

1. Pie charts
2. Bar graphs
3. Time series graphs

Pie Charts

A **pie chart** is a circular chart split into segments, with each showing the percentages of parts relative to the whole.

Understanding pie charts is a piece of cake. A **pie chart** is a circular chart split into segments to show the percentages of parts relative to the whole. Put another way, pie charts are used to describe how a single variable is broken up into different categories, or "slices." Economists often use pie charts to show important economic variables, such as sources of government tax revenue or the targets of government expenditure, which we discuss in Chapter 10.

For example, consider the race of the students in our experiment. In Exhibit 2A.1, we learn that 59 percent of ninth-graders in the experiment are African-American. We therefore differentiate 59 percent of our pie chart with the color blue to represent the proportion of African-Americans relative to all participants in the experiment. We see that 15 percent of the students are non-Hispanic whites, represented by the red piece of the pie. We continue

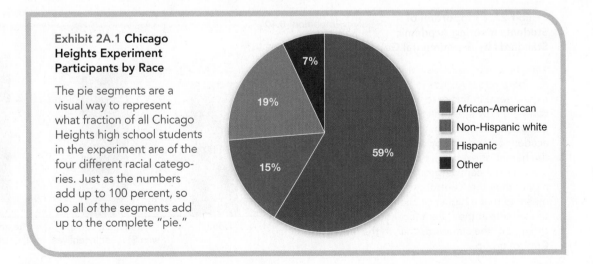

Exhibit 2A.1 Chicago Heights Experiment Participants by Race

The pie segments are a visual way to represent what fraction of all Chicago Heights high school students in the experiment are of the four different racial categories. Just as the numbers add up to 100 percent, so do all of the segments add up to the complete "pie."

African-American
Non-Hispanic white
Hispanic
Other

breaking down participation by race until we have filled in 100 percent of the circle. The circle then describes the racial composition of the participants in the experiment.

Bar Charts

Another type of graph that can be used to summarize and display a variable is a bar chart. A **bar chart** uses bars (no surprise there) of different heights or lengths to indicate the properties of different groups. Bar charts make it easy to compare a single variable across many groups. To make a bar chart, simply draw rectangles side-by-side, making each rectangle as high (or as long, in the case of horizontal bars) as the value of the variable it is describing.

For example, Exhibit 2A.2 captures the overall success rates of students in the various experimental groups. In the exhibit we have the **independent variable**—the variable that the experimenter is choosing (which treatment a student is placed in)—on the horizontal or x-axis. On the vertical or y-axis is the **dependent variable**—the variable that is potentially affected by the experimental treatment. In the exhibit, the dependent variable is the proportion of students meeting the academic standards. Note that 100 percent is a proportion of 1, and 30 percent is a proportion of 0.30.

We find some interesting experimental results in Exhibit 2A.2. For instance, we can see from the bar graph that 28 percent of students in the Control group (students who received no incentives) met the standards. In comparison, 34.8 percent of students in the Parent Incentive group met the standards. This is a considerable increase in the number of students meeting the standards—important evidence that incentives can work.

Time Series Graphs

With pie charts and bar graphs, we can summarize how a variable is broken up into different groups, but what if we want to understand how a variable changes over time? For instance, how did the proportion of students meeting the standards change over the school year? A **time series graph** can do the trick. A time series graph displays data at different points in time.

As an example, consider Exhibit 2A.3, which displays the proportion of students meeting the standards in each month in the Control and Parent Incentive groups. Keep in mind that although there are multiple months and groups, we are still measuring only a single variable—in this case, the proportion meeting the standard. As Exhibit 2A.3 makes clear, the number of students meeting the standard is higher in the Parent Incentive treatment group than in the Control group. But notice that the difference within the Parent Incentive and Control groups changes from month to month. Without a time series, we would not be able to appreciate these month-to-month differences and would not be able to get a sense for how the

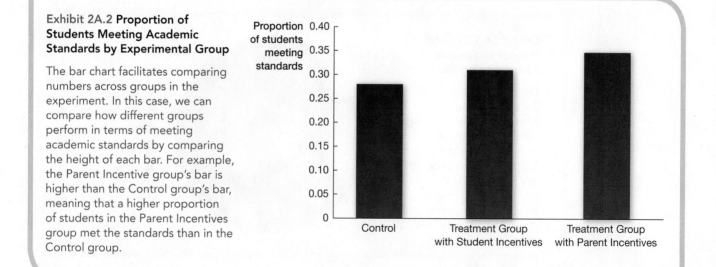

Exhibit 2A.2 Proportion of Students Meeting Academic Standards by Experimental Group

The bar chart facilitates comparing numbers across groups in the experiment. In this case, we can compare how different groups perform in terms of meeting academic standards by comparing the height of each bar. For example, the Parent Incentive group's bar is higher than the Control group's bar, meaning that a higher proportion of students in the Parent Incentives group met the standards than in the Control group.

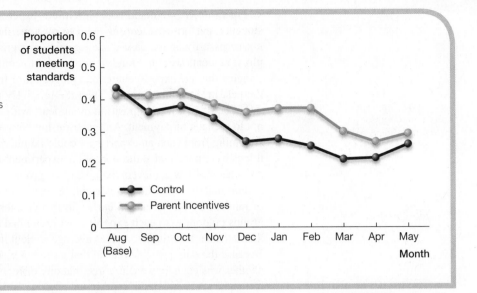

Exhibit 2A.3 Participants Meeting All Standards by Month

The time series graph takes the same information that was in the bar chart, but shows how it changes depending on the month of the school year during the experiment. The points are connected to more clearly illustrate the month-to-month trend. In addition, by using a different color or line pattern, we can represent two groups (Control and Parent Incentives) on the same graph, giving the opportunity to compare the two groups, just as with the bar chart from before.

effectiveness of the incentive varies over the school year. As you read this book, one important data property to recognize is how variables change over time; time series graphs are invaluable in helping us understand how a variable changes over time.

Scatter Plots

A **scatter plot** displays the relationship between two variables as plotted points of data.

You might ask yourself, without such monetary incentives is education worth it? In this chapter we showed you how wages and years of education are related. Another way to show the relationship is with a **scatter plot**. A scatter plot displays the relationship between two variables as plotted points of data. Exhibit 2A.4 shows the relationship between years of education and average weekly income across U.S. states in September of 2013. For example, the point 10.4 years of education and $800 in weekly earnings is from New Jersey. This means that the average years of education for New Jersey adults is 10.4 and the average weekly earnings is $800.

Cause and Effect

We've written a fair amount about causation and correlation in this chapter. Economists are much more interested in the former. Causation relates two variables in an active way—*a* causes *b* if, because of *a*, *b* has occurred.

Exhibit 2A.4 Relationship Between Education and Earnings

Each point in Exhibit 2A.4 is the average years of education and the median weekly earnings for one state in the United States. The exhibit is constructed using Current Population Survey (CPS) data from September 2013. The exhibit highlights the positive relationship between years of education and weekly earnings.

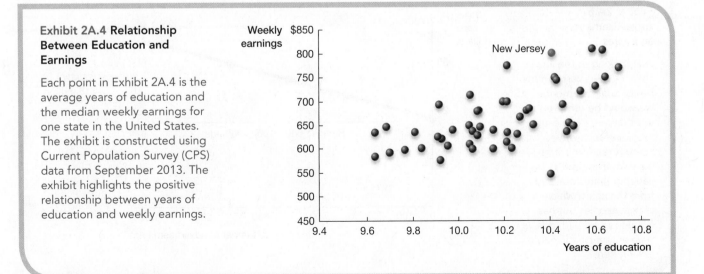

For example, we could conclude in our experimental study that paying money for the students' performance *causes* them to improve their academic performance. This would not necessarily be the case if the experiment were not properly implemented—for example, if students were not randomly placed into control and treatment groups. For instance, imagine that the experimenters had placed all of the students who had achieved poorly in the past in the control group. Then the relatively poor performance of the control group might be due to the composition of students who were assigned to the control group, and not to the lack of payment. Any relationship between academic achievement and payment stemming from such an experiment could be interpreted as a correlation because all other things were not equal at the start of the experiment—the control group would have a higher proportion of low achievers than the other groups.

Fortunately, the Chicago Heights Experiment was implemented using the principle of randomization, discussed earlier in this chapter. The experimenters split students into groups randomly, so each experimental group had an equal representation of students and their attributes (variables such as average student intelligence were similar across groups). Because the only possible reason that a student would be assigned to one group instead of another was chance, we can argue that any difference between the groups' academic performance at the end of the experiment was due to the difference the experimental treatment imposed, such as differences in financial incentives.

This means that we can claim that the cause of the difference between the performance of the Student Incentive group and the Control group, for example, is that students in the Student Incentive group were given an incentive of $50 whereas students in the Control group received no incentive for improvement.

Correlation Does Not Imply Causality

Often, correlation is misinterpreted as causation. You should think of correlation between two variables as providing a reason to look for a causal relationship, but correlation should only be considered a first step to establishing causality. As an example, not long ago, a high-ranking marketing executive showed us Exhibit 2A.5 (the numbers are changed for confidentiality reasons). He was trying to demonstrate that his company's retail advertisements were effective in increasing sales: "It shows a clear positive relationship between ads and sales. When we placed 1,000 ads, sales were roughly $35 million. But see how sales dipped to roughly $20 million when we placed only 100 ads?! This proves that more advertisements lead to more sales."

Before discussing whether this exhibit proves causality, let's step back and think about the basic characteristics of Exhibit 2A.5. In such an exhibit we have:

1. The *x*-variable plotted on the horizontal axis, or *x*-axis; in our figure the *x*-variable is the number of advertisements.

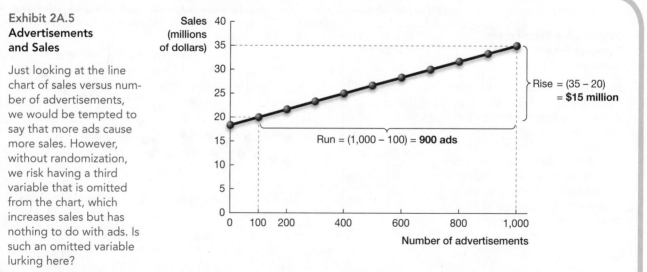

Exhibit 2A.5
Advertisements and Sales

Just looking at the line chart of sales versus number of advertisements, we would be tempted to say that more ads cause more sales. However, without randomization, we risk having a third variable that is omitted from the chart, which increases sales but has nothing to do with ads. Is such an omitted variable lurking here?

Rise = (35 − 20) = **$15 million**

Run = (1,000 − 100) = **900 ads**

2. The y-variable plotted on the vertical axis, or y-axis; in our figure the y-variable is the sales in millions of dollars.

3. The origin, which is the point where the x-axis intersects the y-axis; both sales and the number of advertisements are equal to zero at the origin.

In the exhibit, the number of advertisements is the independent variable, and the amount of sales is the dependent variable. When the values of both variables increase together in the same direction, they have a positive relationship; when one increases and the other decreases, and they move in opposite directions, they have a negative relationship.

So in Exhibit 2A.5, we find a positive relationship between the two variables. What is the strength of that positive relationship? This is called the slope. The **slope** is the change in the value of the variable plotted on the y-axis divided by the change in the value of the variable plotted on the x-axis:

The **slope** is the change in the value of the variable plotted on the y-axis divided by the change in the value of the variable plotted on the x-axis.

$$\text{Slope} = \frac{\text{Change in } y}{\text{Change in } x} = \frac{\text{Rise}}{\text{Run}}.$$

In this example, the increase in the number of advertisements from 100 to 1,000 was associated with an increase in sales from \$20 million to \$35 million. Thus, the rise, or the change in sales (y), is \$15 million and the run, or change in x, is 900. Because both are rising (moving in the same direction), the slope is positive:

$$\text{Slope} = \frac{\$35,000,000 - \$20,000,000}{1000 \text{ ads} - 100 \text{ ads}} = \frac{\$15,000,000}{900 \text{ ads}} = \$16,667 \text{ per ad}.$$

Thus, our exhibit implies that one more advertisement is associated with \$16,667 more in sales. But, does this necessarily mean that if the retailer increases the number of advertisements by one, this will cause sales to increase by \$16,667?

Unfortunately, no. While it is tempting to interpret the sales increasing with ads as a causal relationship between the two variables, because the number of advertisements was not randomly determined with an experiment, we cannot be sure that this relationship is causal. In this case, the marketing executive forgot to think about *why* they so drastically increased their advertisement volume to begin with! They did so because of the holiday season, a time when sales would presumably have been high anyway.

So, after some further digging (we spare you the details), what the data actually say is that the retailer placed more ads during times of busy shopping (around Thanksgiving and in December), but that is exactly when sales were high—because of the holiday shopping season. Similar to what happened in the Walmart red/blue ad example in this chapter, once we recognize such seasonal effects and take them into account, the causal relationship between ads and sales disappeared!

This example shows that you should be careful when you connect a few points in a graph. Just because two variables move together (a correlation), they are not necessarily related in a causal way. They could merely be linked by another variable that is causing them both to increase—in this case, the shopping season.

To see the general idea of what is happening more clearly, let's instead graph the quantity of ice cream produced versus the number of monthly drownings in the United States. Using data across months in 2011, we constructed Exhibit 2A.6. In Exhibit 2A.6, we see that in months when ice cream production is relatively high, there are a lot of drownings. Likewise, in months when there is relatively little ice cream production, there are many fewer drownings. Does this mean that you should not swim after you eat ice cream?

Indeed, parents persuaded by such a chart might believe that it's causal, and never let their kids eat ice cream near swimming pools or lakes! But luckily for us ice cream lovers, there is an omitted variable lurking in the background. In the summertime, when it is hot people eat more ice cream *and* swim more. More swimming leads to more drowning. Even though people eat more ice cream cones in the summer, eating ice cream doesn't *cause* people to drown.

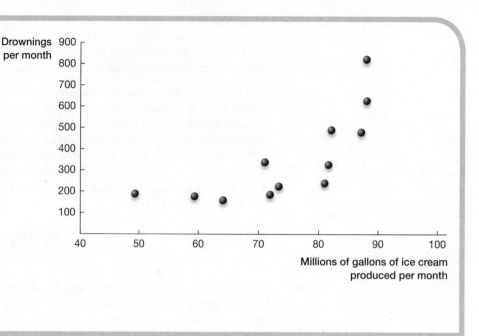

Exhibit 2A.6 Ice Cream Production and Drownings in the United States

We depict the relationship between monthly ice cream production and monthly drownings. Each of the 12 points represents a single month in 2011. Is this relationship causal or is there an omitted variable that is causing these two variables to move together? Hint: the point in the upper right-hand corner of the exhibit is July and the point in the lower left-hand corner of the exhibit is December!

Sources: Centers for Disease Control and Prevention, and Brian W. Gould, University of Wisconsin Dairy Marketing and Risk Management Program.

Just as a heightened shopping season was the omitted variable in the retailer advertisement example, here the omitted variable is heat—it causes us to swim more *and* to eat more ice cream cones. While the former causes more drownings (as we would all expect), the latter has nothing to do with drowning even though there is a positive correlation between the two as shown in Exhibit 2A.6.

Beyond an understanding of how to construct data figures, we hope that this appendix gave you an appreciation for how to interpret visual displays of data. An important lesson is that just because two variables are correlated—and move together in a figure—does not mean that they are causally related. Causality is the gold standard in the social sciences. Without understanding the causal relationship between two variables, we cannot reliably predict how the world will change when the government intervenes to change one of the variables. Experiments help to reveal causal relationships. We learned from the Chicago Heights experiment that incentives can affect student performance.

Appendix Key Terms

pie chart *p. 35*

bar chart *p. 36*

independent variable *p. 36*

dependent variable *p. 36*

time series graph *p. 36*

scatter plot *p. 37*

slope *p. 39*

Appendix Problems

A1. How would you represent the following graphically?

   a. Income inequality in the United States has increased over the past 10 years.

   b. All the workers in the manufacturing sector in a particular country fit into one (and only one) of the following three categories: 31.5 percent are high school dropouts, 63.5 percent have a regular high school diploma, and the rest have a vocational training certificate.

   c. The median income of a household in Alabama was $43,464 in 2012 and the median income of a household in Connecticut was $64,247 in 2012.

A2. Consider the following data that show the quantity of coffee produced in Brazil from 2004 to 2012.

Year	Production (in tons)
2004	2,465,710
2005	2,140,169
2006	2,573,368
2007	2,249,011
2008	2,796,927
2009	2,440,056
2010	2,907,265
2011	2,700,440
2012	3,037,534

   a. Plot the data in a time series graph.

   b. What is the mean quantity of coffee that Brazil produced from 2009 to 2011?

   c. In percentage terms, how much has the 2012 crop increased over the 2009–2011 mean?

A3. Suppose the following table shows the relationship between revenue that the Girl Scouts generate and the number of cookie boxes that they sell.

Number of Cookie Boxes	Revenue ($)
50	200
150	600
250	1000
350	1400
450	1800
550	2200

   a. Present the data in a scatter plot.

   b. Do the two variables have a positive relationship or do they have a negative relationship? Explain.

   c. What is the slope of the line that you get in the scatter plot? What does the slope imply about the price of a box of Girl Scout cookies?

3 Optimization: Doing the Best You Can

How does location affect the rental cost of housing?

Suppose you have just landed a job near the center of a city and you now need to decide where to live. If you live close to the city center, your round-trip commute will be 15 minutes. If you live in the distant suburbs, your round-trip commute will be 60 minutes. If there are lots of workers like you who work downtown, where will the apartments be relatively less expensive? How will you choose where to live? How should you make the best decision given the trade-offs you face?

In this chapter, we'll dig into the concept of optimization—choosing the best feasible option. You will learn how to optimize by using cost-benefit analysis. And we will apply this knowledge to a single example that we revisit throughout the chapter—choosing an apartment.

CHAPTER OUTLINE

3.1
Two Kinds of Optimization: A Matter of Focus

3.2
Optimization in Levels

3.3
Optimization in Differences: Marginal Analysis

EBE
How does location affect the rental cost of housing?

- When an economic agent chooses the best feasible option, she is optimizing.

- *Optimization in levels* calculates the *total* net benefit of different alternatives and then chooses the best alternative.

- *Optimization in differences* calculates the *change* in net benefits when a person switches from one alternative to another, and then uses these *marginal* comparisons to choose the best alternative.

- Optimization in levels and optimization in differences give identical answers.

3.1 Two Kinds of Optimization: A Matter of Focus

In Chapter 1, we described economics as the study of choice. Economists believe that people usually make choices by trying to select the best feasible option, given the available information. In other words, people optimize. Recall that this is the first principle of economics.

> **Economists believe that optimization describes most of the choices that people, households, businesses, and governments make.**

Economists believe that optimization describes most of the choices that people, households, businesses, and governments make. To an economist, seemingly unrelated decisions—for example, where a college student will travel on spring break, which apartment a worker will rent, or what price Apple charges for an iPhone—are all connected by the unifying principle of optimization. Whatever choices people face, economists believe that they are likely to try to choose optimally. Economists don't assume that people *always* successfully optimize, but economists do believe that people try to optimize and usually do a pretty good job with whatever information they have.

In other words, economists believe that people's behavior is *approximated* by optimization. People aren't *perfect* optimizers because optimization is usually not easy, and it is often quite complex. To illustrate the complexity, consider the choice of an apartment. In large cities there are hundreds of thousands of rental apartments. And each apartment has many different characteristics to consider, such as location, views, and neighborhood amenities.

At the heart of this complexity are trade-offs. For example, how do you compare two apartments, one of which has the virtue of lower rent and one of which has the virtue of a shorter commute? How would you determine which apartment is a better choice for you? In this chapter, we are going to see how to optimally evaluate such trade-offs. We will introduce you to the most important optimization tools that economists use.

We have a lot to say about choosing a rental apartment, but we want you to remember that the choice of an apartment is just one illustration of the general concept of optimization.

Optimization can be implemented using either of two techniques of cost-benefit analysis. Both techniques emphasize the concept of net benefit—benefit minus cost—which we introduced in Chapter 1.

1. **Optimization in levels** calculates the *total* net benefit of different alternatives, and then chooses the best alternative.
2. **Optimization in differences** calculates the *change* in net benefits when a person switches from one alternative to another and then uses these marginal comparisons to choose the best alternative.

As you'll see in the examples that follow, optimization in levels and optimization in differences should always yield answers in perfect agreement. These techniques are two sides of the same coin.

To get a taste for these two methods, take a peek at the Halloween bag after this paragraph. Think about how much you would enjoy eating the contents of this bag—the bag's benefit to you.

Now think about how much you would enjoy eating the contents of a second bag of candy:

In principle, the bag that offers the greatest total enjoyment is the bag you would choose if you were asked to choose between them. This kind of analysis is an example of optimization in levels. You calculated the benefit of each bag, and then you chose the best bag.

Now consider a second version of *exactly the same decision*. We'll take the same two bags of candy and put them side by side. We'll now reorder the candy bars to highlight the similarities and differences. In this case, all of the bars match except the first bag

Optimization in levels calculates the *total* net benefit of different alternatives and then chooses the best alternative.

Optimization in differences calculates the *change* in net benefits when a person switches from one alternative to another and then uses these marginal comparisons to choose the best alternative.

has a Milky Way and the second bag has a 3 Musketeers. Since all of the candy bars except one are the same, it's natural to focus on this one difference. Does this difference—3 Musketeers replacing Milky Way—increase the value to you of the Halloween Bag? If this one difference increases the value, you should pick the second bag. If this one difference decreases the value, you should pick the first bag.

This is an example of optimization in differences. Optimization in differences analyzes the *change* in net benefits when a person switches from one bag to another and then uses this marginal comparison to choose the best alternative.

We asked you to make the same choice twice—we used the same pair of bags in both choices. The first time you chose, you analyzed each of the Halloween bags in isolation. The second time you chose, you analyzed the difference between the two bags. *This change in focus is all that distinguishes optimization in levels and optimization in differences.* If you choose optimally, this shift in focus shouldn't have changed your final decision, but it might have speeded things along. In many cases, optimization in differences is faster and easier, because you focus on the *key* differences between the options.

Behavioral economics jointly analyzes the economic and psychological factors that explain human behavior.

🖐 CHOICE & CONSEQUENCE

Do People Really Optimize?

Economists believe that the framework of optimization approximates how people make most economic choices. But economists don't take optimization for granted. A large body of economic research studies the question: do people really optimize?

Thousands of research papers have been written on this question. This research has broadly concluded that optimization is a good model of economic behavior in most, though not all, situations. One field of economics—**behavioral economics**—identifies the specific situations in which people fail to optimize. Behavioral economists explain these optimization failures by combining economic and psychological theories of human behavior.

Several special situations are associated with behavior that is not optimal. For example, when people have self-control problems—like procrastination, or, far worse, addiction—optimization is not a good description of behavior.

People also tend to fail as optimizers when they are new to a task. For instance, the first time someone plays poker they tend to play poorly—they make rookie mistakes. On the other hand, optimization is a good description of choices when people have lots of experience. For example, as a consumer gains a few years of experience with a new credit card, they become half as likely to miss their monthly payment deadline.

Because people aren't born perfect optimizers, optimization is a useful skill to develop. Economists show people how to be better optimizers—such advice amounts to normative economic analysis.

We hope that you use the concept of optimization in two ways: it is a good description of the behavior of experienced decision makers and it provides an excellent toolbox for improving decision making that is not already optimal.

3.2 Optimization in Levels

Let's explore optimization in levels in more depth. To illustrate ideas, we return to our opening example in which you are an apartment hunter.

Imagine that you have narrowed your choices to four leading candidates—your "short list." Exhibit 3.1 summarizes this short list, including two key pieces of information for each apartment—the monthly rent and the amount of commuting time per month. In Exhibit 3.1, rents fall the farther you are from work. Later in this chapter, we explain why the economic model predicts this relationship between rents and distance from work. We'll also show you empirical evidence that confirms this prediction.

You might wonder about everything that was left out of the summary of information in Exhibit 3.1. What about *other* differences among these apartments, like how long it takes to walk to the neighborhood laundromat or whether there is a park nearby? We also omitted commuting costs other than time, like the direct dollar cost of public transportation or, if you drive yourself, gasoline and tolls. Shouldn't all of these considerations be part of the comparison?

To keep things simple, we will omit other factors for now, even though they *are* important in practice. We omit them to keep the calculations simple and so that the basic economic concepts are easier to see. As you'll discover in the problems at the end of the chapter, once you understand the basic ideas, it is easy to add more details. For now, we will assume that the four apartments—*Very Close, Close, Far*, and *Very Far*— are identical except for the differences in Exhibit 3.1.

Note, too, that we are focusing only on costs in this example—the cost of commuting time and the cost of rent. We are assuming that the benefits of these apartments are the same—for instance, proximity to shopping or public transportation. If the benefits are the same, then cost-benefit analysis becomes simpler. In normal cost-benefit analysis the decision maker finds the alternative with the highest value of *net benefit*, which is benefit minus cost. When the benefits are the same across all the alternatives, cost-benefit analysis simplifies to finding the alternative with the lowest cost. That's what we are going to do next.

Exhibit 3.1 Apartments on Your Short List, Which Differ Only on Commuting Time and Rent and Are Otherwise Identical

Many cities have a single central business district—which is often referred to as the city center—where lots of employers are concentrated.

In most cities, apartments near the city center cost more to rent than otherwise identical apartments that are far away. Why is this so?

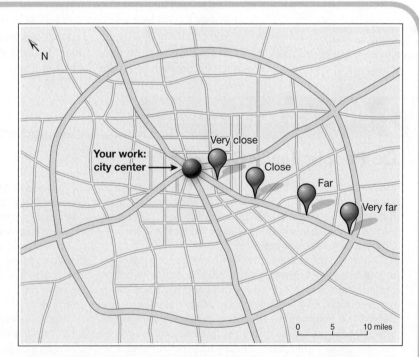

Apartment	Commuting Time (hours per month)	Rent ($ per month)
Very Close	5 hours	$1,180
Close	10 hours	$1,090
Far	15 hours	$1,030
Very Far	20 hours	$1,000

The proximity of local amenities should also go into a complete optimization analysis, because these amenities change the net benefits.

Exhibit 3.1 contains the information that we need, but on its own, it does not enable us to choose the best apartment. We do not yet have a way to add up the costs of rent and commuting time. We need to sum these costs to calculate the *total* cost of each apartment. The total cost includes the *direct* cost of rent and the *indirect* cost of commute time.

To sum these two costs, we first need to decide on a common unit of account. Let's pick dollars per month for now. Because rent is already expressed in dollars per month, half of our work has been done for us. All that remains is to translate the indirect cost—commuting time—into the same unit of measurement.

To do this, we use the concept of opportunity cost, which we introduced in Chapter 1. Let's begin by assuming that the opportunity cost of commuting time is $10/hour. This is the hourly value of the alternative activity that is crowded out when you spend more time commuting. The fact that it is a dollar value doesn't imply that this time would have been spent at work if it weren't spent commuting. An extra hour of time has value to you whatever you would do with that time, including napping, socializing, watching videos, taking longer showers, or working.

If the round-trip commute takes 20 hours per month and the opportunity cost of time is $10/hour, then the dollar cost of that commute is

$$\left(\frac{20 \text{ hours}}{\text{month}}\right)\left(\frac{\$10}{\text{hour}}\right) = \left(\frac{\$200}{\text{month}}\right).$$

The first term on the left is commute time per month, which is expressed in *hours* per month, just as it is in Exhibit 3.1. The term just before the equal sign is the opportunity cost of time, which is expressed as dollars per *hour*. The units in *hours* cancel, leaving a final cost expressed as dollars per month.

Now we are ready to rewrite Exhibit 3.1. Using the calculations that we just illustrated for 20 hours of monthly commuting time, we can calculate costs for a commute of any duration. Exhibit 3.2 reports this commuting cost in dollars per month for all four apartments.

Exhibit 3.2 gives us the answer to our optimization problem. Apartment Far is the best apartment for a consumer with an opportunity cost of time of $10/hour. This apartment has the lowest total cost —$1,180—taking into account both direct rent costs and indirect time costs of commuting.

We can also see this result by plotting the total costs. Exhibit 3.3 plots the total cost of each of the four apartments. It is easy to see that Apartment Far is the best. Economists call the best feasible choice the **optimum**, which you can see labeled on the total cost curve.

To sum up our discussion so far, optimization in levels has three steps:

The **optimum** is the best feasible choice. In other words, the optimum is the optimal choice.

1. Translate all costs and benefits into common units, like dollars per month.
2. Calculate the *total* net benefit of each alternative.
3. Pick the alternative with the highest net benefit.

Exhibit 3.2 Commuting Cost and Rental Cost Expressed in Common Units, Assuming an Opportunity Cost of Time of $10/hour

To optimize, it is necessary to convert all of the costs and benefits into common units. In this example, the common unit is $ per month. The optimum—in bold—is Apartment Far, which has the lowest total cost.

Apartment	Commuting Time (hours per month)	Commuting Cost ($ per month)	Rent ($ per month)	Total Cost: Rent + Commuting ($ per month)
Very Close	5 hours	$50	$1,180	$1,230
Close	10 hours	$100	$1,090	$1,190
Far	**15 hours**	**$150**	**$1,030**	**$1,180**
Very Far	20 hours	$200	$1,000	$1,200

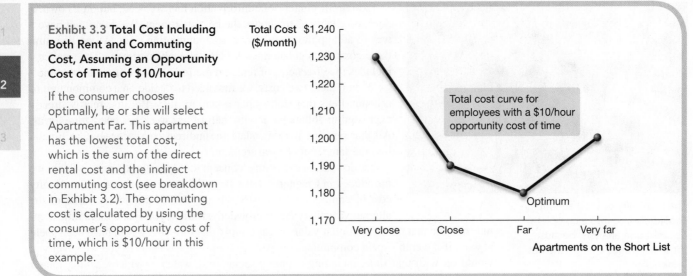

Exhibit 3.3 Total Cost Including Both Rent and Commuting Cost, Assuming an Opportunity Cost of Time of $10/hour

If the consumer chooses optimally, he or she will select Apartment Far. This apartment has the lowest total cost, which is the sum of the direct rental cost and the indirect commuting cost (see breakdown in Exhibit 3.2). The commuting cost is calculated by using the consumer's opportunity cost of time, which is $10/hour in this example.

Comparative Statics

Comparative statics is the comparison of economic outcomes before and after some economic variable is changed.

Economic models predict how a person's choices change when something in the environment changes. **Comparative statics** is the comparison of economic outcomes before and after some economic variable is changed. For example, some consumers will choose to drive more expensive cars if their wealth increases. In this example, the car choice is the economic behavior that changes when the variable of consumer wealth changes.

We now return to the example in the previous subsection to conduct a comparative statics analysis. Specifically, we ask what happens when the opportunity cost of time is changed.

Recall that we studied the choice of an apartment assuming that the opportunity cost of time was $10/hour. Let's instead assume that the opportunity cost of time is $15/hour. Why might opportunity cost rise? For example, a freelance worker's opportunity cost of time would rise if their hourly wage rose.

How does this increase in the opportunity cost of time change the predicted behavior? Before we take you through it step-by-step, try to use your intuition. How would a change in the value of time affect the optimal decision of where to live? Should commuters with a higher value of time move closer to where they work or farther away?

To answer this question, we again need to translate the indirect cost—commuting time—into the same units as the direct cost of rent, which is dollars per month. Accordingly, we rewrite Exhibit 3.2, assuming instead a $15/hour opportunity cost of time. Exhibit 3.4 reports this commuting cost in dollars per month for all four apartments.

Exhibit 3.4 provides the answer to our new optimization problem. The best apartment for a consumer with an opportunity cost of time of $15/hour now shifts to Apartment Close

Exhibit 3.4 Commuting Cost and Rental Cost Expressed in Common Units, Assuming an Opportunity Cost of Time of $15/hour

To optimize, it is necessary to convert all of the costs and benefits into common units. In this example, the common unit is $ per month. The optimum—in bold—is Apartment Close, which has the lowest total cost.

Apartment	Commuting Time (hours per month)	Commuting Cost ($ per month)	Rent ($ per month)	Total Cost: Rent + Commuting ($ per month)
Very Close	5 hours	$75	$1,180	$1,255
Close	**10 hours**	**$150**	**$1,090**	**$1,240**
Far	15 hours	$225	$1,030	$1,255
Very Far	20 hours	$300	$1,000	$1,300

from Apartment Far. Apartment Close has the lowest total cost—$1,240—taking into account both direct rent costs and indirect time costs of commuting.

Exhibit 3.5 plots the total cost of each of the four apartments assuming a $15/hour opportunity cost of time. Apartment Close is the best choice—the optimum.

The higher opportunity cost of time caused the optimal choice to change from Apartment Far to Apartment Close. When the opportunity cost of time increases from $10/hour to $15/hour, it becomes more valuable for the commuter to choose an apartment that reduces the amount of time spent commuting. So the optimal choice switches from a relatively inexpensive apartment with a longer commute to a relatively expensive apartment with a shorter commute—Apartment Close.

Exhibit 3.6 takes the two different cost curves from Exhibits 3.3 and 3.5 and plots them in a single figure. The purple line represents the total cost curve for the commuter with an opportunity cost of $10/hour. The orange line represents the total cost curve for the commuter with an opportunity cost of $15/hour. Two key properties are visible in Exhibit 3.6.

1. The $10/hour cost curve lies below the $15/hour cost curve. The $10/curve has lower commuting costs for each apartment, so the total cost, which takes into account both the direct cost of rent and the indirect cost of commuting, is lower for all apartments.
2. The $10/hour curve has a minimum value for Apartment Far, while the $15/hour curve has a minimum value for Apartment Close. In other words, the optimal apartment switches from Apartment Far to Apartment Close when the opportunity cost of time rises from $10/hour to $15/hour.

Exhibit 3.5 Total Cost Including Both Rent and Commuting Cost, Assuming an Opportunity Cost of Time of $15/hour

Given the opportunity cost of $15/hour, the optimal choice is Apartment Close. This apartment has the lowest total cost, which is the sum of the direct rental cost and the indirect commute cost.

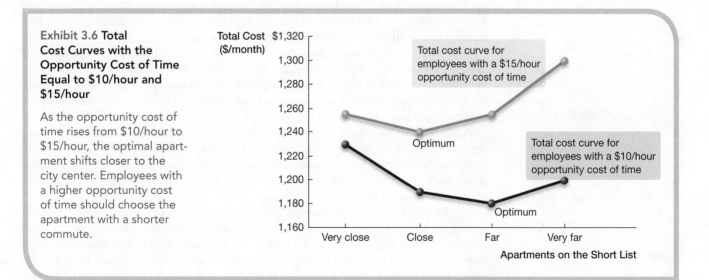

Exhibit 3.6 Total Cost Curves with the Opportunity Cost of Time Equal to $10/hour and $15/hour

As the opportunity cost of time rises from $10/hour to $15/hour, the optimal apartment shifts closer to the city center. Employees with a higher opportunity cost of time should choose the apartment with a shorter commute.

3.3 Optimization in Differences: Marginal Analysis

Until now, we have studied the apartment-hunting problem by calculating the *total* cost of each apartment. As explained above, we call that approach *optimization in levels*. We are now going to discuss an alternative optimization technique: *optimization in differences*. Optimization in differences is often faster to implement than optimization in levels, because optimization in differences focuses only on the way that alternatives differ.

Optimization in differences breaks an optimization problem down by thinking about how costs and benefits *change* as you hypothetically move from one alternative to another. For example, consider two alternative vacations at the same hotel in Miami: a four-day trip versus a five-day trip. Suppose that you are choosing between these two options. If you optimize in levels, you would evaluate the *total* net benefit of a four-day trip and compare it to the *total* net benefit of a five-day trip. Alternatively, you could think about only the *differences* between the two trips. In other words, you could think *only* about the costs and benefits of the *extra* day. An optimizer will take the five-day vacation if the benefit of vacationing for the fifth day exceeds the cost of the fifth day. In choosing between the four- and five-day options, the optimizer doesn't actually need to worry about the first four days, since those four days are shared by both the four-day trip and the five-day trip. The optimizer can focus on the one thing that differentiates the two vacations: the fifth day.

Economists use the word *marginal* to indicate a difference between alternatives, usually a difference that represents one "step" or "unit" more. The fifth day of vacation is the difference, or margin, between a four-day vacation and a five-day vacation.

A cost-benefit calculation that focuses on the difference between a feasible alternative and the next feasible alternative is called **marginal analysis**. Marginal analysis compares the consequences—costs and benefits—of doing one step more of something. Thinking back to our apartment example, marginal analysis can be used to study the costs and benefits of moving one apartment farther away from the city center.

Marginal analysis will *never* change the ultimate answer to the question "what is optimal?" but it will change the way that you think about optimizing. Marginal analysis forces us to focus on what is changing when we compare alternatives. Marginal analysis is the way that we implement optimization in differences. Marginal analysis is one of the most important concepts in economics.

> **Marginal analysis** is a cost-benefit calculation that studies the difference between a feasible alternative and the next feasible alternative.

> Marginal analysis will *never* change the ultimate answer to the question "what is optimal?" but it will change the way that you think about optimizing.

Marginal Cost

Let's return to the problem of choosing the best apartment. We go back to this problem to preserve continuity with our earlier analysis. Though it may appear otherwise, we are not personally obsessed with apartment-hunting. Our analysis illustrates techniques that will enable you to optimize in any situation.

When we studied the problem of choosing a rental apartment, we did *not* use marginal analysis. Instead, we solved the problem by calculating and comparing the *total* cost—including direct and indirect costs—of the four apartments. We'll now solve the same apartment-selection problem using marginal analysis. The optimum won't change—we'll confirm that below—but the way that you think about the problem will.

Again consider the commuter with a $10/hour opportunity cost of time. Instead of thinking about each of the apartments in isolation, let's now think about the apartments comparatively. Specifically, let's focus on what changes as we hypothetically "move" from one apartment to the next, stepping farther away from the city center. What is the difference between each pair of apartments?

Exhibit 3.7 helps you think about these changes. The "Commuting Cost" column reports the monthly commuting cost for each apartment assuming a $10/hour opportunity cost of time. The "Marginal Commuting Cost" column reports the value of the extra monthly commuting time that is generated by moving one apartment farther from the city center. For example, to move from *Apartment Close* to *Apartment Far* generates additional

Exhibit 3.7 Relationship Between Levels and Differences (Margins), Assuming a $10/hour Opportunity Cost of Time

We can break the problem down by studying the marginal costs of moving farther from the city center. At what point does it make sense to stop moving farther from the city center?

Apartment	Commuting Cost	Marginal Commuting Cost	Rent Cost	Marginal Rent Cost	Total Cost	Marginal Total Cost
Very Close	$50		$1,180		$1,230	
		$50		−$90		−$40
Close	$100		$1,090		$1,190	
		$50		−$60		−$10
Far	$150		$1,030		$1,180	
		$50		−$30		$20
Very Far	$200		$1,000		$1,200	

Marginal cost is the extra cost generated by moving from one feasible alternative to the next feasible alternative.

commuting costs of $50 per month. In other words, the "Marginal Commuting Cost" column reports the difference between two commuting costs in adjacent positions on the list. In this particular example, the marginal commuting cost is always the same—the commuting cost rises by the same amount with each move farther away from the city center. This won't generally be the case, but we've set it up this way in this problem to keep things simple. In general, **marginal cost** is the extra cost generated by moving from one feasible alternative to the next feasible alternative.

Now turn to the column labeled "Rent Cost," which reports the monthly rent for each apartment. The "Marginal Rent Cost" column reports the change in the rent cost generated by moving from one apartment to the next apartment—one step farther from the city center. For example, to move from *Apartment Very Close* to *Apartment Close* would save you $90 per month, so the marginal rent cost is a negative number, −$90. Likewise, if you moved from *Apartment Close* to *Apartment Far*, you would save an additional $60 per month, so the marginal rent cost is −$60.

Finally, we'd like to know the marginal value of total cost. It turns out that we can calculate the marginal value of total cost in two alternative ways. First, we can add up the marginal commuting cost and the marginal rent cost to obtain the marginal total cost. For example, look at the first row of marginal cost numbers and confirm that $50 + −$90 = −$40. In other words, a move from *Apartment Very Close* to *Apartment Close* raises commuting costs by $50 and changes rent by −$90, producing a combined change of −$40.

Alternatively, we could calculate total cost itself. This is done in the column labeled Total Cost. For instance, for *Apartment Very Close,* the commuting cost is $50 and the rent cost is $1,180, so the total cost is $1,230. For *Apartment Close*, the commuting cost is $100 and the rent cost is $1,090, so the total cost is $1,190. Total cost *falls* by $40 when we move from *Apartment Very Close*, with total cost $1,230, to *Apartment Close*, with total cost $1,190.

Both methods confirm that the marginal total cost is −$40 when moving from *Apartment Very Close* to *Apartment Close*.

$$\text{Marginal commuting cost} + \text{Marginal rent cost} = \$50 + -\$90 = -\$40$$
$$\text{Total cost of } \textit{Close} - \text{Total cost of } \textit{Very Close} = \$1,190 - \$1,230 = -\$40$$

The fact that we calculated −$40 in both cases is no accident. The exact match reflects the fact that it doesn't matter how we decompose costs to calculate marginal total cost. It doesn't matter whether we calculate marginal total cost by summing marginal costs category by category or whether we calculate marginal total cost by subtracting the *total* cost of one apartment from the other. Because the answer is the same, you should calculate marginal total cost whichever way is easier for you.

The last column of Exhibit 3.7—marginal total cost—contains all of the information that we need to optimize. Start at the top of the column and think about how each "move" away from the city center affects the worker. The first move, from *Very Close* to *Close*, has a marginal cost of −$40 per month, so it is cost cutting. That move is worth it.

The second move, from *Close* to *Far*, has a marginal cost of −$10 per month. That move is also cost cutting and consequently it is also worth taking.

The third move, from *Far* to *Very Far*, has a marginal cost of $20 per month. So that move is not worth taking, because it represents an increase in costs.

To sum up, the first two moves paid for themselves and the final move did not. *Very Far* can't be an optimum, since moving from *Far* to *Very Far* made the worker worse off. *Very Close* can't be an optimum, since moving from *Very Close* to *Close* made the worker better off. Finally, *Close* can't be an optimum, since moving from *Close* to *Far* made the worker better off.

We conclude that *Far* is the optimum—the best feasible choice. Moving from *Close* to *Far* made the worker better off. But moving from *Far* to *Very Far* made the worker worse off. *Far* is the only apartment that satisfies the following property: moving to the apartment makes the worker better off and moving away from the apartment makes the worker worse off. In other words, *Far* has the virtue that it is a better option than its "neighbors."

The **Principle of Optimization at the Margin** states that an optimal feasible alternative has the property that moving to it makes you better off and moving away from it makes you worse off.

The optimizer's goal is to make himself as well off as possible. An optimum is the point at which the optimizer cannot do any better. The apartment that is better than all its feasible alternatives is also the apartment that minimizes total costs. This is an example of the **Principle of Optimization at the Margin**, which states that an *optimal* feasible alternative has the property that moving to it makes you better off and moving away from it makes you worse off.

It helps to visualize these ideas. Exhibit 3.8 plots the total cost of each apartment and the marginal cost of moving one apartment at a time farther away from the center of town. For instance, moving from *Very Close* to *Close* lowers total cost by $40. The dashed red line shows a change of −$40 between the total cost of *Very Close* and the total cost of *Close*.

Optimization using marginal analysis will always pick out a single optimal alternative when the total cost curve has the bowl-like shape in Exhibit 3.8. Where the *total* cost (in purple) is falling, marginal cost (in red) will be negative and marginal analysis will recommend moving farther away from the city center, thereby lowering total cost. After total cost bottoms out, marginal cost will afterwards be positive, implying that the renter should move no farther out.

When the total cost curve is *not* bowl-shaped, the analysis gets more complicated, but even in this case, optimization in differences ultimately identifies the same optimum as optimization in levels.

Since optimization in levels and optimization in differences pick out the same optimum, you can use whichever method is easier for the particular problem that you are

Exhibit 3.8 Total Cost of Each Apartment and the Marginal Cost of Moving Between Apartments, Assuming an Opportunity Cost of $10/hour

The cost-minimizing choice is Apartment Far. We can see this by looking at total cost (in purple) or by looking at marginal cost (in red). Total cost is falling when marginal cost is negative. Total cost is rising when marginal cost is positive. Apartment Far is the only apartment that is better than all of its neighbors. Marginal cost is negative when moving to Apartment Far and marginal cost is positive when moving away from Apartment Far. Thus, Apartment Far is the only apartment that satisfies the Principle of Optimization at the Margin.

analyzing. However, it is important to understand why economists mostly use optimization in differences—in other words, optimization at the margin. Optimization at the margin is simple because you can ignore everything about two alternatives that are being compared except the particular attributes that are different. Marginal analysis reminds you not to analyze information that will turn out to be irrelevant to your decision.

To sum up, optimization in differences has three steps:

1. Translate all costs and benefits into common units, like dollars per month.
2. Calculate the marginal consequences of moving between alternatives.
3. Apply the Principle of Optimization at the Margin by choosing the best alternative with the property that moving to it makes you better off and moving away from it makes you worse off.

Evidence-Based Economics

Q: How does location affect the rental cost of housing?

Throughout this chapter, we've been assuming that rental prices are higher near the city center, holding the quality of the apartment fixed. You may have wondered whether we had our facts right.

People often imagine *dingy* apartments downtown and *nice* houses out in the country. If we want to isolate the effect of location, we need to hold apartment quality constant and vary *only* location.

Economists Beth Wilson and James Frew assembled a database that contains information on many apartments that were available for rent in Portland, Oregon.[1] They used statistical techniques to effectively compare apartments near the city center to similar apartments that were farther away. Such analysis reveals a strong negative relationship between distance and rent, which is plotted in Exhibit 3.9.

Exhibit 3.9 was calculated for apartments that all have the following features—one bedroom, one bathroom, laundry unit in the apartment, covered parking, cable, and air-conditioning—and have none of the following features—a fireplace, access to an exercise room, or access to a pool. The analysis compares the rent of these apartments, holding all of their features constant *except* for the distance to the city center.

Exhibit 3.9 Apartment Rent in Portland, Oregon, Depends on Distance from the City Center

This plot is drawn for apartments that are identical, except for their distance from the city center. The blue line is the approximate location of a ring of highways that encircle most of Portland.

Approximate location of highways that ring the city center

Evidence-Based Economics *(Continued)*

Exhibit 3.9 confirms that proximity to the city center raises rents. The closer you get to the city, the higher the rent goes. For example, at a distance of 6 miles from the city center, the typical rent for an apartment with the specified features is nearly $1,000. For an apartment that is 1 mile from the city center, the rent for the "same" apartment is $1,500.

Exhibit 3.9 also displays a noticeable flattening around 12 miles from the city center. Can you guess why rents stop changing in this region? The answer follows from considerations about the opportunity cost of time and the structure of Portland's highway system. Like most large cities, Portland has a ring of fast highways—a "ring road"—about 12 miles from the center of the city. People who live within a few miles of the ring road have the advantage of being near a highway system that speeds up travel time. Because of the ring roads, commute times change relatively little as you go from 9 miles to 14 miles away from the city center.

Scarcity, Prices, and Incentives

We can now come full circle and return to an important question that we asked previously. *Why* do rental prices fall as you move farther from the city center? What does this have to do with the topic of this chapter: optimization?

Ring Road System Around Portland, Oregon

Like most large cities, Portland has a ring of fast highways—a "ring road"—about 12 miles from the center of the city.

Mt. Hood rises to the east of Portland and presents a beautiful view to apartment dwellers lucky enough to face that way. But not everyone has such spectacular views. Some apartments are on low floors and some apartments face the less awesome views to the west. Eastern-facing apartments on high floors rent for about 20 percent more than similar apartments that don't have the killer views. To an economist, this price differential is a good way of measuring the dollar value of a scarce resource: a room with a view.

We've shown that many optimizing commuters would love to live in the city center *if* the rental prices were the same downtown as they are in distant neighborhoods. But everyone can't live downtown. Everyone can't have a short commute. There just aren't enough downtown apartments for everyone who would like one. That is an example of economic scarcity—one of the first concepts we studied in Chapter 1.

The market for apartments resolves the question of who gets to have the short commute. Markets allow optimizing landlords and optimizing renters to freely negotiate the rental price of an apartment. In the marketplace, the rental price of apartments is determined by market forces rather than by politicians or regulators. The optimizers with the highest opportunity cost of time push up the rental price of apartments with the shortest commutes.

Market prices—here the rental price of apartments—provide incentives that implicitly allocate economic resources. As the price of downtown apartments rises, only workers with the highest opportunity cost of time will be willing to rent them. Most other workers will choose to move farther away and accept the consequences of a longer commute. That's a trade-off—more time commuting in exchange for a lower monthly rent.

Market prices have the effect of allocating the downtown apartments to the people who are willing to pay the most for them. This allocation mechanism implies that mostly highly paid workers—and others with a high opportunity cost of time—tend to rent the apartments with the best locations.

Some critics of markets complain that markets are unfair—why should the highest-paid workers also get the apartments with the best locations? The defenders of markets respond that people are paying for the privilege of having a good apartment—the apartments with the best locations have higher rents—and the market allocation mechanism guarantees that people who are willing to pay the most for the best apartments get them.

Understanding how the market allocation process works is the subject of our next chapter and many other chapters in this book. As we begin to discuss these issues, we want you to think about how society *should* determine the price of scarce resources, like downtown apartments. Should we have a system that allows optimizing landlords and optimizing renters to negotiate freely to determine rental prices for apartments? What if this produces a system in which the highest-paid workers are the only ones who can afford to live in the most convenient apartments? Is that inequitable? Can you think of a better way to allocate apartments?

Question	Answer	Data	Caveat
How does location affect the rental cost of housing?	In most cities, though not all, the farther you are from the city center, the more rental costs fall (holding apartment quality fixed). For example, in Portland, Oregon, rents fall by 33 percent as you move from the city center to otherwise identical apartments 6 miles out of town.	Rental prices in Portland, Oregon.	Though the analysis uses special statistical techniques to compare similar apartments located at different distances from the city center, it is possible that some important apartment characteristics were not held fixed in the comparison. This would bias the calculations.

Summary

✱ Economists believe that optimization describes, or at least approximates, many of the choices economic agents make. Economists believe that most people optimize most of the time. But economists don't take optimization for granted. Economic research attempts to answer the question: Do people optimize? Using optimization to describe and predict behavior is an example of positive economic analysis.

✱ Optimization also provides an excellent toolbox—especially, cost-benefit analysis and marginal analysis—for improving decision making that is not already optimal. Using optimization to improve decision making is an example of normative economic analysis.

✱ Optimization in levels has three steps: (1) translate all costs and benefits into common units, like dollars per month; (2) calculate the *total* net benefit of each alternative; (3) pick the alternative with the highest net benefit.

✱ Optimization in differences analyzes the change in net benefits when you switch from one alternative to another. The most important example is marginal analysis, a cost-benefit calculation that focuses on the difference between one alternative and the next alternative. Marginal analysis compares the consequences of doing one step more of something. Marginal cost is the extra cost generated by moving from one alternative to the next alternative.

✱ Optimization in differences has three steps: (1) translate all costs and benefits into common units, like dollars per month; (2) calculate the marginal consequences of moving between alternatives; (3) apply the Principle of Optimization at the Margin by choosing the best alternative with the property that moving to it makes you better off and moving away from it makes you worse off.

✱ Optimization in levels and optimization in differences yield answers in agreement. These techniques are two sides of the same coin.

Key Terms

optimization in levels *p. 44*
optimization in differences *p. 44*
behavioral economics *p. 45*

optimum *p. 47*
comparative statics *p. 48*
marginal analysis *p. 50*

marginal cost *p. 51*
Principle of Optimization at the
   Margin *p. 52*

Questions

1. What is meant by optimization? How does optimization in levels differ from optimization in differences?

2. Does the principle of optimization imply that people always make the best choices?

3. What is meant by comparative statics? Explain with an example.

4. Some people choose to live close to the city center; others choose to live away from the city center and take a longer commute to work every day. Does picking a location with a longer commute imply a failure to optimize?

5. Suppose you had information on the sales of similar homes just east and just west of the boundary between two school districts. How could you use those data to estimate the value parents place on the quality of their children's schools?

6. There is a proverb "anything worth doing is worth doing well." Do you think an economist would agree with this proverb?

7. Why do economists mostly use optimization in differences, as opposed to optimization in levels?

8. Explain how the market for apartments allocates the scarce supply of apartments near the city center.

9. Is optimization analysis positive or normative, or both? Explain your answer.

Problems

1. Suppose the government in a certain country wants to reduce urban sprawl. What measures could it take to ensure that people choose to live closer to the central business district? (Urban sprawl refers to the development of residential and commercial areas in the suburbs around the periphery of a city. One of the main problems with urban sprawl is that it leads to increased traffic congestion and air pollution as commuters travel to the city every day.)

2. Suppose you are accepted at all of the three business schools to which you applied. Consider the factors that could matter when it comes to choosing a business school.

   a. How would you go about making an optimal decision about which school to attend?

   b. Suppose you have to give up a job that pays you $40,000 a year to attend business school. How would this affect your calculation of which business school to attend?

3. Determine if the following statements better describe optimization in levels or optimization in differences.

   a. John is attempting to decide on a movie. He determines that the new Batman movie provides him with $5 more of a benefit than the new Spiderman movie.

   b. Marcia finds that the net benefit of flying from Chicago to Honolulu on a non-stop United Airlines flight is $400, and the net benefit for the same trip flying on a one-stop American Airlines flight is $200.

   c. Nikki decided to take the first available parking space as she entered the student lot. She felt that the first available space had a $5 premium compared with all other possible spaces because she did not want to risk being late for her exam.

   d. Reagan determined that the net benefit of taking the combination of two lecture courses and an online lecture course was $100. The same three courses online gave her a net benefit of $80, and all three in a lecture-based format gave her a net benefit of $90.

4. You are taking two courses this semester, biology and chemistry. You have quizzes coming up in both classes. The following table shows your grade on each quiz for different numbers of hours studying for each quiz. (For the purposes of this problem, assume that each hour of study time can't be subdivided.) For instance, the table implies that if you studied one hour on Chemistry and two hours on Biology you would get a 77 on Chemistry and a 74 on Biology.

Hours of Study	Chemistry	Biology
0	70	60
1	77	68
2	82	74
3	85	78

Your goal is to maximize your average grade on the two quizzes. Use the idea of optimization in differences to decide how much time you would spend studying for each quiz if you had only one hour in *total* to prepare for the two exams (in other words, you will study for one hour on one exam and zero hours on the other exam). How would you allocate that single hour of study time across the two subjects? Now repeat the analysis assuming that you have two hours in *total* to prepare for the two exams. How would you allocate those two hours across the two subjects? Finally, repeat the analysis assuming that you have three hours in *total* to prepare for the two exams. How would you allocate those three hours across the two subjects?

5. Your total benefits from consuming different quantities of gas each week are shown in the following table.

Gallons per Week	Total Benefit (dollar equivalent)	Marginal Benefit
0	0	X
1	8	
2	15	
3	21	
4	26	
5	30	
6	33	
7	35	
8	36	

a. Complete the marginal benefit column starting with the step from 0 gallons to 1 gallon per week.

b. The price of gasoline is $4 per gallon. Use the Principle of Optimization at the Margin to find an optimal number of gallons of gas to consume each week.

c. Some people have suggested a tax of $2 per gallon of gasoline as a way to reduce global warming. (Burning fossil fuels such as gasoline releases greenhouse gases, which are a cause of global warming.) Suppose the price of gasoline (including the tax) rises to $6 per gallon. Use the Principle of Optimization at the Margin to find an optimal number of gallons of gasoline given this new tax on gasoline.

6. Scott loves to go to baseball games, especially home games of the Cincinnati Reds. All else equal, he likes to sit close to the field. He also likes to get to the stadium early to watch batting practice. The closer he parks to the stadium the more batting practice he is able to watch (the garages all open simultaneously). Find Scott's optimal seat type and parking garage using the information that follows.

Location/Seat	Price	Scott's Value of View
Diamond Seats	$235	$200
Club Home	$95	$130
Club Seating	$85	$125
Scout Box	$79	$120
Scout	$69	$100

Parking Location	Parking Fee (game night)	Missed Batting Practice	Benefit of Arrival Time
Westin parking garage	$5	60 min	$0
Fountain Square South Garage	$10	50 min	$10
West river parking	$17	25 min	$35
East river parking	$25	10 min	$50
Under stadium parking	$45	0 min	$60

7. Suppose the total benefit and total cost to society of various levels of pollution reduction are as follows:

(1) Pollution Reduction	(2) Total Benefit	(3) Total Cost	(4) Total Net Benefit	(5) Marginal Benefit	(6) Marginal Cost
0	0	0		X	X
1	20	9			
2	38	20			
3	54	33			
4	68	48			
5	80	65			
6	90	84			

a. Complete column (4).

b. Use optimization in levels to show that if the U.S. Environmental Protection Agency (EPA) wants to maximize total net benefit, then it should require 3 units of pollution reduction.

c. Complete columns (5) and (6), starting with the step from 0 to 1 unit of pollution reduction.

d. Show that the Principle of Optimization at the Margin would also tell the EPA to require 3 units of reduction.

8. Assume that your country's income tax structure has the following tax rates: if your income is $30,000 or less you pay no income tax; if your income is above $30,000, you pay 30 percent of the amount above $30,000. And so, for example, someone who earns $60,000 would pay 30% × ($60,000 − $30,000) = $9,000.

Your marginal tax rate is defined as the taxes you pay if you earn one more dollar. Your average tax rate is defined as the total taxes you pay divided by your income. And so, to continue with this example, someone who earns $60,000 would have a marginal tax rate of 30 percent and an average tax rate of $9,000/$60,000 = 15%.

You have three alternatives. You could not work at all, you could work half time, or you could work full time. If you do not work at all, you will earn $0; if you work half-time you will earn $30,000; and if you work full-time, you will earn $60,000. Any time you do not work, you can spend surfing. You love to surf: surfing full-time is worth $50,000 per year to you, surfing half-time is worth $25,000 per year to you, and not surfing at all is worth nothing to you. As you are making your decision about how much to work, should you pay attention to your average tax rate or to your marginal tax rate? Explain your answer carefully.

9. Consider the total cost of traveling from point A to point B. The cost of traveling by car would include the cost of gasoline and the opportunity cost of time; the cost of hopping on a bus would include the bus ticket and the opportunity cost of time. Assume that the bus ticket costs less than the gasoline. Does this imply that using a bus to get to the destination involves lower total costs than getting there by car? What if the bus doesn't take the fastest route from point A to point B?

4 Demand, Supply, and Equilibrium

How much more gasoline would people buy if its price were lower?

During 2013, the retail price of a gallon of gasoline in the United States fluctuated between $3 and $4 per gallon. How much gasoline do you buy now? How much would you buy if the price were lower—say, $1 per gallon? How low would it have to go to tempt you to take lots of road trips? What if the price were $0.04 per gallon, so that gasoline was practically free? Amazingly, that's what Venezuelans paid for gas in 2013, due to an extraordinary government subsidy.

In this chapter, we study how buyers and sellers respond to the changing price of goods and services, and we use the energy market and gasoline as our leading example. How does the price of gas affect the decisions of gas buyers, like households, and gas sellers, like ExxonMobil? How do the decisions of buyers and sellers jointly determine the price of gas when it isn't dictated by government policies?

☀ In a perfectly competitive market, (1) sellers all sell an identical good or service, and (2) any individual buyer or any individual seller isn't powerful enough on his or her own to affect the market price of that good or service.

☀ The demand curve plots the relationship between the market price and the quantity of a good demanded by buyers.

☀ The supply curve plots the relationship between the market price and the quantity of a good supplied by sellers.

☀ The competitive equilibrium price equates the quantity demanded and the quantity supplied.

☀ When prices are not free to fluctuate, markets fail to equate quantity demanded and quantity supplied.

4.1 Markets

Every year over one billion drivers pull into gas stations around the world. These drivers almost never find that gas stations are "sold out." Most of the time, it takes less than 10 minutes to fill the tank and pull back on the road.

The efficiency of this system is amazing. Nobody tells the companies that run the gas stations how many drivers to expect, and nobody tells the drivers where to fill their tanks. No "fill 'er up" tickets are presold by Ticketmaster or Live Nation. But somehow, there is almost always enough gas for every driver who wants to fill the tank. Drivers get the gas they are willing to pay for, and gasoline companies make enough money to pay their employees and send dividends to their shareholders.

> A **market** is a group of economic agents who are trading a good or service, and the rules and arrangements for trading.

This chapter is about how the gasoline market and other markets like it work. A **market** is a group of economic agents who are trading a good or service, and the rules and arrangements for trading. Agricultural and industrial goods like wheat, soybeans, iron, and coal are all traded on markets. A market may have a specific physical location—like Holland's Aalsmeer Flower Auction—or not. For example, the market for gasoline is dispersed—located on every corner you find a gas station. Likewise, Monster.com (a Web-based job market) operates wherever there's a computer and an Internet connection. To an economist, dating Web sites like okcupid.com or christianmingle.com are markets, too.

> **Prices act as a selection device that encourages trade between the sellers who can produce goods at low cost and the buyers who place a high value on the goods.**

We focus the discussion on markets in which all exchanges occur voluntarily at flexible prices. This chapter explains how markets use prices to allocate goods and services. Prices act as a selection device that encourages trade between the sellers who can produce goods at low cost and the buyers who place a high value on the goods.

We will illustrate all of this by studying the market for gasoline, which is refined from crude oil, as well as the broader market for energy. You'll see that the price of gasoline is set in a way

This warehouse in Aalsmeer, Holland, covers an area larger than 100 football fields and hosts thousands of daily auctions for wholesale (bulk) flowers.

If all sellers and all buyers face the same price, it is referred to as the **market price.**

In a **perfectly competitive market**, (1) sellers all sell an identical good or service, and (2) any individual buyer or any individual seller isn't powerful enough on his or her own to affect the market price of that good or service.

A **price-taker** is a buyer or seller who accepts the market price—buyers can't bargain for a lower price and sellers can't bargain for a higher price.

When two gas stations are located at the same intersection, their prices tend to be very close, and sometimes are exactly the same.

that implies that gas stations are ready to sell a quantity of gasoline that is equal to the quantity of gasoline that drivers want to buy.

Competitive Markets

Think of a city filled with hundreds of gas stations, each of which has an independent owner. The gas station on your block would lose most of its business if the owner started charging $1 more per gallon than all of the other stations. Likewise, you wouldn't be able to fill your tank if you drove around town offering gas station attendants $1 less per gallon than they were charging their other customers. Gas station attendants usually don't cut special deals with individual customers. Drivers of Cadillacs and Kias pay the same price for a gallon of regular unleaded.

To prove that pleading poverty and haggling for a better gas price won't work, try bargaining for a discount the next time you need to fill your tank. Try this only if you have enough gas to reach the next station.

If all sellers and all buyers face the same price, that price is referred to as the **market price**. In a **perfectly competitive market**, (1) sellers all sell an identical good or service, and (2) any individual buyer or any individual seller isn't powerful enough on his or her own to affect the market price. This implies that buyers and sellers are all **price-takers**. In other words, they accept the market price and can't bargain for a better price.

Very few, if any, markets are perfectly competitive. But economists try to understand such markets anyway. At first this sounds kind of nutty. Why would economists study a thing that rarely exists in the world? The answer is that although few, if any, markets are perfectly competitive, many markets are nearly perfectly competitive. Many gas stations do have nearby competitors—often right across the street—that prevent them from charging more than the market price. There are some gas stations that don't have such nearby competitors—think of an isolated station on a country road—but such examples are the exception. If sellers have nearly identical goods and most market participants face lots of competition, then the perfectly competitive model is a good approximation of how actual markets work.

On the other hand, there are some markets in which large market participants—like Microsoft in the software market—can single-handedly control market prices; we'll come to markets like that in later chapters.

In this chapter, our goal is to understand the properties of markets that have flexible prices and are perfectly competitive (identical goods and market participants who can't influence the market price). Along the way, we'll ask three questions.

1. How do buyers behave?
2. How do sellers behave?
3. How does the behavior of buyers and sellers jointly determine the market price and the quantity of goods transacted?

Each of the next three sections addresses one of these fundamental questions.

4.2 How Do Buyers Behave?

We start by studying the behavior of buyers. We assume that these buyers are price-takers: they treat the market price as a take-it-or-leave-it offer and don't try to haggle to lower the price. We want to study the relationship between the price of a good and the amount of the good that buyers are willing to purchase. At a given price, the amount of the good or service that buyers are willing to purchase is called the **quantity demanded**.

Quantity demanded is the amount of a good that buyers are willing to purchase at a given price.

To illustrate the concept of quantity demanded, think about your own buying behavior. When gas prices rise, do you tend to buy less gas? For example, if gas prices rise, a student who lives off campus might bike to school instead of driving. She might join a carpool or shift to public transportation. If gas prices rise high enough, she might sell her gas guzzler altogether. Even a student who lives on campus might cut back her gasoline consumption. During spring break, she might take the bus from Boston to her parents' home in Washington, D.C., rather than driving her car.

Let's quantify these kinds of adjustments. Take Chloe, a typical consumer who responds to increases in gasoline prices by reducing her purchases of gasoline. Chloe may not be able to adjust her gasoline consumption immediately, but in the long run she will use less gas if the price of gas increases—for instance, by switching to public transportation. The relationship between Chloe's purchases of gasoline and the price of gasoline is summarized in the shaded

From 2005 to 2008, gasoline prices rose by 30 percent and Hummer sales fell by 50 percent. At that time, no other car brand experienced sales declines that were this steep. Hummer demand fell so quickly that General Motors shut down the brand in 2010.

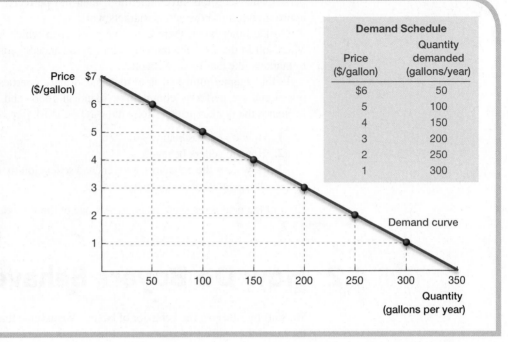

Exhibit 4.1 Chloe's Demand Schedule and Demand Curve for Gasoline

The lower the price of gasoline, the more gasoline that Chloe chooses to buy. In other words, her quantity demanded increases as the price of gasoline decreases. Demand curves are downward-sloping—the height of the curve falls as we move from left to right along the horizontal axis.

Demand Schedule

Price ($/gallon)	Quantity demanded (gallons/year)
$6	50
5	100
4	150
3	200
2	250
1	300

A **demand schedule** is a table that reports the quantity demanded at different prices, holding all else equal.

Holding all else equal implies that everything else in the economy is held constant. The Latin phrase *ceteris paribus* means "with other things the same" and is sometimes used in economic writing to mean the same thing as "holding all else equal."

The **demand curve** plots the quantity demanded at different prices. A demand curve plots the demand schedule.

Two variables are **negatively related** if the variables move in the opposite direction.

Law of Demand: In almost all cases, the quantity demanded rises when the price falls (holding all else equal).

box in the upper-right corner of Exhibit 4.1. This table reports the quantity demanded at different prices and it is called a **demand schedule**. Chloe's demand schedule for gasoline tells us how Chloe's gasoline purchases change as the price of gas changes, **holding all else equal**. The phrase "holding all else equal" implies that everything other than the price of gas is held constant or fixed, including income, rent, and highway tolls. The demand schedule reveals that Chloe increases the quantity of gasoline that she purchases as the price of gasoline falls.

Demand Curves

We'll often want to plot a demand schedule. That is what the demand curve does. The **demand curve** plots the relationship between prices and quantity demanded (again, holding all else equal). In Exhibit 4.1, each dot plots a single point from the demand schedule. For example, the leftmost dot represents the point at which the price is $6 per gallon and the quantity demanded is 50 gallons of gasoline per year. Similarly, the rightmost dot represents the point at which the price is $1 per gallon and the quantity demanded is 300 gallons of gasoline per year. Notice that the horizontal axis (the *x*-axis) represents the quantity demanded. The vertical axis (the *y*-axis) represents the price per gallon. Economists always adopt this plotting convention—quantity demanded on the horizontal axis and price on the vertical axis. Economists usually "connect the dots" as we have in Exhibit 4.1, which implies that prices and quantities demanded don't always have to be round numbers.

The demand curve has an important property that we will see many times. The price of gasoline and the quantity demanded are **negatively related**, which means that they move in opposite directions. In other words, when one goes up, the other goes down, and vice versa. In Chloe's case, a gas price of $6/gallon generates a quantity demanded of 50 gallons per year, and a price of $1/gallon generates a much greater quantity demanded of 300 gallons per year. The price of gas and the quantity demanded move in opposite directions.

Almost all goods have demand curves that exhibit this fundamental negative relationship, which economists call the **Law of Demand**: the quantity demanded rises when the price falls (holding all else equal).

In this book all demand curves, demand schedules, and graph labels related to demand are in blue.

Willingness to Pay

Chloe's demand curve can also be used to calculate how much she is willing (and able) to pay for an additional gallon of gasoline. One extra gallon of gasoline is called a marginal gallon. The height of her demand curve at any given quantity is the amount she is willing to pay for that marginal unit of the good. In other words, the height of her demand curve is the value in dollars that Chloe places on that last gallon of gasoline.

For example, Chloe is willing to pay $4 for her 150th gallon of gasoline. In other words, with 149 gallons already at her at her disposal in one year, Chloe's willingness to pay for an additional gallon of gasoline is $4. **Willingness to pay** is the highest price that a buyer is willing to pay for an extra unit of a good.

On the other hand, Chloe is willing to pay only $3 for a marginal gallon of gasoline if she already has 199 gallons (for use that year). Chloe's willingness to pay for an additional gallon is negatively related to the quantity that she already has—this is the quantity on the horizontal axis in Exhibit 4.1. The more gasoline that she already has, the less she is willing to pay for an additional gallon. For most goods and services, this negative relationship applies. The more you have of something—for instance, slices of pizza—the less gain there is from acquiring another unit of the same good.

This is an example of a concept called **diminishing marginal benefit**: as you consume more of a good, your willingness to pay for an additional unit declines. An easy way to remember this concept is to think about donuts. My first donut in the morning is worth a lot to me so I am willing to pay a lot for it. My fourth donut in the same sitting is worth much less to me, so I am willing to pay less for it. In general, the more donuts I eat, the less I am willing to pay for an extra donut.

From Individual Demand Curves to Aggregated Demand Curves

So far we've talked about a single consumer, Chloe. But we can easily extend the ideas that we have discussed to all buyers of gasoline, including consumers and firms.

Think about the worldwide market for energy. Chloe's demand curve implies that she will increase her use of gasoline when the price of gasoline goes down. Other gasoline users will also increase their consumption of gasoline as its price falls.

Though all individual demand curves are downward-sloping, that's about all they have in common. For example, a schoolteacher in Kenya may earn $1,000 per year. For any given price of gasoline, the schoolteacher probably won't consume nearly as much gasoline as a typical worker in the United States (who has about 50 times as much income to spend).

This leaves us with a challenge. How do we account for the gasoline demand of billions of consumers worldwide? All of their demand curves will obey the Law of Demand, but otherwise they won't look alike. To study the behavior of the worldwide energy market, economists need to study the worldwide demand curve for gasoline, which is equivalent to the sum of all the individual demand curves. Economists call this adding-up process the **aggregation** of the individual demand curves.

We'll begin by showing you how to add up the demand of just two individual buyers. We'll first teach you how to do it with demand schedules. Then we'll show you what that implies for plotted demand curves. Remember that these different ways of thinking about demand are equivalent. Each method reinforces the other.

Exhibit 4.2 contains two individual demand schedules and a total demand schedule. To calculate the total quantity demanded at a particular price, simply add up Sue's and Carlos's quantity demanded at that price. For example, at a price of $4 per gallon, Sue has a quantity demanded of 200 gallons per year. At that same price, Carlos has a quantity demanded of 400 gallons per year. So the aggregate level of quantity demanded at a price of $4/gallon is 200 + 400 = 600 gallons per year.

Conceptually, aggregating quantity demanded means fixing the price and adding up the quantities that each buyer demands. It is important to remember that quantities are being added together, not prices. Here's an example to help you remember this point. Consider a bakery selling donuts at $1 each. Suppose that two hungry students walk into the bakery and each wants a donut. The total quantity demanded by the two students would be two donuts at a price of $1 per donut. Remember this tale of two donuts and you'll avoid getting confused when you calculate total demand schedules.

Exhibit 4.2 also contains plotted demand curves. When a demand curve is a straight line, as in this exhibit, the relationship between price and quantity demanded is said to

Willingness to pay is the highest price that a buyer is willing to pay for an extra unit of a good.

Diminishing marginal benefit: As you consume more of a good, your willingness to pay for an additional unit declines.

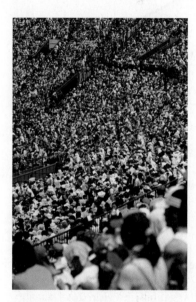

The process of adding up individual behaviors is referred to as **aggregation**.

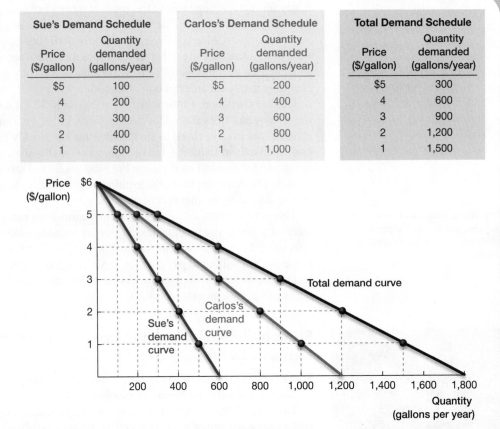

Exhibit 4.2 Aggregation of Demand Schedules and Demand Curves

Demand schedules are aggregated by summing the quantity demanded at each price on the individual demand schedules. Likewise, demand curves are aggregated by summing the quantity demanded at each price on the individual demand curves.

Sue's Demand Schedule	
Price ($/gallon)	Quantity demanded (gallons/year)
$5	100
4	200
3	300
2	400
1	500

Carlos's Demand Schedule	
Price ($/gallon)	Quantity demanded (gallons/year)
$5	200
4	400
3	600
2	800
1	1,000

Total Demand Schedule	
Price ($/gallon)	Quantity demanded (gallons/year)
$5	300
4	600
3	900
2	1,200
1	1,500

be linear. Economists often illustrate demand curves with straight lines because they are easy to explain and easy to express as equations. On the other hand, real-world demand curves don't tend to be perfectly straight lines, so the linear model is mostly used as an illustrative case.

The plotted demand curves in Exhibit 4.2 can be aggregated the same way that the demand schedules are aggregated. Again, look at the quantities demanded at a single price, say $4/gallon. Sue's demand curve has a quantity demanded of 200 gallons per year. Carlos's demand curve has a quantity demanded of 400 gallons per year. Total quantity demanded at a price of $4 per gallon is the sum of the two individual quantities demanded: 200 + 400 = 600 gallons per year.

Building the Market Demand Curve

Exhibit 4.2 shows you how to add up demand curves for just two buyers. We would like to study the demand of all buyers in a market. Economists refer to this as the **market demand curve**. It is the sum of the individual demand curves of all the potential buyers. The market demand curve plots the relationship between the total quantity demanded and the market price, holding all else equal.

Over 1 billion economic agents purchase gasoline every year. If we added up the total quantity of gasoline demanded at a particular market price, we could calculate the market demand for gasoline at that price. But economists rarely study the market demand for gasoline. Economists who study energy markets recognize that the gasoline market is very closely tied to all of the other markets for products produced from crude oil. Jet fuel, diesel fuel, and automobile gasoline are all produced from oil. Accordingly, when economists study the market for gasoline, we aggregate to the total market for oil. Exhibit 4.3 reports a rough approximation of the worldwide demand curve for billions of "barrels of oil" (there are 42 gallons per barrel), which is the unit of measurement that is commonly used in this market.

The **market demand curve** is the sum of the individual demand curves of all the potential buyers. It plots the relationship between the total quantity demanded and the market price, holding all else equal.

Exhibit 4.3 Market Demand Curve for Oil

The price of a barrel of oil averaged about $100 per barrel from 2011 to 2013. At that price, worldwide demand for oil was around 35 billion barrels per year. This demand curve plots the relationship between the price of oil and the quantity demanded.

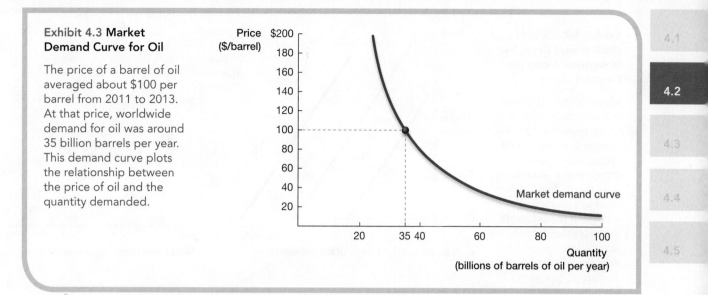

Finally, note that the demand curve in Exhibit 4.3 is not a straight line, and therefore looks a bit different from the straight demand curves that you saw earlier. This serves as a reminder that the key property of a demand curve is the negative relationship between price and quantity demanded. Demand curves can exhibit this negative relationship without being straight lines.

Exhibit 4.3 also contains a horizontal dashed line that represents the market price of oil from 2011 to 2013: $100 per barrel. The horizontal price line crosses the demand curve at a point labeled with a dot. At this intersection the buyers' willingness to pay (the height of the demand curve) is equal to the market price of oil. Buyers keep purchasing oil as long as their willingness to pay is greater than or equal to the price of oil. At a market price of $100 per barrel, the demand curve implies that buyers will keep purchasing oil until they reach a quantity demanded of 35 billion barrels of oil per year.

Shifting the Demand Curve

When we introduced the demand curve, we explained that it describes the relationship between price and quantity demanded, holding all else equal. It's now time to more carefully consider the "all else" that is being held fixed.

The demand curve shifts when these five major factors change:

- Tastes and preferences
- Income and wealth
- Availability and prices of related goods
- Number and scale of buyers
- Buyers' beliefs about the future

Changing Tastes and Preferences   A change in tastes or preferences is simply a change in what we personally like, enjoy, or value. For example, your demand for oil products would fall (holding price fixed) if you became convinced that global warming was a significant global problem and it was your ethical duty to use fewer fossil fuels. Because your willingness to buy oil products decreases as a result of your growing environmental worries, your demand curve shifts to the left. We refer to this as a "left" shift in the demand curve because a lower quantity demanded for a given price of oil corresponds to a leftward movement on the horizontal axis. If many people have experiences like this—say an environmental documentary convinces millions of drivers to buy hybrids—then the market demand curve will experience a shift to the left. See Exhibit 4.4 for an example of a left shift in a demand curve.

Naturally, a taste change could also shift a demand curve to the right, corresponding to an increase in the quantity demanded at a given market price. For example, this would happen to your individual demand curve if you started dating someone who lives a few towns away, thereby increasing your transportation needs. Exhibit 4.4 also plots a right shift in a demand curve.

Exhibit 4.4 Shifts of the Demand Curve vs. Movement Along the Demand Curve

Many factors other than a good's price affect the quantity demanded. If a change in these factors reduces the quantity demanded at a given price, then the demand curve shifts left (panel (a)). If a change in these factors increases the quantity demanded at a given price, then the demand curve shifts right (panel (a)). On the other hand, if only the good's own price changes, then the demand curve does not shift and we move along the demand curve (panel (b)).

(a) Left and right shifts of the demand curve

(b) Movement along the demand curve

The **demand curve shifts** only when the quantity demanded changes at a given price.

If a good's own price changes and its demand curve hasn't shifted, the own price change produces a **movement along the demand curve.**

This example illustrates two key concepts:

- The **demand curve shifts** only when the quantity demanded changes at a given price. Left and right shifts are illustrated in panel (a) of Exhibit 4.4.
- If a good's own price changes and its demand curve hasn't shifted, the own price change produces a **movement along the demand curve**. Movements along the demand curve are illustrated in panel (b) of Exhibit 4.4.

It is important to master these terms, because they will keep coming up. Use Exhibit 4.4 to confirm that you know the difference between a "shift of the demand curve" and a "movement along the demand curve." It helps to remember that if the quantity demanded changes at a given price, then the demand curve has shifted.

We now continue with a discussion of the key factors, other than tastes and preferences, that shift the demand curve.

Changing Income or Changing Wealth A change in income or a change in wealth affects your ability to pay for goods and services. Imagine that you recently got your first full-time job and went from a student budget to a $40,000 annual salary. You might buy a car and the gas to go with it. You'd probably also start taking more exotic vacations: for instance, flying to Hawaii rather than taking the bus to visit your friends in Hackensack. Your willingness (directly and indirectly) to buy fuel will now be higher, holding the price of fuel fixed, implying that your demand curve shifts to the right. For a **normal good**, an increase in income causes the demand curve to shift to the right (holding the good's price fixed).

On the other hand, consider a good like Spam, which is canned, precooked meat. In the developed world, as people's incomes rise, they are likely to consume fewer canned foods and more fresh foods. If rising income shifts the demand curve for a good to the left (holding the good's price fixed), then the good is called an **inferior good**. This seemingly insulting label is actually only a technical term that describes a relationship between increases in income and leftward shifts in the demand curve.

For an inferior good, rising income shifts the demand curve to the left. No insult intended to Spam lovers.

Changing Availability and Prices of Related Goods A change in the availability and prices of related goods will also influence demand for oil products (holding the price of

For a **normal good,** an increase in income causes the demand curve to shift to the right (holding the good's price fixed).

For an **inferior good,** an increase in income causes the demand curve to shift to the left (holding the good's price fixed).

Two goods are **substitutes** when the fall in the price of one leads to a left shift in the demand curve for the other.

Two goods are **complements** when the fall in the price of one, leads to a right shift in the demand curve for the other.

oil fixed), thereby shifting the demand curve for oil. For example, if a city cuts the price of public transportation, drivers are likely to partially cut back use of their cars. This produces a left shift in the demand curve for gas. Two goods are said to be substitutes when the fall in the price of one leads to a left shift in the demand curve for the other. Public transportation and gas are **substitutes**, because a fall in the price of public transportation leads people to drive their cars less, producing a left shift in the demand curve for gas.

On the other hand, there are some related goods and services that play the opposite role. For example, suppose that a ski resort located 200 miles from where you live decreases its lift ticket prices. The price cut will lead some people to increase their visits to the ski resort, thereby increasing their transportation needs and shifting right their demand curve for gas. Two goods are said to be **complements** when the fall in the price of one good, leads to a right shift in the demand curve for the other good.

Changing Number and Scale of Buyers   When the number of buyers increases, the demand curve shifts right. When the number of buyers decreases, the demand curve shifts left. The scale of the buyers' purchasing behavior also matters. For example, if the mayor of a small town switches all of the town buses from gasoline to battery power, this will have a much smaller impact on worldwide gasoline demand than a switch by the mayor of the world's largest city, Tokyo.

Changing Buyers' Beliefs About the Future   Changing buyers' beliefs about the future also influence the demand curve. Suppose that some people begin losing their jobs during the first months of an economy-wide slowdown. Even if you hadn't lost your job, you might still be worried. You could lose your job at some point in the near future, and anticipating this possibility might lead you to build up a rainy-day fund right now. To do this, you might cut your spending by carpooling or eliminating weekend trips to local ski resorts. Such belt-tightening tends to reduce gas usage and shifts the demand curve for oil to the left.

> ## Summary of Shifts in the Demand Curve and Movements Along the Demand Curve
>
> **The demand curve shifts when these factors change:**
> 1. Tastes and preferences
> 2. Income and wealth
> 3. Availability and prices of related goods
> 4. Number and scale of buyers
> 5. Buyers' beliefs about the future
>
> **The *only* reason for a movement along the demand curve:**
> A change in the price of the good itself

Evidence-Based Economics

Q: How much more gasoline would people buy if its price were lower?

We've explained that the quantity of gasoline demanded falls as the price rises. We're now ready to study empirical evidence that backs this up.

Brazil and Venezuela share a border, and they have similar levels of income per person. Both are also large oil producers—each produced about 3 million barrels per day in 2013. However, they have radically different energy policies. Like most countries, Brazil heavily taxes the sale of gasoline. In contrast, Venezuela aggressively subsidizes the sale of gasoline. To compare their policies, we report the U.S. dollar price of gasoline in 2013, when Brazilian drivers paid $5.58 per gallon and Venezuelan drivers paid only $0.04 per gallon. The Venezuelan government provided enough of a subsidy to make

Evidence-Based Economics *(Continued)*

gasoline practically free. The Venezuelan government is a major oil producer and supplies enough gas to meet consumer demand, even when the price was $0.04 per gallon.

The Law of Demand predicts that a lower price should be associated with a higher quantity demanded, all else held equal. In fact, per person gasoline consumption is almost five times higher in Venezuela than in Brazil.

Exhibit 4.5 plots the price of gasoline on the vertical axis (including taxes and subsidies) and the quantity of gasoline demanded on the horizontal axis. As you can see, there is a negative relationship between price and quantity demanded. We've also added Mexico to this figure to give you a sense of how another Latin American country (with similar per person income) compares. Mexico provides a small subsidy on gasoline and consequently falls between the other two countries. The Law of Demand predicts a negative relationship between price and quantity demanded, and the data confirms that prediction.

Exhibit 4.5 The Quantity of Gasoline Demanded (per person) and the Price of Gasoline in Brazil, Mexico, and Venezuela

There is a negative relationship between price and quantity demanded in the gasoline market. Quantity demanded is from the OECD. After-tax, after-subsidy gasoline prices are from AIRINC.

Question	**Answer**	**Data**	**Caveat**
How much more gasoline would people buy if its price were lower?	Venezuelans, who paid only $0.04 per gallon of gas, purchased five times as much per person as Brazilians, who paid $5.58 per gallon.	We compare the quantity of gasoline demanded in Latin American countries with similar levels of income per person and very different gas prices. The variation in gas prices is caused by differences in taxes and subsidies.	Though income levels per person are similar in these countries, the countries have other differences that are not accounted for in this analysis.

4.3 How Do Sellers Behave?

You now understand the behavior of buyers. To understand the complete picture of a market, we also need to study sellers. The interaction of buyers and sellers in a marketplace determines the market price.

We want to analyze the relationship between the price of a good and the amount of the good that sellers are willing to sell or supply. At a given price, the amount of the good or service that sellers are willing to supply is called the **quantity supplied**. Note that in this book, all supply curves, supply schedules, and graph labels relating to supply are in red.

Quantity supplied is the amount of a good or service that sellers are willing to sell at a given price.

To build intuition for the concept of quantity supplied, think about a company like ExxonMobil. As the price of oil goes up, ExxonMobil increases its willingness to supply oil that is relatively expensive for the company to discover and extract. Some oil is in deep-water locations where the ocean depth is 2 miles and the oil is another 8 miles below the seafloor. Such wells are drilled by specialized ships two football fields long, which are staffed by hundreds of workers and equipped with robotic, unmanned submarines. Because of the enormous expense, such wells are only drilled when the price of oil is over $70 per barrel.

Drilling for oil from offshore platforms above the Arctic Circle is even more costly. If a single small iceberg could sink the *Titanic*, imagine the challenge of building and protecting oil rigs in areas where tens of thousands of large icebergs pass each year. Offshore oil wells within the Arctic Circle are only drilled when the price of oil is over $80 per barrel.

The higher the price of oil goes, the more drilling locations become profitable for ExxonMobil. Many observers talk about oil and warn that we are running out of it. In fact, companies like ExxonMobil are only running out of cheap oil. There is more oil under the surface of the earth than we are ever going to use. The problem is that much of that oil is very expensive to extract and deliver to the market.

Drilling from offshore platforms above the Arctic Circle is not profitable unless the price of oil exceeds $80 per barrel. At the other extreme, oil from the deserts of Saudi Arabia costs less than $20 per barrel to extract.

Supply Curves

A **supply schedule** is a table that reports the quantity supplied at different prices, holding all else equal.

ExxonMobil responds to increases in the price of oil by developing new oil fields in ever more challenging locations. The relationship between ExxonMobil's production of oil and the price of oil is summarized in the boxed supply schedule in Exhibit 4.6. A **supply schedule**

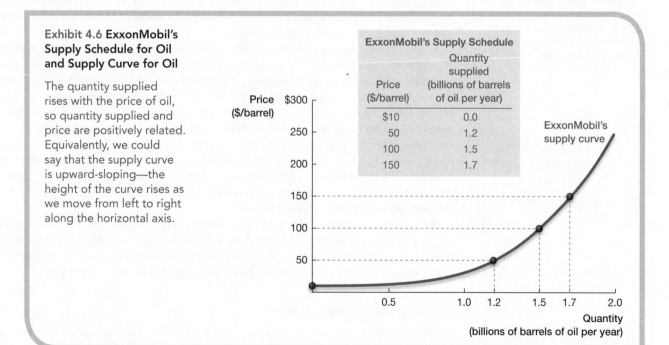

Exhibit 4.6 ExxonMobil's Supply Schedule for Oil and Supply Curve for Oil

The quantity supplied rises with the price of oil, so quantity supplied and price are positively related. Equivalently, we could say that the supply curve is upward-sloping—the height of the curve rises as we move from left to right along the horizontal axis.

ExxonMobil's Supply Schedule

Price ($/barrel)	Quantity supplied (billions of barrels of oil per year)
$10	0.0
50	1.2
100	1.5
150	1.7

The **supply curve** plots the quantity supplied at different prices. A supply curve plots the supply schedule.

Two variables are **positively related** if the variables move in the same direction.

Law of Supply: In almost all cases, the quantity supplied rises when the price rises (holding all else equal).

Willingness to accept is the lowest price that a seller is willing to get paid to sell an extra unit of a good. Willingness to accept is the same as the marginal cost of production.

The **market supply curve** is the sum of the individual supply curves of all the potential sellers. It plots the relationship between the total quantity supplied and the market price, holding all else equal.

is a table that reports the quantity supplied at different prices, holding all else equal. The supply schedule shows that ExxonMobil increases the quantity of oil supplied as the price of oil increases. Exhibit 4.6 also plots ExxonMobil's **supply curve**, which plots the quantity supplied at different prices. In other words, a supply curve plots the supply schedule.

The supply curve in Exhibit 4.6 has a key property. The price of oil and the quantity supplied are **positively related**. By positively related we mean that the variables move in the same direction—when one variable goes up, the other goes up, too. In almost all cases, quantity supplied and price are positively related (holding all else equal), which economists call the **Law of Supply**.

ExxonMobil starts to produce oil when the price exceeds a level of $10 per barrel. An oil price of $50 per barrel generates a quantity supplied of 1.2 billion barrels per year. A higher oil price of $100 per barrel generates a higher quantity supplied of 1.5 billion barrels per year. At the highest price of oil listed in the supply schedule, the quantity supplied rises further to 1.7 billion barrels per year.

Willingness to Accept

If ExxonMobil is optimizing, the firm should be willing to supply one additional barrel of oil if it is paid at least its marginal cost of production. Recall from the chapter on optimization (Chapter 3) that marginal cost is the extra cost generated by producing an additional unit. As long as an oil producer is paid at least its marginal cost per barrel, it should be willing to supply another barrel of oil.

For an optimizing firm, the height of the supply curve is the firm's marginal cost. For example, ExxonMobil's supply curve implies that if the price of oil is $100, then the quantity supplied is 1.5 billion barrels per year. We can turn this around and say it another way—ExxonMobil is willing to accept $100 to produce its 1.5 billionth barrel of oil. That's what the supply curve tells us. Economists call this ExxonMobil's **willingness to accept**, which is the lowest price that a seller is willing to get paid to sell an extra unit of a good. For an optimizing firm, willingness to accept is the same as the marginal cost of production. ExxonMobil is willing to accept $100 for an additional barrel, because $100 is ExxonMobil's marginal cost when it produces its 1.5 billionth barrel in a year.

From the Individual Supply Curve to the Market Supply Curve

When we studied buyers, we summed up their individual demand curves to obtain a market demand curve. We're now ready to do the same thing for the sellers. Adding up quantity supplied works the same way as adding up quantity demanded. We add up quantities at a particular price. We then repeat this at every possible price to plot the **market supply curve**. The market supply curve plots the relationship between the total quantity supplied and the market price, holding all else equal.

Let's start with an aggregation analysis that assumes there are only two oil companies, ExxonMobil and Chevron. Assume that they have the supply schedules listed in Exhibit 4.7. At a price of $100 per barrel, the quantity supplied by Chevron is 1 billion barrels of oil per year and the quantity supplied by ExxonMobil is 1.5 billion barrels of oil per year. So the total quantity supplied at the price of $100 per barrel is 1 billion + 1.5 billion = 2.5 billion barrels of oil per year. To calculate the total supply curve, we repeat this calculation for each price. The resulting total supply curve is plotted in Exhibit 4.7.

Of course, the market contains thousands of oil producers, not just ExxonMobil and Chevron. The market supply curve is the sum of the individual supply curves of all these thousands of potential sellers, just as the market demand curve is the sum of the individual demand curves of all the potential buyers.

Aggregating the individual supply curves of thousands of oil producers yields a market supply curve like the one plotted in Exhibit 4.8. We've included a dashed line at $100/barrel, which is the approximate market price that prevailed in the world oil market from 2011 to 2013. At this price, the total quantity supplied is 35 billion barrels of oil per year.

Shifting the Supply Curve

Recall that the supply curve describes the relationship between price and quantity supplied, holding all else equal. There are four major types of variables that are held

Exhibit 4.7 Aggregation of Supply Schedules and Supply Curves

To calculate the total quantity supplied at a particular price, add up the quantity supplied by each supplier at that price. Repeat this for each price to derive the total supply curve.

Chevron's Supply Schedule		ExxonMobil's Supply Schedule		Total Supply Schedule	
Price ($/barrel)	Quantity supplied (billions of barrels of oil per year)	Price ($/barrel)	Quantity supplied (billions of barrels of oil per year)	Price ($/barrel)	Quantity supplied (billions of barrels of oil per year)
$10	0.0	$10	0.0	$10	0.0
50	0.8	50	1.2	50	2.0
100	1.0	100	1.5	100	2.5
150	1.1	150	1.7	150	2.8

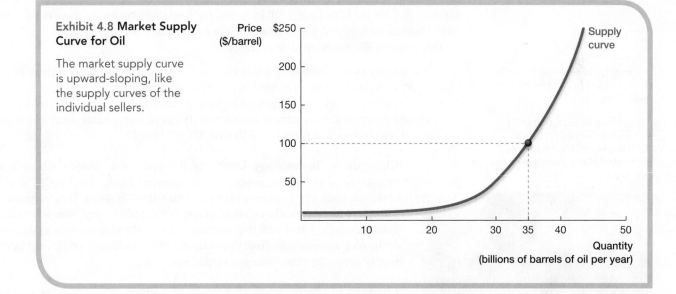

Exhibit 4.8 Market Supply Curve for Oil

The market supply curve is upward-sloping, like the supply curves of the individual sellers.

fixed when a supply curve is constructed. The supply curve shifts when these variables change:

- Prices of inputs used to produce the good
- Technology used to produce the good
- Number and scale of sellers
- Sellers' beliefs about the future

Changing Prices of Inputs Used to Produce the Good Changes in the prices of inputs shift the supply curve. An **input** is a good or service used to produce another good or service. For instance, steel is used to construct oil platforms, to create oil drilling machinery,

An **input** is a good or service used to produce another good or service.

Exhibit 4.9 Shifts of the Supply Curve vs. Movement Along the Supply Curve

Many factors other than a good's price affect the quantity supplied. If a change in these factors decreases the quantity supplied at a given price, then the supply curve shifts left (panel (a)). If a change in these factors increases the quantity supplied at a given price, then the supply curve shifts right (panel (a)). On the other hand, if only the good's own price changes, then the supply curve does not shift and we move along the supply curve (panel (b)).

(a) Left and right shifts of the supply curve

(b) Movement along the supply curve

to build pipelines, and to construct oil tankers. Hence, steel is a critical input to oil production. An increase in the price of steel implies that some opportunities to produce oil will no longer be profitable, and therefore optimizing oil producers will choose not to supply as much oil (holding the price of oil fixed). It follows that an increase in the price of steel shifts the supply curve of oil to the left. In other words, holding the price of oil fixed, the quantity of oil supplied falls. On the other hand, a fall in the price of steel shifts the supply curve of oil to the right. Panel (a) of Exhibit 4.9 plots these left and right shifts in the supply curve.

This example illustrates two key concepts:

The **supply curve shifts** only when the quantity supplied changes at a given price.

If a good's own price changes and its supply curve hasn't shifted, the own price change produces a **movement along the supply curve.**

- The **supply curve shifts** only when the quantity supplied changes at a given price. Left and right shifts are illustrated in panel (a) of Exhibit 4.9.
- If a good's own price changes and its supply curve hasn't shifted, the own price change produces a **movement along the supply curve**. Movements along the supply curve are illustrated in panel (b) of Exhibit 4.9.

Changes in Technology Used to Produce the Good Changes in technology also shift the supply curve. In recent years, "fracking" (induced hydraulic fracturing) has revolutionized the energy industry. This technology uses pressurized fluids to create fractures in the underground rock formations that surround a drilled well. The fractures enable oil and natural gas to seep out of the rock and be drawn from the well. Fracking has caused a right shift in the supply curves for petroleum and natural gas.

Changes in the Number and Scale of Sellers Changes in the number of sellers also shift the supply curve. For example, in 2011 Libyan rebels overthrew Muammar Gaddafi, a dictator who had controlled the country for 42 years. Gaddafi loyalists defended his regime and the fighting dragged on for 6 months. During this period, Libya essentially stopped oil production. Before the war, Libyan wells had been producing about 1.5 million barrels per day. This is the scale of Libyan production. During the Libyan civil war, the worldwide supply curve shifted to the left by 1.5 million barrels per day.

A photograph of a Libyan oil refinery burning during the 2011 civil war that overthrew Colonel Muammar Gaddafi. During the war almost all of Libya's oil production was shut down, shifting the world oil supply curve to the left.

Changes in Sellers' Beliefs About the Future Finally, changes in sellers' beliefs about the future shift the supply curve. For example, consider the market for natural gas. Every winter, natural gas usage skyrockets for home heating. This creates a winter spike in

Summary of Shifts in the Supply Curve and Movements Along the Supply Curve

The supply curve shifts when these factors change:

1. Prices of inputs used to produce the good
2. Technology used to produce the good
3. Number and scale of sellers
4. Sellers' beliefs about the future

The *only* reason for a movement along the supply curve:

A change in the price of the good itself

natural gas prices. Expecting such price spikes, natural gas producers store vast quantities during the summer (when prices are low by comparison). In other words, natural gas producers use much of their summer natural gas production to build up stockpiles instead of selling all of the summer production to the public. This implies that natural gas suppliers shift the supply curve to the left in the summer. This is an optimization strategy. By pulling supply off the (low-price) summer market and increasing supply in the (high-price) winter market, natural gas suppliers obtain a higher average price. Summarizing this strategy, natural gas producers adjust their supply throughout the year in response to expectations about how the price of natural gas will move in the future.

4.4 Supply and Demand in Equilibrium

Up to this point, we have provided tools that explain the separate behavior of buyers and sellers. We haven't explained how to put the two sides of the market together. How do buyers and sellers interact? What determines the market price at which they trade? What determines the quantity of goods bought by buyers and sold by sellers? We will use the market demand curve and the market supply curve to answer these questions. We'll continue to study a perfectly competitive market, which we'll refer to from now on as a "competitive market."

> Competitive markets converge to the price at which quantity supplied and quantity demanded are the same.

Competitive markets converge to the price at which quantity supplied and quantity demanded are the same. To visualize what it means to equate quantity supplied and quantity demanded, we need to plot the demand curve and supply curve on the same figure. Exhibit 4.10 does this.

Exhibit 4.10 Demand Curve and Supply Curve for Oil

In a competitive market, the market price is the point at which the demand curve intersects the supply curve.

The **competitive equilibrium** is the crossing point of the supply curve and the demand curve.

The **competitive equilibrium price** equates quantity supplied and quantity demanded.

The **competitive equilibrium quantity** is the quantity that corresponds to the competitive equilibrium price.

When the market price is above the competitive equilibrium price, quantity supplied exceeds quantity demanded, creating **excess supply.**

When the market price is below the competitive equilibrium price, quantity demanded exceeds quantity supplied, creating **excess demand.**

In Exhibit 4.10, the demand curve (in blue) and the supply curve (in red) for the oil market cross at a price of $100 per barrel and a quantity of 35 billion barrels. Because the demand curve slopes down and the supply curve slopes up, the two curves have only one crossing point. Economists refer to this crossing point as the **competitive equilibrium**. The price at the crossing point is referred to as the **competitive equilibrium price**, which is the price at which quantity supplied and quantity demanded are the same. This is sometimes referred to as the market clearing price, because at this price there is a buyer for every unit that is supplied in the market. The quantity at the crossing point is referred to as the **competitive equilibrium quantity**. This is the quantity that corresponds to the competitive equilibrium price.

At the competitive equilibrium price, the quantity demanded is equal to the quantity supplied. At any other price, the quantity demanded and the quantity supplied will be unequal. To see this, draw a horizontal line at any other price. Only the horizontal line at the competitive equilibrium price equates quantity demanded and quantity supplied.

Exhibit 4.11 illustrates a case in which the market is not in competitive equilibrium because the market price is above the competitive equilibrium price. The higher price makes selling more desirable and buying less desirable, raising the quantity supplied above its competitive equilibrium level and lowering the quantity demanded below its competitive equilibrium level. When the market price is above the competitive equilibrium price, quantity supplied exceeds quantity demanded, creating **excess supply**. For example, Exhibit 4.11 shows that at a market price of $140 per barrel for oil, the quantity supplied of 38 billion barrels of oil per year exceeds the quantity demanded of 29 billion barrels of oil per year.

If the market stayed in this situation, sellers would pump 38 billion barrels of oil per year, but buyers would purchase only 29 billion of those barrels, leaving the difference—9 billion barrels—unsold each year. This would push down oil prices, as enormous stockpiles of oil started to build up around the world. Because existing oil storage tanks are limited in scale and expensive to build, sellers would start undercutting each other's prices to get rid of the rising inventory of unsold oil. Prices would fall. As a result, the situation in Exhibit 4.11 normally wouldn't last for long. Sellers, who are selling nearly identical barrels of oil, would compete with one another for customers by cutting prices. This would continue until the market price fell back to the competitive equilibrium price. This competitive process plays an important role in pushing the market toward the aptly named competitive equilibrium.

Exhibit 4.12 illustrates the opposite case. When market price is below the competitive equilibrium price, quantity demanded exceeds quantity supplied, creating **excess demand**. In Exhibit 4.12 the quantity demanded of 44 billion barrels of oil per year exceeds the quantity supplied of 30 billion barrels of oil per year. Buyers want 44 billion barrels of oil, but there are only 30 billion barrels available on the market.

Exhibit 4.11 Excess Supply

When the market price is above the competitive equilibrium level, quantity demanded is less than quantity supplied. This is a case of excess supply. In this particular example, the excess supply is 38 − 29 = 9 billion barrels of oil per year.

Exhibit 4.12 Excess Demand

When the market price is below the competitive equilibrium level, quantity demanded is greater than quantity supplied. This is a case of excess demand. In this case, the excess demand is 44 − 30 = 14 billion barrels of oil per year.

The situation in Exhibit 4.12 also normally won't last long. Buyers who aren't getting the goods they want will compete with one another by offering to pay higher prices to get the limited quantity of oil. This will continue until the market price rises to the competitive equilibrium price of $100 per barrel.

Curve Shifting in Competitive Equilibrium

We are now ready to put this framework into action. We'd like to know how a shock to the world oil market will affect the equilibrium quantity and the equilibrium price of oil.

For example, what would happen if a major oil exporter suddenly stopped production, as Libya did in 2011? This causes a left shift of the supply curve, as illustrated in Exhibit 4.13. Since oil has become more scarce, the price of oil needs to rise from its old level to equate quantity supplied and quantity demanded. The rise in the equilibrium oil price is associated with a movement along the demand curve (which hasn't shifted). Because the demand curve is downward-sloping, a rising price causes a reduction in the quantity demanded. In fact, the outbreak of full-scale fighting in Libya and the consequent shutdown of the Libyan oil fields did correspond with an increase in the world price of oil.

Exhibit 4.13 A Left Shift of the Supply Curve

A left shift in the supply curve raises the equilibrium price and lowers the equilibrium quantity. The original equilibrium is located at the grey dot. The new equilibrium is marked by the black dot, where the original demand curve and the new supply curve intersect.

Exhibit 4.14 A Left Shift of the Demand Curve

A left shift in the demand curve lowers the equilibrium price and lowers the equilibrium quantity. The original equilibrium is located at the grey dot. The new equilibrium is marked by the black dot, where the original supply curve and the new demand curve intersect.

We can also predict the effect of a shift in the demand curve. For example, what would happen if rising environmental concerns led consumers to cut back their carbon footprint by using less oil? This change in consumer tastes shifts left the demand curve for oil, which is plotted in Exhibit 4.14. Oil demand has decreased, so the price of oil needs to fall from its old level to equate quantity supplied and quantity demanded. The decrease in the equilibrium oil price is associated with a movement along the supply curve (which hasn't shifted). Because the supply curve is upward-sloping, a falling price causes a reduction in the quantity supplied.

Using demand and supply curves to study markets enables economists to resolve puzzles. For example, in Exhibit 4.14, the market price of oil drops and people buy less oil! Hearing those two facts might sound perplexing. Shouldn't a drop in the price of oil lead to an increase in oil buying? In Exhibit 4.14, you can see that the drop in the price of oil is caused by a shift of the market demand curve to the left. This left shift causes the price to fall and the fall in price causes the quantity supplied to fall. So the fall in price and the fall in the equilibrium quantity are both consequences of the left shift in the demand curve.

So far we have studied examples in which only one curve—either the demand or supply curve—shifts at a time. But life isn't always this simple. Sometimes both curves shift at the same time. For example, a revolution in Libya might shift the supply curve for oil to the left at the same time that rising environmental consciousness shifts the demand curve for oil to the left.

We would also like to know what happens in mixed cases. Exhibit 4.15 shows how simultaneous shifts in the supply and the demand curves translate into changes in the market price and the quantity of transactions. As you can imagine, there are many possible combinations of shifts. These figures and their captions take you through one group of cases. The problems at the end of the chapter take you through other cases.

In all three panels of Exhibit 4.15 the demand curve shifts left and the supply curve shifts left. The three panels graph three different special cases. We represent the old demand curve in light blue and the new demand curve in dark blue. Likewise, the old supply curve is light red and the new supply curve is dark red. The grey dot marks the old competitive equilibrium, where the old demand curve and the old supply curve intersect. The black dot marks the new competitive equilibrium, where the new demand curve and the new supply curve intersect. The old competitive equilibrium price is P_1 and the new

Exhibit 4.15 Both the Demand Curve and the Supply Curve Shift Left

When both supply and demand shift left, the competitive equilibrium quantity will always decrease (Q_2 is always less than Q_1). On the other hand, the competitive equilibrium price may decrease (P_2 less than P_1), stay the same (P_2 equal to P_1), or increase (P_2 greater than P_1).

competitive equilibrium price is P_2. The old competitive equilibrium quantity is Q_1 and the new competitive equilibrium quantity is Q_2.

In all three panels, the equilibrium quantity falls: Q_2 is less than Q_1. However, the equilibrium price responds differently depending on the relative size of the shifts in the demand and supply curves. In the first panel, the left shift in demand dominates and the equilibrium price falls from P_1 to P_2. In the second panel, the equilibrium price stays exactly the same: $P_1 = P_2$. In the third panel, the left shift in supply dominates and the equilibrium price rises from P_1 to P_2. Summing up, when both supply and demand shift left, the competitive equilibrium quantity will always decrease, but the competitive equilibrium price may move in either direction or stay the same.

4.5 What Would Happen If the Government Tried to Dictate the Price of Gasoline?

Our analysis has concluded that competitive markets will end up at the competitive equilibrium—the point where the supply and the demand curves cross. But this can happen only if prices are allowed to respond to market pressures.

However, some markets have prices that are set by laws, regulations, or social norms. Economists are interested in the way that all markets work, even markets that are not allowed to reach a competitive equilibrium. We illustrate these issues by considering markets without a flexible price.

Take another look at Exhibit 4.12. When the market price of gasoline is artificially held below the level of the competitive equilibrium price, the quantity of gasoline demanded exceeds the quantity supplied. Accordingly, many drivers who would like to buy gas at the market price won't be able to do so.

In a situation like this, the allocation of gasoline is determined by something other than who is willing to pay for it. During the U.S. oil crisis of 1973–1974, the U.S. government

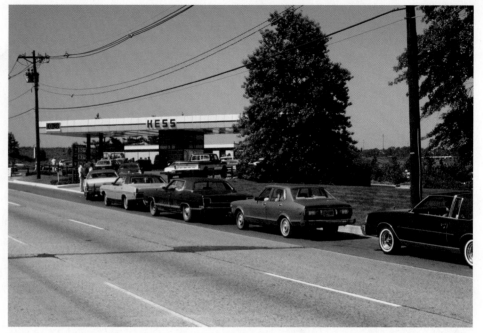

At the end of 1973, the U.S. government effectively capped the price of gasoline, creating a situation of excess demand.

effectively capped the price of gasoline, causing quantity demanded to exceed quantity supplied. This is referred to as a price ceiling. Drivers soon realized that there was excess demand at the capped price, leading them to show up early to get whatever gas was available. Lines began to form earlier and earlier in the day.

A New York Times reporter wrote, "Everywhere lines seemed to be the order of the day. In Montclair, N.J., Mrs. Catherine Lee got up at 4:20 one morning and drove to her filling station to be first on line. She had to settle for second place—No. 1 had gotten there at 3:15. Mrs. Lee fluffed up the pillow she had brought, threw two comforters over herself, and slept for three hours until the station opened." Some drivers devised ingenious means of getting around the system. "In Bedford, Massachusetts, a businessman drove his auto into a Hertz car rental lot, ordered a car, received it complete with a full tank of gas, siphoned the gas into his own car, paid Hertz their daily rental fee—no mileage charge, of course—and drove home in his car to enjoy his full tank of gas."[1]

The lines were an optimal response by buyers who understood that there was excess demand. Because quantity demanded exceeded quantity supplied, gas stations frequently ran out of gas. During the peak of the crisis, 20 percent of stations ran out of fuel. Getting in line early—very early—was an optimal way of assuring that you'd be able to fill your own tank.

Some folks didn't like waiting in long lines, particularly when they suspected that the station was going to run out of fuel before they got their turn at the pump. "They're out of their minds, they're turning sick. They'll kill you. They're fighting amongst themselves. They'll shoot you with a gun. They're all sick." Does this sound like a scene from World War Z? It's actually a gas station attendant describing his customers during the gasoline crisis of 1973–1974. An owner of another station put it this way: "It was mayhem. They were fighting in the streets and one customer pulled a knife on another one. And that was *before* we opened."

Economic history is filled with stories of governments that try to fix the price of goods instead of letting the market generate an equilibrium price. Price controls often do not work out well and governments keep forgetting this lesson.

The following Choice & Consequence feature details one more example of a failed effort to fix a price. As you read it, ask yourself how the goods in question could have been allocated differently.

This photograph was taken in 1974. Why don't we see signs like this today?

The Unintended Consequences of Fixing Market Prices

What would happen if your town announced a first-come, first-served sale of 1,000 Apple laptops for $50 each? Would the residents form an orderly line and patiently wait their turn?

In Henrico County, Virginia such a laptop sale was actually conducted. County residents began lining up at 1:30 A.M. on the day of the sale. When the gates opened at 7 A.M., more than 5,000 people surged into the sale site, pushing and shoving their way to get to the computers. Elderly people were trampled underneath the human tidal wave, and a baby's stroller was crushed. Eventually, about 70 police officers were called in to restore order. Seventeen people were injured and four landed up in the hospital. And after the uproar died down, over 4,000 people were left with nothing to show for all the trouble. Of those that did manage to obtain one of the computers, many later sold them.[2]

The Henrico County computer sale resulted in a situation of excess demand. At the fixed price set by the county, $50 per laptop, the quantity demanded of 5,000 exceeded the quantity supplied of 1,000. Exhibit 4.16 illustrates the fact that there were not enough laptops to go around. The people who got laptops were not necessarily the ones who were willing to pay the most.

Instead, the consumers who got the laptops were the ones who were able and willing to fight their way through the crowd. Even if we assume that the laptops were subsequently resold to other people who valued the laptops more, the stampede itself caused many injuries. A stampede is a bad way to allocate society's resources.

Economists are often asked to provide advice on how to design markets that will work well. Naturally, a flexible price would have made this market work better and it would have raised far more revenue for Henrico County.

Alternatively, the market could have been organized as an auction with bids received by phone or e-mail. The county could have auctioned off the 1,000 laptops to the 1,000 highest local bidders.

Even a random lottery would have worked much better than the stampede. The stampede allocated the laptops to the people who were the strongest and the pushiest and led to numerous injuries. A random lottery would allocate the laptops to the people who get lucky. And these lucky winners would be free to sell their laptop to anyone who valued it more than they did.

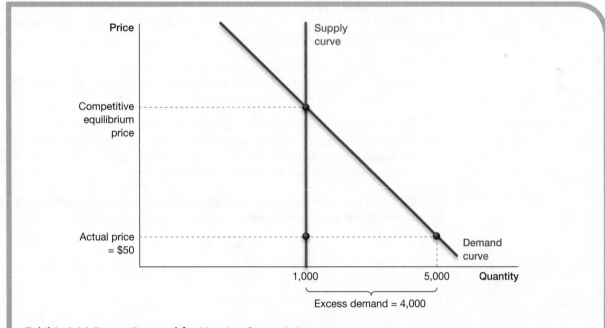

Exhibit 4.16 Excess Demand for Henrico County's Laptops

By fixing the price at $50 per laptop, Henrico County created a situation of excess demand. At this price, the quantity demanded (5,000 laptops) exceeded the quantity supplied (1,000 laptops). To equate the quantity demanded and the quantity supplied, a much higher price was needed: the competitive equilibrium price. The vertical supply curve reflects the fact that the supply of laptops at the $50 sale was fixed at 1,000 units.

Summary

❖ A market is a group of economic agents who are trading a good or service, and the rules and arrangements for trading. In a perfectly competitive market, (1) sellers all sell an identical good or service, and (2) individual buyers or individual sellers aren't powerful enough on their own to affect the market price of that good or service.

❖ Quantity demanded is the amount of a good that buyers are willing to purchase at a given price. A demand schedule is a table that reports the quantity demanded at different prices, holding all else equal. A demand curve plots the demand schedule. The Law of Demand states that in almost all cases, the quantity demanded rises when the price falls (holding all else equal).

❖ The market demand curve is the sum of the individual demand curves of all the potential buyers. It plots the relationship between the total quantity demanded and the market price, holding all else equal.

❖ The demand curve shifts only when the quantity demanded changes at a given price. If a good's own price changes and its demand curve hasn't shifted, the own price change produces a movement along the demand curve.

❖ Quantity supplied is the amount of a good or service that sellers are willing to sell at a given price. A supply schedule is a table that reports the quantity supplied at different prices, holding all else equal. A supply curve plots the supply schedule. The Law of Supply states that in almost all cases, the quantity supplied rises when the price rises (holding all else equal).

❖ The market supply curve is the sum of the individual supply curves of all the potential sellers. It plots the relationship between the total quantity supplied and the market price, holding all else equal.

❖ The supply curve shifts only when the quantity supplied changes at a given price. If a good's own price changes and its supply curve hasn't shifted, the own price change produces a movement along the supply curve.

❖ The competitive equilibrium is the crossing point of the supply curve and the demand curve. The competitive equilibrium price equates quantity supplied and quantity demanded. The competitive equilibrium quantity is the quantity that corresponds to the competitive equilibrium price.

❖ When prices are not free to fluctuate, markets fail to equate quantity demanded and quantity supplied.

Key Terms

market *p. 61*
market price *p. 62*
perfectly competitive market *p. 62*
price-taker *p. 62*
quantity demanded *p. 63*
demand schedule *p. 64*
holding all else equal *p. 64*
demand curve *p. 64*
negatively related *p. 64*
Law of Demand *p. 64*
willingness to pay *p. 65*
diminishing marginal benefit *p. 65*

aggregation *p. 65*
market demand curve *p. 66*
demand curve shifts *p. 68*
movement along the demand curve *p. 68*
normal good *p. 68*
inferior good *p. 68*
substitutes *p. 69*
complements *p. 69*
quantity supplied *p. 71*
supply schedule *p. 71*
supply curve *p. 72*

positively related *p. 72*
Law of Supply *p. 72*
willingness to accept *p. 72*
market supply curve *p. 72*
input *p. 73*
supply curve shifts *p. 74*
movement along the supply curve *p. 74*
competitive equilibrium *p. 76*
competitive equilibrium price *p. 76*
competitive equilibrium quantity *p. 76*
excess supply *p. 76*
excess demand *p. 76*

Questions

All questions are available in MyEconLab *for practice and instructor assignment.*

1. What is meant by holding all else equal? How is this concept used when discussing movements along the demand curve? How is this concept used when discussing movements along the supply curve?

2. What is meant by diminishing marginal benefits? Are you likely to experience diminishing marginal benefits for goods that you like a lot? Are there exceptions to the general rule of diminishing marginal benefits? (*Hint*: Think about batteries that you would use in a flashlight that requires two batteries.) Explain your answer.

3. How is the market demand schedule derived from individual demand schedules? How does the market demand curve differ from an individual demand curve?

4. Explain how the following factors will shift the demand curve for Gillette shaving cream.
    a. The price of a competitor's shaving cream increases.
    b. With an increase in unemployment, the average level of income in the economy falls.
    c. Shaving gels and foams, marketed as being better than shaving creams, are introduced in the market.

5. What does it mean to say that we are running out of "cheap oil"? What does this imply for the price of oil in the future?

6. What does the Law of Supply state? What is the key feature of a typical supply curve?

7. What is the difference between willingness to accept and willingness to pay? For a trade to take place, does the willingness to accept have to be lower, higher, or equal to the willingness to pay?

8. Explain how the following factors will shift the supply curve for sparkling wine.
    a. New irrigation technology increases the output of grapes of a vineyard.
    b. Following an increase in the immigration of unskilled labor, the wages of wine-grape pickers fall.
    c. The government sets a minimum wage for seasonal employment.

9. How do the following affect the equilibrium price in a market?
    a. A leftward shift in demand
    b. A rightward shift in supply
    c. A large rightward shift in demand and a small rightward shift in supply
    d. A large leftward shift in supply and a small leftward shift in demand

10. Why was a fixed price of $50 not the best way of allocating used laptops? Suggest other possible ways of distributing the laptops that would be efficient.

Problems

All problems are available in MyEconLab for practice and instructor assignment.

1. Suppose the following table shows the quantity of laundry detergent that is demanded and supplied at various prices in Country 1.

P ($)	Quantity Demanded (million oz.)	Quantity Supplied (million oz.)
2	65	35
4	60	40
6	55	45
8	50	50
10	45	55
12	40	60
14	35	65

   a. Use the data in the table to draw the demand and supply curves in the market for laundry detergent.

   b. What is the equilibrium price and quantity in the market?

   c. The following tables give the demand and supply schedules for two of its neighboring countries, Country 2 and Country 3. Suppose these three countries decide to form an economic union and integrate their markets. Use the data in the table to plot the market demand and supply curves in the newly formed economic union. What is the equilibrium price and quantity in the market?

   Country 2

P ($)	Quantity Demanded (million oz.)	Quantity Supplied (million oz.)
2	35	5
4	30	10
6	25	15
8	20	20
10	15	25
12	10	30
14	5	35

   Country 3

P ($)	Quantity Demanded (million oz.)	Quantity Supplied (million oz.)
2	40	10
4	35	15
6	30	20
8	25	25
10	20	30
12	15	35
14	10	40

2. In 1999, the Coca-Cola Company developed a vending machine that would raise the price of Coke in hot weather. Present a supply-and-demand diagram for soft drinks to explain the logic behind this machine.

3. Explain how simultaneous shifts in demand and supply curves could explain these situations:

   a. The price of insulin injection kits, used by diabetic patients, increases from $45 to $52, but the equilibrium quantity remains the same.

   b. A pest attack on the tomato crop increases the cost of producing ketchup. A mild winter causes cattle herds to be unusually large, causing the price of hamburgers to fall. The equilibrium quantity of ketchup is unchanged.

4. Suppose people who are thinking about buying a home (demanders in the housing market) and current home owners who are thinking about selling their homes (suppliers in the housing market) suddenly believe that home prices are likely to be significantly higher next year than this year.

   a. Will this change in expectations cause the demand curve for housing this year to shift to the left or shift to the right? Explain.

   b. Will this change in expectations cause the supply curve for housing this year to shift to the left or shift to the right? Explain.

   c. Will these shifts in the demand and supply curves lead to an increase or a decrease in the price of housing this year? Use supply and demand curves to explain your answer.

5. Brazil is the world's largest coffee producer. There was a severe drought in Brazil in 2013–14 that damaged Brazil's coffee crop. The price of coffee beans doubled during the first three months of 2014.

   a. Draw and discuss a supply and demand diagram to explain the increase in coffee prices.

   b. Are coffee and tea substitutes or complements? Explain.

   c. What do you think the impact of this drought has been on the equilibrium price and quantity of tea? Draw a supply and demand diagram for the tea market to explain your answer.

6. There is a sharp freeze in Florida that damages the orange harvest and as a result, the price of oranges rises. Will the equilibrium price of orange juice rise, fall, or remain constant? Will the equilibrium quantity of orange juice rise, fall, or remain constant? Present a supply-and-demand curve diagram to explain your answers.

7. An appendectomy is an operation to have your appendix removed. To simplify analysis, assume that everyone has health insurance, so that anybody who needs an

appendectomy will have one. (a) Show that the demand curve for appendectomies is vertical. (b) There is a technological breakthrough that allows surgeons to perform appendectomies at a much lower cost. Will the equilibrium price of appendectomies rise, fall, or remain constant? Will the equilibrium quantity of appendectomies rise, fall, or remain constant? Present a supply-and-demand curve diagram to defend your answers.

8. Land in Sonoma, California, can be used either to grow grapes for pinot noir wine or to grow Gravenstein apples. The demand for pinot noir shifts sharply and permanently to the right. What will be the effect of the rightward shift in demand for pinot noir on the equilibrium price and quantity of Gravenstein apples?

9. Suppose one of your friends offered the following argument:

A rightward shift in demand will cause an increase in price. The increase in price will cause a rightward shift of the supply curve, which will lead to an offsetting decrease in price. Therefore, it is impossible to tell what effect an increase in demand will have on price.

Do you agree with your friend? If not, what is the flaw in your friend's reasoning?

10. The UK government is contemplating introducing a minimum price for alcohol to reduce binge drinking and the consumption of alcohol in general. Suppose the following diagram shows the alcohol market in the UK. The current price of alcohol is 23 pence per unit, and 8 units of alcohol are consumed each week. What happens in the market if the government sets a minimum price of 30 pence per unit of alcohol? Will there be an excess supply or an excess demand for alcohol if the government adopts this policy? Explain.

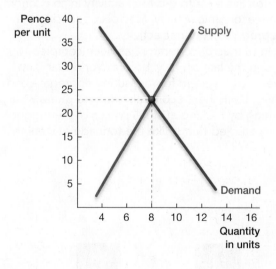

11. Lobsters are plentiful and easy to catch in August but scarce and difficult to catch in November. In addition, vacationers shift the demand for lobsters further to the right in August than in any other month. Compare the equilibrium price and quantity of lobsters in August to the equilibrium price and quantity of lobsters in November. Present and discuss a supply-and-demand diagram to explain your answers.

12. The market price of rice in Thailand is 100 baht. The Thai government offers to buy rice for 140 baht.

   a. How is this likely to affect other buyers in the domestic market for rice?

   b. Present a supply and demand diagram to show how much rice the Thai government will have to purchase under this program.

13. As part of U.S. sugar policy (in 2013), the government offered to buy raw sugar from domestic sugarcane mills at an average price of 18.75 cents per pound. This government offer was made for as much raw sugar as the sugarcane mills produced. Any raw sugar purchased by the government was not sold in the domestic market, as this might have caused raw sugar prices to fall.

   a. Under this policy, what do you think the government's demand curve for sugar looks like?

   b. What impact does this policy likely have on domestic sugar prices? Explain your reasoning with a supply-and-demand diagram.

14. *Note: This problem requires some basic algebra.* The demand for computers is $Q_D = 15 - 2P$, where P is the price of computers. Initially, the supply of computers is $Q_S = P$.

   a. Find the original equilibrium price and quantity.

   b. Suppose the prices of memory chips and motherboards (two important components in computers) rise and as a consequence, the supply curve for computers becomes $Q_S = -3 + P$. Find the new equilibrium price and quantity.

5

The Wealth of Nations:
Defining and Measuring Macroeconomic Aggregates

In the United States, what is the total market value of annual economic production?

Beginning with this chapter we focus on the economy as a whole. Economists refer to the *total* activity in an economy as *aggregate* economic activity. *Macroeconomics* is the study of *aggregate* economic activity.

The field of macroeconomics has been completely transformed in the last century. Before World War I, no country even had a system for measuring aggregate economic activity. Back then, economists had to guess what was happening by looking at small pieces of the bigger picture. They studied things like the tonnage of steel that

CHAPTER **OUTLINE**

☀ Macroeconomics is the study of aggregate economic activity.

☀ National income accounting is a framework for calculating gross domestic product (GDP), which is a measure of aggregate economic output.

☀ GDP can be measured in three different ways, and in principle these three methods should all yield the same answer: Production = Expenditure = Income.

☀ GDP has limitations as a measure of economic activity and as a measure of economic well-being.

☀ Economists use price indexes to measure the rate of inflation and to distinguish nominal GDP from real GDP (which holds prices fixed).

was manufactured or the volume of freight that was shipped on rail lines. These indicators were used to make educated guesses about aggregate economic activity. If freight shipments were booming, it probably meant that the aggregate economy was booming too, but nobody could be certain.

Today, we no longer have to guess what is happening in the economy. Modern economies have a sophisticated system that measures the level of aggregate activity. Careful measurement has made it possible to study the aggregate economy and to design policies that improve its performance.

In this chapter, we set the stage by answering a foundational question: How does it all add up? How do we calculate the total market value of aggregate economic production?

5.1 Macroeconomic Questions

Until now we've been studying microeconomics: how individuals, households, firms, and governments make choices, and how those choices affect the allocation of resources, the well-being of other agents, and the prices of specific goods and services. Now it's time to turn to macroeconomics. Recall from Chapter 1 that macroeconomics is the study of economic aggregates and economy-wide phenomena, like the annual growth rate of a country's total economic output, or the annual percentage increase in the total cost of living. Macro, which is shorthand for macroeconomics, is our new topic.

Macroeconomic analysis explains past patterns in aggregate economic activity and tries to predict future changes. For example, macroeconomists are interested in the enormous differences in income across countries and the creation of policies that would enable the countries with lower income to catch up.

Income per capita—in other words, income per person—in the United States is more than twice the level in Portugal, seven times the level in China, and over one-hundred times the level in Zimbabwe. How do we measure these cross-country differences? What causes them? How long will they persist?

Income per capita is income per person. This is calculated by dividing a nation's aggregate income by the number of people in the country.

China has been catching up to the United States very quickly. China's economy has been growing four times as fast as the U.S. economy for over 30 years. Will China eventually match the level of U.S. income per capita? Will China surpass the United States? Or, will something else happen? For example, Japan experienced a long-run slowdown in economic growth starting around 1990, when its income per capita was about to overtake that of the

Zimbabwe has spectacular natural resources like Victoria Falls but has not succeeded in developing a healthy economy or a robust tourism industry. Today, most of the visitors to the Falls stay on the Zambian side of the border.

Recessions are periods (lasting at least two quarters) in which aggregate economic output falls.

A worker is officially **unemployed** if he or she does not have a job, has actively looked for work in the prior four weeks, and is currently available for work.

The **unemployment rate** is the fraction of the labor force that is unemployed.

United States. Over two decades later, the United States is still ahead. Why do growth rates slow down as income per capita rises?

What can be done to improve living conditions in impoverished nations like Zimbabwe? Annual income per capita in Zimbabwe was $369 per year in 2010, barely enough for survival. Figuring out how to make low-income countries grow faster is a question of enormous importance for human well-being. Malnutrition and lack of health-care cause tens of millions of annual deaths worldwide. If low-income countries could raise their annual growth by five percentage points, economists estimate that 50 million lives would be saved over the next 20 years.

To understand how to achieve long-run economic prosperity, we need to understand how different government policies augment or undermine economic growth. Corruption and confusion can lead policymakers down the wrong path. What are the bad policies, and will we avoid them in the future?

Macroeconomists also study the year-to-year, or "short-run," fluctuations in economic activity. Why does economic growth sometimes stall, or turn negative? We call an economic downturn lasting at least two quarters a **recession** (a quarter is one-fourth of a year).

During recessions the *unemployment rate*, one of the most important macroeconomic variables, rises. A person is officially **unemployed** if three conditions are satisfied: he or she (1) does not have a job, (2) has actively looked for work in the prior four weeks, and (3) is currently available for work. Fluctuations in the **unemployment rate**—the fraction of the labor force that is unemployed—are covered in detail in Chapter 9.

To see an example of economic fluctuations, consider the period from 2007 to 2009, when the U.S. economy shrank by 4.3 percent and the unemployment rate rose from 5 percent to 10 percent. At the same time, the world experienced a series of financial crises, including stock market crashes, collapsing housing prices, mortgage defaults, and bank failures. Why did these events occur, and what should governments have done to reduce their severity? What caused worldwide stock markets to lose over half their value in a year's time? Why did so many major banks suddenly become insolvent?

Though the financial crisis of 2007–2009 was calamitous, it does not hold a candle to the Great Depression, which stretched from 1929 to 1939. From 1929 to 1933, production fell by nearly 30 percent and the unemployment rate rose from 3 percent to 25 percent of the labor force. In July 1932, the U.S. stock market reached the bottom

During the peak of the Great Depression 25 percent of the U.S. workforce didn't have a job. Some towns put up signs discouraging job seekers from looking for employment in the area.

of an 87 percent roller-coaster plunge from its peak in September, 1929. Are there policies that will enable us to avoid such disasters in the future? Or are we only able to respond after the fact? Could the 2007–2009 financial crisis have turned into another Great Depression?

These are all important questions. To answer them, we need some special tools and new models. The first thing that we must do is measure the thing we are studying: a country's aggregate economy. This is a seemingly impossible task. How can we measure the total activity of millions of economic agents? A hundred years ago, nobody knew how to do this. Fortunately, economic science has progressed. Today, we have a framework called the **national income accounts**, which we use to measure the entire economy. In the United States, the formal name for this system of national accounts is the **National Income and Product Accounts (NIPA)**. Once we understand how the national income accounts works, we will be ready to start answering the interesting and important questions posed above.

> **National income accounts** measure the level of aggregate economic activity in a country.
>
> The **National Income and Product Accounts (NIPA)** is the system of national income accounts that is used by the U.S. government.

5.2 National Income Accounts: Production = Expenditure = Income

To measure aggregate economic activity, we will need to take both quantities and prices into account. Let's start by considering the hypothetical nation of Fordica. Fordica is a small country with only one employer, the Ford Motor Company, hereafter Ford, which produces 5 million cars each year. We'll assume that Fordica has 200,000 citizens who happen to be the workers in Ford's factories and also the owners of Ford's stock. We'll look at three different ways of thinking about Fordica's economy—a production approach, an expenditure approach, and an income approach.

Production

As economists, we want to measure the total market value of annual production in the nation of Fordica. To keep things simple, we'll assume that Ford only needs its own machines and the labor of Fordica's citizens to build cars. We won't worry right now about other inputs like steel and plastic. In fact, we'll momentarily assume that these other inputs don't exist.

To determine the market value of production in Fordica, we multiply the quantity of cars produced by the market price of each car. For example, if the market price of a Ford is $30,000, then Fordica has total annual production of:

$$(5 \text{ million cars}) \times (\$30,000/\text{car}) = \$150 \text{ billion.}$$

By multiplying production quantities and market prices, we have a measure that reflects the market value of the goods produced in the economy during a particular period of time—in this example, one year. So the economy of Fordica produces goods with a market value of $150 billion per year.

Economists call this measure of aggregate economic activity **gross domestic product,** or **GDP**. We define GDP as the market value of the final goods and services produced within the borders of a country during a particular period of time. GDP is always associated with a particular period of time, usually either a year or a quarter. For example, "GDP in 2015" is the market value of the final goods and services produced during the year 2015. "GDP in Q1:2015" is the market value of the final goods and services produced during the first quarter of the year 2015. When talking about aggregate economic activity, the first quarter begins in January (January–March). The second quarter begins in April (April–June). The third quarter begins in July (July–September). The fourth quarter begins in October (October–December).

The definition of GDP includes the word *final*, which signifies that we are interested in valuing the end product in a chain of production. Components that are put together to make a final product—for instance, a car engine is a

> **Gross domestic product (GDP)** is the market value of the final goods and services produced within the borders of a country during a particular period of time.

The real-life Ford Motor Company employs about 200,000 workers worldwide. It manufactures 5–6 million cars per year, generating annual sales of $150 billion.

component of a car—don't get counted separately because that would imply double-counting. The engine is implicitly counted when we value the final good, which is the complete car.

GDP is a measure of production, not a measure of sales to consumers. So something that is produced is counted in GDP even if it is not sold to a customer. For example, Ford will increase its inventory of (unsold) cars if it manufactures a car in 2015 but doesn't sell it in 2015. Production that goes into inventories counts as part of GDP.

Expenditure

There's a *second* way to think about the level of aggregate activity in the economy of Fordica. This second method yields exactly the same answer as the previous production-based method. Households and firms, some of whom reside in Fordica and some of whom reside in foreign countries, are going to buy all of the cars produced in this economy. If we add up all of these car purchases, we will find that the total expenditure on Fordica's output is exactly $150 billion (again).

You might object by asking, "What if some of the goods don't get sold?" Economists reply that those unsold goods are *owned* by a firm and those goods are therefore counted as part of the firm's inventory. In the accounting system that we are describing here, that inventory is coded as having been "purchased" by the firm. Including both household car expenditures and firm inventory car expenditures, total expenditures sum to $150 billion.

Income

Let's pause for a moment and ask why we are focusing on the goods and services that are produced by Fordica and purchased from producers in Fordica. We could instead have focused on what households and firms located in Fordica earned—in other words, their income. Isn't that really what matters? Let's consider that alternative approach, which happens to be the *third* way to think about the level of aggregate activity.

We've already calculated that Ford generates $150 billion of revenue. It pays $X to its workers, and it keeps ($150 billion − $X) for its owners. So the total income of all the workers and all of the owners in the nation of Fordica is

$$\$X + (\$150 \text{ billion} - \$X) = \$150 \text{ billion}.$$

Note that this is the identical amount—$150 billion—that we determined the economy *produced* in our earlier calculations. It is also the value of expenditures on goods and services produced in Fordica.

The fact that we keep coming up with the amount $150 billion is not a coincidence. Because of the way we've set up the system of national income accounts, every dollar of revenue must either go to some worker or be retained by the firm. So the total value of revenue *must* equal the total value of income received by workers and owners. This necessary equivalence is referred to as an *identity*. Two variables are related by an **identity** when the two variables are defined in a way that makes them mathematically identical. The equivalence of the value of production, the value of expenditure, and the value of income may not be apparent at first glance, but the three concepts have been defined so that they are necessarily identical.

You can now understand the following aggregate accounting identity:

$$\text{Production} = \text{Expenditure} = \text{Income}.$$

This identity is the key conceptual point of this chapter and the foundation on which most macroeconomic analysis is built. Now let's delve more deeply into the system of national income accounts.

Two variables are related by an **identity** when the two variables are defined in a way that makes them mathematically identical.

Production = Expenditure = Income, is the key conceptual point of this chapter and the foundation on which most macroeconomic analysis is built.

Circular Flows

Factors of production are the inputs to the production process.

Factors of production are the inputs to the production process. Factors of production come in two key forms: *capital* and *labor*. We'll have more to say about capital below, but for now it is helpful to simplify analysis by thinking of capital as physical capital—for instance, land, factories, and machines. Both physical capital and labor are "owned" by households. Households own most of the physical capital in the economy, either directly or indirectly, because firms are owned by shareholders and most shareholders are households.

To understand how the three parts of the national income accounts—production, expenditure, and income—relate to one another, we need to think about the connections between households and firms. Firms, like the aircraft manufacturer Boeing, demand physical capital and labor and supply goods and services, like airplanes. Households demand goods and services, like air travel, and supply physical capital and labor.

We can explain the connections between households and firms with a circular flow diagram of the type displayed in Exhibit 5.1. This diagram highlights four kinds of economic flows that connect households and firms. It includes the three kinds of flows that we discussed in the Fordica example (Production = Expenditure = Income) and adds a fourth category, Factors of Production.

1. Production
2. Expenditure
3. Income
4. Factors of Production

Exhibit 5.1 is admittedly a simplification of the economy because it leaves out important institutions like governments, markets, banks, and foreign countries. But the circular flow diagram provides a useful way of understanding the basic structure of a modern economy.

Exhibit 5.1 Circular Flow Diagram

Economists have designed national income accounts that measure GDP in four equivalent ways: production, expenditure, income, and factors of production. The circular flow diagram provides a visual way of remembering the relationships among these four equivalent systems. Firms on the left produce goods and services (<u>Production</u>). Households on the right pay to buy those goods and services (<u>Expenditure</u>). Firms pay households to use households' physical capital and labor (<u>Income</u>). Physical capital and labor are factors of production, which are put to use by firms (<u>Factors</u>). The national income accounting system is set up so that all four sets of flows are equal in market value.

Production and expenditure. A Ford Mustang is produced by Ford (production) and it is purchased by Ford's customers (expenditure).

The circular flow diagram presents two main decision makers—firms and households—and it shows the four types of flows that we listed a moment ago.

Production represents the goods and services that are produced by firms. These goods and services are ultimately sold to households. We therefore draw an arrow from the firm sector to the household sector when talking about production. For example, a Ford Mustang starts life on the factory floor and ends up in someone's garage.

Expenditure represents the payments for goods and services. These payments are made by households to firms. So we draw an arrow from the household sector to the firm sector when talking about expenditure. Continuing our earlier example, the household pays Ford $30,000 for a Mustang. Note that production and expenditure both involve goods and services, so these two flows are grouped together. They jointly represent the market for goods and services.

Income represents the payments that are made from firms to households to compensate the households for the use of their physical capital and labor (in other words, the use of the households' factors of production). These payments include things like wages, salaries, interest, and dividends. We therefore draw an arrow from the firm sector to the household sector when talking about income. For instance, the average labor compensation received by Ford's employees is $65,000 per year.

Factors of production represent the productive resources that are owned by households and used by firms in the production process. Because factors of production—both labor and physical capital—are directly or indirectly owned by households, we draw an arrow from the household sector to the firm sector when talking about factors of production.

The remarkable thing about these four types of transactions or "flows" is that they must all be *exactly* the same in market value. That's where the system of national income accounts comes in. If we do the accounting correctly, the market value of expenditure *must* equal the market value of production. Likewise, the market value of expenditure *must* equal the market value of income of the households in the economy. In the same way, the market value of income *must* equal the market value of the factors of production—labor and physical capital—that are receiving those income payments. These relationships are just mathematical consequences of the ways that we define the system of national income accounts.

Although the circular flow diagram contains four sets of flows with identical market values, in the discussion that follows we return to our earlier three-part system of national income accounts: Production = Expenditures = Income. In practice, these are the three parts of the national income accounts that government statisticians actually measure.

National Income Accounts: Production

We now revisit each of the methods for calculating national income and dig a little deeper. First, let's consider production-based national income accounts. Production-based accounts sum up the market value that is added by each domestic firm in the production process. More formally, production-based accounts measure each firm's **value added**,

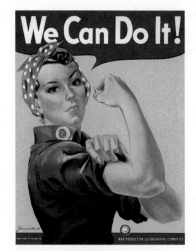

A factor of production and a source of income. This famous image of a factory worker appeared in a poster designed to boost worker morale during World War II.

Production-based accounting measures each firm's **value added,** which is the firm's sales revenue minus the firm's purchases of intermediate products from other firms.

which is the firm's sales revenue minus the firm's purchases of intermediate products from other firms.

For example, consider the Dell computer company. Two decades ago, Dell assembled almost all of its computers in the United States. These days, Dell buys almost all of its computers from foreign manufacturers. When a customer orders a Dell computer, Dell instructs a foreign producer—usually one in Asia, Mexico, or Ireland—to assemble the computer. Dell then imports the machine from the foreign factory and sends the machine to its U.S. customer. The laptop that Dell purchases from a foreign producer is an intermediate product in Dell's production.

Dell has also shifted its business strategy on the retail side. Dell now markets some, though by no means all, of its computers through other companies. For example, you can buy a Dell computer at BestBuy, Staples, or Walmart.

Exhibit 5.2 puts all of these pieces together. As the exhibit shows, consumers buy about $50 billion worth of Dell computers in the United States each year. About $15 billion of sales of Dell computers comes from customers who buy at third-party retailers, like Walmart. About $35 billion of sales comes from customers who buy directly from Dell.

Retailers like Walmart pay Dell about two-thirds of the revenue that Walmart receives from the sale of Dell's computers. So Dell receives $10 billion from third-party retailers and another $35 billion from direct-sale customers: $45 billion in total. Dell pays its foreign suppliers $30 billion for assembling Dell computers. That leaves Dell with $15 billion in net revenue from its U.S. operations. Out of that revenue, Dell pays its domestic costs, such as employee wages and construction costs for building warehouses.

Let's determine what value Dell (including its domestic employees) has added to the production process. That amount will be Dell's contribution to U.S. gross domestic product (GDP). The answer is $15 billion, which is a lot less than the $50 billion that U.S. consumers spent on Dell computers. We came to $15 billion by taking the revenue that Dell itself

Exhibit 5.2 Dell's Value Added

U.S. consumers spend $50 billion annually on Dell computers, but Dell's value added to U.S. GDP is only $15 billion. Dell receives revenue of $45 billion from third-party retailers ($10 billion) and from direct sales to retail customers ($35 billion). Dell pays its suppliers (foreign producers) $30 billion. The difference, $45 billion − $30 billion = $15 billion, is the value added of Dell and its employees.

Retail customers

Retail customers

$15 billion

Walmart

STAPLES
The Office Superstore

BEST BUY

Third-party retailers

$10 billion

$35 billion

DELL

$30 billion

Foreign producers of Dell's computers

received, $45 billion, and subtracting Dell's payments of $30 billion to foreign suppliers for intermediate goods.

Total sales of Dell computers to retail customers:

$15 billion through other retailers + $35 billion in direct sales = $50 billion.

Revenue received by Dell:

$10 billion from third-party retailers + $35 billion from direct sales = $45 billion.

Revenue received by Dell minus purchases of intermediate products = Dell's value added:

$45 billion received by Dell − $30 billion paid for intermediate products = $15 billion.

We could go on to ask what else would get counted as U.S. GDP in this chain of economic activity (even if it isn't counted as part of Dell's contribution). The foreign factories don't count toward U.S. GDP. The production of the foreign laptop factories is part of a foreign country's GDP because the factories are within the boundaries of those foreign countries.

The production-based accounting system implies that importing some good from abroad and selling it to a U.S. consumer at the exact same import price doesn't add value. However, importing something for $1 and reselling it for $1.50 is a source of production—$0.50 of value added to be precise. Dell's ability to mark up its price relative to the import cost comes from a combination of marketing, corporate reputation, customer convenience, and bundled services like access to call centers.

Likewise, Walmart's ability to sell Dell's computers is another source of U.S. value added. Walmart isn't making anything in a factory, but its ability to buy goods at wholesale prices and sell those goods at higher retail prices reflects its value added and consequently its contribution to GDP. Walmart's value added is not the revenue that Walmart receives from its customers. Walmart's value added is the difference between the revenue that Walmart receives when it sells Dell's computers and the amount that Walmart pays Dell for the laptops. Dell's laptops are Walmart's intermediate goods. In our example, all of the third-party retailers receive $15 billion in revenue from selling Dell's computers and pay Dell $10 billion for those computers. Through this chain of transactions, the third-party retailers generate value added of $5 billion ($15 billion − $10 billion), which is counted as part of production-based U.S. GDP.

National Income Accounts: Expenditure

Let's now turn to the second, mathematically equivalent, way of measuring GDP. Expenditure-based national income accounts measure the purchases of goods and services produced in the domestic economy. These purchases can be assigned to five categories.

(1) Consumption. This is the market value of consumption goods and consumption services that are bought by domestic households. Such consumption expenditures cover everything from Frisbees to foot massages. This category includes all consumption expenditures except expenditures that are made on residential construction (which is part of the next category).

(2) Investment. This is the market value of new physical capital that is bought by domestic households and domestic firms. This is technically called *private investment* but is usually just referred to as investment. Such new physical capital includes residential houses, business inventories (for example, the Camaro waiting to be bought at a Chevrolet dealership), business structures (for example, office towers and factories), and business equipment (for example, computers and freight trains). When macroeconomists talk about investment, they are referring only to purchases of *new physical capital* and *not* to financial investments like purchases of stocks or bonds. This difference in usage generates lots of confusion, because noneconomists are more familiar with the everyday financial meaning of "making an investment" (for instance, buying a mutual fund or contributing money to an Individual Retirement Account), which is not what macroeconomists have in mind. In the

Consumption is the market value of consumption goods and consumption services that are bought by domestic households.

Investment is the market value of new physical capital that is bought by domestic households and domestic firms.

language of macroeconomics, investment is only the purchase of new physical capital, like a new supertanker or a new factory or a new house.

Government expenditure is the market value of government purchases of goods and services.

(3) Government expenditure. This is the market value of government purchases of goods and services. Tanks and bridges are two examples of government expenditure. For the purposes of the national income accounts, government expenditure *excludes* transfer payments (for example, Social Security payments to retirees) and also *excludes* interest paid on government debt. These categories are omitted because they represent payments to other agents in the economy who will use those payments to buy goods and services. To avoid double-counting, these government payments to other agents are not counted as government expenditure on goods and services.

Exports are the market value of all domestically produced goods and services that are purchased by households, firms, and governments in foreign countries.

(4) Exports. This is the market value of all domestically produced goods and services that are sold to households, firms, and governments in *foreign* countries.

These first four categories are nonoverlapping. In other words, there is no double-counting. Each purchase appears in only one of the four categories above.

Imports are the market value of all foreign-produced goods and services that are sold to domestic households, domestic firms, and the domestic government.

(5) Imports. This is the market value of all foreign-produced goods and services that are sold to domestic households, domestic firms, and the domestic government. Note that imports are already part of consumption expenditures, investment expenditures, and government expenditures. Hence, imports overlap with the first three categories in our list. We'll explain why this overlap is useful in a moment.

We are now ready to use these five categories to calculate gross domestic product (GDP). Let Y represent the total market value of goods and services that are produced in the domestic economy, which is GDP. We'll use C to represent consumption: household expenditures on consumption of goods and services, including expenditure on consumption of goods and services produced domestically and abroad. Variable I will represent investment: expenditures on investment goods by private agents (excluding the government), including investment goods produced domestically and abroad. We'll let G represent goverment expenditure: government purchases of goods and services, including goods and services produced domestically and abroad.

We need to adjust for the fact that exports (goods produced in the United States, which are sold to households, firms, and governments in foreign countries) count as part of U.S. GDP. On the other hand, imports (domestic expenditures on goods and services produced abroad) don't count as part of U.S. GDP.

> **The GDP equation says that the market value of domestic production is equal to the total expenditure of domestic economic agents ($C + I + G$), plus the expenditure of foreign agents on exports (X) minus the value of domestic expenditure that was imported (M).**

Let X represent exports: the value of goods and services produced in the domestic economy and purchased by economic agents in foreign countries. Let M represent imports: the value of goods and services produced in foreign countries and purchased by economic agents in the domestic economy. Finally, note that exports minus imports, or $X - M$, is the trade balance. When X is greater than M, exports are greater than imports, so the country runs a trade surplus. When X is less than M, exports are less than imports, so the country runs a trade deficit.

We can now calculate the total value of expenditures on goods and services produced in the domestic economy:

$$Y = C + I + G + X - M \quad \text{(National Income Accounting Identity)}.$$

The **national income accounting identity,** $Y = C + I + G + X - M$, decomposes GDP into consumption + investment + government expenditure + exports − imports.

The GDP equation says that the market value of domestic production is equal to the *total* expenditure of domestic economic agents, $C + I + G$, plus the expenditure of foreign agents on exports, X, minus the value of domestic expenditure that was imported, M. We subtract imports because expenditure on foreign production is included in the terms C, I, and G. To *remove* this expenditure on foreign production, we subtract imports, M.

This identity, which decomposes GDP into ($C + I + G + X - M$), is so important that we give it a name: the **national income accounting identity**. We'll use it many times in our study of the macroeconomy.

Evidence-Based Economics

Q: In the United States, what is the total market value of annual economic production?

Government statisticians measure gross domestic product, the total market value of economic output. In the United States, this work is conducted by the Bureau of Economic Analysis in the Department of Commerce. In 2013, the Bureau of Economic Analysis reported that U.S. GDP was $16.8 trillion. That year, the U.S. population was 316.4 million people. So GDP per person—in other words, GDP *per capita*—was about $53,100.

It is also valuable to study the components of GDP using the national income accounting identity that we just discussed. Exhibit 5.3 reports this data for the United States in 2013. We can observe several important properties. First, the overwhelming share of GDP is represented by household consumption. In 2013, consumption represented 69 percent of GDP. Government expenditure comes in far behind, with only 19 percent of GDP. Investment follows next with 16 percent. Exports account for 14 percent of GDP and imports account for 16 percent of GDP. Notice that imports appear in Exhibit 5.3 with a negative sign, reminding you that when calculating GDP, imports are subtracted out after we add up all of the other components. Confirm that the items in Exhibit 5.3 add up to GDP (with a bit of rounding error).

The fraction of GDP in each category—these are called GDP shares—has been relatively constant over the past 80 years. Exhibit 5.4 reports the GDP shares from 1929 to 2013. In other words, Exhibit 5.4 reports the ratio of each expenditure category to GDP. The sum of these shares, minus the import share, must sum to one. Exhibit 5.4 shows that consumption has consistently represented about two-thirds of economic activity.

Government expenditures have consistently hovered around 20 percent of economic activity, with two exceptions. First, at the very beginning of the sample period, government expenditures accounted for only 10 percent of GDP. Large governments did not become the norm in the modern world until after World War II.

Second, government expenditures temporarily absorbed a particularly large share of GDP during World War II. The high point was nearly 50 percent of GDP. It is natural

MyEconLab Real-time data

	Trillions of Dollars	Share of GDP
Gross domestic product	16.8	100.0%
Consumption	11.5	68.5%
+ Investment	2.7	15.9%
+ Government expenditure	3.1	18.6%
+ Exports	2.3	13.5%
− Imports	−2.8	−16.4%

Exhibit 5.3 U.S. 2013 GDP and GDP Shares (Expenditure-based Accounting)

U.S. gross domestic product in 2013 was $16.8 trillion. Each component of GDP is expressed as a percentage of GDP, or a GDP "share" (component/GDP). Rounding causes the components to fail to sum to total GDP. Rounding also causes small discrepancies between the column in dollars and the column in shares.

Source: Bureau of Economic Analysis, National Income and Product Accounts.

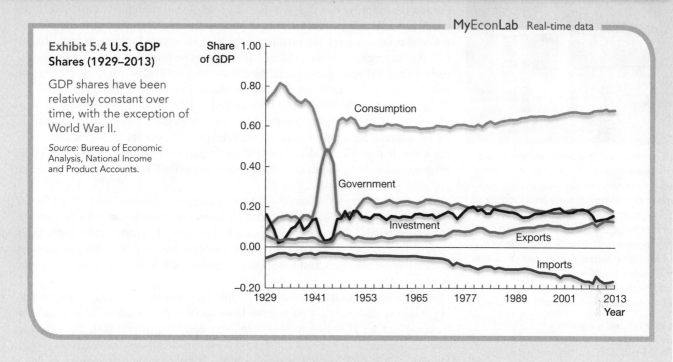

Exhibit 5.4 U.S. GDP Shares (1929–2013)

GDP shares have been relatively constant over time, with the exception of World War II.

Source: Bureau of Economic Analysis, National Income and Product Accounts.

that during major wars the government accounts for a much larger share of a country's economic output because a war effort is run almost exclusively by the government. The rise in government activity during World War II is mirrored by a fall in consumption and a fall in (private) investment.

There is one final property that is important to note in Exhibit 5.4: the export and import shares have both been getting larger in absolute value over the past 80 years. Transportation technology has made it less expensive to ship goods anywhere in the world. Information technology has also made it easier for residents of one country to provide services to residents of other countries (think of call centers in India). Falling transportation and telecommunication costs have fueled an ongoing rise in trade, as optimizers look beyond their national borders to buy the goods and services that they want. Rising exports show up as a rising share of exports. Because imports appear as a negative number in the GDP identity, rising imports show up as a movement in the import share further below zero.

Question

In the United States, what is the total market value of annual economic production?

Answer

In 2013, the Bureau of Economic Analysis reported that U.S. GDP was $16.8 trillion, or $53,100 per capita.[1]

Data

National Income and Product Accounts compiled by the Bureau of Economic Analysis.

Caveat

National income accounts omit many types of economic production, an issue that we discuss later in this chapter.

Home ownership is an important source of capital income. If you own your home, you don't need to pay rent (though you may need to pay interest on a mortgage). Economists consider the "nonpayment" of rent to be a form of capital income to homeowners. The implied income from home ownership is the amount of money the owner would have needed to spend had he or she been renting the same kind of residence from a landlord.

Labor income is any form of payment that compensates people for their work.

Capital income is any form of payment that derives from owning physical or financial capital.

National Income Accounting: Income

So far, we've taken a detailed look at the economy by studying GDP as a production concept—that was the discussion of value added—and then by studying GDP as an expenditure concept—that was the discussion of the national income accounting identity, $Y = C + I + G + X - M$. As we explained at the start of the chapter, we can also study GDP as an income concept. Recall that income-based national accounts track the income of the various agents in the economy. Recall, too, that aggregate income is identical to aggregate production and aggregate expenditure. So if aggregate expenditure was $16.8 trillion in 2013, then aggregate production and aggregate income were also each $16.8 trillion in 2013.

Income payments come in two key categories. First, there is *income paid for people's work*. We call this **labor income**. This category includes familiar items like wages, salary, workers' health insurance, and workers' pension benefits. It also includes every other way that people are directly or indirectly paid for their labor, including signing bonuses, free parking spaces at work, and the value to the CEO of being able to use the company jet on weekends.

The second category of income payments is income (or benefits) realized by the owners of physical capital (for instance, a house) or financial capital (for instance, stocks and bonds). We refer to this as **capital income**. This category includes many things: for example, dividends paid to shareholders, interest paid to lenders, earnings retained by corporations, rent payments made to landlords, and the benefits of living in your own house!

This division into labor income and capital income may encourage the misleading intuition that people who receive labor income are different from those who receive capital income. However, most people in the economy receive both. For example, a 50-year-old worker with a job, a house, and a retirement savings account will receive labor income from her job, capital income from her house (the implicit value of having a roof over her head), and capital income from her retirement savings account (dividends).

It is also important to remember that firms are owned by households. Firms can't own themselves. When a firm earns income, it is the owners of the firm who are the ultimate

LETTING THE DATA SPEAK

Saving vs. Investment

Economists use the national income accounting identities to study saving and investment. To derive an equation for saving, start with GDP, which is equivalent to national income, and subtract the things that households and the government consume. In other words, subtract consumption expenditures and government expenditure. We then find that

$$Saving = Y - C - G$$
$$= (C + I + G + X - M) - C - G$$
$$= I + X - M.$$

To get from the first equation to the second equation, we replaced Y with its components from the national income accounting identity: $C + I + G + X - M$. The final equation in our derivation can be written out in words:

$$Saving = Investment + Exports - Imports.$$

In most countries, exports and imports are relatively close in magnitude. In that case, exports minus imports will be close to zero, enabling us to further simplify our expression:

$$Saving = Investment.$$

This simplified expression is just an approximation, since exports and imports are never exactly the same when a

country trades with other countries. However, this equation will be *exactly* true for a closed economy, which is an economy that does not trade with other countries. In a closed economy, exports and imports are both equal to zero.

Let's now take the last equation and divide both sides by GDP. You'll then see that the saving rate (saving divided by GDP) is equal to the investment rate (investment divided by GDP):

$$\frac{Saving}{GDP} = \frac{Investment}{GDP}.$$

Using U.S. data from 1929 to 2013, we can compare the saving rate and the investment rate, year-by-year. Exhibit 5.5 graphs a scatter plot of these two ratios. Each point plots a single year of data: the saving rate for that year is on the horizontal axis and the investment rate is on the vertical axis. As you can see, the saving rate and the investment rate move together very closely and the cloud of data points stays relatively close to the 45 degree line (which is plotted in red).

Exhibit 5.5 implies that saving is roughly equal to investment. We'll use this fact in the next chapter when we start to discuss the determinants of economic growth, including investment in physical capital.

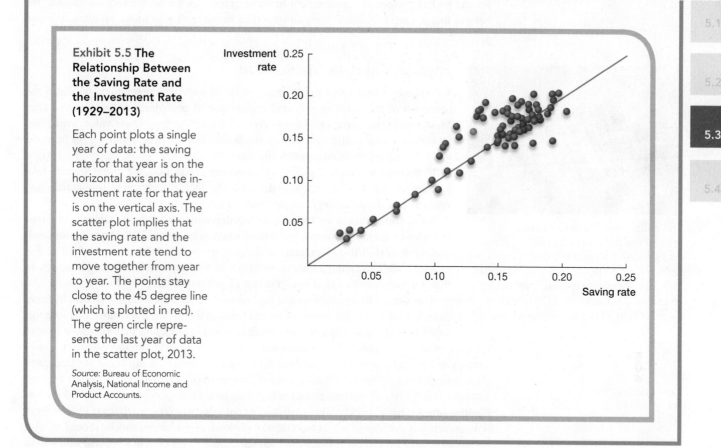

Exhibit 5.5 The Relationship Between the Saving Rate and the Investment Rate (1929–2013)

Each point plots a single year of data: the saving rate for that year is on the horizontal axis and the investment rate for that year is on the vertical axis. The scatter plot implies that the saving rate and the investment rate tend to move together from year to year. The points stay close to the 45 degree line (which is plotted in red). The green circle represents the last year of data in the scatter plot, 2013.

Source: Bureau of Economic Analysis, National Income and Product Accounts.

beneficiaries. Most large firms have shares that are traded on the stock market. In this case, the firm is owned by hundreds of millions of shareholders around the globe. The beneficiaries of capital income are these shareholders.

Finally, it is interesting to ask what fraction of income payments are labor payments and what fraction of income payments are capital payments. In the United States and other developed economies, nearly two-thirds of income payments goes to labor and one-third goes to capital.

This is a simplified, but useful summary of the weather. Likewise, GDP is a simplified, but useful summary of the economy.

5.3 What Isn't Measured by GDP?

Before leaving our homes in the morning, many of us go to the Web to look up the current weather conditions. Some weather Web sites report a single temperature and a simple picture.

This weather report leaves a lot of details out. Humidity, haze, wind speed, and hundreds of other factors all contribute to the actual conditions that we experience as we walk to work or sprint for the train. Nevertheless, commuters are grateful for a simple summary that tells them most of what they need to know about the local weather.

Likewise, GDP and national income accounting is a useful system for taking the temperature of the economy. It's not perfect, and it necessarily leaves out a lot of details. Nevertheless, GDP does a good job of telling us much of what we need to know about the level, fluctuations, and long-run trends in economic activity. With this tool in hand, we are ready to try to measure and predict the behavior of the entire economy.

But it's important to discuss what GDP leaves out, so we know what GDP can and can't do. GDP has many quirks that limit its value as a measure of societal well-being or even of overall economic activity.

Economists are a bold breed. Measuring the production of an entire economy can't be done exactly right, but we do it *anyway*. Sticking our collective heads in the sand and waiting for the perfect system of measurement to be invented is not a satisfactory alternative. We believe that it's much better to have an imperfect measure than to throw up our hands and give up.

Physical Capital Depreciation

We start by noting that GDP omits physical capital depreciation, which is the reduction of the value of physical capital due to obsolescence or wear and tear. Most productive processes cause physical capital to lose some value over time. Driving a tractor trailer wears down the brakes and the tires. Pumping oil from the ground depletes remaining petroleum reserves.

If we want a complete picture of economic production, we might want to take account of the physical capital depreciation that accompanies production and *subtract* that depreciation from the value of total production.

Most governments *do* try to measure depreciation in their national accounts, though they do *not* subtract depreciation when calculating GDP. Depreciation analyses tend to find that depreciation is equal to about 10–15 percent of GDP. For example, the U.S. national accounts estimate that depreciation is large enough so that *if* it were subtracted, it would offset 13 percent of GDP.

This sounds like a problem that has been solved, but the situation is actually more complicated. First, the depreciation estimates in the national accounts are more like sophisticated guess work—"guesstimates"—than something that we know how to measure precisely. Second, the depreciation estimates don't even attempt to cover lots of hard-to-analyze categories like oil reserve depreciation. Third, thinking about physical capital depreciation raises many related questions. For example, changes in our health are also left out of the GDP calculations completely. Some productive processes make workers less healthy—for example, backbreaking work in a coal mine or exposure to toxic chemicals in a manufacturing process. If we take account of physical capital depreciation, should we also try to calculate depreciation of health and *human capital* (a concept that we will return to in the next chapter)?

In sum, trying to measure depreciation is a complicated conceptual issue and the standard measure of GDP does not account for any type of depreciation.

Home Production

GDP also stumbles when it comes to home production, which is not included anywhere in the national income accounts. If you grow your own flowers (without buying seeds or shovels from a plant store), the bouquet you create is not measured in GDP, but if you buy domestically grown flowers from the local florist, every dollar is included in GDP. If you knit your own wool cap using wool from the sheep that you keep on your farm, nothing shows up in GDP, but if you knit a cap from the same wool and sell it to your neighbor, every dollar counts in GDP. Sometimes the accounting rules are laughable. For example, GDP goes down if you marry your gardener.

All economists agree that excluding home production is a flaw in the GDP accounts, but we do not yet have a way to measure home production. There is no market transaction, market price, or measurable quantity that accompanies home production. What is the market value of a home-cooked meal? Families have been debating that philosophical question for a long time.

If we were only talking about a home-cooked meatloaf here and there, this omission would not be a big deal. But a large fraction of economic activity takes place in the home. Most families maintain their own homes by personally dusting, vacuuming, mopping, and polishing them. People often mow their own grass, rake their own leaves, and weed their own flower beds. Most families eat most of their meals at home.

Finally, there is the very important category of childcare, which is illustrated by the following example. Suppose there are two parents in *different* households, Avery and Micah. Suppose that they each have kids. If Avery and Micah stay home to care for their *own* kids, there is no market transaction and the childcare is not recorded in GDP. On the other hand, if Avery takes care of Micah's kids and is paid a salary of $40,000, and Micah takes care of Avery's kids and receives a salary of $40,000, then annual GDP rises by the sum, $80,000. Note that the children are being cared for regardless of whether this

The cruise ship *Costa Concordia* hit a reef off the Italian coast in 2012. Thirty-two people died and the ship, which cost $600 million to build, was sold for scrap. The loss of physical capital is an example of capital depreciation. GDP does not take account of capital depreciation.

Should childcare be measured in GDP, even when it is not a market-based activity?

care is measured by GDP. When each parent cares for his or her own kids, childcare is produced without a market transaction and childcare is omitted from GDP. When each parent takes care of the *other* family's kids, childcare generates a market transaction and GDP is $80,000 higher.

There are two reasons why economists lose sleep worrying about all of this. First, a large fraction of the adult population does stay at home to work. We know from surveys of time use that people who are not officially employed are doing a lot more than watching reruns of *Breaking Bad*. Second, even people with formal jobs are engaged in some home production. If you hold down a day job, it is likely that you also do some cleaning or cooking or childcare when you get home from work.

Let's quantify these effects. In the United States, where the total population was 316.4 million in 2013, there were approximately 144 million working-age adults with formal jobs and another 52 million working-age adults without formal jobs.

Many of the people without formal jobs are engaged in a considerable amount of home production, including food preparation, household maintenance, and childcare. Suppose that the working-age adults without formal jobs have an average annual home production of $20,000 per person. That number averages over people with different amounts of home production. Some people who aren't in the formal labor force care for newborn triplets and others watch YouTube all day.

In addition, suppose that the people *with* formal jobs outside the home also do home production of $10,000 per year.

Adding up all of these different sources of home production we get annual home production in the United States of $2.5 trillion:

$$\text{(52 million people)} \times (\$20,000/\text{person})$$
$$+ \text{(144 million people)} \times (\$10,000/\text{person}) = \$2.5 \text{ trillion.}$$

In an economy with $16.8 trillion of market-based production, $2.5 trillion represents nearly 15 percent of additional economic production that has been overlooked in the GDP calculation. Many other estimates of home production are even higher.

The Underground Economy

The *underground economy*—transactions that are intentionally hidden from government statisticians—represents another hole in the GDP accounts. This includes the plumber who asks to be paid in cash and the taxicab driver who negotiates a lower rate if you would just agree to let him turn off the meter. Plumbing and cab driving are perfectly legal, but some workers hide income to avoid paying taxes. Earnings from legal professions may also be hidden for other reasons, for instance, an acrimonious divorce or the lack of a work visa.

The underground economy also includes markets in illegal professions. Drug dealing and prostitution top the list (though some communities have legalized some of these activities). Illegal drug sales alone are estimated to be equal in magnitude to 1 percent of GDP. For the U.S. economy, that is equivalent to the value of *all* agricultural production.

In developed economies with excellent law enforcement systems—think of countries like Switzerland, Japan, Hong Kong, and the United States—transactions in the underground economy add up to about 10 percent of GDP. In developing countries, the fraction of underground economic activity is generally much higher. For example, in Mexico, the underground economy is estimated to be half of measured GDP.

Some countries, including Ireland, Italy, and the United Kingdom have recently started to include underground economic activity, including illicit drug purchases and prostitution, in their GDP calculations.

Negative Externalities

Negative externalities occur when an economic activity has a spillover cost that does not affect those directly engaged in the activity. Positive externalities occur when an economic activity has a spillover benefit that does not affect those directly engaged in the activity. Externalities—both negative and positive—are usually omitted from the GDP calculations. Consider a coal-powered electrical plant generating power for thousands of

The societal cost of pollution is not subtracted from GDP.

Gross national product (GNP) is the market value of production generated by the factors of production—both capital and labor—possessed or owned by the residents of a particular nation.

homes and simultaneously belching out a continuous stream of toxic airborne pollutants. GDP counts the electricity produced, but fails to subtract the cost of the pollution.

Sometimes negative externalities even get counted as *positive* contributors to economic output. For example, property crimes, like theft, lead people to purchase locks and other security devices. In some cases, property owners hire guards to safeguard their possessions. All of this preventive activity counts as positive contributions to GDP.

Gross Domestic Product vs. Gross National Product

As we've already explained, GDP is the market value of everything produced within the borders of a country during a particular period of time. So GDP includes both the production of a country's residents and the production of visitors. For example, if a U.S. worker spends two months working in Singapore, her production will be counted in the GDP of Singapore and omitted from U.S. GDP. Likewise, if a Japanese auto company—like Honda —opens a plant in Alabama, the value added of this plant will be counted in U.S. GDP and not in Japanese GDP. This would be the case even if the plant were operated entirely by robots and didn't have one U.S. employee. The plant is operating within the borders of the United States, so its value added is counted in U.S. GDP.

At first glance, you might wonder if cross-border activities amount to much. In fact, there are large amounts of such activity. For example, about 70 percent of the "Japanese" cars that are sold in the United States are now manufactured at plants in Canada, Mexico, and the United States.

With facts like this in mind, economists have constructed a measure of aggregate economic activity that includes only the output of factors of production owned by residents of a particular country: **gross national product (GNP)**. U.S. GNP includes the production of a worker who normally resides in the United States, even if the production occurred when the worker was temporarily working abroad. For example, if a U.S. professor gives a summer course at the National University of Singapore, her two-month salary, which was paid by the National University of Singapore, would be included in U.S. GNP and excluded from Singapore's GNP.

Likewise, U.S. GNP would exclude the value added of machines owned by a Japanese car manufacturer, even if those machines operate in Alabama. On the other hand, U.S. GNP would include the value added of U.S. workers who are employed in a Japanese auto plant in Alabama. U.S. GNP is carefully constructed to count only the value added of factors of production possessed or owned by U.S. residents, no matter where those factors of production operate in the world.

GNP is therefore a measure of national production, where the word *national* signifies the factors of production—like capital and labor—possessed or owned by the residents of a particular nation. To calculate GNP, begin with GDP and first add in the production of U.S.-owned factors of production that operate within the borders of foreign countries. Then subtract the production of foreign-owned factors of production that operate within the borders of the United States.

Gross national product = (Gross domestic product)
  + (Production of U.S.-owned capital and labor within the borders of foreign countries)
  − (Production of foreign-owned capital and labor within U.S. borders).

Plugging in the actual (rounded) numbers for 2013, we find that U.S. GNP ($17.1 trillion) is higher than U.S. GDP ($16.8 trillion). Specifically, the market value of production of U.S. capital and labor within the borders of foreign countries ($0.8 trillion) exceeds the market value of production of foreign capital and labor within U.S. borders ($0.6 trillion). In 2013, U.S. GNP was 1.5 percent larger than U.S. GDP.

For a few countries, GNP and GDP diverge much more substantially. For example, Kuwait—a wealthy oil exporter in the Persian Gulf—owns a very large portfolio of foreign assets, and residents of foreign countries own comparatively few assets inside Kuwait. The income from Kuwait's foreign assets is counted in Kuwait's GNP but excluded from Kuwait's GDP. Accordingly Kuwait's GNP is substantially larger—generally about

10 percent larger—than its GDP. However, Kuwait's situation is uncommon. For most countries, GNP and GDP are nearly the same.

Leisure

Leisure is another sore spot in the GDP system. The GDP accounts give an economy no credit for producing leisure. However, most people would agree that leisure is a key ingredient in human well-being. For example, in time-use surveys, people report that they are happiest when they are socializing.[2] Likewise, people report that they are the least happy when they are at work or commuting to and from work. When you think about GDP comparisons across countries, you need to remember that different countries are working at different levels of intensity. Of course, the goal in life is *not* to maximize your income by working every moment that you can. If that were our goal, nobody would ever retire or take a vacation. A more reasonable goal is to maximize human well-being—this is another example of optimization. GDP tells us how many material goods are being produced by an economy, but it does not tell us whether all of those material achievements are being used to optimize human happiness.

Does GDP Buy Happiness?

Despite the omission of leisure, GDP per capita is often used as a summary measure of the well-being of a society. We would like to know whether GDP per capita is *actually* a good predictor of human happiness. Social scientists do not have a foolproof way of measuring happiness, but we do have a crude way of gauging whether a person is satisfied with life: ask them. It's not an ideal method—for instance, people may not tell the truth: "I'm fine, how are you?"—but it's a start. When survey researchers ask about happiness in millions of interviews around the world, some remarkable patterns appear in the data.

GDP per capita turns out to be an excellent predictor of life satisfaction. Exhibit 5.6 displays a positive relationship between GDP per capita and self-reports of life satisfaction in a large sample of countries. The countries with higher levels of GDP per capita report higher levels of life satisfaction. The exhibit plots GDP per capita on the horizontal axis and average life satisfaction on the vertical axis. Life satisfaction was measured with a 10-point scale. Each circle represents a different country, and the size of the circle reflects the size of the population in that country. The large circle on the right is the United States. The two large circles on the left are India and China.

> **GDP per capita turns out to be an excellent predictor of life satisfaction.**

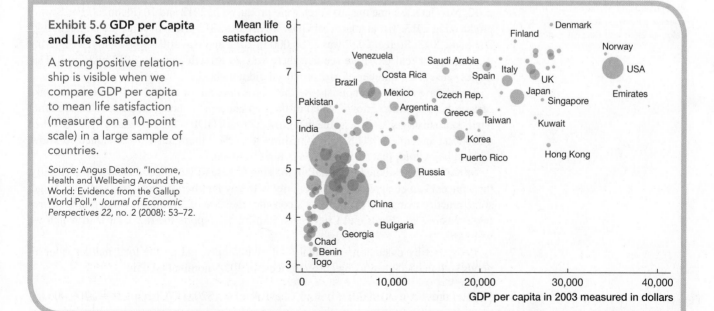

Exhibit 5.6 GDP per Capita and Life Satisfaction

A strong positive relationship is visible when we compare GDP per capita to mean life satisfaction (measured on a 10-point scale) in a large sample of countries.

Source: Angus Deaton, "Income, Health and Wellbeing Around the World: Evidence from the Gallup World Poll," *Journal of Economic Perspectives* 22, no. 2 (2008): 53–72.

The same relationship also shows up within each country. In other words, when economists study household-level data on income and life satisfaction, we find that low-income households within a country report substantially lower life satisfaction than higher-income households within the same country.[3]

5.4   Real vs. Nominal

GDP is particularly useful as a tool for determining how the overall economy is growing. To implement this growth analysis, we would like to separate the increase in the value of GDP that is due to overall price increases (in other words, inflation, a concept we will define below) from the increase in the value of GDP that is due to increases in the quantity and quality of goods and services.

For example, suppose the country of Fordica makes 10 cars in 2012 and 10 identical cars in 2013. Here we'll make the simplifying assumption that the quality of the cars hasn't changed over time. Economists have sophisticated tools for handling improvements in quality, but we'll sidestep those issues to keep the analysis as simple as possible. Holding quality fixed, assume that the price of each car rises from $30,000 to $40,000 from 2012 to 2013. In this case, GDP in 2012 would be (10 cars $\times$ $30,000/car) = $300,000 and GDP in 2013 would be (10 cars $\times$ $40,000/car) = $400,000. At first glance, the economy has grown by 33 percent, or

$$\frac{(\text{GDP in 2013}) - (\text{GDP in 2012})}{\text{GDP in 2012}} = \frac{(\$400,000) - (\$300,000)}{\$300,000} = \frac{1}{3} = 0.33 = 33\%.$$

But the actual number of cars produced hasn't grown at all. It's still 10 cars. If we counted the *number* of cars, rather than their market value, the growth rate of the economy from 2012 to 2013 would have been 0 percent. We don't want to pat ourselves on the back because prices have gone up (holding car quality fixed as we are in this example).

Naturally, we would like to separate the growth that is due simply to price increases from the growth that is due to increases in the production of goods and services. To do this, we contrast the concepts of *nominal GDP* and *real GDP*. Nominal GDP is the standard GDP measurement that we've been discussing throughout this chapter. **Nominal GDP** is the total market value of production, using *current* prices to determine value per unit produced.

Real GDP is based on the same idea as nominal GDP—summing up the market value of the quantities of final goods and services—but real GDP uses prices from a base year that may be different from the year that the quantities were produced. To illustrate this idea, let's take 2012 as the base year. In our example, the price of a Ford was $30,000 in 2012. Now let's assume that 10 Fords were produced in 2012 and 10 (identical) Fords were produced in 2013. To calculate real GDP, we use the 2012 prices to value the output in *both* 2012 and 2013. So real GDP was $300,000 in 2012 and was still $300,000 in 2013. Using the concept of real GDP, we see that there was no growth between 2012 and 2013. That makes sense—the number of cars produced did not change.

To increase clarity, economists use the words *nominal* or *real* in their analysis to make certain that the reader knows which of the two concepts is being discussed. On the other hand, journalists generally assume that growth of *real* GDP is the only game in town. When a headline announces, "U.S. Growth Slows to 2.2%," the readers are assumed to know, without being told, that real growth is being discussed.

So far we have studied real GDP in the simple case of a one-good economy. Naturally, this concept can be applied to an economy with any number of goods and services. To get some practice using this concept, let's consider the case of an economy that manufactures two types of cars: Fords and Chevrolets. Exhibit 5.7 reports the raw data with which we will work.

Let's start by calculating nominal GDP. We simply add up the total market value of goods sold in each year, using current prices. In 2012, nominal GDP is

(10 Fords) $\times$ ($30,000/Ford) + (5 Chevrolets) $\times$ ($20,000/Chevrolet) = $400,000.

Nominal GDP is the total value of production (final goods and services), using current market prices to determine the value of each unit that is produced.

Real GDP is the total value of production (final goods and services), using market prices from a specific base year to determine the value of each unit that is produced.

In 2013, nominal GDP is

(10 Fords) × ($40,000/Ford) + (20 Chevrolets) × ($25,000/Chevrolet) = $900,000.

Check these totals against the values in the column of Exhibit 5.7 labeled Nominal GDP.

To calculate real GDP, we will use 2012 as the base year. That means that we keep using 2012 prices in the calculation of *both* 2012 and 2013 real GDP. This doesn't rock the boat for 2012. Real GDP for 2012 is calculated with 2012 quantities and 2012 prices (exactly matching our calculation of nominal GDP in 2012):

(10 Fords) × ($30,000/Ford) + (5 Chevrolets) × ($20,000/Chevrolet) = $400,000.

The boat rocking comes when we calculate real GDP in 2013, using 2012 as the base year. Now we need to use quantities from 2013 and prices from 2012. In 2013, real GDP is

(10 Fords) × ($30,000/Ford) + (20 Chevrolets) × ($20,000/Chevrolet) = $700,000.

By holding prices constant—using prices from a single base year, 2012—we are able to make meaningful comparisons across years. Economists say that such analysis uses *constant dollars*. In this case, the constant dollars are based on prices from 2012. To make the base year clear to their audience, economists say that the analysis uses "constant 2012 dollars."

Now that you understand how to calculate real GDP, we are able to talk about the growth rate of real GDP, which is usually referred to as **real GDP growth**. For example, the formula for real GDP growth in 2013 is given by

Real GDP growth is the growth rate of real GDP.

$$\text{Real GDP growth in 2013} = \frac{(\text{Real GDP in 2013}) - (\text{Real GDP in 2012})}{\text{Real GDP in 2012}}.$$

By focusing on real GDP growth—which holds prices fixed across time—we compare the total value of real output in 2012 ($400,000 in our example) and the total value of real output in 2013 ($700,000 in our example). In this example, real GDP has grown by 75 percent:

$$\frac{(\$700,000 - \$400,000)}{\$400,000} = \frac{3}{4} = 0.75 = 75\%.$$

The concept of real GDP growth lets us focus on the thing that we care the most about—how much the economy is producing at different points in time—without letting price movements muddy up the comparison.

Finally, don't let this teaching example mislead you. Unfortunately, *actual* growth rates for real GDP are much lower than they are in our illustration. Since 1929, when reliable national income accounts were first created, real GDP growth in the United States has averaged 3.3 percent per year. Even rapidly growing developing countries achieve average real GDP

	Ford		Chevrolet			
	Quantity	Price	Quantity	Price	Nominal GDP	Real GDP using 2012 Base Prices
2012	10	$ 30,000	5	$ 20,000	$ 400,000	$ 400,000
2013	10	$ 40,000	20	$ 25,000	$ 900,000	$ 700,000

Exhibit 5.7 Quantities (Q) and Prices (P) in an Economy with Two Goods

The yellow box contains Ford's quantities and prices in years 2012 and 2013. The orange box contains Chevrolet's quantities and prices. Nominal GDP is the total value of production using prices and quantities from the same year. Real GDP in 2012 using 2012 prices is the same as nominal GDP in 2012. Real GDP in 2013 using 2012 prices is the total value of quantities in 2013 using prices from 2012.

growth of only 5 percent to 10 percent per year. We'll analyze long-run real GDP growth in Chapter 7, and we'll study short-run fluctuations in real GDP growth in Chapter 12.

The GDP Deflator

We can also use real GDP to study the level of prices in the overall economy. Specifically, if we divide nominal GDP by real GDP in the same year and multiply the resulting ratio by 100, we end up with a measure of how much prices of goods and services produced in a country have risen since the base year. This ratio is called the **GDP deflator**:

$$\text{GDP deflator} = \frac{\text{Nominal GDP}}{\text{Real GDP}} \times 100.$$

To understand why this ratio is a measure of rising prices, it helps to write out the formula. Consider again the example in Exhibit 5.7, in which we treat 2012 as the base year for calculations of real GDP. To get our feet wet, let's first evaluate the GDP deflator for 2012. We've written out the expressions for nominal GDP and real GDP below, putting the quantities in blue and the prices in red. Using the data in Exhibit 5.7, you can confirm the numbers in the formula below:

$$\text{GDP deflator (2012)} = \frac{\text{Nominal GDP (2012)}}{\text{Real GDP (2012)}} \times 100$$

$$= \frac{\text{Cost of buying everything produced domestically in 2012 using 2012 prices}}{\text{Cost of buying everything produced domestically in 2012 using base-year prices}} \times 100$$

$$= \frac{10 \times 30{,}000 + 5 \times 20{,}000}{10 \times 30{,}000 + 5 \times 20{,}000} \times 100$$

$$= 100.$$

This first calculation reminds us that in the base year (2012 in this example), nominal GDP matches real GDP. Consequently, in the base year, the GDP deflator is exactly equal to 100.

Now let's consider 2013, the year after the base year. Once again, you can use the data in Exhibit 5.7 to confirm the numbers in the equation below:

$$\text{GDP deflator (2013)} = \frac{\text{Nominal GDP (2013)}}{\text{Real GDP (2013)}} \times 100$$

$$= \frac{\text{Cost of buying everything produced domestically in 2013 using 2013 prices}}{\text{Cost of buying everything produced domestically in 2013 using base-year prices}} \times 100$$

$$= \frac{10 \times 40{,}000 + 20 \times 25{,}000}{10 \times 30{,}000 + 20 \times 20{,}000} \times 100$$

$$= \frac{900{,}000}{700{,}000} \times 100$$

$$= 128.6.$$

In the formula for the 2013 GDP deflator, the numerator and the denominator have exactly the same quantities (in blue): 10 Fords and 20 Chevys. These are the quantities that are sold in 2013. The only things that change between the numerator and the denominator are the prices (in red). The numerator (top) has the 2013 prices, which are used to calculate nominal GDP in 2013. The denominator (bottom) has the 2012 prices that are used to calculate real GDP for 2013—recall that the 2012 prices are the base-year prices.

The numerator shows what it would cost to purchase everything that the economy produced in 2013 using 2013 prices. The denominator shows what it would cost to purchase everything that the economy produced in 2013 using 2012 prices. The GDP deflator is the ratio that reflects the rising cost of buying everything produced in 2013, holding the goods and services produced in 2013 fixed, but changing the prices from the 2013 prices (in the numerator) to the 2012 prices (in the denominator).

The 2013 GDP deflator is telling us how the 2013 prices (in red in the numerator) compare with the 2012 prices (in red in the denominator), holding the quantities fixed in the numerator and the denominator. You can think of the (blue) quantities as weights. The higher the 2013 quantity, the more weight that good or service gets in determining the overall ratio. This makes sense. Goods or services with large quantities *should* get more weight when we form an overall measure of the price level.

Economists study the percentage change in the GDP deflator from year to year. For example, the percentage change in the GDP deflator in 2013 is given by

Percentage change in GDP deflator in 2013

$$= \frac{(\text{GDP deflator in 2013}) - (\text{GDP deflator in 2012})}{\text{GDP deflator in 2012}}.$$

The percentage change in the GDP deflator is a measure of the percentage change in the overall level of prices. In our illustrative example, the GDP deflator was 100 in 2012, and it was 128.6 in 2013. So an economist concludes that prices have risen 28.6 percent:

$$\frac{(128.6 - 100)}{100} = \frac{28.6}{100} = 0.286 = 28.6\%.$$

Note that this overall rate of price inflation is between the rate of price inflation for Fords ($30,000 to $40,000, or a 33 percent increase) and the rate of price inflation for Chevrolets ($20,000 to $25,000, or a 25 percent increase). The relative weights of Ford and Chevy prices is determined by their quantity weights.

Exhibit 5.8 plots the value of the *actual* U.S. GDP deflator from 1929 to 2013, using 2009 as the base year. Because 2009 is the base year, the GDP deflator is exactly 100 in

MyEconLab Real-time data

Exhibit 5.8 The Value of the GDP Deflator from 1929 to 2013, Using 2009 as the Base Year

Because 2009 is the base year, the GDP deflator is exactly 100 in 2009. Notice that the GDP deflator is less than 100 before 2009 and greater than 100 after 2009. The deflator is an indicator of the overall level of prices in the economy. In an economy with rising prices, the deflator rises over time. The only period of sharp declines in the GDP deflator was the period from 1929 to 1933, which was the Great Depression. The series is plotted on a scale with constant proportionality, implying that changes of equal size on the printed page represent equal proportional movements. For example, going from the level of 4 to 20 (a multiple of 5) has the same step size on the printed page as going from the level of 20 to 100 (another multiple of 5).

Source: Bureau of Economic Analysis, National Income and Product Accounts.

2009. The GDP deflator is less than 100 before 2009 and greater than 100 after 2009. From 1929 to 2013 the GDP deflator increased on average 2.9 percent per year, which is a measure of how quickly prices rose on average during this period.

There are many different ways to measure overall movements in prices, which causes some degree of confusion. In fact, the general public is largely unaware of the GDP deflator and its usefulness as a tool for measuring price movements. The most well-known price measure is the Consumer Price Index, which we come to next.

The Consumer Price Index

As you now know, the GDP deflator is the ratio

$$\text{GDP deflator (2013)} = \frac{\text{Nominal GDP (2013)}}{\text{Real GDP (2013)}} \times 100$$

$$= \frac{\text{Cost of buying everything produced domestically in 2013 using 2013 prices}}{\text{Cost of buying everything produced domestically in 2013 using base-year prices}} \times 100.$$

For example, if the base year were 2009, then the prices that are used in the denominator are the prices that existed in the economy in 2009.

The Bureau of Labor Statistics calculates a related formula called the **Consumer Price Index (CPI)**. As you can see, the CPI looks almost identical to the formula for the GDP deflator:

The **Consumer Price Index (CPI)** is 100 times the ratio of the cost of buying a basket of consumer goods using 2013 prices divided by the cost of buying the same basket of consumer goods using base-year prices.

$$\text{CPI (2013)} = \frac{\text{Cost of buying a particular basket of consumer goods using 2013 prices}}{\text{Cost of buying a particular basket of consumer goods using base-year prices}} \times 100.$$

As you can see, the GDP deflator and CPI formulas are nearly indistinguishable:

1. Both formulas use 2013 prices in the numerator and base-year prices in the denominator.
2. Both formulas contain a ratio that compares what it would cost to buy "stuff" in 2013 (in the numerator) to what it would have cost to buy "the same stuff" using base-year prices (in the denominator).
3. Both formulas also have the same interpretation: a higher ratio implies a greater price increase from the base year to 2013.

The key difference between the formulas is the basket of goods that is being bought. The GDP deflator studies the basket of goods that is produced domestically. In other words, the GDP deflator studies the basket of goods that represents the total production of the domestic economy. We'll call this the GDP basket.

The CPI studies a particular basket of consumer goods. This basket is constructed to reflect the types and quantities of goods that are purchased by a typical U.S. household. We'll call this the consumer basket.

There are three key differences between the two baskets:

(1) The GDP basket includes things that households don't purchase, like coal-fired power plants, locomotives, subway stations, city buses, aircraft carriers, and nuclear submarines. Consumers use services provided by governments and firms that purchase these items, but no consumer purchases them directly, so they appear in the GDP basket (in the year they are purchased) but not in the consumer basket.

(2) The consumer basket includes things that households purchase but are not counted in GDP. For example, GDP only counts *domestic* production, so it does not count imports, such as a laptop manufactured abroad. A Chinese laptop that is purchased by a U.S. consumer does not get counted in the U.S. GDP basket but would get counted in the U.S. consumer basket.

(3) Even if a product is included in both the GDP basket and the consumer basket, it is likely to have a different weight in the two baskets. For example, housing-related expenditures are in both the GDP basket and the consumer basket, but housing has a larger role in the consumer basket. Housing—including the cost of shelter, utility bills, and household furnishings—represents over 40 percent of the consumer basket, but these items jointly represent less than 20 percent of the GDP basket.

With all of these differences, it's natural to wonder whether the GDP deflator and CPI tell very different stories about the evolution of prices in the overall economy. In fact, in practice it almost makes no difference, as we demonstrate next.

Inflation

The rate of increase in prices is the **inflation rate**. It is calculated as the year-over-year percentage increase in a price index. For example, to calculate the overall U.S. inflation rate in 2013, we use the following formula, with either the GDP deflator or the CPI as the "price index":

$$\text{Inflation rate in 2013} = \frac{(\text{Price Index in 2013}) - (\text{Price Index in 2012})}{\text{Price Index in 2012}}.$$

The rate of increase in prices is the **inflation rate.** It is calculated as the year-over-year percentage increase in a price index.

It turns out that the choice of the price index doesn't have a large impact on the resulting rate of inflation. Exhibit 5.9 plots the historical rate of inflation calculated with either the GDP deflator (blue) or the CPI (dashed red line). As you can see, the two inflation series move very closely together.

This similarity may partially explain why there are relatively few news stories about the GDP deflator. The GDP deflator doesn't have much to add once we know the CPI. Moreover, CPI is released on a monthly basis, so it is more timely than the GDP deflator, which is released quarterly. Finally, CPI describes inflation that matters the most for households. In this sense, CPI has more personal relevance for the typical consumer.

Adjusting Nominal Variables

You can't make meaningful comparisons across time without adjusting nominal variables. For example, William Howard Taft was paid $75,000 per year for his service as president. He was inaugurated in 1909. In 2013, the U.S. president was paid $400,000. So who was paid more?

When we ask that question, we don't mean "Who received more dollars?" We really mean "Whose salary was worth more?" or, in the language of economics, "Who had more buying power?" There has been a lot of inflation between 1909 and 2013, so a dollar paid out in 1909 bought much more than a dollar in 2013. To compare Taft's salary to a modern presidential salary, we need to translate Taft's salary into current dollars.

There's a formula that enables us to do this:

$$\text{Value in 2013 dollars} = \frac{\text{Price index in 2013}}{\text{Price index in 1909}} \times \text{Value in 1909 dollars}.$$

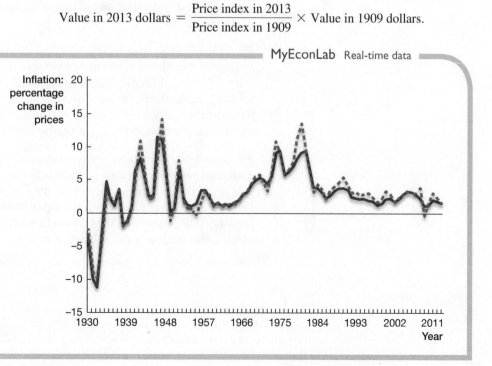

Exhibit 5.9 The Annual U.S. Inflation Rate from 1930 to 2013

The annual percentage change in the GDP deflator from 1930 to 2013 is plotted in blue; it is one measure of inflation. The exhibit also plots the annual percentage change in the Consumer Price Index over the same period (dashed red line). This is another measure of inflation. The two measures have a very similar historical pattern.

Source: Bureau of Economic Analysis, National Income and Product Accounts; and U.S. Bureau of Labor Statistics.

The ratio on the right-hand-side of this equation tells us how much prices have risen, enabling us to transform value expressed in 1909 dollars into value expressed in 2013 dollars. We can fill in these numbers using the 2013 CPI and an historical estimate of what the CPI was in 1909 (official government CPI calculations do not start until 1913).

$$\text{Value in 2013 dollars} = \frac{\text{Price index in 2013}}{\text{Price index in 1909}} \times \text{Value in 1909 dollars}$$

$$= \frac{233}{9} \times \$75{,}000$$

$$= \$1.9 \text{ million.}$$

The ratio of price indices tells you that, on average, prices rose by a factor of 233/9 = 25.89 over this time period, so having \$1 in 1909 is equivalent to having \$25.89 in 2013. Scaling Taft's annual salary of \$75,000 in 1909 by this ratio of price levels implies that his 1909 salary has equivalent purchasing power to \$1.9 million in 2014. Taft's salary was worth more than 4 times Barak Obama's presidential salary.

We can use this simple formula to express any historical price (or value) in dollars for a more recent year (say, 2013). We generally have a good intuition for what 2013 dollars can buy, and we generally have a poor intuition for a dollar's buying power in 1909. Therefore, this type of transformation can come in very handy. We'll use it many times throughout this textbook.

Summary

✹ Macroeconomics is the study of economic aggregates and the economy as a whole. An aggregate is a total. Macroeconomics studies total economic activity.

✹ Gross domestic product (GDP) is the market value of the final goods and services produced within the borders of a country during a particular period of time (for instance, a year). GDP is defined in three equivalent ways: Production = Expenditure = Income. The circular flow diagram explains these identities and adds a fourth identical way of measuring economic activity: factors of production.

✹ Like a short weather report—"92 degrees and partly cloudy"—GDP is just a summary measure of economic activity and economic well-being. GDP leaves many details out, including depreciation, home production, the underground economy, externalities, leisure, and cross-border movements of capital and labor. Nevertheless, residents of countries with relatively high levels of GDP per capita report relatively high levels of life satisfaction.

✹ Economists distinguish nominal values and real values. Real GDP measures the market value of economic production holding prices fixed at a particular base year. The GDP deflator is a measure of the overall level of prices in the economy. The Consumer Price Index (CPI) is another measure of the overall level of prices. Both the GDP deflator and the CPI can be used to measure the overall rate at which prices are rising: the inflation rate.

Key Terms

Questions

All questions are available in MyEconLab for practice and instructor assignment.

1. Find and list three recent stories in the media that would typically be studied in macroeconomics. (Cite the date and source of the stories you choose.) Discuss why they would fall within the subject matter of *macroeconomics*.

2. How is gross domestic product defined?

3. What is an accounting identity? Explain the accounting identity Production = Expenditure = Income.

4. Use the circular flow diagram to show how expenditure, production, and income relate to one another.

5. How is production-based accounting used to estimate GDP? Discuss the role of value-added.

6. How is GDP calculated using expenditure-based accounting?

7. Which category of expenditure accounts for the highest share of GDP in the United States?

8. How is the level of economic activity calculated using the income method?

9. If the level of aggregate expenditure was $16.8 trillion in 2013, what was the level of aggregate income? Explain your answer.

10. What is meant by capital depreciation?

11. Explain three important factors that GDP leaves out.

12. You decide to cook your own meal rather than eat in a restaurant. How will this affect GDP?

13. When would a country's gross domestic product exceed its gross national product?

14. Nobel laureate Simon Kuznets, who did significant work on national income accounts in the 1930s, said that the welfare of a nation can scarcely be inferred from a measurement of national income. Would you agree with him? Why or why not?

15. Why is it essential to differentiate between real and nominal growth rates of GDP?

16. What are the key differences between the Consumer Price Index (CPI) and the GDP deflator?

17. How is the Consumer Price Index similar to the GDP deflator?

Problems

All problems are available in MyEconLab for practice and instructor assignment.

1. Which of the following would be considered a final good in the calculation of U.S. GDP? Explain your answers.

   a. Processors manufactured in California for Apple's new range of laptops (that will be sold in the US).

   b. Foot massages at spas in California

   c. Defense equipment purchased by the federal government

2. By how much would GDP change as a result of each of the following changes. Briefly explain your answers.

   a. A parent switches from buying pre-made ham and cheese sandwiches for a family dinner, which would have cost $20, to buying the raw ingredients, which cost only $6, and making the same ham and cheese sandwiches at home.

   b. On the rebound again, a famous rock star marries her butler, whom she formerly paid $50,000 a year. After they are married, her husband continues to wait on her as before, and she continues to support him as before—but as a husband rather than as an employee, that is, not with a regular salary.

3. Suppose that there are only two small countries in the world: Ascot, with a population of 30,000 people, and Delwich, with a population of 20,000 people. Ascot's GDP is equal to $150 million while Delwich's GDP is $250 million. Delwich's GNP has been estimated to be equal to $280 million. Use this information to calculate Ascot's GNP, the GDP per capita in Ascot, and the GNP per capita in Delwich.

4. The following table gives data for a small country, Magnolia:

Component	Expenditure (in thousands)
Social Security payments	$250
Depreciation	$ 47
Private investment	$630
Exports	$260
Imports	$300
Salaries earned by foreigners working in Magnolia	$160
Household consumption	$850
Purchases of raw materials	$270
Government purchases	$900
Capital income	$290
Salaries earned by Magnolian residents working abroad	$350

a. Use the data to calculate GDP for this economy using the expenditure method.

b. Calculate the value of Magnolia's GNP. Does Magnolia's GDP differ from its GNP? Why?

5. In 2013, the value of the Consumer Price Index (CPI) in a certain country, Polonia, was 230 index points and median (nominal) household income was $31,200. In 1950, the CPI was 51 index points and median (nominal) household income was $9,500.

a. Calculate median real household income in 1950 and in 2013, using 2013 as the base year.

b. In which year was life satisfaction likely to be higher? Explain your answer.

6. Most products we buy go through a lengthy series of intermediate steps before they are available for us to purchase. For this problem, say we are tracing the stages, and the associated transaction values, involved in the production of a hypothetical loaf of bread:

Farmer sells wheat to miller	$0.50
Miller grinds wheat into flour, and sells to baker	$1.00
Baker bakes the loaf, and sells to a grocery wholesaler	$2.00
Wholesaler sells loaf to various chain retail outlets	$2.50
Retailer sells loaf to public	$3.25

a. Which expenditure category of GDP increased as a result of the production and sale of the loaf?

b. Calculate the addition to GDP contributed by this loaf, using all three methods covered in the text: expenditure-based accounting, income-based accounting, and production-based accounting.

7. The country of Sylvania produces and consumes only three goods: Red Bull, pizza, and T-shirts. The quantity produced and price of each good in 2011 and 2012 are given in the following table:

	2011		2012	
	Quantity	Price	Quantity	Price
T-Shirts	100	$25	110	$25
Red Bull (cans)	500	$1	500	$1.50
Pizza (slices)	1000	$2	900	$4

a. Calculate nominal GDP for 2011 and 2012.

b. Using 2011 as the base year, calculate real GDP for 2011 and 2012.

c. Based on your answer from part b, by what percentage did real GDP grow between 2011 and 2012?

d. Now, calculate real GDP for 2011 and 2012 using 2012 as the base year.

e. Based on your answer from part d, by what percentage did real GDP grow between 2011 and 2012?

f. Using 2011 as the base year, what was the GDP deflator in 2011 and 2012?

g. Based on your answer from part f, by what percentage did prices change between 2011 and 2012?

8. A typical resident of the country of Collegia consumes a simple basket of goods consisting of life's essentials: soda, pizza, and Advil. A year's basket contains 1,000 sodas, 100 pizzas, and 50 bottles of Advil. The price of these goods in each of the past 8 years is given in the following table:

	Soda	Pizza	Advil
2005	$1.00	$ 8.00	$10.00
2006	$1.50	$ 8.00	$10.00
2007	$1.50	$ 8.50	$11.00
2008	$2.00	$ 8.50	$11.50
2009	$2.50	$ 9.00	$11.00
2010	$2.50	$ 9.00	$10.00
2011	$2.00	$10.00	$12.00
2012	$3.00	$10.00	$13.00

Using 2008 as the base year,

a. calculate the CPI for each year.

b. calculate the rate of inflation for each year from the previous year, starting with 2006.

9. Social Security payments in the United States are currently linked to the Consumer Price Index for Urban Wage Earners and Clerical Workers (CPI-W). This means that as the CPI-W shows an increase in the price level, Social Security payments will also increase, keeping the real value of the payment constant. The following table shows the weighting given to the different components in the CPI-W consumption basket.

Item	Weight
Food and beverages	15.948
Housing	39.867
Apparel	3.623
Transportation	18.991
Medical care	5.767
Recreation	5.528
Education and communication	6.766
Other goods and services	3.510
Total	**100.000**

It has been suggested that using the CPI-W to adjust Social Security payments understates inflation for seniors. Do you agree? Why might this be the case?

10. Recall the method of calculating real GDP detailed in the chapter. As you may already have noticed, this method has a problem: in calculating aggregate output, this method weights the output of the various goods and services by their relative prices in the base year.

Say, for example, a textbook cost $100 in the base year, and a laptop cost $2,000. This means that the laptop would have 20 times the weight of a book in calculating aggregate output.

But, what happens when relative prices change? As you know, the prices of most high-tech items, including laptops, have generally been decreasing over time. Suppose the price of a laptop declined from $2,000 to $1,000 in the period from the base year to the current year. Now a laptop costs only 10 times as much as the book. So, using base-year relative prices would overweight laptops in calculating real GDP in the current year.

In response to this problem, in 1996 the BEA switched to what is called a *chain-weighted* method of calculating real GDP. Say the base year is 2008. To calculate the growth rate of real GDP between 2008 and 2009, for example, the BEA calculates real GDP for 2008 using 2008 as the base, and then real GDP for 2008 using 2009 as the base. Then, the Bureau calculates real GDP for 2009 using 2009 as the base, and real GDP for 2009 using 2008 as the base. For each base, the growth rate is then calculated as: $\dfrac{2009 \text{ GDP}_{(2008\ Base)} - 2008 \text{ GDP}_{(2008\ Base)}}{2008 \text{ GDP}_{(2008\ Base)}}$,

$\dfrac{2009 \text{ GDP}_{(2009\ Base)} - 2008 \text{ GDP}_{(2009\ Base)}}{2008 \text{ GDP}_{(2009\ Base)}}$.

So, they end up with two different growth rates, which are then averaged. Given this averaged growth rate, and the level of GDP in 2008 at 2008 prices, the Bureau then calculates real GDP for 2009 as 1 plus the average growth rate previously calculated, times 2008 output in 2008

dollars. The growth rate between 2009 and 2010 is then calculated similarly.

Suppose that laptops, economics textbooks, and energy drinks are the only three goods produced in the United States. The following table gives the quantity of each produced (in millions) and their price in the years from 2011 to 2013:

	P Laptops	Q Laptops	P Texts	Q Texts	P Eng. Drnk	Q Eng. Drnk
2011	1500	7	100	7	2	25
2012	1200	9	110	9	4	30
2013	1000	9	120	10	4	35

a. Calculate nominal GDP and real GDP (using 2011 as the base year) for each year.

b. Calculate real GDP for 2012 and 2013 using the chain-weighted method outlined above.

11. On May 22, 2013, *Forbes* magazine reported that Bill Gates had overtaken Mexican businessman Carlos Slim as the "richest man in the world." Gates's fortune on that date was estimated at $70 billion, whereas Slim's was a mere $69.86 billion. (http://www.forbes.com/sites/erincarlyle/2013/05/22/bill-gates-is-worlds-richest-bumps-slim/)

But, does this make Gates the richest American who ever lived?

John D. Rockefeller, the founder of Standard Oil, is usually credited with this distinction. At the time of his death in 1937, the founder of the Standard Oil empire had an estimated net worth of $1.4 billion.

a. Go to the BLS CPI site at http://data.bls.gov/cgi-bin/surveymost?cu. Under "Consumer Price Index-All Urban Consumers," select "US All Items, 1982–84 = 100" and click the "Retrieve data" button at the bottom of the page. Adjust the years to retrieve data from 1937 through 2013.

   Use the data under the "Annual" column to calculate Gates's 2013 net worth measured in 1937 dollars. You should find that Gates's wealth does have more buying power than Rockefeller's wealth.

b. Some analysts say that Rockefeller's net worth was economically equivalent to $250 billion today. However, this figure is arrived at in a particular way. First, his net worth in 1937 is calculated as a *percentage* of total U.S. GDP in 1937. That percentage is then multiplied by the current level of GDP to arrive at the equivalent figure in current dollars. See if you can approximate the $250 billion figure. You can find the relevant GDP figures at http://research.stlouisfed.org/fred2/data/GDPA.txt.

c. What are the pros and cons of the two different methods—reviewed in the previous parts of this question—of adjusting Rockefeller's net worth to make it comparable to the wealth of business leaders today?

6 Aggregate Incomes

Why is the average American so much richer than the average Indian?

We live in a world of great disparities. Standards of living, educational opportunities, health services, and infrastructure differ tremendously across countries. Poverty is endemic in many parts of the world, particularly in sub-Saharan Africa, South Asia, and parts of South America, while most people in the United States, Canada, Western Europe, and a few other fairly rich countries live in relative comfort, even abundance. These differences are so great that if you travel around the globe, you will be struck by the contrast of how different living conditions are in some parts of the world from those back home. The realization that there are such great disparities may have been one of the factors that sparked your interest in economics in the first place. They are also the reason why many people from all over the world emigrate to richer countries, where standards of living are higher.

CHAPTER OUTLINE

6.1	6.2	6.3	EBE
Inequality Around the World	Productivity and the Aggregate Production Function	The Role and Determinants of Technology	Why is the average American so much richer than the average Indian?

Macroeconomics provides a useful conceptual framework for studying these issues and explains why such disparities exist. In this and the next two chapters, we study questions related to economic inequalities across countries and economic growth (sometimes called "long-run macroeconomics") before turning to the study of economic fluctuations (sometimes called "short-run macroeconomics") in the subsequent five chapters. In particular, in this chapter, we explain how we can measure differences in standards of living across countries and why such disparities exist. In the next chapter, we turn to the study of economic growth, that is, how and why an economy grows and becomes more prosperous over time. In our last chapter in this series, Chapter 8, we discuss the fundamental factors that keep poor countries poor.

6.1 Inequality Around the World

Before we can understand the variation of income across the world, our first step is to define our measurements. How do we quantify the differences in standards of living and economic conditions across countries? Income per capita is one robust measure.

Measuring Differences in Income per Capita

We learned in the last chapter how to measure aggregate income or GDP. We can do so by approaching it from the production side, from the expenditure side, or from the income side. From the national income accounting identity, all three give exactly the same answer: gross domestic product, or GDP for short. Dividing GDP by the total population in the country gives us **income per capita** (per person) or **GDP per capita**.

Income per capita or **GDP per capita** is GDP divided by total population.

We use the two terms interchangeably in this textbook because they represent the same number. (Often we use income per capita when we wish to emphasize that the number is the average income of the citizens of a country and GDP per capita when we wish to emphasize that the number is what the economy produces per person.)

More formally, we have:

$$\text{Income per capita} = \text{GDP per capita} = \frac{\text{GDP}}{\text{Total population}}.$$

For example, the United States in 2010 had GDP equal to about $14.45 trillion. With a total population of approximately 310 million, income per capita was approximately $46,613.

How does this compare to the income per capita of other countries? Let us look to a neighboring country: Mexico. Income in Mexico is, of course, not calculated in U.S. dollars but in pesos. Thus with a similar computation, we find income per capita in Mexico in the same year, 2010, to be approximately 116,036 pesos. This number is not directly comparable to the $46,613 for the United States because it is expressed in different units. But we can convert it to the same units by using the exchange rate. For example, on January 1, 2010 one U.S. dollar was worth 12.9 pesos, or one peso was worth 1/12.9 = 0.078 dollars. Using this ratio, we can convert the average income in Mexico into dollars as follows (where p.c. stands for "per capita"):

$$\text{Mexican income p.c. in \$} = \text{Mexican income p.c. in pesos} \times \text{\$/peso exchange rate}$$
$$= 116{,}036 \times 0.078$$
$$= \$9{,}051$$

So the average Mexican had an income per capita of approximately $9,051. This number would be useful if you wanted to think about how much an individual with the average Mexican income per capita, all of which was earned in Mexico, would be able to consume in the United States.

Using this exchange-rate-based measure, we can compute income per capita in every country for which we have data on GDP and population. For example, in 2010, income per capita in Sweden was $50,549 and in Switzerland it was $69,167. While income per capita in Sweden and Switzerland is similar to that in the United States, large disparities emerge when we compare the United States to several other countries. For example, we have already seen that the U.S. income per capita is about 5 times that of Mexico. It is also 30 times greater than income per capita in India, 43 times greater than income per capita in Senegal, and approximately 155 times greater than income per capita in Ethiopia.

Exchange rates allow us to compare GDP across countries using the same units, but we favor a tool that provides even better comparisons of income per capita across countries: purchasing power parity (PPP). Exchange rates convert currencies into the same units but fail to account for the fact that the *prices* of many goods and services will differ across countries. For example, some things—like phone calls—are cheaper in the United States than in Mexico because better technology is available in the United States and because there is a telecommunications monopoly in Mexico, keeping prices relatively high. But other goods—like guacamole and haircuts—are cheaper in Mexico, often because labor and other inputs are cheaper.

We saw in the previous chapter how to adjust economic variables like GDP to correct for changes in prices over time (which led to the notion of *real GDP*). We should make a similar adjustment when comparing GDP between countries. But the exchange rate between dollars and pesos doesn't do this. To see why, recall that the exchange rate between the peso and the dollar was 12.9 on January 1, 2010. If instead we had used the exchange rate on January 1, 2009, which was 13.8 pesos per dollar, the average income in Mexico would have been $8,408 rather than $9,051. But this fluctuation has little to do with changes in prices households face in Mexico or the United States. Rather, it is just a consequence of converting Mexican income into dollars using the current exchange rate, which (as we will see in Chapter 15) fluctuates for a variety of reasons unrelated to differences in the cost of living.

Purchasing power parity provides a better way to convert GDP in domestic currencies into common units. The idea here is very similar to the adjustment we developed for converting nominal GDP into real GDP in the previous chapter. Specifically, the **purchasing power parity (PPP)** constructs the cost of a representative bundle of commodities in each country and adjusts GDP so that a dollar in each country can purchase this representative bundle. The resulting measure is a country's GDP in PPP-adjusted U.S. dollars. For example, this representative bundle cost $1 in the United States and 8.64 pesos in Mexico in 2010. On this basis, the PPP factor between U.S. dollars and pesos is $1 for 8.64 pesos or 1 peso for 0.116 = 1/8.64 U.S. dollars.

Using this procedure, income per capita in Mexico in PPP would be:

$$\text{Mexican income p.c. in PPP \$} = \text{Mexican income p.c. in pesos} \times \text{\$/peso PPP}$$
$$= 116{,}036 \times 0.116$$
$$= \$13{,}460$$

Comparing this result for Mexico with the $9,051 obtained using the peso/$ exchange rate, we see that there is often a significant difference between exchange-rate-based measures and PPP-based measures of income per capita, with the gap between the United States

The **purchasing power parity (PPP)** constructs the cost of a representative bundle of commodities in each country and uses these relative costs for comparing income across countries.

LETTING THE DATA SPEAK

The Big Mac Index

In 1986, *The Economist* magazine proposed the Big Mac index as an alternative measure of exchange rates. This index would simply be the ratio of prices of a Big Mac in two countries. There were already McDonald's restaurants in many countries in 1986, so the price of a Big Mac could be computed for a large number of countries, giving an alternative measure of the exchange rate between any two of them. Though proposed tongue-in-cheek, the Big Mac index caught on and is now commonly used. In fact, there is a good reason for this. The Big Mac index is a simple example of a purchasing power parity adjustment. Its shortcoming is that instead of a representative bundle of diverse goods, this index only compares a bundle consisting of a single good, the Big Mac, which is only a small fraction of people's consumption. Thus, its price will not reflect true cost-of-living differences across countries.

economy and poorer economies generally being smaller when we use PPP-based measures. This pattern reflects the lower cost of living in countries with lower income per capita—that is, the fact that exchange-rate-based measures of GDP ignore the fact that many commodities are cheaper in poorer countries.

Inequality in Income per Capita

There are still very large disparities across countries when we use PPP-based measures. Exhibit 6.1 shows a graph of PPP-adjusted income per capita across countries in 2010 (expressed in terms of 2005 constant dollars, where the notion of constant dollars was defined in the previous chapter). Note that there are 19 countries with less than $1,000 per capita, including the Democratic Republic of Congo, Ethiopia, Liberia, Madagascar, and Togo, and another 23 with incomes of between $1,000 and $2,000, including Afghanistan, Haiti, Kenya, Tajikistan, Uganda, and Zambia. These measures contrast sharply with those of the United States ($41,365), France ($31,299), and Germany ($34,089) in the same year.

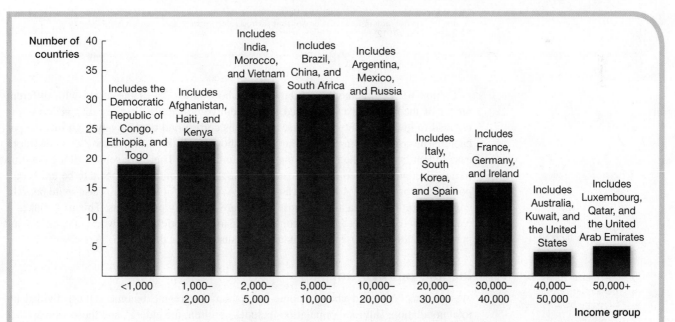

Exhibit 6.1 Income per Capita Around the World in 2010 (PPP-adjusted 2005 Constant Dollars)

There are wide disparities in income per capita across countries. Nineteen countries had income per capita less than $1,000 in 2010 (in PPP-adjusted 2005 constant dollars) while only a few countries had income per capita above $40,000.

Source: Data from Penn World Table; Alan Heston, Robert Summers and Bettina Aten, Penn World Table Version 7.1, Center for International Comparisons of Production, Income and Prices at the University of Pennsylvania (Nov 2012).

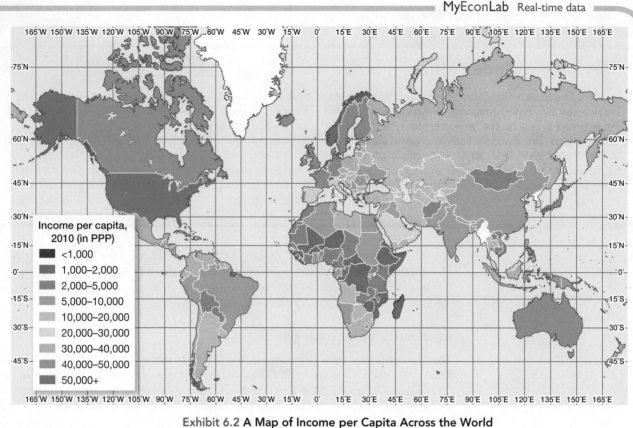

Exhibit 6.2 A Map of Income per Capita Across the World

The large disparities in income per capita across countries are easily visible on this map, which also shows that the poorest countries are concentrated in Africa, parts of Asia, Central America, and the Caribbean.

Source: Data from Penn World Table; Alan Heston, Robert Summers and Bettina Aten, Penn World Table Version 7.1, Center for International Comparisons of Production, Income and Prices at the University of Pennsylvania (Nov 2012).

Exhibit 6.2 complements Exhibit 6.1 by showing a map of the world with different ranges of income per capita shaded in different colors. Reds, oranges, and yellows correspond to lower income per capita, and greens correspond to relatively high income per capita. The overall picture is similar to that shown in Exhibit 6.1, yet we can now more easily identify where the rich and the poor countries are. There are some striking patterns to the differences in incomes. For example, the African continent appears to be uniformly poorer, except for a few spots. Much of South Asia and Latin America is also quite poor. In contrast, North America and Western Europe are relatively prosperous. This map makes it clear that there are indeed major economic disparities throughout the world, and one of our purposes in this chapter is to understand the causes behind them.

Income per Worker

We have so far talked about income per capita—aggregate income (GDP) divided by total population. But total population includes children, the elderly, and those who are not employed, who do not take part in production (though in many less developed economies, child labor is quite common). This raises the possibility that part of the variation in income per capita across countries might be due to differences in what fraction of the population works. Therefore, a natural alternative that avoids this problem is to focus on **income (or GDP) per worker**, defined as GDP divided by "workers," meaning those in employment. That is:

Income (or GDP) per worker is defined as GDP divided by the number of people in employment.

$$\text{Income per worker} = \frac{\text{GDP}}{\text{Number of people in employment}}.$$

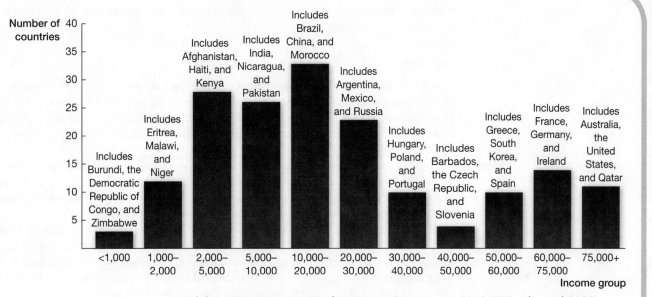

Exhibit 6.3 Income per Worker Across Countries in 2010 (PPP-adjusted 2005 Constant Dollars)

The distribution of countries by income per worker looks similar to the distribution by income per capita shown in Exhibit 6.1. One visible difference is that it is shifted to the right compared to Exhibit 6.1, because every country has higher income per worker (GDP divided by the number of people in employment) than income per capita (GDP divided by total population).

Source: Data from Penn World Table; Alan Heston, Robert Summers and Bettina Aten, Penn World Table Version 7.1, Center for International Comparisons of Production, Income and Prices at the University of Pennsylvania (Nov 2012).

This measure gives us a better picture of how much each worker produces on average by excluding those who do not work.

Exhibit 6.3 is similar to Exhibit 6.1, but uses (PPP-adjusted) income per worker. If there were large differences in the ratio of workers to the total population, this exhibit would look very different from Exhibit 6.1. A direct comparison shows that the overall patterns are very similar, though naturally income per worker is higher for every country than income per capita because the denominator is always smaller for income per worker. For example, PPP-adjusted income per capita in 2010 (in 2005 constant dollars) for Mexico is $11,939 (we saw that this was equal to 13,460 in *current* dollars), whereas PPP-adjusted income per worker for Mexico in 2010 (again in 2005 constant dollars) is $27,625. For India, the two corresponding numbers are $3,477 and $9,010. As a reflection of this, the group of countries with the highest income per worker now corresponds to $75,000+ instead of $50,000+ as in Exhibit 6.1.

Productivity

Productivity refers to the value of goods and services that a worker generates for each hour of work.

The main reason why income per capita or income per worker varies across countries is because productivity varies across countries. **Productivity** here refers to the value of goods and services that a worker generates for each hour of work. From our discussion of the national income accounting identity in Chapter 5, you will recall that the value of goods and services produced in a country, GDP, is equal to the total income in that country. Thus productivity also measures income per hour of work. Income per worker and productivity are very closely related and thus vary across countries for the same reasons. (The only reason why the two concepts differ is that the total number of hours of work per worker may also vary across countries, but in practice, this variation is small.)

It is useful to focus on productivity differences across countries because it emphasizes that to understand the huge differences in

> To understand the huge differences in income per capita across countries, we have to look at the production side.

income per capita across countries, we have to look at the production side. In particular, we need to study the factors that make labor much more productive in some countries than in others.

Incomes and the Standard of Living

A natural question is whether income per capita or income per worker is the quantity we should focus on. The answer depends on what we are trying to measure. Income per worker is particularly informative when we would like to understand why some economies are more productive than others, because it focuses directly on differences in GDP relative to those in employment.

Another reason why we care about disparities in income across countries is that we would like to measure differences in the standards of living across countries. For this purpose, income per capita is a natural first step because the conditions of the whole population, including children and the elderly, are conveyed by this measure.

However, there is much that is left out of income per capita, as you have already seen in the previous chapter. Even though, again as shown in the previous chapter, income per capita is a fairly good predictor of average life satisfaction in a country, we cannot capture the diverse dimensions of well-being and the standards of living of an entire population by looking at a single number. For example, income can vary widely within countries as well as across them. In the United States, the coasts are richer than the middle of the country. In Mexico, there are great differences between the north and the south. High income inequality in general prevents measures of average income (like GDP per capita) from giving a complete picture of how comfortably most people in a country actually live. Finally, as already mentioned in the previous chapter, people do not just care about income and consumption, but also about factors such as pollution, the quality of healthcare, and public safety. Variations in these factors across countries are not captured by income per capita numbers (as you learned at the end of the last chapter).

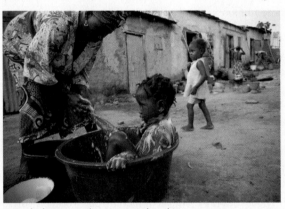

People living at the poverty level.

The **one dollar a day per person poverty line** is a measure of absolute poverty used by economists and other social scientists to compare the extent of poverty across countries.

All of this implies that we should refrain from making sweeping generalizations about the welfare of a country's citizens based on its income per capita alone. Nevertheless, there is quite a bit we can learn from income per capita about the standards of living. In the previous chapter, we saw the relationship between income per capita and average life satisfaction. In addition, one of the things we care about when discussing a particular country is whether there are many people living in extreme poverty. Researchers at the World Bank have come up with the notion of *absolute poverty*, corresponding to living on less than $1.08 per day in 1993—a measure commonly referred to as the **one dollar a day per person poverty line**. This measure has now been updated to $1.25 per person per day (in 2005 U.S. dollars), though it is still sometimes referred to as one dollar a day. For most of us, it is difficult to imagine how anybody could survive on such a tiny sum, but more than 1.4 billion

CHOICE & CONSEQUENCE

Dangers of Just Focusing on Income per Capita

A common error in comparing standards of living across countries is to focus only on income per capita, without thinking about its composition. This error is most clearly illustrated by looking at the situation in South Africa. Until 1994, South Africa was ruled by a minority white population under a repressive system of racial segregation known as *apartheid*—a word meaning "separateness." The apartheid regime prevented blacks from political participation and regulated their economic activities. It also created a

variety of repressive arrangements intended to keep the wages of black workers low. According to the economic historian Charles Feinstein, the result was that although the South African economy became more prosperous as a whole during much of the twentieth century, the incomes of its black citizens did not increase during this entire period.[1] So if we were to look at just income per capita in South Africa, it would not inform us about the very low incomes and poor living conditions of most of its black citizens.

Exhibit 6.4 The Relationship Between Poverty and Income per Capita in 2010 (PPP-adjusted 2005 Constant Dollars)

Absolute poverty, measured here by the fraction of the population living on less than $1.25 per day, is higher among countries with lower income per capita. In the exhibit, when you focus on countries with income per capita above $10,000, this relationship disappears because relatively few people in these relatively prosperous countries actually live on less than $1.25 per day.

Source: Data from the Penn World Table and World Bank DataBank; Alan Heston, Robert Summers and Bettina Aten, Penn World Table Version 7.1, Center for International Comparisons of Production, Income and Prices at the University of Pennsylvania (Nov 2012).

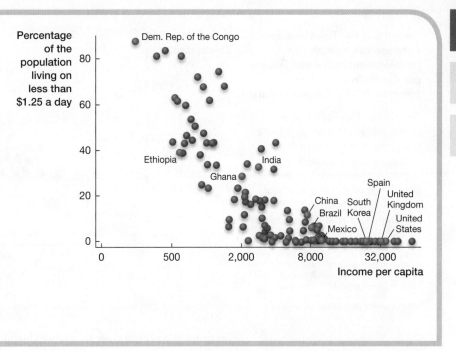

people in 2005 did in fact try to make do with less than $1.25 per day. Exhibit 6.4 shows a scatter plot with the fraction of a nation's population living in poverty (according to this definition) on the *y*-axis and its income per capita on the *x*-axis. The exhibit shows a strong association, indicating that income per capita gives us a fairly good idea of which countries have populations suffering from extreme poverty.

Note that in this and similar exhibits, the horizontal axis is stretched, so that a 10 percent change in income per capita represents the *same* absolute distance on the horizontal scale, whether we're starting from a lower level, like $500, or a higher level, like $8,000. For example, at the point labeled $500, a 10 percent increase takes the same horizontal distance as a 10 percent increase at the point labeled $8,000. This is the same strategy we used for the vertical axis in Exhibit 5.8 in the previous chapter, and why this is an informative way of representing variables such as income or GDP per capita will become clearer when we discuss economic growth in the next chapter.

Another reason why we care about income per capita is that poverty often brings poor health. One way to measure the health of a nation is by looking at the average life expectancy at birth. Exhibit 6.5 shows a scatter plot with life expectancy on the *y*-axis and income per capita on the *x*-axis, and again there is a strong association, indicating that this non-income-based measure of the standard of living also correlates strongly with income per capita.

Exhibit 6.5 The Relationship Between Life Expectancy at Birth and Income per Capita in 2010 (PPP-adjusted 2005 Constant Dollars)

This exhibit shows that people in countries with higher income per capita also have higher life expectancy at birth, meaning that on average, people in richer countries tend to live longer lives.

Source: Data from the Penn World Table and World Bank DataBank; Alan Heston, Robert Summers and Bettina Aten, Penn World Table Version 7.1, Center for International Comparisons of Production, Income and Prices at the University of Pennsylvania (Nov 2012).

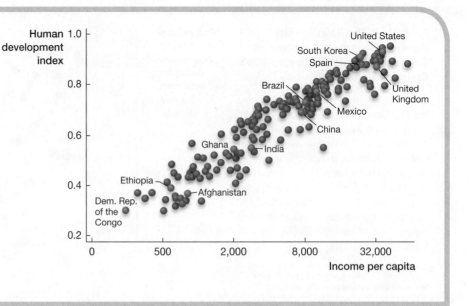

Exhibit 6.6 The Relationship Between the Human Development Index and Income per Capita in 2010 (PPP-adjusted 2005 Constant Dollars)

The Human Development Index combines information on income per capita, life expectancy, average years of schooling for those above age 25, and the enrollment of children in school. This exhibit shows that countries with higher income per capita tend to have higher levels of this index.

Source: Data from Penn World Table (Alan Heston, Robert Summers, and Bettina Aten, Penn World Table Version 7.1) and United Nations Development Programme.

There are also several other factors we should take into account when measuring the standards of living across countries. One alternative is the United Nations' Human Development Index, which combines income per capita, life expectancy, and measures of education to more holistically measure the standard of living. Exhibit 6.6 presents a scatter plot with the Human Development Index on the *y*-axis and income per capita on the *x*-axis. It shows that there is once again a strong association between income per capita and this measure.

Overall, the relationship between income per capita and several measures of the standard of living, including poverty, life expectancy, and the Human Development Index, suggests a simple strategy: first focus on income per capita and then look in greater detail at issues related to health, education, poverty, and inequality within and across countries. This is the strategy we adopt here.

6.2 Productivity and the Aggregate Production Function

As we noted above, to understand differences in income per capita or income per worker across countries, we need to understand differences in productivity. To do so, we first outline the main sources of variation in productivity across countries. Then, we turn to a more systematic analysis of these factors using the aggregate production function.

Productivity Differences

There are three main reasons why productivity differs across countries, each of which we now explain in turn.

(1) *Human capital:* Workers differ in terms of **human capital**, which is their stock of skills to produce output or economic value. For example, a worker with a university degree in computer science will be much more productive in computer programming or Web page design than a worker with just a high school degree. Suppose, for example, that in one day the computer scientist can do the same tasks as two workers with high school degrees. In this case, we say that she has twice the human capital as the workers with high school degrees. But this also implies that she is twice as *productive*.

(2) *Physical capital:* **Physical capital** is any good, including machines (equipment) and buildings (structures), used for production. For example, in agriculture, aggregate production will depend on agricultural machinery, the equipment used for transporting inputs and outputs, and the buildings in which the output is stored. Though these inputs are all

Human capital is each person's stock of skills to produce output or economic value.

Physical capital is any good, including machines and buildings, used for production.

The **physical capital stock** of an economy is the value of equipment, structures and other non-labor inputs used in production.

An economy with better **technology** uses its labor and capital more efficiently and achieves higher productivity.

different, we can aggregate them into a single measure and obtain the **physical capital stock** of the economy using their dollar value. Workers will be more productive when the economy has a bigger physical capital stock, enabling each worker to work with more (or better) equipment and structures.

(3) *Technology:* An economy with better **technology** uses its labor and capital more efficiently and thus achieves higher productivity. We will see below that an economy can have better technology either because it uses superior knowledge in production (for example, new manufacturing techniques not available to other economies) or because it organizes production more efficiently.

The Aggregate Production Function

Human capital, physical capital, and technology each play a part in determining how productive workers in an economy are. The aggregate production function is our tool for understanding how these three ingredients all come together to generate GDP in an economy.

> **Human capital, physical capital, and technology each play a part in determining how productive workers in an economy are.**

In the previous chapter, we saw how we can aggregate tens of thousands of commodities into a single measure of GDP. For our analysis here, we can go one step further. Once we have made the simplification of aggregating everything into GDP, we can just think of GDP as if it were a single commodity. Even though this simplification ignores the *composition* of GDP, it allows us to more clearly look at what determines the *level* of GDP, which is our main purpose in this chapter.

The advantage of looking at GDP in this way is that once we start thinking of the world in terms of a single commodity, we can study the aggregate production function of the economy, which describes the relationship between GDP and its various inputs. This is similar to how we study the relationship between the output of a single firm and the inputs that it uses. For example, if we wanted to understand how much corn a farm produces, we would first specify the relationship between total corn production and its key inputs, for example, the number of workers on the farm and the equipment that the farm uses.

A key concept in our study of the aggregate production function is *factors of production*. You will recall from the previous chapter that factors of production are the inputs to the production process—goods or services purchased in the market for producing other goods, in this case for producing GDP. To understand a nation's output, we will look at a production function that describes how the factors of production are combined to produce GDP. But differently from the case in which we study a single firm, our focus is not specific commodities, such as T-shirts or iPhones, but all of GDP, and we therefore refer to this function as the **aggregate production function**.

An **aggregate production function** describes the relationship between the aggregate GDP of a nation and its factors of production.

The aggregate production function is useful for understanding not only how GDP is determined but also why productivity varies across countries.

Labor

The first and most important factor of production is labor. A nation can increase output by employing more workers. For example, more workers can be deployed for tilling the soil and harvesting corn.

Remember, though, that not all workers are the same. Some will have greater human capital than others and will be able to produce more output or economic value (and this is the reason why, as we have seen, human capital is a major determinant of productivity). Such differences in workers' human capital make looking at the total number of workers in an economy a poor indicator of how much the economy can produce. Instead, we need to know the total efficiency units of labor. **Total efficiency units of labor** is defined as the product of the total number of workers and the average human capital (efficiency) of (employed individuals) workers. For example, suppose a computer science graduate can perform the same job as two high school graduates. Then, it would be natural to give twice the weight to her labor than that of high school graduates. Now applying the same idea more broadly, we can compute the total efficiency units of labor, denoted by H, as the

Total efficiency units of labor is the product of the total number of workers in the economy and the average human capital of each worker.

product of the total number of workers in the economy, *L,* and the average efficiency or human capital of workers, *h.* Thus, we write:

$$H = L \times h.$$

This equation implies that the total efficiency units of labor in the economy can be increased either if more workers take part in the production process (for example, because employment increases) or if each worker becomes more productive. Acquiring more skills through formal schooling is one way for a worker to increase productivity.

Physical Capital and Land

The second major factor of production is physical capital, typically denoted by *K* (corresponding to the first letter of "Kapital," the German spelling of capital). When an economy has more physical capital, or equivalently, a greater physical capital *stock*, its workers can work with more and better equipment and structures, and thus the economy will produce more GDP.

A third factor of production is land. For example, if we think of an economy in the eighteenth century, land and other natural resources would be the key factors of production. Yet other factors of production include natural resources and the entrepreneurial talent of the economy (the skills and capabilities of its entrepreneurs and businesspeople). To simplify the discussion, we focus only on physical capital and labor (specifically, total efficiency units of labor). When we do so, the value of land and natural resources can be included in the physical capital stock (the same way that the value of buildings is). We will return to the role of entrepreneurial talent in the context of our discussion of technology below.

Representing the Aggregate Production Function

Let us represent the aggregate production function as follows:

$$Y = A \times F(K,H).$$

When we read an expression like the one above aloud, we say, "Y is a function of K and H." We read our notation as follows:

1. *Y* stands for GDP.
2. *K* is the physical capital stock of the nation.
3. *H* is the efficiency units of labor that the economy uses in production.
4. The function *F* signifies that there is a relationship between physical capital, labor, and GDP. In particular, GDP is generated through a combination of physical capital and the efficiency units of labor.
5. *A* is an index of technology. A higher *A* implies that the economy produces more GDP with the same level of physical capital stock and total efficiency units of labor. We discuss the role of technology in greater detail below.

As we have already emphasized, this aggregate production function is similar to the production function of an individual firm for producing a specific type of commodity. In particular:

(1) Just like the production function of a specific firm, the aggregate production function will show that GDP is increasing in both physical capital and labor—put differently, more is better. Holding labor constant, if we have a greater physical capital stock, we will be able to produce more GDP. Holding physical capital constant, if we have more labor, we will also be able to produce more GDP.

(2) The aggregate production function is also subject to the Law of Diminishing Marginal Product (which is related to our discussion of diminishing marginal benefit in Chapter 4). The **Law of Diminishing Marginal Product** states that the marginal contribution of a factor of production to GDP diminishes when we increase the quantity used of that factor of production (holding all other factors of production constant). We can illustrate the aggregate production function graphically by holding the total efficiency units of labor constant, as in Exhibit 6.7, or by holding the physical capital stock constant, as in Exhibit 6.8. Let's start with Exhibit 6.7.

The **Law of Diminishing Marginal Product** states that the marginal contribution of a factor of production to GDP diminishes when we increase the quantity used of that factor of production (holding all others constant).

Exhibit 6.7 The Aggregate Production Function with Physical Capital Stock on the Horizontal Axis (with the Total Efficiency Units of Labor Held Constant)

Holding the total efficiency units of labor constant, the aggregate production function shows the relationship between the physical capital stock and GDP in the economy. As the physical capital stock increases, so does GDP. But the relationship becomes less and less steep as the physical capital stock of the economy increases because of the Law of Diminishing Marginal Product. For the same one-unit increase in the physical capital stock, the increase in GDP is greater at point A (with lower physical capital stock) than at point B (with greater physical capital stock).

This exhibit shows both the increasing relationship between physical capital and output, and the Law of Diminishing Marginal Product. In particular, the marginal contribution of an additional unit of physical capital to output—how much output increases as a result of a unit increase in the physical capital stock—is decreasing in the total physical capital stock. We see this by comparing the increase in output for a unit increase in physical capital stock at two different points of the aggregate production function in Exhibit 6.7. Consider a unit increase close to the origin (point A). When there is less physical capital in the economy, the corresponding increase in output is large. When we have the same unit increase farther to the right, corresponding to more physical capital (point B), the resulting increase in output is smaller, as shown by the smaller vertical increase at B than at A. This visual difference captures the Law of Diminishing Marginal Product.

Exhibit 6.7 holds the efficiency units of labor, H, constant and looks at the relationship between the physical capital stock and GDP. Exhibit 6.8 does the opposite, holding the physical capital stock, K, constant and looking at the relationship between the efficiency units of labor of the economy and GDP. This relationship also satisfies the Law of Diminishing Marginal Product.

Exhibit 6.8 The Aggregate Production Function with the Efficiency Units of Labor on the Horizontal Axis (with Physical Capital Stock Held Constant)

Holding the physical capital stock constant, the aggregate production function shows the relationship between the total efficiency units of labor and GDP. Once again, as the total efficiency units of labor increase, so does GDP, but consistent with the Law of Diminishing Marginal Product, the relationship becomes less and less steep as the total efficiency units of labor increase.

6.3 The Role and Determinants of Technology

We now discuss how technology affects the aggregate production function and the factors that influence the level of technology of an economy.

Technology

A third determinant of GDP is technology. The aggregate production function specifies that technology is a way of summarizing the relationship between the factors of production and GDP. A better technology means that the economy can generate more output from the same set of inputs. Exhibit 6.9 shows the implications of better technology for the aggregate production function: again holding the efficiency units of labor, H, constant, the relationship between GDP and the physical capital stock shifts left. Therefore, for every level of the efficiency units of labor, a better technology implies that the economy will produce more GDP.

Our study of the aggregate production function thus clarifies why productivity depends on human capital, physical capital, and technology. Holding the total number of workers constant, greater human capital, a larger stock of physical capital, and better technology will all increase GDP. Because the total number of workers (and hours of work per worker) is constant, this also corresponds to an increase in productivity.

Dimensions of Technology

Technology, as we have defined it, is rather broad, and in fact has two very distinct components. The first is *knowledge*. Today, we know how to produce many new goods, such as smart phones and tablets, which were not available previously. In addition, this knowledge also enables us to perform certain tasks more efficiently. For example, when you use a computer for writing an essay or doing computations for a class, you are making use of the computing power, which comes from the knowledge that society has acquired and has applied to its production process. Part of this knowledge is in the human capital of the workers: workers today can perform a range of tasks more productively than their grandparents could. But an important part of this knowledge is embodied in the physical capital stock of firms: the computers that firms are using are part of the physical capital stock of the economy.

Nevertheless, there is also a sense in which technology is different from the physical capital stock of the economy. Your great-grandparents, however much they may have wished to pay for a computer, would not have been able to do so, because computers were not yet commercially sold. Your grandparents would have had to pay an enormous price for a computer with fewer capabilities than the one you are using now, and it would have likely been a

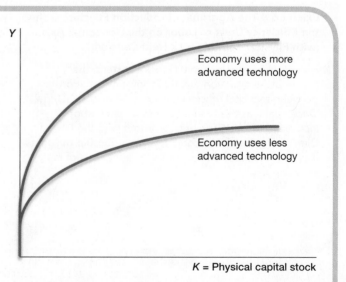

Exhibit 6.9 The Shift in the Production Function Resulting from More Advanced Technology

As technology improves, the aggregate production function shifts upwards, indicating that with the same amount of physical capital stock and total efficiency units of labor, more output can be produced. In this exhibit, the total efficiency units of labor are held constant, and for a given level of physical capital stock, the economy with more advanced technology has a higher level of GDP.

Economy uses more advanced technology

Economy uses less advanced technology

K = Physical capital stock

LETTING THE DATA SPEAK

Moore's Law

A long-term trend of rather remarkable regularity in the development of computer microprocessors has been observed since 1965. It's dubbed Moore's Law after Intel cofounder Gordon Moore, who predicted in that year that the number of transistors on a chip would double approximately every 2 years.[2] The number of transistors is a key determinant of how fast a computer processor is. So roughly speaking, Moore's Law implies that computer processor power should double approximately every 2 years. So far, this seems to have been borne out by developments in computer technology, as illustrated in Exhibit 6.10. Several other measures of technological advances in computing have also behaved according to Moore's Law. For example, the number of pixels in digital cameras and RAM storage capacity have also doubled every 2 years or so, while power consumption of computer nodes and hard disc storage costs appear to have been halved approximately every 2 years.

Naturally, there is nothing predetermined about the relationship between time and progress in technology that would make this into an actual "law." This progress results from the investments of several companies in new computer technologies, which are in turn driven by the profitability of these investments. It also relies on government support for university and private research and on the ability of the United States and other advanced and developing nations to attract increasing numbers of young, talented students into science, engineering, and related fields. Things can change in the future, halting this rapid progress in technology. Fewer college students could choose to major in science and engineering in the future, or governments could decide to limit or even stop their support for private or university research, weakening incentives for further technological advances. Moreover, even without a major cutback in funding or a change in the profitability of research in this area, the rate of advance may slow down from its current breakneck pace. Nevertheless, the relationship so far has been very accurate and, assuming it continues in the years to come, the implications for lives are enormous.

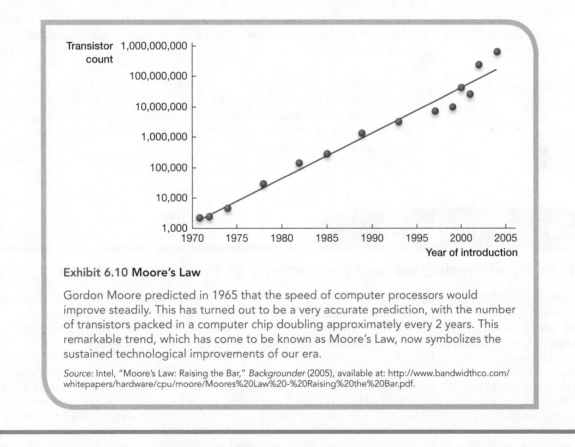

Exhibit 6.10 Moore's Law

Gordon Moore predicted in 1965 that the speed of computer processors would improve steadily. This has turned out to be a very accurate prediction, with the number of transistors packed in a computer chip doubling approximately every 2 years. This remarkable trend, which has come to be known as Moore's Law, now symbolizes the sustained technological improvements of our era.

Source: Intel, "Moore's Law: Raising the Bar," *Backgrounder* (2005), available at: http://www.bandwidthco.com/whitepapers/hardware/cpu/moore/Moores%20Law%20-%20Raising%20the%20Bar.pdf.

Research and development (R&D) refers to the activities directed at improving scientific knowledge, generating new innovations, or implementing existing knowledge in production in order to improve the technology of a firm or an economy.

giant machine rather than the small notebooks that many of you are using. Thus advances in technology—in this specific instance, in computer technology—directly increase the number of tasks we can perform and the speed at which we can accomplish them.

Advances in technology sometimes happen by chance, but more often, they result from the purposeful, optimizing decisions of economic agents. For example, society achieves such advances with **research and development (R&D)**, which involves a wide range of activities like research on new scientific ideas in universities and private labs, research directed at finding

Advances in technology sometimes happen by chance, but more often, they result from the purposeful, optimizing decisions of economic agents.

Efficiency of production refers to the ability of an economy to produce the maximal amount of output from a given amount of factors of production and knowledge.

new ways of applying science to production on the factory floor, and development activities geared at commercializing existing knowledge and products. R&D is a major activity in the United States economy. Almost 1.41 million people worked as researchers in 2007 (the most recent year for which this information is available), and $430 billion—2.77 percent of total GDP—was spent on research and development. Of this amount, about $270 billion was spent by businesses, while the remaining portion was spent by the U.S. government, universities, and other institutions.

Economists often use the term *technology* more broadly than to describe advances in our knowledge about production processes. To see this, imagine two economies. In one, the allocation of resources is determined by the market, and in the other, resources are allocated randomly across individuals and firms. As a specific example, say that both of these economies have two types of workers, economics professors and basketball players, and two types of tasks, teaching and basketball.

The first economy relies on the market for allocating workers to tasks. Basketball players who are better at basketball than teaching will play basketball, and economics professors will do the teaching. In the second, allocation takes place randomly. Suppose that economics professors are assigned to do the basketball playing and the basketball players do the teaching. There are no differences in the knowledge available for production between the two economies, and both have the same human capital. But the first economy will be much more successful (especially in basketball), and will produce more output (more and better basketball and perhaps even better teaching).

What is the difference between the two economies? This difference has to do with the **efficiency of production**—the ability of society to produce the maximal amount of output at a given cost or for given levels of the factors of production and knowledge. When the economy is able to increase the efficiency of production, there will be a shift in the aggregate production function similar to that shown in Exhibit 6.9. We therefore include efficiency of production as part of our definition of technology because it captures the differences in how much output an economy can generate with given amounts of inputs.

The importance of technology for GDP is the reason why we include A and represented the aggregate production function as:

$$A \times F(K,H).$$

🗨 LETTING THE DATA SPEAK

Efficiency of Production and Productivity at the Company Level

Economist James Schmitz Jr. studied the experience of the iron ore industries in the United States and Canada in the face of competition from Brazilian producers.[3] His findings provide a particularly clear illustration of how changes in the organization of firms can lead to improvements in the efficiency of production—or "technology"—and thus increase productivity significantly.

Schmitz documents that productivity—for example, measured as output of iron ore per hour—was constant since at least 1970 in the Canadian and the U.S. iron ore industries when they faced little foreign competition. In the early 1980s, however, Brazilian producers entered the U.S. market and started to deliver iron ore to Chicago and other central markets. Schmitz shows that in the course of the next decade, productivity in the U.S. and Canadian iron ore industries, which had been flat for a long time, doubled. He shows that this was not

due to more intensive use of capital or materials, nor was it driven by the use of new production techniques. Rather, it resulted from a significant reorganization of production.

Iron ore production plants were heavily unionized—a fact that, according to Schmitz, prevented the plants from efficiently allocating labor across different tasks. For example, despite industry studies suggesting that there was an excess number of repair workers for a large variety of equipment, union contracts did not permit reduction in repair staff. Following the increase in competition, these work rules were changed, enabling a more productive use of labor. Schmitz provides a variety of additional evidence showing that these and other changes in work rules allowed a more flexible allocation of labor across tasks and therefore better utilization of equipment, resulting in the dramatic increase in productivity.

Greater *A* corresponds to better technology and increases GDP for given levels of efficiency units of labor and physical capital stock, which shifts the aggregate production function left, as shown in Exhibit 6.9. But note that *A* is *not* a factor of production. Although it designates the technology available to the economy, it does not correspond to an input that the producer can purchase in the marketplace.

Entrepreneurship

A particularly important reason why efficiency of production and productivity might differ across economies relates to entrepreneurship. As we discuss in greater detail in Chapter 8, various factors might influence whether the individuals with a comparative advantage for entrepreneurship become entrepreneurs. When they fail to do so, the efficiency of production of an economy is lower—in the same way as the mismatch between basketball players and economics teachers, though perhaps more importantly.

LETTING THE DATA SPEAK

Monopoly and GDP

When Mexico entered the North American Free Trade Agreement, NAFTA, with the United States in 1994, many economists predicted that Mexico's economy would grow rapidly. But in the first 15 years after signing NAFTA, Mexico's growth was much less than most analysts expected. Monopolies and barriers against the entry of new companies are just some of the reasons why the country has not achieved more significant growth.

Consider the telecommunications sector in Mexico, which was for a long time operated as a state monopoly. It subsequently was privatized, but turned into a private monopoly under the ownership of Carlos Slim, who has now become one of the richest people in the world. In contrast, the telecommunications sector in the United States is very competitive, with many firms competing in both wireless and broadband. The Mexican telecommunications sector not only charges higher prices than other countries but also invests less than other comparable countries, as shown in Exhibit 6.11.

Removing monopolies and entry barriers that prevent the efficient allocation of resources is one important way of increasing GDP.

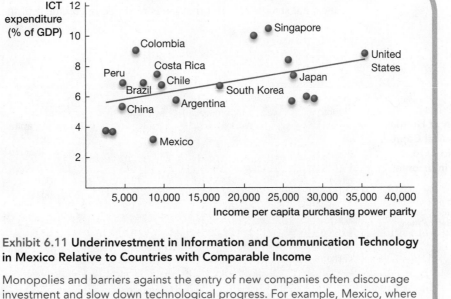

Exhibit 6.11 Underinvestment in Information and Communication Technology in Mexico Relative to Countries with Comparable Income

Monopolies and barriers against the entry of new companies often discourage investment and slow down technological progress. For example, Mexico, where the telecommunications sector is monopolized, invests in information and communication technology less than other countries with similar income per capita.

Source: World Bank DataBank.

Evidence-Based Economics

Q: Why is the average American so much richer than the average Indian?

To understand the variation in productivity and income per worker between the United States and India (and other countries), it is useful to focus on three factors: human capital, physical capital, and technology. To see the relative importance of any one of these factors in explaining differences in income (GDP) per worker across countries, we can compare a country's actual income per worker with what *would be* if the country had access to the same human capital, physical capital stock, or technology of another country. This is exactly what we do in Exhibit 6.12, specifically with technology.

Using data on education attainment (a key aspect of human capital) and employment, we calculate the efficiency units of labor. Column 3 records the average years of schooling per worker of each country. It shows that most countries have significantly lower levels of average schooling than the United States.

Then, using data on investment over several decades, we calculate the physical capital stock for each country. Column 4 shows the ratio of the physical capital stock per worker of each country relative to the physical capital stock per worker in the United States. Most countries have a significantly lower physical capital stock per worker than the United States (but there are also countries like Norway, not shown in the exhibit, that have higher levels than the United States).

Using estimates of the shape of the aggregate production function (we provide details of this estimation in the appendix to this chapter), we can then see how the efficiency units of labor and physical capital stock are translated into income per worker. Comparing these contributions of human capital and physical capital with *actual* income per worker (recorded in column 2 of Exhibit 6.12), we can then infer how much of a contribution technology makes to income per worker. Specifically, any GDP that cannot be accounted for by physical capital and labor, we assume to be accounted for by technology.

Given the estimates of the aggregate production function, we can now compute what the income level of all of these countries would have been if they had had access to exactly the same technology as the United States (using their actual efficiency units of labor and physical capital stock). This information is recorded in column 5 of the exhibit. The difference

Exhibit 6.12 The Contribution of Human Capital, Physical Capital, and Technology to Differences in Income per Worker

Source: Data from Penn World Table (Alan Heston, Robert Summers, and Bettina Aten, Penn World Table Version 7.1).

Country	Income per Worker in 2010	Average Years of Schooling	% of U.S. Physical Capital Stock per Worker in 2010	Income per Worker If Technology Were at U.S. Level
(1)	(2)	(3)	(4)	(5)
United States	82,359	13.1	100.0	SAME
United Kingdom	67,025	9.8	65.8	61,548
South Korea	54,315	11.8	87.7	74,496
Spain	54,539	10.4	83.9	68,684
Mexico	27,625	9.1	33.5	47,725
Brazil	15,975	7.5	16.9	35,045
China	12,961	8.2	14.9	34,881
India	9,010	5.1	8.9	24,071
Ghana	4,928	7.1	4.2	21,502
Afghanistan	3,980	4.2	3.7	16,818
Dem. Rep. of the Congo	628	3.5	0.8	9,625

between actual incomes and these hypothetical numbers illustrates the contribution of technology.

The exhibit reveals some powerful facts. Consistent with the patterns we have already seen in Exhibits 6.1–6.3, income per worker in the United States is about 9 times that in India (82,359/9,010 $\simeq$ 9). We also see that Indians have average years of schooling of 5.1 compared to 13.1 in the United States and that the physical capital stock per worker in India is about 9 percent of that of the United States.

So how much would a typical Indian worker produce with this amount of human capital and physical capital if he, hypothetically, had access to the U.S. level of technology?

Column 5 shows that the answer is $24,071. This implies that the hypothetical income per Indian worker if India's technology were at the U.S. level is nearly 3 times as much as its current income per worker: 24,071/9,010 $\simeq$ 2.7, suggesting a sizable impact of technology differences. If, in addition, India also increased its human capital and physical capital per worker to U.S. levels, it would increase its income per worker to the U.S. level. (This is by construction: if India has the same level of human capital and physical capital per worker, and the same technology as the U.S., it would have the same income per worker as the U.S.). In the Indian case this would correspond to an increase by another 3½ times (82,359/24,071 $\simeq$ 3.5).

Recall, however, that the technology differences that appear so important (roughly as important as total efficiency units of labor and physical capital combined) are not just differences in the knowledge available to the economy and to firms for production. They also reflect differences in the efficiency of production, as our example of economics professors and basketball players illustrated, and if there is any mismeasurement in factors of production, this will appear as technology differences. For example, in practice, human capital across countries differs not only because of average years of schooling but also because of major differences in the quality of schooling. If rich countries have a systematically higher quality of schooling, our methodology can lead to exaggerated technology differences.

Question

Why is the average American so much richer than the average Indian?

Answer

Differences in total efficiency units of labor and physical capital are important. If India had access to the same technology as the United States (including differences in the efficiency of production), its income (or GDP) per worker would be $24,071 instead of $9,010, almost 3 times as high. Increasing India's total efficiency units of labor and physical capital to U.S. levels would increase its income per worker by another 3½ times.

Data

Cross-country data on PPP-adjusted income per worker, schooling, and investment.

Caveat

Technology differences include differences in the efficiency of production and may also reflect mismeasurement.

Summary

✳ Income per capita, defined as aggregate income or gross domestic product (GDP) divided by total population, varies greatly across countries, with some nations such as the United States and Norway having more than 40 times the income per capita of some other nations such as Afghanistan, Niger, and the Democratic Republic of Congo.

✳ Income (or GDP) per capita across countries can be compared using exchange-rate-based measures, which rely on current exchange rates, or purchasing power parity-based measures, which compare estimates of the cost of the representative bundle of commodities in each country. The latter tends to be more reliable as it more appropriately captures differences in relative prices across countries, and is not subject to fluctuations resulting from changes in exchange rates. Though income per capita omits a wealth of other important information about a country (health, schooling, inequality, and poverty), it provides a good summary of prosperity and is typically correlated with higher life expectancy, greater schooling, and lower poverty.

✳ The aggregate production function links the GDP of a nation to its total efficiency units of labor, physical capital stock, technology, and efficiency of production. Greater efficiency units of labor and physical capital, as well as better technology and efficiency of production, increase GDP.

✳ Though the total efficiency units of labor and physical capital stock matter a great deal for GDP, the most important determinant of cross-country differences in income (or GDP) per worker appears to be differences in technology and the efficiency of production.

Key Terms

income per capita or GDP per capita *p.* 115
purchasing power parity (PPP) *p.* 116
income (or GDP) per worker *p.* 118
productivity *p.* 119
one dollar a day per person poverty line *p.* 120

human capital *p.* 122
physical capital *p.* 122
physical capital stock *p.* 123
technology *p.* 123
aggregate production function *p.* 123
total efficiency units of labor *p.* 123

Law of Diminishing Marginal Product *p.* 124
research and development (R&D) *p.* 127
efficiency of production *p.* 128

Questions

All questions are available in MyEconLab *for practice and instructor assignment.*

1. Suppose you are comparing the income per capita in the United States and Ghana. You first convert the values into U.S. dollars using the current exchange rate between the U.S. dollar and the Ghanaian cedi. You also convert both values to U.S. dollars using the purchasing power parity-adjusted exchange rate. Which measure is likely to give you a more accurate picture of the living standards in both countries? Explain your answer.

2. What are the disadvantages of using Big Macs to measure purchasing power parity?

3. Suppose that country A has higher income per capita than country B. Explain why this does not imply that most citizens of country A have higher income than most citizens of country B. Try to construct an example in which both countries have 10 citizens to demonstrate this point.

4. Is income per capita more relevant in understanding differences in international living standards than income per worker?

5. What is the correlation between income per capita and welfare measures like absolute poverty and life expectancy? What does this suggest about income per capita as a measure of welfare?

6. What does the Human Development Index measure? What is the correlation between this index and income per capita in a country?

7. What is productivity? Why does it vary across countries?

8. What are the two components of technology?

9. What are factors of production? What does the aggregate production function describe?

10. What are the total efficiency units of labor? What is the relationship between this concept and human capital?

11. Use the following diagram to explain the relationship between a country's physical capital stock and GDP.

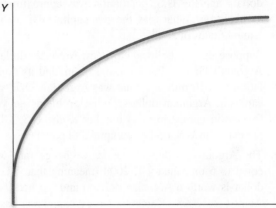

12. Explain the difference between the terms "physical capital" and "human capital."

13. Explain what distinguishes physical capital from natural resources.

14. How do increases in technology affect the aggregate production function?

15. What does Moore's Law state? Is Moore's Law borne out by historical data?

16. Why is the average American so much richer than the average Indian?

17. What policies can be used to raise GDP in a country?

Problems

All problems are available in MyEconLab *for practice and instructor assignment.*
Problems marked 🌐 *update with real-time data.*

1. You read a newspaper report that compares wages paid to employees at Starbucks in India and in the United Kingdom. At the time, 1 pound was equal to 87 rupees. The report says that Starbucks baristas in India are paid a mere 56 pence an hour, which is lower than the cheapest coffee that Starbucks sells in the United Kingdom. A friend of yours who read the report is appalled by this information and thinks that Starbucks ought to raise its salaries substantially in India. Is your friend necessarily correct? Explain your answer.

🌐 2. The following table lists 2012 GDP per capita for four countries. The data are given in the national currencies of the countries. It also lists the price of a Big Mac burger in local currency in each country in 2012.

	2012 GDP per Capita	2012 Big Mac Price
Norway (krone)	579,162	41 krone
Poland (zloty)	41,398	9.1 zloty
Turkey (Turkish lira)	19,580	6.6 Turkish lira
United Kingdom (British pound)	24,740	2.49 pounds

Source for GDP: UNECE Statistical Database, compiled from national and international (CIS, EUROSTAT, IMF, OECD) official sources.

Source for Big Mac Prices: http://bigmacindex.org/2012-big-mac-index.html

The price of a Big Mac in the United States in 2012 was $4.20.

Using the Big Mac burger as a representative commodity common to the countries, calculate the purchasing power parity (PPP)-adjustment factor for each country, and then the PPP level of per capita GDP in each country.

3. Let us use what we have learned in the first part of the chapter to compare living standards in the United States and a hypothetical country, Argonia, in 2008.

   a. The U.S. GDP in 2008 was approximately 14 trillion dollars and the U.S. population was approximately 300 million. What was the per capita GDP in the United States in 2008?

   b. Suppose that in the local currency, Argonian dollars, Argonia's GDP in 2008 was 1 trillion, and its population was 10 million. What was Argonia's GDP per capita in Argonian dollars? What problems do you foresee in comparing this number to the U.S. GDP per capita in U.S. dollars computed in part a?

   c. The Argonian dollar/U.S. dollar exchange rate was equal to 6 on January 1, 2008 (meaning that 1 U.S. dollar is worth 6 Argonian dollars) and reached 9 on August 1, 2008. Compute an exchange-rate-based measure of the GDP per capita in Argonia in U.S. dollars on these two dates. Do you think the change in Argonia's exchange-rate-based measure of GDP per capita between these two dates reflects a true change in living standards?

   d. McDonald's has a thriving business in Argonia and sold a Big Mac for 7 Argonian dollars in 2008, while at the same time, a Big Mac sold for $3.50 in the United States. Using this information, provide an alternative estimate of GDP per capita in Argonia. Would you trust this estimate better than the one based on exchange rates? Why or why not?

4. Suppose you are given the following information for the country Lusitania:

	2011
Population; total in Lusitania	190 million
Employment	80 million
Gross Domestic Product (GDP)	2,476 billion U.S. dollars

   a. What is the income per capita in Lusitania?

   b. What is the income per worker in Lusitania?

The following table gives you the same information for the country Arctica.

	2011
Population; total in Arctica	80 million
Employment	40 million
Gross Domestic Product (GDP)	3,600 billion U.S. dollars

   c. What is the income per capita in Arctica?

   d. What is the income per worker in Arctica?

   e. Based on the given information, would Arctica be considered more productive than Lusitania? Explain your answer.

   f. How would you use the information given in both these tables to compare living standards in Lusitania and Arctica?

5. Suppose that the GDP in current dollars for Polonia is higher than Ruritania's GDP. However, using purchasing power parity-adjusted dollars, Ruritania's GDP is higher than Polonia's GDP. Based on this information, what would you conclude about living standards in Polonia and Ruritania?

6. In 2011, China revised its poverty line upward to 2,300 yuan per year, or 6.3 yuan per day. At the prevailing exchange rate, this was equal to a little less than a single U.S. dollar. Some commentators felt that China's poverty line fell short of the World Bank's poverty line of $1.25 per day, in 2005 purchasing power parity (PPP) U.S. dollars. Would you agree? What other information would you need to evaluate this claim?

7. In this question, we will use what you learned in the second part of the chapter to compare the performance of an economy in two different time periods, as its physical capital stock and efficiency units of labor change.

   a. Suppose that from period 1 to period 2, the unemployment rate in the economy increases. Everything else remains unchanged. What happens to the total efficiency units of labor? Express your results formally as an inequality, using the formula for total efficiency units of labor presented in the chapter (in particular, recall that total efficiency units of labor in two periods can be written as $H_1 = L_1 \times h_1$ and $H_2 = L_2 \times h_2$; where L is the total number of employed workers).

   b. What are the consequences of this increase in unemployment for GDP? Express your results formally as an inequality, using the aggregate production function presented in the chapter.

   c. What are the consequences for GDP per capita and GDP per worker?

   d. Suppose that there is a technological advance from period 1 to period 2 but, at the same time, a decrease in physical capital stock. Can you say whether GDP will increase or decrease? Why or why not?

8. The following table shows the change in GDP in Lithasia with changes in efficiency units of human capital.

GDP (in Millions of Dollars)	Stock of Physical Capital (Units)	Efficiency Units of Labor
100	15,000	16,000
150	15,000	20,000
180	15,000	24,000
200	15,000	28,000
210	15,000	32,000

a. Comment on the rate of change in GDP as the economy uses more efficiency units of labor.

b. How would the aggregate production function of this economy look if GDP is measured along the vertical axis and efficiency units of labor on the horizontal axis?

c. What explains the shape of this aggregate production function?

Links: http://www.worldbank.org/depweb/english/beyond/global/chapter15.html; http://data.worldbank.org/indicator/NY.GNP.PCAP.PP.CD; http://www.worldbank.org/depweb/english/beyond/global/chapter2.html

9. The old Soviet Union devoted enormous resources exclusively to increasing its physical capital stock, and yet eventually the increase in the country's GDP came to an end. Based on the discussion in the chapter, explain why this was inevitable.

10. Draw a graph showing the aggregate production function, assuming diminishing marginal returns to physical capital. Label the axes.

11. Redraw your graph from Problem 10. Now show what would happen if there is a technological advance. Make sure to label the axes once again, and indicate clearly the direction of any changes to your graph.

12. First Japan, then Korea, and now China have managed to grow very rapidly without devoting many resources to research and development (R&D). Given the importance noted in the text of technological advance as an engine of growth, this seems to be a contradiction.

Explain how rapid growth in these countries (and others as well) could have been achieved without a substantial R&D commitment on their part.

13. Give an algebraic and an intuitive explanation of the concept of "efficiency of production." Why is efficiency of production so important to GDP?

Appendix

The Mathematics of Aggregate Production Functions

How did we compute, in Exhibit 6.12, what the average income per worker in India would have been if India had access to the U.S. level of technology?

We worked with the aggregate production function $Y = A \times F(K,H)$ using the following form, which is often estimated as an empirical approximation to data:

$$Y = A \times F(K,H) = A \times K^{1/3} \times H^{2/3}.$$

It is referred to as a Cobb-Douglas function and has several attractive features.[4] For one, the coefficients to which K and H are raised to add up to 1 ($\frac{1}{3} + \frac{2}{3} = 1$). This ensures that the production function exhibits *constant returns to scale*: that is, increasing K and H by 1 percent would lead to a 1 percent increase in Y. Moreover, this functional form is consistent with the empirical fact that, roughly speaking, about two-thirds of national income goes to labor and one-third to physical capital.

Let us now divide both sides of the above equation by the total number of workers in the economy, L, to obtain:

$$Y \times \frac{1}{L} = A \times K^{1/3} \times H^{2/3} \times \frac{1}{L}.$$

This can be rewritten as:

$$y = \frac{Y}{L} = A \times K^{1/3} \times H^{2/3} \times \frac{1}{L^{1/3} \times L^{2/3}},$$

where y is income per worker, or GDP divided by the number of workers in the economy. The last term simply rewrites $1/L$ differently to derive the next equation.

Now rearranging the previous equation, we obtain

$$y = A \times \left(\frac{K}{L}\right)^{1/3} \times \left(\frac{H}{L}\right)^{2/3}.$$

Finally, recalling that $H = L \times h$, this can be rewritten as

$$y = A \times \left(\frac{K}{L}\right)^{1/3} \times h^{2/3}.$$

Stated differently:

GDP per worker = Technology $\times$ *(Capital per worker)*$^{1/3}$ $\times$ *(Human capital per worker)*$^{2/3}$.

This derivation also shows why there is a very tight relationship between cross-country differences in GDP per worker and cross-country differences in productivity. For simplicity, assuming that each worker works the same number of hours in every country, the left-hand side of this equation is also GDP per hour worked and thus the productivity of a country. The equation therefore demonstrates that productivity is determined by the three ingredients we have emphasized in the text: technology, physical capital, and human capital.

We next use data on GDP per worker together with data on the physical capital stock (K), or physical capital per worker, and data on human capital per worker (h). Data on GDP are available from various sources (with original information coming from national income accounts). These sources also provide information on investment, which we can use to compute physical capital stocks. Finally, we can compute human capital differences across nations from differences in average years of schooling. In particular, we know how much more a worker with one more year of schooling earns. We can use this information to create an index, h—on the basis of differences in average years of schooling—that captures differences in human capital across nations. For example, say college graduate workers will typically have 16 years of schooling and earn twice as much as workers with 6 years of schooling. Then if we set $h = 1$ for a country with 6 years of schooling on average, we would have $h = 2$ for a country with 16 years of schooling on average.

Now let us start by computing the technology for the United States, denoted by A_{US} Using the previous equation, we arrive at:

$$A_{US} = \frac{y_{US}}{\left(\dfrac{K_{US}}{L_{US}}\right)^{1/3} \times h_{US}^{2/3}}.$$

As we have seen, the U.S. GDP per worker is given by

$$y_{US} = A_{US} \times \left(\frac{K_{US}}{L_{US}}\right)^{1/3} \times h_{US}^{2/3}.$$

The expression above is obtained simply by rearranging this.

In the same fashion, we can find the contribution of technology to the GDP of India, which is A_{INDIA}:

$$A_{INDIA} = \frac{y_{INDIA}}{\left(\dfrac{K_{INDIA}}{L_{INDIA}}\right)^{1/3} \times h_{INDIA}^{2/3}}.$$

We can then ask how the GDP of India would be different if instead of A_{INDIA} we used A_{US} in the preceding expression. We can calculate the hypothetical GDP per worker of India in the situation in which India has the same technology term, A_{US}, as the United States:

$$y_{INDIA \text{ WITH US TECHNOLOGY}} = A_{US} \times \left(\frac{K_{INDIA}}{L_{INDIA}}\right)^{1/3} \times h_{INDIA}^{2/3}.$$

Using our estimates of A_{US}, K_{INDIA}, L_{INDIA}, h_{INDIA}, for example, we can compute the hypothetical GDP per worker of India, if India were able to use American technology, as $24,071. In the same way, we can plug in the U.S. technology terms into the aggregate production function of any country, which enables us to do the rest of the computations in Exhibit 6.12.

7 Economic Growth

Why are you so much more prosperous than your great-great-grandparents were?

The United States was not always as prosperous as it is today. Its (real) GDP per capita today is about 25 times what it was in 1820. At that time, only a small fraction of the population lived in cities; most people worked in agriculture. People could not even imagine, let alone have access to, many of the goods, services, and technologies that we take for granted, including radio, television, indoor plumbing, shopping malls, cars, planes, or even trains.

The United States and several other countries have vastly increased their GDP (income) per capita over the last 200 years, developing new goods, services, and technologies. We call this process *economic growth*. The key questions we address in this chapter are how and why the United States and several other countries have managed to achieve such notable economic growth over the past two centuries.

CHAPTER OUTLINE

⚙ Economic growth measures how much (real) GDP per capita grows over time.

⚙ Today's high levels of GDP per capita in many nations are a result of rapid economic growth over the last two centuries.

⚙ Sustained economic growth relies on technological progress.

⚙ There are sizable differences in the historical growth rates of different economies, which are largely responsible for their differences in the levels of GDP per capita.

⚙ Economic growth is a powerful tool for poverty reduction.

7.1 The Power of Economic Growth

We saw in Chapter 6 how aggregate incomes (GDP) are determined. We can now start using these ideas to understand why several countries, including the United States, have managed to become so much richer over the past 200 years and in the process, gain a new perspective on the differences across countries that we documented in the previous chapter. Throughout this chapter, by GDP we refer to *real* GDP which uses market prices from a specific base year (in this chapter generally 2005) to express the value of production in the economy, as we discussed in Chapter 5.

MyEconLab Real-time data

Exhibit 7.1 GDP per Capita in the United States (2005 Constant Dollars)

The growth of GDP per capita in the United States has been relatively steady and sustained, except during the Great Depression and its aftermath. Note that the vertical axis has a proportional scale so that the vertical distance between 500 and 2,500 is the same as that between 2,500 and 12,500.

Source: Data from Maddison Project (1820–1959) and World Bank DataBank: World Development Indicators (1960–2012); J. Bolt and J. L. van Zanden, The First Update of the Maddison Project; Re-Estimating Growth Before 1820. Maddison Project Working Paper 4 (2013).

A First Look at U.S. Growth

As a first step, Exhibit 7.1 depicts GDP per capita in the United States over the past 200 years. In Chapter 6, we adjusted incomes in terms of the cost of a given basket of commodities in order to compare them meaningfully across countries. Similarly, we saw in Chapter 5 how to make a similar adjustment for inflation to obtain *real GDP* (or real income), which can be meaningfully compared over time. Recall that this involves adjusting GDP or incomes according to a base-year dollar value, which we call *constant dollars*. This is what we do in this chapter also. Exhibit 7.1, for example, plots the level of GDP per capita in the United States in 2005 constant dollars, so the income for the year 1967, for example, is expressed as what it would be equal to in year 2005 dollars.

Exhibit 7.1 clearly illustrates the *economic growth* in the U.S. economy between 1820 and 2012. **Economic growth**, or simply **growth**, refers to the increase in GDP per capita of an economy. The exhibit shows this type of economic growth and a marked increase in GDP per capita in the U.S. economy over the last 200 years, though the increase is not entirely steady and there are some jagged movements, corresponding to economic fluctuations. One of these stands out: the Great Depression, which started in 1929 and recorded a major contraction in U.S. GDP per capita. Despite its importance and its impact on the lives of millions, the Great Depression was a temporary event—sustained and steady growth of GDP per capita characterizes the U.S. economy both before and after it. In this chapter, we focus on such longer-run movements, returning to economic fluctuations like the Great Depression in subsequent chapters.

As a result of the continued economic growth depicted in Exhibit 7.1, U.S. GDP per capita and standards of living are much higher today than they were in 1820. For example, GDP per capita has increased from $1,858 in 1820 to $13,056 in 1950 and to $45,336 in 2012 (all numbers in 2005 constant dollars). (Notice that the vertical axis of this exhibit has a proportional scale, similar to those we have used in several exhibits in Chapters 5 and 6, and ensures that the distance between $500 and $2,500 is the same as that between $2,500 and $12,500. We explain why this is a good way of presenting the data shortly.)

Let us first specify the measurement of growth in a little more detail. A **growth rate** is defined as the change in a quantity—here, GDP per capita—between two dates, relative to the baseline (beginning of period) quantity. Let's choose two dates, say t and $t + 1$, and denote GDP per capita in these two dates by y_t and y_{t+1}, respectively. Then the growth rate of GDP per capita between these two dates is defined as

$$\text{Growth}_{t,t+1} = \frac{y_{t+1} - y_t}{y_t}.$$

Let us focus on annual differences, so that, for example, t and $t + 1$ correspond to the years 2005 and 2006, respectively. The U.S. economy had GDP per capita of $42,482 in 2005 and $43,215 in 2006, so the growth rate between 2005 and 2006 can be computed as

$$\text{Growth}_{2005,2006} = \frac{\$43,215 - \$42,482}{\$42,482} = 0.017$$

(or equivalently, $0.017 \times 100 = 1.7\%$). Using this formula, we can compute growth rates of GDP for any country.

Exhibit 7.2 depicts the annual growth rate of GDP per capita of the U.S. economy between 1950 and 2012, which is computed using this formula. It shows that the average growth rate is positive, at approximately 2.03 percent, but economic fluctuations are also visible here, including the one starting in 2008, the "Great Recession" which we discuss in greater detail in Chapter 12.

Exponential Growth

Central to our discussion of economic growth is the idea of **exponential growth**, which refers to the process by which a quantity grows at an approximately constant growth rate. This results because the increase in the value of a variable ($y_{t+1} - y_t$ in terms of the above equation) is proportional to its current value (y_t in terms of the above equation). As we will next see, exponential growth results because new growth builds on past growth and its

Economic growth, or **growth**, is the increase in GDP per capita of an economy.

The **growth rate** is the change in a quantity, for example, GDP per capita, between two dates, relative to the baseline (beginning of period) quantity.

Exponential growth refers to a situation in which the growth process can be described by an approximately constant growth rate of a variable such as GDP or GDP per capita.

[Exponential growth results because new growth builds on past growth and its effects compound.]

Exhibit 7.2 The Annual Growth Rate of GDP per Capita in the United States Between 1950 and 2012 (2005 Constant Dollars)

The (annual) growth rate of GDP per capita shows the short-run fluctuations around the average growth rate.

Source: Data from Penn World Table (1950–1959) and World Bank DataBank: World Development Indicators (1960–2012); Alan Heston, Robert Summers and Bettina Aten, Penn World Table Version 7.1, Center for International Comparisons of Production, Income and Prices at the University of Pennsylvania (Nov 2012).

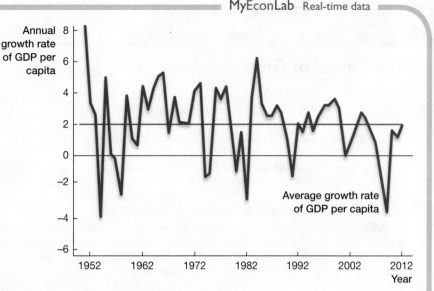

effects compound. This implies that relatively modest differences in growth rates translate into large differences in the level of a quantity after many years of growing.

The exponential nature of economic growth is one of the major reasons why there are such large differences in GDP per capita across countries like the ones we saw in the previous chapter.

To understand both exponential growth and its implications, consider a simple example, where a variable Y_t starts out with the value 1 in the year 2000 and has a constant growth rate of 5 percent (0.05) in subsequent years. What will be the value of this variable in the year 2015? A first guess might be obtained by adding the increment of $1 \times 0.05 = 0.05$ to the base value 15 times (once for every year between 2000 and 2015). This would give us an increase of $15 \times 0.05 = 0.75$, thus producing the value $Y_{2015} = 1.75$.

But this is not a correct depiction of how growth takes place because the power of compounding has to be factored in. Let's see why this is so by starting with 2001. With a growth rate of 5 percent, we will have $Y_{2001} = 1.05$. What about in 2002? The key here is that the additional 5 percent growth between 2001 and 2002 will start from 1.05—not from the initial level of 1.00. Hence, we will have $Y_{2002} = 1.05 \times 1.05 = 1.1025$. Similarly, $Y_{2003} = 1.1025 \times 1.05 = 1.1576$, and by continuing like this, we obtain $Y_{2015} = 2.0789$.

The reason why this number is greater than the naive guess of 1.75 is because of compounding, the root cause of exponential growth. Exponential growth results because current growth builds on past growth. For example, to obtain Y_{2003} we started from the level at 2002, $Y_{2002} = 1.1025$, and built on it, so the incremental growth between 2002 and 2003 was more than 0.05.

One implication of exponential growth is that to depict variables that have exponential growth (approximately constant growth rates), it is much more convenient to use an axis with a proportional scale, like the vertical axis in Exhibit 7.1. This is intuitive: a 10 percent growth rate starting from a base of 1,000 will take us to 1,100, but if we had started with 100,000, it would have taken us to 110,000. The increment is very different in two cases (100 vs. 10,000), but it is the same as a *proportion* of the base value—10 percent. As a result, it is more instructive to show this change on a proportional scale where the 10 percent growth corresponds to the same distance on the vertical axis regardless of whether we start from a base of 1,000 or 100,000. Exhibit 7.3, on the other hand, shows how Exhibit 7.1 would look if we were to use the usual nonproportional scale. You can see that this exhibit creates a misleading impression that GDP per capita in the United States was accelerating, whereas with a proportional scale in Exhibit 7.1, we can clearly distinguish the approximately constant rate of growth of U.S. GDP per capita.

To see the power of exponential growth on economic growth, consider two countries with the same level of GDP per capita in 1810, say $1,000 (in 2005 constant U.S. dollars). Furthermore, suppose that growth is exponential and, in particular, that GDP per capita in one of these countries grows at 2 percent per year while in the other one it grows at just 1 percent. At first glance, this difference seems small. And it is true that such a difference in growth will have only small implications over one or two years.

CHOICE & CONSEQUENCE

The Power of Growth

You have two choices. You can either start a job with a salary of $1,000 per month and a 6 percent increase in your salary every month. Or you can start with a salary of $2,000, but never get a raise. Which one of these two options do you prefer?

The answer might naturally vary from person to person. If you have an immediate need for money, you may be attracted by the prospect of a $2,000 paycheck. But before you rush to sign on the dotted line for the $2,000-per-month job, think of the implications of the 6 percent monthly increase. With a 6 percent-per-month increase, your monthly salary will already exceed $2,000 after only a year. After 4 years, it will be approximately $16,400 a month. So if you were thinking of staying in this job for more than a year, starting with a lower salary might be a much better idea.

The first option is attractive, at least for those of you intending to stay with it for a while, precisely because of exponential growth. The 6-percent-per-month increases

in salary do not apply to the base salary (if they did, this would have increased your salary by $60 every month). Rather, they compound, meaning that each 6 percent applies to the amount that has accumulated up to that point. Thus after 1 month, your salary will be $1,060. After 2 months, it is $1,060 × 1.06 = $1,123.60. After 3 months, it is $1,123.60 × 1.06 = $1,191.02, and so on. We will next see that exponential growth plays the same role in countries' growth trajectories as in your potential income in these two hypothetical jobs.

MyEconLab Real-time data

Exhibit 7.3 GDP per Capita in the United States with a Nonproportional Scale (2005 Constant Dollars)

Source: Data from Maddison Project (1820–1959) and World Bank DataBank: World Development Indicators (1960–2012); J. Bolt and J. L. van Zanden, The First Update of the Maddison Project; Re-Estimating Growth Before 1820. Maddison Project Working Paper 4 (2013).

But the implications of this difference 200 years later will be quite impressive. The country growing at 1 percent per year will achieve GDP per capita of approximately $7,316 in 2010. In contrast, because of the exponential nature of growth, the country growing at 2 percent per year over the same period will reach a GDP per capita of $52,485. Thus, there will be a more than sevenfold difference between these two countries resulting from "just" a 1 percent difference in growth rates.

If instead of 1 percent growth per year, the second country had no growth (that is, 0 percent growth rate), then it would remain at the same level of GDP per capita, $1,000, in 2010.

The gap between the two countries, in this case, would be a truly striking fifty-two-fold! This example again illustrates the power of exponential growth—or, in this case, the lack thereof.

Patterns of Growth

Exponential growth is largely responsible for how the large differences in GDP per capita that we observe today (and discussed in the previous chapter) emerged over time. The nations that are relatively rich today have grown steadily over the past 200 years, whereas those that are poor have failed to do so.

To see these effects of economic growth on economies in the real world, we now turn to Exhibit 7.4, which shows the patterns of growth in GDP per capita across a number of countries between 1960 and 2010 (in PPP-adjusted 2005 constant dollars, where PPP again stands for "purchasing power parity"). The third column of the exhibit summarizes growth between 1960 and 2010. Instead of showing the growth rate between these two dates using the formula we described above, this column provides the *implied* annual growth rate, which shows how much on average each country needed to grow each year to reach the 2010 level starting with the 1960 number. (Exactly how this number is computed is explained in the appendix to this chapter.)

What do these comparisons tell us? For one thing, we see that GDP per capita has increased significantly in the United States, the United Kingdom, and France; the growth rates in the last column confirm this. For example, both the United States and the United Kingdom show an average annual growth rate of about 2 percent between 1960 and 2010.

The exhibit also tells us that there has been an even greater increase in GDP per capita and correspondingly higher growth rates for Singapore, Spain, South Korea, Botswana, and China. All five of these countries were significantly poorer than the United States in 1960, but they closed some or almost all the gap with the United States by 2010. Such success is reflected in the higher growth rates for these countries. For example, the average annual growth rates of GDP per capita in Botswana, South Korea, and Singapore during this period were above 5 percent, and China's was 4.72 percent.

The exhibit also shows other countries that have *not* closed the gap between themselves and richer countries, or have done so only to a limited extent. These nations include Mexico, Brazil, and India, which show similar or only slightly higher growth rates than the United States. Guatemala, Kenya, Ghana, Rwanda, and Haiti had even lower growth rates than the United States over this time period and thus have become relatively poorer. In fact, we see from the data in this exhibit that GDP per capita in Kenya has essentially been stagnant over this almost 50-year period, and GDP per capita in Haiti has declined at the rate of 0.14 percent a year. As a result, Haiti was much poorer at the end of 2010 than it was in 1960. Things have only gotten worse for Haiti since its devastating earthquake in 2010, which not only killed over 200,000 Haitians but also destroyed the country's already crumbling infrastructure.

How has GDP per capita evolved in these countries relative to the United States? Exhibit 7.5 illustrates this by taking some of the countries from Exhibit 7.4 and plotting their levels of GDP per capita divided by GDP per capita in the United States, all in PPP-adjusted 2005 constant dollars.

The overall patterns are consistent with those shown in Exhibit 7.4, but the growth of these economies over time also reveals some interesting facts. For example, GDP per capita in the United Kingdom has remained at about 70 to 80 percent of the GDP per capita of the United States since the 1950s. Spain and South Korea showed early spurts of rapid growth, even though they started with very different income levels at the beginning of the period. By the 1980s, both countries had closed much of the gap between themselves and the

Exhibit 7.4 GDP per Capita and Growth in Selected Countries (PPP-adjusted 2005 Constant Dollars)

GDP per capita in 2010 is determined both by GDP per capita in 1960 and the average annual growth rate of GDP per capita in between these two years. We see how Botswana is much richer than Kenya and Ghana today, even though Botswana started out poorer, because Botswana grew on average at 5.47 percent while the average annual growth was only 0.40 percent for Kenya and 0.98 percent for Ghana. For the same reasons, today South Korea is richer than Brazil and Singapore is richer than Spain.

Source: Data from Penn World Table; Alan Heston, Robert Summers, and Bettina Aten, Penn World Table Version 7.1, Center for International Comparisons of Production, Income and Prices at the University of Pennsylvania (Nov 2012).

	GDP per Capita		Implied (Average) Annual Growth (%)
	1960	2010	
United States	15,398	41,365	2.00
United Kingdom	11,204	34,268	2.26
France	10,212	31,299	2.27
Spain	6,316	27,332	2.97
Mexico	4,914	11,939	1.79
Singapore	4,383	55,862	5.22
Guatemala	2,930	6,091	1.47
Brazil	2,483	8,324	2.45
South Korea	1,656	26,609	5.71
Haiti	1,513	1,410	−0.14
Ghana	1,286	2,094	0.98
Kenya	1,020	1,247	0.40
China	772	7,746	4.72
Rwanda	760	1,025	0.60
India	720	3,477	3.20
Dem. Rep. of the Congo	696	241	−2.10
Botswana	674	9,675	5.47

MyEconLab Real-time data

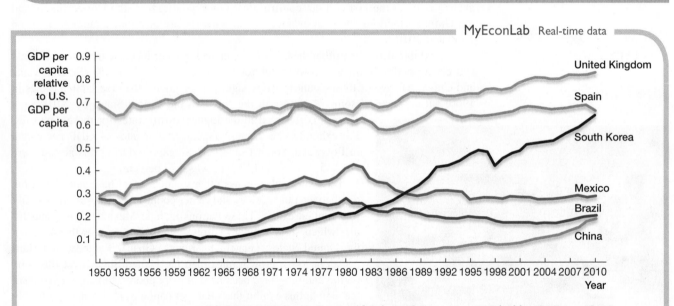

Exhibit 7.5 GDP per Capita of Selected Countries Divided by GDP per Capita of the United States (PPP-adjusted 2005 Constant Dollars)

Plotting the evolution of GDP per capita in selected countries relative to GDP per capita in the United States shows how countries such as South Korea and China have been catching up with the United States relatively steadily, while Mexico and Brazil have not.

Source: Data from Penn World Table; Alan Heston, Robert Summers, and Bettina Aten, Penn World Table Version 7.1, Center for International Comparisons of Production, Income and Prices at the University of Pennsylvania (Nov 2012).

United States, though they both also show periods of relative decline. Brazil also experienced relatively rapid growth in the 1950s and 1960s, closing some of the gap with the United States. But around 1980, this process went into reverse, and by 2010, GDP per capita in Brazil was about 20 percent of the GDP per capita of the United States—not much above where it started, in relative terms, in the 1950s. Finally, although there was a huge gap between the United States and China during the communist dictatorship of Mao Tse-tung (Mao Zedong), this gap started narrowing rapidly following Mao's death in 1976 and the opening of the Chinese economy in 1978.

LETTING THE DATA SPEAK

Levels versus Growth

Is China now poorer relative to the United States than it was in 1980? We saw in Exhibit 7.5 how Chinese GDP per capita relative to that of the United States has increased greatly over the past 30 years. Yet now consider Exhibit 7.6, which plots GDP per capita in China and the United States since 1950. This picture creates the impression that the gap between the United States and China is opening up and that China is becoming relatively poorer. This is not the case, however. In fact, trying to decide whether China is becoming poorer or richer compared to the United States from a figure such as Exhibit 7.6 is an example of a common error: comparing *levels* of variables exhibiting exponential growth. You will have noticed that precisely to avoid this type of fallacy, in Exhibit 7.5 we do not simply plot the GDP per capita levels of different countries; rather, we look at these levels divided by GDP per capita in the United States. By doing so, we directly examine the ratio between GDP in the given country and in the United States.

To see the advantage of this procedure, consider two hypothetical countries. Say that the first one is twice as rich as the second and has GDP per capita of $20,000, while the second has GDP per capita of $10,000. Now suppose that they both grow by 10 percent. The first country will then have GDP per capita of $22,000 and the second one will have GDP per capita of $11,000. The ratio between the two has not changed, but the absolute gap in incomes has increased by $1,000. Thus, comparing levels of GDP is not enlightening when there is exponential growth. In the presence of exponential growth, when relative GDP remains stable, absolute gaps will increase. For this reason, looking at ratios is the right thing to do in Exhibit 7.5. It is an oft-repeated error to compare levels of variables exhibiting exponential growth such as GDP or investment rather than ratios.

MyEconLab Real-time data

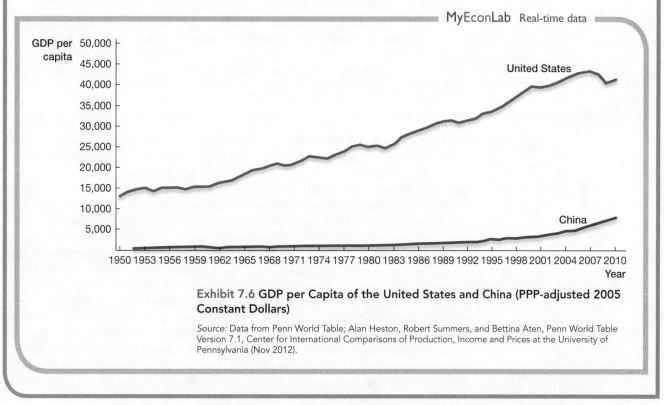

Exhibit 7.6 GDP per Capita of the United States and China (PPP-adjusted 2005 Constant Dollars)

Source: Data from Penn World Table; Alan Heston, Robert Summers, and Bettina Aten, Penn World Table Version 7.1, Center for International Comparisons of Production, Income and Prices at the University of Pennsylvania (Nov 2012).

To convey a more complete picture of growth patterns over the last 50 years, Exhibit 7.7 shows a graph of the growth rates of all countries for which we have data between 1960 and 2010. It shows that there is a wide range of growth rates. Some countries, such as Haiti and the Democratic Republic of Congo, have grown at negative rates during this period, while others, such as South Korea and Singapore, have achieved very high growth rates.

Using historical data, we can compare growth across countries even further back in time than 1960. To show these growth patterns in a simple way, Exhibit 7.8 lists levels of GDP per capita for several countries (in PPP-adjusted 1990 constant dollars) in 1820, 1870, 1920, 1970, and 2010 and their annual growth rates between 1820 and 2010 and between 1920 and 2010.

We see that income levels are not all that different across countries in 1820. For example, the United States was only about twice as rich as Mexico (U.S. GDP per capita

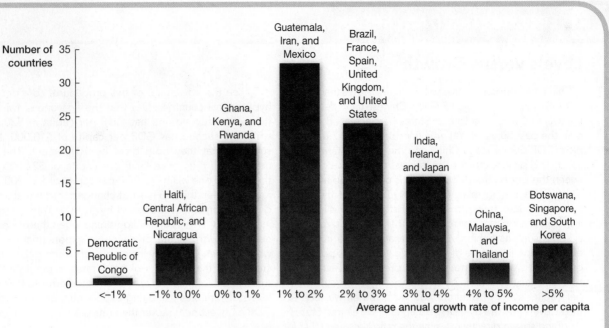

Exhibit 7.7 Average Growth Rates of GDP per Capita from 1960 to 2010 (PPP-adjusted 2005 Constant Dollars)

A few countries, in particular Botswana, Singapore, and South Korea, have grown very rapidly, with average growth rates above 5 percent, while others, such as Haiti, the Democratic Republic of Congo, and Nicaragua have had negative growth since 1960.

Source: Data from Penn World Table; Alan Heston, Robert Summers, and Bettina Aten, Penn World Table Version 7.1, Center for International Comparisons of Production, Income and Prices at the University of Pennsylvania (Nov 2012).

of $1,361 vs. Mexico's $627). But by 2010, there was a sizable gap between these two countries, which can be accounted for by their different growth rates. The average growth rate of the United States between 1820 and 2010 was 1.65 percent a year, while Mexico grew at an average rate of only 1.33 percent a year. The contrast between the United States and India is even starker. India started out with a little less than half of the GDP per capita of the United States in 1820. But by 2010, the gap was nearly tenfold. Once again, this is a direct consequence of the difference in the two countries' growth rates in GDP per capita.

This exhibit also shows that in 1820, the United Kingdom was significantly richer than the United States. Yet by 2010, the United States was about 30 percent richer than the United Kingdom. This change is because of differences in growth rates: while the United States grew at 1.65 percent a year, the United Kingdom grew at only 1.29 percent a year. This relatively small difference in growth rates was sufficient for the United States to overtake the United Kingdom and become about 30 percent richer by 2010. We can also see from this exhibit how several other countries, including Spain, South Korea, and China, became poorer relative to the United States by 1970. Yet it also shows that these countries grew faster than the United States over the past 40 years, closing the gap that had opened up previously.

Catch-up growth refers to a growth process whereby relatively poorer nations increase their incomes by taking advantage of knowledge and technologies already invented in other, technologically more advanced countries.

Part of this growth is what we call **catch-up growth**, meaning that these nations are catching up with the income and technology leader of the world, in this case the United States. Countries undergoing catch-up growth do so mostly by benefiting from available technologies, but also by increasing their saving, efficiency units of labor, and efficiency of production. Catch-up growth is very important in practice, though as the examples of slow growth and stagnation in Exhibit 7.8 demonstrate, it is far from automatic. In the next chapter, we discuss in greater detail why many countries have failed to take advantage of this type of catch-up growth.

Sustained growth refers to a growth process where GDP per capita grows at a positive and relatively steady rate for long periods of time.

Finally, Exhibit 7.8 drives home yet another important idea. The United States and several other countries—for example, the United Kingdom, France, and Spain—demonstrate **sustained growth** between 1820 and 2010 in the sense that there is a positive and relatively steady growth rate in every 50-year period, and the growth rate for the entire period is significantly positive for these countries. Our next task is to understand how this type of sustained growth emerges and what factors determine the growth rate of an economy.

Exhibit 7.8 GDP per Capita since 1820 in Selected Countries (PPP-adjusted 2005 Constant Dollars)

Countries had fairly similar levels of GDP per capita in 1820. Since then, differences in GDP per capita have grown because some countries, such as the United States and the United Kingdom, have grown steadily, while others have not.

Sources: Data from Maddison Project and Bureau of Economic Analysis, National Income and Product Accounts Table 1.1.9; J. Bolt and J. L. van Zanden, The First Update of the Maddison Project; Re-Estimating Growth Before 1820. Maddison Project Working Paper 4 (2013).

	1820	1870	1920	1970	2010	Average Growth (1820–2010)	Average Growth (1920–2010)
UK	2,854	4,390	6,259	14,817	32,722	1.29%	1.85%
U.S.	1,873	3,365	7,641	20,684	41,961	1.65%	1.91%
France	1,562	2,582	4,441	15,702	29,556	1.56%	2.13%
Spain	1,387	1,661	2,996	8,696	23,116	1.49%	2.30%
Brazil	940	981	1,325	4,207	9,467	1.22%	2.21%
Mexico	863	896	2,509	5,945	10,619	1.33%	1.62%
China	826	729	760	1,071	11,054	1.37%	3.02%
India	734	734	874	1,195	4,640	0.98%	1.87%
Morocco	592	775	977	2,224	5,542	1.18%	1.95%
South Korea	461	464	839	2,982	29,865	2.22%	4.05%
Ghana	–	604	1,075	1,960	2,645	–	1.01%
Haiti	–	–	–	1,265	944	–	–
Kenya	–	–	–	1,259	1,570	–	–

7.2 How Does a Nation's Economy Grow?

The aggregate production function, which we studied in the previous chapter, gives us a first answer to this question. Recall that the aggregate production function, $Y = A \times F(K, H)$, links GDP to the two factors of production, the physical capital (K) and total efficiency units of labor (H). The aggregate production function also depends on the level of technology (A), which captures the knowledge available to the economy and the efficiency of production. When A changes, the aggregate production function shifts.

A nation can increase its GDP by increasing its stock of physical capital, K; by increasing the total efficiency units of labor, H (for example, by increasing the human capital of workers); and by improving its technology, A. In this section, we look more closely at these three areas.

Let us consider the physical capital stock, K, which represents the value of all of the equipment (for example, machines, cars, planes, and computers) and structures (like buildings) of the economy. The physical capital stock (and therefore GDP) can be increased by investment, a process also known as *physical capital accumulation*.

You will recall from Chapter 5 that the national income accounting identity implies that $Y = C + I + G + X - M$, where C is consumption (household expenditures on consumption of goods and services), I is investment (expenditures on investment goods by private agents), G is government purchases of goods and services, X is exports, and M is imports. Recall that in a closed economy, there are no exports or imports, and if we also ignore the government (as we have done here), then we have $G = X = M = 0$. Therefore, the national income accounting identity implies

$$Y = C + I.$$

In other words, GDP is equal to the sum of aggregate consumption and investment. This also implies that investment comes directly from aggregate saving. This is because in our closed economy without government spending, all income will be either consumed or saved, so GDP is also equal to aggregate consumption plus aggregate saving or, in other words, $Y = C + S$. Thus

$$I = S.$$

Interpreted differently, this relationship says that all the resources households decide to save will be allocated to firms that will use them for investment (for example, by banks that will take money deposited by households and lend it to firms for investment). Consequently, a nation with a high saving rate will accumulate physical capital rapidly—that is, increase its physical capital stock rapidly—and, by the aggregate production function, increase its GDP. Thus to determine whether and how rapidly an economy will increase its physical capital stock, we need to understand the saving decisions of households, which we turn to next.

Optimization: The Choice Between Saving and Consumption

Consider the U.S. economy in 2008, when its GDP (aggregate income) stood at 14.44 trillion dollars. Naturally, not all of this output was consumed. Firms and the government invested some portion of it in the physical capital stock of the nation—for example, in new machines, roads, and bridges. But the resources for this investment come from the savings of households. For example, in a closed economy without the government, we have just seen that $I = S$.

Thus to understand how the GDP of a nation is divided between consumption and investment, we need to study the preferences of consumers, who decide how much of their income will be allocated to savings. This involves studying how households trade off consumption today versus consumption tomorrow, because saving is a way of allocating some of today's resources for consumption tomorrow (or more generally, consumption in the future). This is yet another example of optimization on the part of individuals and households. Each household typically faces different priorities and needs that influence its decisions to consume its income today versus save it for tomorrow. For example, those preparing to send their children to college may save more today.

As with all optimization problems, such choices are affected by prices. In this case, the relevant price is the *interest rate*, which determines the rate of return that households expect on their savings. (How the interest rate is determined will be discussed in detail in Chapter 10.) Higher interest rates typically encourage more saving. In addition, expectations of future income growth and perhaps taxes will have an impact on the saving decision. For instance, households that expect rapid income growth in the future may have less reason to save to finance future consumption (because future income growth will enable them to do this) or even to save "for a rainy day" (against potential future hardships). Conversely, if they expect high taxes in the future, households may save more in order to be able to pay these taxes without reducing future consumption.

The **saving rate** designates the fraction of income that is saved.

These trade-offs determine the **saving rate** of the economy, which corresponds to the fraction of income that is saved. (In practice, in addition to households, firms and the government also save, and we include these in the total saving of the economy.) We can compute the saving rate by dividing total saving by GDP (aggregate income). For example, in 2013, the level of total saving in the U.S. economy was $2.18 trillion, while GDP was $16.80 trillion (both in current dollars). Then the saving rate is

$$\text{Saving rate} = \frac{\text{Total saving}}{\text{GDP}} = \frac{\$2.18 \text{ trillion}}{\$16.80 \text{ trillion}} = 12.98\%.$$

What Brings Sustained Growth?

Can physical capital accumulation by itself generate sustained growth—where GDP per capita grows at a positive and relatively steady rate for an extended period of time? The answer to this question is "no" for a simple reason: *the diminishing marginal product of physical capital.*

Let's look a little more closely at this reasoning. As Exhibit 6.7 from the previous chapter shows, because of the diminishing marginal product of physical capital, more and more physical capital will translate into smaller and smaller increases in GDP. This precludes the possibility of sustained growth by just accumulating more and more physical capital.

What about steadily raising the efficiency units of labor in the economy? Can't the efficiency units of labor be raised just by increasing the number of workers in the economy? Can't we raise GDP steadily by increasing human capital?

First consider increasing the workforce—the number of people taking part in the production process. Holding all other factors of production and technology constant, every additional worker will increase GDP by less and less because of *diminishing marginal product*

CHOICE & CONSEQUENCE

Is Increasing the Saving Rate Always a Good Idea?

Suppose that you control the saving rate in a country and your objective is to improve the standard of living of the citizens of this country. Is it always a good idea to increase the saving rate? We have seen that greater saving increases the physical capital stock of the economy and consequently raises GDP. But this doesn't mean that increasing saving is always good for society. Imagine the extreme case where as the supreme ruler of a country, you are able to encourage saving so much that every dollar earned in the country is saved. This will indeed increase GDP. But it will not improve the standard of living of the citizens because it will require them to consume little or nothing. In the extreme case where the saving rate reaches 100 percent, consumption drops to zero. This implies that there must exist an optimal level of saving for a society, where saving above this level would make the society worse off because it would significantly reduce consumption.

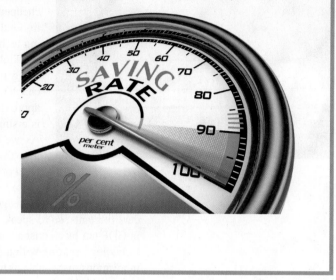

of labor (or diminishing marginal product of total efficiency units of labor). Therefore, we cannot guarantee a steady increase in GDP per capita by just increasing the workforce either.

Note that we can also increase the efficiency units of labor for a given workforce by increasing the human capital of workers—for example, by raising their educational attainment or skill level. Although such changes will indeed increase GDP, they will, by themselves, not achieve *sustained* growth. Because each individual has a finite life, there is a limit to how many years of schooling he or she can obtain, and, of course, more and more schooling would also imply fewer and fewer years in the workforce where an individual actively takes part in production. Thus, achieving greater and greater levels of efficiency units by continuously increasing the years of schooling of the workforce does not appear feasible.

"But hold on," you might say. "What about continuously upgrading the quality of education? Wouldn't that work toward increasing the efficiency units of labor?" Not really. Empirically, the extent to which such improvements can ensure steady growth also appears to be limited, as we will see in greater detail in the Evidence-Based Economics section of this chapter. Therefore, even though investments in education and skills do play a major role in increasing GDP per capita, we cannot achieve sustained growth of about 1.5–2 percent a year just by continuously increasing the educational achievement of the workforce.

These considerations imply that in order to achieve sustained growth, we need something else. And that something else is *technology*—particularly advances in the technical knowledge used in production.

Knowledge, Technological Change, and Growth

You will recall that Moore's Law, which we first encountered in the previous chapter (Exhibit 6.10), claims that the number of transistors on memory microchips will double every 2 years, thereby increasing the computational power of computers. This trend has been true for at least the last 50 years and probably for longer. For example, around 1900, before microprocessors and extra mechanical devices, it was prohibitively expensive to make anything but the most trivial calculations. By 1950, with the technologies associated with the vacuum tube, society had access to the technology to make one relevant computation per second at a cost of $1,000 (in today's dollars). By the 1970s, with the advent of the transistor, we could make up to 100 calculations per second for $1,000. And by the late 1990s, with the widespread use of integrated circuits, almost 10 million calculations per second could be performed for the same cost. Moore's Law is an example of *technological change*.

Technological change is the process of new technologies and new goods and services being invented, introduced, and used in the economy, enabling the economy to achieve a

Technological change is the process of new technologies and new goods and services being invented, introduced, and used in the economy, enabling the economy to achieve a higher level of GDP for given levels of physical capital stock and total efficiency units of labor.

higher level of GDP for given levels of its factors of production, physical capital stock, and total efficiency units of labor.

Consider another example of technological change—the reduction in the cost of light over the past 200 years—as shown in Exhibit 7.9.[1] Obtaining lighting, both for firms and households, has become much cheaper over the past two centuries because of the invention of the lightbulb and ongoing improvements in the quality of lightbulbs, lighting technology, and the transmission of energy.

Technological change, as it turns out, is exponential. In particular, using the same definition of exponential growth from earlier in this chapter, this means that improvements in technology take place at an approximately constant rate—rather than by constant increments. There is a simple reason for this exponential nature of technological change. As we have seen, growth in GDP per capita is exponential because growth compounds—that is, it takes place on the basis of the current level of GDP whose increase is already a result of past growth. There is a similar logic to technological change. New innovations and technologies build on the knowledge stock resulting from past innovations—building on the shoulders of giants, so to speak. This ensures that innovations improve our productive capacity in GDP not by a constant amount but by a constant *proportional* amount. So if we improve technology starting with a technology level that produces a GDP per capita of $1,000, then innovations that enable us to be more productive by a certain amount—say 10 percent—will raise GDP per capita from $1,000 to $1,100. But if we instead start with a technology level that produces $100,000 of GDP per capita, similar innovations bringing a 10 percent improvement will take us to $110,000.

> **New innovations and technologies build on the knowledge stock resulting from past innovations—building on the shoulders of giants, so to speak.**

The exponential nature of technological change illustrated by these two examples is also responsible for the fact that improvements in technology need not necessarily run into diminishing marginal product (whereas, as we have seen, increases in the use of factors of production run into diminishing marginal product). For this reason, improvements in technology appear to be the most plausible engine of sustained growth.

By now, you will have realized that there is a nice symmetry between our treatment of cross-country differences in GDP per capita in the previous chapter and of over-time differences, corresponding to growth, in this chapter. In both, the physical capital stock and efficiency units of labor play important roles, but they are insufficient to explain the major differences. Both across countries and over time, technology instead plays the central role.

Exhibit 7.9 The Real Price of Light over Time

The source of sustained growth is technological progress, which continuously increases the amount that an economy can produce. Here we see one reflection of this technological progress, showing how improvements in lighting technology, the quality of lightbulbs, and transmission of energy have reduced the cost of lighting over time.

Source: William D. Nordhaus, "Do Real-Output and Real-Wage Measures Capture Reality? The History of Light Suggests Not," Cowles Foundation Discussion Papers 1078, Cowles Foundation for Research in Economics (1994).

Evidence-Based Economics

Q: Why are you so much more prosperous than your great-great-grandparents were?

The theoretical discussion in the previous section supports the central role of technology in explaining sustained growth. We will now see that empirical evidence also bolsters the conclusion that technology plays a key role.

To evaluate the sources of U.S. economic growth, we follow the same strategy as in the previous chapter. There, we used the aggregate production function and estimates of the physical capital stock and the efficiency units of labor across different countries to evaluate their contributions to cross-country differences in GDP. The only major difference here is that higher-quality U.S. data enable us to conduct the analysis for GDP per hour worked rather than GDP per worker, thus allowing us to measure the labor input more accurately. We start the analysis in 1950.

Exhibit 7.10 records average GDP per hour worked (in 2005 constant dollars), the average value of the physical capital stock per hour worked, and the most important component of the human capital of workers—the average years of schooling—for 10-year periods starting in 1950. (To remove the short-term effects of the last recession from our calculations on long-term growth, the last period is 2000–2007.) The exhibit shows the steady increase in GDP per hour worked, physical capital stock per hour worked, and educational attainment in the United States between 1950 and 2007.

We then use a methodology similar to that in the previous chapter to compute the contribution of physical capital, human capital (efficiency units of labor), and technology to the growth of GDP in the United States. The results are recorded in columns 4, 5, and 6 of the exhibit (in percentages). Column 7 then gives the annual growth rate of GDP per hour worked, which is the sum of the contributions of physical capital, human capital, and technology.

This exhibit highlights the central role that technology has played in U.S. growth. Let's examine the 1960s, shown in the second row. The 0.17 percent recorded as the contribution of human capital indicates that if the human capital of U.S. workers had remained constant in the 1960s, then the growth rate of GDP per hour worked in the 1960s would have been lower by 0.17 percent (3.09 percent instead of 3.26 percent). In

Time Period	GDP per Hour Worked (2005 Constant Dollars)	Physical Capital Stock per Hour Worked (2005 Constant Dollars)	Average Years of Schooling	Growth (%) Resulting from Physical Capital (K)	Growth (%) Resulting from Human Capital (H)	Growth (%) Resulting from Technology (A)	Annual Growth Rate of GDP per Hour Worked
	(1)	(2)	(3)	(4)	(5)	(6)	(7)
1950–1959	8.30	102,548	9.38	0.89	0.28	2.37	3.54%
1960–1969	11.50	119,593	10.16	0.89	0.17	2.20	3.26
1970–1979	14.96	128,591	11.15	0.88	0.01	1.22	2.11
1980–1989	17.46	137,637	12.07	0.86	0.30	0.45	1.61
1990–1999	20.95	144,354	12.77	0.84	0.36	0.87	2.07
2000–2007	27.06	158,755	13.22	0.99	0.19	1.29	2.47

Exhibit 7.10 Contribution of Technology, Physical Capital, and Human Capital to the Growth of GDP per Hour Worked in the United States between 1950 and 2007. Column 6 is computed by subtracting columns 4 and 5 from column 7.

Sources: Data from Bureau of Labor Statistics, Bureau of Economic Analysis, and United States Census Bureau.

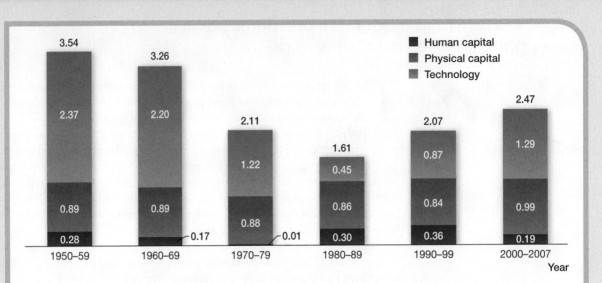

Exhibit 7.11 Share of Technology, Physical Capital, and Human Capital in the Growth of GDP per Hour Worked in the United States Between 1950 and 2007

This exhibit shows the contribution of physical capital, human capital, and technology to growth of GDP per hour worked in the United States. The sum of the three numbers is the growth rate in the period, indicated at the top. It is clear that technology is the single most important contributor to economic growth in the United States.

Sources: Data from Bureau of Labor Statistics, Bureau of Economic Analysis, United States Census Bureau.

contrast, if technology had stayed constant, the annual growth rate of GDP per hour worked would have been lower by 2.20 percent. The other rows of the exhibit paint a similar picture. Mirroring our findings on the role of technology in accounting for cross-country differences in the previous chapter, technology accounts for the bulk of growth in U.S. GDP per hour worked in most periods.

Exhibit 7.11 presents the same information as the last four columns of Exhibit 7.10 in a bar chart, more clearly showing the decomposition of growth between the two factors of production and technology. It also highlights the central role of technology. The total height of each bar is the annual growth of GDP per hour worked during the corresponding period, while the orange part of the bar shows the contribution of technology. It shows that, except between 1980 and 1989, technology was the most important contributor to U.S. growth.

The contribution of technology was somewhat lower during the 1970s and 1980s, which were decades of relatively low growth in GDP per hour worked, while the stock of physical capital in the economy continued to increase—partly because there was considerable investment in information technology capital during these decades.

An important caveat to the conclusions supported by Exhibits 7.10 and 7.11 is worth noting. As pointed out in the previous chapter and in Exhibit 7.10, the contribution of technology is obtained as the fraction of growth in GDP not explained by physical capital and human capital. This implies that if we understate the contribution of physical capital or human capital to GDP growth, which could happen, for example, because we do not fully take into account the improved quality of our physical capital stock, then the contribution of technology may be somewhat exaggerated.

Question

Why are you so much more prosperous than your great-great-grandparents were?

Answer

It is mostly due to better technology, though greater physical capital and greater human capital of workers have also contributed.

Data

Estimates of GDP per hour worked, physical capital stock per hour worked, average educational attainment, and average professional experience of the workforce in the United States between 1950 and 2007.

Caveat

If we understate the contribution of physical capital or human capital to GDP, the contribution of technology may be somewhat exaggerated.

7.3 The History of Growth and Technology

Exhibit 7.8 depicted economic development in several countries since 1820. This 200-year period is sometimes referred to as "modern times." But what about before then? Did patterns of growth before the nineteenth century look similar to those we have documented so far in this chapter? If not, what changed?

Growth Before Modern Times

Humanity had, of course, a long history before the nineteenth century, during which there were several major achievements in science, technology, and the arts. But from an economic point of view, the period before 1800 is distinguished by one thing: a lack of sustained growth. Looking back at Exhibits 7.1 and 7.2, we see that the U.S. economy has had some downturns and one big setback during the Great Depression, but on the whole, it has experienced relatively steady economic growth in GDP per capita.

Though the world before 1800 was certainly not stagnant, it did not experience the type of sustained growth we see in Exhibit 7.1. There were a few notable periods of economic growth and even technological improvements, some of which continued for as long as a century or even more. The periods that are most well known are those in ancient Greece, ancient Rome, and Venice. During the heydays of these civilizations, standards of living improved and economic activity increased significantly. But this growth didn't last. Ancient Rome may have grown, although relatively slowly, for over 300 years, but its growth ultimately came to an end. The situation was similar in Venice.

Even though there was some economic growth during all of these eras, *sustained* economic growth was rare or even absent. There is a simple way to see why growth in these ancient civilizations could not have been sustained. The World Bank's definition of absolute poverty as living off the equivalent of $1.25 per day, which we discussed in the previous chapter, is not an entirely arbitrary one. An individual needs to consume a certain amount of calories in order to live, and, of course, people need shelter and clothing. Though estimates vary, it is practically impossible for a country to have income (GDP) per capita

The **subsistence level** is the minimum level of income per person that is generally necessary for the individual to obtain enough calories, shelter, and clothing to survive.

of much less than $500 or so per year, because this would imply that a large fraction of the population would be living on much less than $500 per person. We call this level of income per capita below which an individual cannot easily survive the **subsistence level** (even if there isn't one unique subsistence level that applies in every environment). The general idea is simple: regardless of the exact level, there exists a minimum level of income per person that is necessary for individual survival and subsistence. When income falls below this level, much of the population will starve.

Of course, there were no national income and product accounts 10,000 years ago, 1,000 years ago, or even 200 years ago. All the same, we know that income per capita in all places in which there were human civilizations could not have been much less than $500 per capita in today's dollars. Moreover, we know from Exhibit 7.8 that at the beginning of the nineteenth century, incomes in much of the world were not much higher than $500 per capita. In the United States, for example, income per capita was about $1,361, and in Western Europe, it was only a little higher. Therefore, there cannot have been much sustained growth before 1800.

There are two reasons for this lack of sustained growth before modern times. The first—the more important one—is related to the major factor that explains sustained growth: technology. Before 1800, though there were some important technological breakthroughs, the pace of technological change was much slower, almost stagnant compared to what came thereafter. Second, whatever improvements in aggregate incomes (GDP) were realized did not typically translate into increases in income per capita. This last point was the basis of the theory of Thomas Malthus, which is sometimes referred to as the Malthusian model. We next discuss the Malthusian model and how the world broke out of it.

Malthusian Limits to Growth

Fertility refers to the number of children per adult or per woman of childbearing age.

Thomas Malthus had a particularly dismal view of the workings of the economy. This was partly because, writing in 1798, he had not seen a period of steady growth like the one Europe experienced in the nineteenth century.[2] Malthus thought that **fertility**—defined as the number of children per adult or per woman of childbearing age—would adjust so that income always would remain close to a subsistence level, a number like the $500 a year we mentioned earlier. In Malthus's theory, couples have more children when the standard of living is above the subsistence level. Then, assuming that aggregate income (GDP) could not grow faster than the population, Malthus concluded that increasing population would push income per capita down toward—and possibly below—the subsistence level. This fall in income per capita in turn would trigger famines or wars that would kill a large fraction of the population. With a given level of aggregate income, a lower population would then cause income per capita to increase again. So in a pattern sometimes referred to as the **Malthusian cycle**, increased aggregate income would raise income per capita above subsistence, fueling population growth, which in turn would put pressure on resources and reduce income per capita back to its initial level or sometimes even below it. This pattern subsequently "corrects" the increase in population through reduced fertility and higher mortality, often due to famines.

The **Malthusian cycle** refers to the preindustrial pattern in which increases in aggregate income lead to an expanding population, which in turn reduces income per capita and puts downward pressure on population.

Dismal though it may be, the Malthusian model seems to be a good representation of how the world actually was before 1800.

Around the same time or shortly thereafter, fertility declined. This process, which has both economic and social causes, is referred to as the **demographic transition**. Economists typically emphasize the importance of the transition from agriculture and rural areas toward industry and cities as a major cause of the demographic transition. Urban families did not need to rely on child labor for help in the field in the same way that rural families did, and the increasing costs of rearing children, particularly when they had to stay in school longer rather than work in the fields, created incentives for smaller families.

The **demographic transition** refers to the decline in fertility and number of children per family that many societies undergo as they transition from agriculture to industry.

Many historians and economists view the demographic transition as a central ingredient to modern growth, because it enabled the economies that experienced reduced fertility to break away from the Malthusian cycle. Until the demographic transition in the nineteenth century, there were recurrent Malthusian cycles. After this date, there was relatively sustained growth in income per capita in many economies, particularly in the Western world.

The Industrial Revolution

But the demographic transition by itself would not have been sufficient to kick-start growth. If all that happened was that fertility declined and stabilized around a lower number, there would not necessarily have been any qualitative changes in the patterns of GDP growth per capita. Instead, sustained growth was due to another major change that occurred around the same time: the *Industrial Revolution*, which opened the way for more steady and rapid technological changes that underpinned modern economic growth.

Contrary to its name, the **Industrial Revolution** was a gradual process rather than a short period of rapid disruption. It is the term coined to designate the arrival of many new machines and methods of production in Britain, starting in textile manufacturing and thereafter spreading into other sectors. The Industrial Revolution is important both as an event in itself (because it was the first time technology and scientific methods were used in production in such a coordinated manner) and also as the starting point of the wave of industrialization that spread to many other countries around the world. We have already seen that the countries that are rich today are those that have managed to achieve steady growth rates over the past 200 years. Those are also the ones that have managed to benefit from the technologies brought about by the Industrial Revolution.

Although clearly new technologies and new knowledge were created before, innovation and the application of new technologies to the production of goods and services became more systematic and pervasive during and in the aftermath of the Industrial Revolution. The available evidence thus suggests that changes in technology that are the root cause of the sustained growth we observe today started with the Industrial Revolution at the end of the eighteenth century in Britain.

Industrial Revolution is the term used for describing the series of innovations and their implementation in the production process that started to take place at the end of the eighteenth century in Britain.

Growth and Technology Since the Industrial Revolution

Many of the technologies that we take for granted today—from railroads to automobiles and airplanes; from radio and TV to telecommunication technologies, computers, the Internet, and social networking; from electricity to almost all of the technologies used on the factory floor to produce the goods we use in our everyday life; from almost all of the drugs that save hundreds of millions of lives every year around the world to basic sanitation including indoor plumbing—have been invented and made available to us over the last 250 years. Such advances are the result of the exponential growth in our knowledge and technology since the Industrial Revolution. An important foundation of this growth has been research and development (R&D) activity, which firms, universities, and governments undertake in order to improve this knowledge base. The United States today spends 365 billion dollars, or 2.79 percent of its GDP, on R&D every year. This number is even higher in some other countries—for example, 4.66 percent in Israel, 3.00 percent in Switzerland, and 3.70 percent in Sweden. To a large extent, our high standards of living today are the return on this R&D investment.

7.4 Growth, Inequality, and Poverty

> The fact that an economy is growing does not necessarily imply that all citizens are benefiting equally from that growth.

The fact that an economy is growing does not necessarily imply that all citizens are benefiting equally from that growth. In fact, in recent decades, rapid growth in the U.S. economy has gone hand-in-hand with increases in inequality. There are almost always some households and individuals with significantly higher-than-average incomes and some with significantly lower-than-average incomes. In fact, economic growth is sometimes associated with increasing inequality because only some workers and businesses benefit from the new technologies that are driving this growth.

Growth and Inequality

There are several reasons why a society might care about inequality. Some may wish to live in a society that does not have great disparities in the living standards of its citizens.

Income Inequality in the United States

Exhibit 7.12 shows a simple measure of inequality in the United States: the share of total U.S. income accruing to the richest 10 percent (the other 90 percent of Americans earned less than individuals in this top decile, and their aggregate earnings correspond to the remaining fraction). The data, compiled by economists Thomas Piketty and Emmanuel Saez, show that until 1940, the top 10 percent earned about 45 to 50 percent of total income.[3] This proportion then declined to about 35 percent, corresponding to a significant decline in income inequality. It then remained there until the late 1970s. Starting in the late 1970s, however, inequality started increasing, and by the end of the 1990s, the share of the top 10 percent is again up to about 50 percent. Piketty and Saez also show another interesting pattern. Before the 1970s, much of the earnings of the very rich came from capital income—that is, income from sources other than wages and salaries, like dividends, accrued wealth, income from ownership, and so on. But over the last 30 years, the contribution of wages to the income of the very rich has changed dramatically, rising to 60 percent in 2000 (though it subsequently fell to 38 percent in 2007). More and more, even the rich have to work.

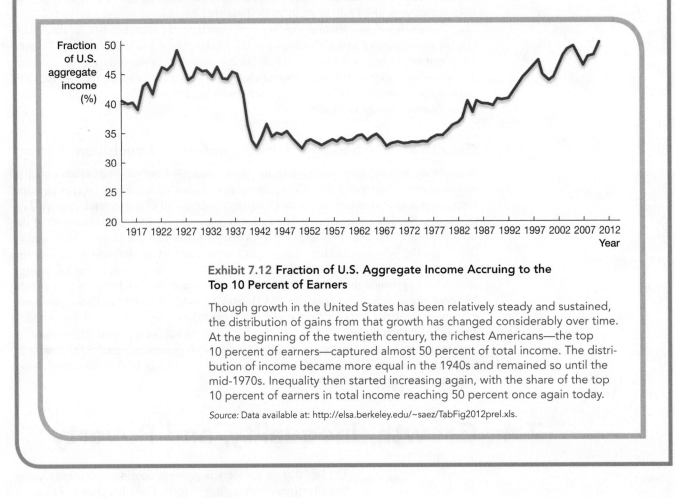

Exhibit 7.12 Fraction of U.S. Aggregate Income Accruing to the Top 10 Percent of Earners

Though growth in the United States has been relatively steady and sustained, the distribution of gains from that growth has changed considerably over time. At the beginning of the twentieth century, the richest Americans—the top 10 percent of earners—captured almost 50 percent of total income. The distribution of income became more equal in the 1940s and remained so until the mid-1970s. Inequality then started increasing again, with the share of the top 10 percent of earners in total income reaching 50 percent once again today.

Source: Data available at: http://elsa.berkeley.edu/~saez/TabFig2012prel.xls.

We may feel that greater inequality leads to more social polarization or even to a greater incidence of crime in society.

So far, we have focused on income (GDP) per capita as the main measure of the productivity and living standards of a nation. But average income per capita of a nation at a particular point in time is not the same as the income of all individuals in that nation. As we already noted in Chapter 6, this distinction cautions us against focusing just on income per capita without taking into account the distribution of income in a given society.

While it is certainly justifiable to care about inequality in and of itself, one reason why many policymakers and citizens are concerned about it is because it is associated with poverty. Poverty, particularly of the extreme sort captured by the $1.25 per day measure of the

CHOICE & CONSEQUENCE

Inequality versus Poverty

Consider a society consisting of just two types of people: rich and poor. Suppose also that half of the population is rich and the other half is poor. Now consider two scenarios. In Scenario 1, the rich have $50,000 each, while the poor have $1,000 each. In Scenario 2, the rich have $5,000, while the poor have $500. Which society would you like to live in?

The answer to this question will naturally depend on several factors. Different people will evaluate inequality and poverty differently. Suppose first that you only care about average income and not at all about equity. Then the comparison is straightforward. You will easily compute that average income in Scenario 1 is $25,500, while it is only $2,750 in Scenario 2. The first scenario clearly dominates.

Suppose, on the other hand, that you only care about equity. One way of thinking about this is to just focus on a measure of inequality and nothing else. In that case, you will see that Scenario 1 has greater inequality because

the ratio of rich-to-poor incomes is 50. In contrast, in Scenario 2, the same ratio is only 10. So if you care only about inequality and nothing else, you may be tempted to say that Scenario 2 is preferable.

There is a fallacy here, however. Most of us would care about inequality because we associate it with poverty and low living standards for part of the population. Yet Scenario 1, despite having greater inequality, also has much less poverty. In Scenario 1, the poor individuals have $1,000 each, whereas in Scenario 2, each poor individual has only $500, regardless of that economy's greater equality. Therefore, even if we strongly care about the welfare of others and the level of poverty in society, just focusing on inequality would be an error. In fact, in this case, Scenario 1 has both greater average income and lower poverty. If, instead of noticing this, we just focused on inequality, presuming that a more equal allocation would also have lower poverty, we would have made an error in judgment.

World Bank, leads to serious economic, health, and social problems. High infant mortality, child malnourishment, lack of access to education, and the inability to take part in several major economic activities are just some of the problems typically associated with extreme levels of poverty. However, it is important to distinguish between inequality and poverty, as we do in the above Choice & Consequence box.

Growth and Poverty

What is the relationship between growth and poverty? We saw in the previous chapter how countries with higher levels of income (GDP) per capita have fewer people living in poverty, as measured by the $1.25 per day measure of the World Bank. Exhibit 7.13

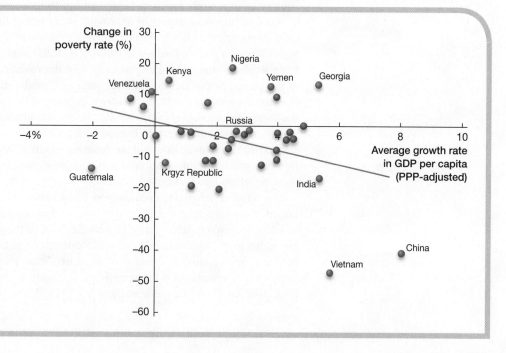

Exhibit 7.13 The Relationship Between Growth and Change in Poverty in the Early 1990s and the Early Twenty-first Century

Economic growth tends to reduce poverty, though the relationship is noisy and less than perfect. Red dots correspond to countries identified by name.

Source: Data from Penn World Table and World Bank DataBank: World Development Indicators; Alan Heston, Robert Summers, and Bettina Aten, Penn World Table Version 7.1, Center for International Comparisons of Production, Income and Prices at the University of Pennsylvania (Nov 2012).

complements this picture by showing that, on average, growth of income per capita is associated with a decline in poverty. For each country in the data, the vertical axis shows the percentage rise or decline in poverty between 1993 and the late 2000s (depending on data availability), while the horizontal axis shows the average growth between the same dates.

Those in the lower-right quadrant are the countries that have experienced positive growth and declines in poverty and include China, India, and Vietnam, among others. Venezuela in the upper-left quadrant is one of only three countries that has a negative growth rate and has also experienced an increase in poverty. The exhibit also includes the line that best fits these points. Although there are some countries where growth and poverty have both increased (such as Yemen, Nigeria, and Georgia), on the whole there is a negative association between growth over the recent decades and the fraction of the population living in poverty. Yet the exhibit also shows that there is quite a bit of dispersion around that best-fit line.

Even though this association does not prove that growth in income per capita is the direct *cause* of declining poverty, it is the type of evidence that bolsters many economists' belief that economic growth is one of the most effective ways of reducing poverty. Nevertheless, it is important to remember that there is no guarantee that economic growth will automatically reduce poverty (as the cases of Georgia, Nigeria, and Yemen in the exhibit show). It will do so only if it is not associated with a significant rise in inequality.

How Can We Reduce Poverty?

Many different policies have been pursued in order to reduce international poverty, and, for reasons that we discuss in greater detail in the next chapter, many have failed. Thus it is quite likely that there are no silver-bullet policies for reducing poverty around the world.

Nevertheless, economic analysis suggests several potentially useful approaches. One solution, which we explore further in Chapter 14, is international trade, which can be beneficial to all countries that take part in it. Although international trade does create losers as well as winners, the overall benefit from international trade is generally positive and significant. This is particularly so for many poor countries that have natural resources and produce agricultural goods that could be exported to the European Union or the United States but are blocked by high tariffs and prohibitive quotas. Reducing tariffs and quotas that wealthy nations impose on poor countries would be one way of creating gains in GDP and perhaps even growth for these nations. In fact, trade might have even further benefits. If international trade also brings with it more interaction with wealthy nations, such cross-country contact might facilitate the transfer of technology.

Another important aspect of improving standards of living around the world is to continue improving the knowledge and technology available in the world economy. The United States spends a sizable fraction of its GDP on R&D, and a significant fraction of its workforce works in science and engineering. The improvements that result from these efforts in the United States and in countries such as Canada, the United Kingdom, France, and Germany improve not only the standards of living in these nations but also those all around the world. For example, improvements in communications technology that originated in the United States and Western Europe now enable cell phones to be used globally, which has helped improve the lives and the business opportunities of billions of people elsewhere. Before wireless communication became available, people in many countries had to rely on wireline telephones for communication.

But wireline telephone industry was often under state control or a private monopoly, and as a consequence, it was very expensive and not widely available. The advances in wireless technology have partly broken the hold of these monopolies on consumers. As the technology improves, wireless telecommunication can be used for better healthcare delivery, and it is already being used as an important part of business deals, starting with improving communication between firms. Similarly, innovations in pharmaceuticals allow lives to be saved around the world, not just in the United States or Germany or France.

LETTING THE DATA SPEAK

Life Expectancy and Innovation

Life expectancy around the world was much lower 70 years ago than it is today.[4] In 1940, child and infant mortality rates were so high and adult diseases, such as pneumonia and tuberculosis, were so deadly (and without any cure) that life expectancy at birth in many nations stood at less than 40 years. For example, the life expectancy at birth of an average Indian was an incredibly low 30 years. In Venezuela, it was 33; in Indonesia, 34; in Brazil, 36. Life expectancy at birth in many Western nations was also low but still considerably higher than the corresponding numbers in the poorer nations. Consider that life expectancy at birth in the United States was 64 years.

In the course of the next three or four decades, this picture changed dramatically. As we saw in the previous chapter, while the gap in life expectancy between rich and poor nations still remains today, health conditions have improved significantly all over the world, particularly before the spread of the AIDS epidemic in sub-Saharan Africa starting in the 1980s. Life expectancy at birth in India in 1999 was 60 years. This was twice as large as the same number in 1940. It was also 50 percent higher than life expectancy at birth in Britain in 1820 (40 years), which had approximately the same GDP per capita as India in 1999. How did this tremendous improvement in health conditions in poor nations take place?

The answer lies in scientific breakthroughs and innovations that took place in the United States and Western Europe throughout the twentieth century. First, there was a wave of global drug innovation, most importantly the development of antibiotics, which produced many products that were highly effective against major killers in developing countries. Penicillin, which provided an effective treatment against a range of bacterial infections, became widely available by the early 1950s. Also important during the same period was the development of new vaccines, including ones against yellow fever and smallpox.

The second major factor was the discovery of DDT (Dichlorodiphenyl trichloroethylene). Although eventually the excess use of DDT as an agricultural pesticide would

turn out to be an environmental hazard, its initial use in disease control was revolutionary. DDT allowed a breakthrough in attempts to control one of the major killers of children in relatively poor parts of the world—malaria. Finally, with the establishment and help of the World Health Organization (WHO), simple but effective medical and public health practices, such as oral rehydration and boiling water to prevent cholera, spread to poorer countries.

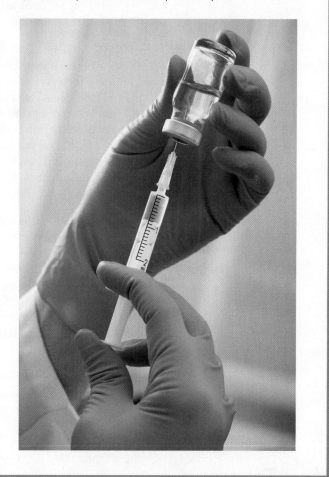

Therefore, although not directly useful for closing the gap between wealthy nations and the rest of the world, continuing with the innovative agenda in the United States and Europe is an important weapon in the fight against international poverty.

In this and the previous chapter, we have focused on how physical capital, human capital, and technology determine the potential for economic growth and cross-country differences in GDP per capita. We have seen how an economy—rich or poor—can grow by investing more in physical capital, upgrading the human capital of its workforce, and improving its technology and efficiency of production. The natural question then is why many countries in the world do not pursue such improvements but remain poor or submit to low growth instead. This is the topic of our next chapter.

Summary

�֍ Many countries, including the United States, have experienced rapid economic growth over the last 200 years, increasing their GDP per capita several times over. For example, current U.S. GDP per capita is about 25 times U.S. GDP per capita in 1820. In addition, U.S. growth has been relatively sustained, meaning that GDP per capita has grown relatively steadily, with the exception of the Great Depression and the decade following it.

✖ Economic growth can sometimes take place rapidly due to catch-up growth, whereby relatively poorer nations increase their GDP per capita by taking advantage of knowledge and technologies already invented in other, more advanced countries.

✖ Economic growth results from an economy increasing its physical capital, raising the human capital of its workers (so that it has greater efficiency units of labor for a given size of the workforce), and improving its technology. Because of the diminishing marginal product of physical capital and limits to how much each worker can invest in his or her human capital before joining the workforce, sustained growth is generally impossible to achieve just by building up physical and human capital. Rather, the most plausible driver of sustained growth is technological progress. Empirical evidence also suggests that technological progress accounts for the bulk of the increase in GDP per capita (or per hour worked) in the United States.

✖ Though the last 200 years have been characterized by sustained economic growth in many parts of the world, the preceding centuries did not experience steady growth. Instead, most economies during these times experienced Malthusian cycles: increases in GDP-fueled population growth, which reduced the standard of living and subsequently acted as a check on further population growth by reducing fertility and survival. The world broke out of the Malthusian cycle through the Industrial Revolution, which started a process of rapid technological progress, underpinning the sustained growth of the last two centuries.

✖ Economic growth has the capacity to significantly reduce poverty, provided that such growth is not associated with much greater inequality.

Key Terms

Questions

All questions are available in MyEconLab *for practice and instructor assignment.*

1. What is meant by economic growth? How has the U.S. economy grown over the past 200 years?

2. What are catch-up growth and sustained growth? Explain with examples.

3. According to the aggregate production function, how does GDP increase?

4. The chapter emphasizes the importance of saving in economic growth.

   a. How is the saving rate in an economy defined?

   b. What factors help households decide whether to consume or save their income?

   c. How do household saving decisions impact investment in the economy?

5. Holding all else equal, will increasing the efficiency units of labor lead to sustained growth? Why or why not?

6. What explains economic growth in the United States over the past few decades?

7. Why was there no sustained economic growth before modern times, that is, before 1800?

8. What did Malthus predict about economic growth? Did his predictions come true? Why or why not?

9. How did the Industrial Revolution affect economic growth?

10. Does an increase in GDP per capita of a nation imply that all its citizens have become richer? Explain.

11. Based on your understanding of the chapter, how can poverty best be reduced?

12. What factors explain the dramatic increases in life expectancy that we saw in most countries in the twentieth century?

Problems

All problems are available in MyEconLab *for practice and instructor assignment.*

1. (Note: All figures in this problem are given in constant, 1990 dollars.)

In 1950, GDP per capita in Germany was only $4,281. GDP per capita in Argentina that same year was $4,987. So, in 1950 Argentina was actually "richer" in per capita terms than Germany.

By 1992, however, GDP per capita in Germany was $19,351, whereas GDP per capita in Argentina was only $7,616.

   a. By what total percentage did per capita GDP in each country increase between 1950 and 1992?

   b. Explain how a country that has a lower GDP per capita than another country in some year can end up with a larger GDP per capita in later years.

2. Currently, some of the fastest-growing countries in the world remain desperately poor. For example, of the top five fastest-growing economies in 2013, three—South Sudan, Sierra Leone, and Turkmenistan—had real per capita GDP that are 144th, 155th, and 95th in the world, respectively. (*Source:* CIA Factbook estimates for 2013, PPP basis.)

This seems like something of a contradiction. Using the equations for growth given in the chapter, explain why a country that has a very low per capita GDP can also have a very high growth rate.

3. The following table lists GDP per capita from 1970 to 2010 for South Korea and the United States. As you can see, both grew substantially over that 40-year period.

Year	South Korea GDP per Capita	U.S. GDP per Capita
1970	317	5247
1980	1778	12598
1990	6642	23955
2000	11948	36467
2010	22151	48358

[Data from the World Bank, *World Development Indicators*]

   a. Plot the five data points for each country on a graph using a nonproportional scale, as in Exhibit 7.3 in the chapter. Connect the points to create a line graph.

   b. Plot the five data points for each country on a graph using a proportional scale, that is, a scale where equal distances represent equal *percentage* changes. Connect the points to create a line graph.

   c. Interpret the differences you see in the two graphs.

4. China's economy is one of the fastest-growing economies in the world. Growth in China is primarily driven by investment and exports. You are discussing the sustainability of China's growth model with your friend. He says that according to the aggregate production function, all China needs to do to ensure sustainable economic growth is to continue to increase its physical capital stock. Do you agree? Explain.

5. The graph below shows an index of world GDP per capita from 1000 BC to the year 2000.

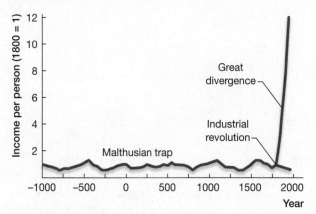

Source: Jeff Speakes, "Economic History of the World," Center for Economic Research and Forecasting, California Lutheran University

   As you can see, over most of that period, global economic growth was virtually nonexistent. While there were periods that experienced some increase in per capita income, sustained growth begins only in the mid-18th century, and explodes after that—by the year 2000, income per capita is 12 times what it had been 250 years before.

Explain what accounts for such a dramatic change in economic growth beginning in the 18th century.

6. Economists have long debated the causes of the slowdown in productivity (GDP per hour worked) in the United States during the 1970s and 1980s. This slowdown can be clearly seen in Exhibits 7.10 and 7.11.

   a. Based on the data in Exhibit 7.10, is it physical capital, human capital, or technology that is most responsible for the overall decline in the annual growth rate of GDP per hour worked in these two decades? Explain your answer with reference to the exhibit.

   b. An interesting study of the slowdown has been done by Yale economist William Nordhaus, which is summarized at http://www.nber.org/digest/jun05/w10950.html. What are the two main conclusions that Nordhaus reaches concerning the 1970s slowdown? Which industries were most affected by the slowdown, and why?

7. The concept of diminishing returns to a factor of production applies not only to physical capital but to labor as well. Use the concept of diminishing returns to labor to explain and illustrate why there was no sustained growth in living standards prior to the Industrial Revolution. Draw a graph to illustrate the relationship between population and GDP, where population is measured on the horizontal axis. Explain how your graph changes after the Industrial Revolution.

8. In 1968, Paul Ehrlich, a Stanford University professor, claimed that overpopulation would lead to famines and starvation in the 1970s and 1980s. In his book *The Population Bomb*, he said that unless population growth was curbed, millions around the world would die. However, as we now know, this did not happen. What do you think was the flaw in Ehrlich's argument?

9. The Letting the Data Speak box on levels versus growth points out how one important index of health—life expectancy—has changed in various countries over time.

   To see a dramatic animation of the data mentioned in the box, go to http://www.gapminder.org/videos/200-years-that-changed-the-world-bbc,/#.U8aTaJRdXTo. Hans Rosling is an expert in global health and is known for his creative presentation of statistics. Watch the brief video, and answer the following questions.

   a. What was the upper limit on life expectancy in almost all countries in 1810? Which two countries were slightly better off?

   b. Which countries failed to improve much in life expectancy and income as a result of the Industrial Revolution?

   c. As of 1948, had disparities in life expectancy and income between countries narrowed or widened? Which were some of the countries that had not made much improvement in either measure by 1948?

   d. As of 2009, what was the general situation regarding the distribution of countries in terms of health and income? What countries still lagged behind?

   e. Based on the video, how can country averages disguise the wide variation in living standards *within* a country? Give an example from the video.

10. Suppose that a 10 percent increase in the physical capital stock increases GDP by 10 percent. Now consider an additional 10 percent increase in the physical capital stock. Will this increase GDP by less than 10 percent, 10 percent, or more than 10 percent? Explain.

11. Challenge Problem: Refer to Exhibit 7.4. If the United States, Mexico, China, Rwanda, and Haiti continue to grow at the rates given in the exhibit, how many years (starting from 2010) would it take each to catch up to the United States in terms of per capita GDP?

Appendix

The Solow Growth Model

The main tool that economists use for formally studying how GDP is determined is the *Solow model*, named after the economist Robert Solow.[5] In this appendix, we present the Solow model to show how it can be used to study the process of economic growth in greater detail. We have placed this material in the appendix rather than in the main body of the chapter because it can be skipped without interfering with the other key ideas in this chapter and elsewhere in the book.

The Three Building Blocks of the Solow Model

The Solow model consists of three building blocks. The first one is the aggregate production function, which we saw in the previous chapter. Recall that the aggregate production function, $Y = A \times F(K,H)$, links GDP to physical capital (K), total efficiency units of labor (H), and the level of technology (A). Technology includes the knowledge available to the economy and the efficiency of production and is a shifter of the aggregate production function.

The second building block is an equation for physical capital accumulation. Most of the equipment and structures making up the physical capital stock of an economy are durable. When you purchase a computer, you will be using it for several years; many household durables are typically used for much longer. Structures—buildings, roads, and bridges—last even longer. But the durability of physical capital is not infinite. Physical capital is subject to *depreciation*, meaning that any equipment or structure goes through "wear and tear" and ultimately becomes obsolete. For example, when you buy a truck and use it for a year, it will have more miles and its brakes may be worn out. As a result of this wear and tear, some of its value will have been lost, and you will get quite a bit less if you try to sell it than you paid last year. Depreciation erodes the value of physical capital, but it can be slowed or reversed by continual investment and upkeep. In the case of your truck, you could also invest in it by having the brakes, oil, or tires changed. This type of investment counterbalances depreciation and increases the value of the truck.

The same is true for the physical capital stock of the economy, as captured by the following physical capital accumulation equation:

$$K_{\text{now}} = K_{\text{last year}} - K_{\text{depreciated}} + I$$

or

$$K_{\text{now}} = K_{\text{last year}} - (\text{Depreciation rate} \times K_{\text{last year}}) + I$$

or

$$K_{\text{now}} = (1 - d) \times K_{\text{last year}} + I.$$

K_{now} is the physical capital stock this year. This directly depends on the physical capital stock last year, $K_{\text{last year}}$, specifically the fraction $1 - d$ of that physical capital stock that doesn't depreciate between the two dates. The remaining $dK_{\text{last year}}$ is the equivalent of the decline in the value of your truck. In the meantime, the firms in the economy undertake investments and purchase new machines to increase the physical capital stock of the economy, in the same way that you may have invested in new gadgets or maintenance to increase the value of your truck. In the above equation, this is represented by the investment amount I.

This equation is not only useful for the Solow growth model, but in fact is one of the key equations that economists use to compute the actual value of physical capital stock in practice, such as in national income accounts.

The third building block of the Solow model is saving by households. Recall from our discussion in the body of this chapter that investment is determined by household saving behavior. Then investment in the economy will be

$$I = s \times Y,$$

where, as you will recall, Y denotes GDP, s is the saving rate, and I is aggregate investment.

Now, using the first building block, the aggregate production function, we can write

$$I = s \times Y = s \times A \times F(K, H).$$

This relationship is drawn in Exhibit 7A.1. The red curve represents the aggregate production function, or more specifically the relationship between GDP and the physical capital stock for given levels of efficiency units of labor and technology. This shows the same shape as Exhibit 6.7 from the previous chapter. The green curve shows the relationship between the level of investment and the physical capital stock given the saving rate of households, s. It is simply given by a downward shift of the aggregate production function—because it represents GDP times the saving rate, s. By definition, therefore, the distance between the green curve and the horizontal axis at a given level of physical capital stock corresponds to aggregate saving or investment, as shown in the exhibit. Because the red curve represents GDP in the economy, as shown in the exhibit, the distance between the red and green curves represents consumption (since $Y = C + I$).

Steady-State Equilibrium in the Solow Model

A natural situation for us to study is one in which the physical capital stock last year and physical capital stock now are equal:

$$K_{\text{now}} = K_{\text{last year}} = K.$$

A **steady-state equilibrium** is an economic equilibrium in which the physical capital stock remains constant over time.

We will refer to such a situation as a **steady-state equilibrium**, which is similar to our usual notion of equilibrium with supply being equal to demand but also requires that the physical capital stock is the same between the two dates.

This equation, combined with the physical capital accumulation equation above, immediately implies that, in order for the physical capital stock to be unchanged between years, we need to have investment equal a fraction d of the physical capital stock, written as follows:

$$I = d \times K.$$

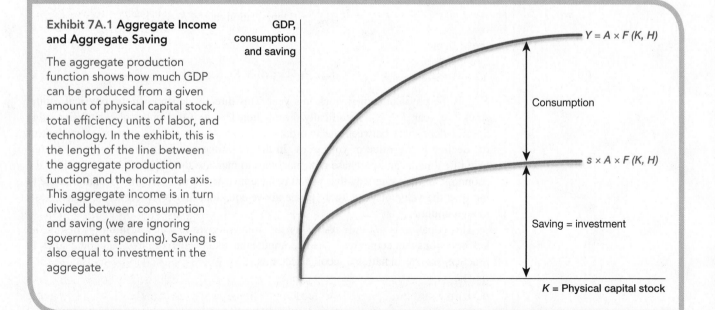

Exhibit 7A.1 Aggregate Income and Aggregate Saving

The aggregate production function shows how much GDP can be produced from a given amount of physical capital stock, total efficiency units of labor, and technology. In the exhibit, this is the length of the line between the aggregate production function and the horizontal axis. This aggregate income is in turn divided between consumption and saving (we are ignoring government spending). Saving is also equal to investment in the aggregate.

GDP, consumption and saving

$Y = A \times F(K, H)$

Consumption

$s \times A \times F(K, H)$

Saving = investment

K = Physical capital stock

Exhibit 7A.2 Steady-State Equilibrium in the Solow Model

The steady-state equilibrium in the Solow model is given as the point of intersection of the curve denoting total saving in the economy (as a function of the physical capital stock) and the line designating the amount of investment necessary to replenish depreciated physical capital. In the exhibit, the steady-state equilibrium corresponds to the physical capital stock of K^* and GDP of Y^*

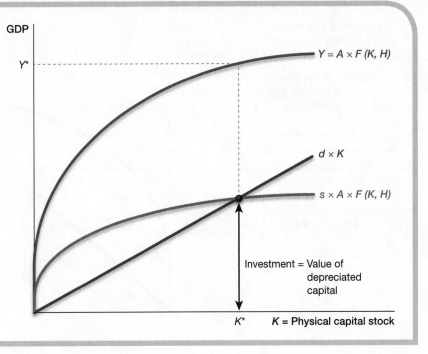

(To see how to derive this, note that in a steady state, the physical capital accumulation equation becomes $K = (1 - d) \times K + I$, and solving this for I gives the desired equation).

In other words, for the physical capital stock of the economy to remain constant over time, the amount of investment must equal the depreciated value of the physical capital stock, which is the depreciation rate of the economy, d, times the physical capital stock, K. Returning to our example above, the value of your truck will remain constant only if the new investment you put in is equal exactly to the depreciation—the reduction in the value of the truck due to wear and tear.

We now put the different ingredients of the Solow model together to determine the steady-state equilibrium. This can be done in Exhibit 7A.2 by also plotting the line representing the value of depreciated physical capital, $d \times K$. The steady-state equilibrium is given by the intersection between this blue line and the green curve (which represents the investment level implied by the saving decisions of households). This follows simply because at this point of intersection, new investment—$I = s \times A \times F(K,H)$—is equal to the value of depreciated physical capital—$d \times K$.

This exhibit shows that there is a unique point where the blue straight line intersects the green curve representing investment. This intersection is the steady-state equilibrium of the Solow model. It gives the steady-state equilibrium level of physical capital stock on the horizontal axis, marked K^*, and the steady-state equilibrium GDP level on the vertical axis, Y^*. The exhibit also shows the level of investment (saving) and the value of depreciated physical capital, which equal each other by definition in a steady-state equilibrium, as well as the level of consumption in this equilibrium.

Once we have the steady-state equilibrium of the Solow model, we can use it to study the determinants of GDP.

Determinants of GDP

Exhibit 7A.2 makes it clear that one of the key determinants of GDP is the saving rate, as we discussed in the text. The impact of a higher saving rate on the steady-state physical capital stock and GDP can be seen in Exhibit 7A.3, where we drop the curve for the aggregate production function, $A \times F(K,H)$, and simply show the investment level given by $I = s \times A \times F(K,H)$.

In this exhibit, we compare two economies that have access to the same aggregate production function and have the same population and same efficiency units of labor, but have different saving rates. The economy with the higher saving rate, $s' > s$, is depicted with the dark green curve, while the one with the lower saving rate, s, is shown with the

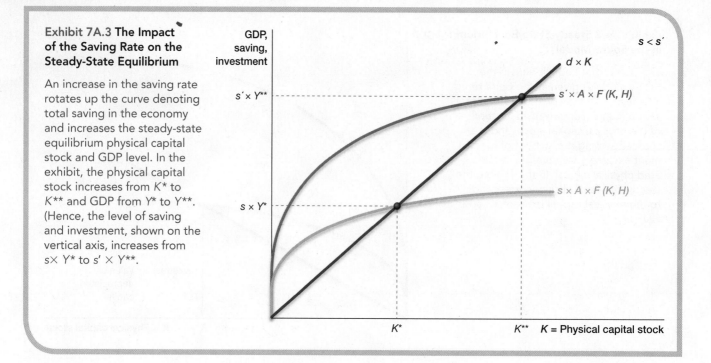

Exhibit 7A.3 The Impact of the Saving Rate on the Steady-State Equilibrium

An increase in the saving rate rotates up the curve denoting total saving in the economy and increases the steady-state equilibrium physical capital stock and GDP level. In the exhibit, the physical capital stock increases from K^* to K^{**} and GDP from Y^* to Y^{**}. (Hence, the level of saving and investment, shown on the vertical axis, increases from $s \times Y^*$ to $s' \times Y^{**}$.

light green curve. (By assumption, both economies have the same rate of depreciation, so the same line represents the value of depreciation). The exhibit shows that the economy with the higher saving rate will have a steady-state equilibrium to the right and above the original one. This corresponds to a greater physical capital stock and hence to greater GDP. Because population is kept constant in this exercise, this also translates into greater GDP per capita.

Both better technology and better human capital of workers also imply that the same amount of physical capital will translate to greater GDP. If the economy has workers that have better human capital, this will increase its efficiency units of labor, H, and given the increasing relationship between efficiency units of labor and GDP shown in Exhibit 6.8 in the previous chapter, we will have greater GDP for a given level of physical capital stock. Therefore, in terms of the relationship between GDP and the physical capital stock, greater human capital of workers implies a shift of the aggregate production function. As a result, aggregate saving shifts to the curve drawn in dark green in Exhibit 7A.4, and the steady-state equilibrium will again be to the right and above the original one, as shown in the exhibit. This implies that higher human capital leads to both higher steady-state equilibrium physical capital stock and higher GDP for the country. Because there has not been any change in the population (or working-age population), the higher GDP again translates into higher GDP per capita.

Exactly the same analysis applies to technology. Recall that better technology corresponds to higher A in terms of our aggregate production function. It can be the result of better knowledge being used in production or of greater efficiency of production. In either case, it will lead to a shift in the aggregate production function that is identical to that in Exhibit 7A.3 (except that it is now the total efficiency units of labor, not the saving rate, that is changing). Consequently, the implications are also identical. There will be a higher steady-state equilibrium level of physical capital stock and a greater steady-state equilibrium level of GDP. Because population is again constant, this will imply greater GDP per capita.

Dynamic Equilibrium in the Solow Model

The Solow model is not only useful for understanding the determinants of steady-state equilibrium but is also the main vehicle that economists use for thinking about economic growth.

As the qualifier "steady-state" hints, we can also imagine an equilibrium that is not a steady-state equilibrium. Such an equilibrium, often referred to as a **dynamic equilibrium**, traces out the behavior of the economy over time. As such, a dynamic equilibrium doesn't correspond to a single point, but to a *path* (of physical capital stock and GDP levels) that will be realized over time.

A **dynamic equilibrium** traces out the behavior of the economy over time.

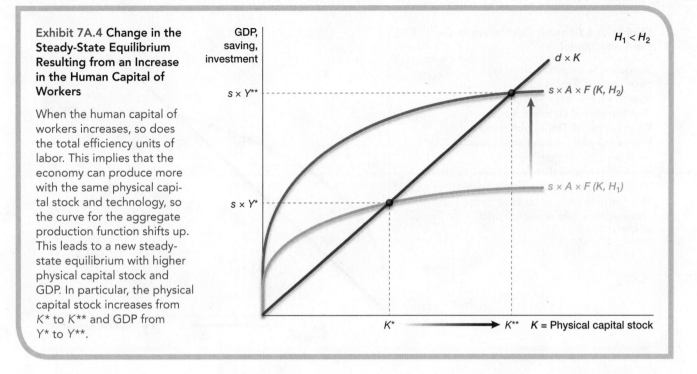

Exhibit 7A.4 Change in the Steady-State Equilibrium Resulting from an Increase in the Human Capital of Workers

When the human capital of workers increases, so does the total efficiency units of labor. This implies that the economy can produce more with the same physical capital stock and technology, so the curve for the aggregate production function shifts up. This leads to a new steady-state equilibrium with higher physical capital stock and GDP. In particular, the physical capital stock increases from K^* to K^{**} and GDP from Y^* to Y^{**}.

To understand this notion, let us look at Exhibit 7A.5, which is the same as Exhibit 7A.2 except without the curve for $A \times F(K, H)$. The steady-state equilibrium again occurs at the point where the blue straight line intersects the curve representing the investment level; thus K^* is the physical capital stock and Y^* is GDP in this steady-state equilibrium.

Now imagine that, starting from K^*, suddenly some of the physical capital in this economy is destroyed, for example, because of war. As a result, the physical capital stock of the economy is now represented by $K_0 < K^*$. Suppose also that nothing else changes; in particular, the aggregate production function, the saving rate, the efficiency units of labor, and technology all remain the same. At this point, even though just one variable has changed, we are no longer in a steady-state equilibrium because physical capital is no longer being replenished precisely at the rate at which it is depreciating.

What will the level of production in the economy be now? Because the physical capital stock is now equal to K_0 but the efficiency units of labor have not changed, GDP will continue to be given by the aggregate production function at Y_0 (and corresponds to the point marked as $s \times Y_0$ on the vertical axis in Exhibit 7A.5). However, this exhibit also makes it clear that at this new point (K_0, Y_0), the economy is above the straight line. Recall that, along this straight line, investment is just equal to the amount of depreciated physical capital. Above it, investment does not just make up for depreciated physical capital, but exceeds it. Recall now the physical capital accumulation equation, which tells us that $K_{\text{now}} = K_{\text{last year}} - K_{\text{depreciated}} + I$. This equation implies that, as investment exceeds depreciated physical capital, we have $I > K_{\text{depreciated}}$, and thus the physical capital stock will increase. Put differently, there will be a dynamic equilibrium path that takes us back toward the steady-state equilibrium at K^*. The dynamic equilibrium path is shown in Exhibit 7A.5 by the green arrows. It starts at (K_0, Y_0) and traces out the path of the economy toward (K^*, Y^*). This highlights both the fact that a dynamic equilibrium corresponds to a path showing the behavior of the economy over time and also the key result that such a dynamic equilibrium will take the economy back toward the steady-state equilibrium (K^*, Y^*).

Sources of Growth in the Solow Model

We can now use the Solow model to return to the discussion of sustained growth in the text. First, Exhibit 7A.6 demonstrates that increases in the saving rate and physical capital accumulation cannot be the source of sustained growth. It shows that, with given levels of total efficiency units of labor and technology, there is a maximum amount of

Exhibit 7A.5 Dynamic Equilibrium in the Solow Model

Suppose the economy starts with a physical capital stock of $K_0 < K^*$, that is, with a physical capital stock less than the steady-state equilibrium. What happens? The exhibit shows that at this point, saving and investment are greater than the amount of physical capital that depreciates, so the physical capital stock increases. This dynamic process takes us to the steady-state physical capital stock of K^*.

Exhibit 7A.6 Three Economies with Different Saving Rates in the Solow Model

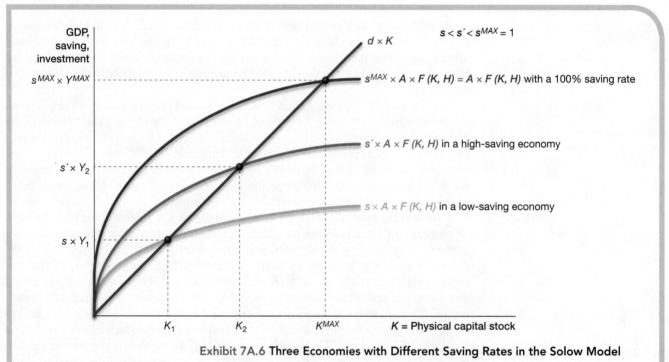

Economies with higher saving rates have higher GDP, but increases in the saving rate cannot be the source of sustained growth. This is because there is a maximum to how much an economy can save and thus a limit to what GDP it can achieve by just saving more.

GDP that an economy can achieve by increasing saving, since we can never go above a saving rate of 100 percent. This determines the level of GDP, Y^{MAX}, beyond which the economy cannot expand with a given aggregate production function and total efficiency units of labor.

The presence of such a maximal level of GDP, Y^{MAX}, implies that sustained growth is not possible by just increasing saving. To see this, note that if an economy grows at a constant

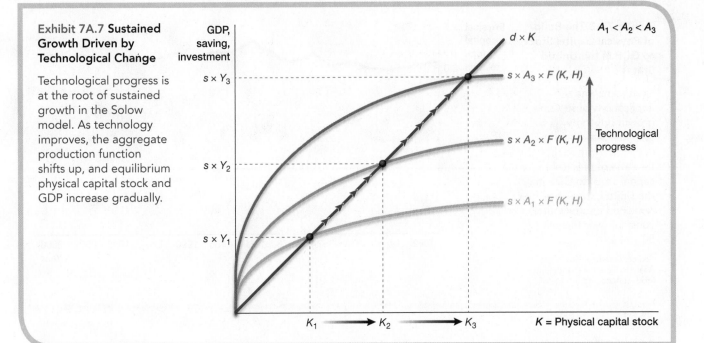

Exhibit 7A.7 Sustained Growth Driven by Technological Change

Technological progress is at the root of sustained growth in the Solow model. As technology improves, the aggregate production function shifts up, and equilibrium physical capital stock and GDP increase gradually.

rate, such as 2 percent per year, it will eventually reach and exceed any fixed level of GDP, such as Y^{MAX}. This is consistent with historical evidence. Over the past 200 years, countries have not achieved steady growth by simply increasing their saving rates. Overall, this discussion and Exhibit 7A.6 show that *increases in the saving rate can increase GDP, but they cannot generate sustained growth.*

To show how technological improvements can lead to sustained growth in the Solow model, Exhibit 7A.7 revisits our by-now familiar figure for the determination of the steady-state equilibrium. It shows that as technology improves, the aggregate production function (and consequently the investment curve) shifts up. This raises the equilibrium levels of physical capital stock and GDP.

Notably, these improvements take place along the straight line of the steady state as shown in the exhibit. Recall that the straight line is given by the equation $d \times K$ and does not shift as a result of technological improvements.

At each point of intersection, we have $s \times Y = d \times K$. Rewriting this gives $K/Y = s/d$, which thus implies that throughout there is a constant ratio of the physical capital stock to GDP. Therefore, the implication of the Solow model for sustained growth is that the *ratio of the physical capital stock to GDP should be constant as the economy grows.*

Exhibit 7A.8 plots the historical evolution of the value of the physical capital stock to GDP in the U.S. economy. The ratio of the physical capital stock to GDP is roughly constant over the last 50 years, with a value of about 2. This pattern is consistent with the implication of the Solow model based on sustained growth driven by technological improvements, which, as we just saw, also implies a constant ratio of physical capital stock to GDP as the economy grows.

What about catch-up growth? In contrast to sustained growth, catch-up growth can result both from the accumulation of physical capital and human capital and from technological change. The nature of catch-up growth can be illustrated by the dynamic equilibrium path of an economy starting with a level of physical capital stock such as K_0 below its steady-state equilibrium K^*, as depicted in Exhibit 7A.5. This dynamic equilibrium path represents the growth trajectory of an economy that is temporarily below its steady-state equilibrium or improves its technology and thus raises its steady-state equilibrium level of physical capital stock and GDP. This exhibit thus shows that, typically, such an economy will rapidly grow toward its steady-state equilibrium. Such rapid growth is a hallmark of the catch-up process as shown by the experiences of several countries depicted in Exhibits 7.4, 7.5, and 7.8.

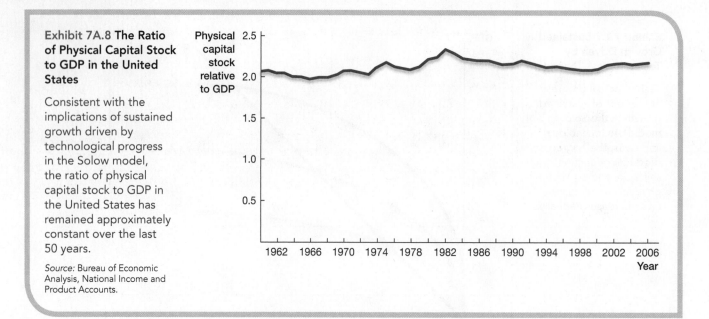

Exhibit 7A.8 The Ratio of Physical Capital Stock to GDP in the United States

Consistent with the implications of sustained growth driven by technological progress in the Solow model, the ratio of physical capital stock to GDP in the United States has remained approximately constant over the last 50 years.

Source: Bureau of Economic Analysis, National Income and Product Accounts.

Calculating Average (Compound) Growth Rates

Now let's discuss how to calculate average growth rates by returning to Exhibit 7.4. Consider the United States. Its GDP per capita was $15,398 in 1960 and $41,365 in 2010 (in PPP-adjusted 2005 constant dollars). We can now compute the 50-year growth rate (between 1960 and 2010) as 168.64 percent, using the formula provided in the text. In particular, this number is obtained as

$$\frac{41{,}365 - 15{,}398}{15{,}398} = 1.6864,$$

corresponding to 168.64 percent growth.

One way of computing the average growth rate is to use the arithmetic average and divide this number by 50 to obtain the average annual growth rate. This would give an annual growth rate of 3.4 percent. The number in Exhibit 7.4 is different—2.00 percent. How is this number obtained, and why is it different?

The answer to this question is related to the importance of the exponential nature of growth, which we discussed earlier in the chapter. Suppose that an economy grows at the rate of $g = 0.034$ (that is, 3.4 percent) every year for 50 years. How much will its GDP per capita have gone up at the end of the 50 years? To compute this, we have to note that after one year its GDP per capita will have increased by $1 + g$. From the second to the third year, it will increase by another $1 + g$, so between the first and third years, it will have gone up by $(1 + g)^2$. Continuing with this reasoning, at the end of 50 years, its GDP per capita will have increased by $(1 + g)^{50}$. If we take $g = 0.034$, we find that its GDP per capita will be 5.32 times higher at the end of the 50 years, which is considerably greater than the numbers for the United States. Instead, these numbers imply that at the end of the 50 years, U.S. GDP per capita was about 2.6864 times higher. (This number can be obtained simply as 41,365/15,398 = 2.6864, that is, GDP per capita in 2010 divided by GDP per capita in 1960, or you can note that it is 1 + 1.6864, where 168.64 percent was the growth rate of the U.S. economy between 1960 and 2010.)

By dividing the total growth between 1960 and 2010 by 50, we have ignored the cumulative effects of growth and overestimated the annual growth rate that would lead to the observed increase in GDP per capita.

This discussion also indicates that a more sophisticated way of computing the average annual growth rate is by using the geometric average. In this case, we would calculate the growth rate as

$$(1 + g)^{50} = 2.6864.$$

We can then use this equation to arrive at the correct average annual growth rate, g. (More technically, we would invert this equation and compute $g = 2.6864^{1/50} - 1$.) This approximately gives the (average) annual growth rate as $g = 0.020$, as recorded in the exhibit. In most cases, using either the arithmetic or the geometric average to compute average growth rates gives similar answers, provided that we are looking at short periods. The reason why there is a sizable difference in this case is because we are considering a long period of time.

Appendix Key Terms

steady-state equilibrium *p. 164*   dynamic equilibrium *p. 166*

Appendix Problems

All problems are available in MyEconLab *for practice and instructor assignment.*
Problems marked 🌐 *update with real-time data.*

A1. Use a diagram to represent the Solow growth model using the aggregate production function and the relationship between the physical capital stock and aggregate saving.

    a. Which point in the figure represents the steady-state equilibrium? Why?

    b. Use the diagram to show the impact of an increase in human capital on GDP.

A2. In the 1980s, the saving rate in Japan was extremely high. Gross savings as a percentage of GDP ranged between 30 and 32%. Can such a high saving rate lead to sustained economic growth? Use the Solow model to explain your answer.

    Data source: http://data.worldbank.org/indicator/NY.GNS .ICTR.ZS/countries/JP?page=5&display=default

🌐 **A3.** India's GDP per capita increased from $310 in 1991 to $1,489 in 2012.

    Data source: http://data.worldbank.org/indicator/NY.GDP .PCAP.CD

    a. Calculate the arithmetic average annual rate of growth of the Indian economy during this period using the arithmetic average.

    b. Calculate the geometric average annual growth rate of India during this period. How does the number you find differ from the number given in Exhibit 7.3? Speculate on what accounts for any difference.

A4. The appendix details the important distinction between arithmetic and geometric averages in determining growth rates.

    a. Using the procedure outlined in the Appendix for *geometric* average growth rates (in the section titled "Calculating Average (Compound) Growth Rates," see if you can reproduce the "Implied (average) annual growth" figures given in the last column of Exhibit 7.4 for the following countries: France, Singapore, Botswana, India and Kenya.

    b. Using the procedure outlined in the Appendix for finding *arithmetic* average growth rates, calculate the arithmetic average growth rate for the five countries. Compare these with the rates you obtained in part a. Does the arithmetic average understate or overstate the actual growth rate? Explain.

Why Isn't the Whole World Developed?

Are tropical and semitropical areas condemned to poverty by their geographies?

If you look back at the map of GDP per capita of the world shown in Exhibit 6.2 in Chapter 6, you will notice a striking regularity: many of the poorest nations are close to the equator in the tropical and semitropical areas of the world. Conversely, countries in the temperate areas away from the equator are much more prosperous. The Democratic Republic of Congo, for example, is cut in the middle by the equator. In 2010, its GDP per capita adjusted for purchasing power was $241 (in 2005 constant dollars). Move up along the map all the way to the sixtieth parallel, and you will find Finland. In that same year, its GDP per capita was $32,989 (in 2005 constant dollars). You can do the same exercise for almost all countries around the equator. Move up the line of longitude to find the corresponding countries at the fortieth, fiftieth, or sixtieth parallels, and almost always you will see that the ones further away from the equator are considerably richer than the ones nearest it. This pattern has led many social scientists to conjecture that there is something particularly pernicious about the economic and

CHAPTER **OUTLINE**

- Proximate causes of prosperity link prosperity and poverty of nations to the levels of inputs, while fundamental causes look for reasons why there are such differences in the levels of inputs.

- The geography, culture, and institutions hypotheses advance different fundamental causes of prosperity.

- Inclusive and extractive economic institutions affect economic development.

- Creative destruction is integral to economic growth through technological change.

- Reversal of fortune evidence provides support for the institutions hypothesis.

social conditions in the areas around the equator. Many have gone so far as to assert that tropical and semitropical areas condemn a nation to poverty.

Can this be true? Can geography determine a nation's prosperity? By the end of this chapter, we provide some answers to this intriguing question. We'll also have developed a much better understanding of why the whole world isn't developed, and why there are wide disparities in GDP per capita across countries.

8.1 Proximate Versus Fundamental Causes of Prosperity

In Chapter 6, we documented the huge differences in GDP per capita and living standards across countries. You may recall the huge gap in GDP per capita between the United States and the Democratic Republic of Congo, Ghana, or Haiti. In that chapter, we emphasized how these gaps can be explained in terms of cross-country differences in physical capital, human capital, and technology.

Yet an explanation based on these causes alone immediately begs the question of why some countries have accumulated more physical capital, invested more in human capital, and developed and adopted better technologies than other countries. After all, if investing in physical and human capital and adopting cutting-edge technologies can lead to major improvements in GDP, wouldn't all countries in the world wish to do so? Why isn't the whole world as developed as the United States or West European nations?

Proximate causes of prosperity are high levels of factors such as human capital, physical capital, and technology that result in a high level of GDP per capita.

These deeper questions make us realize that differences in physical capital, human capital, and technology are only *proximate causes* of economic performance. We call them **proximate causes of prosperity** because they link high levels of prosperity to high levels of the inputs to production, but without providing an explanation for why the levels of those inputs are high.

To get at the reasons why some countries are either unable or unwilling to invest in different amounts of physical capital, human capital, and technology, we have to dig deeper. Causation can be complex, as we discussed in Chapter 2. We sometimes have to see what lies beneath the surface to understand the true causes of an observed phenomenon. We refer to these underlying factors as the **fundamental causes of prosperity**, which are defined as those causes that are at the root of the differences in the proximate causes of prosperity. The relationship between the fundamental and the proximate causes of prosperity is shown in Exhibit 8.1.

Fundamental causes of prosperity are factors that are at the root of the differences in the proximate causes of prosperity.

Exhibit 8.1 Fundamental and Proximate Causes of Prosperity

Societies become prosperous when they have abundant human and physical capital and use advanced technology efficiently in production. But these are proximate causes because they are in turn shaped by other, deeper factors. Fundamental causes, such as geographic, cultural, and institutional factors, have an impact on prosperity by affecting proximate causes such as investment in human capital, physical capital, and technology.

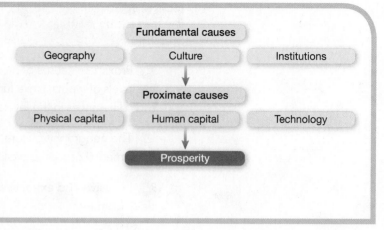

To see the distinction between proximate and fundamental causes more clearly, it is useful to consider an analogy. Say you are experiencing some symptoms of flu—sore throat, fever, and headache—that might motivate you to take drugs, such as throat decongestants or aspirin. In this example, the proximate cause of why you take these drugs is that you have a sore throat, a high fever, and a headache. But the fundamental cause—the reason why you have the symptoms in the first place—is that you have the flu. The flu thus induces both the symptoms and your response of taking drugs. Similarly, if a country underinvests in human capital, physical capital, and/or technology, we should ask why. Both proximate and fundamental causes have to be considered for a complete understanding of why some nations are prosperous and others aren't.

Although there are many different theories about the fundamental causes of poverty and prosperity—theories about why poorer nations around the world have worse technologies and do not invest in physical and human capital as much as rich ones—it is useful to classify them into three categories: theories of geography, culture, and institutions. We next describe these hypotheses and then discuss whether they are consistent with empirical evidence.

Geography

The **geography hypothesis** claims that differences in geography, climate, and ecology are ultimately responsible for the major differences in prosperity observed across the world.

One approach, which we will refer to as the **geography hypothesis**, claims that differences in geography, climate, and ecology ultimately determine the large differences in prosperity across the world. According to this hypothesis, some countries have highly unfavorable geographical, climactic, or ecological circumstances that are outside of their control. Some are situated in areas where much of the soil may be inhospitable for agriculture, daytime temperatures are very high, or a lack of navigable rivers makes transport prohibitively costly. These conditions, some argue, make it impossible or unlikely for such countries to accumulate or effectively use the factors of production.

Many leading thinkers throughout the ages have advocated the geography hypothesis. One of its great proponents was the famous French philosopher Montesquieu, who argued that climate was a key determinant of work effort and thus prosperity.[1] He wrote:

> The heat of the climate can be so excessive that the body there will be absolutely without strength. So, prostration will pass even to the spirit; no curiosity, no noble enterprise, no generous sentiment; inclinations will all be passive there; laziness there will be happiness. . . . People are . . . more vigorous in cold climates. The inhabitants of warm countries are, like old men, timorous; the people in cold countries are, like young men, brave.

Another major proponent of this view was Alfred Marshall, who was the first economist to write a book (just like ours) aimed at making the principles of economics accessible to a broad population of students.[2] He stated:

> Vigor depends partly on race qualities: but these, so far as they can be explained at all, seem to be chiefly due to climate.

These views emphasizing the effect of climate on work effort and vigor are outdated (and sometimes tinged with racist overtones). But other versions of the geography hypothesis are still popular. Today, many believe that geographic characteristics determine the technology available to a society, especially in agriculture. The economist Jeffrey Sachs has been a strong proponent of this view in his academic writings.[3] Using it as the basis of his influential policy recommendations to the United Nations and the World Health Organization, Sachs, for example, argues:

> By the start of the era of modern economic growth, if not much earlier, temperate-zone technologies were more productive than tropical-zone technologies. . . .

Jeffrey Sachs and others also argue that many parts of the world, particularly sub-Saharan Africa, are disadvantaged economically because infectious diseases, such as malaria and dengue fever, spread there more easily. When it is serious and widespread, an illness can indeed destroy a large amount of a country's human capital.

> **If geography is the major fundamental cause of prosperity (or its absence), then the poor nations of the world have little reason to expect much improvement in living standards.**

If geography is the major fundamental cause of prosperity (or its absence), then the poor nations of the world have little reason to expect much improvement in living standards. They are permanently disadvantaged, and we should not expect them to catch up with the rest of the world and become economically developed anytime soon—or so the thinking goes.

Not all variations of the geography hypothesis are equally pessimistic. In some, large-scale investments in transport technology or disease eradication may partially redress these geographic disadvantages.

Culture

The **culture hypothesis** claims that different values and cultural beliefs fundamentally cause the differences in prosperity around the world.

Another potential fundamental cause of differences in economic performance has to do with cultural differences. According to the **culture hypothesis**, different societies respond differently to incentives because of specific shared experiences, religious teachings, the strength of family ties, or unspoken social norms. Culture is viewed as a key determinant of the values, preferences, and beliefs of individuals and societies and, the argument goes, these differences play a key role in shaping economic performance. For example, some societies may have values that encourage investment, hard work, and the adoption of new technologies, while others may nurture superstition and suspicion of new technologies and discourage hard work.

The most famous link between culture and economic development was proposed by the German sociologist Max Weber, who argued that the origins of industrialization in Western Europe could be traced to Protestantism.[4] In his view, the Protestant worldview was crucial to the development of a market economy and economic growth because it encouraged hard work and saving (and thus investment).

Another common version of the culture hypothesis contrasts the Anglo-Saxon culture of the United States and the United Kingdom, which is viewed as conducive to investment and the adoption of technology, with the supposedly less dynamic and more closed-minded Iberian culture of peoples with Spanish and Portuguese origins. Many social scientists have attempted to explain the contrast between North and South America in these terms.

Almost 20 years ago, the Harvard political scientist Samuel Huntington coined the term "clash of civilizations" to capture what he thought would be the defining conflict of the twenty-first century—the conflict between the West and Islam.[5] More broadly, Huntington has supported the view that culture plays a central role in shaping prosperity. For example, his explanation for why South Korea grew rapidly in the twentieth century and Ghana did not summarizes his overall approach:[6]

> Culture had to be a large part of the explanation. South Koreans valued thrift, investment, hard work, education, organization, and discipline. Ghanaians had different values.

Of course, a society's culture is not immutable: cultures change, though they do so slowly.

Institutions

Institutions are the formal and informal rules governing the organization of a society, including its laws and regulations.

A third potential fundamental cause for the differences in prosperity involves **institutions**, the formal and informal rules governing the organization of a society, including its laws and regulations. For example, economic historian Douglass North, who was awarded the Nobel

Prize in economics largely because of his work emphasizing the importance of institutions in the historical development process, offers the following definition of institutions:[7]

> Institutions are the rules of the game in a society or, more formally, are the humanly devised constraints that shape human interaction.

This definition captures three important elements that define institutions:

1. They are determined by individuals as members of a society.
2. They place constraints on behavior.
3. They shape behavior by determining incentives.

First, institutions are "humanly devised." In contrast to geography, which is largely outside of human control, and culture, which changes very slowly, institutions are determined by man-made factors. That is, institutions do not just appear out of thin air, but develop due to the choices members of a society make over how to organize their interactions.

Second, institutions place constraints on individual behavior. On the positive side, institutions constrain the ability of an individual to steal from others or to walk away from debts that he has built up. On the negative side, they might prevent people from entering into occupations or opening new businesses. Such constraints need not be absolute. Individuals around the world break laws and skirt regulations every day. For example, Apple did not own a license to sell iPads in Taiwan in 2010, so selling the device was illegal. Through online auctions, however, people were able to purchase iPad *cases* for more than $1,000, which happened to include a "free" iPad.[8]

Policies, regulations, and laws that punish or reward certain types of behavior will naturally have an effect on behavior. Though some citizens can circumvent a law that bans, for example, the adoption of certain technologies, such a law still discourages their adoption.

This observation leads us to the third important element in North's definition—institutions affect incentives. The constraints that institutions place on individuals—whether formal constraints such as banning certain activities or informal ones discouraging certain types of behavior through customs and social norms—shape human interaction and affect incentives. In some sense, institutions, much more than the other candidate fundamental causes, are about the importance of incentives.

The **institutions hypothesis** maintains that the differences in the way that humans have chosen to organize their societies—differences that shape the incentives that individuals and businesses in the society face—are at the root of the differences in their relative prosperity. For example, when markets allocate individuals to the occupations in which their productivity is highest, laws and regulations encourage firms to invest in physical capital and technology and the educational system enables and encourages people to invest in their human capital, the economy will generate higher GDP and achieve greater prosperity than when its institutions fail to do so.

To sum up, the institutions hypothesis relies on the following chain of reasoning:

1. Different societies typically have different institutions.
2. These different institutions create different types of incentives.
3. The incentives help determine the degree to which societies accumulate the factors of production and adopt new technology.

The idea that the prosperity of a society depends on its institutions is not a new one. It goes back at least to Adam Smith, the father of economics, who, in *The Wealth of Nations*, emphasized the importance of markets in generating prosperity through the workings of the invisible hand and warned how constraints on markets—for example, in the form of restrictions on trade—could destroy such prosperity.[9]

A Natural Experiment of History

The Korean peninsula is divided in two by the thirty-eighth parallel. To the south is the Republic of Korea, also known as South Korea. We saw in Chapter 7 how South Korea has had one of the fastest-growing economies in the last 60 years and has by now achieved living standards comparable to many countries in Europe.

To the north of the thirty-eighth parallel there is another Korea: the Democratic People's Republic of Korea, or simply North Korea. Living standards in North Korea are similar to those in a sub-Saharan African country. The best estimate suggests that in 2010 GDP per capita (in PPP-adjusted 2005 constant dollars) was $1,612 in the North, making its

The **institutions hypothesis** claims that differences in institutions—that is, in the way societies have organized themselves and shaped the incentives of individuals and businesses—are at the root of the differences in prosperity across the world.

inhabitants worse off than the citizens of Sudan or Yemen. In contrast, in that same year GDP per capita (in PPP-adjusted 2005 constant dollars) in the South was $26,609. What explains these large differences? Could it be geography? Culture? Highly unlikely. The North and South share the same geography, essentially the same climate, the same access to the ocean, and the same disease environments. There are also no noticeable differences between their cultures, certainly not before 1947 when the country was split into two. Korea was at that point an unusually homogeneous country, both ethnically and culturally. If we were to believe that geography or culture were important factors in determining South Korea's economic development after 1947, we would then expect a similar process of economic development in North Korea. Nothing of the sort happened.

In fact, the great disparities between the two nations did not exist before World War II when the two parts of Korea were united. They emerged only when the two were separated and adopted very different institutions.

The separation of Korea into two halves was not something to which its citizens willingly agreed. It was an outcome of a geopolitical deal between the Soviet Union and the United States, who agreed at the end of World War II that the thirty-eighth parallel would be the dividing line for their spheres of influence in Korea and set up different governments in the North and the South.

These governments adopted very different ways of organizing their economies. In North Korea, Kim Il-Sung, a leader of anti-Japanese communist partisans during World War II, established himself as dictator. With the help of the Soviet Union, Kim Il-Sung introduced a rigid form of communism, the *Juche* system. Resources in North Korea were allocated through central planning, private property was outlawed, and markets were banned. Freedoms were curtailed not only in the marketplace but also in every sphere of North Koreans' lives—except for those that happened to be part of the very small ruling elite around Kim Il-Sung. This cronyism persisted under his son Kim Jong-Il, who ruled until his death in 2011, and continues today under Kim Il-Sung's grandson, Kim Jong-Un.

> **If institutions are a major determinant of economic prosperity, then the sharply divergent institutions of the two Koreas should have led to divergent economic fortunes. And that's exactly what happened.**

In the South, institutions were shaped by the Harvard- and Princeton-educated, staunchly anti-communist Syngman Rhee, with significant support from the United States. Though Rhee and his successor, General Park Chung-hee, were autocrats, they supported a market-based economy, providing incentives to businesses for investment and industrialization and investing in the education of South Koreans. South Korea did eventually become democratic in the 1990s and further liberalized its economy.

If institutions are a major determinant of economic prosperity, then the sharply divergent institutions of the two Koreas should have led to divergent economic fortunes. And that's exactly what happened. Exhibit 8.2 shows how GDP per capita in North and

Exhibit 8.2 GDP per Capita in North and South Korea (in PPP-adjusted 2005 Constant Dollars)

The economic fortunes of North and South Korea, starting from parity in the 1940s when they were united, have diverged sharply. South Korea, with institutions mostly based on a market economy, has reached a high level of GDP per capita. In contrast, North Korea, under a communist dictatorship, has failed to grow and has less than 1/16th of the level of the GDP per capita of the South.

Source: Data from Maddison Project (1820–2010); J. Bolt and J. L. van Zanden, "The First Update of the Maddison Project; Re-Estimating Growth Before 1820." Maddison Project Working Paper 4 (2013).

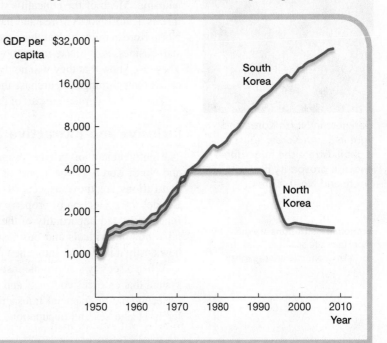

South Korea has sharply diverged over the last 60 years to arrive at the great disparities that we observe today.

The Korean case depicts what we often call a natural experiment or an experiment of history. A country was split in half by a military outcome. The two newly formed, culturally identical, and geographically similar countries proceeded to develop very different institutions. While the South remained a market economy, the North adopted a very rigid form of communist rule with little room for markets, private property, or entrepreneurship. The reason this episode approximates a natural experiment is that while institutions were changing in this radical way, geography and culture remained largely unchanged. It was the changes in institutions that led to massive changes in economic prosperity, as shown in Exhibit 8.2. The Korean example thus provides strong support for the institutions hypothesis (but it does not provide direct evidence against geography and culture because these were held fixed in this comparison).

8.2 Institutions and Economic Development

Teenagers in South Korea grow up just like us. Many obtain a good education, and face incentives that encourage them to exert effort and excel in their chosen vocation. South Korea is a market economy. South Korean teenagers know that, if successful, one day they can enjoy the fruits of their investments and efforts. They can buy computers, clothes, cars, houses, and healthcare. They can start businesses and bequeath their property to their offspring.

This is in large part because the South has well-enforced **private property rights**, meaning that its citizens can hold property like businesses, houses, cars, and many other things without fearing that the government or anyone else will arbitrarily take it away. Just as in the United States, if you own a business in South Korea, you know that the income it generates is yours, other than the taxes you pay, which are often used to provide public goods and services valued by the citizens of the country. Your property is well protected because the state upholds law and order, and if you write business contracts, the courts enforce them. It is possible for entrepreneurs to borrow money from banks and financial markets, for foreign companies to enter into partnerships with South Korean firms, and for individuals to obtain mortgages to buy houses.

Teenagers in North Korea face vastly different lives from those in the South. They grow up in poverty, without high-quality education to prepare them for skilled work or entrepreneurship. Much of the education they receive at school is pure propaganda about foreign threats against North Korea and the benevolent leadership of their supreme leader and the North Korean military. But these teenagers know that they will not be able to own property, start businesses, or make much money because there is no private property in North Korea. They also know that they will not have access to markets where they can deploy their skills or use their earnings to purchase the goods that they need and desire.

These different rules are part of the institutions under which North and South Koreans live.

Private property rights mean that individuals can own businesses and assets and their ownership is secure.

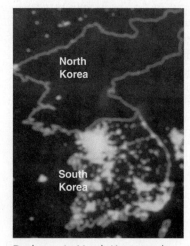

Darkness in North Korea and light in South Korea: lights at night illustrate the huge differences in prosperity between South and North Korea.

Economic institutions are the aspects of the society's rules that concern economic transactions.

Inclusive and Extractive Economic Institutions

The enforcement of private property rights, which differs so sharply between South and North Korea, is one aspect of what we refer to as economic institutions. **Economic institutions** are those aspects of a society's rules that concern economic transactions. Besides the protection of property rights, economic institutions include such things as the functioning and impartiality of the judicial system, the financial arrangements that determine how individuals and businesses can borrow money, and the regulations that shape how costly it is to enter into a new line of business or a new occupation.

When a society's economic institutions provide secure property rights, set up a judicial system that enforces contracts and upholds the law, allow private parties to sign contracts for economic or financial transactions, maintain relatively open and free entry into different businesses and occupations, and enable people to acquire the education and skills

Inclusive economic institutions protect private property, uphold law and order, allow and enforce private contracts, and allow free entry into new lines of business and occupations.

to take part in such businesses and occupations, we say that they are **inclusive economic institutions**. The economic institutions in South Korea approximate these types of inclusive economic institutions. They are inclusive in the sense that they encourage the participation of the great majority of the population in economic activities in a way that best makes use of their talents and skills.

As we have seen, inclusive economic institutions do *not* describe the situation in North Korea. Economic institutions to the north of the thirty-eighth parallel fail to enforce property rights or contracts, erect prohibitive entry barriers, and all but destroy the workings of the markets. We refer to such arrangements as **extractive economic institutions**. This terminology stems from the fact that such institutions are often shaped by those who control political power to *extract resources from the rest of the society*. Extractive economic institutions are not just associated with communist North Korea. Societies ruled by monarchs, dictators, and juntas as well as several that hold elections for their parliaments and presidents have had, and still have, extractive economic institutions. In fact, most societies throughout history have had economic institutions that are closer to the extreme extractive economic institutions of North Korea than to the ideal of inclusive economic institutions we have defined here.

Extractive economic institutions do not protect private property rights, do not uphold contracts, and interfere with the workings of markets. They also erect significant entry barriers into businesses and occupations.

Examples of market economics that have extractive economic institutions include former Soviet republics, such as Azerbaijan, Turkmenistan and Uzbekistan, Myanmar, and Pakistan in Asia, Argentina, Guatemala, and Peru in Latin America, and the Democratic Republic of Congo, Egypt, and Kenya in Africa. Even if the specific forms of these institutions differ from the extreme form of central planning in North Korea, they share the fact that they fail to enforce property rights and instead privilege a few at the expense of the many.

Extractive economic institutions do not exist in a vacuum. It is no accident that North Korea is a repressive dictatorship. Without the political elite's tight control of the state, North Korea would not be able to maintain a system that condemns tens of millions to poverty. This meshing of political and economic power underscores the important role of **political institutions**, which determine who holds political power and what types of constraints exist on the exercise of that power. Extractive economic institutions tend to be supported by certain types of political institutions, which concentrate political power in the hands of the political elite and put little constraint on how political power can be used. Similarly, inclusive economic institutions tend to coexist with different types of political institutions, which tend to distribute political power more equally in society so that no single individual or group is able to use that political power for its own benefit at the expense of the rest of society.

Political institutions are the aspects of the society's rules that concern the allocation of political power and the constraints on the exercise of political power.

How Economic Institutions Affect Economic Outcomes

The contrast between South Korea and North Korea, and between Austria and Czechoslovakia discussed in the next Letting the Data Speak box, illustrates a general principle: *inclusive economic institutions foster economic activity, productivity growth, and economic prosperity, while extractive economic institutions generally fail to do so.*[10] Property rights are central to this principle because only those who have secure property rights will be willing to invest and increase productivity. A farmer who expects his output to be expropriated—meaning stolen, taken away, or entirely taxed away—will have little incentive to work, let alone any incentive to undertake investments and innovations. Extractive economic institutions distort incentives in exactly this fashion. Farmers, traders, businessmen, and workers will be discouraged from investing and producing when they have no property rights. On top of that, firms will not be able to form the trust-based relationships that are necessary to productively do business when private contracts are worth little more than the paper they are written on or when some contractual agreements are banned outright. Finally, because they erect market entry barriers rather

Heck. I thought you were kidding. I guess you really do want democracy.

Divergence and Convergence in Eastern Europe

Between 1948 and 1989, citizens of Central and Eastern European countries, just like those of North Korea, lived under a communist dictatorship. Large, state-owned enterprises were the norm in these economies. These firms did not compete in the market but instead worked toward arbitrary targets set by Communist Party officials (which they almost always failed to meet). As a consequence, shortages of food and consumer goods were common. In a market economy, companies that fail to motivate workers, produce goods of reasonable quality, or meet their production targets are ultimately driven out of the market. But state-owned enterprises under communism did not have to worry about competition or about being driven out of the market, because there was no competition, and it was the state that set prices and footed the bill if these enterprises lost money.

In 1948, Austria and Czechoslovakia, two neighbors in central Europe, each had GDP per capita of about $4,000. But in Czechoslovakia, farms were subsequently taken forcibly from their owners and collectivized, a command economy was established, and political freedoms that existed before World War II were abolished. In Austria, a market system, along with economic institutions much more inclusive than those in communist Eastern Europe, flourished. The consequences were similar to what we have seen in the case of North and South Korea. Not surprisingly, Czechoslovakia kept falling behind its neighbor, Austria, for 40 years.

The two countries, which had very similar histories, geographies, and cultures, had achieved vastly different levels of prosperity by 1989 when the communist regime finally collapsed. Those Central and Eastern European societies that had been under communist rule transitioned to democracy and a market economy, became more inclusive, and started to grow rapidly as the share of the private sector in the economy increased from 5 percent to 80 percent. Exhibit 8.3 shows the divergence between Austria and Czechoslovakia during the communist period and the convergence that started after Czechoslovakia transitioned to a market economy in the 1990s.

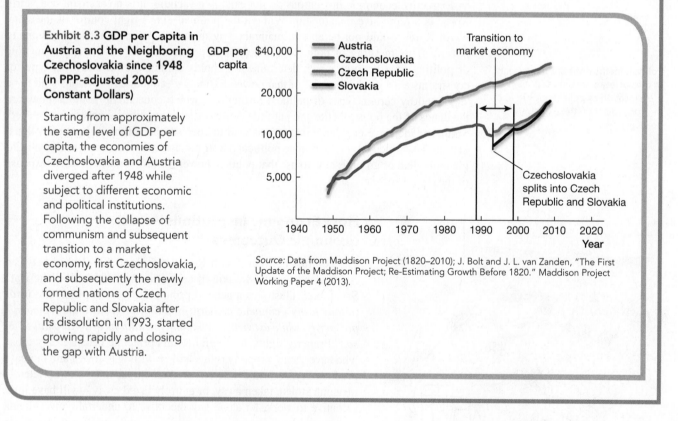

Exhibit 8.3 GDP per Capita in Austria and the Neighboring Czechoslovakia since 1948 (in PPP-adjusted 2005 Constant Dollars)

Starting from approximately the same level of GDP per capita, the economies of Czechoslovakia and Austria diverged after 1948 while subject to different economic and political institutions. Following the collapse of communism and subsequent transition to a market economy, first Czechoslovakia, and subsequently the newly formed nations of Czech Republic and Slovakia after its dissolution in 1993, started growing rapidly and closing the gap with Austria.

Source: Data from Maddison Project (1820–2010); J. Bolt and J. L. van Zanden, "The First Update of the Maddison Project; Re-Estimating Growth Before 1820." Maddison Project Working Paper 4 (2013).

than create an environment that would encourage entry, extractive economic institutions tend to support inefficient firms and prevent entrepreneurs with new ideas from entering into the right lines of business and workers from working in occupations to which their skills are best suited.

Exhibit 8.4 is helpful for illustrating why extractive economic institutions discourage economic activity. There, in a hypothetical economy, we rank potential entrepreneurs in descending order according to the return they will make if they enter and start a business.

Exhibit 8.4 How Extractive Economic Institutions Reduce the Number of Entrepreneurs

Panel (a): The return-to-entrepreneurship curve shows the number of entrepreneurs with at least the return indicated on the vertical axis. It is obtained by ranking potential entrepreneurs from higher to lower return to entrepreneurship. The opportunity cost schedule indicates the value to a potential entrepreneur of her best alternate activity. The intersection of the two curves gives the equilibrium number of entrepreneurs. For example, in panel (a), all potential entrepreneurs with return greater than or equal to $50,000 choose entrepreneurship.

Panel (b): Extractive economic institutions shift the return-to-entrepreneurship curve to the left, as shown in panel (b). Two reasons this shift might occur are the following: first, weak property rights prevent entrepreneurs from capturing their full returns, and second, with a lack of legal backup, entrepreneurs cannot easily form reliable contracts with business partners, which can reduce profitability by making supplies more expensive and revenues more precarious.

Panel (c): Extractive economic institutions also shift the opportunity cost schedule upward because they erect entry barriers that make entry into entrepreneurship more expensive. Panel (c) shows the overall impact of extractive economic institutions on the equilibrium number of entrepreneurs resulting from a leftward shift of the return-to-entrepreneurship schedule and an upward shift of the opportunity cost schedule.

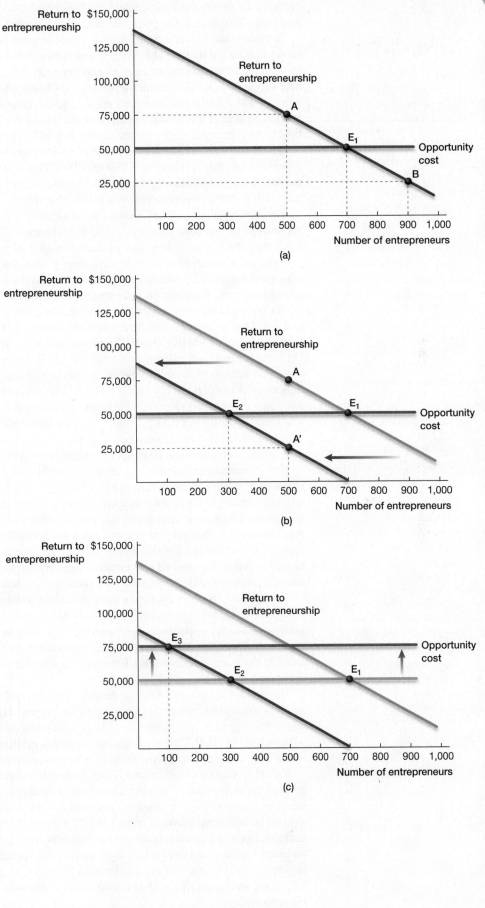

The return-to-entrepreneurship curve in the exhibit (shown in blue) plots these returns. The vertical axis shows the return, while the horizontal axis depicts the number of entrepreneurs who have at least the given rate of return (or higher).

To understand how the figure works, consider point A in panel (a). The vertical axis shows that we are looking at a return to entrepreneurship of $75,000. The horizontal axis, in turn, indicates that the number of entrepreneurs with at least this return to entrepreneurship is 500. As we consider a point with a lower return to entrepreneurship, such as point B, which corresponds to a return of $25,000, naturally there will be more entrepreneurs with at least this return—in this exhibit, 900 of them. This is because, in addition to the 500 entrepreneurs with a return greater than $75,000, there are also 400 entrepreneurs with a return between $25,000 and $75,000, so the total number of entrepreneurs with a return greater than or equal to $25,000 is 900. This reasoning immediately implies that the return-to-entrepreneurship curve is downward-sloping—as we consider a lower return, there will be more entrepreneurs with at least that return.

The horizontal line in red shows the opportunity cost of entrepreneurship, which is assumed to be the same for all potential entrepreneurs. This could be, for example, how much they would earn if they were to choose another occupation.

Panel (a) of the exhibit considers the general question of entry into entrepreneurship, which is determined by whether one's returns to entrepreneurship are above or below one's opportunity cost. Consider an entrepreneur in panel (a) with a return given by point A, whom we will call Entrepreneur A. Because this point is above the horizontal line, this individual has a greater return from entrepreneurship ($75,000) than her opportunity cost, which is at $50,000 in this exhibit. Therefore, she will choose to become an entrepreneur. On the other hand, an entrepreneur with a return given by point B (Entrepreneur B) will not do so because this point is below the horizontal line, and thus the return ($25,000) falls short of her opportunity cost ($50,000). This reasoning establishes that there will be entry into entrepreneurship until the point marked E_1 is reached. At this point, the return to entrepreneurship and the opportunity cost are both $50,000, so any additional entrepreneur will be indifferent between entering into or exiting entrepreneurship. Thus, point E_1 determines the equilibrium level of entrepreneurship in our economy.

How do extractive economic institutions change this picture? First consider the implications of insecure property rights, which are investigated in panel (b). Under insecure property rights, an entrepreneur will not be able to capture all of the returns that he or she creates; for example, the government or some other group may expropriate the returns of his or her enterprise. Suppose, for example, that insecure property rights imply that Entrepreneur A will be able to keep only $25,000 out of her $75,000 return, and that the remaining $50,000 will be expropriated or paid as bribes. Because all entrepreneurs similarly can keep less of what they make under insecure property rights, the return-to-entrepreneurship schedule will shift to the left.

Entrepreneur A also illustrates how extractive economic institutions affect overall entrepreneurship in the economy. This individual's return to entrepreneurship, $75,000, was initially above the opportunity cost schedule. But with insecure property rights, she can make only $25,000, which is less than her opportunity cost of $50,000, as indicated by the fact that the new point describing Entrepreneur A's situation, point A′, now lies below the opportunity cost line.

We can then see that as a result of the shift, the new equilibrium will be at point E_2, which involves strictly less entrepreneurship. Less entrepreneurship implies less business creation, less technology adoption, lower returns to education and capital accumulation, and therefore a lower level of GDP. Thus one effect of extractive economic institutions, working in this instance through insecure property rights, is to reduce entrepreneurship and GDP.

Extractive economic institutions distort economic activity not only by creating insecure property rights but also by making it more costly or impossible to write contracts with suppliers, to borrow money, or to use the courts to uphold business arrangements. For example, say that an entrepreneur would make $75,000 if she could engage the right supplies for her business. But without courts to uphold her contracts, she cannot make the deals necessary for obtaining supplies, and this lack of legal backup will reduce her returns from entrepreneurship by $50,000. These effects will also shift the return-to-entrepreneurship schedule to the left, as shown in panel (b), with the same result of depressing entrepreneurship and GDP in the economy.

Finally, extractive economic institutions can create entry barriers, preventing otherwise profitable businesses from being founded, and may also encourage entrepreneurs to engage in other, nonproductive activities rather than entrepreneurship (for example, joining the underground economy). These factors thus increase the opportunity cost of entrepreneurship, as shown in panel (c) of the exhibit. Using the same numerical example as in panel (b), we can see that without entry barriers, entrepreneurs who can generate returns greater than $50,000 will open businesses (see the light red line on the graph). But if each entrepreneur also has to get a license that costs $25,000, only entrepreneurs who have returns greater than $75,000 will find it profitable to enter (see the dark red line on the graph, now shifted upward). We interpret this additional $25,000 as shifting the opportunity cost upward because it is a cost that entrepreneurs have to pay before they enter, therefore making their second-best alternative more attractive by $25,000. Thus panel (c) of the exhibit simultaneously shows two possible implications of extractive economic institutions:

1. By creating insecure property rights and limiting legal backup, they make entrepreneurship less profitable and shift the return-to-entrepreneurship schedule to the left.
2. By erecting entry barriers, they make entry more costly and shift the opportunity cost schedule upward.

The resulting equilibrium, shown at E_3, now corresponds to even less entrepreneurship. As before, an economy at point E_3, with less entrepreneurship, will have lower prosperity than point E_1 because—as more potential entrepreneurs are discouraged—investment, business creation, and technological development are held back, and the economy generates a lower level of GDP.

The Logic of Extractive Economic Institutions

Exhibit 8.4 shows how extractive economic institutions tend to reduce entrepreneurship and economic activity, thus adversely affecting economic outcomes. It clarifies how there may be large differences in prosperity between two otherwise similar societies that differ in terms of their institutions—one having inclusive economic institutions similar to those in South Korea, and the other one having extractive economic institutions as in North Korea.

But why would a society adopt extractive economic institutions in the first place, particularly as they seem to lead to relative poverty and a lack of economic development? It might seem obvious that everyone should have an interest in creating the type of economic institutions that will bring prosperity. Wouldn't every citizen, every politician, and even a predatory dictator want to make their countries as wealthy as they could?

Unfortunately for the citizens of many countries in the world, the answer is no. To understand why, we turn to a concept first proposed by the famous Austrian economist Joseph Schumpeter.[11] Schumpeter emphasized the notion of *creative destruction* as a central element of technological change. **Creative destruction** refers to the process in which new technologies replace old ones, new businesses replace old ones, and new skills make old ones redundant. The process of creative destruction implies that technological change, which, as we saw in Chapter 7, is the main driver of economic growth, also creates economic losers as it replaces otherwise profitable firms or technologies with new ones. Because creative destruction is an inseparable part of the process of technological change and economic growth, there will be firms and individuals that will lose as a result of this process and will be opposed to it, and this opposition to technological change can provide support for the continuation of extractive economic institutions.

Extending Schumpeter's ideas, we can also introduce the notion of **political creative destruction**, which refers to the process in which economic growth destabilizes existing regimes and reduces the political power of rulers. This might be because new technologies will also bring new actors on the scene who will make political demands, or because new economic activities may fall outside of the control of existing rulers. If the process of economic growth is also associated with political creative destruction, then we would expect that the politically powerful who fear losing their privileged positions will be opposed to this process.

In the context of North Korea, for example, the communist elites are powerful and enjoy a privileged position. The current leader, Kim Jong-Un, and his cronies could open up the

Creative destruction refers to the process in which new technologies replace old ones, new businesses replace existing businesses, and new skills make old ones redundant.

Political creative destruction refers to the process in which economic growth destabilizes existing regimes and reduces the political power of rulers.

> **Fear of creative destruction and political creative destruction makes many rulers . . . explicitly ban the adoption of new technologies and block the process of economic development.**

economy, let markets work, allow citizens to open businesses and import technologies, and start strengthening their ties with South Korea and the West. All these initiatives would kick-start economic growth and lift millions of North Koreans out of poverty. But this process would also allow new leaders to emerge—and perhaps also discredit the old leadership that has kept the country in poverty for so long. Because Kim and his allies put their own interests ahead of those of ordinary North Koreans, they prefer to maintain the status quo rather than reform economic institutions to enhance economic growth.

In fact, fear of creative destruction and political creative destruction makes many rulers, not just communist dictators, explicitly ban the adoption of new technologies and block the process of economic development.

Inclusive Economic Institutions and the Industrial Revolution

We saw in Chapter 7 how the process of technological change gathered speed during the Industrial Revolution in Britain, which first involved a series of major innovations in textiles that then spread to other areas—for instance, resulting in the famous advances in the steam engine, which laid the foundation of modern production as well as the railroad.

LETTING THE DATA SPEAK

Blocking the Railways

A key technology fueling the process of economic growth during the nineteenth century was the railroad. Rapid railway construction reduced transport costs and permitted greater and cheaper trade within and between countries. By 1860, Britain had laid 9,073 miles of railways, Germany 6,890 miles, and the United States 30,626 miles.

While many countries were investing in railways rapidly, two of the most powerful empires in continental Europe—Russia and Austria-Hungary—did not. Russia started doing so only after its bitter defeat in the Crimean war in 1856. Even in the early twentieth century, the number of railway journeys per inhabitant per year was 21.9 in Britain, but only 1.7 in Central and Eastern Europe.

Why did Russia and Austria-Hungary not invest in railways?

The answer is related to political creative destruction. The monarchs in both countries feared that railways and the accompanying process of industrialization would undermine their power and destabilize their regimes. For example, Francis I, who ruled Austria-Hungary in the early nineteenth century, and his right-hand man, Klemens von Metternich, were opposed to industrialization and railways. When the English philanthropist Robert Owen tried to convince the government of Austria-Hungary that some social reforms were necessary to improve the living standards of the citizens, one of Metternich's assistants, Frederick Gentz, replied:

> We do not desire at all that the great masses shall become well off and independent. . . . How could we otherwise rule over them?

This attitude is likely what made Francis I and Metternich oppose railway construction because it would make their subjects more difficult to rule.

This was also the view of Nikolai I, who ruled the Russian Empire between 1825 and 1855. He thought that the railways were the harbinger of worker unrest, industrial demands, and instability, so he opposed them. Austria-Hungary and Russia thus blocked technology adoption and economic development because they feared the political instability that they would bring.

The blocking of productive technologies is not something that just happened in history. The Internet is one of the most important technologies of today and offers a huge amount of information to individuals and firms, as well as a platform for the expression of ideas and media. But according to the organization Reporters Without Borders, Bahrain, Belarus, Myanmar, Cuba, Iran, North Korea, Saudi Arabia, Syria, Turkmenistan, and Uzbekistan seriously curtail the use of the Internet or suppress online expression. As was the case with Russia and Austria-Hungary in the nineteenth century, oftentimes these policies are related to political creative destruction: limiting the content that can be accessed online is a strategy to control dissent and maintain political power.

Economic historians have long debated why the Industrial Revolution took place in Britain rather than in France or some other European nation or in China, and why it started in the second half of the eighteenth century instead of some other time in history.

A complex social and economic process such as the Industrial Revolution seldom has a single cause. Economic historians have come up with scores of explanations for why it occurred. Despite this variety, though, many of these explanations either depend on Britain's relatively inclusive economic institutions or simply take them as given. This is because it would be next to impossible to imagine how the Industrial Revolution could have taken place in Britain without such inclusive economic institutions.[12] The defining characteristic of the Industrial Revolution was that new technologies were being developed and implemented by businessmen for profit. Without secure property rights, these businessmen would not have been encouraged to seek and undertake such innovations. The innovations were profitable, in turn, because Britain already had a well-developed market system, and those who could adopt new technologies to improve quality and reduce costs in textiles and other areas could reach a larger market and make sizable profits.

Britain also had a patent system that allowed the inventors of new technologies to protect their property rights not only in tangible assets but also in ideas. In fact, the protection of new ideas and innovations, just like the protection of other economic assets, was a major impetus to innovation and technological change in Britain.

Britain, in contrast to many other countries in the eighteenth century, also allowed relatively free entry into different lines of business. Although different interests tried to block entry of competitors and were sometimes successful in this endeavor (as when woolen manufacturers temporarily convinced Parliament to ban cotton imports), these entry barriers were often short-lived. By international standards, Britain gradually created a much more level playing field for its potential businesspeople. These institutional features of British society were the key prerequisites for the Industrial Revolution.

Notably, British economic institutions were also supported by the appropriate political institutions. The development of these economic institutions was preceded by major political reforms, in particular the Glorious Revolution of 1688, which introduced a constitutional monarchy and considerable constraints on the political powers of the monarch. The political institutions enshrined in the Glorious Revolution and further developed in the subsequent century were the bulwarks upon which the inclusive economic institutions that underpinned the Industrial Revolution were built.

Evidence-Based Economics

Q: Are tropical and semitropical areas condemned to poverty by their geographies?

How do we determine whether tropical geographic conditions condemn a nation to poverty? We cannot do this by varying a nation's geography and seeing whether this affects its long-run economic development because, by definition, geographic conditions are largely immutable.

To gauge the importance of geographic factors in differences in prosperity and poverty, we can look at whether countries with the same geographic conditions have significantly changed their relative prosperity as their institutions have changed. We have already seen one example of the profound effect of institutions on prosperity in this chapter: North Korea and South Korea. In this section, we answer our opening question by looking at another interesting historical episode.

Europeans came to dominate much of the world starting in the late fifteenth century after they went around the southern end of Africa to reach the Indian Ocean and they discovered the New World. These events led to the process of colonization, in which European nations built new colonies around the world and came to conquer many

Are the more than one billion poor people in tropical and semitropical parts of the world condemned to poverty by the climate and geography of the countries they live in?

existing empires and states. Many of the non-European parts of the world were under their command at one point or another during the 500 years between the end of the fifteenth century and the middle of the twentieth century.

Europeans set up very different institutions in various parts of the world. We in the United States live in a former European colony, and the strength of our institutions today has a lot to do with the fact that Europeans set up a very different system in North America than in other colonies. Political participation quickly became relatively broad in North America and, equally importantly, production came to be supported by fairly inclusive economic institutions. Small agricultural holders were the main producers in the early stages of the American colonies. Though many Europeans first came to North America as indentured servants who were obliged to supply their labor at a very low wage to those who brought them to the new continent, they soon largely acquired economic and political rights and became citizens with relatively secure property rights.

The situation could not have been more different in other colonies. Like North America, Barbados and Jamaica were British colonies. But the British did not set up inclusive economic institutions in these islands. Rather, they developed as clear exemplars of extractive economic institutions: they were plantation economies, with a small minority dominating a majority brought over as slaves from Africa. Slaves had no political rights and essentially no economic rights. They were forced to work for very long hours. Their situation was so terrible that many of them died from the onerous work and the unsanitary conditions in which they were kept. These people could not effectively defend their interests because under the law of the land, the plantation owners controlled all of the power and all of the guns.

These types of extractive economic institutions were not just confined to the Caribbean islands, where the majority of the population consisted of imported slaves. The living conditions of the native population areas that now correspond to Mexico, Guatemala, Peru, and Bolivia were only a little better. The descendants of the Mayas, Incas, and Aztecs were stripped of all rights (not that they had many before the Europeans arrived) and were forced to work in mines and on agricultural estates for low wages and under violent threats. These people also did not have any political representation, and their property rights were far from secure.

In sum, Europeans set up widely different economic institutions. In some places, they were inclusive; in others, highly extractive. Given this variation in institutions, we can try to evaluate whether it is the institutions that matter or whether some parts of the world are condemned to poverty by their geography. In particular, we can achieve this by examining how relative prosperity has changed after European colonization in different areas that were part of the European empire.

But there is a problem. How do we measure the GDP per capita and prosperity of places 500 years ago? Today, we can use the national income accounts, as we saw in Chapter 5. But the inhabitants of the Caribbean islands or the Aztecs and the Incas, let alone the Native Americans occupying the North American plains, did not have national income accounts.

Fortunately, we can use measurements of urbanization (the fraction of the population living in urban centers with 5,000 or more inhabitants) as a fairly good proxy for measuring the prosperity of a nation. This is because only countries that can generate sufficient agricultural surplus and develop a transportation and trading network to bring this surplus to cities can support a large urban population. Much historical evidence documents a causal relationship between urbanization and prosperity. Even in the late twentieth century, when many nations around the world had long been industrialized, there was still a very strong association between GDP per capita and urbanization.

Exhibit 8.5 The Relationship Between Urbanization and GDP per Capita in 2010

This exhibit shows the relationship between urbanization (as measured by the fraction of the population living in urban centers with more than 5,000 inhabitants) and GDP per capita (in PPP-adjusted 2005 constant dollars) in 2010 together with the best-fit line. It suggests that even today, urbanization is a good proxy for prosperity.

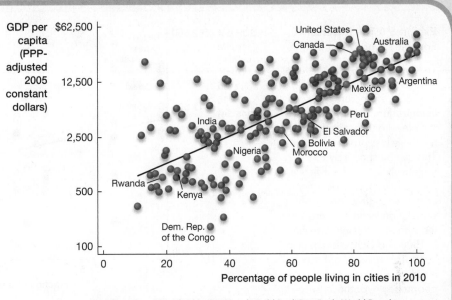

Sources: Data from Penn World Table (2010) and World Bank DataBank: World Development Indicators (2010). Alan Heston, Robert Summers and Bettina Aten, Penn World Table Version 7.1, Center for International Comparisons of Production, Income and Prices at the University of Pennsylvania (Nov 2012).

Exhibit 8.5 shows this relationship in 2010. On the vertical axis, we have GDP per capita (in PPP-adjusted 2005 constant dollars) and on the horizontal axis, we have the fraction of the population living in urban centers with 5,000 or more inhabitants. The exhibit shows that even today there is a fairly strong positive association between urbanization and GDP per capita.

Exhibit 8.6 shows the relationship between urbanization in 1500, estimated from various historical sources, and GDP per capita today. The remarkable thing that the exhibit reveals is what we call "the reversal of fortune," as shown by the best-fit line in this figure. This reversal differs from the pattern of persistent prosperity that we are generally used to seeing around the world. As we saw in Chapter 7, most of the countries that are rich today are those that were rich 50 years ago or even 100 years ago. Thus, holding all else equal, we expect to see the persistence of relative prosperity over time. We would therefore expect areas that were highly urbanized centuries ago to still be the ones that are relatively prosperous today, even if some of their advantage may have been eroded.

But Exhibit 8.6 shows something very different. The areas that were relatively more urbanized in 1500, and thus relatively more prosperous, today are generally poorer. In 1500, places like Mexico, Peru, North Africa, and India were relatively more prosperous than the parts of North America that were later to become the United States and Canada, Australia, New Zealand, and Argentina, which were sparsely populated and scarcely urbanized. Today, the picture has changed. There is a sharp reversal.

Admittedly, Exhibit 8.6 uses a limited sample that excludes sub-Saharan African countries, for which we do not have urbanization data in 1500. But we can extend the sample by using another proxy. The same reasoning that led to the use of urbanization rates as a proxy for prosperity also suggests that we can use population density as a proxy. Only areas with sufficient agricultural surplus, a developed trading and transport structure, and sufficiently healthy living conditions can support a high population density. We therefore adopt this approach in Exhibit 8.7 to include data from places like sub-Saharan Africa. Even with this larger sample, the reversal of fortune persists: areas that were relatively more prosperous as measured by their population density in 1500 are today relatively less prosperous.

Evidence-Based Economics *(Continued)*

Exhibit 8.6 The Reversal of Fortune Using Urbanization

The former European colonies that were more prosperous in 1500, before European colonization, as proxied by their level of urbanization, are relatively less prosperous today. This can be shown by the negatively sloped best-fit line for the relationship between urbanization (fraction of the population living in towns with more than 5,000 inhabitants) in 1500 and GDP per capita in 2010. This reversal of fortune is strong evidence against the geography hypothesis because the relative prosperity of these nations has changed greatly while potential geographic determinants of prosperity haven't.

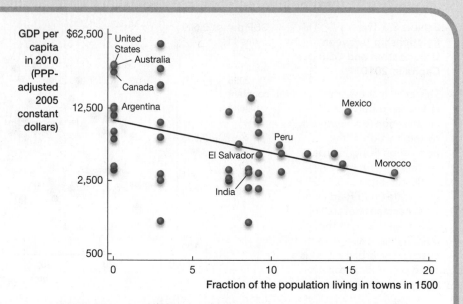

Sources: Data from Penn World Table (2010) and Acemoglu, Johnson, and Robinson (2002). Alan Heston, Robert Summers and Bettina Aten, Penn World Table Version 7.1, Center for International Comparisons of Production, Income and Prices at the University of Pennsylvania (Nov 2012); and Daron Acemoglu, Simon Johnson, and James A. Robinson, "Reversal of Fortune: Geography and Institutions in the Making of the Modern World Income Distribution," *Quarterly Journal of Economics* 117, no. 4 (2002): 1231–1294.

Exhibit 8.7 The Reversal of Fortune Using Population Density

There is also a strong negative relationship between population density in 1500, another potential proxy for prosperity before European colonization, and prosperity today. Colonized areas that were capable of supporting larger populations (per acre of arable land) in 1500 are less prosperous today. This pattern is another piece of evidence against the geography hypothesis and is consistent with the role of institutions in shaping prosperity. That is, the reversal in the relative rankings of countries by prosperity since 1500 is largely a result of the fact that Europeans set up more extractive economic institutions in colonies that had greater population densities.

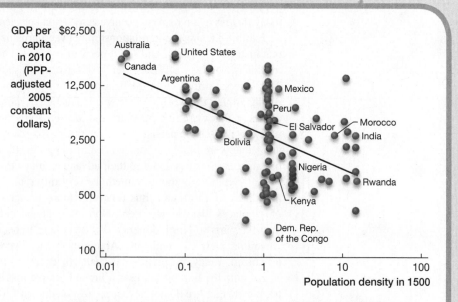

Sources: Data from Penn World Table (2010) and Acemoglu, Johnson, and Robinson (2002). Alan Heston, Robert Summers and Bettina Aten, Penn World Table Version 7.1, Center for International Comparisons of Production, Income and Prices at the University of Pennsylvania (Nov 2012); and Daron Acemoglu, Simon Johnson, and James A. Robinson, "Reversal of Fortune: Geography and Institutions in the Making of the Modern World Income Distribution," *Quarterly Journal of Economics* 117, no. 4 (2002): 1231–1294.

Understanding the Reversal of Fortune

How do we explain this reversal of fortune? One possibility could have been to appeal to geography. In fact, if we had found that places such as Mexico, India, and sub-Saharan Africa were much poorer than North America and Australia 500 years ago, it may have been plausible to think that these differences were due to geography. It could have been argued that agriculture was more productive in the temperate soils of North America and Australia than in the semitropical soils of Peru or India, and these differences were the reason why North America and Australia were richer than South America and South Asia.

But the pattern in the data shows the opposite. Five hundred years ago, many parts of South America, South Asia, North Africa, and sub-Saharan Africa were more developed than North America, Australia, and New Zealand, but today they are much poorer. Thus a geographic explanation cannot account for the patterns that we are seeing in Exhibits 8.6 and 8.7. Geographic conditions are fixed. Therefore, if the geographic conditions of Peru, India, the Caribbean, and African nations condemn them to low agricultural productivity and poverty, we should see that same poverty in 1500 as well as today. But the fact that these places were relatively more prosperous back then suggests that we must look to what actually changed between 1500 and today to understand the root of their reversal of fortune. And what changed was not these countries' geography but their institutions after European colonization.

To be fair, one could come up with more sophisticated geographical hypotheses that could account for such a reversal. For example, we could argue that geography has a time-varying effect. Perhaps the geographic characteristics that were conducive to economic growth in 1500 have become a burden.

Although this supposition is, in theory, possible, it is not plausible in practice. Today, most countries' wealth is generated by industry, trade, and services. And these are precisely the kind of economic activities that depend less on climate and more on institutions. Diseases matter today, but we are much better at controlling them, and many semitropical areas have been able to eradicate deadly diseases such as malaria. Thus, if anything, geographic handicaps such as poor soil quality, a worse disease environment, and more adverse transport conditions should have mattered much more 500 years ago than today. To the extent that sub-Saharan Africa and the tropical parts of Asia and Latin America have adverse geographic conditions, these should have disadvantaged them 500 years ago, not today. If such a sophisticated geography hypothesis were correct, today we should see them having a comparative advantage in industry and trade (the very opposite of what we see, where these poor nations are still largely agricultural).

These observations lead us to conclude that geographic characteristics are *not* the main reason why tropical and semitropical parts of the world are today much poorer than North America and Australia.

Instead, we can view the reversal of fortune as the consequence of an institutional reversal in the sense that *Europeans established more extractive economic institutions in places that were previously more developed and set up more inclusive economic institutions in places that were previously less developed.* This pattern resulted from a simple logic. European colonialism was driven by a profit motive, and in places where Europeans encountered relatively developed civilizations, it was profitable for them to set up extractive economic institutions to funnel gold, silver, and agricultural surplus to their countries and to themselves. Most importantly, they were able to use the labor in these relatively densely populated areas to achieve their objectives, often taking over the existing institutions of the empires they dominated and setting up their own extractive economic institutions.

In contrast, in areas where they did not encounter such developed civilizations and the land was sparsely settled, such as North America, Europeans themselves went in to colonize and develop institutions under which they themselves would live. They had the incentives and the ability to structure these institutions in a more inclusive fashion. As a result, the lands of the former Aztec and Inca empires—Mexico, Peru, and their surroundings—ended up with extractive economic institutions, while Europeans who settled in the lands that were later to become the United States and Canada ended up with more inclusive economic institutions. This institutional reversal then led to the reversal of prosperity. Areas under inclusive economic institutions rapidly developed, particularly in the nineteenth century when they could readily adopt the new technologies of industry, while those under extractive economic institutions stagnated and grew much less rapidly.

We can now suggest an answer to the question posed in the title of this chapter: *Why isn't the whole world developed?* The answer is that inclusive economic institutions are at the root of the wealth of nations because when market participants are not harassed by excessive regulations or paralyzed by uncertainty about the future that extractive economic institutions create, they will work, invest, innovate, and create a vibrant economy where opportunities for success feed on each other. While luck does inevitably play some role in the fate of individuals even in countries with inclusive economic institutions, an uncorrupt justice system that protects life and property and an environment where risk taking and experimentation are not frowned upon are the pillars that provide economic and social incentives that enrich individuals and nations.

> **Inclusive economic institutions are at the root of the wealth of nations.**

Question	Answer	Data	Caveat
Are tropical and semitropical areas condemned to poverty by their geographies?	No. Many of these countries were relatively more prosperous 500 years ago than countries further from the equator that have become prosperous today. This reversal of fortune is not a reflection of changing geographic features but of different institutional structures (extractive versus inclusive) being imposed during European colonization.	Urbanization rates and data on population density in the 1500s and data on GDP per capita and urbanization rates in 2010.	The evidence presented here does not deny that geographic factors could play a role in economic development. Rather, it suggests that these are not the main cause of the poverty of tropical and semitropical areas today.

8.3 Is Foreign Aid the Solution to World Poverty?

In the chapter on economic growth, we discussed certain policies that can help poor countries grow. But what about foreign aid?

Many in the Western world think that, if at all feasible, we should take steps toward improving the lives of the hundreds of millions of people who live in poverty. This conviction has led to a substantial effort over the past 60 years to provide foreign aid—in fact "development aid"—to poor nations. Development aid, given by charitable organizations, the World Bank, and the United Nations, or sometimes by bilateral deals between countries, is meant to alleviate or even fundamentally eradicate poverty around the world.

A solution to world poverty? Angelina Jolie is one of many Hollywood celebrities devoting their time and money to humanitarian efforts aimed at alleviating poverty. Are these efforts likely to eradicate poverty?

Many in the international community—for example, high-level officials of the World Bank and the United Nations and several journalists and commentators—have much hope pinned on development aid. But has this type of foreign aid been effective in reducing poverty around the world?

You might at first be surprised, but economists' overall verdict is that foreign aid has been on the whole ineffective in alleviating poverty. For example, over the past 50 years, hundreds of billions of dollars have been given to Africa as development aid, but as we have seen, African nations are still much poorer than the United States or Western Europe. Why is that the case?

Though surprising at first, once we use economics to understand how foreign aid might work and recognize the difficulties faced, this conclusion turns out to be quite reasonable for three reasons. First, we know from our analysis so far that GDP per capita can be increased and economic growth can be triggered if the levels of a country's physical capital, human capital, and/or technology can be increased significantly. Although generous from the viewpoint of the donor nations, the amount of foreign aid given to even the poorest countries is not large enough to lead to a sizable increase in physical capital or to significantly increase the educational attainment of the countries' population. It also generally does not have an impact on technology or the efficiency of production. In view of this, the fact that foreign aid hasn't made significant progress in increasing GDP per capita among the poorest nations in the world shouldn't be too surprising.

Second, in practice, much of foreign aid does not even get invested in new technology or education. Problems related to corruption and political economy imply that money given to governments or other organizations in poor countries is often captured

CHOICE & CONSEQUENCE

Foreign Aid and Corruption

In the 1990s, the government of Uganda spent a fifth of its budget on primary education. A sizable fraction of this money was provided by the international community as developmental aid.

When policymakers and academics evaluate the effectiveness of spending, they generally ask whether initial objectives were met and whether the benefits of a project exceeded its costs. But in the case of foreign and governmental aid, the money often does not even reach its intended target, precluding the chance to even try to use the money effectively. A survey by economists Ritva Reinikka and Jakob Svensson has revealed that only 13 percent of schools in Uganda actually received the grants to which they were entitled in the period studied.[13]

The study found that a large portion of the money intended for schools was stolen by local officials. Interestingly, the schools located in the richer regions typically received more money than the schools located in the poorer areas. This disparity appears to be partly due to the fact that schools in richer areas have more resources to start with and better connections. So they may have been able to secure more of the money that was intended for them. Very little of the intended resources for students

in the poorest regions actually reached their destination. This type of corruption and siphoning off of government resources and aid money is unfortunately all too common and poses a formidable obstacle to the effective distribution of foreign aid in many countries. As in the Ugandan case, it may often also contribute to greater inequality of resources across regions and schools within a country.

and distributed to corrupt officials. Studies indicate that only about 15 percent of any money given to foreign aid actually reaches its destination, and often it does so in a rather distorted manner.

There is also a third, and a more fundamental, reason for why foreign aid has a limited impact in alleviating poverty. If the root of poverty is the extractive economic institutions of many countries around the world, then foreign aid working within the framework of these same institutions will not fix the fundamental causes. In fact, in some instances, foreign aid funneled to dictators sitting atop of these extractive economic institutions might strengthen or enrich them, as suggested by the Choice & Consequence box on the previous page.

All of the evidence on the costs and limits of foreign aid doesn't mean that foreign aid is bad or useless. Often, foreign aid is a transfer to some of the poorest people in the world and helps alleviate their hardships, albeit temporarily, and as such serves a useful, even if limited, role. Still, we must also devote our energy to developing policies that address the fundamental causes of prosperity—like institutions—if we wish to enduringly improve living conditions in the world's impoverished countries.

Summary

✸ Physical capital, human capital, and technology are proximate causes of prosperity in the sense that, though they determine whether a nation is prosperous or not, they are themselves determined by other, deeper factors. Put differently, if we want to understand why some nations are poor, we have to ask why they do not sufficiently invest in physical capital or human capital and why they do not adopt the best technologies and organize their production efficiently.

✸ The fundamental causes of prosperity include factors that potentially influence the physical and human capital investment and technology choices of nations and, via this channel, shape their prosperity.

✸ Three leading fundamental causes of prosperity are geography, culture, and institutions. According to the geography hypothesis, geographic aspects such as climate, topography, or disease environment determine whether or not a nation can be prosperous. According to the culture hypothesis, it is the cultural values of the country's people that powerfully determine its potential for prosperity. According to the institutions hypothesis, it is the institutions, in particular the formal and informal rules governing the organization of society and economic interactions therein, that are central to prosperity.

✸ Inclusive economic institutions are those that provide secure property rights, and a judicial system that allows and facilitates private contracting and financial transactions and maintain relatively open and free entry into different businesses and occupations. Extractive economic institutions, by contrast, create insecure property rights, a partial judicial system, and entry barriers that protect the businesses and incomes of a small segment of society at the expense of the rest. According to the institutions hypothesis, inclusive economic institutions tend to generate prosperity, while extractive economic institutions do not.

✸ Though the inequalities in GDP per capita around the world have multiple causes, the evidence from the economic experiences of former European colonies suggests that institutional factors, and not geography, are central to explaining these disparities. In fact, the major patterns—for example, the reversal of fortune, whereby areas that were relatively prosperous became relatively less prosperous after European colonization—cannot be explained by geographic factors.

✸ Foreign aid can be useful to temporarily alleviate extreme poverty or manage crises but is unlikely to be a solution to low economic development in many parts of the world. This is because aid largely fails to address the institutional roots of poverty.

Key Terms

proximate causes of prosperity *p. 173*
fundamental causes of prosperity *p. 173*
geography hypothesis *p. 174*
culture hypothesis *p. 175*
institutions *p. 175*

institutions hypothesis *p. 176*
private property rights *p. 178*
economic institutions *p. 178*
inclusive economic institutions *p. 178*
extractive economic institutions *p. 179*

political institutions *p. 179*
creative destruction *p. 183*
political creative destruction *p. 183*

Questions

All questions are available in MyEconLab *for practice and instructor assignment.*

1. How are the proximate causes of prosperity different from the fundamental causes of prosperity?

2. What does the geography hypothesis state?

3. According to the geography hypothesis, what could be done in order to improve incomes in poor countries?

4. What does the culture hypothesis state?

5. In the context of this chapter, what is meant by an institution? What are the three important elements that define institutions?

6. How does the institutions hypothesis explain the difference in prosperity among nations?

7. What does it mean to say that private property rights are well-enforced in an economy? How does it foster economic development?

8. How do inclusive economic institutions differ from extractive economic institutions?

9. What does the return-to-entrepreneurship curve show? What is meant by the opportunity cost of entrepreneurship?

10. How does the existence of extractive institutions discourage entrepreneurship in an economy?

11. Suppose a country has well-enforced private property rights for entrepreneurs, but a large fraction of the population does not have access to education and thus cannot become entrepreneurs. Moreover, their productivity as workers is low. Would you say that this country has inclusive economic institutions? Is it likely to achieve a high level of economic development?

12. What is meant by political creative destruction? How would this concept explain the existence of extractive institutions?

13. Parts of the world that were relatively more prosperous 500 years ago have experienced a reversal of fortune and are relatively poorer today. What factors could explain this?

Problems

All problems are available in MyEconLab *for practice and instructor assignment.*

1. The chapter discusses Max Weber's argument that the origins of industrialization in Western Europe could be traced to Protestantism. According to Weber, the Protestant work ethic was crucial to the development of a market economy and economic growth. Weber, however, also claimed that religions like Confucianism in China and Hinduism in India were not conducive to the development of capitalism. Given that India and China are now among the fastest-growing economies in the world, how effective do you think the culture hypothesis is in explaining economic development?

2. After the Second World War, Germany was divided into two parts, East Germany and West Germany. East Germany was controlled by the former Soviet Union, while West Germany was controlled by the other Allied governments: the United States, the United Kingdom, and France. The war had destroyed most of Germany's economy. The Soviet Union as well as the Allied occupation forces sought to rebuild the economies of their respective parts. Before the fall of the Berlin Wall reunited East and West Germany in 1990, West Germany's economy grew at an annual average growth rate of 4.4 percent, which was about 3 times higher than East Germany's rate. Draw the parallel between the natural experiment discussed in the chapter and the case of East and West Germany. Based on the information given in the question and your own research, why do you think two otherwise similar areas had such divergent growth rates?

3. Suppose the country of Burondo is one of the poorest countries in the world. Its economy is heavily reliant on income from the export of oil. There are only two oil-extracting companies in Burondo. Both are owned by the government. A large part of the earnings from oil exports goes toward financing the president's lifestyle and entourage. Burondo has not had a single democratic election ever since it gained independence 50 years ago. Although Burondo is said to have abundant oil resources, only a small proportion is extracted every year because the extraction process is so inefficient. Transporting goods in and out of the country is costly, as Burondo is surrounded by lofty mountain

ranges. School enrollment in this country is very low and as a result, most of the adult population is illiterate. Life expectancy is also quite low. Agriculture is collectivized in Burondo and so food shortages are common in the country.

Using the information given, distinguish between the fundamental and proximate causes of prosperity (or its absence) in Burondo.

4. Look at the following map of Nogales, a twin city that is divided by the U.S. border.

One part of Nogales lies in the United States, in Arizona, and the other part lies in Sonora, Mexico. Life in Nogales, Mexico is very different from life in Nogales, Arizona. The average income in Nogales, Mexico is about one-third the average income in Nogales, Arizona. Education levels, life expectancy, and health conditions are better in Nogales, Arizona than in Nogales, Mexico. Unlike Nogales in Arizona, Nogales in Mexico has only recently adopted political reforms, bringing it closer to functioning as a democracy. Crime rates are also lower in Nogales, Arizona than in Nogales, Mexico. Since both cities are located so close to each other, they share similar geographical conditions and climate. The inhabitants of both cities also share a common ancestry and enjoy the same types of food and music.

Based on this information and your own research, what factors do you think can explain why Nogales, Arizona is so much more prosperous than Nogales, Mexico?

5. Zimbabwe, formerly known as Rhodesia, was a British colony for around ninety years. It became independent in 1980. The prime minister of newly formed Zimbabwe, Robert Mugabe, implemented a forced land redistribution policy, in which commercial farms were confiscated from white farmers. Mugabe also proceeded to confiscate shares in companies owned by whites. In the following years, agricultural production in the country fell sharply. Zimbabwe, the country that used to be called the breadbasket of Africa, is now seeing food shortages in certain parts of the country.

a. Would Zimbabwe be considered to have extractive or inclusive institutions? Explain your answer.

b. Why would a government undertake policies that would adversely affect the lives of its citizens? Explain your answer with reference to the Zimbabwean situation.

6. The chapter points out how important entrepreneurship is to economic growth, and discusses the factors that foster or exhibit the activities of entrepreneurs.

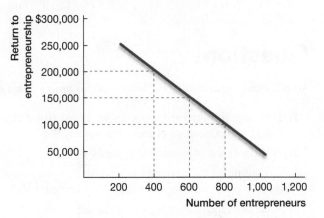

a. The above graph shows the return-to-entrepreneurship curve in a certain country. If the opportunity cost of entrepreneurship in this country is $150,000, find the equilibrium level of entrepreneurship in the economy.

b. Suppose the government of this country decided to expropriate the assets of private firms. Expropriation here means that the government is either taking away the assets of private firms or forcing their owners to sell at low prices. What do you think will happen to the equilibrium level of entrepreneurship in the economy? Use the graph to explain your answer.

c. Suppose the government reduces the fee that needs to be paid to obtain a trade license in this country. Other things remaining the same, how will this policy affect entrepreneurship? Use your graph from part a to explain your answer.

7. Using a graph like the one in the chapter showing returns to entrepreneurship and the opportunity cost of entrepreneurship, illustrate how each of the following historical events shifted one (or both) of the curves.

a. Between 1959 and 1963, the Cuban government passed a series of laws called the Agrarian Reform Laws. These laws expropriated any landholdings above a certain size and turned them over to peasants and cooperatives.

b. From independence in 1947 until the 1990s, there was in place in India that came to be known as the "Paper Raj." The term referred to a series of rules and regulations that put strict controls on business, and forced business owners to navigate a bureaucratic labyrinth in order to start and run their companies. For example, one entrepreneur complained that simply to import a computer, he had to make 50 trips to New Delhi to get the necessary permits. Starting in the 1990s, many of these restrictions were abolished. A series of reforms made it much easier for firms to conduct business. (Based on the series *Commanding Heights*, PBS, 2002.)

c. In 2007 and 2008, the Venezuelan dictator Hugo Chavez nationalized many large firms in several key sectors of the country's economy, including telecommunications, electric utilities, steel, and banking. Subsequently, taxes on banking and other activities were also raised significantly.

8. Suppose the return and cost of entrepreneurship curves are described by the following equations (with numbers measured in the thousands):

$$R = 250,000 - 50,000N,$$
$$C = 50,000 + 150,000N,$$

where

R = returns to entrepreneurship,

C = cost of entrepreneurship,

N = number of entrepreneurs.

a. Based on the equations given, how does the cost of entrepreneurship curve differ (in overall shape) from the one drawn in the chapter? Explain how this difference might arise.

b. Find the equilibrium number of entrepreneurs in this economy and the equilibrium returns to entrepreneurship.

c. The government enacts a license fee of $50,000 to file the paperwork necessary to start a firm. What is now the equilibrium number of entrepreneurs and the equilibrium returns to entrepreneurship?

9. Jointly published by the *Wall Street Journal* and The Heritage Foundation, "The Freedom Index" gives an annual ranking of most of the countries of the world based on their level of economic freedom. Factors considered in the rankings include the status of property rights, the extent of corruption, and the ease of starting and running a business. The index can be found at http://www.heritage .org/index/.

a. Go to http://www.heritage.org/index/ranking and find three countries in each of the freedom categories ("Free," "Mostly Free," etc.). Click on the country name in the table for each country you select, and read about the rationale for their ranking. Provide a summary for the nations you selected.

b. Now go to http://www.heritage.org/index/explore? view=by-variables. Note the per capita GDP of the three countries you selected in each category, and calculate the average of the three you selected in each category.

What pattern do you notice? What preliminary conclusions can you draw concerning the relationship between economic freedom and economic development? Which of the three hypotheses mentioned in the chapter do your results tend to support? Explain.

c. Sub-Saharan Africa is known to be one of the poorest regions of the world. Go to the "Interactive Freedom Heat Map" at http://www.heritage.org/index/heatmap. Into which freedom categories do the majority of countries of the region fall? Which two countries are the exceptions to the overall pattern?

10. Initial phases of the growth process are often accompanied by increasing income inequality within a country. Using the concepts developed in the chapter, explain why this might be the case.

11. Which of the three hypotheses developed in the chapter would be most likely to view foreign aid as essential for economic development? Explain.

12. In his book *The Elusive Quest for Growth*, development economist William Easterly discusses the relationship between foreign aid and investment in poor countries. He posits that to establish the effectiveness of aid in promoting investment, two tests should be passed: First, there should be a positive statistical association between aid and investment; second, aid should pass into investment 1 for 1, that is, a 1 percent (of GDP) increase in aid should result in a 1 percent (of GDP) increase in investment. Using a dataset of 88 countries from 1965 to 1995, he finds that only 17 of 88 countries pass the first test, and of them, only 6 pass the second.

Based on the information in the chapter, and perhaps your own reading, explain why foreign aid designed to spur investment usually does not work.

9 Employment and Unemployment

What happens to employment and unemployment if local employers go out of business?

Economic shocks frequently hit local communities. A weak car market causes Ford to shutter an assembly plant. A weak regional economy causes a big-box-retailer—like JCPenney, Kmart, or Sears—to shut one of its megastores. Falling coal prices cause a mining company to mothball an open-pit coal mine. Competition from new suppliers causes a clothing company to close a textile factory. Do the workers who lose these jobs quickly find new ones? Do the local labor markets quickly bounce back? Or do these communities experience persistent unemployment?

In this chapter, we study the determinants of employment and unemployment, and investigate how various economic shocks affect the labor market equilibrium.

CHAPTER OUTLINE

9.1 Measuring Employment and Unemployment

After 17 months of unsuccessful job applications, one unemployed worker wrote in a letter to the *New York Times* that "nothing stops the omnipresent feeling of loneliness, worthlessness and desperation."[1] For most people, enduring a long period of unemployment takes a terrible toll on their well-being. Long-term unemployment generates three simultaneous traumas: a loss of income, a loss of skills, and a loss of perceived self-worth.

> **Because of its enormous economic and social costs, politicians and policymakers try to limit the amount of unemployment in an economy.**

Because of its enormous economic and social costs, policymakers try to limit the amount of unemployment in an economy. To do so, they must have a way of measuring and tracking unemployment over time. Unfortunately, just measuring unemployment is challenging. For example, it seems reasonable that a 30-year-old without a job who is actively looking for work should count as unemployed. But should we also count another 30-year-old who has lost a job but has decided *not* to look for work? What about full-time college students or stay-at-home parents: people who are busy and work hard but don't receive a paycheck for their labor?

Economists have agreed on a standard, though nevertheless controversial, way of defining employment and unemployment. In the United States, this standard is set by the Bureau of Labor Statistics (BLS) in the Department of Labor, which tracks the official employment statistics for the U.S. economy. We describe the BLS definition here.

Classifying Potential Workers

Potential workers includes everyone in the general population with three exceptions: children under 16 years of age, people on active duty in the military, and institutionalized people, like those in nursing homes or jail.

To determine who is employed and unemployed, we start by identifying the population of workers whose employment behavior we want to measure. This group includes everyone in the general population with three exceptions: children under 16 years of age, people on active duty in the military, and institutionalized people, like those in nursing homes or jail. The BLS calls the remaining population the *civilian non-institutional population ages 16 and over*. For simplicity, we'll refer to them as **potential workers**. In January 2014, the United States had 246.9 million potential workers.

Exhibit 9.1 The U.S. Population of Potential Workers (January 2014)

The population of potential workers is 246.9 million people—otherwise known as the civilian non-institutional population ages 16 and over. Potential workers can be divided into three subgroups: employed workers (145.2 million), unemployed workers (10.2 million), and those not in the labor force (91.5 million). The labor force is the combination of the employed and unemployed workers (155.5 million with rounding).

Source: U.S. Bureau of Labor Statistics.

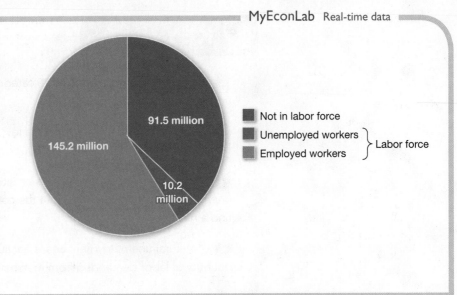

Within the population of potential workers, people are classified into one of three categories: "employed," "unemployed," or "not in the labor force." Those holding full-time or part-time *paid* jobs are officially classified as **employed**. In other words, as long as a person works for pay at least part-time, she is classified as employed. Using the official definition, in January 2014, there were 145.2 million employed workers in the United States.

Potential workers are classified as **unemployed** if they do not have a paid job, have actively looked for work in the prior four weeks, and are currently available for work. This definition of unemployment makes it easy to classify the workers we had trouble considering above. Laid-off workers will only be considered unemployed if they are actively looking for a new job. Similarly, students and parents who don't have a paid job and aren't looking for one will not count as unemployed. In January 2014, there were 10.2 million unemployed workers in the United States.

The **labor force** is the sum of all employed and unemployed workers:

$$\text{Labor force} = \text{Employed} + \text{Unemployed}.$$

Finally, all potential workers who don't fit the criteria for being employed or unemployed are classified as "not in the labor force." People in this category include the stay-at-home parents and students as well as disabled workers, retirees, and any other potential workers who don't have a paid job and aren't looking for one. In January 2014, 91.5 million potential workers were not in the labor force. Exhibit 9.1 depicts the relationship between potential workers, employed workers, unemployed workers, and those not in the labor force.

Calculating the Unemployment Rate

Using these classifications, economists calculate a number of statistics to describe the labor market. The **unemployment rate** is defined as the percentage of the labor force that is unemployed:

$$\text{Unemployment rate} = 100\% \times \frac{\text{Unemployed}}{\text{Labor force}}$$

$$= 100\% \times \frac{\text{Unemployed}}{\text{Employed} + \text{Unemployed}}$$

Similarly, the **labor force participation rate** is defined as the percentage of potential workers that are in the labor force:

$$\text{Labor force participation rate} = 100\% \times \frac{\text{Labor force}}{\text{Potential workers}}$$

A person holding a full-time or part-time paid job is **employed.**

A worker is **unemployed** if she does not have a job, has actively looked for work in the prior four weeks, and is currently available for work.

The **labor force** is the sum of all employed and unemployed workers.

The **unemployment rate** is the percentage of the labor force that is unemployed.

The **labor force participation rate** is the percentage of potential workers that are in the labor force.

Using these equations and our numbers from before, we can calculate what the labor force, unemployment rate, and labor force participation rate were in January 2014. The components are rounded, which explains why the first sum doesn't match exactly.

$$\text{Labor force} = \text{Employed} + \text{Unemployed} = 145.2 \text{ million} + 10.2 \text{ million}$$
$$= 155.5 \text{ million}.$$

$$\text{Unemployment rate} = 100\% \times \frac{\text{Unemployed}}{\text{Labor force}} = 100\% \times \frac{10.2 \text{ million}}{155.5 \text{ million}} = 6.6\%.$$

$$\text{Labor force participation rate} = 100\% \times \frac{\text{Labor force}}{\text{Potential workers}} = 100\% \times \frac{155.5 \text{ million}}{246.9 \text{ million}}$$
$$= 63.0\%.$$

While these calculations reflect the main way that economists measure unemployment, it's important to note that they are just summaries and therefore leave out many important details. In particular, the way we officially count unemployed workers omits two important categories of workers who are frustrated by the lack of jobs: discouraged workers and underemployed workers.

Discouraged workers are potential workers who would like to have a job but have given up looking for one. Because they are not actively looking for work, these workers are not included in the unemployment rate as we defined it above. Instead, discouraged workers will be counted as out of the labor force. There were 837,000 discouraged workers in the United States in January 2014, representing 0.5 percent of the labor force.

Similarly, we count all paid workers as employed, even if they would like to work more hours. Many workers in difficult economic circumstances would like to work more hours to support themselves and their families but don't have the option to do so. Although such workers are *underemployed*, they are not included in the official unemployment statistic. There were 7.3 million underemployed workers in the United States in January 2014, representing 4.7 percent of the labor force.

Trends in the Unemployment Rate

As the overall economy fluctuates, so does the unemployment rate. When the overall economy suffers a *recession*—a period in which GDP falls—the unemployment rate tends to rise. During typical U.S. recessions the unemployment rate reaches a level between 6 percent and 9 percent. When the economy is healthy and expanding, the unemployment rate tends to fall to around 5 percent.

Severe recessions produce the largest increases in the unemployment rate. For example, in early 2007—before the start of the recession later that year—the U.S. unemployment rate hovered around 4.5 percent. The 2007–2009 recession led to a sharp rise in the unemployment rate and a peak rate of 10.0 percent in October 2009. During the Great Depression of the 1930s—the most severe contraction of the U.S. economy in the twentieth century—the unemployment rate reached 25 percent.

Exhibit 9.2 shows the evolution of the monthly unemployment rate in the U.S. economy since 1948. The unemployment rate is relatively high during and following recessions—the shaded areas on the exhibit correspond to recessions. For example, the unemployment rate was high following the oil price shocks in the mid-1970s and then again during the recession of 1981–1982. Since World War II, the peak in unemployment, 10.8 percent, occurred during the 1981–1982 recession. This peak is even higher than the 10.0 percent peak during the severe 2007–2009 recession.

> **Some amount of unemployment—usually around 4 percent or 5 percent—is a necessary attribute of a well-functioning modern economy.**

It is also noteworthy that the unemployment rate is never close to zero. Since 1948, the U.S. unemployment rate has gone below 3 percent during only one period in the early 1950s. Even during the economic boom in the 1990s, the unemployment rate reached a low of only around 4 percent. Later in this chapter, we'll explain why some amount of unemployment—usually around 4 percent or 5 percent—is a necessary attribute of a well-functioning modern economy, while an unemployment rate of 10 percent is a national crisis that policymakers actively try to avoid.

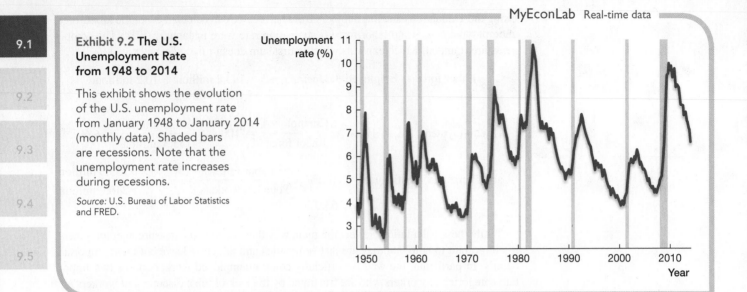

Exhibit 9.2 The U.S. Unemployment Rate from 1948 to 2014

This exhibit shows the evolution of the U.S. unemployment rate from January 1948 to January 2014 (monthly data). Shaded bars are recessions. Note that the unemployment rate increases during recessions.

Source: U.S. Bureau of Labor Statistics and FRED.

Who Is Unemployed?

The prevalence of unemployment varies widely across different segments of the labor force. One of the most noticeable disparities is that unemployment is much higher among those with low levels of education. Exhibit 9.3 shows, for example, that the unemployment rate among those in the labor force with less than a high school diploma was 11.0 percent in 2013. For people in the labor force with a college degree, the unemployment rate was only 3.7 percent.

There are many factors that explain why more educated workers tend to have lower rates of unemployment. The principle of optimization provides part of the answer. When people lose a job, they tend to spend some of their time looking for a new job and some of their time engaged in production at home. There are many "home production" activities, like cleaning out the attic or painting the house, and most of them do not require high levels of formal education. People with higher levels of education aren't necessarily more skillful in these home production activities.

However, more educated workers tend to earn higher wages than less educated workers when working *outside* the home (and this is a consequence of the fact that there is greater demand for their labor because of their additional human capital, as we have seen in Chapter 6). More educated workers therefore have a higher *opportunity cost of time*. An unemployed cab driver might be indifferent between driving a cab and staying home for a few weeks to paint his house. An unemployed engineer might be just as good at house painting as the taxi driver, but the engineer would be much better off getting back to

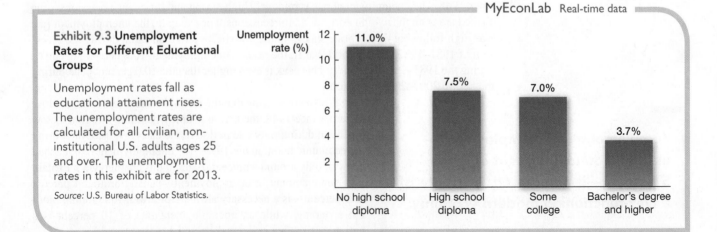

Exhibit 9.3 Unemployment Rates for Different Educational Groups

Unemployment rates fall as educational attainment rises. The unemployment rates are calculated for all civilian, non-institutional U.S. adults ages 25 and over. The unemployment rates in this exhibit are for 2013.

Source: U.S. Bureau of Labor Statistics.

work designing robotic assembly lines, earning a relatively high income, and using some of that income to hire someone *else* to paint her house. Higher wages make the cost of unemployment higher for workers with more education. Similarly, unemployment is often much lower among middle-aged workers, who tend to have more experience and skills—and therefore higher wages—than younger workers.

9.2 Equilibrium in the Labor Market

To study how employment and unemployment are determined, we first need to understand how the labor market works. Like any other market, supply and demand play the key roles. We develop the demand curve for labor and the supply curve for labor separately and then put them together to describe the labor market equilibrium.

The Demand for Labor

When we first studied demand curves in Chapter 4, we discussed households demanding goods and services. Now that we are studying the *labor market*, the role of households flips. In the labor market, households supply labor and firms demand labor. Firms are now on the demand side because they need to hire workers for production.

Optimizing firms try to maximize profits, so they demand the quantity of labor that produces the greatest feasible *profit* (defined as revenues minus costs). How does a firm determine the profit-maximizing quantity of labor? By comparing the revenue that a worker produces with the cost of employing that worker.

To see how this works, consider a barbershop. If the barbershop has only one barber, let's assume that he'll almost always be busy cutting hair and that he'll generate revenue of $25 per hour. Let's also assume that the market wage for barbers is $15 per hour. So the barbershop earns $10 per hour by employing this first barber: $25 − $15 = $10 per hour. If the shop adds a second barber, the barbershop will sell more haircuts, but from time to time, there won't be enough customers to keep both barbers busy. So the addition of the second barber does not double sales at the barbershop. Suppose instead that the second barber increases sales by only $20 per hour. Because the market wage for barbers is $15 per hour, employing the additional barber will still increase profits by $20 − $15 = $5 per hour. So an optimizing barbershop will also hire the second barber.

Now consider what will happen if the barbershop adds a third barber. The third barber will increase sales a bit more, but will do so by even less than the addition of the second barber because it will rarely be the case that the shop has enough customers to simultaneously keep all three barbers busy. Suppose that this third barber increases sales by only $10 per hour. Because the market wage is $15 per hour, hiring this third barber will actually *lower* the profits of the barbershop ($10 − $15 = −$5), so the shop will refrain from hiring a third barber. Thus, the barbershop optimizes—in other words, maximizes its profits—by employing only two barbers.

The barbershop scenario demonstrates two important facts about labor demand. First, as we have also seen in Chapters 6 and 7, firms typically experience *diminishing marginal product* of labor. Recall that the marginal product is the amount of output that one additional worker produces. Diminishing marginal product of labor means that each additional worker creates less marginal output than the workers who were hired before. For example, additional barbers will increase the haircuts that the barbershop offfers, but each additional barber won't be as productive as the last one because there won't be enough customers to keep them all busy. Economists call the market value of a worker's marginal product the *value of the marginal product of labor*. In the barbershop, the first barber creates $25 of additional revenue, the second $20, and the third only $10. Because the value of the marginal product of each additional barber is diminishing, hiring more barbers increases the *total* revenue of a firm by less and less.

Even if a customer just walked in the door, the marginal product of the second and third barbers is still zero.

Exhibit 9.4 The Value of the Marginal Product of Labor Is the Labor Demand Curve

Because the marginal product of labor diminishes as the quantity of labor increases, the curve that plots the value of the marginal product of labor is downward-sloping. Profit maximization implies that the firm should hire workers up to the point where the market wage is equal to the value of the marginal product of labor. The value of the marginal product of labor schedule is also the labor demand curve.

The **labor demand curve** depicts the relationship between the quantity of labor demanded and the wage. The value of the marginal product of labor is also the labor demand curve, because they both show how the quantity of labor demanded varies with the wage.

The second important fact illustrated by the barbershop example is that a firm hires workers until it cannot increase profits by hiring an additional worker. The firm keeps hiring as long as the revenue that an additional worker brings in for the firm—the value of the marginal product of labor—is at least as great as the cost of employing that worker, which is the *market wage*. To see why this is the case, consider Exhibit 9.4, which plots the value of the marginal product of labor against the number of workers employed. Because the value of the marginal product decreases as the number of workers employed increases, the curve is downward-sloping.

If the firm employs fewer workers than the optimal quantity shown in Exhibit 9.4, then it can increase profits by hiring more workers, because the revenue those workers bring in (the value of their marginal product) is greater than the cost of employing them (the market wage). Similarly, if the firm employs more workers than the optimal quantity, the firm can increase profits by laying off workers, because the revenue those workers bring in is less than the market wage, the cost of employing them.

Therefore, *the profit-maximizing firm will hire the amount of labor that makes the value of the marginal product of labor equal to the market wage.* As we change the market wage, the quantity of labor demanded moves *along* the curve depicting the value of the marginal product—the firm adjusts the number of workers it employs to make the value of the marginal product equal to the wage. Thus, the downward-sloping curve in Exhibit 9.4—the value of the marginal product of labor—is also the **labor demand curve**, because it shows how the quantity of labor demanded varies with the wage.

Shifts in the Labor Demand Curve

The labor demand curve depicts the relationship between the quantity of labor demanded and the wage. A *movement along the labor demand* curve occurs when the wage changes and no other economic variables change other than the quantity of labor demanded. On the other hand, there are many factors that cause the entire labor demand curve to shift to the left or right—as depicted in Exhibit 9.5.

Any change that affects the schedule relating the quantity of labor and the value of the marginal product of labor will shift the labor demand curve. We discuss four shifters in this section:

- **Changing output prices:** When the price of haircuts goes down, the value of the marginal product of barbers also declines. This implies that the firm would like to hire fewer barbers at any given wage, shifting the labor demand curve to the left.
- **Changing demand for the output good or service:** When the demand for haircuts declines, this will impact the value of the marginal product of barbers even if it does not directly change the price of haircuts. Falling demand for haircuts lowers the number of customers coming to the barbershop, leading each barber to spend more time waiting idly rather than cutting hair. Such declines in demand for output will shift the labor demand curve to the left.

Exhibit 9.5 Downward-Sloping Labor Demand Curve

The labor demand curve, which shows the relationship between the quantity of labor demanded and the wage, is downward-sloping. The exhibit depicts left and right shifts in the labor demand curve. The labor demand curve shifts when the quantity of labor demanded changes at a given value of the wage.

Technological innovation in the hair business. The technology for permanent waves—now called perms—was first developed in the nineteenth century and has continuously advanced since then.

- **Changing technology:** When the value of the marginal product of labor increases, the labor demand curve shifts to the right. For example, technology that was developed in the late nineteenth century first enabled hair stylists to straighten or curl hair: "perms." The ability to offer perms increased the marginal product of hair stylists and shifted the demand curve for hair stylists to the right. Technological progress and increases in productivity typically shift the labor demand curve to the right, but in rare cases the opposite can happen. For example, machines sometimes substitute for labor and shift the labor demand curve to the left. We discuss one such example later in the chapter.

- **Changing input prices:** Businesses use labor and *other* factors of production, like machines and tools, to produce goods and services. When the cost of these other factors goes down, businesses purchase more of those other factors. This usually increases the marginal product of labor, shifting the labor demand curve to the right. For example, mechanical hair clippers enable barbers to cut hair more quickly. If a barbershop acquires more hair clippers (because the cost of hair clippers falls), the barbers will increase the number of customers that they can serve per hour.

Until now, we've illustrated most ideas with the labor demand curve of a single barbershop or hair stylist. To study the level of employment and unemployment in the *total* economy, we need to derive the labor demand curve of the entire economy. To derive this economy-wide, or "aggregate," labor demand curve, we proceed in two steps. First, we derive the labor demand curve for each industry. For example, this is done by adding together the labor demand curves of every barbershop. If there were 100,000 barbershops in the economy, and each hired two barbers when the wage for barbers is $15 per hour, then the total quantity of labor demanded at that wage would be 200,000 barbers. To derive the rest of the labor demand curve for this industry, we repeat this summation at every wage.

Once we have derived the labor demand curve of each industry, we can sum these industry labor demand curves to obtain the aggregate labor demand curve. In principle, we will also need to account for spillover effects among the different industries and also between workers and firms. For example, expansion in one industry might create additional demand for the products of another industry. In addition, changing the overall level of wages and employment will affect workers' demand for the products of firms. When more workers are employed, they have more income to buy the products that other workers produce. We return to these issues in Chapter 12.

Notice that we are simplifying our model by treating the economy as if it contains a *single* aggregate labor demand curve. In practice, workers have different skills and receive different wages. Nevertheless, the simplifying assumption

The **labor supply curve** represents the relationship between the quantity of labor supplied and the wage.

enables us to generate key insights about how the overall economy functions without having to specify how different segments of the labor market function, even if it also means that we are omitting some interesting details about the performance of these segments.

The Supply of Labor

The **labor supply curve** represents the relationship between the quantity of labor supplied and the wage. Like the labor demand curve, the labor supply curve is derived from the principles of optimization. In this case, workers optimally allocate their limited time between paid work, leisure, and other activities, which might include home production like childcare, home maintenance, cooking, or cleaning. When market wages are higher, it makes sense for workers to spend more time working outside the home. For instance, if you are paid by the hour and your employer is running overtime shifts, you can get paid 1.5 times your normal hourly wage in those special shifts. For many workers this is a tempting arrangement, leading them to work more outside the home and accordingly have less time for chores at home or for leisure.

This kind of reasoning implies that as the wage increases, the quantity of labor supplied rises. Accordingly, the labor supply curve is upward-sloping, as shown in Exhibit 9.6.

Shifts in the Labor Supply Curve

As we have noted, the labor supply curve is the relationship between the quantity of labor supplied and the wage. A *movement along the labor* supply curve occurs when the wage changes and no other economic variables change (other than the quantity of labor supplied).

On the other hand, there are many factors that cause the entire labor supply curve to shift to the left or right (both shifts are depicted in Exhibit 9.6). *Any change that affects the entire schedule relating the quantity of labor supplied and the wage will shift the labor supply curve.* We discuss three potential changes here:

- **Changing tastes:** Changing tastes or social norms affect people's willingness to take a paid job. For example, before World War II, married women working for pay outside the home were frowned upon. However, during World War II, most governments encouraged women to work in armaments factories as an act of patriotism. Factory work during the war was one early step in a worldwide shift toward acceptance of female labor force participation. As a result of this shift in social norms, female labor force participation in the United States rose from 25 percent in 1940 to almost 60 percent in the 1990s, corresponding to a large rightward shift in the labor supply curve.
- **Changing opportunity cost of time:** Devices like vacuum cleaners, dishwashers, laundry machines, and lawnmowers lower the opportunity cost of working outside the home by freeing up time that was previously needed for home production. This encourages people to shift more time out of home production into paid employment,

Exhibit 9.6 Upward-Sloping Labor Supply Curve

The labor supply curve, which shows the relationship between the quantity of labor supplied and the wage rate, is upward-sloping. As the wage rises (holding all else equal), people's willingness to work rises. The exhibit also depicts left and right shifts in the labor supply curve. The labor supply curve shifts when the quantity of labor supplied changes at a given value of the wage.

generating a rightward shift in the labor supply curve. This sort of technology-induced change in the opportunity cost of time has also been a factor contributing to the rise in female labor force participation.

- **Changes in population:** Increases in the size of the population, corresponding to increases in the number of potential workers in the economy, also shift the labor supply curve to the right. One factor increasing population is immigration. For example, each year, the United States experiences a net immigration inflow of roughly 1 million people, implying that the population grows one-third of 1 percent per year due to immigration. This inflow shifts the domestic U.S. labor supply curve to the right.

As with the labor demand curve, the labor supply curve of the entire economy (the "aggregate" labor supply curve) can be derived by summing over the labor supply of each potential worker in the economy.

Equilibrium in a Competitive Labor Market

Recall from Chapter 1 that we define an *equilibrium* as a situation in which nobody would benefit by changing his or her own behavior. Moreover, recall from Chapter 4 that a *competitive equilibrium* is given by the intersection of the supply and demand curves. Equilibrium in a competitive labor market works the same way. In particular, the equilibrium in a competitive labor market is given by the point of intersection between the labor supply and labor demand curves, as shown in Exhibit 9.7. At the competitive equilibrium wage, w^*, the quantity of labor supplied is equal to the quantity of labor demanded. At a wage above w^*, the quantity of labor supplied would exceed the quantity of labor demanded and push the wage down. At a wage below w^*, the quantity of labor demanded would exceed the quantity of labor supplied and push the wage up. Thus w^* is the unique wage that equates the quantity of labor supplied and the quantity of labor demanded. This *equilibrium quantity of labor*, shown by L^* in Exhibit 9.7, is also referred to as *equilibrium employment*.

We refer to the competitive equilibrium wage as the **market-clearing wage**. The label market-clearing should remind you that every worker that wants a job can (eventually) find one: the wage has adjusted so that the quantity of labor demanded matches the quantity of labor supplied. This distinguishes the market-clearing wage from the wage that results from wage rigidities, which prevents the wage from adjusting to equate the quantity of labor demanded and the quantity of labor supplied. As we'll see later in this chapter, such rigidities will generate unemployment.

We will use the labor market equilibrium depicted in Exhibit 9.7 to model the *overall* level of employment in an economy. As mentioned above, we are simplifying our analysis by focusing on a single type of labor. But the labor market equilibrium shown in Exhibit 9.7 can be readily applied to study equilibrium in a specific segment of the market or in a local

We refer to the competitive equilibrium wage as the **market-clearing wage.** At this wage, every worker that wants a job can find one: the quantity of labor demanded matches the quantity of labor supplied.

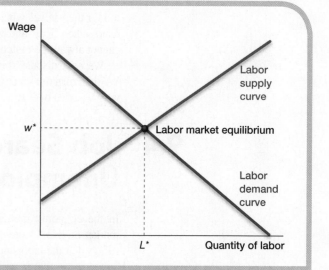

Exhibit 9.7 Equilibrium in the Labor Market

The upward-sloping labor supply curve and the downward-sloping labor demand curve intersect at the market-clearing wage, w^*, and the quantity of labor L^*. At the market-clearing wage, the quantity of labor supplied is equal to the quantity of labor demanded.

labor market as well. For example, we could consider the supply of and demand for workers with computer programming skills (or doctors or gardeners, etc.) and derive the equilibrium wage and employment level in that specific labor market.

It is useful to note that the labor market depicted in Exhibit 9.7 is what is sometimes referred to as a *frictionless* labor market. In a frictionless market, firms can instantly hire and fire workers, both workers and firms have complete information about each other, and the wage adjusts instantly to clear the market (setting the quantity of labor supplied equal to the quantity of labor demanded). We will see next why departures from this frictionless labor market are often useful for understanding real-world labor markets and unemployment.

9.3 Why Is There Unemployment?

At the market-clearing wage w^* in Exhibit 9.7, the labor supply and labor demand curves intersect. Accordingly, the quantity of labor demanded equals the quantity of labor supplied—every worker who wants to work at wage w^* has a job. There are people who are not working—represented by the segment of the labor supply curve that lies *above* the market-clearing wage. The people on this part of the labor supply curve are only willing to work for wages *above* the market-clearing wage w^*.

In the economy depicted in Exhibit 9.7, there are employed workers and workers who are not employed because they are unwilling to work at the market-clearing wage w^*. In a competitive equilibrium, there should be no workers looking for work (they are either employed or unwilling to work at the market-clearing wage). This implies that in a competitive equilibrium there shouldn't be people who are not employed and looking for work. But then, how would we explain the fact that there were 10.2 million *officially* unemployed Americans in January 2014, who are thus counted as not employed and looking for work?

A first possibility is that the official unemployment statistics are probably counting *some* workers who are only willing to work for a wage above the market-clearing wage w^*. Because unemployment survey questions do not specify that the workers should be looking for work at the *current prevailing market wage*, some people might be counted as unemployed even though they are looking only for jobs that pay more than the current prevailing market wage.

However, the available evidence suggests that most unemployed workers *would* be willing to work at the prevailing market wage but are unable to find employers that are willing to hire them at this wage.[2] Thus, we must find another way to explain why 10.2 million Americans couldn't find a job in January 2014.

When economic models do not predict what we observe in the world, we must ask ourselves whether the assumptions we made in our model are correct. In our model of the labor market, we made an assumption that might not actually hold.

We assumed that workers and firms have full information about the job market. For instance, we assumed that they know what the equilibrium wage is, what qualifications employers are looking for, and where the jobs are. This means that workers can instantly find the right job for themselves whenever it is available and no open job will be left unfilled. On the other hand, when firms and workers lack important information about the labor market, workers cannot always be matched to open jobs, and this mismatch will cause unemployment.

We next discuss this type of unemployment, which we call frictional unemployment. We then turn to two other economic factors that explain why unemployment exists and also why it varies over time.

9.4 Job Search and Frictional Unemployment

In the economy described by Exhibit 9.7, any worker wishing to be employed at the market-clearing wage w^* can do so. Up until this point, our analysis of the labor market assumes that the labor market is frictionless, which implies that the worker can *instantly* find an employer that is willing to hire her. Yet if you've ever looked for a job, you've probably discovered that finding the right job is not simple and might take a lot of legwork. It might be simple to find a summer job at McDonald's, but it's hard to land a job that is a good fit for your particular skills and capabilities.

To find the right job, you need to determine which firms are hiring and try to learn how pay, benefits, and other job characteristics vary among them. You have to line up references and send out résumés. It also helps to network with family and friends to find some acquaintance of an acquaintance who happens to work where you are applying. You need to set up interviews and survive them. Finally, you wait for the people who conduct those interviews to finish interviewing the other leading candidates. In most cases, someone else gets chosen and then you start all over again.

> **Because each person has specific capabilities, experience, and job preferences, finding the right match between an unemployed person and a firm usually takes time.**

Job search refers to the activities that workers undertake to find appropriate jobs.

Economists refer to job-hunting activities as **job search**. Because each person has specific capabilities, experience, and job preferences, finding the right match between an unemployed person and a firm usually takes time.

Search frictions arise both because of the time-consuming logistics of finding, applying, and interviewing for jobs and because firms and workers have imperfect information about each other and the state of the economy. Imagine a Detroit autoworker who loses his $40/hour job during the 2007–2009 recession. Shortly afterward, he hears about job offers in the service sector for $20/hour. Instead of pursuing those jobs, he keeps looking for higher-paying jobs in the auto industry. Only after months of unsuccessful searching in the auto sector, does he have enough information to conclude that his best options are the $20/hour jobs in the service sector. Examples like this illustrate that gathering information and searching for the right job takes time.

Frictional unemployment refers to unemployment that arises because workers have imperfect information about available jobs and need to engage in a time-consuming process of job search.

Unemployment resulting from imperfect information about available jobs and from the time-consuming process of job search is **frictional unemployment**.

Though it might at first seem strange, you can think about the dating market in the same way that you think about the job market. It takes a long time to find a person who is a good match as a romantic partner. In this sense, people who are not in a relationship, but looking for one, are romantically unemployed. We don't expect single people to find a new romantic partner overnight and we shouldn't expect unemployed workers to instantly find a job either.

9.5 Wage Rigidity and Structural Unemployment

> **Holding the market wage above the market-clearing wage causes some workers who would like to work at the market wage to be unemployed.**

Frictional unemployment resulting from job search activities is a normal and necessary feature of every labor market. However, unemployment also arises because wages are sometimes above the market-clearing level w^*, meaning that the quantity of labor supplied is greater than the quantity of labor demanded. When wages are held fixed above the competitive equilibrium level that clears the labor market, this is referred to as **wage rigidity**. **Structural unemployment** arises when the quantity of labor supplied persistently exceeds the quantity of labor demanded. Wage

Wage rigidity refers to the condition in which the market wage is held above the competitive equilibrium level that would clear the labor market.

Structural unemployment arises when the quantity of labor supplied persistently exceeds the quantity of labor demanded.

rigidity is a key factor in leading to such a persistent gap. Wage rigidity can occur for many reasons, which we discuss next but the economic effects are all the same: holding the market wage above the market-clearing wage causes some workers who would like to work at the market wage to be unemployed. To illustrate how wage rigidity impacts the labor market, we start with minimum wage laws because it is easy to understand their effect using the supply and demand framework. However, other causes of wage rigidity are much more important in the U.S. labor market and we study those in turn.

Minimum Wage Laws

In most countries, legislation specifies a minimum level for the hourly wage. Such legislated wage floors, often called *minimum wage laws*, can prevent the market wage from

CHOICE & CONSEQUENCE

The Luddites

Does technology cause unemployment? In a Phillips electronics factory in China, hundreds of employees work on an assembly line that manufactures electric shavers. Meanwhile, in the Netherlands, the same shavers are assembled by an army of 128 robotic arms. With video cameras for eyes and computer-calibrated hydraulics, these robots tirelessly go about their work. Robot-filled factories raise the possibility that technology can reduce a firm's demand for labor. Throughout history, workers have complained about technological innovation that reduces employment.

The most famous episode began in 1811, when gangs of British textile workers started burning down factories and smashing newly invented mechanized looms. The rioters also targeted inventors and mill owners, burning down their homes and in one instance conducting an assassination. These so-called Luddites—named after the worker Ned Ludd, who was reputed to have smashed textile machines several decades earlier—opposed the mechanization of production. The riots became so frequent and so destructive that the British army was called in to restore order. Dozens of rioters were hanged and the movement faded in 1813. Ultimately, the Luddites could not stop the mechanization of textile manufacturing.

Were new machines really destroying the livelihoods of the textile workers in 1811? The likely answer is yes. The new machines enabled workers to complete tasks in minutes that had previously taken hours. Consequently, the mills needed to employ fewer workers. Many skilled artisans lost their jobs and their families suffered. So the Luddites were not mistaken in believing that the machines were putting some of them out of work.

Technological progress *can* destroy jobs in a single industry such as textiles. However, historical evidence shows that technological progress does not produce unemployment in a country as a *whole*. Technological progress increases productivity and incomes in the overall

A drawing of workers smashing a mechanized loom in Britain during the period of the Luddite riots (1811–1813).

economy, and higher incomes lead to higher demand for goods and thus higher demand for labor. As a result, workers who lose jobs in one industry will be able to find jobs in others, although for many of them this might take time and some of them, like the Luddites, will end up with lower wages in their new jobs.

Today, the term *Luddite* is synonymous with opposition to new technology. The British textile workers of 1811 were unlucky. They were victims of technological progress. For most people, however, ongoing technological progress improves their lives by raising their productivity and lowering the cost of the goods and services they buy.

falling to the market-clearing wage that equates the quantity of labor supplied with the quantity of labor demanded. In the United States, the federal government chooses a national minimum wage and state legislatures can choose even higher minimum wages for in-state jobs. In January 2014, for example, the federal minimum wage was $7.25, while the highest state minimum wage was $9.32, which applied in Washington State.

Minimum wages might prevent the quantity of labor supplied from equaling the quantity of labor demanded, as depicted in Exhibit 9.8. In this exhibit, the minimum wage is labeled with a line beneath it to signify that the minimum wage is a wage floor: $\underline{w}$. In Exhibit 9.8, the minimum wage, $\underline{w}$, is above the market-clearing wage, w^*. At the minimum wage, $\underline{w}$, the quantity of labor demanded by employers is less than the quantity of labor supplied by workers. Consequently, some workers—represented by the gap between the quantity supplied and the quantity demanded at $\underline{w}$—aren't able to find jobs. These unemployed workers are willing to work at the going wage, $\underline{w}$, and would even be willing to work at wages lower than $\underline{w}$. The minimum wage legislation prevents employers from

Exhibit 9.8 Labor Supply and Labor Demand in a Market with a Minimum Wage

When the minimum wage ($\underline{w}$) is above the market-clearing wage (w^*), the quantity of labor supplied exceeds the quantity of labor demanded, creating unemployment (quantity of labor supplied minus quantity of labor demanded).

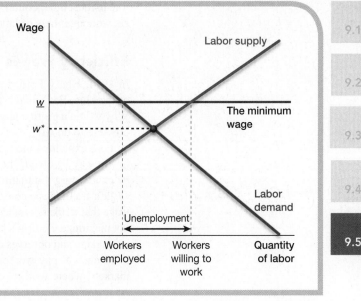

hiring these workers at wages that would equalize the quantity of labor supplied and the quantity of labor demanded.

Minimum wage laws are an example of a policy that creates winners and losers. The winners are the workers who get jobs at wages above the wage that equates quantity supplied and quantity demanded. The losers are the firms that have to pay the higher wage and the unemployed who would like to work but can't find a job at the prevailing wage, $\underline{w}$. The costs and benefits of the minimum wage are actively debated, with economists divided on the question of whether the United States should raise its minimum wage.

The minimum wage produces structural unemployment, but it cannot be the only cause of unemployment. For example, in January 2014, there were 1.6 million college graduates who were unemployed. The median hourly wage for a college graduate was $29.85 per hour in 2013, four times the level of the minimum wage. Because almost all college graduates are paid far more than the minimum wage, it is not the minimum wage that prevents the labor market for college graduates from clearing.

In the overall workforce, including all education levels, 1.0 percent of workers are paid the minimum wage. Accordingly, the impact of the minimum wage on the labor market is modest. The minimum wage does prevent the market for some types of low-skilled workers from clearing but has little impact on the general labor market.

Labor Unions and Collective Bargaining

Another source of wage rigidity is **collective bargaining**, which refers to the contract negotiations that take place between firms and labor unions. A labor union is an organization of workers that advocates for better working conditions, pay, and benefits for its members. Unions use the threat of going on strike—a mass work stoppage—as a bargaining chip in these negotiations. Collective bargaining often leads to equilibrium wages and benefits that are greater than what workers would have received under the market-clearing wage. Collective bargaining has the same effect on unemployment as minimum wage laws that we saw in Exhibit 9.8. By keeping the equilibrium wage above the market-clearing wage, unions cause the quantity of labor supplied to be greater than the quantity of labor demanded, thus creating structural unemployment. Through such collective bargaining, unions benefit their members but make it difficult for non-members to find work.

However, just like the minimum wage, collective bargaining is unlikely to be the most important factor causing wage rigidity in the U.S. labor market because union membership is relatively low in the United States. For example, in 2011, 10.6 percent of employed workers in the United States were members of labor unions. Unions play a more important

In October 2010, striking teachers, postal workers, and transport workers protested the French government's proposal to raise the retirement age from 60 to 62.

Collective bargaining refers to contract negotiations between firms and labor unions.

role in most other countries. For example, in Italy, in 2011, 35.2 percent of employed workers were members of labor unions.

Efficiency Wages and Unemployment

In 1914, Henry Ford, founder of the Ford Motor Company, seemed to go bonkers. Out of the blue, Ford increased the daily wage of most of his employees from $2.34 to $5.00. Why would a profit-maximizing employer double his employees' pay without any external pressure to do so?

Ford explained the wage of $5 per day as an act of *self*-interest. There was "no charity in any way involved," he said. "We wanted to pay these wages so that the business would be on a lasting foundation. We were building for the future."

In a frictionless, competitive labor market, paying an above-market wage (or above the wage that workers would accept) would not be optimal for a firm—in other words, it would not maximize the firm's profits. In such a "perfect" market, the firm knows everything about its workers and observes everything that they do at work. In this idealized environment, there is no need to pay workers more than the market wage to obtain their labor. But in actual markets, where workers can shirk (slack off) on the job, paying *more* than the going wage can have benefits for the firm. Ford's wage premium is an example of what economists call **efficiency wages**. By paying wages above the wage that workers were willing to accept (and in fact above the market wage), Ford was able to increase the productivity and profitability of his company.

Efficiency wages increase productivity and firm profitability for a number of reasons. First, efficiency wages reduce worker turnover. Working on an assembly line is monotonous, causing a relatively high level of turnover. Recruiting and training new workers is costly to the company. If workers are paid more than the prevailing market wage by their employer, they are more motivated to keep their job because they would face lower wages if they needed to find a job elsewhere. Second, the fear of losing a high-paying job motivates employees to work harder than they otherwise would, increasing their hourly output. Third, there is the possibility that employees would be grateful for an above-market wage, leading them to reciprocate this apparent generosity by working harder—another boost to their hourly output. Finally, efficiency wages also improve the quality of the pool of workers who apply for a job in the first place.

If efficiency wages increase productivity, employers like Henry Ford might find it profitable to pay a higher wage than the market-clearing wage. Like minimum wage laws and collective bargaining, this results in a form of wage rigidity. As before, this will cause the quantity of labor supplied to be greater than the quantity of labor demanded, leading to structural unemployment, just as we saw in Exhibit 9.8. One difference is worth noting, however. The minimum wage and collective bargaining force employers to pay a wage above the market-clearing wage level, whereas with efficiency wages, the equilibrium wage is above the market-clearing level because profit-maximizing firms voluntarily prefer to pay such wages.

Downward Wage Rigidity and Unemployment Fluctuations

Another type of wage rigidity results from the fact that workers are highly averse to reductions in their wage, resulting in what economists call **downward wage rigidity**. Cuts in the wage hurt worker morale and lower productivity. As a result, most firms would rather fire workers than cut their wages. Typically, only firms on the brink of bankruptcy attempt to talk their workers into accepting wage reductions.

Downward wage rigidity, like the other forms of wage rigidity we have studied so far, causes wages to remain above the market-clearing level and causes structural unemployment. To see this, consider the following scenario, depicted in Exhibit 9.9. Assume that the labor market begins in a competitive equilibrium with no unemployment (at the point labeled E_1). Next, imagine that the labor demand curve shifts to the left because the economy slows down (we'll have much more to say about why the economy fluctuates in Chapter 12).

Efficiency wages are above the wage that workers would accept, where the extra pay increases worker productivity and improves the profitability of the firm.

Downward wage rigidity arises when workers resist a cut in their wage.

Exhibit 9.9 Shifts in Labor Demand Affect Equilibrium in the Labor Market

With flexible wages, a shift to the left in the demand for labor reduces the equilibrium wage and employment (the economy moves from point E_1 to point F). With a downward rigid wage, the same leftward shift has a larger impact on employment (the economy moves from point E_1 to point E_2). Employment now falls all the way to L_2 instead of L_F, because none of the impact of the leftward shift in the labor demand curve is absorbed by the wage, which remains at its original (rigid) level. Moreover, downward wage rigidity causes unemployment: because the wage does not change, the quantity of labor supplied remains the same, but the quantity of labor demanded falls to L_2. The gap between the quantity of labor supplied and the quantity of labor demanded (at the rigid wage) corresponds to unemployment.

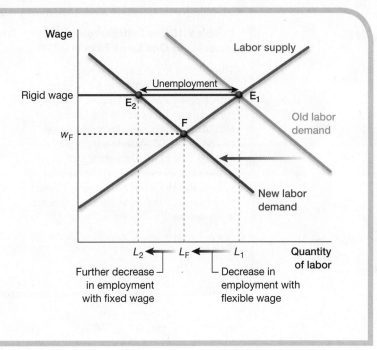

When the wage is flexible, the leftward shift in labor demand moves the market to a new equilibrium (point F) in which the equilibrium wage is w_F as shown in Exhibit 9.9, and the quantity of labor demanded falls to L_F. The exhibit also shows that at this new equilibrium, the quantity of labor supplied is equal to the quantity of labor demanded and so unemployment is still equal to zero.

However, when the wage is rigid, it won't fall to its market-clearing level and will instead stay at its initial level, marked in Exhibit 9.9. This downward wage rigidity causes the quantity of labor supplied, which is still at L_1, to be greater than the quantity of labor demanded, which has now fallen to L_2, thus leading to (structural) unemployment, as shown in Exhibit 9.9.

As we will see in more detail in Chapter 12, the downward wage rigidity depicted in Exhibit 9.9 is one of the causes of unemployment fluctuations. Recessions are periods of leftward (adverse) shifts in labor demand. This, combined with downward wage rigidity, increases the rate of unemployment.

The effect of downward wage rigidity can be seen in Exhibit 9.10, which shows the wage growth of workers in a large company for 2008, right in the middle of the 2007–2009 recession.[3] Each bar shows the fraction of workers whose wage grew by the percentage depicted on the horizontal axis. We see a large bulge in the distribution at zero, meaning that wages were frozen instead of being cut. Wage cuts were so infrequent (only 46 out of 15,000 employees) that they are not even visible on the graph. Although the extent of downward wage rigidity does vary from company to company and industry to industry, this type of rigidity is overall quite pervasive throughout labor markets and can have a significant effect on unemployment, especially during recessions, as we will see in greater detail in Chapter 12.

The Natural Rate of Unemployment and Cyclical Unemployment

As we noted earlier, the U.S. economy always has some unemployment. In addition, the unemployment rate fluctuates considerably as shown in Exhibit 9.2. To distinguish the "normal" rate of unemployment from fluctuations around that normal rate, economists use the concept of the *natural rate of unemployment*. The **natural rate of unemployment** is the rate around which the actual rate of unemployment fluctuates. In practice, the natural rate of unemployment is calculated by averaging the unemployment rate over an extended

The **natural rate of unemployment** is the rate around which the actual rate of unemployment fluctuates.

Exhibit 9.10 The Distribution of Wage Increases at One Large Firm in 2008

The vertical height of each bar represents the fraction of all workers with a particular pay increase. The pay increase can be read off the horizontal axis. At this firm, only 46 workers out of about 15,000 experienced a pay cut in 2008. These 46 workers are plotted in the exhibit, but the bars to the left of zero are too small to be seen. Over 50 percent of the workers experienced a pay freeze.

Source: Nathan Hipsman, "Downward Nominal Wage Rigidity: A Double-Density Model," Harvard University Working Paper (2012).

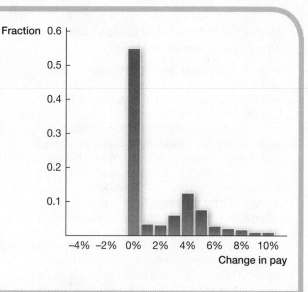

Cyclical unemployment is the deviation of the actual unemployment rate from the natural rate of unemployment.

time period. For example, in Spain, the unemployment rate has averaged 16.1 percent from 1977 to 2013. In the United States, the unemployment rate has averaged 6.5 percent over the same period.

Cyclical unemployment is defined as the deviation of the unemployment rate from its natural rate. Cyclical unemployment usually rises in recessions (when the labor demand curve shifts to the left) and falls in economic booms (when the labor demand curve shifts to the right). Chapter 12 discusses the relationship between unemployment and economic fluctuations in depth.

In 2013, the Spanish unemployment rate was 26.1 percent, implying that cyclical unemployment was 10.0 percent (using the natural rate of 16.1 percent). In 2013, the U.S. unemployment rate was 7.4 percent, implying that cyclical unemployment was 0.9 percent (using the natural rate of 6.5 percent).

The natural rate of unemployment includes frictional unemployment, which is a necessary part of any well-functioning labor market. But the natural rate of unemployment also includes long-term structural unemployment, which is generally considered to be economically inefficient. Accordingly, the natural rate of unemployment should not be confused with the rate of unemployment that is socially optimal or desirable—so some might say there is nothing "natural" about it. To see this, consider an economy that is subject to a significant level of downward wage rigidity. As Exhibit 9.9 shows, this economy will have a relatively high level of structural unemployment and this will increase the long-term average rate of unemployment. This is not a desirable state of affairs, because many potential workers who could have been gainfully employed are out of work and are unable to use their labor productively. This example illustrates that the long-term average rate of unemployment—the natural rate of unemployment—includes some inefficient sources of unemployment.

Just as the natural rate of unemployment has both frictional and structural components, so does cyclical unemployment. During recessions, fewer firms try to hire new workers, and this increases the difficulty that workers face in locating a suitable job, raising frictional unemployment. In addition, as Exhibit 9.9 shows, in the presence of downward wage rigidity, the leftward shift of the labor demand curve during a recession leads to a rise in structural unemployment as the rigid wage remains above the market-clearing wage.

Evidence-Based Economics

Q: What happens to employment and unemployment if local employers go out of business?

From 1990 to 2007, the unemployment rate in Pittsburgh fell by 1.8 percentage points. Pittsburgh had both good and bad economic news during this period, but one particularly lucky factor is that economic activity in Pittsburgh was concentrated in industries that were not highly exposed to Chinese imports. Pittsburgh specialized in industries such as paper, print, and metal products that had "low exposure" to competition from Chinese imports, meaning that across the entire U.S. economy these sectors experienced relatively slow growth of Chinese imports.

The experience of the Raleigh-Durham area in North Carolina, shown in a map of Eastern United States together with the Pittsburgh area in Exhibit 9.11, was very different between 1990 and 2007. In the Raleigh-Durham area, unemployment *increased* by 1.9 percentage points. In addition, many workers in this area are now out of the labor force because they have stopped looking for jobs entirely. One factor contributing to Raleigh-Durham's weakening labor market was its specialization in industries such as textiles and apparel, electrical products, and computers that have "high exposure" to competition from Chinese imports.

By comparing *hundreds* of regions with different levels of exposure to Chinese imports (of which Pittsburgh and Raleigh-Durham are just two examples), economists David Autor, David Dorn, and Gordon Hanson were able to identify leftward shifts in labor demand caused by high exposure to Chinese imports, similar to the shift in Exhibit 9.9.[4] Their analysis shows that high-exposure communities experienced sharper declines in manufacturing employment than low-exposure communities. The rate of unemployment also rose more in the areas with high exposure than those with low exposure.

The study confirms the model of labor market analysis depicted in Exhibit 9.9, in which a leftward shift in the labor demand curve, combined with downward wage

Exhibit 9.11 A Tale of Two Cities

Pittsburgh and Raleigh-Durham have had very different changes in their local unemployment rate between 1990 and 2007. Pittsburgh saw its unemployment rate decline from 7.3 percent to 5.5 percent, while Raleigh-Durham experienced an increase in its unemployment rate from 4.0 percent to 5.9 percent. This difference arose at least partially because Raleigh-Durham has high exposure to Chinese imports, meaning that it specialized in manufacturing industries, which experienced relatively rapid growth in competition from Chinese imports. In contrast, Pittsburgh has low exposure to Chinese imports.

Pittsburgh, PA
Low exposure
Local unemployment rate:
7.3% (1990) → 5.5% (2007)

Raleigh-Durham, NC
High exposure
Local unemployment rate:
4.0% (1990) → 5.9% (2007)

rigidity, reduces the number of jobs and increases the rate of unemployment. Consistent with the model's predictions about wage rigidity, the authors found no decline in manufacturing wages despite the leftward shifts in labor demand. It is therefore likely that some of the higher unemployment in high-exposure areas was due to wage rigidity, as in Exhibit 9.9. However, the authors also find a significant decline in non-manufacturing wages in high-exposure areas, confirming that wage rigidity only applies to a worker's existing job and does not carry over to the new jobs that unemployed workers find. Laid-off manufacturing workers are offered lower wages when they search for new jobs, and they are willing to accept those lower wages to find work.

This analysis might lead you to conclude that the United States should ban Chinese imports to increase U.S. employment, but doing so would generate far more problems than it would solve. Chinese imports are beneficial to most U.S. households, which enjoy the lower prices of the imported goods. Nevertheless, it is true that some domestic workers lose their jobs due to international trade, and much of the debate about trade revolves around the personal and economic dislocation caused by these job losses and the policies that can be used to mitigate these costs. We return to these important issues in Chapters 14 and 15, where we provide a full discussion of the effects of international trade.

Question

What happens to employment and unemployment if local employers go out of business?

Answer

Communities with a high level of exposure to competition from Chinese imports between 1990 and 2007 experienced an increase in the local rate of unemployment relative to communities with a low level of exposure to competition from Chinese imports.

Data

Community-level data on employment, unemployment, and industry composition. National U.S. data on industry-by-industry growth in Chinese imports. The study covers the period from 1990 to 2007.

Caveat

Many factors other than competition from Chinese firms contribute to movements in unemployment rates.

Summary

❂ Potential workers are defined as the civilian non-institutional population ages 16 and older. Those holding a paid full-time or part-time job are classified as employed, while those without a paid job who have actively looked for work in the prior 4 weeks and are currently available for work are unemployed. Potential workers who are employed and unemployed make up the labor force, while the rest of the potential workers are classified as out of the labor force. The unemployment rate is the percentage of the labor force that is unemployed.

❂ The unemployment rate fluctuates significantly over time. It is higher during and in the immediate aftermath of recessions.

❂ Different demographic groups have different unemployment rates. For example, more educated workers tend to have lower unemployment rates.

✹ Employment is determined by labor demand and labor supply. The labor demand curve is downward-sloping because of the diminishing marginal product of labor and profit maximization by firms. The labor supply curve, on the other hand, tends to be upward-sloping because higher wages generally encourage workers to supply more hours to the labor market.

✹ The competitive labor market equilibrium is given by the intersection of the labor demand and labor supply curves. The competitive equilibrium wage is also called the market-clearing wage.

✹ In a competitive labor market equilibrium in which all workers know the market-clearing wage, there will be no unemployment because every worker willing to work at the market-clearing wage can find a job. Workers who are not willing to work at the market-clearing wage will stop searching and will therefore not be counted as unemployed.

✹ Frictional unemployment exists because workers need to learn about the condition of the labor market and search for a job that suits them. Even in a healthy labor market, there will always be some unemployed workers in the process of changing jobs, or finding a new job after losing their previous one, or finding their first job after entry into the labor market. Structural unemployment results when the market wage is above the market-clearing level, causing the quantity of labor supplied to be greater than the quantity of labor demanded. This is often referred to as wage rigidity and can result from institutional features of the labor market like minimum wage legislation or collective bargaining. More importantly, it can result from efficiency wages or from downward wage rigidity.

✹ Efficiency wages arise when employers pay wages higher than the market-clearing wage to increase worker productivity. Downward wage rigidity arises because of the unwillingness of workers to accept wage cuts and prevents wages from immediately falling in response to a leftward shift of the labor demand curve.

✹ The most important cause of unemployment fluctuations is a shifting labor demand curve. When wages are flexible, a shift to the left of the labor demand curve reduces both employment and wages but does not increase unemployment because the labor market clears. When wages are rigid, the same leftward shift creates a larger decline in employment because the wage does not decline and unemployment increases.

✹ The natural rate of unemployment is the long-term average rate of unemployment. Cyclical unemployment is the difference between the current rate of unemployment and the natural rate of unemployment. Cyclical unemployment is positive in recessions and negative in economic booms.

Key Terms

Potential workers *p. 197*
Employed *p. 198*
Unemployed *p. 198*
Labor force *p. 198*
Unemployment rate *p. 198*
Labor force participation rate *p. 198*

Labor demand curve *p. 202*
Labor supply curve *p. 204*
Market-clearing wage *p. 205*
Job search *p. 207*
Frictional unemployment *p. 207*
Wage rigidity *p. 207*

Structural unemployment *p. 207*
Collective bargaining *p. 209*
Efficiency wages *p. 210*
Downward wage rigidity *p. 210*
Natural rate of unemployment *p. 211*
Cyclical unemployment *p. 212*

Questions

All questions are available in MyEconLab for practice and instructor assignment.

1. Unemployment statistics are measured and released by the Bureau of Labor Statistics (BLS), a division of the U.S. Department of Labor.

   a. When does the Bureau of Labor Statistics (BLS) officially classify a person as being employed? When are potential workers classified as being unemployed?

   b. What do the following terms mean and how are they calculated?

   i. The unemployment rate

   ii. The labor force participation rate

2. Explain whether each of these individuals will be counted as a part of the labor force.

   a. Jane is working full-time toward a Ph.D. in philosophy but volunteers at nursing homes during her spare weekends.

   b. Kristen left her full-time job as a journalist to spend more time with her kids and now makes some income working part-time for a children's magazine.

   c. In the past four weeks, Harry did not respond to a call from a firm seeking to interview him for a job opening. But he recently applied for another job that he feels will better suit his qualifications.

3. Consider Exhibit 9.2. What were the two highest rates of unemployment since 1948? When did they occur?

4. What could explain why unemployment is lower among workers with a relatively higher level of education?

5. What is the value of the marginal product of labor? Explain how it is computed with an example.

6. List two factors that can cause a shift in the labor demand curve. Explain why a change in each factor can lead to a shift of the curve.

7. Why does the labor supply curve slope upward and what can cause the labor supply curve to shift?

8. Should a country with a healthy economy have a zero unemployment rate?

9. What is meant by job search? How does it lead to frictional unemployment?

10. What is the difference between frictional and structural unemployment?

11. Sometimes new technology in production reduces the time that a worker takes to complete a task. Technological innovations can also completely replace a factory worker. Does this mean that technological progress will lead to large-scale unemployment? Explain your answer.

12. What is wage rigidity? List and explain two factors that can increase wage rigidity in the labor market.

Problems

All problems are available in MyEconLab for practice and instructor assignment.
Problems marked ⊕ update with real-time data.

⊕ 1. The following table shows the annual averages of the employment level, unemployment level, and the labor force participation rate in the United States in the years from 2001 to 2011. Use the given data to complete the table and answer the following questions. (*Note*: Adult population is for individuals 16 years and over, not in the military, and not institutionalized. All rates are in percent.)

Year	Number Unemployed (in thousands)	Number Employed (in thousands)	Labor Force Participation Rate	Employment Rate	Unemployment Rate	Labor Force	Adult Population
2001	6,830,000	136,939,000	66.8%				
2002	8,375,000	136,481,000	66.6%				
2003	8,770,000	137,729,000	66.2%				
2004	8,140,000	139,240,000	66.0%				
2005	7,579,000	141,710,000	66.0%				
2006	6,991,000	144,418,000	66.2%				
2007	7,073,000	146,050,000	66.0%				
2008	8,951,000	145,370,000	66.0%				
2009	14,301,000	139,888,000	65.4%				
2010	14,815,000	139,070,000	64.7%				
2011	13,743,000	139,873,000	64.1%				

Note: Annual averages based on data from the Bureau of Labor Statistics (Series: LNS12000000, LNS11300000, LNS13000000).

a. In which year did the economy witness the sharpest change in the unemployment rate? What could possibly explain this?

b. Use the data on the size of the labor force and potential workers to compute the percentage of adults out of the labor force for the year 2002. Verify that your calculation is equal to one minus the labor force participation rate.

c. What are the general trends that you observe in the data?

2. In April 2012, The Bazanian Daily, a leading newspaper in the country of Bazania, carried a report titled "20,000 jobs added in the last quarter; unemployment rate shoots up from 5 percent to 6.7 percent." How could the unemployment rate in Bazania increase even when new jobs were created?

3. In macroeconomics, a "leading indicator" is defined as a measurable economic variable that changes prior to when the economy as a whole starts to follow a given trend. Conversely, a "lagging indicator" is a measurable variable that only changes in the latter phases of an overall trend in the economy—or even afterwards.

Study Exhibit 9.2 carefully. Would you describe unemployment as a leading or lagging indicator of an economic downturn? Explain.

4. Suppose Die Cast Aluminum Co. is a subcontractor for the auto industry and makes specialized auto parts. There is a bracket it manufactures that it sells for $1.50. The following table shows the number of brackets that can be produced from a given number of labor hours. Assume that the company cannot hire labor for a fraction of an hour.

Hrs. Labor	Q
0	0
1	50
2	90
3	120
4	140
5	150
6	155
7	157

a. Find the marginal product (in brackets), and the value of the marginal product (in dollars), of each hour of labor.

b. If the wage paid to workers in Die Cast's plant is $25/hour, how many hours of labor should the firm employ? How many hours will be employed if the wage increases to $35/hour? Explain.

c. How many hours will be employed if the wage is $35/hour, but the price of a bracket declines to $1?

5. In a recent study for the National Bureau of Economic Research (NBER), four researchers looked at the effect of generous unemployment benefits on the local unemployment rate. They compared the unemployment situation in adjoining counties, which happened to lie in two different states with different laws regarding the amount and duration of unemployment benefits.

The authors of the study found that the unemployment rate "rises dramatically in the border counties belonging to the states that expanded unemployment benefit duration" during the Great Recession. Why might this be so? (Based on Hagedorn, Karahan, et al., "Unemployment Benefits and Unemployment in the Great Recession: The Role of Macro Effects." NBER working paper 19499, October 2013.)

6. Every month, statistics on employment and unemployment are compiled by the Bureau of Labor Statistics.

a. The unemployed worker whose frustration was discussed at the beginning of section 9.1 had been unemployed for 17 months. Go to www.bls.gov and consult Table A-12. Find the average (mean) duration of unemployment (seasonally adjusted) in the most recent month. Based on what you find, is 17 months higher or lower than average?

b. List some possible reasons for the quoted worker's unemployment that would make his joblessness qualify as frictional unemployment. List reasons that would fall in the category of structural unemployment.

7. Suppose the equilibrium wage in the market for food service workers is $11 per hour. The government then establishes a minimum wage at $9 per hour. What will be the effect of the minimum wage on the market for labor in the food service industry? Explain.

8. The following graph shows the demand for and supply of labor in a market with a minimum wage set at $8 per hour. Use the graph to answer the following questions.

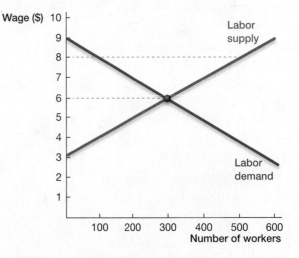

a. How many workers will be unemployed due to the minimum wage? What kind of unemployment is this?

b. What would happen to the quantity of labor demanded and supplied if the minimum wage were less than $6?

c. Who are the winners and the losers when the minimum wage is $8?

d. In the United States, does minimum wage legislation have a significant impact on unemployment in the overall labor force? Why or why not?

9. In response to high unemployment, the Spanish government enacted a series of labor market reforms in 2012. Among other measures, the government reduced severance pay and the influence of unions in setting wages and hours of work. What could be the rationale behind using these measures to boost employment?

10. According to salary.com, the average salary for a software engineer level III (a higher-level position in software design and implementation) in the Silicon Valley area of California is $108,244. However, Google pays its level III software engineers an average salary of $124,258. Explain why Google would pay a salary higher than the equilibrium salary for equivalent positions in the same area.

11. The following figure shows the demand and supply curves in the market for workers in Starbucks coffee shops (called "baristas"). The hourly wage in this market has been fixed at $6 and cannot be changed.

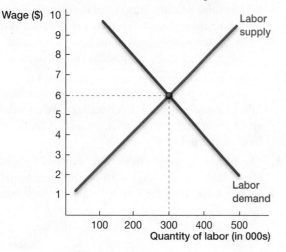

a. Suppose that, due to concerns about the high number of calories in many Starbucks drinks, the demand for Starbucks products declines. Use a graph to explain what will happen to employment in the market for baristas.

b. Now suppose the wage is flexible. How would your answer to part (a) change?

12. The period from 2007 to 2009 was a time of economic contraction that some called the "Great Recession." During periods of recession, most firms experience a decline in demand for their product. All other things being equal, macroeconomic theory predicts that the wage of most workers should decline in recessionary periods. However, this was not the case in the 2007–2009 recession, or during many other economic downturns throughout recent history.

Based on the discussion in the chapter, explain why this might be so, and what the implications are for unemployment.

10 Credit Markets

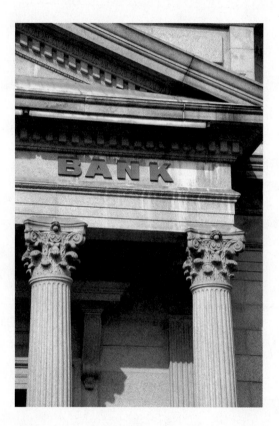

How often do banks fail?

Financial service companies, such as banks, insurance companies, and investment companies, want you to believe that they are rock-solid. They try to convey that message with stone pillars and marble lobbies. Sometimes they choose names that imply indestructibility, like Northern Rock, Blackrock, and Blackstone. Prudential, a leading insurance company, nicknamed itself "The Rock" and adopted the Rock of Gibraltar, a mountain fortress, as its corporate symbol. Those are encouraging words, but are financial institutions really impregnable?

CHAPTER **OUTLINE**

10.1
What Is the
Credit Market?

10.2
Banks and
Financial
Intermediation:
Putting Supply
and Demand
Together

10.3
What Banks Do

How often do
banks fail?

⚙ The credit market matches borrowers (the source of credit demand) and savers (the source of credit supply).

⚙ The credit market equilibrium determines the real interest rate.

⚙ Banks and other financial intermediaries have three key functions: identifying profitable lending opportunities; using short-run deposits to make long-run investments; and managing the amount and distribution of risk.

⚙ Banks become insolvent when the value of their liabilities exceeds the value of their assets.

10.1 What Is the Credit Market?

You've got your first business idea and you can't think about much else. You are going to be the founder and CEO (chief executive officer) of your own company. OK. Catch your breath. And get down to work. Most new businesses fail within 5 years, and you are going to do everything that you can to avoid becoming one of those casualties.

You want to create a taxi and limo company that uses only vehicles that are 100 percent battery powered, just the sort of thing you reckon would appeal to your fellow New Yorkers. You call your new firm BatteryPark. Everyone you know loves the idea and promises to use your start-up if you manage to get it off the ground. You've even been able to convince numerous local companies to sign up for your service for their employees and clients.

Now you need to raise money to buy or rent the necessary equipment and buildings: licenses, electric vehicles, battery-charging systems, a reservation office with computers, and a few garages spread around the city so that your taxis can easily get a fresh battery when they run out of juice. You also need to hire staff, train them, and advertise. You figure you need about $500,000 to start your business and quickly reach an efficient scale of operation. That's not a trivial amount by any stretch of the imagination, but you think it's worth taking the risk, considering what you expect to make from your new business.

But how will you raise $500,000? You certainly don't have it in your checking account, and neither do any of your friends. You think of asking your parents and grandparents, but then you imagine how you would feel if your business went south and a family member lost his or her life savings. So what's the solution?

Borrowers and the Demand for Loans

The good news is that you are not alone in your quest for funds. Every year, hundreds of thousands of entrepreneurs in the United States and millions around the world borrow money to start new businesses. Many, many more businesses that are already in operation also borrow funds to expand their existing operations or simply to pay their bills.

Consumers, too, borrow to purchase big-ticket items like automobiles and houses. Some households borrow to sustain their quality of life during a temporary period of unemployment. Many people borrow to put themselves or their children through college. Almost everyone who pursues graduate studies in business, law, or medicine borrows to pay some of their bills. We refer to economic agents who borrow funds—including entrepreneurs, home buyers, and medical students—as **debtors**. And the funds that they borrow are referred to as **credit**.

Debtors, or borrowers, are economic agents who borrow funds.

Credit refers to the loans that the debtor receives.

The **interest rate** (also referred to as the **nominal interest rate**), i, is the annual cost of a one-dollar loan, so $i \times L$ is the annual cost of an $\$L$ loan.

Most businesses and individuals obtain credit from banks, but the credit market is much broader than banks. It includes several non-bank institutions, as well as the market for commercial debt, where well-established, large businesses obtain large loans.

Of course, borrowed money is not lent for free. You need to pay *interest*. The original amount of borrowed money is referred to as principal. The **interest rate** is the additional payment, above and beyond the repayment of principal, that a borrower needs to make on a *one-dollar* loan (at the end of one year). We can also say that the interest rate is the annual cost of a one-dollar loan.

Let's now scale up that one-dollar loan into an $\$L$ loan. The total interest payment a borrower needs to make for an $\$L$ loan is the loan amount multiplied by the interest rate. Put differently, if you borrow $\$L$ with a one-year loan at an annual interest rate of i, at the end of one year you pay back the L dollars of principal *plus* $i \times L$ dollars in interest. To distinguish it from the real interest rate, which we define next, we'll also refer to the interest rate, i, as the **nominal interest rate**.

Let's now return to your blockbuster business idea. You have enough confidence in your plans that you would be willing to pay a 10 percent interest rate to get your loan. That means you would be willing to make an annual interest payment of $50,000 to get a $500,000 loan ($500,000 \times 0.10 = $50,000). In fact, you are so confident that you would take the loan even if you had to pay 20 percent interest.

But what if the interest rate were 50 percent? An interest payment of $250,000 per year on a $500,000 loan is a bit steep. At that interest rate, there won't be much profit left for you. Perhaps you should scale back your plans and take a smaller loan. Instead of hiring a large team of 20 employees, you might want to start with just a few coworkers.

And what if the interest rate were 100 percent? Principal plus interest one year later would then be $500,000 + $500,000 = $1,000,000 on a $500,000 loan. That is, you would need to pay back twice as much as you borrowed. If so, it might make sense for you to forget about this new idea altogether. It's hard to imagine that any business could make money if it had to finance itself this way.

In reality, most businesses do not need to pay 50 percent or 100 percent interest rates on loans. We present such cases to explain why a rise in the interest rate causes a fall in the quantity of credit demanded. As the interest rate goes up, fewer firms and individuals are willing to pay the high price to acquire credit.

Real and Nominal Interest Rates

The real interest rate is given by the nominal interest rate minus the inflation rate.

The *real* annual price of your loan isn't simply given by the *nominal interest rate* you pay, for example the 10 percent, 20 percent, 50 percent, or 100 percent we have just mentioned. Instead, it is given by the **real interest rate**, r. The real interest rate is the nominal interest rate minus inflation. The inflation rate measures how much less valuable one dollar becomes because of the increase in the overall price level.

The relationship between the nominal and real interest rate is very similar to the relationship between nominal and real GDP growth, which we studied in Chapter 5. To turn nominal GDP growth into real GDP growth, we need to subtract the inflation rate from nominal GDP growth. Similar logic applies to the relationship between the nominal and the real interest rate:

$$\text{Real interest rate} = \text{Nominal interest rate} - \text{Inflation rate}.$$

Or using symbols,

$$r = i - \pi,$$

Optimizing economic agents will use the real interest rate, *r*, when thinking about the economic cost of a loan.

where r is the real interest rate, i is the nominal interest rate, and π denotes the rate of inflation. Economists call this the Fisher equation, naming it after Irving Fisher (1867–1947) whose research emphasized the distinction between the nominal and real interest rates.[1] Here is an example of the Fisher equation in action. If the nominal interest rate is 5 percent and the inflation rate is 2 percent, then the real interest rate is

$$3\% = 5\% - 2\%.$$

Why will optimizing economic agents use the real interest rate, r, when thinking about the economic cost of a loan? If you borrow one dollar for a year, you will need to pay back $(1 + i)$ dollars in a year. Inflation implies that each dollar that you borrowed (and spent) at the beginning of the year has the same purchasing power as $(1 + \pi)$ dollars a year later because the inflation rate is π. It would be misleading to compare a dollar paid back at the end of the year to a dollar with more purchasing power borrowed at the beginning of the year. Optimizers recognize that they should compare what they pay back at the end of the year to what they borrowed at the beginning of the year, adjusting the dollars they borrowed for a year's worth of inflation. In essence, the relevant *real* price of the loan is the difference between what the borrower pays back $(1 + i)$ and the inflation-adjusted value of the dollar he or she originally borrowed, $(1 + \pi)$:

$$(1 + i) - (1 + \pi) = i - \pi.$$

Recall that the real interest rate is $i - \pi$, which appears on the right-hand side of the last equation. We have shown that the real interest rate is equal to the difference between what the borrower pays back and the inflation-adjusted value of the dollar he or she originally borrowed. The real interest rate is the real (inflation-adjusted) cost of a $1 loan. (In the next chapter we will return to this equation and discuss the role of inflationary expectation in thinking about the real interest rate.)

The Credit Demand Curve

The **credit demand curve** is the schedule that reports the relationship between the quantity of credit demanded and the real interest rate.

Because it is the real interest rate, r, that matters for business and individual decisions, the demand for credit will also be a function of this real interest rate. The **credit demand curve** is the schedule that reports the relationship between the quantity of credit demanded and the real interest rate.

Exhibit 10.1 plots the credit demand curve, with the quantity of credit demanded on the horizontal axis and the real interest rate on the vertical axis. The credit demand curve slopes downward because the higher the real interest rate, the lower the quantity of credit demanded. As BatteryPark's demand for credit illustrates, the higher the interest rate a firm pays to borrow money, the lower the borrower's profit. So, fewer borrowers will be willing to obtain a loan at a higher interest rate. This is conceptually the same as other demand curves: when the price of any good—like carrots or caviar—goes up, consumers tend to buy less of it. Credit works the same way, where the real "price" of credit is the real interest rate. The steepness of the credit demand curve tells us about the sensitivity of the relationship between the real interest rate and the quantity of credit demanded.

1. When the credit demand curve is relatively steep, the quantity of credit demanded doesn't change that much in response to variation in the real interest rate.
2. When the credit demand curve is relatively flat, the quantity of credit demanded is relatively sensitive to variation in the real interest rate.

Exhibit 10.1 The Credit Demand Curve

The quantity of credit demanded is plotted on the horizontal axis and the real interest rate is plotted on the vertical axis. As the real interest rate rises, the quantity of credit demanded falls. This is a movement along the credit demand curve.

Having emphasized that the *real* interest rate is the price that appears on the vertical axis of Exhibit 10.1—you can think of it as the price of borrowing money—it is important to remember that almost all loans are made at a *nominal* interest rate. For example, banks quote a nominal interest rate when you apply for a mortgage. Businesses also borrow at a nominal interest rate when they take out a loan. However, what is relevant for the decisions of an optimizer is the implied real interest rate. The real interest rate will play a central role in macroeconomic analysis in the next several chapters, especially the real interest rate for long-term borrowing (like 30-year mortgages or 10-year corporate loans). For now, we focus on the relationship between the real interest rate and the demand for credit. We return to the nominal interest rate and its relationship to the real interest rate in the next chapter. When using the credit demand curve it is important to draw a very careful distinction between *movements along* the credit demand curve, as in Exhibit 10.1, and *shifts* of the credit demand curve. You have already encountered this distinction when we first introduced it in Chapter 4, and it still applies here. Exhibit 10.2 illustrates shifting demand curves. Many factors cause the demand curve to shift:

- **Changes in perceived business opportunities for firms.** Businesses borrow to fund their expansions. For example, if an airline like United Airlines notices that more and more travelers are trying to buy plane tickets, then United's demand for airplanes will increase. United will then have to borrow money to buy or lease more planes, so its credit demand curve will shift to the right. If other businesses are experiencing similar trends and increasing their demand for credit at a given real interest rate, then the market (or aggregate) credit demand curve will shift to the right.

- **Changes in household preferences or expectations.** Households borrow for many reasons: buying a home, a car, that gargantuan flat-screen TV, or paying college tuition bills. If household preferences change so that they would like to consume more of these goods and services, they will tend to borrow more. Likewise, they'll be more willing to borrow when they grow more optimistic about the future, for example, because they expect that they'll be in a good position to pay back those loans later. Such changes in household preferences or expectations shift the market credit demand curve to the right. Likewise, if households become more pessimistic about the future, then they will cut their desired borrowing at each interest rate, shifting the market credit demand curve to the left.

- **Changes in government policy.** Government borrowing in the credit market can swing violently from year to year. For example, in 2007 the U.S. federal government ran a deficit of $0.4 trillion, which implies that it borrowed $0.4 trillion on the credit market. As the 2007–2009 recession deepened, household and business income fell; this situation in turn reduced tax revenues collected by the government. At the same time, government spending rose both to help out struggling families and to stimulate the contracting economy. By 2009, the government deficit was $1.5 trillion. Holding all else equal, an increase in government borrowing shifts the market credit demand curve to the right. (By 2013, the federal government deficit had shrunk to $0.8 trillion, representing a substantial reversal from 2009.) Finally, the government's tax policies can also shift the credit demand curve. Sometimes the government stimulates investment in physical capital by lowering taxes on profits or explicitly introducing subsidies for physical capital investment, thereby shifting the market credit demand curve to the right.

Saving Decisions

Banks provide credit to businesses and households that wish to borrow. But where do banks obtain the money that they lend out?

> **Banks play the role of middlemen, matching savers and borrowers.**

Other economic agents with excess cash have deposited their money in the bank. In this sense, banks play the role of middlemen, matching savers and borrowers. Banks aren't the only middlemen in the market for credit. Many different kinds of institutions—we provide a partial list later in this chapter—play the critical role of linking people with savings to people or firms who want to use those savings.

Let's momentarily ignore the institutions that serve as the middlemen and focus on the depositors—in other words, the savers—who are the initial source of the funds that

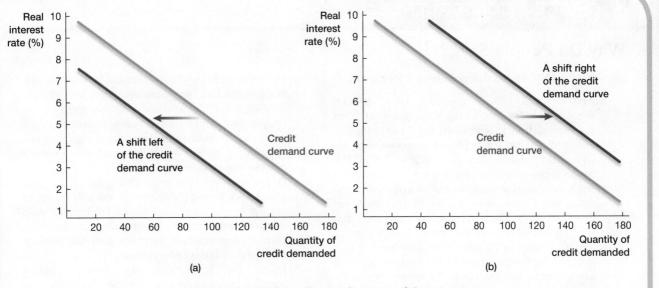

Exhibit 10.2 **Shifts in the Credit Demand Curve**

Changes in perceived business opportunities for firms, changes in household preferences or expectations, and changes in government policy may decrease the quantity of credit demanded for a fixed level of the real interest rate, shifting the credit demand curve to the left (panel (a)). When they increase the quantity of credit demanded for a fixed level of the real interest rate, the credit demand curve shifts to the right (panel (b)).

Buried treasure earns no interest. Savings accounts do.

borrowers will ultimately receive. Savers have money that they are willing to lend out because they prefer to spend it in the future rather than today. Of course, they could keep their money under a mattress or bury it under a palm tree on a deserted island. But buried treasure doesn't pay interest.

The Credit Supply Curve

People and firms with saved money obtain interest by lending the money to a bank or some other financial institution. In some cases, this "lending" takes the form of depositing the money at the bank in return for interest on a savings account. How much money are the savers willing to lend in this way? To answer this question, we need to understand the optimizing behavior of savers.

Saving results from a natural trade-off: people can spend their income on consumption today or can save it for consumption in the future. Because saving requires giving something up—current consumption—people will only save if they get something worthwhile in return. The real interest rate is the compensation that people receive for saving their money because a dollar saved today has $1 + r$ dollars of purchasing power in a year, where r is the real interest rate. Put differently, the real interest rate is the opportunity cost of current consumption—what you are giving up in terms of future purchasing power. Consequently, a higher real interest rate increases the opportunity cost of current consumption and encourages a higher level of saving.

On the other hand, a higher real interest rate might actually *lower* the saving rate. For example, if the real interest rate is relatively high, savings put aside when a person is young will grow relatively quickly, enabling a young worker to save *less* while still achieving a long-run goal of accumulating a retirement nest egg of a certain targeted size. Note, though, in most situations this negative effect on saving is thought to be weaker than the (positive) opportunity cost effect discussed above. In other words, for most people, a higher real interest rate induces a higher saving rate.

Section 10.1 | What Is the Credit Market? **225**

CHOICE & CONSEQUENCE

Why Do People Save?

There are five key reasons that people save for the future.

1. First and foremost, people save for retirement. When you retire, you'll only receive a fraction of the income that you received during working life. For example, the Social Security program pays the typical U.S. household a bit less than half of the household's preretirement income. If you don't want your consumption to fall sharply when you retire, you'll need to save some of your preretirement income. Most advisers recommend that working households in the United States contribute 10 percent to 20 percent of their income to a retirement savings account—for instance a 401(k) account or an IRA (Individual Retirement Account).

2. People save "for their kids," for example, for their weddings or their future educational investments like college and postgraduate school. A small fraction of parents also leave significant amounts of money to their kids in their wills. (Such gifts are called *bequests*.)

3. People save to pay for predictable large expenses, like a home purchase, *durable goods* (for instance, a washing machine or a car), and vacations.

4. People save so they can invest in a personal business. Small businesses sometimes can't obtain loans from banks. The bank's loan officer might not believe in your latest, greatest business idea. (If you were a bank's loan officer, would you give a loan to a recent college graduate with a plan to open a new taxi and limo service like BatteryPark?) In cases where outside funding can't be obtained, small business owners must use their own savings to fund their breakthrough ideas.

5. People save for a "rainy day." Your roof might spring a leak and require an expensive repair. You might lose your job. You might have a large medical expense that is not covered by insurance. In situations like these, you'll need a fund that you can lean on to get through hard times.

The **credit supply curve** is the schedule that reports the relationship between the quantity of credit supplied and the real interest rate.

This leads us to conclude that the **credit supply curve**, which is the schedule that reports the relationship between the quantity of credit supplied and the real interest rate, is upward-sloping. Specifically, a higher real interest rate encourages more saving, increasing the amount of funds that banks can lend and thereby increasing the quantity of credit supplied. Exhibit 10.3 plots the credit supply curve.

As before, it's important to carefully distinguish between movements along the credit supply curve, as in Exhibit 10.3, and shifts of the credit supply curve, as in Exhibit 10.4. Movements along the supply curve correspond to savers' response to changes *only* in the

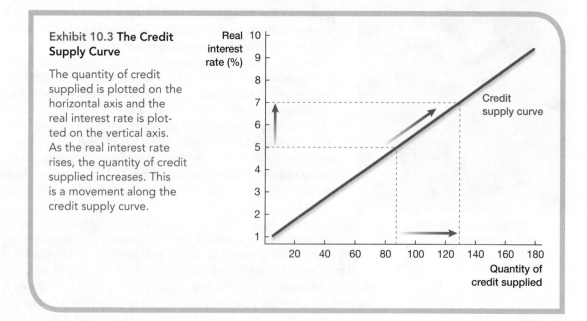

Exhibit 10.3 The Credit Supply Curve

The quantity of credit supplied is plotted on the horizontal axis and the real interest rate is plotted on the vertical axis. As the real interest rate rises, the quantity of credit supplied increases. This is a movement along the credit supply curve.

(a)   (b)

Exhibit 10.4 Shifts in the Credit Supply Curve

Changes in the saving motives of households or firms may decrease the quantity of credit supplied for a fixed level of the real interest rate, shifting the credit supply curve to the left (panel (a)). When households and firms increase the quantity of credit supplied for a fixed level of the real interest rate, the credit supply curve shifts to the right (panel (b)).

real interest rate. Shifts in the credit supply curve are driven by changes in the saving motives of optimizing economic agents, holding fixed the real interest rate.

- **Changes in the saving motives of households.** As discussed above, households save for many reasons—like retirement—but these motives change over time, shifting the credit supply curve. For example, if households start to predict economic hard times ahead, they will save more because they want to build up a store of wealth to be better prepared. This shifts the credit supply curve to the right. Likewise, demographic trends can change the savings behavior of households. For example, as households approach the age of retirement their saving rate tends to rise.
- **Changes in the saving motives of firms.** A firm has positive earnings if its expenses—including the cost of paying employees—are less than the firm's revenue. Some firms pass such earnings back to their stockholders—for example, by paying shareholder dividends. But some firms retain these earnings, depositing them in the firm's bank account and saving them for future investment. The magnitude of such *retained earnings* shifts over time. When firms are nervous about their ability to fund their business activities in the future, they tend to hold on to more retained earnings instead of paying them out as dividends. This shifts the credit supply curve to the right, another form of saving for a rainy day.

Equilibrium in the Credit Market

The **credit market** is where borrowers obtain funds from savers.

Exhibit 10.5 plots *both* the credit supply curve and the credit demand curve. This completes our picture of the **credit market**, where borrowers obtain funds from savers. It is sometimes referred to as the *loanable funds market*.

We've simplified the credit market by assuming that different borrowers all have identical risks of defaulting on their loan. In other words, all borrowers have the same risk of not repaying their loan. This simplification implies that there will be a single equilibrium real interest rate in the credit market. (In actual markets, borrowers with different risks of defaulting face different real interest rates to compensate lenders for these differential default risks.)

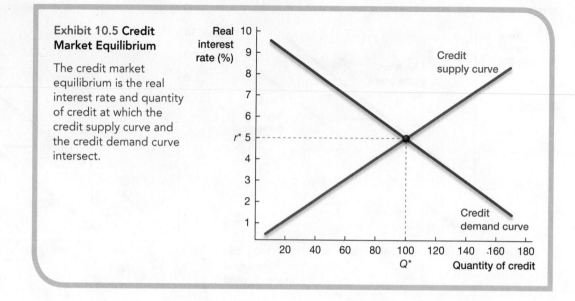

Exhibit 10.5 Credit Market Equilibrium

The credit market equilibrium is the real interest rate and quantity of credit at which the credit supply curve and the credit demand curve intersect.

Like other markets represented by a supply curve and a demand curve, the equilibrium in the credit market is the point at which the curves intersect. This intersection determines both the total quantity of credit in the market (Q^*) and the equilibrium real interest rate (r^*). At the equilibrium real interest rate, the quantity of credit demanded is equal to the quantity of credit supplied. A real interest rate above this level would lead to an excess supply of credit, which would typically put downward pressure on the real interest rate. A real interest rate below the equilibrium level would lead to an excess demand for credit, creating upward pressure on the real interest rate.

To see this in action, consider how a shift in the credit demand curve affects the credit market equilibrium, as shown in Exhibit 10.6. For example, assume that the government introduces a tax credit for business investment expenditures so that every dollar a firm invests by building plants or purchasing equipment reduces the taxes that it owes by 30 cents. Such a tax credit reduces the cost of investment to firms and thus raises the net benefit—benefits minus costs—of investment. As a consequence, an optimizing firm's willingness to borrow in the credit market (to fund investment in plants and equipment) will increase. Consequently, the credit demand curve shifts to the right. The new equilibrium point has a higher real interest rate (r^{**}) and a greater quantity of credit supplied and demanded (Q^{**}).

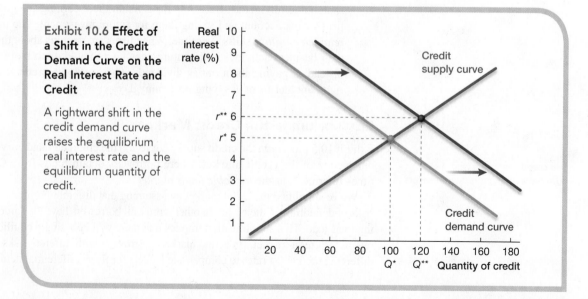

Exhibit 10.6 Effect of a Shift in the Credit Demand Curve on the Real Interest Rate and Credit

A rightward shift in the credit demand curve raises the equilibrium real interest rate and the equilibrium quantity of credit.

> By enabling savers to lend their excess money to borrowers, the credit market improves the allocation of resources in the economy.

Credit Markets and the Efficient Allocation of Resources

Credit markets play an extremely valuable social role. By enabling savers to lend their excess money to borrowers, the credit market improves the allocation of resources in the economy.

There is a simple way of seeing this. Suppose there was no credit market and you had $1,000 you wanted to save for next year. What could you do with it? You could put it in a safe box in your house—"putting the money under your mattress"—in which case you would just have $1,000 next year. With no inflation, you will have received a real interest rate of zero. If there is inflation, say 5 percent, then the real interest rate you will have received is much worse, -5 percent, because inflation eroded 5 percent of the purchasing power of your money.

We can also work through these examples by using the Fisher equation, which gives the formula for the real interest rate: $r = i - \pi$. If you receive no nominal interest (so $i = 0$), then the real interest rate is $r = 0 - \pi$. When the inflation rate is zero (so $\pi = 0$ percent), the real interest rate is $r = 0 - 0 = 0$ percent. When the inflation rate is 5 percent (so $\pi = 5$ percent), then the real interest rate is $r = 0 - 5 = -5$ percent.

You might do better than a 0 percent nominal interest rate by lending your money to your uncle who has some business venture in mind. But unless your uncle happens to be a good businessman, this choice might be worse than the mattress option.

Unknown to you, there could be several borrowers (possibly more reliable than your uncle!) who need that $1,000 for their investment. Without credit markets, they would also suffer because many of them would not be able to raise the necessary funds.

The valuable social role of credit markets is to match savers like you with borrowers. When credit markets work, you will get a reasonable return on your $1,000 saving (typically an average real return of 1 percent to 5 percent depending on how much risk you take), and worthy potential borrowers will be able to raise the funds they need.

10.2 Banks and Financial Intermediation: Putting Supply and Demand Together

Banks and other financial institutions are the economic agents connecting supply and demand in the credit market. Think of it this way: when you deposit your money in a bank account, you do not know who will ultimately use it. The bank pools all of its deposits and uses this pool of money to make many different kinds of loans: credit card loans to households; mortgages to home buyers; small loans to entrepreneurs; and large loans to established companies like General Electric, Nike, and Ford. Banks even make loans to other banks that need cash.

Running a bank is a complicated operation, and, so far, we've taken it all for granted. When we talked about the market for credit in the last section, we assumed that the lenders and borrowers could easily find each other. But in real life, matching lenders and borrowers is complex. Banks are the organizations that provide the bridge from lenders to borrowers, and because of this role, they are called *financial intermediaries*. Broadly speaking, **financial intermediaries** channel funds from suppliers of financial capital, like savers, to users of financial capital, like borrowers.

Financial intermediaries channel funds from suppliers of financial capital to users of financial capital.

Financial capital comes in many different forms, including credit (which is also referred to as debt) and equity. When a saver turns her savings into *credit*, she loans her savings to another party in exchange for the promise of repayment of her loan with interest. When a saver turns her savings into *equity*, she uses her savings to become a shareholder in a company, which means that she has obtained an ownership share and a claim on the future profits of the company. These profits are paid out as dividends to the company's shareholders.

Many different types of financial institutions act as financial intermediaries, channeling funds from suppliers of financial capital—in other words, savers—to users of financial capital. In addition to banks, financial intermediaries include, but are not limited to, asset management companies, hedge funds, private equity funds, venture capital funds, bank-like businesses that comprise the "shadow banking system," and even pawnshops and shops that give payday loans.

Asset management companies, like Blackrock, Fidelity, and Vanguard, enable investors to use their savings to buy financial **securities** like *stocks* and *bonds*. When you buy a company's stock, you are buying a share of ownership in that company. When you buy a bond, you are effectively lending money to the company that issued the bond. These stock and bond investments are often made through mutual funds, which are large, diversified pools of securities. The value of all mutual funds in the United States in 2012 was approximately $13 trillion.

Hedge funds are investment pools gathered from a small number of very wealthy individuals or institutions, like university endowments. Hedge funds tend to follow risky, nontraditional investment strategies, like buying large tracts of land that can be used to grow timber, or buying stock in companies that are in financial trouble and have recently experienced large drops in their stock value. Hedge funds charge fees that are much higher than those of mutual funds. The value of all hedge funds in the United States in 2012 was approximately $2 trillion.

Private equity funds are investment pools that also typically involve a small number of wealthy investors. Private equity funds hold securities that are not publicly traded, so you can't buy them on a stock exchange. For instance, private equity funds might buy a company that is privately owned, like a family business. Alternatively, they might take a publicly traded company private by buying all of the shares in the company. The value of all private equity funds in the United States in 2012 was approximately $3 trillion.

Venture capital funds are a particular kind of private equity fund. They invest in new companies that are usually just starting up and therefore have no track record. For instance, in 1999, two venture capital funds—Kleiner-Perkins and Sequoia Capital—invested $25 million in a start-up company with a funny name—Google—founded the previous year. That single investment is now worth over $25 billion, implying a 1,000-to-1 return on every dollar invested. However, venture capital is a highly risky type of financial intermediation, and the typical venture capital firm didn't make any money in the decade after the tech bubble burst in 2000. The value of all venture capital funds in the United States in 2012 was about $200 billion.

The *shadow banking system* is comprised of thousands of institutions that are not officially banks because they don't take deposits, but nevertheless act like banks in the sense that they raise money and then make loans with those funds. Lehman Brothers, whose bankruptcy fueled the 2008 financial crisis, was one example of a shadow bank. Instead of taking common deposits, Lehman would take loans from large investors like insurance companies and use them to trade stocks and bonds, to make loans to businesses, and to create new financial products that they could sell to other institutions and wealthy investors.

Securities are financial contracts. For example, securities may allocate ownership rights of a company (stocks), or promise payments to lenders (bonds).

Assets and Liabilities on the Balance Sheet of a Bank

To understand what banks do, it helps to first look at a bank's balance sheet, which summarizes both its *assets* and its *liabilities*. Assets include the investments the bank has made, government securities the bank holds, and the money the bank is owed by borrowers, including households and firms that have taken loans from the bank. The bank's liabilities include claims that depositors and other lenders have against the bank. For example, when a household deposits $10,000 at a bank, that deposit is a liability for the bank—money that the bank owes to the depositor.

Accountants call this statement of assets and liabilities a *balance* sheet because it is set up so that the assets and liabilities are balanced one for one. Think of the words *own* and *owe* to clarify the balance sheet—the balance sheet states what the bank owns (assets) and what it owes (liabilities).

Exhibit 10.7 summarizes some key features of the balance sheet of Citibank at the end of 2013, following the convention of listing assets in the left-hand column and liabilities in the right-hand column. The right-hand column also lists stockholders' equity, which is defined as total assets minus total liabilities and represents the value of the owners' (stockholders') stake in the company. Let's look in a bit more detail at the key categories that make up the assets and liabilities of the balance sheet.

Assets   Citibank's assets are simplified by being divided into three categories: reserves, cash and cash equivalents, and long-term investments.

10.1
10.2
10.3

> Official **bank reserves** consist of vault cash and deposits at the Federal Reserve Bank.

1. **Bank reserves** include vault cash (dollars and coins held by Citibank in its own vault) and its holdings on deposit at the Federal Reserve Bank, often called the Fed, which is a special bank that is an agency of the government and is used to regulate the entire monetary system. We have much, much more to say about the Fed in the next chapter. In Exhibit 10.7, Citibank's reserves account for $294 billion of Citibank's total assets.
2. *Cash equivalents* are riskless, liquid assets that Citibank can immediately access, like deposits with other banks. An asset is riskless if its value doesn't change from day to day. An asset is liquid if it can quickly and easily be converted into cash, with little or no loss in value. In Exhibit 10.7, cash equivalents account for $192 billion of Citibank's total assets.
3. *Long-term investments* mostly comprise loans to households and firms but also include things like the value of the real estate that the bank uses for its operations, such as its bank branches and corporate headquarters. Long-term investments account for $1,398 billion of Citibank's total assets.

Liabilities and Stockholders' Equity   In Exhibit 10.7, Citibank's liabilities and stockholders' equity are divided into four categories: demand deposits, short-term borrowing, long-term debt, and stockholders' equity.

> **Demand deposits** are funds that depositors can access on demand by withdrawing money from the bank, writing checks, or using their debit cards.

1. **Demand deposits** are funds "loaned" to the bank by depositors. Most depositors don't think of this as a loan to a bank, but rather as a deposit to a checking account. These deposits are referred to as *demand deposits* because the depositor can access the funds on demand—meaning, at any time—by withdrawing the money from an ATM or bank teller, writing a check, or using a debit card to make a store purchase. Even though demand deposits are "cash in the bank," so to speak, they are liabilities from the perspective of Citibank, because it owes this money to its depositors. Citibank owes depositors $938 billion in demand deposits. We look at these more closely in the next section.

Exhibit 10.7 Citibank's Balance Sheet, June 2013 (billions of dollars)

Citibank's balance sheet from June 2013 summarizes the assets that the bank owns, as well as the claims that depositors and other financial intermediaries have against the bank—the bank's liabilities. Stockholders' equity is defined as the difference between total assets and total liabilities, so liabilities plus stockholders' equity is exactly equal to the value of total assets.

Source: Citigroup Inc., 2013 Second Quarter Form 10-Q.

Assets		Liabilities and stockholders' equity	
Reserves	294	Demand Deposits	938
Cash equivalents	192	Short-term borrowing	527
Long-term investments	1,398	Long-term debt	221
		Total Liabilities	1,686
		Stockholders' equity	198
Total assets	1,884	Total Liabilities + Stockholders' equity	1,884

2. *Short-term borrowing* comprises short-term loans that Citibank has obtained from other financial institutions. All of these loans need to be repaid in the next year, and many of these loans are overnight loans that Citibank needs to repay the next day! Usually, such overnight loans are rolled over from one day to the next, meaning that Citibank repays its overnight loans and then instantly arranges new overnight loans with the same lenders. Unfortunately, heavy reliance on short-term debt generates some fragility in the banking system. If lenders suddenly start to worry that Citibank will have difficulty paying back short-term debt, Citibank might have trouble borrowing new funds and would therefore lack the funds it needs to conduct its day-to-day operations. Despite these risks, Citibank funds its operations by borrowing $527 billion of such short-term debt.

3. *Long-term debt* is defined as debt that is due to be repaid in a year or more. Citibank has $221 billion in long-term debt, representing 13 percent of its liabilities. This proportion contrasts sharply with the asset side of the balance sheet, where nearly 75 percent of the assets are long-term. The difference between long-term debt and long-term assets introduces a source of risk for the bank—a topic that we explore later in this chapter.

4. **Stockholders' equity** is defined as the difference between the bank's total assets and total liabilities.

Stockholders' equity is the difference between a bank's total assets and total liabilities.

$$\text{Stockholders' equity} = \text{Total assets} - \text{Total liabilities}.$$

This difference is equal to the estimated value of the company, or what the total value of Citibank's shares should be worth if the accountants got everything right.

We can rearrange the identity for stockholders' equity to find that

$$\text{Total assets} = \text{Total liabilities} + \text{Stockholders' equity}.$$

Looking at this equation, you can see that the two sides (left and right) of the balance sheet match up. Given the way in which accountants define stockholders' equity, the liability side of the balance sheet and the asset side of the balance sheet are always perfectly balanced.

10.3 What Banks Do

We can use the bank's balance sheet to identify three interrelated functions that banks perform as financial intermediaries.

1. Banks identify profitable lending opportunities.
2. Banks transform short-term liabilities, like deposits, into long-term investments in a process called *maturity transformation*.
3. Banks manage risk by using diversification strategies and also by transferring risk from depositors to the bank's stockholders and, in some cases, to the U.S. government.

We discuss each of these three functions in turn.

Identifying Profitable Lending Opportunities

One of the main roles of banks is to find creditworthy borrowers and channel savings of depositors to them. Thus, banks bring together the two sides of the credit market. Banks are in a good position to do this because, given their willingness to lend, they attract a large number of would-be borrowers and choose the more creditworthy among them. Banks employ armies of investment specialists and loan officers trained in identifying the best loan applications.

Maturity Transformation

Recall from Exhibit 10.7 that 87 percent of Citibank's liabilities, which are shown on the right-hand side of its balance sheet, are short-term (made up of demand deposits and short-term borrowing), while nearly 75 percent of its assets, shown on the left-hand side, are long-term investments. Citibank has transformed its short-term liabilities into long-term assets.

Maturity is the time until debt must be repaid. Demand deposits have a 0-year maturity, because the depositor can take back her money at any time. In contrast, when banks lend

Maturity refers to the time until debt must be repaid.

to borrowers, such loans usually have a maturity ranging from several years up to 30 years. The transfer of short-term liabilities like demand deposits into long-term investments is called **maturity transformation**.

10.1

Maturity transformation is the process by which banks take short-maturity liabilities and invest in long-maturity assets (long-term investments).

Maturity transformation is what enables society to undertake significant long-term investments. But it also implies that banks wind up with a mismatch between the short-term maturities of their deposits and the long-term maturities of their loans. This maturity mismatch could get them into trouble if lots of depositors were to simultaneously ask to make withdrawals. Banks can't simply recall their long-term loans if their short-term depositors want their money back. To ensure that they can fulfill demands for withdrawals, banks do not lend out all of their deposits. They hold back some fraction of the deposit pool as *reserves* or some other form of cash-like security.

10.2

10.3

Banks have a large number of depositors, and typically only a tiny fraction of depositors demand their funds on any given day. Banks are also able to exploit the fact that withdrawals of existing deposits and inflows of new deposits are roughly offsetting on most days. Banks therefore usually need only a small pool of reserves to meet the net withdrawals of deposits. This enables them to commit most of their demand deposits to long-term investments.

Management of Risk

A bank promises that depositors will never lose a penny. This is a striking promise, since the bank makes risky loans with the depositors' savings. For example, banks often invest in *mortgages*—loans to households to purchase houses—which are risky. About 12 percent of the mortgages held by banks at the beginning of the 2007–2009 financial crisis ended up late on payments or in default.

Banks manage risk in two ways. First, they hold a *diversified* portfolio: a typical bank invests not only in mortgages but in a diverse set of assets, including business loans, loans to other financial institutions, and government debt. A diversified portfolio is useful because all the diverse assets of the bank are unlikely to underperform at the same time.

But diversification by itself isn't sufficient to manage risks because sometimes a large fraction of even a diverse set of assets may underperform. Most types of assets lost value during the 2007–2009 financial crisis. But even then, depositors remain safe, because of banks' second strategy of risk management: shifting risk to stockholders, and ultimately, during severe financial crises, to the U.S. government.

To understand how risk is transferred, consider what happens to a simplified bank balance sheet after its long-term investments lose 10 percent of their value. To keep things simple, we analyze a bank with exactly $11 billion in assets, which is allocated to $1 billion in *reserves and cash equivalents* and $10 billion in *long-term investments*.

Panel (a) of Exhibit 10.8 reports an original balance sheet, while panel (b) of Exhibit 10.8 reports a new balance sheet with two changes. First, the value of long-term assets has

Exhibit 10.8 Illustrative Balance Sheet

In panel (a), the bank has $11 billion in assets and stockholders' equity of $2 billion. In panel (b), a $1 billion reduction in the value of the bank's assets reduces stockholders' equity to $1 billion, as stockholders' equity is defined as total assets minus total liabilities.

Panel (a) Before Investment Loss (Billions of Dollars)			
Assets		**Liabilities and stockholders' equity**	
Reserves & cash equivalents	1	Demand deposits	9
Long-term investments	10		
		Total liabilities	**9**
		Stockholders' equity	2
Total assets	**11**	**Total liabilities + stockholders' equity**	**11**

Panel (b) After $1 Investment Loss (Billions of Dollars)			
Assets		**Liabilities and stockholders' equity**	
Reserves & cash equivalents	1	Demand deposits	9
Long-term investments	10 − 1 = 9		
		Total liabilities	**9**
		Stockholders' equity	2 − 1 = 1
Total assets	**11 − 1 = 10**	**Total liabilities + stockholders' equity**	**11 − 1 = 10**

decreased by 10 percent, or $1 billion. Second, the value of stockholders' equity has been reduced by $1 billion. Recall that stockholders' equity is defined as the difference between the value of assets and liabilities. Since the value of the demand deposits has not changed—these are contractual promises from the bank to its depositors—but the value of the assets has declined by $1 billion, the value of stockholders' equity must also fall by $1 billion.

This example illustrates that stockholders bear all of the risk that the bank faces, *as long as stockholders' equity is greater than zero.* In other words, as long as the bank's assets exceed its liabilities, every change in the value of the assets is absorbed one-for-one by stockholders.

When the value of the bank's assets falls below the value of its liabilities, stockholders' equity goes to zero. Now the bank owes more than it owns. At about that moment, the government shuts down the bank. The government bank regulator—the Federal Deposit Insurance Corporation (FDIC)—steps in and takes control of the bank. The FDIC will either (1) shut down the bank's operations and make payouts to depositors or (2) transfer the bank to new ownership.

In the payout scenario, the FDIC takes over the assets of the bank and makes full payouts to all individuals with deposits at that bank up to a cap of $250,000; deposits up to $250,000 are "FDIC-insured." The FDIC may also make payouts for deposits in excess of $250,000 if sufficient funds are available. However, most other creditors and all of the stockholders of the bank will be wiped out, meaning that they will receive nothing.

More often, however, the FDIC does not pay out to depositors, but instead arranges for a speedy takeover by a healthy bank. Bank takeovers usually protect *all* deposits—even those greater than $250,000—but in most cases, the stockholders are still wiped out. The next business day the bank opens for business as usual, though it might have a different name on the front door. If the failed bank's depositors aren't paying attention, they may miss the fact that anything has happened at all.

These maneuvers don't always come cheap. In most cases, the failed bank has liabilities, principally demand deposits, that exceed the value of its assets. In technical terms, the failed bank is **insolvent**, meaning that the value of its assets is less than the value of its liabilities. On the other hand, the healthy bank that is taking over the failed bank is **solvent**, meaning that the value of its assets is greater than the value of its liabilities. The healthy bank needs some financial inducement to take over the operations of the failed bank. The FDIC has to provide this sweetener.

Bank failures during the financial crisis of 2007–2009 cost the FDIC over $100 billion. And the buck doesn't stop there. Depositors at *all* U.S. banks implicitly pay for these bank failures because the FDIC raises its funds by charging all banks deposit insurance premiums. *All* bank depositors, not just those at failed banks, end up indirectly paying to clean up the mess left in the wake of a bank failure.

Bank Runs

Though socially useful, the maturity and the risk transformation roles played by banks also create some risks. Most importantly, maturity transformation causes many of the bank's assets to become *illiquid*—that is, by turning short-term liabilities into long-term, illiquid assets, the bank effectively locks up money that it might need to give back to depositors or other creditors on short notice.

During a banking panic, a substantial fraction of depositors may try to withdraw their deposits at the same time. If the bank has mostly long-term, illiquid assets, the bank may have a hard time coming up with the cash that it will need to pay out those withdrawals. As word gets out that the bank's cash is running low, more depositors will try to make withdrawals in the hope that they can get what little cash remains.

In this way a banking panic can be self-fulfilling—it feeds on itself. An unusually large amount of withdrawals reduces the bank's cash, and this cash shortage begets even *more* withdrawals as depositors race to withdraw their deposits before the bank runs out of cash. Even if a bank was healthy before the panic, it might no longer be healthy after losing many of its depositors and being forced to sell its illiquid assets in "fire sales" where the bank doesn't get a good price for the assets because it doesn't have enough time to find the buyers who are willing to pay the highest price. The expanding panic and rising flood of withdrawals is called a **bank run**.

Bank runs have various economic costs. Most importantly, a run forces a bank to liquidate its long-term, illiquid assets prematurely. This sometimes involves abandonment

Seal of the U.S. Federal Deposit Insurance Corporation. The FDIC was founded in 1933. Today, it insures deposits at over 7,000 banks in the United States.

A bank becomes **insolvent** when the value of the bank's assets is less than the value of its liabilities.

A bank is **solvent** when the value of the bank's assets is greater than the value of its liabilities.

> **A banking panic can be self-fulfilling— it feeds on itself.**

A **bank run** occurs when a bank experiences an extraordinarily large volume of withdrawals driven by a concern that the bank will run out of liquid assets with which to pay withdrawals.

Northern Rock, a U.K. bank that specialized in mortgage lending, found it increasingly difficult to raise funds in late 2007. This triggered the first U.K. bank run in 150 years. A few months later, Northern Rock failed and was taken over by the U.K. government.

or inefficient liquidation of long-term investments in physical capital such as construction projects. In addition, since banks are key participants in the credit market, bank runs also disrupt the smooth working of the credit market.

Bank runs occurred in different forms during the most recent financial crisis, although some of the bank runs were hard for the public to see. The most visible bank run occurred in 2007 at Northern Rock, a U.K. bank that specialized in mortgage lending. Northern Rock's depositors were worried that the bank was insolvent, so they started to withdraw their deposits from the bank. These withdrawals snowballed into the first U.K. bank run in 150 years. Northern Rock desperately tried to find a stronger bank that would buy it out and instill confidence in its depositors. No such sale could be arranged, and Northern Rock was subsequently taken over by the U.K. government.

Bank Regulation and Bank Solvency

If bank runs were a frequent occurrence, the banking system would be quite unstable. Fortunately, bank runs like the one on Northern Rock—with tens of thousands of jittery depositors rushing to withdraw their money—have been relatively rare since the 1930s because of deposit insurance. If a bank fails for any reason, depositors' balances are protected up to some cap. All deposits at or below the cap are paid out in full by the relevant (government) insurance agency (the FDIC in the United States).

Deposit insurance didn't stop the bank run at Northern Rock, since the caps were relatively low in 2007 in the U.K. and many depositors had balances above the cap. Even depositors with fully insured accounts also withdrew their money, as they were afraid that the failure of Northern Rock would temporarily prevent them from accessing their money.

But households aren't the only economic agents depositing money at banks. Firms like Nike and Microsoft also hold bank accounts. Moreover, a bank might borrow money from other banks. When large firms and the general banking community lose confidence in a weak bank, an institutional bank run may ensue, in which firms and banks withdraw their deposits (and short-term loans) from the weak bank. FDIC insurance won't prevent institutional bank runs because institutions make deposits and short-term loans that are far too large to be fully insured by the FDIC. Institutional bank runs occurred frequently during the 2007–2009 financial crisis. However, because it is impossible to take a photograph of an institutional bank run, it is hard to know exactly when one of them is occurring.

We do know that the collapse of the investment bank Lehman Brothers in 2008 was preceded by an institutional bank run. Investment banks specialize in helping firms and governments make large financial transactions, especially for clients that need to raise financial capital to make investments. Investment banks are not FDIC-insured and do not take any deposits the way your neighborhood bank does. Instead, *all* of the liabilities on an investment bank's balance sheet are loans from other institutions, including other banks.

Many of the largest institutions that lent money to Lehman Brothers decided to stop making such short-term loans in the two weeks before Lehman went bankrupt. In other words, Lehman experienced an institutional bank run just before it failed. We now know that Lehman was insolvent at this time—its liabilities exceeded its assets. No wonder smart banks were unwilling to extend new loans to Lehman in the weeks before Lehman's bankruptcy.

Naturally, banks are very eager to avoid such financial meltdowns. They have many strategies at their disposal, though some of these strategies work better than others. As always, prevention is the ideal cure. The ultimate source of strength is to have lots of stockholders' equity, implying that a bank has assets that far exceed the value of its liabilities. When a bank owns far more than it owes, it is said to be well capitalized. In this case, the public should have no doubt about a bank's solvency, which reduces the likelihood of a bank run.

If a bank is running short of reserves, it can stop making new loans and it can sell its long-term investments. However, these efforts can backfire, because they may actually reveal that a bank is in trouble and can intensify the panic that may already have begun. In addition, if a bank stops lending, it reduces its ability to act as a financial intermediary and reduces its earnings at exactly the time when it needs those earnings the most.

Evidence-Based Economics

Q: How often do banks fail?

Banks work very hard to create the impression that they are bedrock institutions. But they haven't proved to be as solid as advertised. In the United States alone, nearly 20,000 banks have failed since 1900. However, most of those failures occurred *before* the establishment of the FDIC in 1933, which created deposit insurance and also enforced strict nationwide bank regulations. Nevertheless, even *since* the FDIC was established, more than 3,000 banks have failed.

Bank failures appear to be a regular feature of modern market economies. The U.S. economy has still observed four major waves of bank failures since the beginning of the twentieth century. The first wave of these bank failures occurred from 1919 to 1928—the decade before the Great Depression—when almost 6,000 banks failed, or 20 percent of all banks in the United States. These failures were concentrated among rural banks that issued mortgages to farms with land values that subsequently fell.

The second wave hit during the Great Depression (1929–1939), when more than 9,000 banks failed. This wave of bank failures was far more severe than the failures of the 1920s. For example, in 1933 *alone*, more than 25 percent of all U.S. banks failed. All told, nearly 50 percent of all U.S. banks failed during the Great Depression.

The third wave occurred during the savings and loan crisis in the 1980s and early 1990s. Savings and loan associations are one type of regional bank. During the savings and loan crisis nearly 3,000 banks failed, comprising about 15 percent of all U.S. banks. The crisis was caused by a boom-to-bust cycle of rising and then falling agricultural and oil prices. During the period of rising prices, the banks made risky investments in local farms and businesses. When agricultural and oil prices turned around, those investments were decimated.

The fourth wave of failures resulted from the 2007–2009 financial crisis. By year-end 2012, there were over 460 bank failures, representing less than 5 percent of all U.S. banks. At first glance, this may seem to be relatively small when compared with the earlier waves. But the 2007–2009 wave included the failure of Washington Mutual in 2008, with more than $300 billion in assets. The largest previous bank failure was Continental Illinois, which collapsed in 1984 with $40 billion in assets, which is equal to $90 billion in 2008 dollars.

Even more importantly, the 2007–2009 financial crisis coincided with the collapse of several (nonbank) financial institutions, like Lehman Brothers. As described earlier, investment banks like Lehman are not regular banks since they don't take deposits and their lenders are not

MyEconLab Real-time data

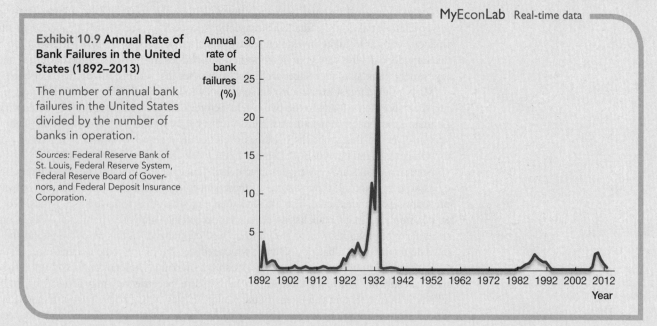

Exhibit 10.9 Annual Rate of Bank Failures in the United States (1892–2013)

The number of annual bank failures in the United States divided by the number of banks in operation.

Sources: Federal Reserve Bank of St. Louis, Federal Reserve System, Federal Reserve Board of Governors, and Federal Deposit Insurance Corporation.

insured by the FDIC. Lehman had $600 billion of loans from other financial institutions, so its balance sheet was nearly twice as large as that of Washington Mutual.

Exhibit 10.9 plots the annual number of bank failures in the United States divided by the total number of banks in operation during that year. Although this measure is not perfect—recall that Washington Mutual counts the same as any other bank, large or small—the data do provide some useful guidance about the pattern of historical bank failures.

Two key facts jump out. First, the Great Depression remains the most severe financial crisis in U.S. history (see the huge peak for 1933 in Exhibit 10.9). Second, after the FDIC regulatory and insurance system was created in 1933, the rate of bank failures plummeted. Note that the FDIC not only insures deposits but also acts as a stringent regulator. Deposit insurance reduces the likelihood of bank runs. Regulation reduces the likelihood that banks take irresponsible risks with their depositors' money. At least so far, the FDIC era has been relatively placid in comparison to the financial mayhem that preceded it.

Question	**Answer**	**Data**	**Caveat**
How often do banks fail?	Although there have been long periods of calm, four waves of bank failures have occurred in the United States since 1900, generating around 20,000 total failures.	Historical banking data from the Federal Reserve and the FDIC.	In some ways, counting bank failures can be misleading, because the failure of one large national bank can be more destructive than the failure of hundreds of small regional banks.

CHOICE & CONSEQUENCE

Too Big to Fail

Many economists worry that extremely large banks have become too powerful. If a bank is large enough, the government will think twice before letting the bank fail, as this failure will reverberate through the economy. If one bank fails, then all of the banks that are owed money by the failed bank will suffer losses. And the dominoes might keep falling, as one bank after another fails and the ripples of financial losses keep spreading through other banks. In theory, the failure of one megabank could bring down the whole financial system.

Regulators call such large financial institutions *systemically important financial institutions* (SIFIs) and agonize about the consequences of the failure of a SIFI. The government faces a devilish problem: if a SIFI is in trouble, even if this is due to the SIFI's own irresponsible decisions, how could a responsible government *not* bail the SIFI out? For instance, the government could lend the bank some funds (at a low interest rate) thereby enabling the bank to keep operating and avoiding the cataclysmic economy-wide consequences of the bank's failure.

Because the SIFI is "too big to fail"—meaning that the government is afraid of letting the megabank fail and will

rescue it if it gets into trouble—the SIFI might knowingly choose to take irresponsible risks. If things *do* go badly, the bank will still be OK, since the government will be forced to offer a bailout. It's the "heads I win, tails you lose" situation, with the winner being the bank's shareholders and the loser being taxpayers, who indirectly bear the losses when the government sends the financial cavalry in to save the day.

To avoid problems like this, bank regulators have adopted two strategies. First, they now require large banks to explain how they could be wound down in an orderly way if they were to become insolvent. These procedures are referred to as "living wills," and they spell out how the bank would sell its assets and pay off its creditors in the event that it needed to end its business operations. Such living wills are designed to make it more credible and easier for a government to shut down a failing bank, including a failing SIFI.

Second, regulators are now requiring banks to take on less risk and hold more stockholders' equity, reducing the likelihood that a large bank will get into trouble in the first place. We return to these issues in the next chapter.

Asset Price Fluctuations and Bank Failures

After hearing about the waves of failures that sometimes engulf the banking industry, you might be wondering how these waves originate. Why do so many banks go belly up at the same time?

Banks fail when they invest in long-term assets that subsequently fall in price. Since different banks tend to invest in the same types of long-term assets, banks' fortunes often rise and fall together. Even a small percentage decline in the value of a bank's long-term assets can wipe out all of a bank's stockholders' equity, causing the bank to become insolvent.

Large changes in asset values are common in economic history. For example, in the late 1920s, stock prices and land prices skyrocketed, only to plummet subsequently during the Great Depression. Likewise, the savings and loan crisis of the late 1980s was caused by a fall in asset values. One of the contributing factors was a roller-coaster ride in the prices of natural resources, particularly oil. From 1972 to 1980, the price of crude oil rose from about \$20/barrel to \$100/barrel (in 2010 constant dollars) and then fell back, ending up in 1986 where it started in 1972 (using constant dollars). When oil prices peaked in 1980, most forecasters predicted steep ongoing increases in oil prices. Consequently, the subsequent fall in oil prices was unanticipated, devastating the oil-producing regions in the United States, particularly towns in Texas, Louisiana, and Oklahoma. Local businesses lost value, and over ten thousand of them went bankrupt. In turn, the slowdown in regional economies decimated housing prices.

The most recent financial crisis (2007–2009) was also associated with falling asset prices. The real value of U.S. stocks halved and the real value of residential real estate fell by over a third.

Why do asset prices fluctuate so much? The most established theory of stock prices links them to *fundamentals*—rational forecasts of the future earnings prospects of companies and the future value of interest rates. This theory, often referred to as *the theory of efficient markets* and associated with Nobel prize-winning economist Eugene Fama, asserts that stock market prices are based exclusively on *fundamentals* and are entirely rationally determined.[2] It implies that all movements in stock prices reflect rational appraisals of new information, not a tendency for investors to let their emotions get in the way. In the efficient markets' view, large fluctuations in asset prices are episodes in which important new information became available to investors, who then use this information to rationally update their beliefs about the future profitability of firms traded on the stock exchange.

An alternative view, gaining more traction over the last three decades and developed by another Nobel prize-winning economist, Robert Shiller, links asset price fluctuations to *asset bubbles*.[3] Bubbles occur when asset prices depart from fundamentals. Some economists believe that substantial asset price bubbles arise on occasion, partly driven by psychological factors and biases, particularly during specific episodes such as extended economic and stock market booms. If bubbles can be identified while they are occurring, then subsequent market crashes would be partially predictable.

Whatever the source of crashes in asset prices, most economists agree that banking regulation plays a useful role in helping the banking sector survive these episodes. Regulators around the world are now drafting new rules that will require banks to have more stockholders' equity—more assets relative to their liabilities—thereby increasing their ability to survive sharp declines in the value of the assets on their balance sheets. The chapters that follow contain extensive discussions about macroeconomic fluctuations—like recessions—and the many different policies that governments use to reduce the severity of these events.

Summary

✳ Credit is essential for the efficient allocation of resources in the economy; for example, credit allows firms to borrow for investment or households to borrow to purchase a house.

✳ The relevant price in the credit market is the real interest rate rather than the nominal interest rate. The real interest rate adjusts the price of borrowing or lending for the effects of inflation, thus reflecting the economic trade-off between the present and the future that borrowers and savers face.

✳ Firms, households, and governments use the credit market for borrowing. The credit demand curve summarizes the relationship between the quantity of credit demanded by borrowers and the real interest rate. The credit demand curve results from optimizing behavior of these borrowers.

⚙ The credit supply curve summarizes the relationship between the quantity of credit supplied and the real interest rate and also results from optimizing behavior, this time of savers. They trade off consumption today for consumption in the future, taking into account the reward for delaying consumption—the real interest rate.

⚙ The intersection of the credit demand curve and the credit supply curve is the credit market equilibrium. At the equilibrium real interest rate, the quantity of credit demanded is equal to the quantity of credit supplied.

⚙ Saving and borrowing in the credit market are intermediated by banks and other financial intermediaries. Banks play three key roles in the economy. First, they find creditworthy borrowers and channel savings of depositors to them. Second, they transform the maturity structure in the economy by collecting money from savers in the form of short-term demand deposits and investing that money in long-term projects. Third, they manage risk by holding a diversified portfolio and by transferring risk from depositors to stockholders and, in economic crises, to the government.

⚙ Governments provide deposit insurance that reduces the likelihood of bank runs, and governments intervene to save failing banks in order to avert widespread crises. The U.S. economy has experienced four major waves of bank failures since 1900.

Key Terms

debtors *p.* 221
credit *p.* 221
interest rate or nominal interest rate
  p. 222
real interest rate *p.* 222
credit demand curve *p.* 223

credit supply curve *p.* 226
credit market *p.* 227
financial intermediaries *p.* 229
securities *p.* 230
bank reserves *p.* 231
demand deposits *p.* 231

stockholders' equity *p.* 232
maturity *p.* 232
maturity transformation *p.* 233
insolvent *p.* 234
solvent *p.* 234
bank run *p.* 234

Questions

All questions are available in MyEconLab *for practice and instructor assignment.*

1. What is the difference between nominal and real interest rates?

2. Firms, households, and governments use the credit market for borrowing. The credit demand curve shows the relationship between the quantity of credit demanded and the real interest rate.

   a. Why does the credit demand curve slope downward?

   b. What can cause a shift in the credit demand curve?

3. What factors explain why people save for the future?

4. Households and firms with savings lend money to banks and other financial institutions. The credit supply curve shows the relationship between the quantity of credit supplied and the real interest rate.

   a. Why does the credit supply curve slope upward?

   b. What can cause a shift in the credit supply curve?

5. What are the key categories on a bank's balance sheet? Illustrate using a table.

6. What is the shadow banking system?

7. What functions do banks perform as financial intermediaries in the economy?

8. What is maturity transformation?

9. What is stockholders' equity? Who bears the risk that a bank faces when stockholders' equity is greater than zero?

10. What is a bank run?

11. What is deposit insurance? Is deposit insurance successful in preventing bank runs?

12. As the Choice and Consequence box on "Too Big to Fail" notes, bank regulators worry about the prospect of the failure of large financial institutions, dubbed "systemically important financial institutions" (SIFIs).

   a. How would the failure of a SIFI affect the economy?

   b. What steps do bank regulators take to prevent SIFIs from failing or to minimize the effect of such failures?

13. Banks fail when they invest in long-term assets that subsequently fall in price. What are the two views on why asset prices fluctuate so much that they lead to financial crises and bank failures?

Problems

All problems are available in MyEconLab *for practice and instructor assignment.*

1. Optimizing economic agents use the real interest rate when thinking about the economic costs and returns of a loan.

   a. Recently, the average rate paid by banks on savings accounts was 0.45%. However, at the same time, inflation was around 1.5%. What was the average saver's real rate of interest on his or her savings?

   b. Banks expect that the rate of inflation in the coming year will be 3%. They want a real return of 5%. What nominal rate should they charge borrowers? Explain using the Fisher equation.

2. The 1970s was a period of high inflation in many industrialized countries, including the United States.

   a. Due to the increase in the rate of inflation, lenders, including credit card companies, revised their nominal interest rates upward. How is the rate of inflation related to the nominal interest rate that credit card companies charge? Why would lenders need to increase the nominal interest rate when the inflation rate increases?

   b. Usury laws place an upper limit on the nominal rate of interest that lenders can charge on their loans. In the 1970s, in order to avoid usury laws, some credit card companies moved to states where there were no ceilings on interest rates. Why would credit card companies move to states without usury laws during a period of high inflation like the 1970s?

3. Imagine two economies—Nervosa and Chillaxia. In Nervosa, consumers and businesses are very apprehensive about higher interest rates. As soon as the real rate of interest increases, they cut back substantially on their borrowing. In Chillaxia, on the other hand, both households and firms have a much more relaxed response to higher rates. Even when the real interest rate increases, people tend not to curtail their borrowing very much.

   Assume the credit supply curve is identical in both countries.

   In which country would the equilibrium real interest rate change more in response to a large increase in the national government's deficit? Explain with reference to a well-labeled graph.

4. In August, 1979, the annual rate of inflation in the U.S. was nearly 12%, and the U.S. short-term nominal interest rate was nearly 10%. Over the next 35 years, both the rate of inflation and short-term nominal interest rate tended to fall. By August 2014, the rate of inflation was about 2% and the short-term nominal interest rate was close to 0%. How has the *real* short-term interest rate changed from 1979 to 2014? Why do the inflation rate and the nominal interest rate tend to move together over the long-run?

5. Explain how the equilibrium real interest rate and the equilibrium quantity of credit would change in each of the following scenarios, and illustrate your answer with a well-labeled graph of the credit market.

   a. As the real estate market recovers from the 2007–2009 financial crisis, households begin to buy more houses and condominiums, and apply for more mortgages to enable those purchases.

   b. Congress agrees to a reduction in the federal deficit, which results in a significant decrease in the amount of government borrowing.

   c. Households begin to fear that the recovery from the 2007–2009 recession will not last, and become more pessimistic about the economy.

   d. Businesses become more optimistic about the future of the economy, and decide to distribute more of their earnings as dividends to their shareholders.

6. Develop a bank balance sheet with assets and liabilities (or series of balance sheets) showing the changes resulting from each of the following events:

   a. A customer deposits $500 in cash into her checking account

   b. A bank makes a student loan of $2,500

   c. A bank is robbed of $5,000

   d. A customer makes a loan payment of $1,000; $800 of the payment represents interest on the balance of the loan, and $200 represents repayment of part of the principal of the loan

   e. A million dollar real estate loan that the bank had made previously unexpectedly defaults (becoming a worthless investment for the bank)

7. Banks that practice *narrow banking* match the maturity of their investments with the term of the deposits that they collect from the public. In other words, narrow banks take short-maturity deposits and invest in assets that carry a low level of risk and are also of short-term maturity, like short-term government debt.

   a. Suppose that all FDIC-insured banks decide to adopt narrow banking. How would narrow banking reduce the level of risk in the banking system?

   b. If narrow banking reduces systemic risk, why do banks still practice maturity transformation?

8. If you have studied microeconomics, you may recall a concept called "moral hazard." Moral hazard occurs when an economic agent is incentivized to take risks because some (or all) of the losses that might result will be borne by other economic agents.

   Discuss how federal deposit insurance, administered by the FDIC as described in the chapter, might lead to moral hazard.

9. Recall from the chapter that banks in the United States hold a fraction of their checking deposits as reserves, either as vault cash or as deposits with the Federal Reserve (where they earn very little interest). Regulations require them to hold a certain percentage (currently 10 percent) of their checking deposits as reserves. However, banks are free to hold additional reserves if they choose. The latter are called *excess reserves*. Ordinarily, banks held very few excess reserves. However, starting in the financial crisis of 2007–2009, the amount of excess reserves held by banks went from virtually zero to over 1.8 trillion dollars.

   a. Explain why banks would be expected to try to minimize the amount of excess reserves that they hold.

   b. Based on what you learned about banking in the chapter, explain why you think that the crisis prompted banks to dramatically expand the amount of excess reserves they held.

10. Lehman Brothers Holdings Inc., an investment bank, experienced a bank run in 2008. There was also a run on Northern Rock, a commercial bank, in 2007.

    a. What were the similarities between these two bank runs? How were they different?

    b. Lehman Brothers was not insured by the Federal Deposit Insurance Corporation (FDIC) but deposits at Northern Rock were insured by the U.K. government. What could explain why there was still a bank run at Northern Rock?

11. The "Choice and Consequence" box on "Asset Price Fluctuations and Bank Failures" discusses the relationship between the prices of things like oil and real estate, and the solvency of lending institutions like banks.

Consider the following two scenarios. Supply the missing entries, and answer the questions that follow.

Assume that Securitas Bank is a large bank in the country of Hyponatremia. The bank's *only* assets and liabilities at the beginning of the year are given in the following balance sheet:

Securitas Bank Balance Sheet

Assets		Liabilities	
Reserves and Cash Equivalents	$20 Billion	Demand Deposits	$200 Billion
Long-term Investments	$330 Billion	Borrowing from Other Banks	$50 Billion
Total Assets	?	**Stockholders' Equity**	?

Philopericulum Bank is another large bank whose only assets and liabilities are summarized in their balance sheet:

Philopericulum Bank Balance Sheet

Assets		Liabilities	
Reserves and Cash Equivalents	$10 Billion	Demand Deposits	$450 Billion
Long-term Investments	$650 Billion	Borrowing from Other Banks	$200 Billion
Total Assets	?	**Stockholders' Equity**	?

Assume now that due to an economic downturn, the value of each bank's long-term investments declines by 10%. Show the resulting situation on each bank's balance sheet. How would you describe the resulting situation for each bank? Relate your answer to the discussion in the chapter of the concept of "Too Big to Fail."

12. The sharpest one-day percentage decline in the Dow Jones Industrial Average (DJIA) took place on October 19, 1987. The DJIA fell 23% on this one day. Foreign exchange markets and other asset markets also exhibit large fluctuations on a daily basis. Based on the information given in this chapter, discuss some factors that could explain why asset prices fluctuate.

What caused the German hyperinflation of 1922–1923?

During a hyperinflation, a country's price level doubles within 3 years. In 1923, the inflation rate in Germany blew past this threshold. At one point, prices were doubling *every three to four days*. At that pace, prices doubled about 8 times in one month. For example, a single egg cost about 1 million German marks on October 1, 1923, and it cost about 256 million marks 30 days later:

8 Doublings: 2, 4, 8, 16, 32, 64, 128, 256

During the entire period of German hyperinflation, prices rose by a factor of roughly 500 *billion*. German currency lost so much value that a briefcase or, in some cases, a wheelbarrow was needed to carry enough paper currency to buy a day's groceries. Paper currency with low denominations had so little value that it was used to make toys, such as the kite on the left.

You might guess that there is something unique about Germany that caused this mass hysteria. But hyperinflations have occurred in many countries over the last century, including Austria, Argentina, Brazil, Chile, China, Hungary, Greece, Poland, and Zimbabwe, to name a few. In this chapter, we examine why hyperinflations occur and explain how they can be avoided. Using these insights, most countries *have* avoided hyperinflations since the end of World War II. Nevertheless, not all policymakers have learned these lessons. For example, since 2011, Belarus, Iran, and Venezuela have suffered from debilitating hyperinflations.

CHAPTER **OUTLINE**

11.1
Money

11.2
Money, Prices, and GDP

11.3
Inflation

EBE
What caused the German hyperinflation of 1922–1923?

11.4
The Federal Reserve

11.1 Money

Money is the asset that people use to make and receive payments when buying and selling goods and services.

The world economy is a phenomenally complex social system. Every year, global GDP totals about $80 trillion of goods and services. **Money** is the asset that people use to conduct these transactions. We can't understand how the world economy works without first understanding how money lubricates the system.

To introduce the role of money, consider a student majoring in English who works part-time in a bookstore; she exchanges her labor for money. Assume she uses her bookstore wages to buy something she wants, say, an iPhone. In this example, money greases the wheels of the exchange: she will give up 20 hours of time in the bookstore to *eventually* obtain an iPhone. Without money, the English major would have a hard time directly trading her labor for an iPhone. It is far more efficient for Apple to take her money than her labor in exchange for the iPhone.

> "Money simultaneously serves three functions in a modern economy. It is a *medium of exchange*. It is a *store of value*. It is a measure of relative value, or a *unit of account*."

The Functions of Money

Money simultaneously serves three functions in a modern economy:

1. It is a *medium of exchange*.
2. It is a *store of value*.
3. It is a measure of relative value, or a *unit of account*.

A **medium of exchange** is an asset that can be traded for goods and services.

A **store of value** is an asset that enables people to transfer purchasing power into the future.

A **medium of exchange** is something that can be exchanged in return for goods and services, thereby facilitating trade. For example, when you hand the cashier $10 for a pepperoni pizza, you are using money—in this case currency—as a medium of exchange. The use of money allows for a convenient, universally acceptable way of buying and selling goods and services.

Money serves as a better medium of exchange when it is also a **store of value**—it enables people to transfer purchasing power into the future. We expect that the $10 bill we receive on Tuesday will be accepted as a form of payment on Wednesday, or even a decade from now. If pizzeria owners didn't trust that the $10 bill would be accepted in the future, they would not accept the $10 bill today.

Money also provides the yardstick for describing prices. What does it cost to buy a pair of jeans? In principle, we could report the price in units of eggs. For example, one pair of jeans might be equal in value to 200 eggs. Alternatively, we could report all prices in units of bananas: one pair of jeans might be worth 100 bananas. But shopping would be difficult if every store used a different yardstick for reporting prices. Life would be easier with a single yardstick for measuring value—a unit of account. Modern economies use money as the **unit of account**—a universal yardstick that expresses the price of different goods and services. We measure the cost of a good by the number of dollars it takes to buy that good, not by the equivalent value in bananas.

Economic transactions are much easier to conduct when there is a medium of exchange, a store of value, and a universal unit of account. Money performs all of these critical tasks simultaneously.

A **unit of account** is a universal yardstick that is used for expressing the worth (price) of different goods and services.

One Benjamin (Franklin)

Fiat money refers to something that is used as legal tender by government decree and is not backed by a physical commodity, like gold or silver.

Types of Money

Paper money was invented around 1,000 AD in China, but *other* forms of money have existed throughout human history. Before the adoption of paper money, people used money that was valuable in and of itself. The most well-known examples are silver and gold, though goats, chickens, and horses were also sometimes used.

Modern societies have switched to using **fiat money**—something that is used as legal tender by government decree and is not backed by a physical commodity, like gold or silver. For example, paper money is valuable only because other people will accept it as money. We don't accumulate Benjamins because we like the fine portrait of Benjamin Franklin on the $100 bill. Rather, $100 bills are useful for exchange, for storing value, and for keeping accounts because we *trust that paper currency will be used for these purposes in the future*.

In theory, any object in limited supply could play the role of fiat money, like used ticket stubs from major league baseball games or cobblestones taken from Peter's Square in the Vatican. But if we used things like ticket stubs or cobblestones for money, there would be a far greater risk of somebody counterfeiting them. This problem is partially resolved by having the government create fiat money that is difficult and illegal to counterfeit (and easy to carry around).

The Money Supply

How much money do you have available to purchase goods and services today? For many people, the answer would be much more than the amount of cash they have in their pocket. Suppose you had $10 of currency in your wallet and a $1,000 balance in your checking account. The minute you pull out your checkbook, the money available to you for purchases jumps from $10 to $1,010. And why stop there? You could increase the balance in your checking account by electronically transferring funds from your savings account.

Money

Hundreds of years ago

Today

CHOICE & CONSEQUENCE

Non-Convertible Currencies in U.S. History

In 1861, at the beginning of the Civil War, the U.S. government paid its soldiers with paper currency that was convertible into gold. However, in 1862 the government ran short of gold and switched to fiat currency, which is not convertible.

You can see the difference in the following pair of images. The top image is paper currency issued in 1861, which is convertible into gold. It was called a Demand Note, because the note could be exchanged for gold "On Demand"—look for those words in the center of the note. The lower image is currency issued in 1862, which could not be exchanged into gold and omits the phrase "On Demand."

When the introduction of fiat money was debated in 1862, the idea was highly controversial. Many politicians believed that money would work only if it were backed by gold or silver. However, once it was issued, the 1862 fiat money quickly gained acceptance and did not generate hyperinflation. Convertibility wasn't reintroduced until 1879.

The Civil War was just one of many periods in which fiat money has been used in the United States. The American colonies temporarily used fiat money during the Revolutionary War. The United States temporarily adopted fiat

A small number of firms now accept payments in bitcoin.

money during the War of 1812. Following each of these episodes, convertibility was eventually reinstated.

Convertibility was gradually eliminated in the twentieth century, and the last vestiges of convertibility were dropped in 1971. Since then, the system of fiat currency has performed well: the buying power of paper currency has been far less volatile than the buying power of gold. Very few economists believe that the United States should return to a "gold standard"—a system in which paper currency is convertible into gold.

In fact, new *non-convertible* electronic currencies are now being introduced by private organizations. Because these new currencies are not endorsed by the government, they are not fiat currencies, and their future success is anyone's guess. These electronic *cryptocurrencies* are protected with computer codes (cryptogaphy) that make theft of the currency difficult, though not impossible. The use of computer codes also hides the identities of the agents who use the currencies. The most famous, and the first, cryptocurrency, is bitcoin.

Cryptocurrencies have had a controversial start. The electronic exchanges on which cryptocurrencies are traded have frequently been used for illegal transactions, such as the sale of cocaine. Moreover, several exchanges have been hacked by rogue computer programmers, resulting in electronic thefts. For example, the bitcoin exchange Mt. Gox declared bankruptcy after $477 million was stolen. Finally, the cryptocurrencies have had volatile valuations, because the public's demand for these new currencies waxes and wanes. For example, during 2013 the value of a bitcoin rose from $13 per bitcoin at the start of the year to a peak of $1,163 per bitcoin on November 30, before falling to $732 by year-end.

Examples of a demand note (top figure), which was convertible into gold, and fiat currency (bottom figure), which was not.

The **money supply** adds together currency in circulation, checking accounts, savings accounts, travelers' checks, and money market accounts. This is sometimes referred to as M2.

When economists talk about money, we include most forms of assets that can be immediately drawn on to purchase goods and services. With this concept in mind, we define the **money supply** as currency in circulation, checking accounts, savings accounts, and most other types of bank accounts. You'll often hear this definition of money supply referred to as M2. Using this definition, the money supply is overwhelmingly comprised of different types of bank accounts.

There are several different definitions of money supply, which go by the related names M1, M2, and M3. To avoid unnecessarily complicating our discussion, we focus on M2.

Exhibit 11.1 plots the evolution of currency in circulation (which does not include currency in bank vaults) and money supply (M2) from 1959 to 2014. To highlight some

Exhibit 11.1 Currency in Circulation Divided by Nominal GDP and Money Supply (M2) Divided by Nominal GDP

Two ratios: (1) currency divided by nominal GDP and (2) money supply (M2) divided by nominal GDP. "Currency" is currency in circulation, which does not include currency in bank vaults. Money supply (M2) is the sum of currency in circulation, checking accounts, savings accounts, travelers' checks, and money market accounts. The exhibit implies that currency in circulation accounts for about 11 percent of the money supply.

Sources: Data from Board of Governors of the Federal Reserve (money supply and currency in circulation) and Bureau of Economic Analysis, National Income and Product Accounts (GDP). Data is quarterly and covers the period from quarter 1 of 1959 to quarter 1 of 2014, or 1959Q1 to 2014Q1.

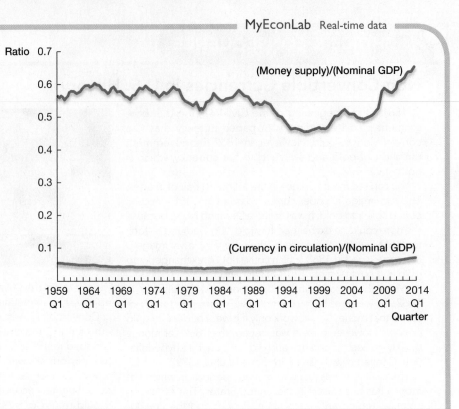

important relationships, we divide everything by the level of nominal GDP. You can see that the ratios have starkly different values. In 2014, there are only about 7 cents of currency in circulation for every dollar of annual GDP. However, there are about 65 cents of total money supply for every dollar of GDP. Hence, the total money supply is about 9 times the magnitude of currency in circulation. This is not surprising once we remember how little cash we carry around compared with the balances in our bank accounts. Moreover, very few of our important financial transactions are conducted with currency. In developed countries, only drug dealers buy a house or a car with a suitcase full of cash. Indeed, even smaller transactions, like paying the rent each month, are rarely conducted with currency.

We can also use Exhibit 11.1 to think about time trends in these ratios. The (Currency in Circulation)/GDP ratio and the (Money Supply)/GDP ratio show no clear long-run time trends, though they do bounce around and they have been rising in recent years.

11.2 Money, Prices, and GDP

We are now ready to study the relationship between money supply, prices, and nominal GDP. Along the way, we will use the fact that the ratio of Money/(Nominal GDP) is relatively stable over the long run.

Nominal GDP, Real GDP, and Inflation

Let's start with a few definitions that we first introduced in Chapter 5. Nominal GDP is the total value of production (final goods and services), using prices from the same year the output was produced. Real GDP is the total value of production (final goods and services), using fixed prices taken from a particular base year, which may or may not be the year the output was produced. Finally, the inflation rate is the growth rate of the overall price level in the economy.

To illustrate these concepts, consider an illustrative economy that only produces soccer balls. Assume that in 2013, this economy produced 10 soccer balls at a market price of $50 per ball, for total sales of $500. In 2014, total sales rise to $550. Therefore, nominal

GDP has risen by $50 = $550 − $500. What has caused the $50 increase? Here are two possibilities:

1. The price of soccer balls is still $50 per ball, and the number of soccer balls produced has risen to 11 balls.
2. The price of soccer balls has risen to $55 per ball, and the number of soccer balls produced has stayed fixed at 10.

Under either Scenario 1 or 2, nominal GDP is $550, 10 percent more than it was the year before.

In Scenario 1 the price hasn't changed, but the number of soccer balls produced has risen from 10 to 11 balls. In this case, we say that inflation is zero and real GDP has grown by 10 percent. For example, using 2013 as the base year for prices, we can see that real GDP rose from 10 × $50 = $500 to 11 × $50 = $550, which is a 10 percent increase.

In Scenario 2 the price has risen from $50 to $55 per ball, but the number of soccer balls produced has stayed fixed at 10 balls in each year. In this case, we say that inflation is 10 percent and real GDP is flat. Using 2013 as the base year for prices, we can see that real GDP held steady at 10 × $50 = $500. In both years, the number of balls produced was 10.

This example illustrates a basic property of nominal GDP. Increases in nominal GDP could arise because of an increase in the price level, an increase in the level of real GDP, or a combination of the two. In fact, we can express the growth rate of nominal GDP as the sum of the growth rate in prices (the inflation rate) and the growth rate in real GDP.

$$\text{Growth rate of nominal GDP} = \text{Growth rate of prices} + \text{Growth rate of real GDP}$$
$$= \text{Inflation rate} + \text{Growth rate of real GDP.}$$

We will now use this basic relationship to derive a theory that describes the connection between the growth rate of the money supply, the inflation rate, and the growth rate of real GDP.

The Quantity Theory of Money

We begin by discussing the relationship between the money supply and nominal GDP. Recall the data from Exhibit 11.1. There we showed that over the long run, the ratio of money supply to nominal GDP is approximately constant.

$$\frac{\text{Money Supply}}{\text{Nominal GDP}} = \text{Constant.}$$

The **quantity theory of money** assumes a constant ratio of money supply to nominal GDP.

The **quantity theory of money** assumes that this ratio is *exactly* constant. In general, that is not the case, as Exhibit 11.1 clearly shows. So in this sense the quantity theory of money is wrong, but it is an *approximation* of how the economy behaves over a few decades, which economists loosely refer to as the *long run*. Look again at Exhibit 11.1, and you will see that although the ratio of money supply to nominal GDP does change over time, it has also been approximately stable over the long run. (The ratio of nominal GDP divided by money supply is referred to as the *velocity* of money— this is the inverse of the ratio plotted in Exhibit 11.1. The concept of the velocity of money does not play a role in our book, but you may encounter it in other courses.)

If the ratio of two variables is constant, then the numerator and the denominator have the same rate of growth. For example, if money supply grows by 10 percent, then nominal GDP also needs to grow by 10 percent to keep the ratio of money supply divided by nominal GDP constant.

So the quantity theory of money implies that the growth rate of money supply and the growth rate of nominal GDP will be the same.

"The quantity theory of money implies that inflation is equal to the gap between the growth rate of the money supply and the growth rate of real GDP."

$$\text{Growth rate of money supply} = \text{Growth rate of nominal GDP.}$$

Using this relationship, we can return to our equation decomposing the growth rate of nominal GDP into (1) the inflation rate and (2) the growth rate of real GDP. Substituting the *inflation rate plus the growth rate of real GDP* for the *growth rate of nominal GDP*, we find that:

$$\text{Growth rate of money supply} = \text{Inflation rate} + \text{Growth rate of real GDP.}$$

We can rearrange this equation to put inflation on the left-hand side. Then we find that

$$\text{Inflation rate} = \text{Growth rate of money supply} - \text{Growth rate of real GDP}.$$

This result is a direct implication of the quantity theory of money. This equation implies that inflation is equal to the gap between the growth rate of the money supply and the growth rate of real GDP. When this gap widens, the inflation rate increases. This equation makes clear predictions that we can test with economic data.

11.3 Inflation

The **deflation** rate is the rate of decrease of a price index.

Recall from Chapter 5 that the inflation rate refers to the rate of increase of a price index. Of course, price movements need not always be positive. If a price level decreases, we call the rate by which it decreases **deflation**. For example, if the inflation rate is negative 1 percent, we say that the deflation rate is 1 percent. Rising price indexes have been much more common than falling prices since World War II, though the United States during the Great Depression and Japan during the last two decades both experienced periods of persistent deflation.

What Causes Inflation?

As we have just seen, the quantity theory of money implies that inflation occurs when the growth rate of money supply exceeds the growth rate in real GDP. This is the implication of the last equation that we derived.

Exhibit 11.2 illustrates this relationship with data from 110 countries over the period 1960–1990. As you can see, the inflation rate (on the vertical axis), is closely related to the growth rate of money supply minus the growth rate of real GDP (this difference is on the horizontal axis). All of these variables are annualized in this exhibit, which means that they are expressed as a rate of increase per year. The quantity theory of money predicts that inflation should rise one-for-one with the growth rate of money supply minus the growth rate of real GDP. That is approximately what you see in Exhibit 11.2: most of the data is close to the 45-degree line, which has a slope of 1. This empirically confirms a key long-run prediction generated by the quantity theory of money.

You might have noticed that some of the countries plotted in Exhibit 11.2 had very high average inflation rates from 1960 to 1990. In the case of Argentina, the most extreme point in Exhibit 11.2, inflation averaged 80 percent per year from 1960 to 1990. Argentina experienced this high average inflation rate during this 30-year period because prices rose extraordinarily quickly in the 1980s, pulling up the three-decade average. At some points in the 1980s, prices rose more than 50 percent *per month*.

Recall from the chapter opener that during a *hyperinflation*, a country's price level doubles within 3 years. Hyperinflationary episodes are always related to extremely rapid growth of the money supply. In almost all cases, such extreme monetary growth is brought about by large government budget deficits. If a government's tax revenues fall short of its expenditures, then it meets its obligations by borrowing from the public and/or printing currency to buy goods and services. When a government prints currency and uses it to make purchases, this increases currency in circulation and thereby increases the money supply. This is also how German policymakers generated the great German hyperinflation of 1922–1923.

The Consequences of Inflation

If relative prices are all that matters for optimization decisions—for instance, the price of a gallon of milk *relative* to a worker's hourly wage—then moderate inflation might not pose a problem. In principle, inflation scales up grocery prices *and* wages, so a worker's ability to buy goods and services is unaffected by economy-wide inflation. Increasing all prices by 5 percent and simultaneously increasing a worker's wage by 5 percent does not change any of the relative prices or the worker's buying power. If inflation simply raised all prices and all wages by the inflation rate, then inflation might not be a big deal.

However, all prices and all wages do not always move in sync (at least not in the short run). An increase in the inflation rate generates windfall losses to some and windfall

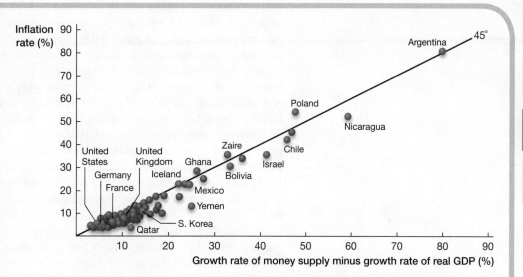

Exhibit 11.2 Testing the Long-Run Prediction of the Quantity Theory of Money

This figure empirically evaluates the long-run predictions of the quantity theory of money, using data from 1960 to 1990 for 110 countries. The vertical axis plots the annualized inflation rate for each country. The horizontal axis plots the annualized growth rate of money supply minus the annualized growth rate of real GDP. Each country is represented by a single point in the figure. We have also plotted the 45-degree line which starts at the origin and has a slope of one, and represents the relationship predicted by the quantity theory of money.

Source: George T. McCandless and Warren E. Weber, "Some Monetary Facts," *Federal Reserve Bank of Minneapolis Quarterly Review* 19, no. 3 (1995): 2–11.

gains to others. Imagine that you have negotiated a 3-year nominal wage contract with your employer. If the inflation rate unexpectedly rises during this 3-year contract, you will be harmed by the unexpected inflation (unless your employer agrees to rewrite the contract). In this example, though you and the other employees of the firm lose out, the shareholders of the firm benefit from the unexpected inflation, because the extra inflation lowers the real (inflation-adjusted) value of the wages that the firm pays its workers.

Next consider a retiree receiving a pension that is not indexed to inflation (in other words, the pension payments do not automatically rise with the overall level of prices). A rise in inflation makes the retiree worse off because the buying power of the pension declines. Here too, there is a winner on the other side of the relationship: the shareholders of the firm that is paying the pension. The real (inflation-adjusted) costs of the pension payments have gone down.

As yet another example, imagine that you have a mortgage at a fixed rate of interest. In other words, you borrowed money from a bank to buy your home and you are repaying that loan back at a fixed (predetermined) interest rate. If the inflation rate rises, your *real* interest rate falls, lowering the real cost of your mortgage. In this case, the consumer is the winner and the bank's shareholders are the losers.

When contracts for wages, pensions, or mortgage payments are *not* indexed to inflation, an increase in inflation hurts some economic agents and helps others.

In these three examples, inflation generates specific winners and losers but no clear *overall* impact on society. However, some consequences of inflation are *generally* socially negative or socially positive. We now turn to those cases.

The Social Costs of Inflation

We first discuss three of the most important reasons that inflation is socially costly.

1. **A high inflation rate creates logistical costs.** In an environment of high inflation, firms need to frequently change their prices. Recall that during the worst months of the German 1923 hyperinflation, prices were doubling every three to four days,

which means they were increasing about 1 percent per hour. Imagine trying to run a business in which you needed to post new prices several times each day! That's an extreme example, but even much lower rates of inflation—for instance, 20 percent per year—necessitate multiple changes to prices over the course of the year. Economists refer to a business's cost of changing its prices as "menu costs," using as a metaphor the new menus that restaurants print when prices change.

2. **A high inflation rate distorts relative prices.** Prices do not stay in sync when the inflation rate is high. Think about a newspaper that charges $1 per paper. Imagine that this newspaper has a cross-town rival that also charges $1 per paper. During a period of high inflation, the real (inflation-adjusted) price of these newspapers falls as long as the papers stick with the $1 price. In other words, the buying power of $1 is falling as the *overall* price level rises. Finally, one of the newspapers acts and doubles its price to $2 (sticking with round numbers to simplify newsstand transactions). After this price change, one newspaper costs *twice* as much as the other, even though the two newspapers pay the same wages to their reporters and have the same printing costs. This newsstand price gap generates a distortion. Two newspapers that should be priced similarly are temporarily priced very differently. During this time, both newspapers might be unprofitable. The lower-priced newspaper isn't charging enough to make money (because its labor and printing costs are rising with the overall price level). The higher-priced newspaper is rapidly losing readers, because its price is twice that of its competitor. Eventually, the lower-priced newspaper will also raise its price to $2, but this might take a few months—complex organizations generally don't make big changes overnight. This is an example of the many ways that inflation causes relative prices to fall out of sync, which reduces the efficiency of economic activity.

3. **Inflation sometimes leads to counterproductive policies like price controls.** Inflation generates voter anger, and politicians sometimes respond by advancing economically destructive schemes, especially price controls. In most of these cases—like the gasoline price controls of the 1970s, which were discussed in Chapter 4—the policy cure is worse than the disease. Price controls cause problems like long lines and supply disruptions. In addition, price controls are partially undone when some of those consumers who are lucky enough to obtain the good at the official capped price resell it at a higher price in the underground economy. Hence, price controls create an inefficient incentive for consumers who don't want to consume the good to buy it anyway, just so they can resell it to someone else at a higher price.

The Social Benefits of Inflation

On the other hand, inflation does generate some social benefits. We mention two here.

1. **Government revenue is generated when the government prints currency.** While printing and spending an *enormous* amount of new currency leads to a hyperinflation, printing/spending a *modest* amount of new currency can be a socially beneficial source of revenue for a government. However, this additional government revenue is a double-edged sword. The citizens gain because their government has more money to spend, but the citizens also lose because the resulting inflation reduces the real value of the currency that the citizens already hold. However, if the amount of money creation is low enough, the net social benefit is positive.

   The government revenue obtained from printing currency is called **seignorage.** This is not a major source of revenue for most governments, though it is relatively important in the United States because there are many people around the globe—especially traders in the underground economy—who hold vast quantities of U.S. currency. Demand for U.S. currency also derives from entirely legal sources, like people in other countries with an unstable local currency who want a stable store of value. Seignorage generates roughly $30 billion of implicit revenue for the U.S. government each year.

   The fact that a government can raise revenue by printing currency makes seignorage a candidate for abuse, and this is the reason why, as we noted above, some governments running large budget deficits often rapidly expand the money supply and cause inflation—as Zimbabwe, Iran, and Venezuela have done recently.

Government revenue obtained from printing currency is called **seignorage.**

Printing a lot of currency has short-term appeal for a government, but in the long run the strategy of printing currency to pay a government's bills often gets out of hand and leads to devastating episodes of hyperinflation.

2. **Inflation can *sometimes* stimulate economic activity.** Assume that a worker's nominal wage is fixed in the short run. This could result from an annual labor agreement or because nominal wages are above their competitive equilibrium level and downwardly rigid (as we discussed in Chapter 9). Because nominal wages are fixed, the higher the rate of inflation, the more the inflation-adjusted wage falls. The inflation-adjusted wage is the wage divided by the overall price index— for instance, the consumer price index (CPI). We refer to this inflation-adjusted wage as the **real wage**. A fall in the real wage increases a firm's willingness to employ workers. Another way to think about this is that a rise in the overall price level shifts the firm's labor demand curve to the right, since the firm can now sell its goods at a higher price. A rightward shift in the labor demand curve, increases employment and GDP.

Inflation also lowers the real interest rate. Recall from Chapter 10 that the real interest rate is the nominal interest rate minus the inflation rate. If the inflation rate rises and nominal interest rates don't respond one-for-one, then the real interest rate falls. Since the real interest rate is the inflation-adjusted cost of borrowing, a fall in the real interest rate stimulates borrowing that funds consumption and investment. An increase in consumption and investment (holding all else equal), increases GDP.

Modest inflation therefore stimulates the economy in the short-run, by cutting real wages (stimulating employment) and cutting real interest rates (stimulating consumption and investment). We explore these channels in more detail in Chapter 13.

The **real wage** is the nominal wage divided by a price index, like the consumer price index (CPI).

In 2010, Zimbabwe was experiencing hyperinflation. For example, it cost 100 billion Zimbabwe dollars to buy lunch.

Evidence-Based Economics

Q: What caused the German hyperinflation of 1922–1923?

At the end of World War I, the Allies imposed heavy financial penalties on the defeated Central Powers, particularly Germany. German reparation payments were specified in the Treaty of Versailles, which was signed in 1919. Postwar Germany, which is referred to as the Weimar Republic, did not make the required payments and France retaliated by occupying the Ruhr, a small German industrial region, in January of 1923. To protest the French occupation, German workers in the Ruhr went on strike. This crippled the German economy along with the finances of the German government. As the economic situation deteriorated, the German government was able to meet only 8 percent of its financing needs with tax collection. The rest was paid by borrowing from the public and printing paper money.

Exhibit 11.3 plots the explosive growth of German currency in circulation during this episode. As implied by the quantity theory of money, the rapid increase in the German money supply (without a simultaneous increase in real GDP) prompted a surge in inflation. Though it is impossible to completely rule out all other explanations, economists believe that the German hyperinflation would not have occurred if the government had reduced its expenditures, borrowed more from the public, or defaulted on its debt so it could avoid printing so much currency to pay its bills.

The collapse of the German economy partially set the stage for the ascent of the Nazi party. On November 8, 1923, coinciding with the height of the hyperinflation, 3,000 members of the Nazi party attempted to conduct a regional coup in Munich. This

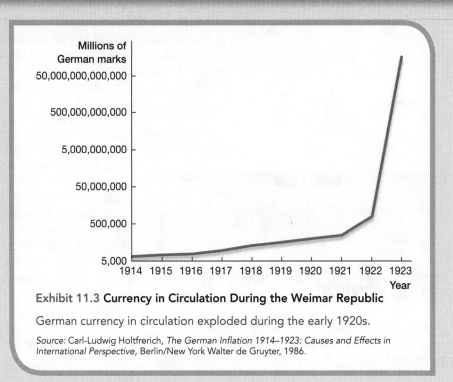

Exhibit 11.3 Currency in Circulation During the Weimar Republic

German currency in circulation exploded during the early 1920s.

Source: Carl-Ludwig Holtfrerich, *The German Inflation 1914–1923: Causes and Effects in International Perspective,* Berlin/New York Walter de Gruyter, 1986.

A plaque commemorating the 1922–1923 German hyperinflation. The inscription reports the price, in German marks, of three basic goods on November 1, 1923: "1 pound of bread, 3 billion; 1 pound of meat, 36 billion; 1 glass of beer, 4 billion." On November, 15, 1923, a new currency, the Rentenmark, replaced the old mark at an exchange rate of 1 new mark for 1 trillion old marks.

coup attempt, which came to be known as the Beer Hall Putsch, ended with Adolf Hitler's arrest and 8-month imprisonment. While in jail, Hitler wrote his autobiography, *Mein Kampf*, or *My Struggle*, which became a rallying point for the Nazi party.

Tragically, Germany's economic nightmare continued 6 years after the 1922–1923 hyperinflation ended. In 1929, the Great Depression enveloped the country and with it came a deep deflation and devastating unemployment. Germany had now experienced three economic catastrophes in little more than a decade: the loss of World War I in 1918 (along with subsequent reparations), hyperinflation in 1922–1923, and depression/deflation in 1929. The Great Depression completed the process of economic impoverishment, catapulting the heretofore unpopular Nazis into power. By 1933, Hitler was chancellor of Germany.

? Question

What caused the German hyperinflation of 1922–1923?

A Answer

The German government could not make reparation payments to the Allies after World War I. As the German economy struggled, the government started to print more and more currency to pay its bills.

Data

Historical money supply data, specifically currency in circulation.

Caveat

Though the German money supply and the German price level rose together in 1922 and 1923, correlation does not always imply causation. Nevertheless, in this case a large body of other supportive evidence implies that the relationship is likely to be causal.

11.4 The Federal Reserve

In each country, the monetary system is run by a central bank. We now introduce the basic operations of the central bank. We will continue this discussion in Chapter 13, when we describe how central banks counteract recessions and other economic fluctuations. In the current chapter, we introduce the most important tools at the disposal of central banks, and describe the "plumbing" of the monetary system.

The Central Bank and the Objectives of Monetary Policy

The **central bank** is the government institution that monitors financial institutions, controls certain key interest rates, and indirectly controls the money supply. These activities are jointly described as **monetary policy**, and central banks are occasionally referred to as the *monetary authority*.

In the United States, the central bank is called the **Federal Reserve Bank**, or simply, the **Fed**. Note that the Fed is *not* the federal government, but rather an independent regulatory agency/bank that operates almost completely autonomously from the rest of the federal government. Exhibit 11.4 shows the locations of the twelve regional Federal Reserve Banks and the Federal Reserve's Board of Governors, which is located in Washington D.C. The Fed's most important policy decisions are made by the Federal Open Market Committee, comprising the presidents of the twelve regional Federal Reserve banks (five of whom vote on a rotating basis) and the seven members of the Board of Governors.

Monetary policy is multifaceted, both in terms of its goals and its policy tools. At the broadest level, the Fed uses monetary policy to pursue two key goals or objectives: (1) low and predictable levels of inflation and (2) maximum (sustainable) levels of employment. These two goals are referred to as the Fed's *dual mandate*.

The goal of low and predictable inflation is sometimes described as "price stability," but this phrase is slightly confusing, since the Fed and almost all other central banks actually interpret "price stability" to mean around 2 percent annual inflation. The term *inflation targeting* refers to the policy of attempting to obtain a specific low level of inflation over the long run. Most central banks have adopted some form of official or unofficial inflation targeting.

> The **central bank** is the government institution that monitors financial institutions, controls certain key interest rates, and indirectly controls the money supply. These activities constitute **monetary policy.**

> The **Federal Reserve Bank,** or the **Fed,** is the name of the central bank in the United States.

> "The Fed uses monetary policy to pursue two key goals or objectives: (1) low and predictable levels of inflation and (2) maximum (sustainable) levels of employment. These two goals are referred to as the Fed's *dual mandate.*"

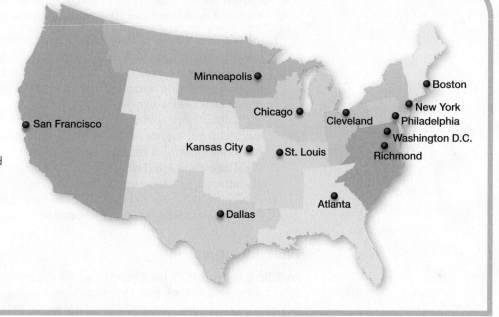

Exhibit 11.4 Geographic Boundaries of the Federal Reserve Districts

The Federal Reserve System was founded in 1913. To avoid political concentration of the central bank's power, the Fed was divided into twelve regional Federal Reserve Banks (color-coded above) and the Board of Governors in Washington D.C. (Alaska and Hawaii are served by the San Francisco district. Puerto Rico is served by the New York district.)

For the European countries that use the euro—the euro-area countries—the European Central Bank (ECB) plays the role of the Fed. But the ECB places greater emphasis on the goal of low and predictable inflation and less emphasis on the goal of maximum employment, partly because of Germany's terrible experience with hyperinflation in the 1920s coupled with its influence on decision making at the ECB.

The Board of Governors of the Federal Reserve System is nominated by the President and confirmed by the Senate. In 2014, the Senate confirmed Janet Yellen's nomination as chair of the Board of Governors.

What Does the Central Bank Do?

The central bank is closely involved in the day-to-day operations of private banks. This involvement takes many forms. First, the central bank is a key regulator of private banks, particularly the largest private banks. The central bank audits the financial statements, or "books," of large private banks, pressing each bank to accurately report the value of assets and liabilities on its balance sheet. The central bank will object if it notices that a private bank is holding a portfolio of assets that is too risky. The central bank also monitors the amount of shareholders' equity in private banks, trying to ensure that it is large enough to absorb possible future losses in the value of the private bank's assets. Such "stress tests" have become an even more important role of central banks since the 2007–2009 financial crisis.

The central bank also oversees interbank payment systems. When one bank transfers money to another—for example, when a depositor writes a check and the recipient of that check deposits the proceeds at a different bank—the central bank processes this transaction. So if a customer at JPMorgan Chase writes a $100 check to a customer at Citibank, then the Fed will clear this check by transferring $100 from JPMorgan Chase to Citibank. In this way, the Fed acts as a *bank for banks*.

The Fed also holds the reserves of private banks (with the exception of vault cash). The management of bank reserves is one of the most important and complex roles that the Fed plays, and this is the focus of the rest of this chapter. As we will see, the Fed's management of bank reserves enables the Fed to do three things:

1. influence short-term interest rates, especially the federal funds rate,
2. influence the money supply and the inflation rate,
3. influence long-term real interest rates.

You may be wondering how employment also comes into this picture. After all, maximizing sustainable employment is one of the two parts of the Fed's dual mandate. Interest rates affect households' and firms' willingness to borrow. *Lowering* interest rates stimulates borrowing, which stimulates spending, thereby shifting the labor demand curve to the right and raising employment. On the other hand, *raising* interest rates discourages borrowing, which reduces spending, thereby shifting the labor demand curve to the left and lowering employment. We'll return to these labor market outcomes in Chapter 13. For now, our task is to understand how the Fed controls bank reserves and why the quantity of bank reserves affects interest rates, the money supply, and the inflation rate.

To understand these issues, we'll proceed as follows:

1. We'll discuss the role of bank reserves in the economy, revisiting some of the issues that we introduced in Chapter 10 when describing the operation of private banks. Bank reserves are traded in a market, and we'll explain the roles of the different participants in that market: private banks, which demand bank reserves, and the central bank, which supplies bank reserves.
2. We'll discuss equilibrium in the market for bank reserves, which pins down a key short-term interest rate (at this interest rate the quantity of bank reserves demanded equals the quantity of bank reserves supplied).
3. We'll then discuss the Fed's influence on the money supply and inflation, which are also affected by the market for bank reserves.
4. Finally, we'll discuss how the short-term interest rate influences long-term interest rates that are directly relevant for households' and firms' investment decisions.

Bank Reserves

As defined in Chapter 10, bank reserves are the combination of deposits that a private bank makes at the central bank plus cash that the private bank holds in its vault—referred to as vault cash. Note that bank reserves are *not* part of M2, which is the money supply that households and (non-bank) firms can use to buy goods and services, but as we will see below, bank reserves can affect the money supply. The quantity of bank reserves plays the key role in the operation of the monetary system. Let's look at how private banks choose the quantity of reserves to hold and how they obtain extra reserves when necessary.

During their regular operations, private banks need to find funds to meet their daily needs. Bank reserves provide this source of funding.

On any given day, a private bank may have more account holders making withdrawals than new deposits coming in. For example, a large corporate account holder at a private bank might pay its employees at the end of the month by withdrawing funds from its corporate bank account. Or a large corporate depositor might withdraw $1 billion of funds from the private bank so the corporation can use those funds for an acquisition of another company.

The private bank may also need funds to make new loans, such as issuing mortgages to home buyers, or making a large commercial loan to a firm building a new plant. Finally, the private bank may need funds to repay other banks from which it has borrowed money in the past.

All of these scenarios imply that the private bank will need **liquidity**, meaning that it will need funds that can be used *immediately* to conduct transactions. We say that a private bank has enough liquidity if it has sufficient funds to conduct its day-to-day business and to meet its regulatory *reserve requirements*. Reserve requirements are set by the central bank. In the United States today, the reserve requirement is 10 percent of a private bank's demand deposits, such as checking accounts and other accounts that can be withdrawn by depositors with no notice ("on demand"). Summing up, the private bank must hold reserves (as vault cash or on deposit at the Fed) that equal 10 percent of the private bank's demand deposits. Reserves in excess of this regulatory minimum are referred to as *excess reserves*.

When a private bank needs funds—liquidity—to conduct transactions, its first line of defense is the reserves that it holds as vault cash or as deposits at the central bank. If the bank has ample reserves, it will use some of these to meet its daily funding needs. However, in some cases, the bank won't have enough reserves to conduct its business. If a bank cannot find a way to raise additional funds at very short notice, it may not be able to make new loans or, in a dire case, it may not be able to pay depositors who wish to withdraw their funds.

Fortunately, banks have a way of obtaining additional liquidity. They can borrow funds from other banks. If some banks face large net withdrawals, then other banks are probably experiencing large net deposits. It is possible that all banks suddenly face large net withdrawals, but most of the time the need for liquidity is not an aggregate phenomenon but specific to a limited set of banks.

To illustrate this point, think about the case of a large employer, like General Electric (GE), on payroll day. GE has 300,000 employees, earning an average salary of about $7,000 per month. To keep things simple, let's assume that GE keeps all of its cash at one bank, pays its employees once per month, and makes all these employee payments electronically. On payroll day, GE's bank account shrinks by 300,000 × 7,000 = $2.1 billion, and the bank accounts of GE's employees swell by $2.1 billion. If GE and its employees all have their accounts at the same bank, this common bank will experience no net withdrawals. Withdrawals and deposits will be offsetting.

But if the accounts are at different banks, which is a more realistic approximation, then GE's bank will receive a net withdrawal of $2.1 billion and the employees' banks will receive net deposits of $2.1 billion. At this moment, GE's bank may be short of reserves, and the employees' banks will be swimming in excess reserves. GE's bank would like to borrow some reserves to address the shortage, and the employees' banks would like to lend out their excess reserves.

Enter the **federal funds market**. This is where banks borrow and lend reserves to one another. In this market banks typically make one-day (24-hour) loans, so the federal funds market is referred to as an overnight market. The loan is typically made in the morning and is repaid the next morning. The term *federal funds* refers to the fact that these are loans of bank reserves held at the Federal Reserve Bank. The interest rate in this market is referred to as the **federal funds rate**.

An overnight loan might sound strange, but large banks are so efficient at making interbank loans that they are happy to make these loans for 24 hours (or less!). *You* wouldn't want a 24-hour mortgage because it would kill you to re-sign all of that paperwork *every* morning for

Liquidity refers to funds available for immediate payment. To express the same concept a slightly different way, funds are liquid if they are immediately available for payment.

The **federal funds market** refers to the market where banks obtain overnight loans of reserves from one another.

The **federal funds rate** is the interest rate that banks charge each other for overnight loans in the federal funds market. The funds being lent are reserves at the Federal Reserve Bank.

Exhibit 11.5 The Demand Curve in the Federal Funds Market

The (net) demand curve for reserves is downward-sloping: a higher federal funds rate increases the cost of holding reserves and reduces the quantity of reserves demanded by optimizing banks. Conversely, a lower federal funds rate increases the quantity of reserves demanded by banks. Movements in the federal funds rate, holding all else equal, correspond to movements along the demand curve. Shifts of the entire demand curve arise because of economic expansion or contraction, a changing deposit base, or changing liquidity needs.

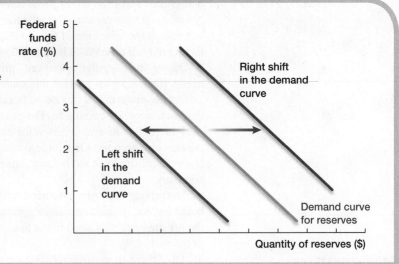

30 years. However, large banks make billions of dollars of loans to one another each morning in the blink of an eye. Every morning, the banks assess their liquidity needs for the coming business day and borrow or lend accordingly. The following morning, the cycle repeats itself.

The Demand Side of the Federal Funds Market

Exhibit 11.5 graphs the demand curve for reserves. To be precise, these are reserves held on deposit by private banks at the Federal Reserve Bank (so we are not including vault cash held in private banks). The federal funds rate is plotted on the vertical axis, and the quantity of reserves is plotted on the horizontal axis. It is important to emphasize that the demand curve for reserves plots the *total* quantity of reserves held by private banks (*not* just the borrowed reserves). So if one bank has $10 billion in reserves and loans $1 billion of reserves to another bank, the net quantity of reserves demanded is:

To avoid double-counting, the $1 billion of loaned reserves is only counted as reserves for the borrowing bank. In this example, the total quantity of reserves held by private banks is $10 billion.

The demand curve relates the total quantity of reserves demanded by private banks for each level of the federal funds rate. The demand curve slopes down because optimizing banks choose to hold more reserves as the cost of holding those reserves—the interest rate that they pay to borrow reserves—falls. Reserves are a safety net for the banks, and they prefer to have a bigger safety net if the cost of that safety net falls.

Hence, a lower interest rate increases the quantity of reserves demanded. Changes in the federal funds rate (holding all else equal) generate movements along the demand curve for reserves.

On the other hand, if some factor *other* than the federal funds rate changes, the entire demand curve shifts. A shift in the demand curve for reserves corresponds to a change in the quantity of reserves demanded at a given federal funds rate. There are five key reasons for such shifts in the demand curve for reserves, and the last two of these reasons are under the direct control of the Fed:

- **Economic expansion or contraction:** In a booming economy, private banks need to obtain liquidity so they can make new loans to their customers—for instance, a manufacturing firm that wishes to expand production by building a new factory. Reserves provide liquidity that can be used to fund these loans. Therefore, an expansion in private banks' loan originations produces a shift to the right in the demand curve for reserves. Likewise, a contraction in private banks' loan originations produces a shift to the left in the demand curve for reserves.

- **Changing liquidity needs:** If banks expect a flood of withdrawals—for instance, a bank run—this also increases the demand for reserves. Paying out depositors requires liquidity, which is exactly what reserves provide. Hence, an anticipated flood of withdrawals shifts the demand curve for reserves to the right.

- **Changing deposit base:** The demand for reserves is proportional to the total value of bank account balances. Recall that the reserve requirement compels each bank in the United States to hold 10 percent of its customers' bank accounts in either vault cash or in reserves held on deposit at the Fed. So an expansion in the quantity of bank account balances produces a shift to the right in the demand curve for reserves. Conversely, the demand curve for reserves shifts to the left as a consequence of a contraction in bank account balances.

- **Changing reserve requirement:** The Fed has the authority to change the 10 percent reserve requirement. Though it rarely uses this authority, the Fed could raise the reserve requirement, thereby shifting the demand curve for reserves to the right. Likewise, the Fed could lower the reserve requirement, thereby shifting the demand curve for reserves to the left.

- **Changing interest rate paid by the Fed for having reserves on deposit at the Fed:** The Fed pays a modest interest rate when private banks deposit money at the Fed—in other words, when private banks hold reserves at the Fed. In 2014, the interest rate paid by the Fed to private banks with reserves on deposit at the Fed was ¼ of one percentage point. When the Fed raises this interest rate, reserves become more beneficial to private banks, shifting the demand curve for reserves to the right. When the Fed lowers this interest rate, reserves become less valuable, shifting the demand curve for reserves to the left.

Exhibit 11.5 plots right and left shifts of the demand curve.

The Supply Side of the Federal Funds Market and Equilibrium in the Federal Funds Market

We're now ready to talk about the supply side of the federal funds market. To understand the day-to-day operations of the Fed, it is useful to model the supply curve of reserves as a vertical line that is set every morning by the Fed. However, from day to day, the Fed may move this vertical supply curve to the right or to the left—as we will see below. Exhibit 11.6 starts with the simple case in which the vertical supply curve does not respond to right or left shifts in the demand curve.

Exhibit 11.6 Equilibrium in the Federal Funds Market

Because the Fed fixes the supply of reserves each day, we represent the supply curve of reserves as a vertical line. The intersection of the downward-sloping demand curve and the supply curve gives the equilibrium in the federal funds market. Assuming that the Fed does not shift the supply curve in response to movements in the demand curve, a shift to the left in the demand curve lowers the federal funds rate, and a shift to the right in the demand curve raises the federal funds rate.

The point where the supply and demand curves cross in the federal funds market is the **federal funds market equilibrium**. Here, the equilibrium quantity of reserves demanded is equal to the equilibrium quantity of reserves supplied by the Fed. The equilibrium federal funds rate is the point at which the demand curve of private banks crosses the vertical supply curve of reserves set by the Fed.

In practice, each dollar of reserves (held at the Fed) is an electronic IOU issued by the Fed to a private bank. Private banks sell the Fed assets in exchange for these reserves. In most cases, the assets that the Fed buys are government bonds, principally bonds issued directly by the federal government or entities sponsored by the federal government, like the Federal National Mortgage Association (informally called Fannie Mae), which provides funding to the mortgage market.

If the Fed wishes to increase the level of reserves that private banks hold, it buys government bonds from the private banks, and in return it gives the private banks more electronic reserves. If the Fed wishes to decrease the level of reserves, it sells government bonds to the private banks and in return the private banks give back some of their reserves. By buying or selling government bonds, the Fed shifts the vertical supply curve in the federal funds market and thereby controls the level of reserves (at the Fed) held by private banks. These transactions are referred to as **open market operations**, and they are the Fed's most important monetary policy tool. The transactions associated with open market operations are illustrated in Exhibit 11.7, and discussed again in chapter 13.

The Fed chooses between two alternative strategies when it implements monetary policy. First, consider again the case in Exhibit 11.6. In this case, the Fed holds reserves fixed, even when the demand curve shifts. When this strategy is adopted, shifts in the demand curve translate into changes in the federal funds rate.

The Federal Reserve's second strategy is to find the level of reserves that achieves a particular level of the federal funds rate. Exhibit 11.8 shows how to find the level of reserves that generates a particular federal funds rate (2 percent in the exhibit). In this case, the Fed first chooses the federal funds rate and then finds that point on the demand curve that corresponds to that federal funds rate. The Fed makes available the exact level of reserves associated with that point on the demand curve. Using a strategy like this, the Fed can hold the federal funds rate at a particular fixed value, even as the demand curve shifts from day to day. When the demand curve shifts to the right, the Fed increases the supply of reserves to keep the federal funds rate from rising. When the demand curve shifts to the left, the Fed reduces the supply of reserves to keep the federal funds rate from falling.

Over the last 30 years, the Fed has gradually shifted towards this second strategy rather than the first strategy depicted in Exhibit 11.6. In particular, starting in 1995, the Federal Open Market Committee began making regular statements about the level (or range) of the federal funds rate that it was targeting.

11.1

11.2

11.3

11.4

The point where the supply and demand curves cross in the federal funds market is the **federal funds market equilibrium.**

If the Fed wishes to increase the level of reserves that private banks hold, it offers to buy government bonds from the private banks, and in return it gives the private banks more electronic reserves. If the Fed wishes to decrease the level of reserves, it offers to sell government bonds to the private banks and in return the private banks give back some of their reserves. By buying or selling government bonds, the Fed shifts the vertical supply curve in the federal funds market and thereby controls the level of reserves. These transactions are referred to as **open market operations.**

Exhibit 11.7 Open Market Operation That Lowers the Federal Funds Rate

An open market operation is an exchange between the central bank and private banks. In the example depicted in Exhibit 11.7, the Fed gives a private bank $1 billion in IOUs, which take the form of reserves held on deposit at the Fed. In exchange, the Fed receives $1 billion in bonds from Bank of America.

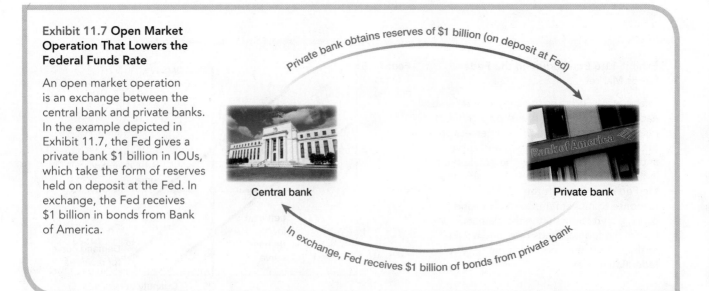

Private bank obtains reserves of $1 billion (on deposit at Fed)

Central bank

Private bank

In exchange, Fed receives $1 billion of bonds from private bank

Exhibit 11.8 Picking Reserves to Keep the Federal Funds Rate Fixed

In response to shifts in the demand curve for reserves, the Fed can adjust the level of reserves to hold the federal funds rate constant. If the blue demand curve for reserves shifts to the right (from D to D_R), the Fed will need to shift the supply curve of reserves to the right by exactly the amount that will make the intersection between the new supply curve and the new demand curve remain at the same federal funds rate (S shifts to S_R). If the demand curve for reserves shifts to the left (from D to D_L), the Fed will need to shift the supply curve of reserves to the left (from S to S_L).

Exhibit 11.8 shows how the Fed can maintain a constant federal funds rate even when the demand curve for reserves shifts. On almost all days since the late 1980s, that is exactly what the Fed has done. But from time to time, the Fed decides to change the federal funds rate in an effort to nudge the economy. As we explain in Chapter 13, raising interest rates will cause economic growth to slow down, whereas lowering interest rates will cause economic growth to speed up. We have a lot to say later in the book about why the Fed raises and lowers interest rates, but for now let's discuss how the Fed makes this happen.

Exhibit 11.9 illustrates how the Fed can raise the federal funds rate by shifting the supply curve for reserves to the left. As we have seen, the Fed can shift the supply curve to the left by selling government bonds to private banks, allowing the private banks to pay for these bonds with their reserves, and thereby lowering the quantity of reserves that private banks hold at the Fed. The shift in the supply curve leads to a new equilibrium with a higher "price" for reserves—a higher equilibrium federal funds rate.

Likewise, Exhibit 11.9 also illustrates how the Fed can lower the federal funds rate by shifting the supply curve for reserves to the right. The Fed can shift the supply curve to the right by buying government bonds from private banks and giving the private banks

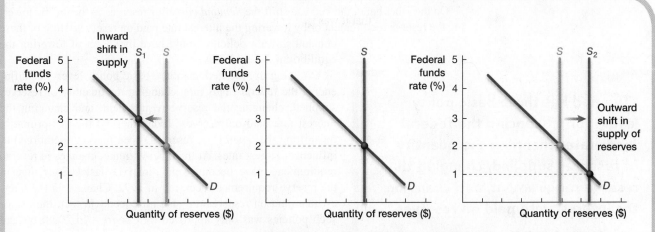

Exhibit 11.9 Shifts in the Federal Funds Rate Induced by a Shift in the Supply of Reserves

The Fed can raise the federal funds rate by shifting the supply curve for reserves to the left. This shift leads to a new equilibrium with a higher equilibrium federal funds rate. Likewise, the Fed can lower the federal funds rate by shifting the supply curve for reserves to the right. This shift leads to a new equilibrium with a lower equilibrium federal funds rate.

Exhibit 11.10 The Federal Funds Rate Between July 1954 and January 2014

The federal funds rate has varied a great deal during the postwar period. During recessions—indicated by the shaded areas in the exhibit—the federal funds rate tends to fall. When the economy is weak, the Fed stimulates the economy by lowering the federal funds rate.

Source: Board of Governors of the Federal Reserve System.

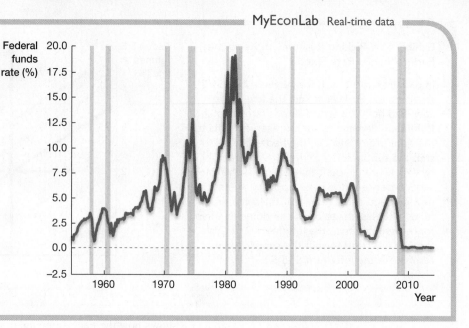

additional reserves in return for these bonds. The shift in the supply curve leads to a new equilibrium with a lower "price" for reserves—a lower equilibrium federal funds rate.

Exhibit 11.10 provides historical perspective on the behavior of the federal funds rate. It depicts fluctuations in the federal funds rate between July 1954 and January 2014. The exhibit shows that the federal funds rate can increase sharply. This volatility arises both from shifts in the supply curve of reserves (as shown in Exhibit 11.9), and from shifts in the demand curve for reserves (as shown in Exhibit 11.6).

Summary of the Fed's Control of the Federal Funds Rate   Drawing together what we've discussed so far, the Fed can influence the federal funds rate either by shifting the quantity of reserves supplied (with open market operations) *or* by shifting the demand curve for reserves. Recall that the Fed can shift the *demand curve* for reserves to the right by raising the reserve requirement (which was 10 percent of demand deposits in June 2014) or by increasing the interest rate paid on reserves (which was ¼ of one percentage point in June 2014). Both of these demand-shifting policies would have the effect of increasing the equilibrium federal funds rate.

On the other hand, the Fed can shift the *demand curve* for reserves to the left by lowering the reserve requirement or by lowering the interest rate paid on reserves. Both of these demand-shifting policies would have the effect of lowering the equilibrium federal funds rate.

Summing up, the Fed has three basic policy levers for influencing the federal funds rate: changing the quantity of reserves supplied, changing the reserve requirement, and changing the interest rate paid on reserves. Today the Fed focuses primarily on shifting the quantity of reserves (open market operations) to influence interest rates. At the other extreme, changes in reserve requirements have become very rare. The last U.S. change in the reserve requirement occurred in 1992. Changes in the interest rate paid on reserves are also infrequent (in fact, the use of such policies was only approved by Congress in 2008) but are expected to become more commonplace in the years ahead.

> "The Fed has three basic policy levers for influencing the federal funds rate: changing the quantity of reserves supplied, changing the reserve requirement, and changing the interest rate paid on reserves."

The Fed's Influence on the Money Supply and the Inflation Rate

We've now completed our discussion of the determination of the federal funds rate—a key short-term interest rate. This was the first of *three* consequences of the Fed's management of bank reserves. We're now ready to turn to the second category: the Fed's influence on the money supply and on the inflation rate.

CHOICE & CONSEQUENCE

Obtaining Reserves Outside the Federal Funds Market

During normal times, the federal funds market operates without a hitch. Banks that need extra reserves borrow them, and banks that have excess reserves lend them out. But during extraordinary times, such as during a financial panic, the federal funds market can break down because banks with excess reserves don't know whom they can trust. They don't know which banks are solvent—those that are able to pay back their lenders—and which banks are not. Accordingly, the banks with excess reserves may be unwilling to lend these reserves out.

In such a crisis, the banks that need reserves may not be able to obtain them. Fortunately, the Fed can step in and provide reserves to the banks that need them. The Fed does this by allowing banks to borrow reserves at the "discount window." Because loans from the discount window have a higher interest rate than loans obtained on the federal funds market, the discount window is usually a private bank's *last resort* for borrowing reserves. Sometimes the Fed is referred to as the "lender of last resort." When all else fails, a bank can go directly to the Fed for a loan of reserves.

In fact, the Fed cannot directly control either the money supply or the inflation rate. Some people mistakenly think that the Fed controls the money supply because the Fed controls the quantity of bank reserves. But bank reserves are actually *not* part of the money supply. Instead, the money supply includes deposits by households and firms at private banks and currency in circulation.

Though the Fed doesn't directly control the money supply or inflation, the Fed does try to influence these important macroeconomic variables. Since inflation is part of the Fed's dual mandate (along with employment) and the money supply is not, the Fed cares a great deal about inflation and only indirectly cares about the money supply. Accordingly, if the annual inflation rate is close to the Fed's target of 2 percent, the Fed won't worry about short-run variation in the growth rate of the money supply.

In the long run, the inflation rate is *approximately* equal to the growth rate of the money supply minus the growth rate of real GDP as we saw in our empirical analysis of the quantity theory of money. Because of this relationship, the Fed will try to slow down the rate of money supply growth if the inflation rate starts to rise above the Fed's inflation target.

Note that the money supply increases when banks make new loans. Consider a home buyer who takes out a $200,000 mortgage from Citibank. The person who is selling the home receives these funds from the buyer and deposits them at her bank, which may or may not be Citibank. This deposit increases the money supply by $200,000. Hence, the origination of this new mortgage increases the money supply by $200,000. Accordingly, the origination of many new loans causes the money supply to grow rapidly. When the Fed attempts to slow down the growth of the money supply, it does this by slowing down the growth of loans from private banks to households and firms.

As we explain in the next subsection, the federal funds rate influences the long-term interest rates that affect the quantity of new loans demanded by households and firms. By raising the federal funds rate, the Fed raises the interest rate that households and firms face, thereby lowering the quantity of loans demanded and lowering the growth rate of the money supply.

Summary of the Fed's Influence on the Money Supply and the Inflation Rate

The Fed raises the federal funds rate with three tools. First, the Fed can reduce the quantity of bank reserves by using open market operations. Second, the Fed can increase the reserve requirement. Third, the Fed can increase the interest rate that it pays on reserves. All of these policies will increase the federal funds rate and the interest rates that households and firms face for borrowing. Consequently, a higher federal funds rate reduces the rate of loan growth to households and firms, reducing the rate at which the money supply grows, and reducing the rate of inflation. Likewise, a lower federal funds rate increases the rate of loan growth to households and firms, increasing the rate at which the money supply grows, and increasing the rate of inflation.

The Relationship Between the Federal Funds Rate and the Long-Term Real Interest Rate

We've now completed our discussion of the first *two* consequences of the Fed's management of bank reserves. We're ready to turn to the third, and final, category. By intervening in the market for bank reserves, the Fed influences both the federal funds rate and *the long-term real interest rate.* Recall that the real interest rate is defined as the real price of a loan, or, in other words, the price of a loan adjusted for inflation. It is defined as

$$\text{Real interest rate} = \text{Nominal interest rate} - \text{Inflation rate.}$$

Consider a firm that borrows \$100 for a year at a nominal interest rate of 5 percent in an economy with a 2 percent inflation rate. One year later, the firm pays back \$100 × (1 + 0.05) = \$105 dollars, but inflation has chipped away at the buying power of this money. If the inflation rate is 2 percent, \$105 in the payback year has buying power of only \$105/(1 + 0.02), or about \$103 in the year the loan was issued. This is just \$3 more than the original loan amount. So the *real* cost to the borrower is only \$3 of buying power, which is 3 percent of the original \$100 loan. In general, the real cost of a loan is the nominal interest rate *minus* the inflation rate. In the current example, the real interest rate can be calculated as 5% − 2% = 3%.

Investment depends on the **long-term real interest rate**, which is the *long-term* nominal interest rate minus the *long-term* inflation rate. When we talk about the long-term, we are referring to horizons that are at least 10 years away. The long-term real interest rate is relevant for the economy because many investments require funding for at least a decade. A home loan lasts 30 years. A major corporate research and development project—like the development of the double-decker, "superjumbo" Airbus A380—can take 20 years between the initial conceptualization and the roll-out of the finished product.

In contrast, the federal funds rate is a *short-term* nominal interest rate. So there is a mismatch between the short-term interest rate that the Fed essentially controls and the long-term real interest rates that matter for most investment decisions. To understand the potential impact of the federal funds rate on the long-term real interest rate, it is also useful to think about the real interest rate that is *anticipated* when the loan is made. This is potentially different from the real interest rate that is *realized* over the life of the loan. It is therefore useful to distinguish between a *realized real interest rate* and an *expected real interest rate.*

The **realized real interest rate** is defined as:

$$\text{Realized real interest rate} = \text{Nominal interest rate} - \text{Realized inflation rate.}$$

For example, if a borrower takes out a loan on December 31, 2010 and repays the loan on December 31, 2020, the realized real interest rate would be the nominal interest rate that the borrower agreed to on December 31, 2010, minus the actual realized inflation rate between December 31, 2010 and December 31, 2020. Note that realized inflation is the inflation that actually occurred over a particular period of time. When the loan is first issued, the borrower doesn't yet know what the *realized* inflation rate will be. So the borrower won't be able to calculate the realized real interest rate until the loan ends on December 31, 2020.

But we do have beliefs, or expectations, about the inflation rate between now and then. We can use those expectations to motivate a closely related concept called the **expected real interest rate**:

$$\text{Expected real interest rate} = \text{Nominal interest rate} - \text{Expected inflation rate.}$$

When making loans, optimizing borrowers and lenders consider the *expected* real interest rate; they do not yet know what the realized inflation rate will be. Because the expected real interest rate plays the key role in people's decisions, its components matter, including *inflation expectations.* Economic agents' **inflation expectations** are their beliefs about future inflation rates.

The **long-term real interest rate** is the long-term nominal interest rate minus the long-term inflation rate.

Development of the A380 was started in 1988. The first aircraft was sold in 2008. Twenty-year research and development projects are **not** funded by 365 × 20 = 7,300 overnight loans.

The **realized real interest rate** is the nominal interest rate minus the realized rate of inflation.

The **expected real interest rate** is the nominal interest rate minus the expected rate of inflation.

Economic agents' **inflation expectations** are their beliefs about future inflation rates.

CHOICE & CONSEQUENCE

Two Models of Inflation Expectations

How do people actually form inflation expectations? Some economists believe that people's inflation expectations are determined by the level of inflation in the recent past. For example, "my forecast of the inflation rate next year is the inflation rate that was realized last year." Such *adaptive expectations* are a backward-looking form of inflation expectations. Such backward-looking inflation expectations are plausible, because it is natural to believe that the future will mirror your recent past experiences.

But believing that what will happen in the future is the same as what happened in the recent past is not maximally rational. Many economists believe that people are more sophisticated than the adaptive expectations theory assumes. These critics of the adaptive expectations

model typically endorse the model of *rational expectations*, which assumes that people have inflation expectations that incorporate all of the information that is available when the inflation expectations are being formed and use that information in the most sophisticated way possible. If agents have rational expectations, they are masterful forecasters who make the best possible forecast using a sophisticated understanding of the workings of the economy.

Critics of the rational expectations model complain that it overestimates the degree of human rationality. For decades, economists have debated which of these models—or yet another model of people's belief formation—best describes the actual inflation expectations of consumers and workers. The jury is still out.

We are now ready to ask how a change in the federal funds rate affects the long-term expected real interest rate. Although there is no universally accepted answer, most economists agree that changing the federal funds rate also tends to change—in the same direction—the long-term expected real interest rate.

A fall in the federal funds rate implies that private banks are able to borrow reserves in the federal funds market at a lower interest rate. Because the private banks, own borrowing costs are falling, they start to offer loans at lower interest rates too. This implies that the supply of credit from private banks shifts to the right.

> **"Although there is no universally accepted answer, most economists agree that changing the federal funds rate also tends to change—in the same direction—the long-term expected real interest rate."**

Moreover, the long-term nominal interest rate falls because a long-term loan is effectively made up of many short-term loans. You can think of a 10-year loan as ten 1-year loans lined up one after the other—like a freight train made up of box cars that are linked together. When the federal funds rate goes down, the first 1-year loan becomes less expensive for the private bank to make. In addition, a change in the federal funds rate is usually not reversed for at least several years, so several of the 1-year loans that are linked together in the first few years of the 10-year loan package are affected. Think of the nominal interest rate for the long-term loan as the average of these ten 1-year loans. Since several of the 1-year loans are affected by a change in the federal funds rate, the long-term nominal rate moves in the same direction.

| One-year loan | One-year loan | One-year loan | One-year loan | One-year loan | One-year loan | One-year loan | One-year loan | One-year loan | One-year loan |

Ten-year loan

To make this concrete, suppose that the Federal Reserve lowers the federal funds rate from 4 percent to 3 percent, and that this decrease is going to last for 2 years, at which point the federal funds rate will revert to its old level. Then, the 10-year nominal interest rate, which can be thought of as the average of ten 1-year loans, will fall from 4 percent to 3.8 percent. To see why, let's take the average of ten 1-year loans, where the first two loans are made at 3 percent and the last eight loans are made at 4 percent:

$$\frac{3\% + 3\% + 4\% + 4\% + 4\% + 4\% + 4\% + 4\% + 4\% + 4\%}{10} = 3.8\%.$$

To complete our analysis, we now need to determine how changes in the long-term *nominal* interest rate—which we just analyzed—affect the long-term expected *real* interest

Exhibit 11.11 Effect of Open Market Operation on the Long-Term Expected Real Interest Rate

An increase in bank reserves at the Fed lowers the federal funds rate, which in turn lowers the long-term nominal interest rate. With constant inflation expectations, the long-term expected real interest rate falls by as much as the long-term nominal interest rate.

Starting point
Federal funds rate: 4%
Long-term nominal interest rate: 4%
Long-term inflation expectations: 2%
Long-term expected real interest rate: 4% − 2% = 2%

Open market operation increases bank reserves

CAUSES

Federal funds rate to fall from 4% to 3%

CAUSES

Long-term nominal interest rate to fall from 4% to 3.8%

(Assume that inflation expectations don't change)

Ending point
Federal funds rate: 3%
Long-term nominal interest rate: 3.8%
Long-term inflation expectations: 2%
Long-term expected real interest rate: 3.8% − 2% = 1.8%

rate. This requires that we study the effect of monetary policy on both the long-term nominal interest rate and the long-term expected inflation rate.

First, imagine what would happen if inflation expectations don't change in response to a fall in the federal funds rate. If inflation expectations don't change, and nominal interest rates fall, then the expected real interest rate falls. Hence, a fall in the federal funds rate lowers the long-term nominal interest rate and lowers the expected long-term real interest rate.

Exhibit 11.11 summarizes these linkages and provides a numerical example. The exhibit begins with an increase in the reserves held at the central bank. This change results from open market operations conducted by the Fed. Specifically, the Fed buys bonds from banks and gives the banks reserves in exchange for the bonds. The rightward shift in the supply of reserves lowers the federal funds rate—in this example, from 4 percent to 3 percent. This in turn lowers the long-term nominal interest rate from 4 percent to 3.8 percent. If the long-term expected inflation rate remains at 2 percent, then the long-term expected real interest rate falls from $4 - 2 = 2$ percent (before the open market operation) to $3.8 - 2 = 1.8$ percent (after the open market operation).

If inflation expectations do change, the analysis gets more complicated, but even in this case, the long-term expected real interest rate often falls in response to a reduction in the federal funds rate.

Summary of the Fed's Influence on Long-term Expected Real Interest Rates   The long-term real interest rate is the long-term nominal interest rate minus the long-term expected inflation rate. When the Fed influences short-term interest rates, such as the federal funds rate, this affects the long-term nominal interest rate. A long-term loan is like a combination of short-term loans. You can think of a 10-year loan as ten 1-year loans lined up one after the other. When the federal funds rate goes down, the interest rate for the first 1-year loan goes down. In addition, a change in the federal funds rate is usually not reversed for several years, so several of the 1-year loans in the 10-year loan package are affected. In most cases, when the Fed lowers the federal funds rate this has little impact on long-term inflationary expectations. Summing this up, the long-term real interest rate tends to fall when the federal funds rate falls because the long-term nominal interest rate falls and inflation expectations tend to stay roughly the same.

This completes our overview of the Fed's activities. We've discussed the Fed's core activities, but we've left some important details out. We'll fill in the rest of the picture in the next two chapters. The current chapter introduced the concept of money and the fundamental "plumbing" of the Fed's operations, especially the Fed's influence over the federal funds market. In the next two chapters, you'll see how the Fed trades off competing policy goals and how the Fed actually conducted policy during and after the financial crisis and recession of 2007–2009.

Summary

✺ Money plays a vital role in our lives. It makes a range of economic transactions possible, simultaneously serving as (1) a medium of exchange that can be traded for goods and services, (2) a store of value that enables us to save and transfer purchasing power into the future, (3) a common unit of account that expresses the price of different goods and services.

✺ The money supply is the quantity of money that individuals can immediately use in transactions. The money supply is defined as the sum of currency in circulation (which excludes currency in bank vaults) and the balances of most bank accounts at private banks. This measure of the money supply is referred to as M2. This measure of the money supply excludes all forms of bank reserves.

✺ The quantity theory of money links the money supply to nominal GDP, which is the value of total output in the economy measured at current prices. The quantity theory of money implies that the long-term inflation rate equals the long-run growth rate of the money supply minus the long-run growth rate of real GDP.

✺ At a fixed growth rate in real GDP, faster growth of the money supply leads to inflation and, in extreme cases, to hyperinflation. Inflationary growth in the money supply generates social costs, which include "menu costs" that firms incur as they make frequent price changes, distortions in relative prices, and price controls. Moderate growth in the money supply, which produces moderate inflation, also generates certain benefits for society, including seignorage and temporarily lower real wages and real interest rates, which stimulate growth of real GDP.

✺ Central banks, such as the Federal Reserve Bank (the Fed) in the United States, attempt to keep inflation at a low and stable level and also try to maximize the sustainable level of employment.

✺ The Fed holds the reserves of private banks (with the exception of vault cash). The management of these private bank reserves is one of the most important roles that the Fed plays. The Fed's management of private bank reserves enables it to do three things: (1) set the federal funds rate, a short-term interest rate; (2) influence the money supply and the inflation rate; and (3) influence long-term real interest rates.

✺ The Fed has many policy levers that enable it to influence the market for bank reserves and, by implication, the federal funds rate, including shifting the quantity of reserves supplied (which is referred to as open market operations), changing the reserve requirement, and changing the interest rate paid on reserves.

Key Terms

Questions

All questions are available in MyEconLab for practice and instructor assignment.

1. List and explain the three functions of money in a modern economy.

2. How does fiat money differ from commodities like gold and silver that were used as money?

3. How is the M2 money supply defined?

4. Recall the discussion in the chapter about the "quantity theory of money."
   a. Explain the quantity theory of money.
   b. Explain how predictions of the quantity theory of money are borne out by historical data.

5. What is the difference between inflation, deflation, and hyperinflation?

6. What is the most common cause of hyperinflation?

7. What are the costs associated with inflation?

8. Does inflation have any benefits? Explain.

9. What is the federal funds rate? What are the factors that would shift the demand curve for reserves?

10. What is an open market operation? Why does the Federal Reserve conduct open market operations?

11. Why is the Federal Reserve referred to as the "lender of last resort"?

12. How does the Federal Reserve influence the long-term real interest rate?

13. What are the two models that are used to describe inflationary expectations?

Problems

All problems are available in MyEconLab for practice and instructor assignment. Problems marked ⊕ *update with real-time data.*

1. Barter is a method of exchange whereby goods or services are traded directly for other goods or services without the use of money or any other medium of exchange.
   a. Suppose you need to get your house painted. You register with a barter Web site and want to offer your car cleaning services to someone who will paint your house in return. What are the problems you are likely to encounter?
   b. Some barter Web sites allow the use of "barter dollars." The registration fee that you pay to a barter Web site gets converted into barter dollars that can be exchanged with other users to buy goods and services. Would the use of barter dollars resolve the problems you listed in part (a)? Explain.

2. Money makes a variety of economic transactions possible. In the following three situations, determine whether money is involved in the transaction.
   a. In prison camps during World War II, and in some prisons today, cigarettes circulate among prisoners. For example, an iPod might cost two cartons of cigarettes, whereas a magazine might cost only two cigarettes. Discuss whether cigarettes are fulfilling all three functions of money in this case.
   b. Over the last 50 years, credit cards have become an increasingly popular way for people to purchase goods and services. Are credit cards money? Explain your reasoning.
   c. Almost every day, many people sign their names to little pieces of paper called checks, which are then accepted in exchange for goods and services. Do these checks constitute money? Why or why not?

3. Yap is a small island in the Pacific Ocean with a total land area of 39 square miles. In the 1900s, there were only three commodities that were traded on this isolated island—fish, coconuts, and sea cucumber. However, the monetary system in Yap was highly sophisticated. The currency that was used on Yap was called "Fei." Fei were large wheels of stone with a hole in the center. These stone wheels were not quarried in Yap but were brought to the island from elsewhere. The value of each wheel as currency depended on its size, which ranged from 1 foot in diameter to 12 feet. Each time a transaction had to be settled in Fei, the ownership of each stone wheel was transferred to the seller, even if the wheel was not physically moved to the seller's house. Explain how Fei fulfilled or failed to fulfill the three functions of money.

4. Bitcoins are defined as a "peer-to-peer decentralized digital currency." The supply of bitcoins is not controlled by the government or any other central agency. The value of each bitcoin is determined on the basis of supply and demand and is defined in terms of dollars. New bitcoins can be generated through a process called "mining." However, new bitcoins will not be created once there are a total of 21 million bitcoins in existence. Some commentators feel that bitcoins can eventually replace most of the major currencies in the world. Would you agree? Explain your answer.

5. Imagine that the chairperson of the Federal Reserve announced that, as of the following day, all currency in circulation in the United States would be worth 10 times its face denomination. For example, a $10 bill would be worth $100; a $100 bill would be worth $1,000, etc. Furthermore, the balances in all checking and savings accounts are to be multiplied by 10. So, if you have $500 in your checking account, as of the following day your balance would be $5,000, etc.

   Would you actually be 10 times better off on the day the announcement took effect? Why or why not?

6. The following four exercises ask you to retrieve and work with macroeconomic data from the FRED Web site of the Federal Reserve Bank of St. Louis.

   a. Go to http://research.stlouisfed.org/fred2/data/GDP .txt. Find the figure for nominal GDP for the latest quarter. (Q1 is January, February, and March; Q2 is April, May, June, etc.) The figure for a given quarter will be listed under the first day of the month beginning the quarter. For example, data for Q1 of 2013 will be listed as of 2013-01-01; for Q2, 2013-04-01; Q3, 2013-07-01; Q4, 2013-10-01.

   b. Go to the following Web page from the Federal Reserve FRED database: http://research.stlouisfed.org/ fred2/data/M2SL.txt. What is the most recent figure for the M2 money stock?

   c. Calculate the average M2 figure for the same quarter you found for GDP in part (a). (Data for a given month is listed under the first day of that month; for example, the data for June of 2013 will be listed under 2013-06-01.)

   d. Divide your answer from part (c) by your answer from part (a), and compare it with the ratios given in Exhibit 11.2. Is it higher, lower, or in line with the data summarized in the graph?

7. According to the BBC, inflation in the country of Zimbabwe reached an annualized rate of 231,000,000 percent in October of 2008. Prices got so high that in January of 2009, the country's central bank—the Reserve Bank of Zimbabwe—introduced a $100 trillion bill.

   (*Sources*: http://news.bbc.co.uk/2/hi/africa/7660569 .stm; http://news.bbc.co.uk/2/hi/africa/7832601.stm.)

   Read the summary of Zimbabwe's experience with hyperinflation in Wikipedia (http://en.wikipedia.org/wiki/ Hyperinflation_in_Zimbabwe). How does the history of hyperinflation in the country illustrate the points made in the chapter regarding the root causes, costs, and benefits of inflation? What were some of the adaptations that citizens of the country used to cope with the situation?

8. The following table shows the cost of producing dollar notes of various denominations. As you can see in the table, it costs only 12.7 cents to produce a $100 bill. Suppose the government decided that it will print new notes to fund its fiscal deficit as well as all its ongoing expenditure. What would be the effects of such a policy?

Note	Cost of Production
$1 and $2	5.4 cents per note
$5	9.8 cents per note
$10 notes	9.0 cents per note
$20 and $50	9.8 cents per note
$100	12.7 cents per note

9. Assume there is an increase in the demand for reserves— in other words, the demand curve for reserves shifts to the right. Suppose also that the Fed did not change the quantity of reserves supplied.

   a. Using a graph of the demand and supply of reserves, show the effect of this increase on the equilibrium federal funds rate and the equilibrium quantity of reserves.

   b. Given your results from part (a), if the Fed wants to restore the federal funds rate to its pre-expansion level, what kind of open market operation would it need to undertake? Show the result of the operation on your graph from part (a).

10. From 2001 to 2006, Japan's central bank, the Bank of Japan (BOJ), engaged in a monetary policy program called quantitative easing. The BOJ increased the value of the excess reserves that commercial banks held with the central bank by buying assets from these commercial banks. Use a graph to show how this policy is likely to have affected the overnight call rate. The overnight call rate in Japan is similar to the federal funds rate in the United States.

11. As the U.S. economy recovered from the recession of 2007–2009, it was widely anticipated that the Fed would raise the federal funds rate.

    Suppose the current federal funds rate is 1 percent, and that this rate is expected to prevail for one more year. Then, the expectation is that the Fed will raise the federal funds rate by 1 percent each year for 4 years, reaching 5 percent in year five and then maintaining the federal funds rate at that level for another 5 years.

    What will be the 10-year nominal interest rate as a result of these expectations? Explain and show your work.

12. The chapter discusses different models of how people form their expectations regarding inflation. Consider the following two investors, who are trying to forecast what inflation will be for next year. Sean reasons as follows: "Inflation was 2.5 percent last year. Therefore, I think it is likely to be 2.5 percent this year." Carlos, on the other hand, thinks this way: "The economy has recovered from recession sufficiently that inflationary pressures are likely to build. Likewise, a weaker dollar means that imports are going to be more expensive. I don't think the Fed will risk slowing the recovery and raising unemployment by raising interest rates to fight inflation. So, in light of all these factors, I expect inflation to increase to 5 percent next year." Using the terminology mentioned in the chapter, explain how you would best describe how each investor is forming his expectations of inflation. Which description better fits your own forecasts of inflation?

12 Short-Run Fluctuations

BANK OWNED
FOR SALE
FORECLOSURE
PRICED 2 SELL
DON'T WAIT
CALL TODAY!

What caused the recession of 2007–2009?

The U.S. economy, like any other, experiences economic fluctuations—in other words, the growth rate fluctuates from year to year. Between 1982 and 2007, the U.S. economy tended to grow quickly and experienced only two mild recessions, achieving average growth in real gross domestic product (GDP) of 3.4 percent per year. But starting at the end of 2007, the economy began a deep contraction. The fall in economic activity caused significant hardship for hundreds of millions of households worldwide. In the United States alone, the number of unemployed workers rose by 7.4 million. Many families also lost a large chunk of their life savings; U.S. housing prices fell by a third and stock prices halved. The recession that started in December 2007 lasted until June 2009, when the economy started growing again.

What caused the recession of 2007–2009? In this chapter, we examine the various factors that contributed to this economic and financial free fall. But first we will explore the characteristics of economic fluctuations in general and possible causes for them. In the process, we will develop a model that can help us better understand the short-run causes and consequences of fluctuations in economic activity.

CHAPTER **OUTLINE**

⚙ Recessions are periods (lasting at least two quarters) in which real GDP falls.

⚙ Economic fluctuations have three key features: co-movement, limited predictability, and persistence.

⚙ Economic fluctuations occur because of technology shocks, changing sentiments, and monetary/financial factors.

⚙ Economic shocks are amplified by downward wage rigidity and multipliers.

⚙ Economic booms are periods of expansion of GDP, associated with increasing employment and declining unemployment.

⚙ Three key factors contributed to the 2007–2009 recession: a collapsing housing bubble, a fall in household wealth, and a financial crisis.

12.1 Economic Fluctuations and Business Cycles

Growth, even for the most developed economies, is never completely steady.

Short-run changes in the growth of GDP are referred to as **economic fluctuations** or **business cycles**.

Modern market economies have demonstrated a remarkable ability to generate long-run growth. As we saw in Chapter 7, the U.S. economy grew substantially over the last 100 years. But growth, even for the most developed economies, is never completely steady. Instead, there are periods of good times and bad, of ups and downs. These fluctuations tend to be hard to predict. We refer to short-run changes in the growth rate of real GDP as **economic fluctuations** or **business cycles**.

Exhibit 12.1 plots the level of real GDP (in blue) in the United States from 1929 to 2013, using 2009 as the base year for prices. Recall that real dollars hold the overall price level fixed, implying that the effects of inflation are removed from plots of *real* variables. The plot of real GDP starts in 1929 because that is when high-quality data were first available.

The exhibit also plots a trend line (in red), which represents the level of real GDP that the economy would attain if we could wave a wand and magically maintain a steady rate of growth, thereby avoiding fluctuations. The trend line in Exhibit 12.1 is derived by drawing a path that grows smoothly over time. Such a fluctuation-free economy is not actually feasible—economic fluctuations are a fact of life. Government policies can only reduce the severity—not the very existence—of fluctuations.

In Exhibit 12.1, two major deviations from trend are apparent: the Great Depression (lasting throughout the 1930s) and the period of U.S. participation in World War II (1941–1945). During the Great Depression, the U.S. economy fell far below trend GDP. Conversely, during World War II, the U.S. economy surged ahead of trend GDP.

Exhibit 12.2 provides an alternative way of looking at the same data by plotting the percent deviation between real GDP and its trend. This corresponds to the percentage difference between the blue and red lines in Exhibit 12.1. Looking at Exhibit 12.2, we can again easily

12.1

12.2

12.3

Exhibit 12.1 Real U.S. GDP and a Trend Line (1929–2013; billions of 2009 constant dollars)

The exhibit plots real GDP (in blue) and a red trend line, which represents the level of real GDP that the economy would attain if we could smooth out the year-to-year fluctuations. The trend line is derived by drawing a path that grows smoothly over time. The figure uses a proportional scale for the vertical axis.

Source: Bureau of Economic Analysis, National Income and Product Accounts (GDP). The trend line is calculated by the authors.

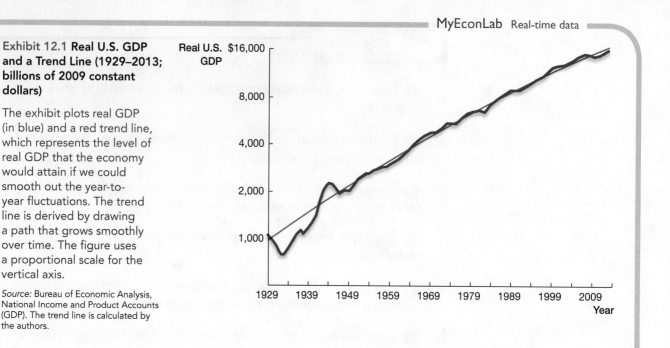

Exhibit 12.2 Percent Deviation Between U.S. Real GDP and Its Trend Line (1929–2013)

Here we show the percent deviation between U.S. real GDP and a trend line for U.S. real GDP (the trend line is plotted in Exhibit 12.1). The percent deviation is calculated as 100 × (Real GDP − Trend)/Trend.

Source: Bureau of Economic Analysis, National Income and Product Accounts (real GDP). The trend line is calculated by the authors.

see two big events standing apart from the rest: the Great Depression and World War II. The most recent recession (2007–2009) is visible at the end of the plot. Even in 2013, 4 years after the end of the recession, real GDP remains well below its trend level.

In addition to comparing economic activity to its trend as we did in Exhibit 12.1, economists focus on fluctuations in the annual growth rate of GDP. They refer to periods of positive growth in GDP as *expansions* or *booms* and to episodes of negative GDP growth as *downturns*, *contractions*, or *recessions*.

As we have seen in Chapter 5, recessions are periods (lasting at least two quarters) in which real GDP falls. Of course, we also care about periods of economic growth. **Economic expansions** are the periods between recessions. Accordingly, an economic expansion begins at the end of one recession and continues until the start of the next recession. During the last century, the average economic expansion has been about 4 times as long as the average recession.

Economic expansions are the periods between recessions. Accordingly, an economic expansion begins at the end of one recession and continues until the start of the next recession.

Exhibit 12.3 U.S. Recessions from 1929 to 2013

Since 1929, a recession has occurred about once every 6 years and each recession has on average lasted about 1 year. The recession trough is the low point for real GDP during a recession, corresponding to the end of the recession. In most recessions, the decline in real GDP from peak to trough is less than 3 percent, though in the Great Depression of 1929–1933, the U.S. economy did experience a 26.3 percent drop in real GDP from peak to trough.

Sources: National Bureau of Economic Research (recession dating) and Bureau of Economic Analysis, National Income and Product Accounts (real GDP).

Starting Month	Ending Month	Duration (Months)	Decline in Real GDP from Peak to Trough
August 1929	March 1933	43	26.3%
May 1937	June 1938	13	3.3%
February 1945	October 1945	8	12.7%[1]
November 1948	October 1949	11	1.5%
July 1953	May 1954	10	1.9%
August 1957	April 1958	8	3.0%
April 1960	February 1961	10	0.3%
December 1969	November 1970	11	0.2%
November 1973	March 1975	16	3.1%
January 1980	July 1980	6	2.2%
July 1981	November 1982	16	2.5%
July 1990	March 1991	8	1.3%
March 2001	November 2001	8	0.3%
December 2007	June 2009	18	4.3%

Exhibit 12.3 reports the dates of the 14 U.S. recessions that have occurred since 1929 and the decline in real GDP from peak to trough in each recession. The peak is the high point of real GDP, just before a recession begins. The trough is the low point of real GDP during the recession, which corresponds to the end of the recession. Since 1929, a recession has occurred about once every 6 years, and the average recession length has been about 1 year.

Patterns of Economic Fluctuations

Economic fluctuations have three key properties:

1. Co-movement of many aggregate macroeconomic variables
2. Limited predictability of fluctuations
3. Persistence in the rate of economic growth

We now look at each of these properties in turn.

Co-Movement Many aggregate macroeconomic variables grow or contract together during economic booms and recessions. Economists refer to this pattern as *co-movement*. Exhibit 12.4 illustrates co-movement, focusing on two key variables: consumption and investment both adjusted for inflation, which are referred to as real consumption and real investment. The horizontal axis plots the growth rate of real consumption in a single year, and the vertical axis plots the growth rate of real investment in the same year. Each plotted point is a single year of historical data, so you can read the growth rates for real consumption and real investment by tracing a point to both horizontal (real consumption) and vertical (real investment) axes.

The exhibit shows that points tend to cluster around an upward-sloping line. This means that consumption and investment co-move. When consumption growth is high, investment growth tends to be high as well. When consumption growth is low (or negative), investment growth tends to be low (or negative). In other words, consumption and investment tend to either grow together or shrink together.

Note also that investment is more volatile than consumption. The vertical axis ranges from −100 percent to +150 percent, while the horizontal axis ranges only from −10 percent to +15 percent. The substantial variation in investment growth occurs because firms often drastically cut investment in response to a weakening economy and then raise it rapidly when the economy is booming. However, it is optimal for households to try to *smooth* consumption over time. For example, unless you actually run out of money, you wouldn't want to postpone replacing your smashed smartphone until the economy recovers from a recession.

Employment and GDP also move together with consumption and investment, and unemployment moves negatively with GDP. This implies, for example, that during

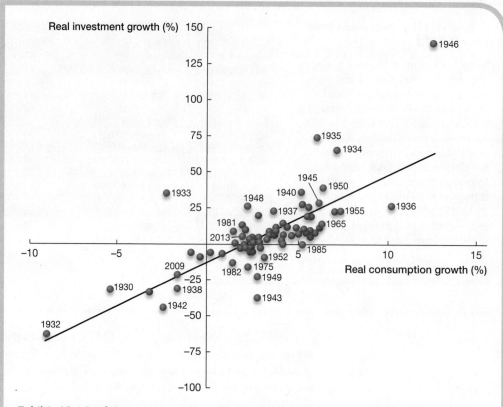

Exhibit 12.4 Real Consumption Growth Versus Real Investment Growth (1929–2013)

The horizontal axis plots the growth rate of real consumption in a single year, and the vertical axis plots the growth rate of real investment in the same year. Each plotted point corresponds to a single year of historical data, so you can read the growth rates for real consumption and real investment by tracing a point to both horizontal (real consumption) and vertical (real investment) axes. For example, on the right-hand side of the exhibit, there is a point marked 1950. That year, real consumption grew about 6 percent (read this off the horizontal axis), and real investment grew about 39 percent (read this off the vertical axis). When consumption growth is relatively high, investment growth also tends to be relatively high. On the left-hand side of the exhibit, there is a point marked 2009. That year, real consumption grew about −2 percent (horizontal axis), and real investment grew about −22 percent (vertical axis). When consumption growth is relatively low, investment growth also tends to be relatively low. Economists say that consumption and investment tend to move together—they exhibit co-movement.

Source: Bureau of Economic Analysis, National Income and Product Accounts.

contractions real consumption, real investment, employment, and real GDP all fall, while unemployment rises.

Limited Predictability The second important feature of economic fluctuations is that of *limited predictability*. If you look back at Exhibit 12.3, showing the duration of recessions in the U.S. economy since 1929, you can see that recessions have been as short as 6 months and as long as 43 months. The 2007–2009 recession was 18 months long. Economic expansions also have highly variable lengths. Since 1929, the shortest expansion was 1 year and the longest was 10 years.

Because recessions and expansions have such variable lengths, it is clear that they do not follow a repetitive, easily predictable cycle. In fact, even with the tools of modern economics, it is impossible to predict far in advance when a recession or an expansion will end. We call this property "limited predictability" rather than "no predictability," because by using sophisticated statistical techniques we can achieve a *small* degree of predictive power. Given the current state of economic science, we are usually able to accurately predict the end of a recession a month or two before the actual end. But it is practically impossible to

An impoverished farm worker and three of her children, photographed in California during the Great Depression.

The **Great Depression** refers to the severe contraction that started in 1929, reaching a low point for real GDP in 1933. The period of below-trend real GDP did not end until the buildup to World War II in the late 1930s.

Although there is no consensus on the definition, the term **depression** is typically used to describe a prolonged recession with an unemployment rate of 20 percent or more.

> The Great Depression . . . came as a complete surprise to most economists, policymakers, and business leaders.

forecast the end of a recession at the time the recession begins. Moreover, it is also impossible to forecast when an expansion will end. Limited predictability is important to acknowledge because many early theories of business cycles assumed that economic fluctuations had a pendulum-like structure with systematic swings in economic growth. Such predictability is very far from the truth.

Persistence in the Rate of Growth   The third noteworthy regularity of economic fluctuations is that of *persistence*. Even though recessions begin and end at somewhat unpredictable times, economic growth is not random. When the economy is growing, it will probably keep growing the following quarter. Likewise, when the economy is contracting— in other words, when growth is negative—the economy will probably keep contracting the following quarter. So if the economy is in a recession this quarter, our best bet is that it will still be in a recession next quarter as well. Thus there is some amount of persistence in the rate of economic growth.

The Great Depression

We've noted that one event stands out like no other in the history of economic fluctuations. This is the **Great Depression**, which is far and away the most severe U.S. economic contraction since modern methods for measuring GDP were developed about 100 years ago. Although there is no consensus on the definition, the term **depression** is typically used to describe a prolonged recession with an unemployment rate of 20 percent or more. Although the U.S. economy has experienced dozens of recessions, only the 1929 contraction qualifies as a depression. For example, unemployment during the 2007–2009 recession peaked at 10.0 percent, less than half the level of peak unemployment during the Great Depression.

The Great Depression started in 1929, coinciding with a crash in the U.S. stock market. From 1929 to 1933, the crisis deepened as stock markets around the world continued to fall. At its bottom in 1933, the U.S. stock market was about 80 percent below its peak 4 years earlier. Millions of U.S. farmers and homeowners went bankrupt. Real GDP fell 26.3 percent below its 1929 level, and unemployment eventually rose from 3 percent in 1929 to 25 percent in 1933. From 1929 to 1933, the number of banks in the United States fell from 23,679 to 14,207. This decline was driven by failing banks that either went out of business altogether or were acquired by stronger competitors. Similar events occurred in almost all developed countries around the world, though the U.S. contraction was among the most severe.

The Great Depression illustrates the three key properties of economic fluctuations that we just discussed. First, it featured strong co-movement in economic aggregates. Panel (a) of Exhibit 12.5 illustrates this co-movement by plotting real GDP, real consumption, and real investment from 1929 to 1939. The three series started to fall in 1929 and bottomed out in 1932 and 1933. Unemployment moved in lockstep in the opposite direction: starting at 3 percent in 1929 and peaking at 25 percent in 1933. The unemployment rate is plotted in panel (b) of Exhibit 12.5. Finally, the financial markets reflected these movements, also co-moving with real GDP. The Dow Jones Industrial Average, an important stock index, fluctuated with the level of economic activity—see panel (c) of Exhibit 12.5.

The Great Depression also featured limited predictability—or in this case, *no* predictability. In fact, it came as a complete surprise to most economists, policymakers, and business leaders.[2] The preeminent economic forecaster of the late 1920s was Irving Fisher, a Yale professor and newspaper columnist, who repeatedly wrote about the strength of the economy and the low likelihood of adverse economic events. Indeed, one week before the stock market's Great Crash of October 24, 1929, Fisher stated that "stock prices have reached what looks like a permanently high plateau." Even after the initial October stock market crash, and after the broader economy had started to contract, Fisher maintained his optimism. On May 19, 1930, Fisher wrote, "It seems manifest that

Exhibit 12.5 (a) The Great Depression started in 1929 and real GDP bottomed out in 1933—the trough. During the contraction and the long recovery, real GDP, real consumption, and real investment moved together, as this exhibit demonstrates.

Source: Bureau of Economic Analysis, National Income and Product Accounts.

(b) The unemployment rate tracks fluctuations in GDP but moves in the opposite direction. Unemployment tends to rise when GDP falls. During the Great Depression, unemployment rose from 3 percent in 1929 to a peak of 25 percent in 1933.

Source: U.S. Census Bureau, Historical Statistics of the United States, Colonial Times to 1970, U.S. Department of Commerce, no. 93 (1975).

(c) Stock prices also tend to move with other measures of economic activity. The Dow Jones Industrial Average is an index that averages together the stock prices of thirty of the most important companies based in the United States.

Source: Global Financial Data.

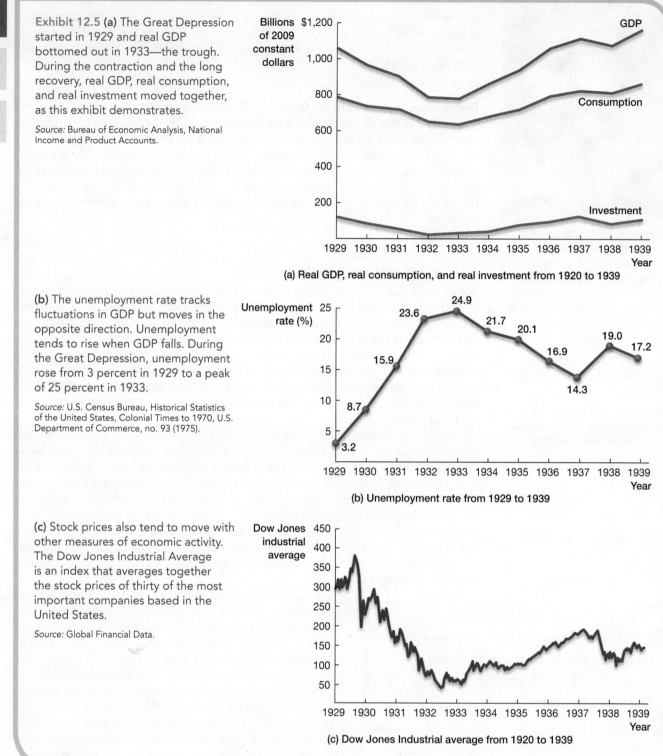

(a) Real GDP, real consumption, and real investment from 1920 to 1939

(b) Unemployment rate from 1929 to 1939

(c) Dow Jones Industrial average from 1920 to 1939

thus far the difference between the present comparatively mild business recession and the severe depression of 1920–1921 is like that between a thunder-shower and a tornado." Unfortunately, unfolding events would soon prove him completely wrong. The contraction of 1920–1921 turned out to be minor when compared to the much deeper contraction that started in 1929.

Fisher's misplaced optimism was common. No leading economic or business forecaster foresaw the Great Depression. Consider this: on January 18, 1930, a group of eminent forecasters at Harvard wrote, "There are indications that the severest phase of the recession is over." In truth, the Great Depression had barely begun.

Finally, the Great Depression featured the third property of economic fluctuations—a great deal of persistence. The period of negative growth in real GDP lasted for 4 years, starting in 1929 and ending in 1933.

12.2 Macroeconomic Equilibrium and Economic Fluctuations

Why are there economic fluctuations? Given the importance of economic fluctuations and the voluminous amount of research on the topic, you might think that we would have a convincing answer—one on which we could all agree. Alas, that is not the case. In fact, there probably isn't another topic that incites as much passionate disagreement among economists. Although this disagreement, often aired in newspaper editorials and blogs, is real, it masks the fact that economists have built up a significant body of shared knowledge about the nature of economic fluctuations. This knowledge forms the basis of the model of economic fluctuations that we will now describe.

Labor Demand and Fluctuations

We begin our analysis by returning to a discussion of the labor market. Recall from Chapter 9 that the intersection of the labor demand and labor supply curves determines the labor market equilibrium. Here we start with a labor market with flexible wages and then show how downward wage rigidity amplifies the impact of labor demand shifts—and thus amplifies the magnitude of economic fluctuations.

Summary of Shifts in the Labor Demand Curve

In Chapter 9, we discussed the most important sources of shifts in the labor demand curve:

1. **Changing output prices:** When the price of the output good goes down, the value of the marginal product of labor also declines. This implies that the firm would like to hire fewer workers at any given wage, shifting the labor demand curve to the left. (When the price of the product the firm produces rises, the value of the marginal product of labor goes up, shifting the labor demand curve to the right.)
2. **Changing output demand:** When the demand for the product the firm produces declines, its price and thus its value of the marginal product of labor goes down, shifting the labor demand curve to the left. (When the demand for the product the firm produces rises, the value of the marginal product of labor goes up, shifting the labor demand curve to the right.) In addition to the factors emphasized in Chapter 9, an expansion in credit (and a decline in the interest rate) can also lead to an increase in output demand, as we have seen in Chapter 10.
3. **Changing technology and productivity:** When the marginal product of labor falls, the labor demand curve shifts to the left. (When the marginal product of labor rises, the labor demand curve shifts to the right.)
4. **Changing input prices:** Businesses use labor and other factors of production, like physical capital and energy, to produce goods and services. When the cost of these other factors goes up, firms purchase less of them. This usually decreases the marginal product of labor, shifting the labor demand curve to the left. (When the cost of these other factors goes down, firms purchase more of them, shifting the labor demand curve to the right.) A change in the credit market equilibrium can also influence labor demand by affecting the firm's cost of financing the acquisition of physical capital.

Panel (a) of Exhibit 12.6, which focuses on the case of flexible wages, reminds you of this relationship by graphing labor demand and labor supply curves and their intersection. Also recall that labor demand reflects profit maximization by firms, and labor supply reflects how households optimally trade off labor and leisure.

Exhibit 12.6 A shift to the left of the labor demand curve leads to a fall in equilibrium employment and a fall in the wage (point "2: Recession"). This example assumes that wages are flexible and consequently fall as a result of the leftward shift in the labor demand curve.

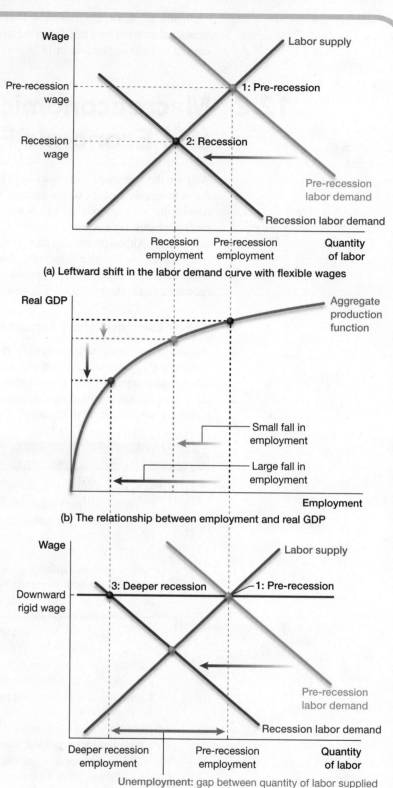

(a) Leftward shift in the labor demand curve with flexible wages

(b) The relationship between employment and real GDP

(c) Leftward shift in the labor demand curve with downward rigid wages

The decline in employment from the pre-recession equilibrium (point 1) to a recession moves the economy along the aggregate production function relating employment to real GDP, causing a decline in real GDP. The decline in employment is smaller when wages are flexible (point 2, which appears in panel (a)) than when wages are downward rigid (point 3, which appears in panel (c)). Consequently, the fall in real GDP is also smaller when wages are flexible than when wages are downward rigid.

When wages are downward rigid, a shift to the left of the labor demand curve leads to a sharp fall in equilibrium employment. In the new equilibrium (point "3: Deeper recession"), there are many workers (denoted by the green line) who would like to work at the market wage but can't find a job. These workers are officially classified as unemployed because they would like to work at the market wage but can't find a job.

The labor market equilibrium, which corresponds to the wage and employment levels given by the intersection of the labor supply and labor demand curves, is the key building block we will use to construct a model of economic fluctuations. Employment fluctuations correspond to changes in this labor market equilibrium, and real GDP and employment fluctuations are linked. Panel (a) of Exhibit 12.6 illustrates these linkages by depicting a leftward shift in the labor demand curve, which reduces the equilibrium quantity of labor employed. Before a recession begins, the original equilibrium is given by the point labeled "1: Pre-recession." After an economic shock has shifted the labor demand curve to the left, the new equilibrium, which features a lower wage and a lower quantity of labor demanded, is at the point labeled "2: Recession."

Panel (b) of Exhibit 12.6 depicts the aggregate production function, which we discussed in Chapter 6. Holding physical capital and technology constant, this curve shows the relationship between employment and GDP (we are holding human capital per worker constant here, so the efficiency units of labor are proportional to employment). We can see in the panel that as employment declines (due to the leftward shift in the demand curve), so does real GDP (because there is less labor producing goods and services). Accordingly, employment and real GDP rise and fall together, which is another illustration of co-movement among economic aggregates.

In practice, the fall in real GDP might exceed what we show in panel (b) of the exhibit because the decline in employment generates other types of economic adjustment. Laying off a worker also makes the physical capital that the worker was previously using—plant and equipment—less productive, leading firms to shutter plants and mothball equipment. The rate of utilization of physical capital is called *capacity utilization*, and recessions are usually accompanied by a reduction in capacity utilization. For example, during the depths of the 2007–2009 recession, capacity utilization in the United States fell to 67 percent from a normal rate of 80 percent, further depressing real GDP.

When firms shed their workers, utilization of physical capital also falls.

As we discussed in Chapter 9, when wages are downward rigid, the impact of a shift in labor demand is amplified. This is shown in panel (c) of Exhibit 12.6. In the case of downward wage rigidity, firms are unable or unwilling to cut wages because of contractual restrictions or because of morale problems that would result from falling wages. As a result, firms end up laying off more workers than they would have if wages were downward flexible. With downward rigid wages, a leftward shift in the labor demand curve causes employment to fall by even more than it does in the flexible wage

> **When wages are downward rigid, the impact of shifts in labor demand is amplified.**

case. Accordingly, with downward rigid wages there is an even deeper recession and a bigger movement along the aggregate production function than in the flexible wage case (panel (b)).

Downward rigid wages are one source of *unemployment*. At the market wage, which is the downward rigid wage, the number of workers who are willing to work exceeds the number of jobs that firms are willing to fill. The number of unemployed workers in this deeper recession—in other words, workers who would like to work at the market wage but can't find a job—is represented by the green bar at the bottom of panel (c).

Although shifts in the *supply* of labor can also cause fluctuations in employment and unemployment, the most important source of fluctuations are shifts in the *demand* for labor. To understand the nature of short-run macroeconomic equilibrium, we need to know why the demand for labor fluctuates.

Sources of Fluctuations

Economists have tried to identify the forces that affect the demand curve for labor. These forces cause recessions and other aggregate economic fluctuations.

In Chapter 9 we provide one breakdown of the factors that shift the labor demand curve: (1) changes in the output price for a firm's products, (2) changes in the demand for a firm's products, (3) changes in productivity or technology, or (4) changes in the costs of a firm's inputs.

We now offer a different breakdown, by discussing three schools of thought within the economics profession. Each school has a different story to tell about the sources of aggregate economic fluctuations.

1. *Real business cycle theory*: emphasizes changing productivity and technology
2. *Keynesian theory*: emphasizes changing expectations about the future
3. *Financial and monetary theories*: emphasize changes in prices and interest rates

LETTING THE DATA SPEAK

Unemployment and the Growth Rate of Real GDP: Okun's Law

Exhibit 12.6 emphasizes that employment and real GDP are tightly connected through the aggregate production function. This linkage is related to an equation called **Okun's Law**, which is named after economist Arthur Okun, who first noticed in the early 1960s that there is a close connection between falling unemployment and the growth rate of real GDP.[3] Employment tends to increase and the unemployment rate tends to decline when the growth rate of real GDP is high.

In particular, let g represent the annual growth rate of real GDP, in percentage points. Then Okun's Law says that:

(Year-to-year change in the rate of unemployment)
$$= -\frac{1}{2} \times (g - 3\%).$$

This equation implies that the unemployment rate holds steady when the growth rate of real GDP is 3 percent. The equation also implies that the unemployment rate falls when g is above 3 percent; and the unemployment rate rises when g is below 3 percent. In other words, the unemployment rate falls when real economic growth is relatively high; and the unemployment rate rises when real economic growth is relatively low. Okun's Law is plotted as a black line in Exhibit 12.7. Although the data don't line up perfectly with the equation, Okun's Law is roughly consistent with the data.

Though the overall relationship between changes in the rate of unemployment and the growth rate of real GDP is clear in the data, these two variables do not *always* move together. Sometimes, a fall in the unemployment rate is delayed by a year or more *after* the growth rate of real

Okun's Law says that the year-to-year change in the rate of unemployment is equal to $-\frac{1}{2} \times (g - 3\%)$, where g represents the annual growth rate of real GDP, in percentage points.

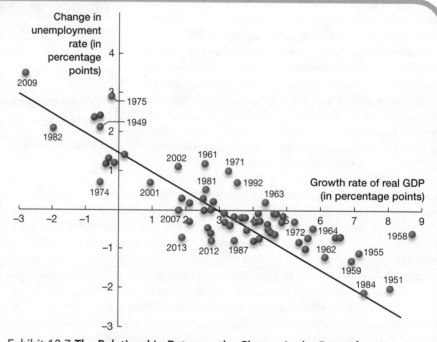

Exhibit 12.7 The Relationship Between the Change in the Rate of Unemployment and the Growth Rate of Real GDP

This exhibit depicts Okun's Law, which shows the relationship between the change in the rate of unemployment and the growth rate of real GDP (g). Okun's Law (the black line) implies that the year-to-year change in the rate of unemployment is

$$-\frac{1}{2} \times (g - 3\%).$$

In other words, unemployment remains constant when the growth rate of real GDP is 3 percent, unemployment declines when the growth rate of real GDP is above 3 percent, and unemployment increases when the growth rate of real GDP is below 3 percent. The exhibit plots annual data from 1948 to 2013.

Sources: Bureau of Labor Statistics (unemployment rate) and Bureau of Economic Analysis, National Income and Product Accounts (real GDP).

GDP picks up at the end of a recession. This delay occurs for several reasons, but the most important one is *labor hoarding*. Because recruiting workers and training them is costly, firms may not want to lay off qualified workers during a temporary slowdown. During a recession some firms will reduce the hours of their workers or even pay those workers to come to jobs at which little gets done, rather than laying the workers off. When the economic recovery comes and these firms increase production, they will not initially need to hire new workers because they can start to ramp up production by fully utilizing the workers they hoarded during the contraction.

Each of these three schools of thought draws upon one or more of the four categories of shifts in the labor demand curve from Chapter 9. Most economists studying business cycles believe each school of thought has generated many key insights, and economists generally don't believe that any one school has all of the answers. The model that we use to describe economic fluctuations expresses the ideas of all of these different schools in a single general framework.

1. Technology Shocks: Explanations from Real Business Cycle Theory In Chapters 6 and 7, we showed that technology differences across firms and workers in different countries help explain differences in cross-country income and growth. Accordingly, one might look for technological reasons to explain economic fluctuations within a given country. For example, imagine that research and development (R&D) leads firms to invent more valuable products (e.g., smartphones replacing traditional cellular phones). This will increase the value of the marginal product of labor, inducing firms to expand their operations, most likely leading them to increase their demand for labor. Firms will also likely seek to increase their productive capacity, raising the level of investment in the economy. These changes will lead to higher household income for three reasons: (1) employment increases, (2) wages rise, and (3) rising corporate earnings make the corporations' stockholders wealthier. For all of these reasons, households will raise their consumption. Thus certain types of technological improvements can lead to increases in labor demand and increases in aggregate economic activity, including investment and consumption.

A version of this view appears in the work of classical economists, most notably, that of Arthur Cecil Pigou.[4] It was revived and extended in the 1980s in what came to be known as **real business cycle theory**—a school of thought that emphasizes the role of technology in causing economic fluctuations.[5]

Real business cycle theory is the school of thought that emphasizes the role of changes in technology in causing economic fluctuations.

But although we know from Chapters 6 and 7 that the rate of technological progress is at the root of long-run variation in economic growth and technological breakthroughs could cause a rapid *increase* in a particular industry's output, purely technological theories have difficulty explaining recessions in which real GDP falls. "Technological regress," in which the technological capabilities of an economy deteriorate, seems an unlikely explanation for recessions. It is unlikely, for example, that a negative technology shock caused the Great Depression.

Nevertheless, the rate of technological progress is believed to play a key role in *long-term* variation in economic growth. As we saw in Chapter 7, countries that consistently develop new technologies, or import cutting-edge technologies from other countries, will attain high rates of growth. So technological progress is a very important determinant of long-term fluctuations in growth—for instance, over several decades—even though it is not the main force driving recessions.

Proponents of real business cycle theory tend to also emphasize the importance of changing input prices—especially the price of oil. We can think of an increase in the price of oil as a decrease in the productivity of firms that use oil. Because almost all firms use oil in one form or another—oil products are a key source of energy—changes in the price of oil function like technology changes. As oil price changes can be abrupt, including large increases in the price of oil, this factor does help to explain recessions.

2. Sentiments and Multipliers: Explanations from John Maynard Keynes Many modern analyses of economic fluctuations build on the insights of the British economist John Maynard Keynes (1883–1946), who was an academic, stock market trader, and a frequent advisor to the British government. (In case you want to talk about him over dinner in your dining hall, Keynes is pronounced "cains.")

Keynes was 46 years old at the start of the Great Depression. As the Depression took hold, Keynes began to develop new theories that attempted to explain its causes. This work culminated in his groundbreaking book *The General Theory of Employment, Interest and Money.*[6] His ideas also had novel implications for government policy. Keynes was highly controversial during his time and remains so today, though few would deny his enormous influence on modern macroeconomics.

Keynes believed in a phenomenon that he dubbed **animal spirits**, which represent psychological factors that lead to changes in the mood of consumers and businesses, thereby affecting consumption, investment, and GDP. In Keynes's view, the animal spirits in an economy could fluctuate sharply even as the underlying fundamental features of the economy changed relatively little. For example, a period of heightened optimism could give way to a period of deep pessimism even though the economic fundamentals—technology, physical capital, and human capital—hadn't changed much at all.

Animal spirits are in fact one example of a broader phenomenon: changing **sentiments**, which include changes in expectations and changes in the (actual or perceived) uncertainty facing firms and households. Changes in sentiments lead to changes in household consumption and firm investment.

For example, consider what happens when firms expect future demand for their products to be low. Such pessimism will have a direct effect on labor demand. When United Airlines becomes pessimistic about future demand for air travel, it cuts back its hiring of flight attendants and pilots. It also cuts back its orders for new planes. This reduces demand for planes at manufacturers like Boeing. Consequently, labor demand both at United Airlines and Boeing shifts to the left.

Consider the effects of this pessimism on GDP. Let's begin by analyzing the fall in investment that occurs when United Airlines cuts back its orders for new planes. Recall the national income accounting identity from Chapter 5:

$$Y = C + I + G + X - M.$$

The change in the behavior of United Airlines causes a decline in investment in the economy (I) and thus also in GDP (Y). But this decline could be at least partially offset by an increase in consumption (C), government expenditure (G), or the difference between exports and imports ($X - M$). With completely *offsetting* movements in C, G, or $X - M$, it is possible for GDP, Y, to remain unchanged despite a sharp decline in investment. For example, if I falls by \$5 billion, C could rise by \$5 billion, offsetting the reduction in I.

When firms are turning pessimistic and cutting back employment and investment, however, households are unlikely to increase their consumption. In fact, households face a heightened risk of losing their jobs because of the fall in investment. Accordingly, in most instances, consumption moves in the same direction as investment (consistent with our discussion of co-movement above).

The implications for employment were displayed in Exhibit 12.6. Particularly when there is downward wage rigidity, a change in labor demand will have a large effect on employment. Hence, a fall in investment will tend to produce a leftward shift in firms' labor demand curves, reducing employment and ultimately reducing GDP.

The implications of households becoming more pessimistic are similar: they will cut their current spending to build up their "rainy-day" savings and thereby prepare for economic problems ahead. This translates into a decline in the current demand for the products of many firms, shifting the labor demand curve of those firms to the left.

This discussion hints at another major element of Keynes's theory: the possibility that a modest shock could hit the economy and generate a cascade of follow-on effects that ultimately cause a much larger contraction. For example, an increase in pessimism among airline executives will have a series of immediate effects—for instance, lower hiring at United Airlines—that might cascade into a series of follow-on effects—lower hiring at aircraft manufacturers, like Boeing. The cascade keeps building as the ripples spread to more and more interconnected firms, which each start to cut back hiring and shift their own labor demand curves to the left. The pessimism might also spread to households, which, sensing fewer opportunities in the labor market, start to reduce their demand for goods and services. The economic mechanisms that cause an initial shock to be amplified by follow-on effects are called **multipliers**.

To illustrate the potential power of multipliers, imagine that a stock market decline causes a drop in consumer confidence and reduces households' willingness to spend. Such an event

---

Animal spirits are psychological factors that lead to changes in the mood of consumers or businesses, thereby affecting consumption, investment, and GDP.

Sentiments include changes in expectations about future economic activity, changes in uncertainty facing firms and households, and fluctuations in animal spirits. Changes in sentiments lead to changes in household consumption and firm investment.

Multipliers refer to economic mechanisms that amplify the initial impact of a shock.

will cause many other dominos to fall. Firms will cut back production and lay off employees. Those newly unemployed workers will be unable to buy goods and services, leading firms that previously sold goods to these consumers to scale back production even more. According to Keynes, such a cycle could have calamitous effects as each round of layoffs further damages the economy, setting off another wave of layoffs. Such cascades of effects will amplify—or multiply—the impact of the initial shock whether the initial shock is negative or positive news. Hence a bit of good economic news can also produce a cascade of positive effects as consumers increase their demand for goods and services and firms respond by shifting the labor demand curve to the right, all of which multiplies the impact of the initial news. Keynes's theory of multipliers plays an important role in many modern economic models.

It is also useful to note that the workings of multipliers involve an element of a **self-fulfilling prophecy**, since the expectation of an event, such as a leftward shift in labor demand in the future, induces actions that lead to the realization of that event, that is, firms cutting their employment now. This is because sentiments can be powerful catalysts of economic change. For example, when a large number of economic actors become pessimistic about the future state of the economy, their resulting actions can indeed reduce the level of future economic activity, partially or even fully justifying their pessimistic beliefs. Consumers might stop buying goods and services. Firms might stop investing in plants and equipment. Labor demand will then shift to the left, reducing employment and raising unemployment. This notion of a self-fulfilling prophecy also highlights that a change in expectations driven by animal spirits might turn out to be "rational"; when households and firms become pessimistic about the economy, the economy will contract as a result of people's pessimistic behavior. So the pessimism ends up justifying itself!

3. Monetary and Financial Factors: Explanations from Milton Friedman

Monetary factors are yet another force that drives business cycles. As we saw in the last chapter, money supply affects nominal GDP. Typically, a fall in nominal GDP, driven by a sharp decline in the money supply, will not only affect the aggregate price level but also real GDP. In this case, changes in the money supply will also drive business cycles. The major proponent of this view has been one of the few macroeconomists to rival Keynes in terms of genius and influence—Milton Friedman.[7]

To understand how monetary factors drive fluctuations in real GDP, consider a scenario in which contractionary monetary policy causes the money supply (M2) to fall sharply.

The fall in the money supply will cause the price level to fall, as predicted by the quantity theory of money (Chapter 11). A fall in the price level reduces employment because of *downward wage rigidity*. To understand why, note that a drop in the aggregate price level implies that firms have cut their output prices reducing their value of marginal product of labor. Consequently, each firm demands a lower quantity of labor at a given wage. In other words, a fall in output prices shifts the labor demand curve to the left. If wages were to fall as much as output prices, then firms would employ as many workers as they had employed before the fall in output prices. However, with a downward rigid wage (recall Chapter 9), wages won't fall and optimizing firms will instead cut back the number of employed workers.

In addition, as we saw in Chapter 11 contractionary monetary policy causes the real interest rate to rise. Recall from Chapter 10 that the real interest rate is the price that a firm pays for another one of its inputs—physical capital. A rise in the real interest rate will therefore make production more costly. Because physical capital is needed by labor, the rising cost of physical capital leads firms to hire less labor, implying a leftward shift in the demand for labor.

Disruptions in the operation of the credit market also cause economic fluctuations. In Chapter 10 we saw how the supply and demand for credit determine the equilibrium interest rate and the amount of credit in the economy. Disruptions in the credit market—for instance, bank failures or other types of financial crises—will reduce the amount of investment and consumption, thereby lowering real GDP and employment. Hence, a leftward shift in the supply of credit will shift firms' labor demand curves to the left.

Multipliers and Economic Fluctuations

Multipliers, which we discussed in the context of changes in sentiment, can amplify the effects of any economic shock, regardless of whether the shock arises from changes in technology, sentiment, or financial markets. Exhibit 12.8 illustrates a simple feedback loop that arises in a contracting economy with multipliers. A shock to consumption causes firms

A **self-fulfilling prophecy** is a situation in which the expectations of an event (such as a left shift in labor demand in the future) induce actions that lead to that event.

Exhibit 12.8 Multipliers in a Contracting Economy

Start the feedback loop at any point in the circle. For example, a shock to consumption causes the firms that produce consumption goods to reduce labor demand, shifting the labor demand curve to the left. The leftward shift in labor demand leads to layoffs, which in turn reduces household income and further reduces household consumption. The cycle continues in the same way, increasing the depth of the economic contraction with each loop around the circle. In this way, the impact of an initial shock is multiplied.

Multipliers . . . can amplify the effects of any economic shock, regardless of whether the shock arises from changes in technology, sentiment, or financial markets.

to reduce labor demand, shifting the labor demand curve to the left. The leftward shift in labor demand leads to layoffs, reducing household income and further reducing household consumption. The cycle continues in this way, increasing the depth of the economic contraction with each loop around the circle.

The effects of multipliers on wages and employment are graphed in Exhibit 12.9 for the case of flexible wages. Labor supply is shown as the red curve and labor demand as blue. The economy begins at the equilibrium labeled "1: Pre-recession." A shock causes the labor demand curve to shift to the left. The economy is now at a new temporary equilibrium, at the point labeled "2: After shock." We refer to this point as a temporary equilibrium because it does not factor in multiplier effects. In particular, the first wave of layoffs leads unemployed workers to cut back their demand for goods and services, leading the businesses that provide those goods and services to further reduce their labor demand—another leftward shift in the labor demand curve. This moves the economy to the full-blown recession equilibrium labeled "3: Trough." A trough is the low point of real GDP in a recession. This exhibit plots two shifts in the labor demand curve:

a. The initial shock to labor demand (the first shift to the left).

b. A second leftward shift of labor demand due to the layoffs resulting from the *initial* shock. This second shift to the left takes into account multiplier effects.

Exhibit 12.9 Multipliers in an Economy with Flexible Wages

The economy begins at the equilibrium labeled "1: Pre-recession." A shock causes labor demand to shift to the left. The economy is now at a new temporary equilibrium, "2: After shock," which does not include multiplier effects. The layoffs lead to additional reductions in labor demand—more leftward shifts of the labor demand curve—moving the economy to the full-blown recession equilibrium "3: Trough." A trough is the low point of GDP in a recession.

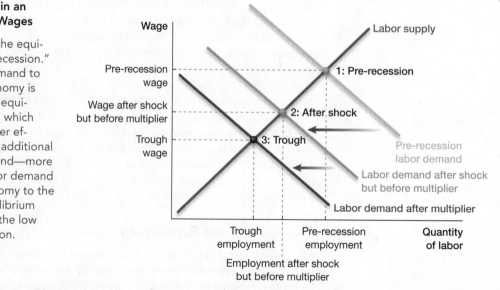

Exhibit 12.10 Additional Multipliers

Start the multiplier loop at any point in the circle. For example, a shock that lowers consumption causes the firms that manufacture consumption goods to reduce labor demand, shifting the labor demand curve to the left. The weak economy leads to layoffs, declining asset prices, mortgage defaults, household bankruptcies, firm bankruptcies, and declining financial intermediation (as banks struggle to survive and some banks fail). All of this in turn reduces consumption and investment. The cycle continues, increasing the depth of the economic contraction with each loop around the circle.

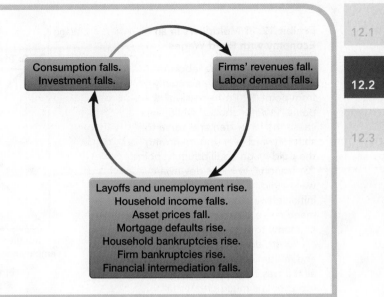

In principle, there could be many more leftward shifts in labor demand, each driven by the last round of layoffs. In practice, economies eventually stabilize and the downward spiral stops. For instance, new businesses replace old firms that have gone bankrupt. If a firm does not have enough demand to remain profitable, the physical and human capital that was employed at that firm will eventually be reallocated to other firms, especially firms in other types of business. The entry of these new firms causes labor demand to stop shifting to the left and eventually start shifting back to the right.

The multiplier loop depicted in Exhibit 12.8 leaves out many of the mechanisms that are important in a modern economy. Exhibit 12.10 adds some of these mechanisms, providing a more complete picture of the factors that multiply the impact of an initial negative shock. These mechanisms include declines in asset prices, such as the value of stocks, bonds, and housing; rising rates of mortgage defaults, which weaken banks' balance sheets; rising rates of household bankruptcies, generating defaults on numerous types of consumer credit including credit card loans; rising rates of firm bankruptcies, causing their lenders to absorb large losses; and falling levels of financial intermediation as banks become unwilling or unable to extend new loans, even to their existing customers. All of these mechanisms create additional multiplier effects and drive down the level of consumption and investment, further depressing labor demand. Falling labor demand leads to additional declines in employment and GDP, further weakening the economy and generating additional rounds of multiplier effects.

Equilibrium in the Short Run, with Multipliers and Downward Wage Rigidity

A more complete picture of recessionary shocks can be seen by combining downward wage rigidity and multipliers. Both of these ingredients amplify the impact of shifts in labor demand on employment. Here is how a shock plays out:

a. An initial shock shifts the labor demand curve to the left.
b. Downward wage rigidity leads firms to adjust to the initial shock by sharply cutting employment rather than reducing both employment and wages by a modest amount.
c. Multipliers cause the labor demand curve to shift leftward even more.

These three factors are illustrated in Exhibit 12.11. Before any shocks, the economy is at the equilibrium labeled "1: Pre-recession." The initial shock causes the economy to move to the new temporary equilibrium labeled "2: After shock." Because we are assuming that the wage is downward rigid, only employment adjusts. When the multipliers kick in, the labor demand curve shifts left again and the economy ends up at the equilibrium labeled "3: Trough." Both the downward wage rigidity and the multipliers have amplified the contractionary impact of the initial recessionary shock. *Without* downward wage rigidity and multipliers, the initial leftward shift of the labor demand curve would have moved the economy to the equilibrium

Exhibit 12.11 Multipliers in an Economy with Rigid Wages

A leftward shift in the labor demand curve takes the economy from point "1: Pre-recession" to point "2: After shock." Multipliers cause the labor demand curve to shift leftward even more, moving the rigid-wage equilibrium to point "3: Trough." Without downward wage rigidity and multipliers, the initial leftward shift of the labor demand curve would have moved the economy to the equilibrium labeled "A." With downward wage rigidity and multipliers, the economy moves all the way to "3: Trough," which represents a much greater fall in employment than Point A.

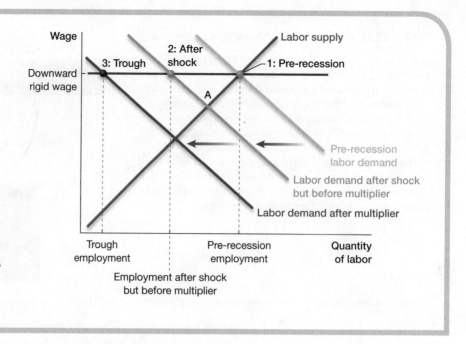

labeled "A." *With* downward wage rigidity and multipliers, the economy moves all the way to "3: Trough," which features a much greater fall in employment than point A.

Equilibrium in the Medium Run: Partial Recovery and Full Recovery

There are many forces—some market-driven and some policy-driven—that tend to reverse the effects of a recession in the course of a few years. We refer to this 2- to 3-year time horizon as the *medium run* to distinguish it from the short run, which corresponds to a few quarters, and the long run, which corresponds to periods of a decade or more. In our discussion, we divide the recovery mechanisms into two categories.

i. The labor demand curve shifts back to the right due to market forces.
ii. The labor demand curve shifts back to the right due to expansionary government policies.

Let's now explore each of these in more detail.

i. *The labor demand curve shifts back to the right due to market forces.* This rebound occurs for many reasons, and here are the most important ones:
   - Labor demand partially recovers (shifts to the right) when excess inventory has been sold off. For example, after an excessive economic boom in housing construction there will be little need for the construction of more new homes, causing the labor demand curve for construction workers to shift to the left. However, the inventory of unsold homes will eventually be sold off, and at that point construction of new homes will start up again, shifting the labor demand curve back to the right. This effect applies to any business that holds an inventory of unsold goods, like car or computer manufacturers. Inventories won't last forever. When they run out, the firm usually increases production. A rightward shift in the labor demand curve is plotted in Exhibit 12.12.
   - Labor demand partially recovers (shifts to the right) when technological advances encourage firms to expand their activities. For example, after the 2007–2009 recession, new drilling technologies enabled energy companies to profitably extract natural gas and oil from oil-shale geological deposits. This led to a rapid expansion in the U.S. energy industry, including drilling activity, pipeline construction, and the growth of industries that have a comparative advantage in regions with ample energy resources.
   - Labor demand partially recovers (shifts to the right) as the banking system—and the rest of the system of financial intermediation—recuperates and businesses are again

Exhibit 12.12 Partial Recovery Due to a Partial Rightward Shift in the Labor Demand Curve

With downward rigid wages, a leftward shift in labor demand to "Labor demand at trough" takes the economy from point "1: Pre-recession" to point "2: Trough." A partial recovery in the labor demand curve takes the economy from point "2: Trough" to point "3: Partial recovery." The economy does not reach the competitive equilibrium (point B) because the wage is downward rigid.

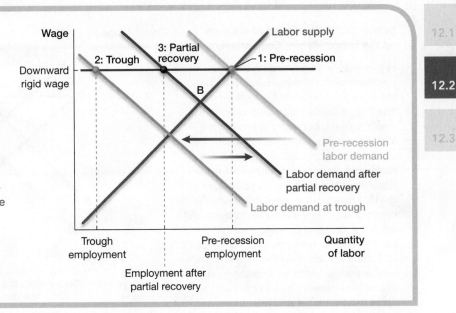

able to use credit to finance their activities. During the 2007–2009 financial crisis, many small firms had a hard time obtaining loans from their banks. When the banks that survived the crisis returned to health, they became more willing to lend to businesses, enabling those businesses to expand their operations and hire more workers. The availability of credit shifted the borrowers' labor demand curve to the right.

ii. *The labor demand curve shifts back to the right due to expansionary government policies.* The next chapter focuses exclusively on these issues. For now, we summarize the key policy levers:

- The central bank can use *monetary policy* to shift labor demand to the right. Lowering interest rates stimulates both firm investment and household consumption.
- Labor demand also shifts to the right as overall *inflation* raises firms' output prices. A rise in output price makes production, and thus increasing employment, more profitable at a given wage. This shifts the labor demand curve to the right. In panel (a) of Exhibit 12.13, we see the implications of this inflation-driven rightward shift of the labor demand curve. With wages pinned down by the downward wage rigidity, the rightward shift of the labor demand curve causes a movement from point A to point B, which corresponds to a partial recovery in employment.

At this point, you might rightly wonder about the labor supply curve. Shouldn't inflation also impact labor supply? As inflation increases output prices, a given wage will buy a smaller consumption bundle. For example, if all prices were to double, a worker who supplied the same hours of work at the same wage would be able to consume only half of what she did before. As a result of inflation, this worker—and, with the same reasoning, all workers—will be willing to supply fewer hours to the market at a given wage. The resulting leftward shift of the labor supply curve is also shown in panel (a) of Exhibit 12.13. The important point, however, is that *as long as we stay at the downward rigid wage,* this shift of labor supply has no impact, and employment is simply given by the intersection of the labor demand curve and the horizontal line representing the downward rigid wage. This brings us to the important conclusion that when wages are pinned down by downward wage rigidity, inflation-driven shifts of the labor demand curve will increase employment.

This analysis also tells us when shifts of the labor supply curve will actually start to matter. If the shifts in question were large enough, which would result from high levels of inflation, then the wage will no longer be pinned down by downward wage rigidity. Rather, the market clearing wage would rise above the downward rigid wage, as shown in panel (b) of Exhibit 12.13. In this case, the equilibrium wage has risen above the downward rigid wage. Once such an

Exhibit 12.13 The Effect of Inflation on the Labor Market Equilibrium

In panel (a), a downward rigid wage (represented by the horizontal line) prevents the labor market from clearing. The "original labor demand curve" and the "original labor supply curve" cross at the point labeled C. At this point, the market clearing wage is below the downward rigid wage. Accordingly, the original labor market equilibrium is point A, where the downward rigid wage intersects the original labor demand curve. Inflation shifts the labor demand curve to the right (firms can sell their output goods at higher prices) and shifts the labor supply curve to the left (a given wage has less purchasing power). Even after these shifts, the market-clearing wage (labeled D) is still below the downward rigid wage. Accordingly, the post-inflation labor market equilibrium is point B, where the downward rigid wage intersects the labor demand curve after inflation.

In panel (b), the original labor market equilibrium is point A, so the downward rigid wage is above the original market-clearing wage (labeled point C). Inflation causes the labor demand curve to shift to the right and the labor supply curve to shift to the left. Now these inflation-induced shifts are large enough to move the market-clearing wage above the downward rigid wage. The final labor market equilibrium is point E. Wages have now risen above the downward rigid wage.

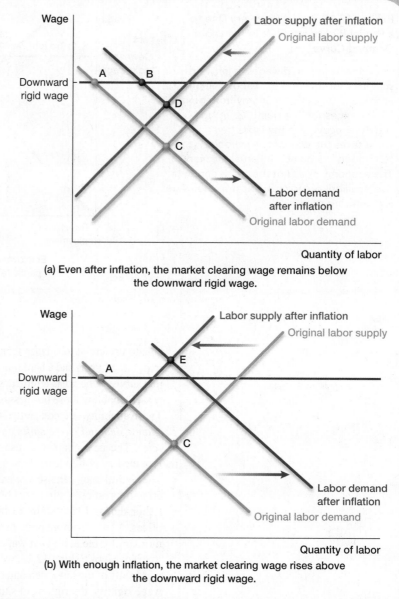

(a) Even after inflation, the market clearing wage remains below the downward rigid wage.

(b) With enough inflation, the market clearing wage rises above the downward rigid wage.

equilibrium wage is reached, further increases in inflation will shift the labor demand and labor supply curves by *equal* amounts, increasing wages but leaving employment unchanged.

- The government also uses *fiscal policy* (government spending and taxes) to shift the labor demand curve to the right. Increasing government spending increases the demand for the products that firms produce, shifting the labor demand curve to the right. Decreasing taxes gives firms and consumers more after-tax income, thereby increasing their purchasing power and increasing demand for the products that firms produce, shifting the labor demand curve to the right.

Exhibit 12.14 puts all of these market-based and policy-driven effects together to illustrate a complete cycle of contraction and recovery. Initially, the economy is at point "1." The combination of downward rigid wages and multipliers creates a rapid contraction in labor demand, which moves the economy to point "2." This is the trough of employment. The labor demand curve then starts to shift back toward its pre-recession level due to both market mechanisms and government intervention. Inflation plays two roles, shifting the labor demand curve to the right and the labor supply curve to the left. At the beginning of the recovery, the equilibrium remains at the rigid wage and the economy shifts from point "2" to point "3."

Exhibit 12.14 Full Recovery

The labor demand curve begins at "Labor demand pre-recession" and then shifts to the left: "Labor demand at trough." Because the wage is downward rigid, it does not fall and the economy transitions from point "1" to point "2." As the labor demand curve shifts back to the right ("Labor demand after partial recovery"), the level of employment partially rebounds to point "3." At this point, the downward rigid wage is still preventing the labor market from clearing. Eventually, the combination of rightward shifts in labor demand and leftward (inflation-driven) shifts in labor supply lead the economy to point "4." At this point, downward wage rigidity is no longer a constraint because the market-clearing wage is above the downward rigid wage.

Eventually, the combination of rightward shifts in labor demand and leftward shifts in labor supply lead the economy to point "4." At this point, downward wage rigidity is no longer a constraint because the market-clearing wage is above the downward rigid wage.

In this particular example, the economy returns to its original level of employment. This won't be the case if the original level of employment was generated by an unsustainable economic boom.

Exhibit 12.14 also shows that the post-recession wage is above the pre-recession wage. This results from the accumulation of price inflation during and after the recession. This inflation has lifted both output prices and wages.

Nominal Wages versus Real Wages

Actual wages are also called **nominal wages,** which distinguishes them from wages adjusted for inflation, or **real wages**. To calculate real wages, economists divide nominal wages by a measure of overall prices, for example the Consumer Price Index (CPI).

In this chapter (as in Chapter 9), we've conducted the analysis using the actual wages that workers are paid. Actual wages are also called **nominal wages**, which distinguishes them from wages adjusted for inflation, or **real wages**. The distinction between nominal and real wages is similar to the distinction between nominal and real GDP. To calculate real wages, we divide nominal wages by a measure of overall prices. Real wages can be interpreted as the (price-level-adjusted) buying power of nominal wages.

The entire analysis of labor demand and labor supply can be equivalently carried out using real wages. The change in variables wouldn't change the conclusions, but it would highlight different elements of the story. If we focus on real wages, we emphasize that firms base their hiring decisions on the ratio of how much they pay their workers (nominal wages) and how much they charge their customers (their output prices). It would also emphasize, as we have noted above, that in their labor supply decisions, workers care about the buying power of their wages—in other words, the real consumption bundles that they can afford with their wages.

Downward rigidity in nominal wages, one of the factors that amplifies negative macroeconomic shocks, plays a similar role when we look at the labor market through the lens of real wages. In particular, downward nominal wage rigidity implies that, because nominal wages cannot fall, real wages do not immediately adjust either. As a result, the labor market does not reach the market-clearing real wage.

But in the presence of inflation, real wages can fall even if nominal wages don't. Because real wages are the ratio of nominal wages to a price index, and because inflation raises the price index, real wages will fall when (1) the price index rises and (2) *nominal* wages are fixed. This is exactly the scenario we have highlighted in panel (a) of Exhibit 12.13. As such, the analysis of real wages provides another way of explaining how modest inflation might help an economy with downward rigid *nominal* wages recover from a recession.

12.3 Modeling Expansions

We have so far focused on recessions. The framework we presented can also be used for studying economic booms. Returning to the same example we used earlier, suppose that now United Airlines becomes optimistic about the demand for its products. This will shift its labor demand curve to the right. When many firms become optimistic about their future demand, the aggregate labor demand curve will shift to the right, as shown in Exhibit 12.15.

One important difference from our analysis of leftward shifts is that there is no issue of rigid wages in this case because, as we emphasized in Chapter 9, workers are often unwilling to accept cuts in their wages, but this has no equivalent for increases in their wages. This implies that there is downward, but not upward, wage rigidity. For this reason, in Exhibit 12.15, following the rightward shift in the labor demand curve, employment changes along a labor supply curve (and not along a horizontal line as in, for example, Exhibit 12.11).

Though the impact of the rightward shift in the labor demand curve is not exacerbated by wage rigidities, multiplier effects will continue to be present, amplifying the initial shift. For example, as United increases its purchases of airplanes and other inputs, this will cause the firms that supply United to shift their labor demand curves to the right. Increases in labor demand will tend to raise household income, causing households to start consuming more, triggering another round of multiplier effects. As a result of these multiplier effects, there is a further shift in the labor demand curve, as shown in Exhibit 12.15.

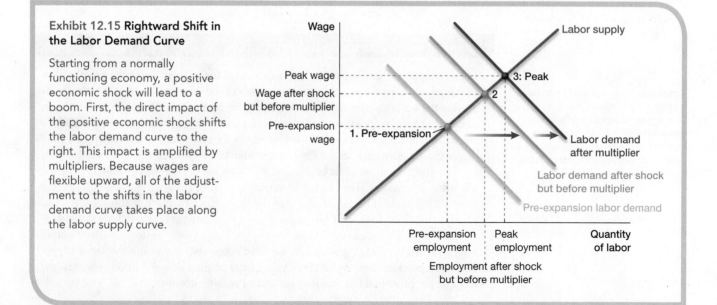

Exhibit 12.15 Rightward Shift in the Labor Demand Curve

Starting from a normally functioning economy, a positive economic shock will lead to a boom. First, the direct impact of the positive economic shock shifts the labor demand curve to the right. This impact is amplified by multipliers. Because wages are flexible upward, all of the adjustment to the shifts in the labor demand curve takes place along the labor supply curve.

Economic booms also have a dark side. If before the beginning of the boom the economy is close to full employment and full capacity utilization (meaning that the unemployment rate is low and firms are employing most of their capacity), there will be relatively little room for the economy to grow. If so, the optimism or other factors that might have originally triggered the boom are likely to get reversed at some point. But such a reversal involves precisely the sort of leftward shift in labor demand we have analyzed in this chapter. These leftward shifts tend to create negative multiplier effects and might take the economy into a recession rather than gently back to its pre-boom level.

This dark side of economic booms raises some of the most difficult challenges for policymakers. Prudent policymaking would involve attempting to control the economic booms in order to limit the potential negative effects when the boom is ultimately reversed. However, the increase in employment and the fall in unemployment accompanying economic booms increase the popularity of policymakers, encouraging them to let economic booms continue or even to fan their flames (especially during election years).

Evidence-Based Economics

What caused the recession of 2007–2009?

The causes of the recession of 2007–2009 can be likened to chains of dominos, with one negative shock setting off another in a sequence of events that cascaded throughout the American and global economies. Three key factors appear to have played the central roles in the crisis: (1) a fall in housing prices, which caused a collapse in new construction; (2) a sharp drop in consumption; and (3) spiraling mortgage defaults that caused many bank failures, leading the entire financial system to freeze up.

Let's first zoom out to take an aerial snapshot:

1. During the pre-recession years of 2000–2006, a run-up in housing prices caused a boom in housing construction, which produced a large stock of newly constructed homes. When housing prices fell sharply from 2006 to 2009, homebuilders rapidly reduced their rate of new construction because they already held a large inventory of new homes and the falling prices made new construction unprofitable. Consequently, their labor demand curves shifted sharply to the left.

2. The decline in housing prices in turn reduced many consumers' wealth and curtailed their ability to borrow more against their homes—a scenario that in turn sharply reduced consumption. The firms that produce the goods and services that consumers buy were suddenly faced with a substantial drop in demand for their products. Accordingly, they cut back production and their labor demand curves shifted to the left.

3. The decline in housing values led to millions of mortgage defaults (for reasons we explain below). These mortgages, which were held on the balance sheets of many large banks, pushed those banks to the brink—and in some cases over the brink—of solvency. As banks failed, or cut their lending activity to increase their reserves and strengthen their balance sheets, credit to the private sector fell, causing borrowing firms to cut their production and shifting their labor demand curves to the left. The decline in credit to households reduced their consumption and triggered another round of adverse demand shifts.

This was the big picture. We now zoom in on each of these economic events and look at the data.

Housing and Construction: A Burst Bubble

Many economists characterize the rapid rise of housing prices between the late 1990s and 2006 as a *bubble*, meaning that the significant increase in asset prices (in this case housing assets) did not reflect the true long-run value of the asset. Exhibit 12.16 plots a

Exhibit 12.16 Index of Real Home Prices in Ten Major U.S. Cities (January 1987–December 2013)

Real U.S. home prices started rising precipitously in the late 1990s, with real prices more than doubling in a single decade: 1996 to 2006. Prices then fell sharply from 2006 to 2009.

Source: S&P/Case-Shiller home price index and Bureau of Labor Statistics (Consumer Price Index).

Exhibit 12.17 Real Investment in Residential Construction (1987 q1–2013 q4; Normalized to 100 in 2009)

The flow of real investment in residential construction nearly doubled from 1995 to 2005, peaking just before housing prices peaked. Residential construction then fell sharply, falling well below its level from 1995. As the excess inventory of newly built homes was sold off, home building slowly picked up again after 2011.

Source: Bureau of Economic Analysis, National Income and Product Accounts.

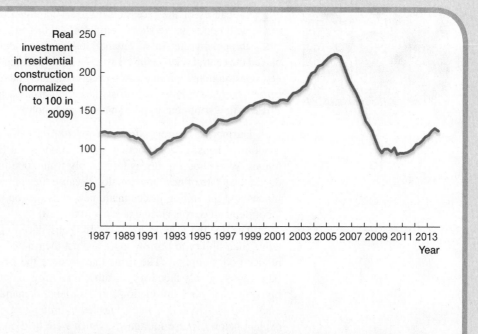

monthly index of housing prices adjusted for inflation in ten major U.S. cities from 1987 to 2013. Notice that the index rose sharply from 100 in January 2000 to 190 in May 2006. Then everything fell apart—the index collapsed to a value of 120 by April 2009 and continued falling a bit more after that. The bubble in housing prices had burst.

Falling housing prices had a devastating effect on the home construction industry. Exhibit 12.17 plots the real value of investments in residential real estate. Note how real investment in new home construction started falling after peaking in the third quarter of 2005. The exhibit shows that when the dust had settled in 2009, the rate of home construction had fallen by nearly 60 percent.

Then the other shoe dropped. As the home construction industry shrank, employment in the industry also plummeted. At its peak in April 2006, there were 3.5 million jobs in the residential construction industry. By 2010, the number of jobs had fallen to 2 million, a 43 percent decline. Related industries also got hit as all real estate prices fell, including commercial real estate, like office buildings and malls. For example, the non-residential construction industry fell from employment of 4.4 million in early 2008—at the start of the recession—to 3.4 million in 2010.

Putting all of the pieces together, the sharp drop in real estate prices caused a large leftward shift in the labor demand curve for construction jobs, which then led to a sharp drop in employment in the construction industry. The key step—a leftward shift in the labor demand curve—was plotted in Exhibit 12.6. Panel (a) of that exhibit plots the flexible wage case. Panel (c) plots the case of downward wage rigidity, which features an even larger fall in employment.

The decline in economic activity in the construction industry also led to multiplier effects. Many construction workers lost their incomes, and many businesses that served those workers—home supply stores like Home Depot—saw demand for their products plummet. Falling home construction and home sales also lowered demand for home appliances—like washing machines and refrigerators. These multiplier effects magnified the effects of the fall in home prices, shifting the aggregate labor demand curve further leftward and deepening the fall in aggregate employment.

Cuts in Consumption

The housing price declines were also associated with large reductions in overall household consumption—the second key factor in the 2007–2009 recession.

During the early 2000s, many households had increased their consumption by using funds that they had borrowed from banks. In most cases, this borrowing took the form of mortgages—for instance, taking out a second mortgage in addition to a first mortgage. "Cash-out" refinancings were also popular—when interest rates fell, homeowners with an existing mortgage would lower their interest rate and increase the size of their mortgage, taking the difference as a cash payout. At the peak of the housing bubble, consumers used second mortgages and "cash-out" refinancing to extract $400 billion of wealth per year from their homes. Even consumers who did not take our more mortgage debt tended to increase their real consumption during the run-up in housing prices from 2000 to 2006, because home price rises increase wealth and consumers' perceptions of what they can afford to consume.

That wealthy feeling started to vanish in 2007. By March 2009, U.S. households had lost about $15 trillion in net worth—both the housing market and the stock market had crashed. Most households cut back their consumption, causing aggregate real consumption to decline by 2.7 percent from the start of the recession in the fourth quarter of 2007 to the end of the recession in the second quarter of 2009. This decline translated into a significantly lower demand for the products of firms, creating another multiplier effect that shifted the labor demand curve further to the left.

Spiraling Mortgage Defaults and Bank Failures

Falling house prices also led mortgage delinquencies to skyrocket: many borrowers stopped making their required mortgage payments. For example, suppose that a family had bought a $300,000 home with almost no down payment in 2006. If we assume that the home's value followed the ten-city index, this home would have fallen to a value of $200,000 by 2009. However, the mortgage debt would not have been affected by the fall in the home value, leaving the borrower owing nearly $300,000 (very little of the initial mortgage would have been paid off within the first 3 years of home ownership). Consequently, the family would find itself with a debt of almost $300,000 on a house worth only $200,000. Owing more on your home than it is worth is referred to as being "upside down" or "underwater." If a household with an underwater mortgage sells their home, they don't receive enough money

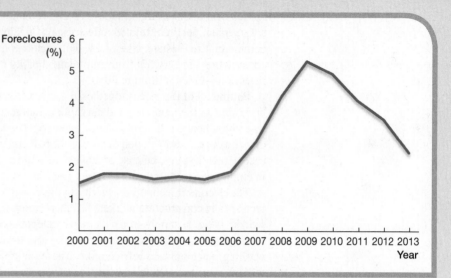

Exhibit 12.18 Percentage of U.S. Home Mortgages That Began Foreclosure Proceedings (2000 to 2013)

This exhibit plots the annual rate of foreclosure filings in the United States. A 2 percent rate of foreclosure filing implies that 2 percent of the homes with a mortgage started foreclosure proceedings in that year.

Source: Mortgage Bankers' Association National Delinquency Survey.

to repay the mortgage. In many U.S. states, households in this situation have a strong incentive to default on their mortgages—that is, stop making their mortgage payments and walk away. This incentive is further strengthened when households face economic hardship (for example, because of unemployment or other negative labor income shocks).

And that is exactly what millions of households did, either because they didn't have a job and couldn't afford to pay their mortgage, or because they recognized that it wasn't optimal to keep paying interest on a mortgage that vastly exceeded the value of the home. Previously, when home prices were rising, foreclosure rates stayed around 1.7 percent per year. In other words, 1.7 percent of U.S. homes with a mortgage entered foreclosure each year. Exhibit 12.18 shows that the foreclosure rate rose to 5.4 percent during the financial crisis. To appreciate the significance of that foreclosure rate, consider that there are approximately 75 million owner-occupied homes in the United States and about two-thirds, or 50 million, have a mortgage. So a foreclosure rate of 5.4 percent translates into almost 3 million foreclosed homes per year at the peak of the crisis. In total, about 10 million foreclosures took place from 2007 to 2012.

Home foreclosures were terrible news not only for homeowners but also for banks. Consider that when a bank seizes a home that is worth $200,000, on which the outstanding mortgage is $300,000, the bank has no way of recouping its money. At best, it can sell the house for $200,000, realizing a $100,000 loss on its $300,000 loan. In practice, the foreclosure sale yields a price significantly *below* $200,000. With so many homes being sold simultaneously, and with no homeowner to put flowers in window pots, mow lawns, or keep vandals from trashing the empty houses or ripping out copper pipes, it's easy to end up selling the house for far less than $200,000.

Consequently, banks suffered enormous losses on their portfolios of mortgages. In 2005, during the run-up in home prices, banks recorded losses in their real estate portfolios equal to only 0.2 percent of the value of their real estate loans. In 2009, banks booked real estate losses that were 40 times greater —8 percent of the total value of their real estate loans.

Many banks could not withstand the extent of the hit they took on their mortgage holdings. Among the 5,000 banks regulated by the FDIC, about 400 failed from 2007 to 2011.

But the biggest story of the 2007–2009 recession was the failure of Lehman Brothers, a bank that was *not* regulated by the FDIC. Lehman did not originate home mortgages of its own, but it did originate commercial mortgages (for businesses) and it did buy mortgages that other banks had issued. As those mortgages lost value in 2008, Lehman Brothers lost huge sums and perhaps more importantly also lost the confidence of its business partners.

Within a two-week period in September of 2008, many of Lehman's biggest institutional trading partners and lenders stopped doing business with the bank. Each new defection bred more uncertainty and a widening loss of confidence in Lehman's future. Lehman experienced an institutional bank run, a special kind of bank run that we discussed in Chapter 10. The bank customers running for the exits were large financial institutions like other large banks and hedge funds. Soon, no institutions would lend money to Lehman, and at that point Lehman was both illiquid and insolvent.

The failure of Lehman Brothers initiated a financial panic that suddenly threatened the prosperity of the world economy. Other major bank crises followed in Iceland, the United Kingdom, Greece, Ireland, Portugal, Switzerland, France, Germany, the Netherlands, Spain, Italy, and Cyprus. Suddenly, many countries teetered on the precipice of another depression.

As financial markets fell, the banking sector cut back on loans to businesses because failed banks obviously couldn't make loans. Even the surviving banks were hesitant to make loans, afraid that these new loans—to households and businesses—would soon end up in default. The retrenchment of the financial sector created yet another multiplier effect, which reduced consumption and investment and shifted the labor demand curve further to the left.

Question

What caused the recession of 2007–2009?

Answer

Real housing prices rose 90 percent from 2000 to 2006 and then fell almost completely back to their 2000 level. Falling house prices led to a collapse in the home building industry, to a sharp decline in real consumption, and to a jump in mortgage defaults. Approximately 10 million U.S. home foreclosures occurred from 2007 through 2012. The defaulting mortgages caused 400 bank failures, including the spectacular failure of the investment bank Lehman Brothers.

Data

Historical data on housing prices (Case/Shiller housing price index), residential investment (NIPA), foreclosure rates (Mortgage Bankers Association), and bank balance sheets (FDIC and Lehman Brothers).

Caveat

Many other factors also contributed to the financial crisis and it is not yet clear what the most important factors were.

Summary

✴ All economies experience economic fluctuations—in other words, the growth rate fluctuates from year to year. During recessions, real GDP contracts and unemployment increases. On rare occasions a recession turns into a depression, like the Great Depression which started in 1929. From 1929 to 1933 real GDP declined by 26 percent, and the rate of unemployment rose from 3 percent to 25 percent.

✴ Economic fluctuations display three key properties:

1. Co-movement: consumption, investment, GDP, and employment generally fall and rise together. Unemployment moves in the opposite direction.
2. Limited predictability: economic fluctuations are not pendulum-like with regular up and down cycles. It is difficult to predict in advance when an economy will enter a recession and when a recession will end.
3. Persistence: when the economy is growing, it will probably keep growing the following quarter. Likewise, when the economy is contracting—when growth is negative—the economy will probably keep contracting the following quarter.

✴ Many factors explain fluctuations in economic activity, most notably:

1. Technology shocks (the theory of real business cycles): changes in firms' productivity translate into shifts in the demand curve for labor, causing fluctuations in employment and real GDP. When the labor demand curve shifts to the left, employment and real GDP fall. When the labor demand curve shifts to the right, employment and real GDP rise.
2. Keynesian factors:
   - Changes in sentiments, including changes in expectations, uncertainty, and animal spirits, influence firm and household behavior. If a firm becomes pessimistic, the demand curve for labor shifts to the left. If a firm's customers become pessimistic, they reduce their purchases, decreasing demand for the firm's products and shifting the firm's labor demand curve to the left.
   - An initial shift in the labor demand curve creates a cascading chain of events, multiplying or amplifying the impact of the initial shock. For example, when firms lay off workers in response to a shock, the laid-off workers cut their own consumption, reducing the demand for the products of other firms and leading to shifts in the labor demand curves of the other firms. Financial factors create additional multiplier effects. Defaults, bankruptcies, and declines in asset prices lead banks to scale back their lending to firms and households, generating another round of adverse shifts in the labor demand curve.
3. Monetary and financial factors: a fall in the price level is contractionary because firms face downward wage rigidities—that is, they are either unable or unwilling to cut wages. Employment declines by more than it would have with flexible wages. In addition, monetary contractions cause the real interest rate to rise, reducing investment. Finally, financial crises reduce the credit available to firms and households. All of these channels will shift the labor demand curve to the left, reducing employment and real GDP.

✹ Multiplier effects help us understand the sharp recession of 2007–2009. Between the late 1990s and 2006, the U.S. housing market experienced a bubble. This bubble burst in 2006 and real housing prices fell by approximately 40 percent. The construction industry, which had been booming until then, began a sharp contraction. Falling housing prices, and by implication falling wealth, led households to cut their consumption. Firms, seeing the demand for their products decline, reduced their labor demand, starting a spiral of layoffs and further reductions in household consumption. The collapse in housing prices also led to mortgage defaults and foreclosures. The defaults and foreclosures generated huge losses for many banks, which either failed or sharply cut lending, further worsening the recession.

✹ Economic booms tend to increase employment and reduce unemployment as the labor demand curve of the economy shifts to the right and the multiplier effects increase employment further. However, economic booms also have a dark side because when they reverse, the economy can sink into a recession. For this reason, some policymakers try to control and dampen economic booms, though other factors might push policymakers and politicians to fan the flames of economic booms rather than follow a prudent course of action.

Key Terms

economic fluctuations or business cycles *p. 269*
economic expansions *p. 270*
Great Depression *p. 273*
depression *p. 273*

Okun's Law *p. 278*
real business cycle theory *p. 279*
animal spirits *p. 280*
sentiments *p. 280*
multipliers *p. 280*

self-fulfilling prophecy *p. 281*
nominal wages *p. 287*
real wages *p. 287*

Questions

All questions are available in MyEconLab *for practice and instructor assignment.*

1. What are economic fluctuations? What is the difference between an economic expansion and a recession?

2. What does it mean to say that an economic fluctuation involves the co-movement of many aggregate macroeconomic variables? Name four variables that exhibit co-movement during an economic expansion.

3. The duration of an economic fluctuation is completely unpredictable. Explain whether this statement is true or false.

4. Does the Great Depression illustrate the three characteristics of economic fluctuations? Explain your answer.

5. How do wage flexibility and downward wage rigidity affect the extent of unemployment in the economy when the demand for labor shifts to the left?

6. How does real business cycle theory explain economic fluctuations?

7. How did John Maynard Keynes use the concepts of animal spirits and sentiments to explain economic fluctuations?

8. The concept of multipliers was one of the key elements of John Maynard Keynes's theory of fluctuations. What is a multiplier? Explain with an example.

9. How can contractionary monetary policy lead to an economy-wide recession?

10. What are two important mechanisms that reverse the effects of a recession in a modern economy?

11. How can the 2007–2009 recession be explained?

12. Between 2000 and 2006, housing prices in the United States increased by about 90 percent. As detailed in the chapter, this increase abruptly reversed.

    a. Why is the rise in housing prices between the late 1990s and 2006 characterized as a bubble by some economists?

    b. How did the fall in housing prices cause the financial system in the United States to freeze up?

Problems

All problems are available in MyEconLab *for practice and instructor assignment.*
Problems marked 🌐 *update with real-time data.*

1. Consider the data in Exhibit 12.3.

   a. List the recessions since 1929 by duration, with the longest recession first and the shortest last.

   b. List the recessions since 1929 according to decline in real GDP from peak to trough, with the greatest decline first and the smallest decline last. Note which recessions are first and second on your list from part (a) and first and third on your list from part (b). Can you think of a reason why the fall in real GDP at the end of World War II (1945; second recession on your list from part (b)) was so deep even though that recession was very short?

🌐 2. Go to http://research.stlouisfed.org/fred2/series/UNRATE, which shows the U.S. unemployment rate since 1948. Every recession during this period is shown by the gray bars on the graph.

   a. Does the behavior of the unemployment rate illustrate the principle of co-movement discussed in the chapter? Why or why not?

   b. Economic variables are sometimes divided into "leading indicators" and "lagging indicators." Leading indicators are variables that start to change before an economic expansion or contraction. Lagging indicators change only when an expansion or contraction is well underway. Based on the graph of the unemployment rate, is unemployment a leading or lagging indicator of recessions? Explain.

3. The Conference Board publishes data on Business Cycle Indicators (BCI). The Composite Index of Leading Economic Indicators is one of the three components of the BCI. Changes in leading economic indicators usually precede changes in GDP. Some of the variables tracked by the index are listed below.

   i. The average weekly hours worked by manufacturing workers

   ii. The average number of initial applications for unemployment insurance

   iii. The amount of new orders for capital goods unrelated to defense

   iv. The number of new building permits for residential buildings

   v. The S&P 500 stock index

   vi. Consumer sentiment

   Consider each variable and explain whether it is likely to be positively or negatively correlated with real GDP.

4. Suppose that the mythical country Moricana has a downward rigid wage. Moricana is in a recession; capacity utilization in the economy is at an all-time low, and surveys show that firms do not expect economic conditions to improve in the coming year.

   a. Firms in the country are cutting back on capital spending and investment. Use a graph to show how this would affect the labor demand curve (ignore the effects of multipliers).

   b. How would the economy move along the aggregate production function curve?

   c. Is unemployment in Moricana likely to be classified as voluntary or involuntary? Explain your answer.

5. Assuming flexible wages, in which case would the change in total employment be greater during a recession:

   Scenario 1: Workers do not increase their labor supply very much in response to an increase in the wage;

   or

   Scenario 2: Workers increase their labor supply substantially in response to an increase in the wage. Explain your answer fully with a graph.

6. Assume that labor supply and labor demand are described by the following equations:

   $$\text{Labor Supply:} \quad L^S = 5 \times w.$$
   $$\text{Labor Demand:} \quad L^D = 110 - 0.5 \times w.$$

   where w = wage expressed in dollars per hour, and L^S and L^D are expressed in millions of workers.

   a. Find the equilibrium wage and the equilibrium level of employment.

   b. Assume that there is a shock to the economy, such that the labor demand curve is now described by the equation:

   $$L^D = 55 - 0.5 \times w.$$

   If wages are flexible, what will be the new equilibrium wage and level of employment? Show your work.

   c. Now assume that wages are rigid at the level you found in part (a). What will employment be at this wage? How many workers will be unemployed?

7. In 1973, the major oil-producing nations of the world declared an oil embargo. The price of oil, a key source of energy, increased. In many countries, this led to a fall in real GDP and employment. Which of the three business cycle theories explained in the chapter—real business cycle theory, Keynesian theory, and monetary theory—would best fit this explanation of the 1973 recession?

8. The Internet boom of the 1990s has changed all of our lives and transformed the way business is conducted. During the late 1990s, the economy was described as the "best of all possible worlds" with quite high employment (and low unemployment). Explain this phenomenon using the real business cycle approach.

9. An old saying goes: "Nothing succeeds like success." Explain how this could relate to Keynes's animal spirits view of economic fluctuations.

10. Use a detailed graph to show the effect of a negative shock on the labor demand curve in an economy. Assume that wages in the economy are rigid and cannot fall in the short run. Compare the point of trough employment on the graph with the point of trough employment if wages were flexible.

11. In the early 1980s, the unemployment rate in the United States rose above 10 percent. The United States was in a severe recession. Both fiscal and monetary policies were used to stimulate the economy. Government spending increased by 18.9 percent, while the Federal Reserve cut interest rates by nearly 11 percentage points. How would these policies affect the labor demand curve? Assuming wages are rigid, use a graph to explain your answer. Be sure to show the pre-recession equilibrium, the situation at the trough of the recession, and the effect of the government policies.

12. The Evidence-Based Economics feature in the chapter identifies three key factors that caused the recession of 2007–2009.

   a. How would Keynes's concept of animal spirits explain the creation of a housing bubble?

   b. What does the national income identity show? Explain how the recession of 2007–2009 affected the consumption and investment components of the national income identity.

13. Some economists stress the role of monetary policy in the period leading up to the recession of 2007–2009. Between 2001 and 2003, the Federal Reserve lowered the target Fed Funds rate from 6.5 percent to 1 percent and kept it there through much of 2004. This resulted in a substantial decline in real interest rates throughout the economy, including mortgage rates.

   Based on the chapter's discussion of monetary and financial factors, explain how the Federal Reserve's policies could have contributed to the economic "bubble" of the pre-recession years of 2000–2006.

Countercyclical Macroeconomic Policy

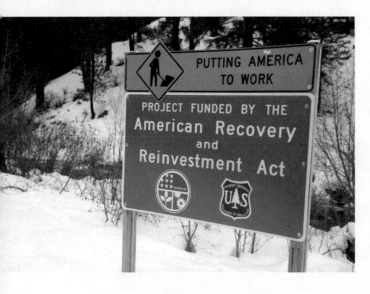

How much does government expenditure stimulate GDP?

You are a key presidential adviser on economic policy: the chairperson of the Council of Economic Advisers (CEA). The CEA consists of three economists who advise the president and help formulate the administration's economic policy. These experts prepare the annual *Economic Report of the President*.

Unfortunately, you happen to be in office during a severe economic downturn. The president asks you, "What would happen if the government increased spending?" How would more government expenditure—for instance, repairing highways, hiring teachers, or building schools—support an economic recovery?

This chapter studies the many ways that policymakers try to smooth out fluctuations in GDP, stimulating the economy during contractions and stepping on the brakes during periods of excessively rapid economic expansion.

CHAPTER **OUTLINE**

13.1	13.2	13.3	EBE	13.4
The Role of Countercyclical Policies in Economic Fluctuations	Countercyclical Monetary Policy	Countercyclical Fiscal Policy	How much does government expenditure stimulate GDP?	Policies That Blur the Line Between Fiscal and Monetary Policy

13.1 The Role of Countercyclical Policies in Economic Fluctuations

Countercyclical policies attempt to reduce the intensity of economic fluctuations and smooth the growth rates of employment, GDP, and prices.

Countercyclical monetary policy, which is conducted by the central bank (in the United States, the Fed), attempts to reduce economic fluctuations by manipulating bank reserves and interest rates.

Countercyclical fiscal policy, which is passed by the legislative branch and signed into law by the executive branch, aims to reduce economic fluctuations by manipulating government expenditures and taxes.

[**Countercyclical monetary and fiscal policies both work by shifting the labor demand curve.**]

In Chapter 12, we discussed the reasons why economic growth fluctuates. In this chapter, we focus on the government and the Fed's efforts to reduce those fluctuations by using what are called *countercyclical policies*. **Countercyclical policies** attempt to reduce the intensity of economic fluctuations and smooth the growth rates of employment, GDP, and prices. (In this chapter, whenever we discuss GDP, we are referring to *real* GDP.)

During a recession, *expansionary policy* aims to reduce the severity of the downturn by shifting labor demand to the right and "expanding" economic activity (GDP). Similarly, *contractionary policy* is sometimes used to slow down the economy when it grows too fast or "overheats."

Countercyclical policies come in two main categories:

1. **Countercyclical monetary policy**, which is conducted by the central bank (in the United States, the Fed), attempts to reduce economic fluctuations by manipulating bank reserves and interest rates.
2. **Countercyclical fiscal policy**, which is passed by the legislative branch and signed into law by the executive branch, aims to reduce economic fluctuations by manipulating government expenditures and taxes.

Though countercyclical monetary and fiscal policies work in different ways and are effective in different circumstances, they also share some common features. Countercyclical monetary and fiscal policies both work by shifting the labor demand curve. During a recession, monetary and fiscal policies are used to stimulate the economy by shifting the labor demand curve to the right. During a runaway boom, monetary and fiscal policies are used to slow the economy by shifting the labor demand curve to the left.

We plot the case of a recession in panel (a) of Exhibit 13.1 where we first study a labor market with flexible wages. Starting from a pre-recession equilibrium (point 1: Pre-recession), a shock shifts the labor demand curve to the left, reducing employment

Exhibit 13.1 The Effect of Countercyclical Policy on the Labor Market Panel

(a) Flexible Wage Case
During a recession, the labor demand curve has shifted to the left and the equilibrium is at the point labeled 2: Trough. Countercyclical policy can partially reverse this situation by shifting the labor demand curve back to the right. With flexible wages, the equilibrium transitions from 2: Trough to 3: Partial recovery. The rightward shift in the labor demand curve translates into an increase in wages and an increase in employment (represented by the green arrow).

(b) Rigid Wage Case
During a recession, the labor demand curve has shifted to the left and the equilibrium is at the point labeled 2: Trough. Countercyclical policy can partially reverse this low-employment equilibrium by pursuing an expansionary policy that will shift the labor demand curve back to the right. With downward rigid wages, the equilibrium transitions from 2: Trough to 3: Partial recovery. Compare the gains in employment (in green) in the "flexible wage" and "rigid wage" panels of Exhibit 13.1. With downward rigid wages the gains in employment are greater, since downward wage rigidity implies that the rightward shift in the labor demand curve translates one-for-one into employment gains.

(a) Flexible wage case

(b) Rigid wage case

and GDP. This takes us to the point marked 2: Trough, where employment and wages are lower. Successful expansionary policy shields the economy from the full impact of the recession by shifting the labor demand curve back to the right, taking the economy to the point labeled 3: Partial recovery.

As in Chapter 12, when wages are downward rigid, the recession has more severe employment consequences. In panel (b) of Exhibit 13.1, the labor demand curve at trough is exactly the same as it was in panel (a). But the drop in employment—from 1: Pre-recession to 2: Trough—is now larger than it was in panel (a). This is because none of the leftward shift of the labor demand curve can be absorbed by a fall in wages.

Downward-rigid wages also imply that countercyclical policy is relatively more effective. We can see this in panel (b) of Exhibit 13.1, where the same countercyclical shift in the labor demand curve increases employment more than it did in panel (a). The full force of the expansionary policy impacts employment, because there is no wage response in this case. This can be seen by comparing the lengths of the green arrows shown underneath the horizontal axis, representing the employment effects of countercyclical policies in the flexible and rigid wage cases.

Just as expansionary policy reduces the severity of a recession, policymakers sometimes use contractionary policy that reduces economic growth during a boom. Why would policymakers ever intentionally adopt a policy that has the effect of *reducing* GDP growth and *reducing* the level of employment? In many situations, the negative effects on GDP and employment are a by-product of another policy goal. For example, when inflation is consistently above the Fed's target, the Fed will raise interest rates to suppress borrowing, thereby slowing growth of the money supply and reducing the rate of inflation. The rise in interest rates will shift the labor demand curve to the left, causing employment to fall as a by-product of the Fed's efforts to reduce inflation.

In other cases, countercyclical policy may be directly targeting economic expansion. Recall from Chapter 12 that factors such as excessively optimistic sentiments about the economy can result in an *unsustainable economic expansion*. Left alone, such expansions may eventually lead to a severe downturn because optimistic sentiments can implode suddenly and severely (due to multiplier effects). In some cases, contractionary policy attempts to reduce the risks of an *extreme* contraction by trying to cool off the economy *before* it overheats. Such cooling off is achieved by putting gradual leftward pressure on the labor demand curve. Contractionary policy is sometimes referred to as "leaning against the wind."

13.2 Countercyclical Monetary Policy

We now discuss countercyclical policies in detail. We first focus on countercyclical monetary policy, which, as we explained in Chapter 11, is conducted by the Fed.

Expansionary monetary policy increases the quantity of bank reserves and lowers interest rates.

The Fed responds to economic contractions by adopting **expansionary monetary policy**, which increases the quantity of bank reserves and lowers interest rates. Let's begin by getting a big-picture view of the impact of such policies.

The Fed influences short-term interest rates, especially the *federal funds rate*. Recall that the federal funds rate is the interest rate that banks use to make loans to one another, using reserves on deposit at the Federal Reserve Bank.

When the Fed wants to stimulate the economy, it lowers short-term interest rates. This, in turn, usually causes long-term interest rates to fall. Recall from Chapter 11 that the long-term interest rate is related to the long-term average of short-term interest rates.

A fall in long-term interest rates encourages households to buy more durable goods, like cars, because a lower interest rate implies a lower cost of a car loan. To satisfy an increase in household demand for durable goods, firms try to hire more workers, shifting the labor demand curve to the right. Likewise, a fall in long-term interest rates causes firms to engage in more investment in plants and equipment, like building a new factory, because a lower interest rate implies a lower cost of a commercial loan that will fund the construction project. Firms need workers to build and operate these new factories, shifting the labor demand curve to the right. In many different ways, expansionary monetary policy shifts firms' labor demand curve to the right and increases the level of employment, as we saw in Exhibit 13.1. Exhibit 13.2 provides a bird's-eye view of this process.

Exhibit 13.2 Expansionary Monetary Policy

These are the core ingredients of expansionary monetary policy. The first half of this chapter explores the various ways in which the Fed implements the top (red) box in this exhibit.

To better understand monetary policy we need to discuss *how* the Fed lowers short-term interest rates and expands access to credit. In essence, we need to fill in the details of the red box in Exhibit 13.2. The Fed's most powerful tool in this process is its control of bank reserves and the federal funds rate, which we review next.

Controlling the Federal Funds Rate

The primary tool of monetary policy is the Fed's control of the federal funds rate. By changing the supply of bank reserves available to private banks, which is called open market operations, the Fed influences the federal funds rate. As explained in Chapter 11, in an open market operation, the Fed transacts with private banks to increase or reduce bank reserves held at the Fed. These transactions influence the federal funds rate.

> **The primary tool of monetary policy is the Fed's control of the federal funds rate.**

For instance, by increasing the supply of bank reserves available to private banks, the Fed decreases the federal funds rate. This mechanism is shown in Exhibit 13.3. You can see in this exhibit that a shift to the right of the supply of reserves held at the Fed drives down the federal funds rate (which is the price that a bank pays to borrow another dollar of reserves).

It helps to describe how open market operations work with a concrete example. Suppose that the Fed wants to raise bank reserves held on deposit at the Fed by $1 billion. To bring this about, the Fed finds a bank—let's say Citibank—that is willing to sell the Fed $1 billion worth of bonds in exchange for $1 billion in bank reserves on deposit at the Fed. The Fed doesn't use paper currency in this transaction. Instead, the Fed creates the $1 billion in bank reserves with the stroke of a computer key. Poof! The Fed has issued an IOU to the private bank. The IOU takes the form of $1 billion of reserves that the private bank holds on deposit at the Fed.

Following these open market operations, Citibank now has $1 billion *more* in bank reserves on deposit at the Fed and owns $1 billion *less* in bonds: those are the bonds that Citibank sold the Fed in this transaction. On the assets side of its balance sheet, Citibank has an extra $1 billion in bank reserves that it received in exchange for the $1 billion in bonds that are now owned by the Fed and appear on the Fed's balance sheet. *Total* assets at Citibank are unchanged, though the *composition* of assets has tilted away from bonds and toward bank reserves. Exhibit 13.4 illustrates this change on Citibank's balance sheet, showing how reserves on the assets side of its balance sheet increase from $100 billion to $101 billion.

The Fed's balance sheet has also changed. The Fed's assets now include $1 billion more in bonds—this amount represents the bonds that the Fed bought from Citibank. The Fed's liabilities also show a corresponding increase. In particular, the Fed's liabilities now include $1 billion more in the form of reserves—these are the reserves that the Fed electronically created and then exchanged with Citibank. Exhibit 13.5 illustrates this change on

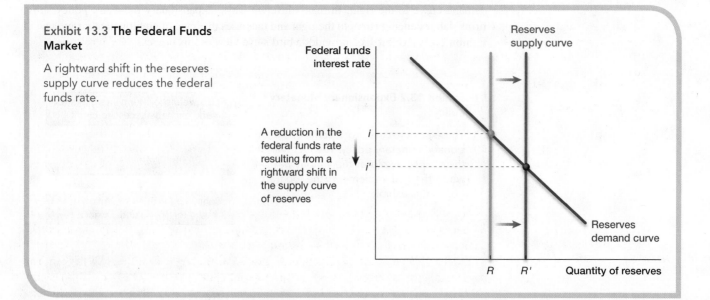

Exhibit 13.3 The Federal Funds Market

A rightward shift in the reserves supply curve reduces the federal funds rate.

Assets		Liabilities and shareholder's equity	
Reserves:	$100 billion	Deposits and other liabilities:	$800 billion
Bonds and other investments:	$900 billion	Shareholder's equity:	$200 billion
Total assets:	$1000 billion	Liabilities + shareholder's equity:	$1000 billion

Before:

Assets		Liabilities and shareholder's equity	
Reserves:	$101 billion	Deposits and other liabilities:	$800 billion
Bonds and other investments:	$899 billion	Shareholder's equity:	$200 billion
Total assets:	$1000 billion	Liabilities + shareholder's equity:	$1000 billion

After:

Exhibit 13.4 Balance Sheet of Citibank Before and After $1 Billion Bond Sale to the Fed

The Fed engages in an open market operation with Citibank. The Fed buys $1 billion in bonds in exchange for $1 billion in reserves that are credited to Citibank. This changes nothing on the liabilities and shareholder's equity side of Citibank's balance sheet. On the assets side, total assets don't change, but the composition of assets does (changes on the assets side are shown in blue). After the trade, Citibank has another $1 billion in reserves on deposit at the Fed and $1 billion less in bonds.

Assets		Liabilities and shareholders' equity	
Treasury bonds:	$1000 billion	Reserves:	$1000 billion
Other bonds:	$1000 billion	Currency:	$1000 billion
Total assets:	$2000 billion	Total liabilities:	$2000 billion

Before:

Assets		Liabilities and shareholders' equity	
Treasury bonds:	$1001 billion	Reserves:	$1001 billion
Other bonds:	$1000 billion	Currency:	$1000 billion
Total assets:	$2001 billion	Total liabilities:	$2001 billion

After:

Exhibit 13.5 Balance Sheet of the Fed Before and After $1 Billion Bond Purchase from Citibank

This exhibit shows the changes in the Fed's balance sheet following its open market operation with Citibank. In return for the $1 billion in bonds, the Fed gives Citibank $1 billion in reserves on deposit at the Fed. On the liabilities and shareholder's equity side of the Fed's balance sheet, the Fed now has another $1 billion of IOUs in the form of reserves, held by Citibank (changes on the liabilities side are shown in red). On the assets side, the Fed has another $1 billion in bonds received from Citibank (changes on the assets side are shown in blue).

the Fed's balance sheet. Note that reserves held at the Fed are an *asset* to Citibank—which can draw on the reserves—and a *liability* to the Fed—which is on the hook to pay out the reserves if asked to do so.

Most of the time, the stock of reserves—including both banks' vault cash and the reserves that banks hold at the Fed—fluctuates between $40 billion and $80 billion. During and after the 2007–2009 recession, however, the Fed *drastically* expanded the quantity of reserves banks held on deposit at the Fed.

Exhibit 13.6 plots this expansion. In August 2008, reserves totaled about $40 billion. You have to squint to see them, because they are hovering close to the horizontal axis. This quantity of reserves was enough to cover banks' reserve requirements, with little left to spare. In other

Exhibit 13.6 Total Reserves on Deposit at the Federal Reserve Bank (Monthly Data from January 1959 through December 2013)

Here we see total reserves of private banks held on deposit at the Fed. Before 2008, reserves fluctuated between $40 billion and $80 billion, which was roughly the minimum amount of reserves that were required to be held— 10 percent of demand deposits at large banks. In 2008, in response to the financial crisis, the Fed drastically increased the amount of reserves held at the Fed, causing total reserves to rise to $2.5 trillion by December 2013. This expansion was designed to drive down interest rates, thereby stimulating GDP.

Source: Board of Governors of the Federal Reserve System.

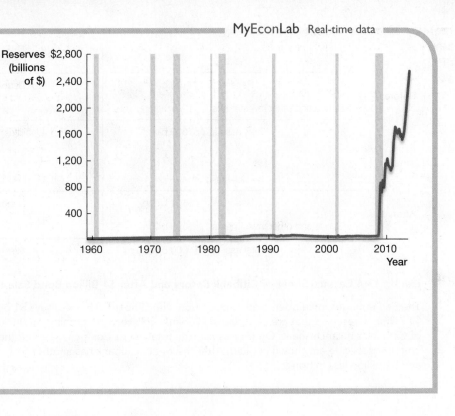

words, the quantity of reserves was roughly equal to the amount of reserves that banks were required to hold—for large banks, 10 percent of the demand deposits of their customers.

Over the next 5 years, the quantity of reserves exploded, exceeding $2.5 trillion. This vast expansion in reserves did not reflect an increase in required reserves, but rather an expansion of reserves far, far above the quantity that was required to be held. Reserves above and beyond the regulatory minimum are referred to as *excess reserves*. The Fed expanded reserves to push the federal funds rate close to 0 and to also lower long-term real interest rates. (Recall how Exhibit 13.3 showed us that a rightward shift in the supply of reserves drives down the federal funds rate.) And this reduction in interest rates is exactly what this policy achieved. In early 2007, before the 2007–2009 recession, the federal funds rate was 5.25 percent. By early 2009, it was only 0.1 percent. The federal funds rate has been kept near 0 from 2009 up to the present day (this textbook went to press in September 2014). Most forecasters expect that the Fed will reverse its policy and start to slowly raise the federal funds rate beginning in 2015.

Other Tools of the Fed

The Fed uses many tools to manipulate interest rates and affect the demand for goods, services, and labor. Like traditional open market operations, which we just discussed, most of these additional tools also work through the Fed's supply of bank reserves. We list these other tools here, many of which will be familiar from Chapter 11.

1. **Changing the reserve requirement.** For large private banks, the current level of required reserves is 10 percent of their customers' demand deposits. The Fed can decrease the quantity of required reserves, which shifts private banks' demand curve for reserves to the left and decreases the federal funds rate. (Likewise, the Fed can increase the quantity of required reserves, which shifts the demand curve for reserves to the right and increases the federal funds rate.)

2. **Changing the interest rate paid on reserves deposited at the Fed.** The Fed currently pays an interest rate of 0.25 percent on reserves deposited at the Fed. The Fed can change this interest rate. A decrease in the interest rate paid on reserves shifts the demand curve for reserves to the left and decreases the federal funds rate. (An increase in the interest rate paid on reserves shifts the demand curve for reserves to the right and increases the federal funds rate.)

3. **Lending from the discount window.** The Fed can lend bank reserves through its *discount window*. For private banks, the discount window is an alternative to the federal funds market as a source of reserves. Lending from the discount window occurs most frequently during financial crises, when private banks are afraid to lend to one another in the federal funds market because they can't be sure that they will be paid back.

4. **Quantitative easing.** The Fed can also change the way that it conducts open market operations. Rather than buying short-term Treasury bonds, which is the usual way that the Fed increases bank reserves in an open market operation, the Fed can buy *long-term* bonds instead. Purchasing long-term bonds in an open market operation pushes up the price on the long-term bonds and thereby drives down long-term interest rates. The interest rate is the (fixed) coupon that the bond pays divided by the price of the bond, so a higher bond price implies a lower interest rate. Quantitative easing occurs when the central bank creates a large quantity of bank reserves to buy long-term bonds, simultaneously increasing the quantity of bank reserves and pushing down the interest rate on long-term bonds. Quantitative easing played a key role in the huge run-up in bank reserves that occurred from 2008 to 2014.

Central banks occasionally invent even more ways of increasing the supply of credit during financial crises by creating specialized lending channels that increase lending in the credit market and thus indirectly stimulate the demand for goods, services, and labor.

For example, immediately after the investment bank Lehman Brothers went bankrupt in September 2008, an even larger financial firm—the American International Group (AIG)—also suffered a cataclysmic liquidity crisis. AIG desperately needed cash because it had to make billions of dollars of immediate payments to hundreds of other financial firms, including many of the largest banks in the United States, Europe, and Asia. AIG was having trouble raising funds because investors feared that AIG was about to declare bankruptcy. The failure of AIG would have triggered a domino effect that could have crippled the global financial system. If AIG declared bankruptcy, any institutions that were owed money by AIG would not immediately receive the funds they were counting on, and some of these *other* firms would be unable to meet their own financial commitments, creating ripples that might cause hundreds of interconnected financial institutions to fail.

The Fed joined forces with the U.S. Treasury Department to prop up AIG by extending AIG loans, credit lines, and other guarantees for a total of nearly $200 billion. AIG eventually recovered, and the Fed and Treasury got back their money. AIG's original shareholders were almost completely wiped out, but AIG was able to pay off its debts to other financial institutions, averting an even worse global financial meltdown.

> **The effectiveness of monetary policy depends on expectations about interest rates and inflation.**

We've now discussed the key tools that the Fed uses in its conduct of countercyclical monetary policy. However, we haven't completed the picture yet. There are several important factors that influence the way the Fed uses these tools. We turn to these issues in the next three subsections.

Expectations, Inflation, and Monetary Policy

The effectiveness of monetary policy depends on expectations about interest rates and inflation. Recall that the federal funds rate, which the Fed directly controls, is the annualized interest rate on overnight loans between banks. In contrast, the interest rate that is relevant for consumers' and firms' investment decisions—for instance, the real mortgage interest rate—is the long-term expected real interest rate:

$$\text{Long-term expected real interest rate} = \text{Long-term nominal interest rate}$$
$$- \text{Long-term expected inflation rate.}$$

For the Fed to lower the long-term real interest rate, it has to either lower the long-term nominal interest rate or raise long-term expectations of the inflation rate (or both). To do this, the Fed can communicate that it will maintain an expansionary monetary policy, holding down the federal funds rate and propping up the inflation rate, for a long period of time.

LETTING THE DATA SPEAK

Managing Expectations

The Fed's desire to influence long-term expectations is apparent in its monthly policy statements. In the fall of 2010, the economy was slowly recovering from the 2007–2009 recession and consequently the Fed wanted to maintain a low long-term expected real interest rate. In its September 2010 policy announcement, the Federal Open Market Committee—the committee that conducts the Fed's open market operations—wrote that the federal funds rate would be held between 0 and 0.25 percent for "an extended period."

In its December 2012 announcement, the Fed announced an even clearer policy rule, by linking changes in the federal funds rate to future changes in the unemployment rate and the inflation rate:

"The committee decided to keep the target range for the federal funds rate at 0 to 1/4 percent and currently anticipates that this exceptionally low range for the federal funds rate will be appropriate at least as long as

• the unemployment rate remains above 6.5 percent,

• inflation between one and two years ahead is projected to be no more than a half percentage point above the Committee's 2 percent longer-run goal,
• and longer-term inflation expectations continue to be well anchored."

(Federal Open Market Committee, 12/2012)

In this statement, the Fed announced a specific policy rule, which increased the public's ability to forecast future interest rates. In essence, the Fed announced that it planned to keep the federal funds rate close to 0 percent as long as the unemployment rate remained above 6.5 percent and inflation remained close to the Fed's 2 percent target. At the time that this announcement was made, the unemployment rate was 7.7 percent and forecasters anticipated that it would take years for the unemployment rate to fall to the 6.5 percent threshold that the Fed set for itself. As this book goes to press (September, 2014), the unemployment rate has fallen below the 6.5 threshold, and the Fed is now actively talking about raising the federal funds rate during the next year.

William McChesney Martin, Jr., a teetotaler in his personal life, was the chairman of the Fed from 1951 to 1970. He described the Fed's role this way: "I'm the fellow who takes away the punch bowl just when the party is getting good."

Contractionary monetary policy slows down growth in bank reserves, raises interest rates, reduces borrowing, slows down growth in the money supply, and reduces the rate of inflation.

If households and firms believe that the federal funds rate will remain low for several years, then the long-term nominal interest rate will also be low. Intuitively, you can think of the 10-year nominal interest rate as being close to the market's expectations of the average interest rate for overnight loans over the next 10 years. If the Fed promises to keep the federal funds rate low for the next decade, then the 10-year (long-term) nominal interest rate will also be low.

A similar analysis applies to long-term expectations of inflation. To many people, inflation is a four-letter word. But as we already mentioned in Chapter 11, the impact of inflationary expectations on the long-term expected real interest rate also implies that the Fed might wish to create expectations of inflation—if it can. In particular, it might promise to conduct expansionary monetary policy for several years. If the market believes this promise, then inflationary expectations will rise, which will lower the long-term expected real interest rate if the nominal interest rate doesn't rise one-for-one with inflation.

Contractionary Monetary Policy: Control of Inflation

Recall from Chapter 11 that stabilizing inflation is one of the Fed's two mandates. The Fed would like the inflation rate to hover around 2 percent per year, neither deviating far above or far below this target.

Expansionary monetary policy can put this inflation target at risk. In normal circumstances, increasing the quantity of bank reserves enables banks to make more loans. Those loans circulate through the economy and return to the banking system as deposits. Rising bank deposits increase the amount of money in the economy, since the stock of money includes customers' bank deposits. The quantity theory of money, which we studied in Chapter 11, implies that over the long run, the inflation rate will equal the growth rate of M2 minus the growth rate of real GDP. Excessively rapid growth in M2 therefore creates a risk of high levels of inflation. We summarize these linkages in Exhibit 13.7. Countercyclical policy is useful for controlling inflation. In particular, when inflation threatens to rise substantially and persistently above the Fed's target of 2 percent, the Fed uses **contractionary monetary policy**, which slows down growth in bank reserves, raises interest rates, reduces borrowing, slows down growth in the money supply, and reduces the rate of inflation.

Contractionary monetary policy is like expansionary monetary policy, but now the Fed runs everything in reverse. The Fed will *shrink* bank reserves—or slow their growth—to

Exhibit 13.7 The Path from Reserves to Inflation

Increasing the quantity of bank reserves deposited at the Fed usually leads banks to make more loans. Those loans circulate through the economy and return to the banking system as deposits. Rising bank deposits enable banks to make even more loans. The resulting total increase in deposits generates an increase in the stock of money (for instance, M2). If the stock of money grows faster than real GDP, the aggregate price level will rise, generating inflation. This only poses a problem when inflation persistently rises above the Fed's 2 percent target.

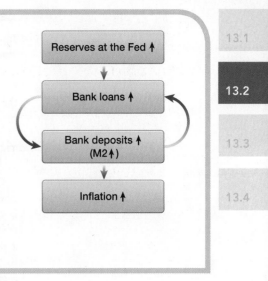

> ## The Fed (plays) a countercyclical role, leaning against the prevailing economic winds.

raise the federal funds rate. It might also attempt to change expectations about future monetary policy, leading households and businesses to anticipate more contractionary policies in the future.

In essence, the Fed can run the engine of monetary policy either forward or backwards. During a recession, the Fed employs expansionary monetary policies to partially offset the economic contraction. During a boom, particularly one that is inflationary, the Fed employs contractionary monetary policy to reduce a rising rate of inflation. In both cases, of course, the Fed is playing a countercyclical role, leaning against the prevailing economic winds.

Though it might sound simple to run the engine of monetary policy backwards, controlling inflation is not always easy. Once prices begin rising quickly—for instance, an inflation rate of 5 percent or more—the public starts to expect a high inflation rate in the future and the central bank has a hard time regaining its reputation as an inflation fighter. Such a loss in reputation occurred during the 1970s—a decade of high and rising U.S. inflation caused in part by expansionary monetary policy. By the end of the 1970s, the Fed's reputation as a careful steward of the monetary system was shattered. In 1979, the U.S. public expected that inflation would remain at a high level for the foreseeable future. This is when a new Fed chairman, Paul Volcker, stepped in with a sharply contractionary monetary policy. To cut inflation, he drastically slowed the growth rate of the stock of money, which raised the federal funds rate to 20 percent. This was the beginning of the 1981 recession that turned out to be one of the most severe U.S. recessions since World War II. Volcker's recession generated a peak unemployment rate of 10.8 percent, even greater than the 10 percent peak during the 2007–2009 recession. Volcker believed that the benefits of lowering the rate of inflation offset the costs of this deep recession. Volcker managed to reclaim the Fed's credibility for fighting inflation, and ever since, the Fed has retained its reputation for being serious about controlling the level of inflation.

With historical episodes like this in mind, central banks work hard to protect their reputation for keeping inflation at a low level—around 2 percent per year. Even the slightest hint that inflation is getting out of control might lead a central bank to end a policy of monetary expansion.

Paul Volcker sharply reduced the growth rate of the money stock in the early 1980s to reclaim the Fed's reputation as an inflation fighter. His actions raised interest rates and started a major recession. Despite national protests against his policies, he stayed the course, and he is now viewed as one of the greatest Fed chairmen. This is one central banker you shouldn't mess with. (He also had the odd quirk of testifying before the Senate while puffing on cigars.[1])

Zero Lower Bound

Japan has experienced four recessions and a very low level of overall growth in real GDP since the early 1990s. Many observers refer to the 1990s and 2000s as "lost decades" for the Japanese economy. In response to these economic conditions, Japan's central bank has responded by increasing the supply of bank reserves, thereby lowering Japan's version of the federal funds rate—the interest rate for interbank loans—nearly to zero. Exhibit 13.8 plots this interbank interest rate.

When an interest rate hits zero, economists say that it has "hit the zero lower bound." This language implies that zero is a barrier—or a boundary line—that nominal interest rates can't cross.

To understand the zero lower bound, it is helpful to explain how bizarre a negative nominal interest rate would be if it arose. A *negative* interest rate would imply that a borrower would eventually repay *less* money than he borrowed. For example, suppose that you go to the bank to borrow $100 million for one year at a *negative* interest rate of 1 percent. Assuming that you can store this money—for example, under a very big mattress or in a safe deposit box—then borrowing at a -1 percent interest rate would present a great profit opportunity for you. You borrow $100 million. You store it for a year and then repay your loan by giving the bank $99 million back and pocketing the remaining $1 million!

Of course, lending money at a negative interest rate is a bad deal for banks; they would rather keep the money in their own vaults than lend it to you. At least then they would have $100 million at the end of the year rather than just the $99 million they would get from you.

CHOICE & CONSEQUENCE

Policy Mistakes

On occasion, policymakers fail to recognize what is happening in the economy. Sometimes they mistakenly adopt policies that increase the magnitude of economic fluctuations instead of policies that smooth things out.

Some economists believe that the severity of the 2007–2009 financial crisis and recession was in part caused by unduly expansionary monetary policy from 2002 to 2005. During this period, the Fed, under Chairman Alan Greenspan, lowered the federal funds rate to 1 percent, even though the economy was growing and the housing market was gripped by what we now realize was an unsustainable speculative bubble. Alan Greenspan's unwillingness to increase the federal funds rate was in part caused by his belief at the time that unsustainable speculative bubbles are extremely rare. After the collapse in housing prices, Greenspan publicly revised his views on the frequency of asset bubbles.

Asset bubbles—like the home price bubble that peaked in 2006—do occur from time to time and are often followed by recessions. In other words, asset bubbles increase, or amplify, economic fluctuations. The Fed's expansionary policies of 2002–2005 greased the wheels of the housing bubble and therefore played a partial role in causing the recession that followed. Sometimes central banks administer the wrong monetary medicine.

Central banks have studied this policy failure and many are now attempting to identify asset bubbles as

they are forming. Some central banks, including the Bank of England, are also implementing policies that are designed to suppress asset price bubbles before they grow destructively large.[2]

Exhibit 13.8 Japan's Interbank Lending Rate from 1987 to 2013

The Japanese central bank has kept the interest rate on interbank loans near zero since 1995. The interbank lending rate is analogous to the federal funds rate in the United States. (Shaded periods are Japanese recessions.)

Source: Board of Governors of the Federal Reserve System.

These arguments explain why banks generally won't lend money at an interest rate that is below zero. Banks will hold onto their money rather than make loans at negative interest rates. It therefore follows that central banks can't push nominal interest rates below zero. And that is the zero lower bound.

The zero lower bound is a problem for monetary policy when the rate of inflation is low or negative, which has also been the case in Japan since the early 1990s. Remember that households and firms make investment decisions based on the expected real interest rate. When the nominal interest rate is stuck at or just above 0 and the inflation rate is negative (also called *deflation*), the real interest rate will be positive. For example, a nominal interest rate of 0 and an expected inflation rate of -1 percent jointly imply an expected real interest rate of

$$\text{Nominal interest rate} - \text{Expected inflation rate} = 0\% - (-1\%) = 1\%.$$

If the inflation rate keeps falling (further below zero), the real interest rate will rise, squelching investment and shifting the labor demand curve to the left.

When the economy is in recession or growing only slowly, the central bank usually wants to lower the real interest rate to stimulate economic growth. But what does it do when nominal interest rates can't be lowered any further because they are already at the zero lower bound? As we discussed earlier, the central bank tries to influence expectations of *future* nominal interest rates and *future* inflation. By promising to keep nominal interest rates low for many years and promising to keep inflation at 2 percent in the long run, the central bank attempts to influence the long-term expected real rate of interest, even if the current federal funds rate is at zero and can't be lowered any further.

Policy Trade-offs

We hope you have concluded that the job of a central banker is not easy. Monetary policy-makers face many conflicting considerations. For example, the Fed would like to stimulate the economy during a recession, but the Fed does not want to risk runaway inflation. How should the Fed make this trade-off?

Many central banks set the federal funds rate in a way that is approximately described by this formula, also called a *Taylor rule* after economist John Taylor who first suggested it[3]:

Federal funds rate = Long-run federal funds rate target + 1.5(Inflation rate − Inflation rate target) + 0.5(Output gap in percentage points).

This equation relates the federal funds rate to its long-run target (about 3.5 percent), the inflation rate, the inflation target (2 percent), and the output gap in percentage points. The *output gap*, which was first discussed in Chapter 5, is the difference between GDP and trend GDP divided by trend GDP:

$$\text{Output gap} = \frac{\text{GDP} - \text{Trend GDP}}{\text{Trend GDP}}.$$

An output gap of -0.05 is expressed in percentage points as -5 percent—in other words, the economy is 5 percent below trend. Recall from Chapter 5 that trend GDP is a smoothed version of actual GDP. You often will see the output gap expressed with trend GDP replaced by *potential GDP*, which represents the level of GDP that would be attained if the labor force and the capital stock were fully employed in production.

It is useful to spell out the two parts of the Taylor rule:

1. It says that the Fed raises the federal funds rate as the inflation rate rises. A greater inflation rate leads the Fed to raise the federal funds rate, thereby reducing the degree of stimulus. Specifically, the formula says that every percentage point increase in the inflation rate (for a given inflation target) will translate into a 1.5 percentage point increase in the federal funds rate.

2. The Taylor rule also says that the Fed sets a higher federal funds rate the higher the output gap. A larger output gap—in other words, a stronger economy—leads the Fed to raise the federal funds rate, thereby reducing the degree of stimulus. The formula says that every percentage point increase in the output gap will translate into a half percentage point increase in the federal funds rate.

To see the Taylor rule in action, consider the state of affairs in early 2014. Inflation was running at about 1.5 percent, and the economy was about 5 percent below its trend GDP level. Plugging these numbers into the Taylor rule (and assuming a 3.5% long-run federal funds rate target and 2% inflation rate target), the recommended level of the federal funds rate was:

$$\text{Federal funds rate} = 3.5\% + 1.5(1.5\% - 2\%) + 0.5(-5\%) = 0.25\%.$$

Hence, the Taylor rule predicted a federal funds rate of only 0.25 percent, far below its long-run target of 3.5 percent. In fact, the actual federal funds rate in early 2014 was 0.1 percent, not far from the level predicted by the Taylor rule.

The Taylor "rule" is really just a rule of thumb. Monetary policy is as much an art as a science—policymakers need to use their intuition and wisdom, not just a simple formula. However, the Taylor rule is a good starting point for their deliberations and a rough-and-ready summary of the trade-offs that central banks have made in the past.

13.3 Countercyclical Fiscal Policy

Countercyclical monetary policy, which is conducted by the central bank and aims to reduce economic fluctuations by manipulating interest rates, has been our focus so far. Countercyclical fiscal policy is the *other* major category of countercyclical policy. Countercyclical fiscal policy, which is passed by the legislative branch and signed into law by the executive branch, reduces economic fluctuations by manipulating government expenditures and taxes.

Expansionary fiscal policy uses higher government expenditure and lower taxes to increase the growth rate of real GDP. Like expansionary monetary policy, expansionary fiscal policy shifts the labor demand curve to the right, as Exhibit 13.1 showed. **Contractionary fiscal policy** uses lower government expenditure and higher taxes to reduce the growth rate of real GDP. Just like contractionary monetary policy, contractionary fiscal policy shifts the labor demand curve to the left.

We now discuss the reasons that macroeconomists view fiscal policy as a useful tool for offsetting macroeconomic fluctuations. We'll also explain some of its limitations.

Expansionary fiscal policy uses higher government expenditure and lower taxes to increase the growth rate of real GDP.

Contractionary fiscal policy uses lower government expenditure and higher taxes to reduce the growth rate of real GDP.

Fiscal Policy Over the Business Cycle: Automatic and Discretionary Components

Fiscal policy can be divided into automatic and discretionary components.

1. *Automatic countercyclical components* are aspects of fiscal policy that automatically partially offset economic fluctuations. These automatic countercyclical components do not require deliberate action on the part of the government. For example, tax collection falls automatically during a recession because unemployed workers don't owe income tax. Moreover, during a recession, government expenditure automatically *increases*, because government transfer payments rise, including

unemployment insurance and food stamps (otherwise known as the Supplemental Nutrition Assistance Program or SNAP). The less households earn, the more government transfers they receive.

These automatic countercyclical fiscal mechanisms are often referred to as **automatic stabilizers** because they stimulate the economy during economic contractions. Such transfers help households cope with economic hardship and are widely believed to stimulate GDP by enabling millions of households to spend more during recessions.

2. *Discretionary countercyclical components* are those aspects of the government's fiscal policy that policymakers deliberately enact in response to economic fluctuations. In most cases, these new policies introduce a package of specific expenditure increases or temporary tax cuts to reduce economic hardship and stimulate GDP. For example, during the recession of 2007–2009 the U.S. Congress passed the Economic Stimulus Act of 2008—signed by President George W. Bush in February 2008—and the American Recovery and Reinvestment Act of 2009—signed by President Barack Obama in February 2009. The first package contained $152 billion in tax cuts, which were received by households in the spring of 2008. The second package cost $787 billion, with a third of the funding supporting new tax cuts and two-thirds of the funding supporting new government expenditure. The new spending was spread out over several years.

We illustrate the behavior of fiscal policy (combining both the automatic and discretionary components) during the 2007–2009 recession in Exhibit 13.9. The rising budget deficit—government revenue minus government expenditure—provides a summary measure of fiscal policy, because the deficit reflects rising expenditures and falling tax collection. In the fourth quarter of 2007, which was the start of the recession, the budget deficit was $416 billion (all numbers are in constant 2009 dollars). By the end of the recession in the second quarter of 2009, the budget deficit had risen to $1,603 billion. Persistent weakness in the labor market coupled with lags in spending from the 2009 American Recovery and Reinvestment Act caused the deficit to remain high following the end of the recession.

Such deficits have consequences. When the government borrows money to pay its bills, future taxpayers are implicitly responsible for paying back the government's debts.

Automatic stabilizers are components of the government budget that automatically adjust to smooth out economic fluctuations.

MyEconLab Real-time data

Exhibit 13.9 U.S. Government Accounts from 2007 to 2010 Combining Federal, State, and Local Governments (Constant 2009 Dollars)

During the 2007–2009 recession (December 2007 to June 2009, which corresponds to the shaded area), fiscal policy was implemented in two major pieces of legislation. The first act was passed in February 2008 and was principally focused on tax cuts that were paid out in the spring of 2008 (the second quarter of 2008). The second act was passed in February 2009 and included both tax cuts and spending increases. Vertical lines identify the quarter that each piece of legislation was passed.

Sources: Bureau of Economic Analysis, National Income and Product Accounts; and National Bureau of Economic Research.

> **The basic idea behind fiscal policy is that higher government expenditure and lower taxation play a useful role in recessions by increasing spending by households, firms, and governments.**

Ultimately, the government will have to pay what it owes. Roughly speaking, the 2007–2009 recession generated $2 trillion of *automatic* fiscal adjustments and $1 trillion of *discretionary* fiscal adjustments, implying that future taxpayers will be on the hook for approximately $3 trillion of new government debt. But all of this debt was accumulated for a reason—to conduct countercyclical fiscal policy. The basic idea behind fiscal policy is that higher government expenditure and lower taxation play a useful role in recessions by increasing spending by households, firms, and governments. This increased spending translates into demand for firms' products, which in turn increases demand for labor, shifting labor demand to the right. To the extent that some of this money goes to state and local governments, it enables them to avoid laying off state and local employees.

The remainder of the chapter explains why more government expenditure and lower taxation increases GDP. We first look at expenditure-based fiscal policy and then at taxation-based fiscal policy.

Analysis of Expenditure-Based Fiscal Policy

Let's begin with the national income accounting identity.

$$Y = C + I + G + X - M.$$

Here, Y is GDP, C is consumption, I is investment, G is government expenditure, X is exports, M is imports, and thus $X - M$ is net exports. To start the analysis of fiscal policy, assume (for the moment) that changing government expenditure does not change any of the other terms on the right-hand side of the equation. Then a $1 increase in government expenditure would cause a $1 increase in GDP, Y:

$$[Y + 1] = C + I + [G + 1] + X - M.$$

If we take the change in GDP (Y) and divide it by the change in government expenditure (G), we have what is known as the **government expenditure multiplier**. If government expenditure rises by $1 and causes GDP to rise by m, then the government expenditure multiplier is $m/$1 = m$. For example, if $m = 1$, then a $1 increase in government expenditure generates a $1 increase in GDP (which is the case in the previous equation). In terms of our analysis of Exhibit 13.1, if $m = 1$, then increased government expenditure of $1 raises the demand for firms' goods and services and shifts the labor demand curve to the right, increasing GDP by $1.

> If a $1 change in government expenditure causes an m change in GDP, then the **government expenditure multiplier** is m.

Let's now revisit the assumption that nothing else on the right-hand side changes. Additional government expenditure might lead to higher levels of household consumption. For example, the government's extra expenditure might encourage additional business activity, which would raise employment and take-home pay and thereby increase household consumption. In this scenario, increased government expenditure levels are creating a multiplier effect of the sort we discussed in Chapter 12. The multiplier effect shifts firms' labor demand curves further to the right and translates into a larger impact of government expenditure on employment and GDP.

We can illustrate this multiplier effect with the national income accounting identity. Assume that the multiplier effect raises household consumption by $1 (in addition to the original $1 increase in government expenditure). In particular:

$$[Y + 2] = [C + 1] + I + [G + 1] + X - M.$$

In this scenario Y rises by $2—remember that the left- and right-hand sides of this equation must be equal. In this case, the government expenditure multiplier would be $2/$1 = 2. This means that GDP rises by $2 for every $1 increase in government expenditure.

Advocates of expenditure-based fiscal policy tend to believe that the government expenditure multiplier lies between 1 and 2.

Crowding Out In addition to its useful role of combatting recessions as part of countercyclical fiscal policy, there is also a negative side to government expenditure. Rising government expenditures leads to more government borrowing, and such borrowing can soak up resources that would otherwise have been used by households and firms. Some

Crowding out occurs when rising government expenditure partially or even fully displaces expenditures by households and firms.

economists believe that rising government expenditure "crowds out" private economic activity like consumption and investment. **Crowding out** occurs when rising government expenditure partially or even fully displaces expenditures by households and firms. In Exhibit 13.1, crowding out results in a smaller effect of countercyclical policy—in other words, crowding out implies that the labor demand curve shifts to the right less than it otherwise would.

For example, suppose that an extra $1 of government expenditure forces the government to borrow an extra $1 to pay its bills, leading $1 of private savings to switch from funding private investment to purchasing government debt. The switch occurs because the government is willing to pay whatever interest rate it takes to borrow funds, whereas private businesses tend to be more responsive to interest rate changes. As the government borrows to pay its bills, the interest rate in the credit market rises, causing a reallocation of savings from private borrowers—like households and firms—to the government. If private investment becomes too expensive for consumers and firms, it might fall by $1 when the government increases its spending by $1. In effect, the private investment is "crowded out" by the government borrowing. In this scenario, countercyclical government expenditure will *not* shift the firms' labor demand curve to the right because the expansionary effect of the additional government expenditure is offset by the contractionary effect of the fall in private investment. Consequently, GDP does not increase, because the $1 increase in government expenditure crowds out $1 of private investment:

$$Y = C + [I - 1] + [G + 1] + X - M.$$

In this case, the government expenditure multiplier is $[-\$1 + \$1]/\$1 = 0$. Critics of fiscal policy emphasize the importance of crowding out and believe that the government expenditure multiplier is well below 1 and might even be close to 0.

At this point you are probably wondering which scenario is "right." Unfortunately, we are not completely sure. Economists hold a wide range of positions on this question, and everyone in this debate has some data that partially support his or her position. Taking into account *both* multipliers and crowding out, the government expenditure multiplier probably lies between 0 and 1.5, depending on the state of the economy.

If the economy is already running at full steam, it is likely that additional government expenditure will substantially crowd out other kinds of economic activity. For example, if all factories are already operating at full capacity, there may be little the government can do in the short run to increase GDP. Consequently, many economists believe that the government expenditure multiplier is close to zero when the economy is already booming. But that's not particularly relevant to the fiscal policy debate because economists don't recommend expansionary fiscal policy when the economy is already growing rapidly.

The interesting question is what we should expect the government expenditure multiplier to be when the economy is contracting. For example, envision an economy suffering from an extreme contraction, and further assume that monetary policy has been rendered less effective because interest rates have already been lowered to zero and can't be lowered any further—the scenario in which monetary policy has hit the zero lower bound.

This was the situation of the U.S. economy in the aftermath of the 2007–2009 recession. In a situation like this there will be substantial slack in productive resources, like factories running below capacity and significant numbers of unemployed workers. Accordingly, additional government expenditure might only weakly crowd out private consumption and investment. Additional government expenditures can then encourage the utilization of some of the idle capacity and unemployed workers. For instance, President Barack Obama's administration assumed a government-expenditure multiplier of 1.57 when developing the American Recovery and Reinvestment Act of 2009.[4] This number was close to, though slightly above, the estimates of other forecasters at that time.

Most economists endorse some additional government expenditures during a deep recession, but there is substantial debate on this issue. Critics of expansionary government expenditure believe that crowding out is strong even during recessions. Accordingly, the appropriate scale of countercyclical government expenditure remains an open policy question.

We'll now show you how to use the government expenditure multiplier to predict the impact of expenditure-based countercyclical policy. We'll assume that the economy is in a deep recession and that the multiplier is 1.5, approximately the top of its range. The American Recovery and Reinvestment Act of 2009 contained about $500 billion of new spending, but this new spending was spread out over many years. Only $120 billion occurred in 2009, implying an impact of

$$1.5 \times \$120 \text{ billion} = \$180 \text{ billion}.$$

Since GDP was approximately $14 trillion in 2009, a $180 billion increase in GDP amounted to an increase of about

$$\frac{\$180 \text{ billion}}{\$14 \text{ trillion}} = 1.3\%.$$

That might not seem like much, but 1.3 percentage points of extra growth does make a difference when talking about the growth rate of the entire U.S. economy. For example, in 2009 real GDP fell by 2.8 percent. A multiplier of 1.5 implies that the economy would have fallen by 4.1 percent without the impact of the new government expenditures in the American Recovery and Reinvestment Act of 2009.

Analysis of Taxation-Based Fiscal Policy

So far, we've been discussing the use of government expenditure to partially offset an economic contraction. Expansionary fiscal policy can also be implemented by cutting taxes. Let's therefore switch gears and assume that the government gives households a $1 tax cut. To illustrate ideas, let's start with the extreme assumption that consumers spend every penny of the tax cut, raising consumption (C) by $1, but nothing else changes on the right-hand side of the national income accounting identity. Then GDP would rise by $1 and the **government taxation multiplier** would be $1/$1 = 1:

$$[Y + 1] = [C + 1] + I + G + X - M.$$

But a $1 tax cut need not increase GDP by $1. If it increases it by m, the government taxation multiplier would be $m/$1 = m$.

For instance, there are many reasons why a $1 tax cut might have an impact that is even greater than $1. The rise in consumption might have multiplier effects, causing a domino effect of rising consumption, rising firm revenues, rising firm hiring, rising household income, and yet more consumption. In addition, a cut in the income tax might lead workers to supply more labor because their *after-tax* wages will have risen (though this effect is estimated to be small in magnitude). In Exhibit 13.1, this would shift the labor supply curve to the right. With these kinds of mechanisms in mind, suppose that a $1 decrease in taxation leads to a $2 increase in households' incomes and a $2 increase in consumption. Suppose that nothing else changes on the right-hand side of the accounting identity. In this case, GDP (Y) would rise by $2, so the government taxation multiplier would be $2/$1 = 2.

$$[Y + 2] = [C + 2] + I + G + X - M.$$

On the other hand, tax cuts might generate crowding out of the sort that we described before. As consumers try to spend more, resources that would have previously gone to investment might now be redirected to consumption. For instance, a car company might shift from manufacturing rental cars (an investment for Hertz and Avis) toward manufacturing cars that households buy:

$$[Y + 1] = [C + 2] + [I - 1] + G + X - M.$$

Likewise, as consumers try to spend more, the extra goods might be provided by an increase in imports, lowering net exports. If imports rise by $1, then net exports will fall by $1, so the national income accounting identity becomes:

$$[Y + 1] = [C + 2] + I + G + X - [M + 1].$$

If crowding-out effects are large, the government taxation multiplier will be significantly reduced. In the last two examples that we have discussed, the government taxation multiplier would be [$2 − $1]/$1 = 1.

Critics of using tax policy to manage short-run economic contractions point out that optimizing consumers might not actually spend much of their tax cut right away. In other words, critics worry that consumption might not rise very much as a result of a tax cut. Why might households hold back on spending their tax cuts? There are at least two reasons.

1. If consumption offers diminishing returns—a fifth slice of pizza might not taste as good as the fourth slice—consumers might try to smooth their consumption by

If a $1 reduction in taxation causes an m increase in GDP, then the **government taxation multiplier** is m.

spreading the "extra" spending over the long term rather than consuming the proceeds of a tax cut all at once.

2. Consumers might recognize that the government will have to raise taxes in the future to pay for the current tax cut. Because of this anticipated future tax hike, they may decide that a current tax cut should be saved so that they will be in a position to pay these higher taxes in the future.

The tendency to save the tax cut will be particularly pronounced among wealthy consumers who don't have an urgent reason to consume the tax cut right away. In summary, if some consumers save some or even all of a tax cut, cutting taxes will have only a small effect on consumption, and the government taxation multiplier will be small.

Economists believe that the government taxation multiplier is between 0 and 2. The administration of President Barack Obama assumed a government-taxation multiplier of 0.99 when developing the American Recovery and Reinvestment Act of 2009.[5] The act created total tax cuts of about \$300 billion, but only \$65 billion of those cuts took effect in 2009. Assuming a government-taxation multiplier of 1, these tax cuts raised 2009 GDP by about \$65 billion, representing about 0.5 percent of GDP in 2009.

We can therefore calculate the total impact of the American Recovery and Reinvestment Act of 2009, *if* the government's estimates of multipliers were correct. Expenditures raised GDP by 1.3 percent (see calculations above) and tax cuts raised GDP by 0.5 percent. Hence, the act raised 2009 GDP by

$$1.3\% + 0.5\% = 1.8\%.$$

Actual growth in real GDP was −2.8 percent from 2008 to 2009. If the act raised GDP by 1.8 percent, then *without* the act, growth in real GDP would have been

$$-2.8\% - 1.8\% = -4.6\%.$$

Viewed this way, the act had a considerable impact on GDP growth.

Fiscal Policies that Directly Target the Labor Market

There are a few specific fiscal policies that are directly targeted at the labor market. For example, in the midst of recessions, when many workers have lost their jobs and are unemployed, governments enact policies to lessen the terrible personal toll of joblessness. In the United States, the government extends eligibility for unemployment insurance from 26 to 52 weeks and, in some severe downturns, even to 99 weeks.

More generous eligibility rules have complex effects on the labor market. Lengthening eligibility reduces the hardships that unemployed workers suffer and gives them more time to find a job that is a good fit for their skills, but lengthened eligibility also partially reduces the incentive for unemployed workers to find new jobs. This shifts the labor supply curve to the left, which, holding all else equal, reduces employment.

However, by increasing the incomes of unemployed workers, lengthened eligibility supports household spending and thus limits the negative multiplier effects that result from falling employment. Hence, lengthened eligibility increases household consumption and this effect shifts the labor demand curve to the right.

Adding up the different considerations, the extension of unemployment benefits probably is good policy, but this is due to the suffering that it alleviates and not its effect on GDP. Because of the multiple effects with opposing implications for employment, lengthening eligibility is likely to have only a limited effect on total employment or GDP.

During recessions another type of fiscal policy reduces unemployment by subsidizing wages and thereby encouraging job creation. Such subsidies might be justified when unemployment remains high for a long period of time—for instance, this was the case during the Great Depression. Wage subsidies might also be justified when traditional monetary and fiscal policy have only limited success in combating unemployment. The last three U.S. recessions have been followed by "jobless recoveries," meaning that the rate of employment growth after these three recessions, although positive, has been lower than after earlier recessions.

We show the effect of a subsidy on labor demand and job creation in Exhibit 13.10. With a \$1 subsidy received by employers, a wage of \$10 per hour would cost employers only \$9 per hour. So the subsidy shifts the labor demand curve right by just enough to create a \$1 *vertical* gap between the old and new labor demand curves (drop a vertical line from one

Exhibit 13.10 The Impact of a $1 Wage Subsidy

If the government introduces a $1 per hour wage subsidy that is paid to firms, the labor demand curve shifts rightward by enough so that the new labor demand curve and the original labor demand curve are separated by a vertical distance of exactly $1. If a firm was willing to hire a worker at a wage of $w per hour without the subsidy, the firm is willing to hire the worker at a wage of $(w + 1) per hour with the subsidy. At the new equilibrium, employment is higher and the wage has risen to w*. Notice that the increase from the original equilibrium wage, w, to the new equilibrium wage, w*, is less than $1. This is because the rise in employment causes a fall in the (unsubsidized) value of the marginal product of labor (point A).

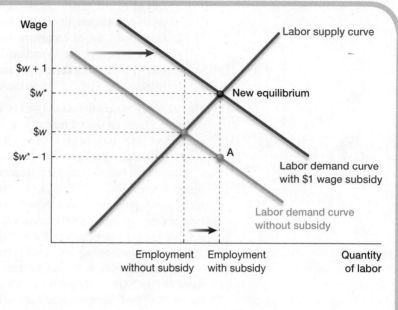

curve to the other to see the $1 gap). An employer who is willing to pay $9 for a worker without the subsidy is willing to pay $10 for that worker once the $1 government subsidy is in effect. Wage subsidies have been used commonly by European governments since the 1990s when their economies were also beset by jobless recoveries.

> **Though the government typically funds socially valuable projects as part of countercyclical fiscal policy, government waste is often a problem.**

Policy Waste and Policy Lags

Though the government typically funds socially valuable projects as part of countercyclical fiscal policy, government waste is often a problem. The government frequently funds *pork barrel spending*, which is the (derogatory) name given to inefficient public spending that politicians value because it increases their popularity with their constituents. For example, a senator has an incentive to obtain federal funding for an infrastructure project in his or her home state, even if the project is expensive and unnecessary, such as a bridge to nowhere. Since the home state residents only pay approximately 1/50th of the cost of the project (through their federal taxes) but get most of the benefits, they are happy to see it built, and the project improves the senator's in-state popularity. In this sense, the senator is personally optimizing when obtaining federal funding for almost any in-state project, even those with total social costs that exceed their total social benefits.

The efficiency of public expenditures further deteriorates when hundreds of billions of dollars of new government expenditures need to be spent quickly. The urgency makes it harder to identify and efficiently implement the projects that are socially beneficial. In addition, many of the projects with the highest social return have been funded already, raising the chance that a new project won't be socially desirable. Finally, politics and special interests sometimes get in the way, increasing the chances that wasteful projects with negative social value get funded.

Another important determinant of the effectiveness of expenditure-based policies is the lag in implementation. Most spending projects are slow out of the starting gate. It takes a long time to build a bridge, a highway, or a school. Plans have to be drawn up. The local community has to be consulted. The relevant zoning boards need to mull over the proposals, request changes, and then evaluate the amended plans. Environmental impact studies have to be conducted. Contractors have to be hired. And only then, construction begins.

For example, when the most recent recession officially ended in June 2009, practically none of the $230 billion in infrastructure spending legislated in the American Recovery and Reinvestment Act of (February) 2009 had yet been spent. In June 2010—almost a full year after the recession was over—only a *quarter* of the infrastructure budget had been

The "Bridge to Nowhere" was a $398 million project to build a road to Gravina Island, Alaska, which has 50 residents and is served by a ferry. After generating a national protest over pork barrel spending, the bridge was cancelled.

spent. Many of the largest infrastructure projects hadn't spent a penny one full year after the end of the recession. Lags like these raise the concern that by the time many of the projects are implemented, the economy might already be past the point where these projects would have been most useful.

In contrast, taxation-based fiscal policy can sometimes advance more quickly, for example because it doesn't take the Treasury Department long to mail every household a check. Taxation-based policies also have the advantage that the additional spending is done by households themselves so that the money is spent on goods and services that they value. (Government expenditure also *ultimately* puts money in households' pockets, but in the process it may lead to the implementation of projects of negative social value.)

Despite these concerns, expenditure-based policies are still a very useful part of countercyclical strategies. Several expenditure-based policies are not plagued by waste and lags. For example, most economists endorse federal transfers that enable state and local governments to reduce layoffs of teachers, firefighters, and police during recessions. Such countercyclical transfers from the federal government to the states are particularly useful because many states have balanced-budget rules that prevent them from borrowing during a recession. Without federal transfers, states would be forced to lay off many public employees, reducing public services and deepening the recession.

Likewise, most economists endorse infrastructure projects—like repairs to bridges and highways—that have already passed rigorous cost-benefit analysis. Such projects are said to be "shovel ready."

Evidence-Based Economics

Q: How much does government expenditure stimulate GDP?

On December 7, 1941, bombers from six Japanese aircraft carriers attacked the U.S. Pacific fleet. The bombers destroyed or damaged 8 battleships, numerous other ships, and 188 aircraft. The attack on Pearl Harbor catapulted the United States into World War II.

The attack also initiated an enormous increase in war-related spending, including the rebuilding and expansion of the Pacific fleet. A few months *before* the attack, when the United States was not yet a combatant, analysts forecast that preparations for a possible war would cost the United States about $100 billion (1941 dollars). Immediately after the attack, estimates for war-related spending rose to $200 billion. The economic magnitude of these numbers is revealed by comparing this war spending to 1941 GDP, which was $129.4 billion.

Though terrible, wars and the expenditures they trigger can be used to identify the economic effects of government expenditure, as economist Valerie Ramey has shown.[6] She studied 63 years of news articles to identify foreign events that caused a change in U.S. government expenditure. Ramey's data includes many war-related events—like the attack on Pearl Harbor—as well as other events like the surprise launch in 1957 of the Soviet satellite *Sputnik*, the first Earth-orbiting satellite, that sparked the space race between the United States and the Soviet Union. Ramey estimated that the launch of *Sputnik* led to an expansion of $10.3 billion (1957 dollars) in the U.S. government's space program.

Evidence-Based Economics *(Continued)*

On December 7, 1941, Japanese bombers attacked Pearl Harbor, catapulting the United States into World War II and drastically raising the expected level of future government expenditure.

The 1957 launch of *Sputnik*, the first Earth-orbiting satellite, kicked off a space race between the United States and the Soviet Union.

Surprising foreign events that change government expenditure present us with a natural experiment—recall the discussion of natural experiments in Chapter 2. In Ramey's study, a foreign shock causes the government to spend more for reasons unrelated to the state of the economy. She then compared the growth of GDP after these large random spending shocks to the growth of GDP in periods that did not experience such shocks.

Using such comparisons, Ramey estimated a government expenditure multiplier between 0.6 and 1.2. In other words, when the government raises expenditure by $1 (because of a surprising foreign event), GDP increases by an amount between $0.60 and $1.2. The range of possible values is large because we don't have enough historical data to pin down a more precise answer.

Question

How much does government expenditure stimulate GDP?

Answer

In this study, the government expenditure multiplier is estimated to lie between 0.6 and 1.2.

Data

National income and product account data from the United States (1939–2008) and historical news coverage in *Business Week*, the *New York Times*, and the *Washington Post*.

Caveat

Ramey's analysis measures the government expenditure multiplier that arises from expenditures that are mostly war-related. The analysis might underestimate the government expenditure multiplier during periods of economic slack, like recessions.

13.4 Policies That Blur the Line Between Fiscal and Monetary Policy

Some countercyclical policies represent a mix of fiscal and monetary effects. For example, some government expenditures are intended to affect the supply of credit.

The 2008 Troubled Asset Relief Program (TARP) is an example of such a mixed policy. At the peak of the 2007–2009 financial crisis, the U.S. Congress passed emergency legislation authorizing the Treasury Department to spend $700 billion to stabilize the financial system. The Treasury Department is a government agency that resides in the executive branch and therefore is *not* part of the Fed. Nevertheless, the TARP legislation was developed jointly by Fed and Treasury officials and the legislation required that the Fed chairman be consulted during TARP's implementation.

Of the $700 billion in TARP funds, $115 billion was used to increase the capital of the eight largest U.S. banks, which were all *forced* to participate. In essence, the banks were required to issue new shares that the government bought. Some of the banks didn't like this plan, since the government became a partial owner. In addition, all eight banks were obligated to limit the compensation of their senior executives. An additional $135 billion was used to increase the capital of smaller banks that applied for TARP support.

These bank capital infusions—totaling $250 billion—gave the participating banks breathing room, and the financial system as a whole stabilized. The financial system came back from the brink of a devastating financial contagion in which banks were falling like dominos, each failure instigating other failures as banks couldn't repay their debts to one another. TARP funding is now viewed as a successful policy, though there remain questions about whether it played a causal role in rescuing the economy or simply appeared to be successful because of coincidental timing.

The bank capital infusions ended up costing the government little, since the government was repaid after the crisis had passed. In fact, the government made a small profit from its TARP investments in the banks. However, there were many government programs other than TARP that benefited banks, so banks were net recipients of government support.

You might be wondering about the $450 billion of TARP funding that was not used to buy bank shares. Dozens of other programs were funded by TARP, including investments in the bankrupt car companies General Motors and Chrysler and the nearly bankrupt insurance company AIG. When the dust settled, the government was able to recoup most of its investment, and the government's support prevented these important companies from shutting down their operations at the peak of the crisis. Such shutdowns would have aggravated the crisis, leading to an even deeper recession.

We do not know what would have happened without TARP and the other countercyclical fiscal and monetary policies that were adopted during the financial crisis. It would be convenient if we could set up numerous *identical* economies to study macroeconomic policy interventions, just like a laboratory scientist would do. In one economy, we would include TARP. In another otherwise identical economy, we would not. We could then see which economy had better performance. Because economists can't run experiments like that, we are stuck with making judgments based on less than perfect data and models of economic behavior. Though most economists think that TARP was a success, it is impossible to be sure.

Summary

� Countercyclical policies attempt to reduce the intensity of economic fluctuations and smooth the growth rates of employment, GDP, and prices.

✸ Countercyclical monetary policy, which is conducted by the central bank (in the United States, the Fed), attempts to reduce economic fluctuations by manipulating bank reserves and interest rates.

✸ Open market operations refer to the Fed's transactions with private banks to increase or reduce bank reserves held on deposit at the Fed. Open market operations influence the federal funds rate—an increase in the supply of bank reserves lowers the federal funds rate, holding all else equal.

✸ Expansionary monetary policy increases the quantity of bank reserves and lowers interest rates, shifting the labor demand curve to the right and increasing the growth rate of GDP.

✸ Contractionary monetary policy slows down the growth in bank reserves and increases interest rates, shifting the labor demand curve to the left and reducing the growth rate of GDP. Contractionary monetary policy is used when inflation is rising above the Fed's long-run target of 2 percent or when the economy is growing excessively quickly.

✸ Countercyclical fiscal policy, which is passed by the legislative branch and signed into law by the executive branch, reduces economic fluctuations by manipulating government expenditures and taxes.

✸ Countercyclical fiscal policies might be automatic or discretionary. Automatic stabilizers are components of the government budget, like taxes owed, that automatically adjust to smooth out economic fluctuations.

✸ Expansionary fiscal policy uses higher government expenditure and lower taxes to increase GDP, shifting the labor demand curve to the right. Crowding out occurs when rising government expenditure partially (or even fully) displaces expenditures by households and firms.

✸ Contractionary fiscal policy uses lower government expenditure and higher taxes to reduce GDP, shifting the labor demand curve to the left.

✸ Some policies, like the 2008 Troubled Asset Relief Program (TARP), blur the line between monetary policy and fiscal policy.

Key Terms

countercyclical policies *p. 299*
countercyclical monetary policy *p. 299*
countercyclical fiscal policy *p. 299*
expansionary monetary policy *p. 301*

contractionary monetary policy *p. 306*
expansionary fiscal policy *p. 310*
contractionary fiscal policy *p. 310*
automatic stabilizers *p. 311*

government expenditure multiplier
  p. 312
crowding out *p. 313*
government taxation multiplier *p. 314*

Questions

All questions are available in MyEconLab *for practice and instructor assignment.*

1. What are the similarities and the differences between monetary and fiscal policies?

2. How do expansionary policies differ from contractionary policies?

3. Briefly explain how expansionary monetary policy shifts the labor demand curve to the right.

4. What is quantitative easing? Why do central banks undertake quantitative easing programs?

5. Other than open market operations and quantitative easing, what tools does the Federal Reserve use to manipulate interest rates in the economy?

6. Does the effectiveness of monetary policy depend on inflation expectations? Explain.

7. Briefly explain how an increase in the quantity of reserves that commercial banks hold at the Federal Reserve could lead to inflation.

8. How does the zero lower bound on interest rates affect the working of monetary policy?

9. When nominal interest rates have hit the zero lower bound, can central banks use interest rates to stimulate the economy? Explain.

10. What does the Taylor rule state?

11. According to the Taylor rule, when should the Federal Reserve lower or raise the federal funds rate?

12. What are the automatic and discretionary components of fiscal policy?

13. How can expansionary expenditure-based fiscal policy lead to crowding out in the economy?

14. What could explain why a decrease in taxes could lead to a less-than-proportionate increase in output?

15. Why is the Troubled Asset Relief Program (TARP) considered an example of a countercyclical policy that represents a mix of fiscal and monetary effects?

Problems

All problems are available in MyEconLab *for practice and instructor assignment.*

1. The former chairman of the Federal Reserve, Alan Greenspan, used the term "irrational exuberance" in 1996 to describe the high levels of optimism among stock market investors at the time. Stock market indexes such as the S&P Composite Price Index were at an all-time high. Some commentators believed that the Fed should intervene to slow the expansion of the economy. Why would central banks want to clamp down when the economy is growing? What policies could the government and the central bank use to achieve the goal of slowing down the economic expansion?

2. The following figures show the Federal Reserve's balance sheet as well as the balance sheet of a commercial bank, BHZ Bank. Suppose the Federal Reserve wants to lower bank reserves by $1 billion. Assuming that BHZ Bank is willing to transact with the Federal Reserve, show how the Fed's as well as BHZ's balance sheet will change.

The Federal Reserve

Assets		Liabilities and Shareholders' Equity	
Treasury Bonds	$1,500 billion	Reserves	$1,500 billion
Other bonds	$500 billion	Currency	$500 billion
Total assets	**$2,000 billion**	**Total liabilities**	**$2,000 billion**

BHZ Bank

Assets		Liabilities and Shareholders' Equity	
Reserves	$200 billion	Deposits and other liabilities	$700 billion
Bonds and other investments	$800 billion	Shareholders' equity	$300 billion
Total assets	**$1,000 billion**	**Liabilities + shareholders' equity**	**$1,000 billion**

3. Suppose the Fed wants to raise the federal funds rate. Explain the available mechanisms that the Fed can use to achieve this goal. In your answer, use a graph of the money market to show how the Fed's action translates into a higher interest rate.

4. You and a friend are debating the merits of using monetary policy during a severe recession. Your friend says that the central bank needs to lower interest rates all the way down to zero. According to him, zero nominal interest rates will boost lending and investment; consumers and firms will surely borrow and spend when interest rates are zero. Would you agree with his reasoning? How does the level of inflation affect your answer? Explain your conclusions.

5. In the following graph, the dashed line shows what the federal funds rate should have been according to the Taylor rule against the actual federal funds rate. At a symposium of central bankers in 2007, John Taylor, after whom the Taylor rule is named, suggested that if the Fed had been following the Taylor rule, the federal funds rate would have been increasing in 2002 and not falling.

   What is likely to happen if the Fed reduces the federal funds rate when it actually should be increasing it?

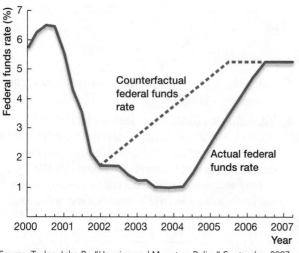

Source: Taylor, John B., "Housing and Monetary Policy" September 2007, http://web.stanford.edu/~johntayl/HousingandMonetaryPolicy--Taylor--JacksonHole2007.pdf

6. The following graph shows actual and projected estimates of potential GDP and GDP. Potential GDP is also a measure of trend GDP. When is the output gap, defined as the percent difference between GDP and potential GDP, negative? According to the Taylor rule, how should a negative output gap affect the federal funds interest rate?

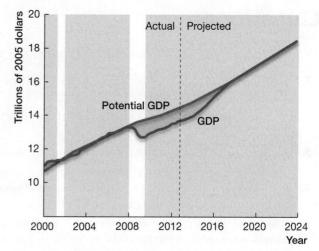

Sources: Congressional Budget Office; Department of Commerce, Bureau of Economic Analysis.

7. Two economists estimate the government expenditure multiplier and come up with different results. One estimates the multiplier at 0.75, while the other comes up with an estimate of 1.25.

   a. What do these different estimates imply about the consequences of government expenditure?

   b. If the current value of GDP is $13.28 trillion and the government is planning to increase spending by $800 billion, what is the percentage increase in GDP for each of the two estimates for the multiplier? Assume the increase in spending occurs all in one year.

8. In 2005, $320 million of the federal government's budget was allocated toward building a "bridge to nowhere" in Alaska that connected two small towns. In 2006, $500,000 was allocated toward a teapot museum in North Carolina, $1 million toward a water-free urinal initiative in Michigan, and $4.5 million toward a museum and park at an abandoned mine in Maine. These projects were requested by specific legislators in order to boost their popularity in their constituencies.

   a. What is this type of expenditure called?

   b. Since government spending increases employment by shifting the labor demand curve to the right, is it always a good idea for the government to increase expenditure? Explain your answer.

9. Milton Friedman, the renowned monetary economist, gave the following analogy about the Fed: "Imagine your house is being heated by a heater. The heater is controlled by a thermostat. The way it's set up, when the house gets a little too warm, the thermostat turns off the heater; if it gets too cold, the thermostat turns the heater back on. If everything

works as planned, the room temperature in the house should roughly be the targeted temperature all the time.

Now suppose the thermostat is not in the same room as the heater. In fact, it's in the last room that is affected by the heater. Say, the attic. And the radiators through which the heater works are really old, and it takes them at least twenty minutes to react. Then, instead of making the temperature more stable, the thermostat would make the temperature swing wildly. For example, if the house is cold, then the thermostat will turn the heater on. But it will turn the heater off only when the attic is warm. By then, the entire house will be scorching hot. When it turns the heater off, it will not turn it back on until the attic is cooler. By then, the house will be freezing."

(In this analogy, the thermostat is the Fed; the house is the entire economy.)

a. What do you think Milton Friedman was trying to say about monetary policy? (*Hint*: You do not need to draw any graphs for this question.)

b. As in the thermostat analogy, what might be some possible unintended consequences of monetary policy? Might there be a similar effect for fiscal policy? If yes, how does it differ from monetary policy?

10. Based on the information in the chapter, discuss the ways in which the 2008 Troubled Asset Relief Program (TARP) had some of the characteristics of monetary policy, and some of the characteristics of fiscal policy.

11. *Challenge Problem.* The chapter mentions that an open market operation by the Fed can increase or decrease the quantity of deposits in banks and therefore the money supply. (See, for example, Exhibit 13.8.)

The expansion in the money supply from a Fed open market operation is given by the following equation (under the simplifying assumption that households don't hold cash so the money supply is equal to demand deposits):

$$\text{Change in money supply} = (\text{Change in reserves}) \times \frac{1}{RR + ER},$$

where RR = the percentage of deposits that banks are required to keep as reserves (expressed as a decimal), and

ER = the percentage of deposits that banks voluntarily hold as excess reserves (expressed as a decimal).

$1/(RR + ER)$ is called the "money multiplier."

Suppose the Fed decides to sell $14 billion in Treasury bonds. Assume that the reserve requirement is 8 percent and banks hold 4 percent in excess reserves, so $RR = 0.08$ and $ER = 0.04$.

What is the total increase or decrease in the money supply that would result from the Fed's action? Explain your answer and show your calculations. Verify that the quantity of new deposits (which is the change in the money supply in this example) is backed up by an adequate quantity of new reserves:

$$(RR + ER) \times (\text{Change in deposits}) = (\text{Change in reserves}).$$

12. *Challenge Problem.* Assume that the public in the small country of Sylvania does not hold any cash. Commercial banks, however, hold 5 percent of their checking deposits as excess reserves, regardless of the interest rate. In the questions that follow, use the "money multiplier" equation from Problem 11.

a. Consider the balance sheet of one of several identical banks:

Assets	Liabilities & Net Worth
Reserves $400	Checking Deposits $2,000
Loans $1,600	Net Worth $0

What is the required reserve ratio in the country of Sylvania?

b. If the total money stock (supply) is $100,000, find the total amount of reserves held in the banking system. Show your work.

c. The Sylvania Central Bank decides that it wants to cut the money stock in half. It is considering an open market operation. How many dollars' worth of bonds should the Central Bank buy or sell? Assume that excess reserves are 5 percent and the required reserve ratio is what you found in part (a). Show your work.

14

Macroeconomics and International Trade

Are companies like Nike harming workers in Vietnam?

Consumers love sneakers. Nike alone sells approximately $15 billion of them each year. Nike conducts much of its production in places like Vietnam, using subcontractors that employ workers with little education who are paid around $4–$5 per day. Some subcontractors even employ children, although it is illegal to do so and Nike officially bans such practices. Employees in many of these factories put in 60-hour work weeks with working conditions that do not come close to meeting U.S. and European safety standards. Critics denounce such sweatshops and student groups have occasionally advocated boycotts of Nike products. Prodded by these protestors, Nike has tried to clean up its act. Even though the Nike subcontractors still pay very little, the factories have become much safer over the past 20 years.

This situation is just the tip of the iceberg of low wages and poor working conditions throughout parts of the interconnected global economy. U.S. consumers are some of the beneficiaries of this trade. Are consumers to blame for buying sneakers manufactured in sweatshops?

CHAPTER **OUTLINE**

⚙ International trade enables countries to focus on activities in which they have a comparative advantage.

⚙ The current account includes international flows from exports, imports, factor payments, and transfers.

⚙ If a country runs a current account deficit, it pays for this by giving its trading partners financial IOUs. If a country runs a current account surplus, it receives financial IOUs from its trading partners.

⚙ The world has become more globalized over the past several decades.

14.1 Why and How We Trade

Trade, both within and between countries, enhances our quality of life by increasing the efficiency of production. In modern economies, goods and services are produced by individuals who specialize in their production. For example, your professor spent years mastering economics. Similarly, the engineers who work for Apple have extensive training in their particular line of work.

An Apple engineer can't produce insightful economics research or teach an economics course. Likewise, an economics professor can't design a miniaturized circuit board and a high throughput factory to manufacture it. In a market system, people choose occupations that suit their talents and interests. Then they develop specialized skills in their chosen industry and trade with others. Trade exploits **gains from specialization**, which are the economic gains that society obtains by having some workers specialize in specific productive activities.

Specialization won't work without trade. Economics professors can't eat economic ideas or live in them. Economists teach, and then get paid with money, and then use the money to buy food and shelter. Apple engineers love the iPhone, but they can't sleep on it or drive it to work. Engineers get paid so they can buy what they want.

Without opportunities for trade, life is bleak. If your economics professor were stranded on an island, he or she would have no students to teach and no policymakers to advise. The professor would have little or no way to put economic knowledge to use. Despite all of that knowledge, day-to-day life would resemble that of a Stone Age hunter-gatherer.

Gains from specialization are the economic gains that society can obtain by having some individuals, regions, or countries specialize in the production of certain goods and services.

> **Without opportunities for trade, life is bleak.**

Absolute Advantage and Comparative Advantage

To gain a deeper understanding of how trade works, consider the late Steve Jobs, the visionary chief executive officer (CEO) of Apple. Jobs was famous for being a great marketer and a brilliant designer.

Because of his knowledge of and love for Apple products, Jobs was a much better salesperson than most of Apple's employees. To illustrate this point, let's assume that Jobs could sell twice as many computers (per time period) compared to the typical Apple storeclerk. In this sense, Jobs had an *absolute advantage* at selling

An economy without trade wasn't great for this castaway.

Exhibit 14.1 Productivity in Sales and Design		Steve Jobs	Chuck Chores
	Sales	2,000 sales/year	1,000 sales/year
	Design	1,000 design ideas/year	1 design idea/year

A producer has an **absolute advantage** in producing a good or service if the producer can produce more units per hour than other producers.

A producer has a **comparative advantage** in producing a good (or service) when the producer has a lower opportunity cost per unit produced compared to other producers.

computers. A producer has an **absolute advantage** in producing a good or service if the producer can produce more units per hour than other producers.

Of course, selling computers isn't the only skill that Jobs had. As CEO, he *designed* revolutionary new products. Relative to a typical salesclerk, Jobs was a superstar designer. Let's assume that if Jobs allocated his time to design, he would generate 1,000 design ideas per year. If a typical salesclerk worked on design, he would generate only one design idea per year.

Let's give the typical Apple salesclerk a name: Chuck Chores. Exhibit 14.1 reports the estimated productivity of Jobs in the first column of data and the estimated productivity of Chores in the final column.

By looking across the rows of Exhibit 14.1, we see that Jobs has an absolute advantage in both tasks: Jobs was capable of producing twice as many sales per year (relative to Chores) and Jobs was capable of producing 1,000 times as many useful design ideas per year (relative to Chores). Which task should Apple have asked him to do?

To answer this question, let's calculate the opportunity cost *per unit of production* or, more precisely, the opportunity cost of a design idea in terms of forgone sales. This calculation will answer the following question: how many sales are given up to produce a design idea? A worker has a *comparative advantage* in design when the opportunity cost of the worker's design idea is lower than the opportunity cost of other workers' design ideas. More generally, a worker has a **comparative advantage** in producing a good (or service) when he has a lower opportunity cost per unit produced compared to other producers.

Exhibit 14.1 implies that Steve Jobs forgoes 2,000 sales for every 1,000 design ideas that he generates, or $2,000/1,000 = 2$ forgone sales per design idea. On the other hand, Chuck Chores forgoes 1,000 sales for every design idea that he generates.

With that calculation in mind, we can determine how production should be optimally organized. Apple can produce design ideas by allocating Jobs to design, with an opportunity cost of 2 forgone sales per design idea. Or Apple can produce design ideas from Chores with an opportunity cost of 1,000 forgone sales per design idea. Since Jobs has a lower opportunity cost for *each* design idea (2 forgone sales for Jobs versus 1,000 forgone sales for Chores), Jobs has a *comparative advantage in design ideas*. Hence, Apple should allocate Jobs to work on design and Chores to work on sales (as long as it needs both types of activities).

You can verify that the same conclusion would have been reached if we calculated the opportunity cost of a sale in terms of forgone design ideas. Using Exhibit 14.1, we find that Jobs forgoes 1,000 design ideas for every 2,000 sales. Because $1,000/2,000 = ½$, Jobs has an opportunity cost of ½ forgone design idea per sale. Chores forgoes 1 design idea for every 1,000 sales, so Chores has an opportunity cost of 1/1,000 forgone design idea per sale. Because Chores has the lower opportunity cost per sale, he should be the one doing sales and Jobs should work on design.

Comparative advantage is the idea that *opportunity cost, not absolute advantage, should be used to determine which producer is assigned to which task*. Just relying on absolute advantage would not have been sufficient for Apple to determine whether Jobs should work in design or in sales: Jobs has an absolute advantage in working as a salesclerk *and* he has an absolute advantage in working as a designer.

Until now, we have assumed that the work allocation decision is being made by Apple. Although such decisions are sometimes made by corporations, in practice they are often the result of choices that individuals make for themselves. Jobs himself decided to found Apple and work as a designer, while many individuals such as Chores apply to become salesclerks, not designers. Why is this?

The career choices that individuals make are also a consequence of comparative advantage, but, in this case, the key economic signals are market prices. In fact, one of the powerful implications of comparative advantage is that market prices will induce individuals to choose occupations and activities that line up with their comparative advantage.

To see this, suppose that Jobs and Chores sell their skills in a competitive labor market in which their wages are equal to their (personal) contribution to value added (recall from Chapter 5 that value added is defined as a firm's sales revenue minus the firm's purchases of intermediate products from other firms). To simplify the analysis, suppose that the economy consists *only* of workers like Jobs and Chores and that the economy needs both design and sales functions to be performed. We will now see that equilibrium prices must be such that workers with productivity similar to Jobs will choose to work in design and those with productivity similar to Chores will choose to work in sales.

Let's start by assuming that the prices in this economy are such that the value added from each computer sale is $50 and the value added from each design idea is also $50. If you multiply output in Exhibit 14.1 by value added per task, you'll generate the results in panel (a) of Exhibit 14.2. These numbers imply that both Jobs and Chores will maximize their own wages if they work in sales: $100,000 for Jobs in sales versus $50,000 for Jobs in design; $50,000 for Chores in sales versus $50 for Chores in design. Hence, workers like Jobs and workers like Chores will both work in sales. But this cannot be a market equilibrium because the economy needs both functions—design and sales—to be performed. If everyone is working in sales, there will be no design ideas in this economy, pushing the value added from design much higher than $50 (there would be a shortage of design, raising the relative wages of designers).

What happens if market prices for design become much higher so that value added from each design idea now shoots up to $100,000 (holding fixed value added from sales at $50)? The resulting wages are shown in panel (b) of Exhibit 14.2. Now we have a situation in which both Jobs and Chores have higher wages in design, thus all workers in this economy will now choose design careers. But this also cannot be a market equilibrium. Now there will be no sales in the economy and a lot of design ideas. Yet again the economy needs both functions to be performed, and this will push the relative wages of salespeople higher.

You have probably already guessed that equilibrium prices will need to settle somewhere between these two extremes. Equilibrium prices should induce some people to do design and some others to do sales. Take another combination of values: $50 of value added per sale and $5,000 of value added per design idea. The resulting wages are shown in panel (c) of Exhibit 14.2. At these wages, it is clear that Chores will choose to work in sales while Jobs focuses on design. Indeed, at these wages Jobs would be greatly misallocating his time if he worked as a salesclerk.

The key insight is that market prices will adjust so that individuals choose occupations consistent with their comparative advantages. This is the sense in which trade in the market supports and reinforces comparative advantage. In fact, without such trade we could not realize the gains from comparative advantage. For example, it is trade that allowed Steve Jobs to hire other people to work as salesclerks in Apple stores, enabling him to focus on his comparative advantage: designing the next beautiful gizmo that everyone wants to have.

At this point, you might be curious about whether one could have picked a value added for each sale and a value added for each design that would make Jobs choose sales while Chores would prefer to do design. Comparative advantage implies that the answer is no.

Exhibit 14.2 Wages in Sales and Design

(a) With Value Added of $50 from Sales and $50 from Design		Steve Jobs	Chuck Chores
	Sales	$100,000/year	$50,000/year
	Design	$50,000/year	$50/year

(b) With Value Added of $50 from Sales and $100,000 from Design		Steve Jobs	Chuck Chores
	Sales	$100,000/year	$50,000/year
	Design	$100,000,000/year	$100,000/year

(c) With Value Added of $50 from Sales and $5,000 from Design		Steve Jobs	Chuck Chores
	Sales	$100,000/year	$50,000/year
	Design	$5,000,000/year	$5,000/year

Steve Jobs, Apple's most productive salesclerk.

If their different opportunity costs lead Jobs and Chores to choose different tasks, comparative advantage always implies it will be Jobs who earns more in design than in sales, and Chores who earns more in sales than in design.

Comparative Advantage and International Trade

To illustrate how *international* trade exploits comparative advantage—much like the division of labor between Steve Jobs and Chuck Chores—consider a particular Apple product, the iPod. In some sense, the iPod is a U.S. product—designed by engineers in the United States by a company headquartered in the United States. However, it is not actually manufactured in the United States. Each iPod is composed of hundreds of parts, most of which are manufactured and assembled outside the United States.

Let's consider some of the key components. The iPod has a hard drive where the songs and videos and photos are stored. This is produced in Japan. It also has a memory card, which is produced in Korea. The central processing unit, on the other hand, is produced in the United States. Specialization explains this proliferation of locations. For example, the Japanese company Toshiba specializes in hard drive manufacturing and has become a world leader in the production of tiny hard drives with very low failure rates. Gains from specialization are realized by delegating production of two of these three key parts to manufacturers outside the United States. Finally, all of the components are combined into the final product on a Chinese assembly line.[1]

Comparative advantage in international trade explains why Chinese workers assemble iPods, even though U.S. workers have an absolute advantage in assembly. Let's begin by considering the hourly productivity of U.S. and Chinese workers in different tasks. For the moment, we'll assume that in terms of their productivity, the U.S. workers are all identical to one another and the Chinese workers are also all identical to one another—a simplifying assumption that we'll revisit later in the chapter.

The first row of Exhibit 14.3 shows that a U.S. worker would assemble 20,000 iPods per year, which is 15,000 more than a Chinese worker would assemble. The difference between U.S. and Chinese workers in their productivity arises for a variety of reasons. Workers in the United States currently have relatively more education and thus greater *human capital* (recall from Chapter 6 that human capital is each person's stock of ability to produce output or economic value). This greater human capital makes U.S. workers more productive in a range of tasks. In addition, U.S. workers currently have access to more physical capital per worker and better technology—for instance, robotic assembly lines—than their Chinese counterparts.

Consider another task, which we refer to as research and development, or R&D. We assume that U.S. workers generate 10 R&D innovations per year. We assume that Chinese workers, who currently don't have as much education as U.S. workers, would be much less effective at this, and we assume that their productivity in R&D is 1 innovation per year.

Looking across the rows in Exhibit 14.3, we see that U.S. workers have an absolute advantage in both assembly and R&D. Considering only absolute advantage, it's tempting to guess that both assembly and R&D should be performed in the United States. But this is the wrong conclusion for the same reason that Steve Jobs shouldn't have been working as a salesclerk.

To determine the optimal allocation across industries, we again need to use the concepts of opportunity cost and comparative advantage. We can verify that U.S. workers have a comparative advantage in R&D. Their productivity in assembly relative to R&D is 20,000/10 = 2,000/1. In other words, U.S. workers forgo the assembly of 2,000 iPods for every R&D innovation they generate. Chinese workers' productivity in assembly relative to R&D is 5,000/1. Chinese workers forgo the assembly of 5,000 iPods for

Exhibit 14.3 Productivity in Assembly and R&D (Research and Development)		U.S. Worker	Chinese Worker
	Assembly	20,000 iPods/year	5,000 iPods/year
	Research and Development	10 innovations/year	1 innovation/year

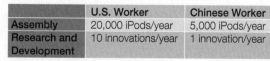

Exhibit 14.4 Wages in Assembly and R&D		U.S. Worker	Chinese Worker
	Assembly	$30,000/year	$7,500/year
	Research and Development	$50,000/year	$5,000/year

14.1

14.2

14.3

every R&D innovation they generate. The U.S. workers thus have a lower opportunity cost per R&D innovation (2,000 forgone iPod assemblies) compared to Chinese workers (5,000 forgone iPod assemblies). This implies that U.S. workers have a comparative advantage in R&D and should focus on R&D, while Chinese workers should (currently) specialize in assembly.

To further illustrate the allocation of tasks between U.S. and Chinese workers, suppose that workers in both economies are paid the value added they generate and that the value added from each iPod assembly is $1.50 and the value added from each R&D innovation is $5,000. If you multiply output in Exhibit 14.3 by value added per task, you'll generate the results in Exhibit 14.4, which describes annual wages of U.S. and Chinese workers in assembly and R&D.

iPod assembly line in China.

Looking at Exhibit 14.4, you can see that the U.S. worker will choose to specialize in R&D and the Chinese worker will specialize in assembly. In fact, for the same reasons that we highlighted in our discussion of the allocation problem of Steve Jobs and Chuck Chores, value added and market prices cannot be such that both U.S. and Chinese workers all have greater value added in assembly or such that they all have greater value added in R&D, because otherwise the world economy would not generate *both* iPod assemblies and R&D ideas. Given the current pattern of comparative advantage (in R&D for U.S. workers and in iPod assembly for Chinese workers), if these workers are choosing different tasks, then it must be the case that it is the U.S. workers who are specializing in R&D and the Chinese workers who are working in assembly.

As in our earlier example, trade is essential to achieve an efficient allocation of resources. If there were no international trade, then U.S. workers would end up spending less time on R&D and more time on assembly, lowering the value of their total output.

Efficiency and Winners and Losers from Trade

By exploiting comparative advantage, international trade increases overall economic efficiency. For example, if Apple could not assemble iPods in foreign countries, it would have to do so in the United States, and the cost of making an iPod would rise. As a result, iPods would likely cost 10 percent or 20 percent more than they do now. Consumers benefit from international trade and the resulting international division of labor.

At this point you might wonder whether foreign iPod production prevents the United States from benefiting from its own innovation. How much of the value added from iPod manufacturing goes to foreign producers and not to the iPod's U.S. inventors? Of course, even if all of the value added went to foreign workers, U.S. consumers would still benefit from the low cost of an iPod. But is a low retail price the only benefit that U.S. residents receive?

A study by economists Greg Linden, Kenneth Kraemer, and Jason Dedrick shows that a large part of the retail price of an iPod is ultimately received by U.S. residents.[2] For iPods sold in the United States through a retailer other than Apple, 41 percent of the value added is generated by U.S. firms other than Apple, including distributors, retailers, and component manufacturers with domestic production facilities. Another 45 percent of the value added goes to Apple, the company that designed the iPod and owns the intellectual property rights. These are not just corporate earnings, since Apple has a large team of in-house engineers, designers, and executives whose salaries are paid with Apple's revenues.

The example of the iPod illustrates that international trade contributes to value added in the United States as well as low prices for U.S. consumers.

The iPod story is not unusual. Other products confirm the same pattern of widely shared benefits from trade. For example, Hewlett-Packard's laptop computers are assembled in low-wage countries like China and Brazil. Nevertheless, over half of the value added from the production of these laptops accrues to residents of the United States.

> **Though international trade achieves a more efficient allocation of resources . . . in any given instance, trade will produce some winners and some losers.**

This doesn't mean that everybody gains from trade. Though international trade achieves a more efficient allocation of resources and creates potential gains for society as a whole, in any given instance, trade will produce some winners and some losers. We can see this by going back to the issue of U.S.-China trade. When we discussed the gains from exploiting comparative advantage, we talked of the typical U.S. worker. In practice, of course, the United States isn't inhabited by "typical" U.S. workers, but by some U.S. workers with high levels of skill, and others with low levels of skill and a comparative advantage in assembly. International trade causes routine assembly jobs to move to developing countries like China, and as a result, there are many fewer assembly jobs performed in the United States today than three decades ago. If they can no longer find assembly jobs, those U.S. workers with a comparative advantage in assembly are made worse off by the outsourcing of assembly jobs to countries like China. This is illustrated by our Evidence-Based Economics feature in Chapter 9, which showed how workers in areas specializing in products competing with Chinese imports have experienced employment losses.

When considering the consequences of opening a country to free international trade, it is important to recognize that within that country there will be winners and losers. The efficiencies achieved by exploiting comparative advantage and specialization are so great that the winners will be far more numerous than the losers. In principle, the winners could compensate the losers so that everyone would be better off as a result of free trade. In practice, however, this is usually not possible, because it is hard for the government to identify how much each person has gained or lost as a consequence of international trade. Hence, the government can't compensate the losers with targeted individual subsidies. With imperfect targeting or no compensating redistribution by the government, many people do end up on the losing side of the ledger. Nevertheless, because many more end up on the winning side, open international trade still tends to be favored by economists.

How We Trade

To realize the gains from comparative advantage and specialization, the United States and China need to trade goods and services. This takes the form of *imports* and *exports*. Recall from Chapter 5 that imports refer to the goods and services that are produced abroad and sold domestically, and exports are the goods and services that are produced domestically and sold abroad. Thus exports from the United States to China are China's imports from the United States.

A **closed economy** does not trade with the rest of the world.

In theory it is possible for a country not to have any exports or imports. Such a country that doesn't trade—that is, does not have any imports or exports—is said to be a **closed economy**. Today, not a single country has an entirely closed economy, but North Korea, a totalitarian dictatorship with mostly closed borders, comes the closest.

An **open economy** trades freely with the rest of the world.

An **open economy** allows international trade, and in most countries such trade amounts to a significant share of GDP. For example, in 2012, the United Kingdom's imports equaled 34 percent of GDP, double the import share in the United States. But neither country could compete with Hong Kong and Singapore, which each had 2012 imports equaling about 200 percent of GDP. Hong Kong and Singapore have such large import shares since many of their imports are later re-exported with only modest value added domestically. For example, if a country imports $200 of electronic parts and assembles them into a $250 smart phone, then the value added is just $50. In this illustrative example, imports are 4 times the level of GDP (because only value added is counted in GDP). If the assembled phone is later exported, then exports ($250) are 5 times the level of value added.

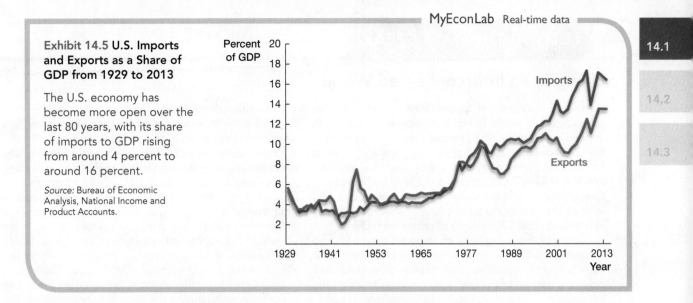

Exhibit 14.5 U.S. Imports and Exports as a Share of GDP from 1929 to 2013

The U.S. economy has become more open over the last 80 years, with its share of imports to GDP rising from around 4 percent to around 16 percent.

Source: Bureau of Economic Analysis, National Income and Product Accounts.

Exhibit 14.5 depicts the evolution of U.S. imports and exports as a share of GDP since 1929. In 1950, imports amounted to 4 percent of GDP. In 2013, the import share was 16 percent. Economically speaking, the United States is now more closely linked to the rest of the world than at any other period in U.S. history.

The increase in imports and exports as a share of GDP is not confined to the United States. Most major economies in the world have been trading more over the last 50 years. Exhibit 14.6 plots the evolution of imports as a share of GDP for Germany, China, India, and the world average, as well as the United States.

Trade Barriers: Tariffs

Because international trade creates winners and losers, there are some opponents to trade. As a result, most countries, including the United States, impose a host of *trade barriers* that reduce their imports. The most common restrictions are tariffs, which are special taxes levied only on imports.

The average U.S. tariff on all imported products was 2.8 percent in 2011, down from over 5 percent in 1990. The average 2011 tariff of 2.8 percent masked an enormous amount of variation across industries. In recent years, the average U.S. tariff on agricultural products has been 62 percent. Tariffs on tobacco have run to approximately 90 percent, while tariffs on sugar have been even higher, sometimes exceeding 100 percent. Such tariffs naturally

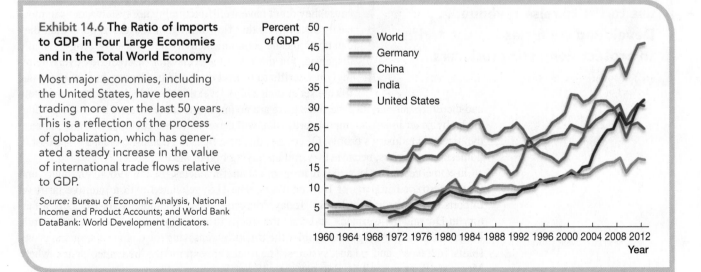

Exhibit 14.6 The Ratio of Imports to GDP in Four Large Economies and in the Total World Economy

Most major economies, including the United States, have been trading more over the last 50 years. This is a reflection of the process of globalization, which has generated a steady increase in the value of international trade flows relative to GDP.

Source: Bureau of Economic Analysis, National Income and Product Accounts; and World Bank DataBank: World Development Indicators.

LETTING THE DATA SPEAK

Living in an Interconnected World

Given the importance of specialization and comparative advantage, the world is highly interconnected through imports and exports. The first and most obvious facet of this interconnection is the array of goods and services we consume. Look at the shelves of your local Walmart and you will find an enormous number of items made in China, Mexico, and Brazil. Two-thirds of the goods sold in Walmart are imported. For example, Walmart annually imports over $30 billion worth of goods from China.

Check out the geography of trade whenever you go shopping. You'll be amazed at the range of countries that manufacture the goods you buy. You may think of Pakistan only as a hotbed of political and religious unrest on the border of Afghanistan. Pakistan also happens to manufacture *half* of the world's hand-stitched soccer balls. Pakistan is also an important exporter of textiles and clothing. Look at the latest fashions on display at Banana Republic or Old Navy, and you will see that much of this clothing is produced in India, Indonesia, Turkey, and Vietnam.

Many people mistakenly believe that international trade can only flow in goods. Services, however, are also getting into the act. In 2013, the United States imported $453 billion in services and exported $682 billion in services. The next time you call a computer company for advice about removing a virus or upgrading software, ask the technician where he or she is located. There's a good chance you are speaking to someone in India, where service representatives carefully hone American accents and adopt American names during working hours. Carol Miller might be Bhumika Chaturvedi.

Many of the services that now flow across international boundaries are very sophisticated. The United States exports entertainment services—music and movies—and financial services—financial advice given by a New York investment bank to an oil exploration company in Brazil.

Even medical services can be traded internationally. An Indian radiologist—a physician specializing in reading X-rays—earns one-eighth of a U.S. radiologist's income. So an Indian radiologist has a lower opportunity cost of time than a U.S. radiologist. There is a small group of Indian teleradiologists who read X-rays for hospitals in the United States, United Kingdom, and Singapore. Here's how it works. A patient who is a resident of the United Kingdom has an X-ray taken at a U.K. hospital. The images are uploaded to a teleradiologist in Bangalore, India. The teleradiologist examines the X-ray for abnormalities, like tumors, writes a report, and then sends it back to the patient's U.K. physician.

> **Some developing countries use tariffs to raise revenue. . . . Developed countries . . . use tariffs to protect domestic producers.**

discourage international trade. Due to tariffs and trade barriers, U.S. sugar imports have fallen 80 percent over the last 30 years.

Some *developing* countries use tariffs to raise revenue, because they don't have well-functioning tax systems and can more easily tax imports that flow through a few urban ports than they can tax domestic economic activity that is widely geographically dispersed. On the other hand, *developed* countries overwhelmingly use tariffs to protect domestic producers. In fact, some tariffs are set at such a high level that they block imports completely and therefore raise no revenue since there are no imports to tax. Powerful domestic producers lobby governments to impose tariffs that will drive out foreign competition and increase the domestic industry's profits. Of course, this benefit to the domestic industry is a cost to domestic consumers, because they end up paying higher prices.

In some cases, trade wars create comical inefficiencies. In the 1960s, Germany and France restricted imports of U.S. chickens. The U.S. retaliated with a punitive tariff on imports of European light trucks. Today, Mercedes-Benz assembles light trucks at a factory in Dusseldorf, Germany and tests the trucks to verify that they drive properly. Then Mercedes-Benz partially disassembles the trucks by removing the engines, bumpers, driveshafts, fuel tanks, and exhaust systems. The trucks are exported to the United States, where Mercedes-Benz doesn't need to pay the U.S. tariff, because the trucks aren't fully assembled. At a warehouse in South Carolina, the disassembled parts are screwed on again.[3]

Tariffs and Votes

In March 2002, President George W. Bush imposed 8 percent to 30 percent tariffs on steel imports. The move was widely viewed as a political decision to shore up support among industrial states that might switch party allegiance in the November midterm election. If you ran for office, would you do the same thing, even if you believe in the benefits of trade?

The U.S. trade representative, Robert B. Zoellick, even admitted during a speech in Brazil that political calculations had motivated the new tariffs: "We are committed to moving forward with free trade, but, like Brazil, we have to manage political support for free trade at home. We have to create coalitions." The administration maintained the tariffs despite a flood of world-wide criticism and threats among many countries to erect punitive tariffs in response. One month after the U.S. election, the administration reversed itself and removed the tariffs.[4]

14.2 The Current Account and the Financial Account

In 2013, U.S. imports amounted to $2,746 billion. Of this amount, $456 billion was imported from China. In most years, approximately 1/7th of U.S. imports come from China.

In 2013, the United States exported goods and services worth $2,271 billion. That year, U.S. exports to China were $157 billion. Approximately 1/20th of U.S. exports go to China.

To some pundits, the fact that the United States imports more from China than it exports to China is a sign of a serious problem. However, there is no reason to expect that U.S. exports to China should equal U.S. imports from China, in the same way that there is no reason to expect your own purchases from the grocery store to equal the grocery store owner's purchases from you. If you own a Ford dealership and the grocery store owner loves Cadillacs, then you'll never get a dollar of her business. But that's OK as long as there are other people who are interested in buying your Fords.

That's generally the way that markets and exchanges work. There is no need to sell our goods and services to the same people from whom we buy goods and services. Now apply that idea to a national economy. There is nothing necessarily wrong with the fact that the United States as a whole sells relatively little *to* China and still buys a lot *from* China. There are other countries, like Brazil, to which the United States sells lots of stuff and from which the United States buys relatively little. These facts lead us to the observation that trade between two specific countries—also referred to as bilateral trade—will rarely be balanced. This does not imply that there is absolutely *nothing* wrong with the United States–China trade relationship, but these arguments do imply that a bilateral trade imbalance is not necessarily a bad thing.

Trade Surpluses and Trade Deficits

There is another important sense in which trade can be imbalanced. Sometimes a country imports more or less than it exports to the world as a whole. We'll see that even this imbalance can also be socially desirable, though it depends on the reasons for the trade imbalance.

When a country as a whole imports more from abroad than it exports abroad, the country runs a trade deficit. This is a case of spending on imports more than the country earns from exports. Exports minus imports is defined as **net exports** or the **trade balance**. When the trade balance is positive, it is referred to as a **trade surplus**. When the trade balance is negative, it is called a **trade deficit**. In 2013, U.S. net exports were negative, so the United States ran a trade deficit:

$$\text{Net exports} = \text{Exports} - \text{Imports}$$
$$= \$2{,}271 \text{ billion} - \$2{,}746 \text{ billion} = -\$475 \text{ billion}.$$

Net exports are the value of the country's exports minus the value of its imports. Net exports are also known as the **trade balance**.

A **trade surplus** is an excess of exports over imports and is thus the name given to the trade balance when it is positive.

A **trade deficit** is an excess of imports over exports and is thus the name given to the trade balance when it is negative.

International Financial Flows

It might appear that knowing the value of the trade balance is sufficient for understanding how payments flow from one country to another. However, a complete understanding of international financial flows requires more details. We need to study *all* the sources of payments from foreign residents to domestic residents, and all the sources of payments from domestic residents to foreign residents. Trade flows represent only *one* source of these financial payments.

The international accounting system is built upon the concept of residency, not the concept of citizenship. In this accounting system, domestic *residents* are people who reside in the United States, whether or not they are U.S. citizens. So a Japanese citizen living in the United States is defined as a domestic resident of the United States in the official international trade accounts. Residents of foreign countries—we'll call them "foreigners"—are people who reside outside the United States (some of whom are U.S. citizens living abroad).

Income-Based Payments from Foreigners Let's start with income-based payments from foreigners. There are three ways that domestic residents receive income-based payments from foreigners:

1. Receiving payments from the sale of goods and services to foreigners—*exports*
2. Receiving income from assets that the domestic resident owns in foreign countries—*factor payments from foreigners*
3. Receiving transfers from individuals who reside abroad or from foreign governments—*transfers from foreigners*

Recall that *exports* are the goods and services that domestic residents produce and then sell in foreign countries. When a foreign resident receives these goods and services, he directly or indirectly makes a payment to the domestic resident who produced them.

Factor payments from foreigners represent the payments that domestic residents receive from assets owned in foreign countries. For example, if a U.S. resident owns stock in Tata Steel, one of the largest companies in India, and Tata Steel pays a dividend, that dividend payment would count as a factor payment from abroad. Likewise, if a U.S. company owns a plant in China and that plant generates earnings, those earnings would count as a factor payment from abroad. Or, if a U.S. engineer who *resides* in the United States spends a day working in Turin, Italy, where she consults for Fiat, the payment that she receives from Fiat would count as a factor payment from abroad. In this consulting example, the relevant factor of production is human capital.

Transfers from foreigners are "gifts" from foreign residents or foreign governments. For example, following Hurricane Katrina in 2005, China sent 104 tons of emergency supplies to New Orleans, including tents and generators, valued at $5 million. All told, foreign governments and citizens of foreign countries sent hundreds of millions of dollars of aid to support the victims of Hurricane Katrina; contributions like these are transfers from abroad.

Income-Based Payments to Foreigners There are also similar types of financial flows that move in the opposite direction. We now list all of the sources of income-based payments *to* foreigners:

1. Making payments to foreigners in return for their goods and services—*imports*
2. Paying income on assets that foreign residents own in the domestic economy—*factor payments to foreigners*
3. Making transfers to individuals who reside abroad or to foreign governments—*transfers to foreigners*

Imports are the goods and services that foreigners produce and then sell to domestic residents. *Factor payments to foreigners* represent the payments made to foreigners who own assets in the domestic economy. *Transfers to foreigners* are "gifts," which include foreign aid from the U.S. government, donations from U.S. citizens to foreign charitable organizations, and remittances from legal and illegal residents of the United States. For example, a Mexican citizen who permanently resides in the United States and periodically transfers money back to family members in Mexico is making a transfer to foreigners. In this case, the transfer is just the money that is sent to family members in Mexico, and not the total earnings that the Mexican citizen receives for work that she does in the United States.

The Workings of the Current Account and the Financial Account

The **current account** is the sum of net exports, net factor payments from abroad, and net transfers from abroad.

The **current account** adds together these different sources of payments into and out of a country. It consists of the sum of net exports, net factor payments from abroad, and net transfers from abroad.

$$\text{Net exports} = (\text{Payments from abroad for exports}) \\ - (\text{Payments to foreigners for imports})$$

$$\text{Net factor payments from abroad} = (\text{Factor payments from abroad}) \\ - (\text{Factor payments to foreigners})$$

$$\text{Net transfers from abroad} = (\text{Transfers from abroad}) - (\text{Transfers to foreigners})$$

The current account is the net flow of payments made to domestic residents from foreign residents.

$$\text{Current Account} = (\text{Net exports}) + (\text{Net factor payments from abroad}) \\ + (\text{Net transfers from abroad}).$$

It is important to bear in mind that any of these net flows could be *negative,* which would correspond to a net flow of payments *to* foreign residents. In fact, in 2013, the United States did run a current account deficit of $379 billion. In other words, U.S. residents paid foreigners $379 billion more than foreigners paid U.S. residents.

Exhibit 14.7 breaks down the current account deficit for the United States in 2013 into its three components. The current account is shown in the top box. We'll discuss the bottom box—the financial account—a bit later. Focusing on the top box, we can see that trade in goods and services led to net payments of $475 billion to foreigners. Factor payments led to net payments of $229 billion from foreigners to U.S. residents. Finally, net transfer payments led to net payments to foreigners of $133 billion. Adding these up, and remembering to use a negative sign when net payments are made to foreigners, we come up with a total current account *deficit* of $379 billion.

MyEconLab Real-time data

	Payments from Foreigners	Payments to Foreigners	Net Payments
Trade in goods and services	2,271	2,746	−475
Factor payments	789	560	229
Transfer payments			−133
Current account			−379
Financial account			379

Exhibit 14.7 The Current Account and the Financial Account of the United States in 2013 (in Billions of 2013 Dollars)

The current account (top box in red) is the sum of net exports, net factor payments from abroad, and net transfers from abroad. (The U.S. government does not break down transfer payments into gross flows, so only the net flow is reported here.) The financial account mirrors the current account and represents the change in IOUs resulting from current account transactions.

Source: Bureau of Economic Analysis, National Income and Product Accounts.

What are the consequences of running a current account deficit? When U.S. residents make $379 billion of net payments to foreigners, the payments are made in U.S. dollars. These dollars enable the foreign residents to buy U.S. assets, which can be exchanged for U.S. goods and services at some point in the future.

To understand what this means in practice, consider a simple current account transaction that we illustrate in Exhibit 14.8. Suppose a U.S. consumer decides to buy a Chinese laptop that costs $1,000. In effect, the U.S. consumer gives the Chinese laptop manufacturer $1,000. In the U.S. current account, this amount would show up as a $1,000 payment to foreigners. Exhibit 14.8 illustrates this current account transaction by showing the purchase of the $1,000 laptop.

Now suppose that there is *no* offsetting transaction in which China buys goods and services from the United States, so the $1,000 payment can be thought of as a current account deficit. Instead of importing $1,000 of goods and services from the United States, China saves the $1,000, thereby preserving that purchasing power for *future* purchases of goods and services. For example, the Chinese company could use the $1,000 to buy a specific U.S. asset from U.S. residents, for instance a U.S. Treasury bond. This is the case depicted in the circular flow of Exhibit 14.8.

Let's summarize the flows in Exhibit 14.8. At the end of the international transactions depicted here, the United States has one new laptop and owns one less Treasury bond. In the current account, the U.S. has imported goods worth $1,000. In the **financial account**, the U.S. has transferred to China a Treasury bond worth $1,000. The financial account is defined as the increase in domestic assets held by foreigners minus the increase in foreign assets held domestically. The financial account is just the accounting system that records the asset purchases that domestic residents and foreigners make. The financial account is defined so that *the net flows in the financial account offset the net flows in the current account.* (To keep the analysis simple, we have omitted a few other details in the accounting rules.)

The following two equations give the definition of the financial account and describe its relationship with the current account:

The **financial account** is the increase in domestic assets held by foreigners minus the increase in foreign assets held domestically.

$$\text{Financial account} = (\text{Increase in domestic assets held by foreigners})$$
$$- (\text{Increase in foreign assets held domestically}).$$

$$(\text{Current account}) + (\text{Financial account}) = 0.$$

When foreigners receive net payments in the current account, they can buy any type of U.S. asset in the financial account. In the example that we already discussed, they bought U.S. Treasury bonds. But they could also just hold the payment in dollars (in a bank account) as a claim against the United States. In either case, the current account deficit is exactly offset by a financial account surplus.

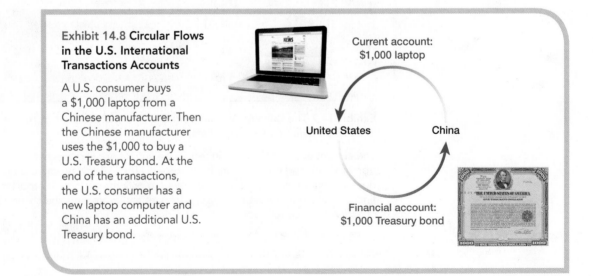

Exhibit 14.8 Circular Flows in the U.S. International Transactions Accounts

A U.S. consumer buys a $1,000 laptop from a Chinese manufacturer. Then the Chinese manufacturer uses the $1,000 to buy a U.S. Treasury bond. At the end of the transactions, the U.S. consumer has a new laptop computer and China has an additional U.S. Treasury bond.

Current account: $1,000 laptop

United States   China

Financial account: $1,000 Treasury bond

Now we are ready to reconsider Exhibit 14.7, which shows the current account for the United States in 2013. As required by the accounting identities, the financial account perfectly offsets the current account. In 2013, foreigners received $379 billion in net payments in the current account, corresponding to a current account deficit. In return, the financial account indicates that U.S. residents gave foreigners $379 billion in assets (including dollar-denominated deposits).

This isn't necessarily bad news for U.S. residents. It was a trade. Residents of the United States got Sony TV sets, Louis Vuitton handbags, BMWs, and hundreds of thousands of other imported goods and services. Foreigners obtained bank deposits and other assets worth $379 billion from residents of the United States.

When a country runs a current account deficit, it is analogous to what takes place when a single household spends more than it earns. To fund this extra spending, the household either borrows or spends down assets that had previously been accumulated. For example, suppose you spend $1,000 more than you earn from all sources, including labor income, asset income, and transfers. If you already have some assets in the bank, say $3,000 in your checking account, you could finance the extra $1,000 of consumption by running down those assets so that at the end of the year you would have only $2,000 left in your checking account. Or if you do not have such assets to spend down, you could borrow. If you start without any assets and without any debt, you would borrow $1,000, so your net asset position would become −$1,000. Notice that regardless of what your asset position was at the beginning, you are financing your $1,000 shortfall by reducing your asset position by $1,000—either from $3,000 to $2,000 or from zero to −$1,000.

> **Just like an individual household, an entire country can only spend more than it earns if it finds a way to fund the extra spending.**

The situation is identical for a country, which must also finance its net exports by running down its assets or borrowing. This fact highlights a central concept in international accounting: just like an individual household, an entire country can only spend more than it earns if it finds a way to fund the extra spending. The country must either sell assets to foreigners or borrow from foreigners.

Hence, current account deficits must match financial account flows. In other words, when a country makes net purchases of goods and services from foreigners, the country must make net asset sales to foreigners to pay the bill.

14.3 International Trade, Technology Transfer, and Economic Growth

International trade benefits countries not just through specialization and comparative advantage. It is also a conduit for the transfer of technology from more advanced to less advanced economies, thus contributing to an increase in the recipient's productive capacity (recall the discussion in Chapter 6 on the importance of technology for productivity and living standards).

The interplay between international trade and technology transfer is illustrated by China's economic development. When the founding father of Communist China, Mao Zedong, died in 1976, Chinese PPP-adjusted GDP per capita was $882 in 2005 dollars. Under Mao, China was organized as a planned economy, so state officials decided how to allocate almost all economic resources. Free markets were banned, international travel was forbidden, international trade was very low by comparison to most other countries, and citizens could not own land or businesses. The Chinese state owned all of the important types of physical capital. From an economic perspective, human capital was also controlled by the Chinese government, because people could not choose where to work and did not receive wages that were commensurate with their value added. The economic consequences of these policies were disastrous, leading to mass starvation under Mao's leadership. Approximately 30 million people died from malnutrition during the Great Famine of 1958–1961.

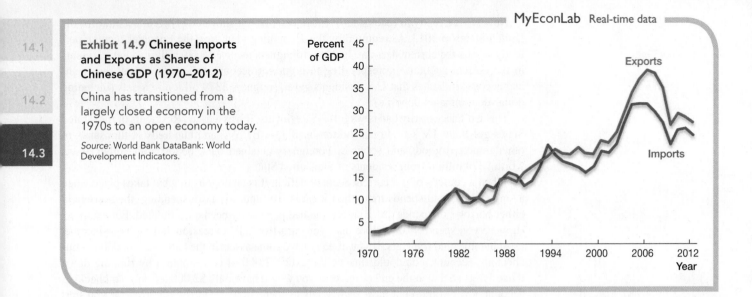

Exhibit 14.9 Chinese Imports and Exports as Shares of Chinese GDP (1970–2012)

China has transitioned from a largely closed economy in the 1970s to an open economy today.

Source: World Bank DataBank: World Development Indicators.

In 1978, two years after Mao's death, Deng Xiaoping became the next powerful leader of China. Under Deng, China began to liberalize the economy, including opening the country to international trade. Exhibit 14.9 plots Chinese imports and exports as shares of GDP since 1970. Under Mao's leadership in the early 1970s, exports represented less than 5 percent of GDP. Over the last 10 years, the export share of the Chinese economy has averaged over 30 percent. Chinese growth over the last 20 years has often been described as "export-led growth."

China achieved an average annual growth rate of real GDP per capita of 6.6 percent between 1979 and 2012. At this pace, Chinese real GDP per capita has *doubled* approximately once every 11 years, implying more than three doublings since 1979. Consequently, Chinese real GDP per capita has increased by more than a factor of $2 \times 2 \times 2 = 8$ since 1979! By comparison, it takes about 40 years for U.S. real GDP per capita to double.

China's spectacular growth is largely due to the shift from central planning—in other words, state control of the economy—towards a market economy. Opening to trade in goods and services was just one part of that transition. Farmers and family businesses were allowed to make their own decisions, own private property, and keep the profits from their economic activity. State-owned industries were privatized and China, which previously banned all kinds of foreign capital inflows, became a major destination for foreign investment. Along the way, China improved its technology greatly, enabling its citizens to work in modern factories, which now export to markets around the world.

Foreign direct investment refers to investments by foreign individuals and companies in domestic firms and businesses. To qualify as foreign *direct* investment, these flows need to generate a large foreign ownership stake in the domestic business.

Technology transfer creates one more type of cross-country interdependence.

Foreign direct investment refers to investments by foreign individuals and companies in domestic firms and businesses. To qualify as foreign *direct* investment, this capital flow must generate a large ownership stake in a local firm for the foreign investors. For example, foreign direct investment in China occurs when a foreign company opens a factory in China. It would also count as foreign direct investment if the Chinese factory were jointly owned by the foreign company and some local Chinese investors or a local Chinese company. China receives more foreign direct investment than any other country in the world.

Foreign direct investment is a major conduit for technology transfer, though in most cases this transfer is not the goal of the foreign firm that is making the investment. When a UK company becomes part of a joint venture or opens a factory in China, it brings its know-how and technology to the country. This type of technology transfer enables recipient countries to improve their productivity.

Technology transfer creates one more type of cross-country interdependence. Countries are not only trading goods and services and having their firms and banks borrow from and lend to each other but they are also technologically interlinked. Innovations and technological improvements in one country will ultimately improve productivity in all countries. Moreover, the more interaction there is between these countries, in particular through foreign direct investment, the faster these improvements will migrate from one to the other. Such transfers are particularly beneficial for countries that start out technologically less advanced, as China did in the late 1970s.

14.1

14.2

14.3

LETTING THE DATA SPEAK

From IBM to Lenovo

In 1980, almost no families had a computer at home. Personal computers did exist, but they were expensive, hard to use, and were primarily used by technology hobbyists and science geeks. The internet did not exist. The kind of entertainment one could get from a computer was a game like Pong. The game of Tetris wouldn't even be invented until 1984.

Between 1980 and 1990, the personal computer reached the mainstream, thanks to gradually improving technology as well as successful marketing. The big bang

was the introduction of the IBM-PC (model 5150) in 1981. This computer was so successful that it quickly became the industry standard. By the mid-1990s, no self-respecting college student in the developed world still wrote term papers on a typewriter.

The first generation of IBM-PCs was manufactured with mostly U.S. parts and assembled in a U.S. plant. However, even the first IBM-PC had a Japanese monitor. Over time, foreign components came to dominate the business. Mass production of hard disks began in Japan and Korea in the 1980s. Eventually, almost all of the key components of the personal computer were manufactured outside of the United States. Eventually, the final assembly also shifted to foreign factories.

Today, IBM is completely out of the business of manufacturing and selling personal computers. The end of IBM's involvement occurred in 2005, when IBM sold its successful laptop business to Lenovo, its Chinese manufacturing partner. So what did IBM do after abandoning its old line of business? IBM did very well by recognizing that its highly skilled U.S. labor force had higher value added—that is, a *comparative advantage*—in providing consulting services rather than in manufacturing machines that low-wage workers could assemble. Today, IBM remains a highly profitable company. Each year it sells proximately $100 billion in consulting and technical services to companies around the world. It has over 400,000 employees, and the company is worth approximately $200 billion.

Evidence-Based Economics

Q: Are companies like Nike harming workers in Vietnam?

Working on a Vietnamese farm is tough. Wages are very low—approximately $1–$3 per *day* for unskilled labor.[5] And the working conditions are miserable. The physical labor on a Vietnamese farm is grueling and injuries are common. Benefits like health insurance or pension plans don't exist in the agricultural sector. If you are injured on the job and can't work the next day, you don't get paid. Some children work in the agricultural sector because their families can't afford to send them to school and need the meager income that the children can earn.

Unskilled workers in the factories that manufacture Nike products earn little more than the Vietnamese minimum wage, which is $4–$5 per day depending on the location of the factory.[6] But this is greater than the wage they would earn in the largely unregulated agri-

cultural sector. Some of the factory workers also have free access to rudimentary health clinics. But working conditions are terrible—cramped, noisy, hot rooms, filled with dangerous chemicals. As in the agricultural sector, the factories offer no job security. Sick or injured employees lose their jobs and do not receive unemployment benefits. Working in a factory that makes Nike shoes is a nightmare by the standards of workers in the developed world.

Defenders of free markets emphasize the gains from international trade. At the moment, many Vietnamese workers, with limited human capital and limited access to modern technology, have a comparative advantage in assembly jobs—like work in sneaker and clothing factories. Preventing them from working in these jobs reduces their income. Defenders of free trade point to the agricultural sector and say that Nike is doing a good thing by giving agricultural workers an alternative job that increases their pay. The factory job provides reliable income and therefore does not depend on the timing of seasonal rains or whether the harvest happens to be good or bad. Famines occur when agricultural production fails, often because of a long stretch of bad weather. Famines generally don't occur in factory towns. Finally, when Nike's subcontractors use foreign direct investment to build new sneaker factories, this facilitates the transfer of new technology to Vietnam.

On the other hand, critics of the factory sweatshops point out that the factory jobs don't even measure up to the jobs that the *worst-off* workers hold in developed countries. A low-wage worker in the United States earns over $50 per day. An unskilled factory worker in Vietnam earns less than a tenth of that wage. The Vietnam factory wouldn't even come close to passing a U.S. safety inspection. Moreover, many of the factory workers are under-age, just like the workers in the agricultural sector.

Almost everyone agrees with these facts. But there is a great deal of disagreement about what should be done. Is it possible for Nike to continue to buy shoes from suppliers in Vietnam but require those suppliers to pay higher wages?

Suppose that U.S. consumers boycotted Nike's products because of the work arrangements at the factories that supply Nike with sneakers. The protestors would like Nike's subcontractors to pay the factory workers more and to improve working conditions in those factories. In principle, such improvements could be implemented without necessitating a very large increase in Nike's sneaker prices.

Would there be unintended negative consequences if Nike paid its subcontractors more and forced them to pass these extra funds on to the workers? Perhaps Nike would lose business because of the need to (modestly) raise its sneaker prices. If Nike does lose some customers, Nike might end up reducing its sneaker purchases from the Vietnamese subcontractors, leading some of its suppliers to shut down. In this case, some of the workers that the U.S. protestors were trying to help might actually be hurt. Perhaps Nike would improve conditions at the existing factories in Vietnam, but the subcontractors would stop building *new* factories in Vietnam, thereby preventing other agricultural workers from transitioning to the relatively well-paid manufacturing sector. Consumers in the United States would like to see the lives of Vietnamese families improve, but it's not clear what would happen if Nike and its subcontractors were forced to raise the wages of workers in Vietnamese sneaker factories.

Though it is not clear what would happen if Nike were forced to pay its Vietnamese workers more, it is clear that globalization in general has been an enormous force for good in Vietnam. Like Deng Xiaoping, who initiated market and trade reforms in China after decades of strict central planning, Nguyen Van Linh pursued a similar policy in Vietnam starting in 1988 (two years after he came to power). As a result of these Vietnamese reforms, trade rapidly expanded, with exports rising from 10 percent of GDP to 75 percent of GDP today. Since the reforms were passed, real GDP per capita has grown at a rate of 5.5 percent (1988–2013), more than a doubling from the pre-reform growth rate.[7] Poverty has fallen precipitously if it is measured with the poverty line of one (U.S.) dollar per day. In 1993, nearly 60 percent of the Vietnamese population fell below that standard of living, but by 2006 (the most recent data available) "only" 16 percent of the population consumed less than a dollar-per-day.[8]

Economists believe that sustained growth is one of the key factors that reduces child labor. Exhibit 14.10 shows that there is a strong negative correlation between child labor and GDP per capita: fewer children are forced to, or choose to, work in countries with higher GDP per capita. Consistent with Exhibit 14.10, rising levels of income in Vietnam have coincided with a sharp fall in child labor, and much of the decline in child labor is credited to Vietnam's opening to trade.[9]

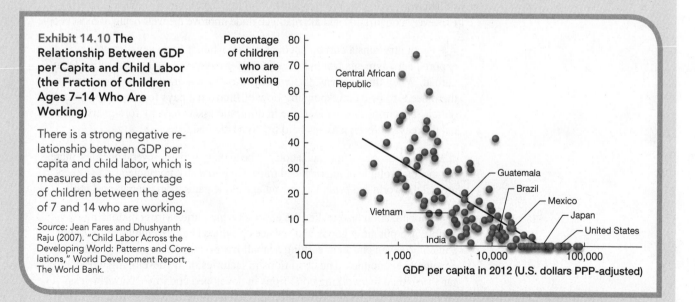

Exhibit 14.10 The Relationship Between GDP per Capita and Child Labor (the Fraction of Children Ages 7–14 Who Are Working)

There is a strong negative relationship between GDP per capita and child labor, which is measured as the percentage of children between the ages of 7 and 14 who are working.

Source: Jean Fares and Dhushyanth Raju (2007). "Child Labor Across the Developing World: Patterns and Correlations," World Development Report, The World Bank.

Evidence-Based Economics *(Continued)*

Question

Are companies like Nike harming workers in the developing world?

Answer

The Vietnamese workers that make Nike's sneakers are paid extremely low wages and work in conditions that are unsafe by the standards of developed countries. However, the next best alternative for many of the workers that produce Nike's sneakers, which is work in the agricultural sector, appears to be even worse.

Data

Agricultural and factory wages in Vietnam, as well as data on trade, growth, poverty, and child labor-force participation.

Caveat

Nike could improve the quality of life of the workers who manufacture its products if it forced its subcontractors to raise the workers' wages.

Summary

✸ The process of globalization has produced a highly interconnected world.

✸ International trade enables us to exploit specialization and comparative advantage. Comparative advantage arises when a person or country has a lower opportunity cost of production than another person or country.

✸ Some individuals are made worse off by international trade, especially low-skilled workers in *developed* countries who lose their jobs to foreign producers. However, globalization and international trade improve the well-being of most people.

✸ A country runs a current account deficit when it has a negative sum of net exports, net payments from abroad for factor payments, and net transfers from abroad. When this happens, the country must have a financial account surplus, as there needs to be a corresponding flow of funds that pays for the current account deficit. This implies a net increase in domestic assets held by foreigners and/or a net decrease in foreign assets held by domestic residents.

✸ A rapid process of globalization has been underway for several decades, increasing the total volume of international trade. Consequently, consumers and workers around the world can better take advantage of the gains from international trade.

✸ Globalization also makes the enormous inequities across nations more visible. We purchase goods and services produced and assembled by workers, sometimes even children, earning a small fraction of the wages of workers in developed economies. The conditions in factories in the developing world are far worse than the working conditions in developed countries. Nevertheless, globalization usually improves the well-being of most of the low-paid factory workers in foreign countries. Their alternative opportunities for employment are usually worse than these factory jobs in the traded goods sector.

Key Terms

gains from specialization *p. 325*
absolute advantage *p. 326*
comparative advantage *p. 326*
closed economy *p. 330*

open economy *p. 330*
net exports or the trade balance *p. 334*
trade surplus *p. 334*
trade deficit *p. 334*

current account *p. 335*
financial account *p. 336*
foreign direct investment *p. 338*

Questions

All questions are available in MyEconLab for practice and instructor assignment.

1. How does comparative advantage differ from absolute advantage?

2. How does trade allow buyers and sellers to exploit gains from specialization?

3. Engaging in trade increases overall economic efficiency. Does this also imply that everyone in an economy gains from trade equally?

4. Explain the following terms:
   a. Open economy
   b. Closed economy
   c. Imports
   d. Exports
   e. Tariffs

5. Has trade been increasing or decreasing over the past few decades? What could explain why the ratio of imports to GDP in the United States fell sharply after 1929 before rebounding shortly thereafter?

6. How is the trade balance defined? When is a country said to be running a trade deficit or a trade surplus?

7. The international accounting system maintains a clear distinction between residency and citizenship.
   a. Who would be considered a domestic resident of the United States, according to the international accounting system?
   b. Suppose a U.S. citizen lives and works in Nigeria. Would he be considered a "foreigner" or a domestic resident in the U.S. international transactions accounts?

8. List the sources of income-based payments that domestic residents make to foreigners and the ways that domestic residents can receive income-based payments from foreigners.

9. What does the current account include? Explain each of its components.

10. What is included in a country's financial account? How is the financial account related to the current account?

11. What is foreign direct investment? Explain with an example. How does foreign direct investment benefit the recipient country?

12. Are multinational companies harming factory workers in the developing world by hiring them at low wages?

Problems

All problems are available in MyEconLab for practice and instructor assignment.

1. The economist Alan Blinder said that any economist who mows his own lawn probably has not understood the concept of comparative advantage. Would you agree with Professor Blinder?

2. You and your roommate are enrolled in the same course: Postmodern Deconstruction of Postmodern Deconstructionism. The course requires a term paper. Since the professor encourages collaboration on the paper, you decide to work on it together, "trading" tasks.

   In 8 hours, you can type 18 pages, whereas your roommate can type only 10. If you do outlining instead of typing, in the same 8 hours you could produce 6 summary outlines of the course readings, while your roommate could produce only 2.

   a. Who has the absolute advantage in typing? In outlining? Explain your answers.

   b. Who should do the typing, and who should do the outlining? Explain.

3. Suppose that the United States and Chile are the only two countries in the world, and that labor is the only productive input. In the United States, a worker can produce 15 bushels of corn or 10 barrels of oil per day. In Chile, a worker can produce 5 bushels of corn or 5 barrels of oil per day.

   a. Which country has the absolute advantage in the production of oil? Of corn? Explain.

   b. Explain in words what comparative advantage means. Which country has the comparative advantage in the production of oil? Of corn?

   c. If free trade is allowed, which commodity will the United States import? Which commodity will Chile import? Explain.

4. Assume that an American worker can produce 5 cars per year or 10 tons of grain per year, whereas a Japanese worker can produce 15 cars per year or 5 tons of grain per year. Assume labor is the only input used in car and grain production.

    a. Which country has the absolute advantage in producing cars? In producing grain?

    b. For the United States, what is the opportunity cost of producing a car? What is the opportunity cost of a ton of grain? Show how you arrived at your numbers.

    c. For Japan, what is the opportunity cost of producing a car? What is the opportunity cost of producing a ton of grain? Show how you arrived at your numbers.

    d. If free trade is allowed, which country will import cars? Which country will import grain? Explain.

5. David Ricardo, the British political economist, used the example of two commodities—wine and cloth—produced by England and Portugal to explain trade. The following table shows the number of labor hours it would take England and Portugal to produce one unit each of wine and cloth:

	Portugal	England
Wine	80	120
Cloth	90	100

Portugal can produce both wine and cloth using fewer labor hours than England. A group of Mercantilists, who believe that nations build their wealth by exporting more than they import, suggest that Portugal has nothing to gain from trading with England. Would you agree? Explain your answer.

6. Tire production in the United States has been on the decline, in both absolute and relative terms. Imported tires are replacing most of the domestically manufactured tires in the market. Trade unions in the United States have claimed that over 7,000 jobs have been lost due to Chinese tire imports. You read a blog post that uses this example to say that this is exactly why countries should not engage in free trade; cheaper imports will flood the domestic market and unemployment in the country will increase. Do you think the blogger's conclusions are entirely correct? Explain.

7. In his book *Where the Right Went Wrong*, commentator and politician Patrick "Pat" Buchanan says that trade between China and the United States must be reciprocal—"If America is to buy 30 percent of China's exports, Beijing must give preference in its purchases to goods made in the USA." According to him, the United States loses the "trade war" unless its imports from China are matched by China's imports of U.S. goods. Based on your understanding of bilateral trade deficits, identify the flaw in Pat Buchanan's reasoning.

8. Suppose the following table shows data on transactions between the United States and the rest of the world for the month of May 2013. Assuming the list is exhaustive, use the information given to fill in the table showing the current and financial accounts for May 2013.

U.S. aid to earthquake-hit Haiti	$8,000,000
Payments made to Indian software companies for services rendered by workers in India to U.S. customers	$850,000
Payments made to U.S. producers for ethanol exports	$3,000,000
Dividend payment from Walmart in China to a U.S. resident	$10,500
Salary earned by a team of IT consultants from the UK who were working in the U.S. for a few days	$120,000
Sale of U.S. Treasury bonds from U.S. Treasury to foreign governments	$15,000,000
Remittances from U.S. residents to other family members in Mexico	$30,000
Payments made to Chinese producers for steel imports	$8,000,000
Purchases of foreign assets by the U.S. government	$1,040,500
A U.S. citizen, who is a resident of Dubai, sends money to a charity in the United States	$30,000

Current and Financial Account for May, 2013

	Payments from Foreigners	Payments to Foreigners	Net Payments
Trade in goods and services			
Factor payments			
Net transfer payments			
Current account			
	Increase in domestic assets held by foreigners	Increase in foreign assets held domestically	
Net sales to foreigners			
Financial account			

9. Recall the national income accounting identity (in Chapter 5): $Y = C + I + G + X - M$, where $X - M$ is net exports, given by exports − imports. We have seen from the chapter that net exports is equivalent to the trade balance, but not to the current account. Hence, aggregate expenditure does not include the current account balance.

    Discuss why the entire current account is not included in the calculation of GDP.

10. Throughout the 1950s and 1960s, many poor countries pursued a policy called "import-substituting industrialization," or ISI for short. India, and many nations in Africa and Latin America, closed themselves off to trade in order to promote the development of domestic industries.

As noted in the *Economist* article "Grinding the Poor" (September 27, 2001), "[o]n the whole, ISI failed; almost everywhere, trade has been good for growth." The article discusses how growth was disappointing in countries that pursued ISI. Nations that were open to trade—primarily in Asia—grew much more rapidly.

Based on the discussion in the chapter, speculate on why ISI was ultimately a failure and why integration with the global economy promotes economic growth and development.

11. Foreign direct investment (FDI) in several sectors in India is still heavily regulated. After much debate, the government of India recently relaxed restrictions on FDI in the retail sector. For purported reasons like national security and possible job losses, many sectors of the economy such as defense, nuclear power, and oil refining are not fully open to foreign direct investment. Suppose you are hired to serve on the government's Working Group on Foreign Direct Investment. What would you suggest to the government? Defend your position.

12. The coffee market is one of the most globalized and volatile commodity markets in existence. In terms of the value of trade, it is second only to oil. Coffee is produced in over seventy countries, primarily lower-income nations in Latin American, Africa, and Asia. In recent years, a movement has developed supporting "fair trade coffee," which seeks to better the conditions and increase the incomes of coffee producers in poor countries.

Read the following online sources and list the main arguments for and against the fair trade coffee movement, as delineated in the articles. Comment on any similarities you see between fair trade coffee policy and the case of Nike in Vietnam (as discussed in the chapter's Evidence-Based Economics feature).

"The Fair Trade Debate," in Wikipedia: http://en.wikipedia.org/wiki/Fair_trade_debate

"Coffee," from Fair Trade International: http://www.fairtrade.net/coffee.html

"Fair Trade Coffee Enthusiasts Should Confront Reality," from the Cato Institute: http://object.cato.org/sites/cato.org/files/serials/files/cato-journal/2007/1/cj27n1-9.pdf

"The Pros and Cons of Fair Trade Coffee" from the Organic Consumers Association: http://www.organicconsumers.org/articles/article_4738.cfm

15 Open Economy Macroeconomics

How did George Soros make $1 billion?

George Soros, one of the world's most renowned investors, challenged the central bank of England in the summer of 1992. In essence, he bet everything he had that the British currency, the pound, would lose value relative to other currencies. Starting in September, the pound plummeted in value. Soros made approximately $1 billion of profits for himself and his investors. How did Soros know that the pound was about to collapse?

CHAPTER OUTLINE

15.1 Exchange Rates

In the previous chapter, we saw that economies around the world are linked through trade and investment. For example, the United States imported about $456 billion of goods and services from China in 2013. But *how* does this trade take place? After all, almost all transactions in the United States are in U.S. dollars, while most transactions in China are in the Chinese currency, the *yuan*, also called the *renminbi*.

Many countries have their own currencies for use in economic transactions: the United Kingdom has the pound, Japan the yen, Mexico the peso, and India the rupee, among others. An exception to the use of a national currency is the euro, a currency used by twenty-four European countries (as of January 1, 2015). The euro, first introduced in 1999, is the second-most-traded currency after the U.S. dollar.

Nominal Exchange Rates

Walmart sells toys imported from China. How does Walmart decide whether to purchase the toys from China rather than purchasing similar toys from some U.S. toy manufacturer?

To answer this question, we need to understand the concept of the *nominal exchange rate*. The **nominal exchange rate** is the price of one country's currency in units of another country's currency. Specifically, the nominal exchange rate is the number of units of foreign currency that can be purchased with one unit of domestic currency. Sometimes you'll see the nominal exchange rate, referred to simply as the "exchange rate" (which is what we did in Chapter 6). In the current chapter, we often use the full name, *nominal* exchange rate, to distinguish the nominal exchange rate from another type of exchange rate that we will discuss later in the chapter.

In the following equation, the nominal exchange rate is represented by the symbol e:

$$e = \frac{\text{Units of foreign currency}}{1 \text{ Unit of domestic currency}}.$$

For instance, if the yuan-dollar exchange rate is 6.05 yuan per dollar, then a person holding 1 dollar can exchange the dollar for 6.05 yuan.

$$e = 6.05 \text{ Yuan per dollar} = \frac{6.05 \text{ Yuan}}{1 \text{ Dollar}}.$$

The **nominal exchange rate** is the rate at which one currency can be traded for another.

Exhibit 15.1 The Nominal Exchange Rates e and $1/e$

The nominal exchange rates e and $1/e$ for several major currencies on January 2, 2014.

Source: Federal Reserve Board of Governors.

	British Pound Versus Dollar	Euro Versus Dollar	Mexican New Peso Versus Dollar	Swiss Franc Versus Dollar	Yuan Versus Dollar
e	0.61	0.73	13.12	0.90	6.05
$1/e$	1.64	1.37	0.08	1.11	0.17

All Chinese currency features a portrait of Mao Zedong, the first leader of modern China.

The higher the value of e, the more units of foreign currency a dollar buys. When a nominal exchange rate goes up, we say that the domestic currency is *appreciating* against the foreign currency. When a nominal exchange rate goes down, we say that the domestic currency is *depreciating* against the foreign currency.

We can also use the yuan-dollar exchange rate to calculate the value of 1 yuan in terms of dollars. When the yuan-dollar exchange rate is e, the number of units of dollars that can be purchased with 1 yuan is $1/e$. Put differently, 1 yuan is worth $1/e = 1/6.05 = 0.17$ dollars.

Notice that the appreciation of a currency—a rise in e—always has a flip side. When the dollar appreciates against the yuan, implying that e is rising, the yuan is depreciating against the dollar, implying that $1/e$ is falling.

Exhibit 15.1 shows e and $1/e$ for some key currencies on January 2, 2014. The above discussion and Exhibit 15.1 clarify that both e (yuan per dollar) and $1/e$ (dollars per yuan) convey the same information. In newspapers, you will see exchange rates sometimes expressed as yuan per dollar or euros per dollar and at other times as dollars per yuan or dollars per euro. In this chapter, to avoid confusion, we will stick to the definition above of the exchange rate, e, expressing it as the number of units of foreign currency that can be purchased by one unit of domestic currency, such as yuan per dollar or euros per dollar.

Now let's return to Walmart's *sourcing* decision—should Walmart purchase toys from a Chinese or a U.S. manufacturer? Walmart needs to decide whether a toy sold by a Chinese manufacturer at a unit price of 20 yuan is less expensive than an identical toy sold by a competing U.S. manufacturer at a unit price of $5 (we are ignoring transportation costs for simplicity). To implement this comparison, Walmart makes the yuan and dollar prices comparable by using the nominal exchange rate. For example, on January 2, 2014, the yuan-dollar exchange rate was 6.05, so the dollar price of the Chinese-manufactured toy was

$$\text{Dollar cost} = \text{Yuan cost} \times \frac{\text{Dollars}}{\text{Yuan}}$$
$$= \text{Yuan cost} \times \frac{1}{e}$$
$$= 20 \times \frac{1}{6.05}$$
$$= \$3.31.$$

As you can see, the dollar price of the Chinese-manufactured toy is just over $3, which is less than the $5 price of the U.S.-manufactured toy, so it is less expensive to purchase the toy from the Chinese manufacturer.

Flexible, Managed, and Fixed Exchange Rates

Exhibit 15.2 shows historical movements in two nominal exchange rates: the yuan-dollar and the euro-dollar nominal exchange rates. Both nominal exchange rates vary over time. However, the yuan-dollar exchange rate has had long periods in which it doesn't move, followed

Exhibit 15.2 Yuan-Dollar and Euro-Dollar Exchange Rates from 1999 to January 2014

The yuan-dollar exchange rate is managed by the Chinese government, so its rate is either held fixed or slowly allowed to drift in one direction. The euro-dollar exchange rate floats freely, so its path is set by market forces that fluctuate from day to day.

Source: Federal Reserve Bank of St. Louis.

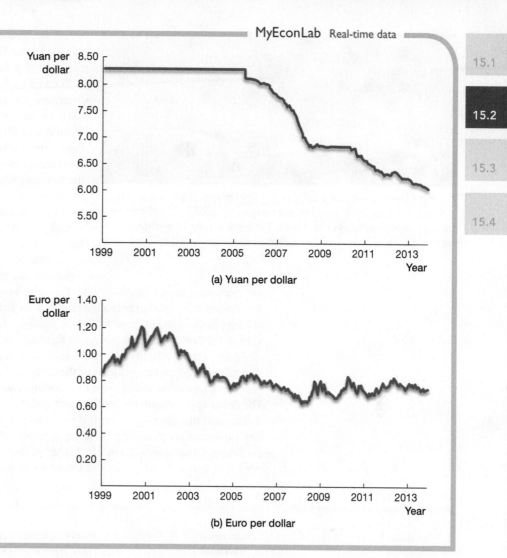

(a) Yuan per dollar

(b) Euro per dollar

If the government does not intervene in the foreign exchange market, then the country has a **flexible exchange rate**, which is also referred to as a **floating exchange rate**.

If the government fixes a value for the exchange rate and intervenes to maintain that value, then the country has a **fixed exchange rate**.

If the government intervenes actively to influence the exchange rate, then the country has a **managed exchange rate**.

by short periods in which it mostly moves down. For example, the yuan-dollar exchange rate was constant—8.28 yuan per dollar—from late 1998 to 2005. Likewise, the yuan-dollar exchange rate was nearly constant at 6.82 yuan per dollar between mid-2008 and mid-2010.

The euro-dollar exchange rate fluctuates much more than the yuan-dollar exchange rate because the euro-dollar exchange rate is determined with little or no government intervention. Each day the exchange rate moves up and down as market forces change. This is referred to as a **flexible exchange rate**, or a **floating exchange rate**.

On the other hand, a government could fix a value for the exchange rate and intervene to maintain that value. In this case, the country has a **fixed exchange rate**.

There is also a middle case. The yuan-dollar exchange rate is not flexible or fixed but is instead a **managed exchange rate**: the Chinese government influences its movement. Managed exchange rates change, but those movements tend to be relatively smooth. For example, the Chinese government has allowed the yuan to slowly appreciate against the dollar since 2005.

We'll explain why a country might adopt a managed or a fixed exchange rate later in the chapter. For now, we only note that there are many reasons, among them the belief that managed or fixed exchange rates provide more economic stability and might facilitate international trade.

15.2 The Foreign Exchange Market

The **foreign exchange market** is the global financial market in which currencies are traded and nominal exchange rates are determined.

The **foreign exchange market** is the global financial market in which currencies are traded and nominal exchange rates are determined. To illustrate the role of this market, suppose Air China would like to add five Boeing Dreamliners, each costing $200 million, to its aircraft fleet. To do this, it needs to pay the Boeing Company in dollars. So Air China will go to the foreign exchange market to buy (demand) a total of $1 billion (= 5 × $200 million), offering yuan in

Boeing's Dreamliner costs $200 million per plane. If a Chinese airline tries to buy one, it will need to exchange (e × $200 million) on the foreign exchange market to obtain $200 million. At an exchange rate of e = 6.05 yuan per dollar, that amounts to 1,210 million yuan.

return. Because the yuan-dollar exchange rate is e = 6.05, this means Air China will be paying 6.05 billion yuan in exchange of dollars.

As with other markets, the supply and demand curves determine the equilibrium price, which is the equilibrium exchange rate in the foreign exchange market. Exhibit 15.3 illustrates the supply and demand curves in the foreign exchange market. The horizontal axis represents the quantity of dollars available for transactions in the foreign exchange market. We'll use the yuan-dollar exchange rate on the vertical axis to represent the value or "price" of a dollar: how many yuan a dollar will buy. Recall that we are expressing the nominal exchange rate as units of foreign currency per U.S. dollar.

In panel (a) of Exhibit 15.3, the dollar demand curve represents the relationship between the quantity of dollars demanded and the exchange rate. The demand curve represents traders who are trying to buy dollars in the foreign exchange market with yuan. So, Air China's demand for dollars is reflected in this demand curve. Of course, millions of other economic agents will also be trying to obtain dollars by selling yuan. All of these agents make up the dollar demand curve.

To understand why the demand curve for dollars in exchange for yuan is downward-sloping, consider an *appreciation* of the dollar—in other words, a *depreciation* of the yuan. A dollar appreciation would move the exchange rate from A to B in panel (a) of Exhibit 15.3. The dollar appreciation implies that each dollar buys more yuan, that each yuan buys fewer dollars, and that the price of each Boeing aircraft is now greater in yuan. The Chinese airline's revenues are paid (largely) in yuan, so the relevant price for Air China is the price of the Boeing Dreamliner in yuan. The higher yuan-denominated price for the Dreamliner leads Air China to reduce the quantity of Dreamliners demanded. This implies that the quantity of

Exhibit 15.3 The Foreign Exchange Market under a Flexible Exchange Rate Regime

The demand for dollars in exchange for yuan in panel (a) is downward-sloping because a dollar appreciation (a movement from A to B) increases the price of U.S. goods faced by Chinese firms and consumers, reducing the quantity of goods they demand and thereby reducing the quantity of dollars they demand. The supply of dollars in exchange for yuan in panel (b) is upward-sloping because a dollar appreciation (a movement from A to B) increases the quantity of goods purchased by U.S. buyers from Chinese producers, thus raising the dollar earnings of Chinese producers and the quantity of dollars that they supply to the foreign exchange market. The intersection of the demand and supply curves in panel (c) gives the equilibrium exchange rate in a flexible exchange rate regime.

dollars demanded will fall—with fewer aircraft demanded, fewer dollars will be demanded. We've just shown how an appreciation of the dollar leads to a reduction in the quantity of dollars demanded. Examples like this imply that the demand curve is downward-sloping, as shown in the exhibit.

The dollar supply curve, shown in panel (b) of Exhibit 15.3, represents the relationship between the quantity of dollars supplied and the exchange rate. Traders who are trying to obtain yuan by selling dollars are represented by this dollar supply curve. For example, Chinese manufacturers that export their products are often paid in dollars and they need to exchange these dollars into yuan so they can pay their workers and suppliers. All of the millions of households and firms supplying dollars in exchange for yuan make up the dollar supply curve.

The reason that the supply curve (for dollars in exchange for yuan) slopes up is related to the reason that the demand curve (for dollars in exchange for yuan) slopes down. When the dollar appreciates (yuan depreciates) and we move from exchange rate A to exchange rate B, each dollar buys more yuan. This implies that the prices of all Chinese products, such as the toys produced by Chinese manufacturers, become less expensive in U.S. dollars—recall that when we draw supply (or demand) curves, we are holding constant all other prices, such as the yuan-denominated price of toys manufactured in China. Because an appreciation of the dollar enables U.S. consumers to pay fewer dollars for each good they import from China, U.S. consumers and companies increase their purchases of Chinese goods. This implies greater dollar revenues for Chinese firms, and thus a greater quantity of dollars supplied by them to the foreign exchange market. To sum up, a rising yuan-dollar exchange rate leads to a greater quantity of dollars supplied, so the supply curve is upward-sloping.

The equilibrium exchange rate under a flexible exchange rate regime is given by the foreign exchange equilibrium, which corresponds to the exchange rate that equates the quantity supplied and the quantity demanded. This intersection of the supply and demand curves is shown in panel (c) of Exhibit 15.3 at quantity q^* and price (yuan-dollar exchange rate) e^*. As we have already noted, the yuan-dollar exchange rate is not flexible but managed, so panel (c) shows what the yuan-dollar exchange rate would be if there were no Chinese government intervention. In fact, the Chinese government has been slowly reducing the scope of its foreign exchange market interventions, leading the yuan-dollar market to move closer to the situation that would arise under a flexible exchange rate regime like that in panel (c).

What happens to the equilibrium exchange rate if Air China unexpectedly faces a higher demand for air travel in China? Air China would need more aircraft. For example, its demand curve for aircraft would shift so that, at unchanged prices, it would now demand 10 Dreamliners instead of 5. In this case, again keeping prices including the exchange rate fixed, Air China's demand for dollars would increase by 5 × $200 million = $1 billion. In terms of Exhibit 15.3, this corresponds to a $1 billion rightward shift of the dollar demand curve, as illustrated in Exhibit 15.4.

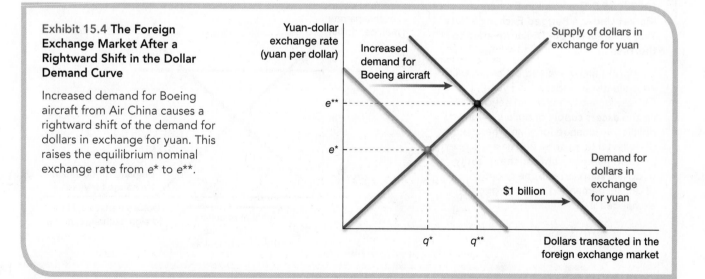

Exhibit 15.4 The Foreign Exchange Market After a Rightward Shift in the Dollar Demand Curve

Increased demand for Boeing aircraft from Air China causes a rightward shift of the demand for dollars in exchange for yuan. This raises the equilibrium nominal exchange rate from e^* to e^{**}.

Under a flexible exchange rate, the rightward shift in the dollar demand curve causes the equilibrium yuan-dollar exchange rate to increase, implying that a dollar will now buy more yuan. Using the terminology we introduced earlier we can see that, with flexible exchange rates, in response to the increased demand for Boeing aircraft, the dollar would appreciate against the yuan or, equivalently, the yuan would depreciate against the dollar.

How Do Governments Intervene in the Foreign Exchange Market?

How does equilibrium work when an exchange rate is not flexible? If a government attempts to control the value of its exchange rate through a managed or fixed exchange rate system, we say that the exchange rate is being "pegged" by the government.

Though this may no longer be the case, Chinese authorities have historically chosen an exchange rate that makes the yuan substantially *undervalued* relative to the dollar. By implication this means that the dollar is somewhat *overvalued* relative to the yuan. Exhibit 15.5 illustrates the yuan-dollar foreign exchange market and reveals what it means for the yuan to be undervalued and the dollar to be overvalued. The exchange rate is pegged at the level shown by the solid purple line. The dollar is overvalued because the dollar is worth more yuan than it would have been under a flexible exchange rate regime. The flexible equilibrium is still represented by e^*. The pegged exchange rate is *above* the market-clearing price at the intersection of the supply and demand curves.

At the exchange rate corresponding to the peg, the quantity supplied exceeds the quantity demanded. If the Chinese authorities simply announce the peg and do nothing else, the forces of supply and demand will lower the yuan-dollar exchange rate below the peg. Recall that the supply curve represents the quantity of dollars supplied to the yuan-dollar foreign exchange market at a particular yuan-dollar exchange rate. If that quantity supplied exceeds the quantity demanded at a particular yuan-dollar exchange rate, there will be an excess supply of dollars, which will drive down the price of dollars. In other words, the price of dollars—the exchange rate—will fall, so the dollar will depreciate against the yuan. This process will lower the yuan-dollar exchange rate from the peg toward the market-clearing price at the intersection of the supply and demand curves.

> **Simply announcing a target exchange rate will have little or no effect on the exchange rate that will prevail in the foreign exchange market.**

This analysis shows that simply *announcing* a target exchange rate will have little or no effect on the exchange rate that will prevail in the foreign exchange market. Because the quantity of dollars supplied exceeds the quantity of dollars demanded at the pegged yuan-dollar exchange rate, Chinese authorities would need to soak up this excess supply by buying dollars and selling yuan. Exhibit 15.5 shows that to maintain the peg above the

Exhibit 15.5 The Foreign Exchange Market Under a Pegged Exchange Rate That Overvalues the Dollar Relative to the Yuan

To support an overvalued dollar (or equivalently an undervalued yuan), the Chinese government would need to soak up the excess supply of dollars by buying dollars in exchange for yuan. The quantity of dollars that must be purchased is given by the difference between the quantity of dollars supplied and the quantity of dollars demanded at the pegged exchange rate.

market-clearing exchange rate—in other words, to keep the dollar overvalued—Chinese authorities would have to continuously purchase dollars and sell yuan.

In fact, this is exactly what they have been doing. Between 1990 and 2013, the Chinese central bank increased its holdings of foreign reserves from about $30 billion to more than $3,800 billion. Most of these reserves are in dollars, but the Chinese central bank has bought other currencies as well. The analysis in Exhibit 15.5 shows why dollar purchases were necessary, given the fact that the yuan has been pegged to the dollar at exchange rates that overvalued the dollar and therefore undervalued the yuan.

Later in this chapter we'll explain why the Chinese government has gone to all this trouble: an overvalued dollar (undervalued yuan) increase the net exports of China.

Defending an Overvalued Exchange Rate

Exhibit 15.5 makes it look easy to defend a fixed exchange rate. The Chinese authorities bought dollars, building up their dollar reserves. In exchange, the Chinese authorities supplied yuan. This was simple to achieve because a country with a national currency, like the Chinese yuan, has the right to print or electronically create as many units of that currency as it wants. So, at least in the short run, defending an *undervalued* yuan appears feasible. However, it is not as easy to defend an exchange rate when your currency is *overvalued*.

In many cases, countries try to peg their exchange rate at a level that overvalues their *own* currency. To see why a country might do so, let's consider the example of Mexico and analyze the peso-dollar exchange rate, with the convention that the exchange rate is measured in pesos per dollar. Why would the Mexican government want the peso to be overvalued and the dollar to be undervalued?

Most countries regularly borrow from foreign lenders. In developing countries like Mexico, these loans are typically denominated in dollars. So the Mexican borrowers receive dollars when they take out their loans and pay back dollars, not pesos, at the end of the loan period. To work through a numerical example, imagine that Mexican borrowers, including the Mexican government and Mexican companies, owe $1 billion to U.S. banks. If the peso-dollar exchange rate is 10, meaning that 10 pesos purchase one dollar, then Mexican borrowers need 10 billion pesos to pay back their dollar-denominated debts.

Now suppose that at the exchange rate of 10 pesos per dollar, the dollar is undervalued and that its market-clearing price under a flexible exchange rate regime would be 20 pesos per dollar instead. What would happen if the Mexican government allowed the *undervalued* dollar to appreciate, which is equivalent to allowing the *overvalued* peso to depreciate? This situation would have several implications, one of which is that Mexican borrowers would now need to give up 20 billion pesos instead of just 10 billion pesos to pay back their debts of $1 billion. Allowing the dollar to appreciate, and hence the peso to depreciate, has suddenly doubled the number of pesos that are needed to pay back the dollar-denominated debts of Mexican borrowers.

Having an overvalued peso also has other benefits for Mexico. An undervalued dollar—hence, an overvalued peso—lowers the cost that Mexican consumers pay in pesos to import goods from the United States. Consequently, the Mexican government can keep prices and inflation low by keeping the dollar undervalued and the peso overvalued. For example, suppose that an iPhone costs $400 to import into Mexico. If the Mexican exchange rate is 10 pesos per dollar, then the local cost will be 4,000 pesos. This is a lower iPhone price (in pesos) than if the peso-dollar exchange rate rises to 20 pesos per dollar. In that case, the local cost of the iPhone doubles to 8,000 pesos. Price increases like this raise the overall inflation rate in Mexico.

Another reason that countries maintain an overvalued exchange rate is because a fall in the value of a currency is often perceived as a failure of government policies. A currency that is depreciating (sometimes confusingly called a "weak currency") is at times perceived to be a sign of a weak government or a weak country. This perception can be a problem for incumbent politicians in democratic countries. For this reason, officials at the U.S. Treasury Department frequently repeat the mantra that they support a "strong dollar policy." The American public doesn't like to hear politicians associate anything "weak" with the United States, including its currency. However, as we have learned, a "weak" currency is exactly what the non-democratic Chinese government has pursued for decades.

Exhibit 15.6 The Foreign Exchange Market Under a Pegged Exchange Rate That Undervalues the Dollar Relative to the Peso

To maintain an undervalued dollar, which is the same thing as an overvalued peso, the Mexican government needs to supply dollars to purchase pesos. The quantity of dollars that must be supplied is given by the difference between the quantity of dollars demanded and the quantity of dollars supplied at the pegged exchange rate.

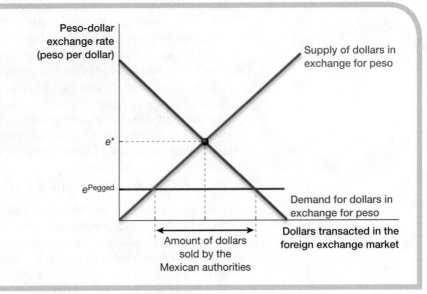

Whatever their motivations, many governments have intervened in the foreign exchange market to maintain an overvalued national currency. But overvaluation is also costly, as we will discuss below. In addition, overvalued currencies are much harder to defend than undervalued ones. Exhibit 15.6 plots the situation for an *overvalued* peso, which implies an *undervalued* dollar. Exhibit 15.6 is very similar to Exhibit 15.5, except that the solid purple line corresponding to the peg value is now *below* the market-clearing price, e^*, at the intersection of the supply and demand curves (again marked with the dotted line in the exhibit). Thus the peso-dollar exchange rate is below what it would have been under a flexible exchange rate regime, and in particular, the dollar is worth fewer pesos than it would be at the market-clearing price. Hence, the dollar is undervalued and the peso is overvalued.

Exhibit 15.6 illustrates how the Mexican authorities would in principle defend an overvalued peso (and thus keep the dollar undervalued). This exhibit differs from Exhibit 15.5, where the quantity of dollars supplied *exceeded* the quantity of dollars demanded. In Exhibit 15.6, the quantity of dollars supplied falls short of the quantity of dollars demanded. To maintain the peso-dollar exchange rate at the value corresponding to the peg, the Mexican authorities have to sell dollars and purchase pesos. The Mexican authorities can certainly do this if they have substantial dollar reserves. But how long can they keep up this policy?

In the situation depicted in Exhibit 15.5, the Chinese authorities can print or electronically create as many yuan as they want, so they could perpetually supply yuan to buy dollars if they wished. Likewise, Mexican authorities can create as many *pesos* as they want, but sustaining an *overvalued* peso relative to the dollar does not rely on the creation of more pesos. Instead, the Mexican authorities need to keep selling dollars to sustain an overvalued peso. Because they can't create new dollars, the Mexican authorities have to use their preexisting dollar reserves, which are limited. If the quantity of dollars they need to supply exceeds their reserves, they won't be able to sustain an overvalued peso. At the moment it becomes clear that their dollar reserves are going to run out, defending the overvalued peso becomes impossible. Whatever their public announcements, the Mexican authorities will then have to give up the peg and allow the peso to depreciate and the dollar to appreciate, which implies that the number of pesos per dollar—the peso-dollar exchange rate—will rise.

This discussion highlights the observation that overvalued exchange rates can be defended for a while—as long as the dollar reserves of the country defending the exchange rate last. But this scenario cannot continue indefinitely. If the peso-dollar exchange rate is too low relative to what supply and demand dictate—meaning that the dollar is undervalued and the peso is overvalued—there will continue to be an excess demand for dollars, and this excess demand will keep draining the dollar reserves of the Mexican authorities who are trying to defend the overvalued peso.

Market pressure often pushes prices in financial markets, including exchange rates, back to their market-clearing levels, no matter what the government tries to do.

CHOICE & CONSEQUENCE

Fixed Exchange Rates and Corruption

Some developing countries with fixed exchange rates announce an *official* exchange rate that overvalues their local currency and then ration who gets the privilege of exchanging the local currency for dollars at the overvalued exchange rate. In particular, the situation has some similarities to Exhibit 15.6, which depicts an undervalued dollar and, by implication, an overvalued foreign currency. As in Exhibit 15.6, at the official pegged exchange rate the supply of dollars falls short of the demand for dollars, but, with rationing, some of the demand for dollars will *not* be met by the government. The government will pick and choose who gets to sell the local currency at the price that undervalues dollars and overvalues the local currency. In cases like this, a *black market*—the name for the underground market, in this case for dollars—comes into existence. A black market is part of the broader underground economy, which includes all transactions that are hidden from the government. The exchange rate on the black market, which is determined by supply and demand, will be less favorable to sellers of local currency than the official pegged exchange rate.

For instance, in Venezuela in 2009, the official exchange rate was 2.15 bolivares to the dollar, but the black market exchange rate was roughly 5 bolivares to the dollar. Hence, a Venezuelan who wanted to sell 1,000 bolivares in exchange for dollars would get 1,000/2.15 = $465 at the official exchange rate, but only 1,000/5 = $200 at the black market exchange rate. As you can see in this case, everybody with bolivares would have liked to purchase dollars at the more advantageous official rate. But the Venezuelan government did not allow this and simply refused to sell dollars at the official exchange rate to all Venezuelans who asked to buy dollars with bolivares. Those who are denied dollars have to either make do without the dollars or pay the much higher price for dollars on the black market—in this case the black market rate was more than twice as high.

To further complicate matters, many people who receive dollars at the official exchange rate are likely to turn around and sell them at the much higher black market rate. Such black market sales are illegal, but in most cases the black market transactions are prosecuted only if they are conducted by political enemies of the government. Can you see who benefits from the system?

Not surprisingly, many governments maintain overvalued exchange rates as a way of rewarding friends, cronies, and themselves. They can benefit directly from having access to the official and artificially cheap dollars. The system ultimately collapses, however, because it is inefficient. But while it lasts, politicians and their buddies make billions in profits.

Market pressure often pushes prices in financial markets, including exchange rates, back to their market-clearing levels, no matter what the government tries to do. In some cases, this pressure works gradually. In other cases, like the example we discuss in our Evidence-Based Economics feature, the pressure ends up generating explosive fallout.

Evidence-Based Economics

Q: How did George Soros make $1 billion?

From 1990 to 1992 the British pound had an exchange rate that was pegged against the German mark, the currency that Germany used before its current currency, the euro. The mark-pound exchange rate was initially pegged at a value that required little government intervention. However, in 1992, changing market forces put pressure on the British pound to depreciate. During the summer of 1992, the British authorities spent about $24 billion of foreign currency reserves to defend the pegged value of the pound. The British authorities were running low on foreign currency reserves when a new wave of pound sales hit the market on September 16, 1992. At the end of that day, the British authorities gave up trying to prop up its currency and accepted a sharp depreciation, as shown in Exhibit 15.7. This day came to be known as Black Wednesday.

Exhibit 15.7 The Mark-Pound Exchange Rate (Marks per Pound) from January 1991 to December 1992

Changes in economic conditions during 1992 implied that the British pound had become overvalued. British authorities spent their foreign currency reserves trying to defend their overvalued currency, leading to a sharp decline in their reserves in August and especially in early September 1992. On September 16, they gave up on their attempts to prop up the British pound, allowing a sharp depreciation.

Source: Federal Reserve Board of Governors.

Journalists referred to George Soros as "the man who broke the Bank of England." He bet against the pound in 1992 and made $1 billion when the pound subsequently fell in value.

The events leading up to Black Wednesday yielded winners and losers. The winners were the currency traders, especially George Soros. He had bet against the pound by borrowing about $10 billion worth of pounds and then using those pounds to purchase German marks. Following Black Wednesday, the German mark became more valuable relative to the pound and, consequently, the $10 billion of pound-denominated debts that Soros owed were cheaper to pay off with appreciated marks. Soros is believed to have made over $1 billion of profits on these transactions. These trading profits benefited Soros and the investors in his hedge fund.

In making these investments, Soros was employing basic economic reasoning. He understood that the British government was running out of foreign currency reserves, like German marks, in the summer of 1992. Soros was able to generate billions of dollars of additional sales of the British government's foreign currency reserves—Soros used pounds to buy $10 billion worth of marks on the foreign exchange market—which helped force the British authorities' hand. Soros's pound sales and mark purchases accelerated the pace of the British government's reserve losses, convincing the government that it couldn't resist the tide of pound selling.

The losers from Black Wednesday included the British government, which suffered enormous losses because it spent billions of dollars of foreign currency reserves to prop up the pound. By selling foreign currency reserves that would subsequently appreciate against the pound, the British government ended up with trading losses of approximately $6 billion worth of pounds.

Question

How did George Soros make $1 billion?

Answer

George Soros bet against an overvalued British pound just before the pound depreciated. Soros borrowed pounds and then used those pounds to buy German marks. On September 16, 1992, a day that came to be known as Black Wednesday, the British authorities succumbed to market pressure and devalued the pound. At this moment, Soros's investments in German marks became more valuable than his pound-denominated debts. Soros was able to forecast the pound's depreciation because British foreign currency reserves were rapidly running down during the summer of 1992.

Data

Exchange rate and reserves data.

Caveat

George Soros and other speculators have made many bets against currencies they thought were overvalued, but these bets have not all been successful because authorities can sometimes successfully defend overvalued exchange rates.

15.3 The Real Exchange Rate and Exports

So far we've focused on the nominal exchange rate. That's the exchange rate that you read about in the newspaper each day and is also the exchange rate that equates quantity supplied and quantity demanded in the foreign exchange market. However, it is a different exchange rate—the so-called real exchange rate—that is actually crucial for the macro-economy and for trade. We now define the concept of the real exchange rate and explain why it plays such an important role in influencing trade flows.

From the Nominal to the Real Exchange Rate

As we have seen, for its sourcing decisions Walmart compares the costs of domestic manufacturers and foreign manufacturers, adjusting for the exchange rate. For example, holding quality fixed, Walmart compares the implied dollar price of the toy manufactured in China to the dollar price of a similar toy manufactured in the United States. In essence, Walmart is interested in the following ratio:

$$\frac{\text{Dollar price of U.S. toy}}{\text{Dollar price of Chinese toy}}.$$

If this ratio is greater than 1, U.S. toys are more expensive than Chinese toys and Walmart buys from the Chinese supplier. On the other hand, if this ratio is less than 1, a U.S. toy is less expensive than a Chinese toy and Walmart buys from the U.S. supplier.

This ratio incorporates two different kinds of information: the prices of the toys in their respective domestic currencies and the yuan-dollar exchange rate that enables Walmart to convert yuan prices to dollar prices. The numerator is just the price that U.S. suppliers quote Walmart. If the U.S. manufacturer will supply toys to Walmart at $5 per toy, then $5 is the numerator.

To calculate the dollar price of the Chinese toy, we need to take the Chinese price (in yuan) and multiply it by the number of dollars per yuan. Recall that e is the yuan-dollar nominal exchange rate, defined as the number of yuan per dollar. The number of dollars per yuan is given by $1/e$. Thus the dollar price of Chinese toys can be calculated as

$$\text{Dollar price of Chinese toy} = (\text{Yuan price of Chinese toy}) \times \frac{\text{Dollars}}{\text{Yuan}}$$

$$= (\text{Yuan price of Chinese toy}) \times \frac{1}{e}.$$

For example, if a Chinese toy has a price of 20 yuan and the nominal exchange rate is 6.05 yuan per dollar, then the dollar price of the Chinese toy is 20/6.05 = $3.31 per toy.

Let's put these pieces together. We can now rewrite our initial ratio this way:

$$\frac{\text{Dollar price of U.S. toy}}{\text{Dollar price of Chinese toy}} = \frac{\text{Dollar price of U.S. toy}}{(\text{Yuan price of Chinese toy}) \times \frac{1}{e}}$$

$$= \frac{\text{Dollar price of U.S. toy} \times e}{\text{Yuan price of Chinese toy}}.$$

This ratio represents the relative price, adjusted for the exchange rate, of U.S. and Chinese toys. All companies make these calculations when sourcing their products.

Because this ratio is at the heart of every firm's sourcing decisions, economists have developed a special name for it. We define this ratio for a general basket of goods and services and refer to it as the *real exchange rate*. The **real exchange rate** for the United States is defined as the ratio of the dollar price of a basket of goods and services in the United States divided by the *dollar* price of the *same* basket of goods and services in a foreign country, for instance, China. Echoing the previous derivation for the toy example, the overall real exchange rate for the United States and China is written as:

> The **real exchange rate** is defined as the ratio of the dollar price of a basket of goods and services in the United States, divided by the dollar price of the same basket of goods and services in a foreign country.

$$\frac{\text{Dollar price of U.S. basket}}{\text{Dollar price of Chinese basket}} = \frac{(\text{Dollar price of U.S. basket}) \times e}{\text{Yuan price of Chinese basket}}.$$

The dollar price of a U.S. basket refers to the price of a basket of goods and services in the United States. The yuan price of a Chinese basket is the price of the *same* basket in China. By using the nominal exchange rate, we make the U.S. basket, priced in dollars, and the Chinese basket, priced in yuan, comparable.

Co-Movement Between the Nominal and the Real Exchange Rates

The previous equation makes it clear that the real exchange rate depends partially on the nominal exchange rate and partially on the ratio of U.S. prices and Chinese prices. If U.S. and Chinese prices don't respond to a change in the nominal exchange rate, then the real exchange rate should move proportionally with the nominal exchange rate. This is indeed the case in the short run but not necessarily in the long run.

Let's first consider the short-run consequences of a change in the nominal exchange rate. Exhibit 15.8 plots both the nominal exchange rate between British pounds and U.S. dollars (pounds per dollar, normalized to 100 in 1950, in blue) and the real exchange rate between the two currencies (dollar prices in the United States

> In most circumstances the nominal and real exchange rates appreciate and depreciate together.

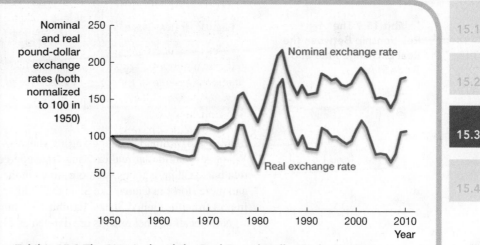

Exhibit 15.8 The Nominal and the Real Pound-Dollar Exchange Rates from 1950 to 2010

This exhibit plots the nominal exchange rate between British pounds and U.S. dollars (pounds per dollar, in blue) and the real exchange rate between the two currencies (dollar prices in the United States divided by dollar prices in the United Kingdom, in red). The pound and the dollar were pegged until 1966, so the nominal exchange rate was constant from 1950 to 1966. However, the real exchange rate fell from 1950 to 1966 because prices were rising faster in the United Kingdom than they were in the United States. After 1967, the nominal and the real exchange rates seem to move up and down together: when the nominal pound-dollar exchange rate rises so that the dollar appreciates, so does the real pound-dollar exchange rate. Over the entire period, the real exchange rate keeps falling further behind the nominal exchange rate because the UK inflation rate has been slightly greater on average than the U.S. inflation rate. Note that both exchange rates are normalized to equal 100 in 1950 (every observation is divided by the value of the same series in 1950 and the result is multiplied by 100).

Source: Alan Heston, Robert Summers, and Bettina Aten, Penn World Table Version 7.1, Center for International Comparisons of Production, Income and Prices at the University of Pennsylvania, July 2012.

divided by dollar prices in the United Kingdom, also normalized to 100 in 1950, in red). The exhibit reveals that, in the short run, the nominal pound-dollar exchange rate moves almost in lockstep with the real exchange rate. In other words, in most circumstances the nominal and real exchange rates appreciate and depreciate together.

However, the exhibit also shows that there are movements in the real exchange rate that are not associated with changes in the nominal exchange rate. This is easiest to see from 1950 to 1966, when the nominal exchange rate was pegged between the two countries. With the nominal exchange rate temporarily *fixed*, movements in the real exchange rate derive solely from different amounts of inflation in the United States and the United Kingdom. During this period, UK inflation was higher than U.S. inflation, causing the ratio of U.S. prices to UK prices to fall. With a fixed nominal exchange rate, a higher inflation rate in the United Kingdom relative to the United States implies that the real exchange rate fell from 1950 to 1966.

Movements in the real exchange rate arising from differences in the U.S. and UK inflation rates have also occurred after 1966 (when the two currencies started floating against one another), but these inflation effects are easy to miss when you look at the exhibit. For floating currencies with modest levels of inflation, most of the year-to-year movement in the real exchange rate derives from movement in the nominal exchange rate and not from cross-country differences in the rate of inflation.

The Real Exchange Rate and Net Exports

The real exchange rate is the key determinant of whether Walmart is stocking its U.S. store shelves with U.S. or Chinese products and whether Shanghai Bailian—a Chinese big-box

Exhibit 15.9 The Relationship Between the Real Exchange Rate and Trade Flows	Yuan-Dollar Real Exchange Rate	China	United States
	Goes up (dollar appreciates and the yuan depreciates)	Import less from United States Export more to United States	Export less to China Import more from China
	Goes down (dollar depreciates and the yuan appreciates)	Import more from United States Export less to United States	Export more to China Import less from China

retailer like Walmart—is stocking its shelves (in China) with U.S. or Chinese products. When the yuan-dollar real exchange rate appreciates, U.S. goods become more expensive relative to Chinese goods, so more stores in the United States prefer to import from China and more stores in China, like Shanghai Bailian, prefer to buy local products rather than to import from the United States. Exhibit 15.9 summarizes these optimizing decisions.

Now recall that net exports are defined as exports minus imports:

$$\text{Net exports} = \text{Exports} - \text{Imports}.$$

Exhibit 15.10 plots the *net exports curve*, denoted by $NX(E)$, which shows the relationship between net exports and the real exchange rate, denoted as E. This relationship is downward-sloping because when the yuan-dollar real exchange rate appreciates (implying a higher value of E), U.S. exports to China tend to fall and U.S. imports from China tend to increase.

Exhibit 15.10 The Real Exchange Rate (E) and Net Exports

When its real exchange rate appreciates, a country imports more from other countries and exports less to other countries, reducing its net exports. This relationship is shown by the downward-sloping net exports curve, denoted by $NX(E)$. For instance, when the real exchange rate rises from E^* to E_1, net exports fall from 0 to NX_1 < 0. Conversely, when the real exchange rate falls from E^* to E_2, net exports rise from 0 to $NX_2 > 0$.

Notice also that there is a particular value of the real exchange rate, marked as E^* in Exhibit 15.10, where net exports are equal to zero. When the real exchange rate is above E^*, net exports are negative (a trade deficit), and when the real exchange rate is below E^*, net exports are positive (a trade surplus). The real exchange rate usually can't stay far above E^*, because large permanent trade deficits tend to be unsustainable. A large permanent trade deficit leads to an ever-rising debt to foreign countries. At some point, foreign countries will get nervous that this debt won't be repaid. When that happens, they will start selling their U.S. assets, driving down the nominal dollar exchange rate, which causes E to fall toward E^*.

15.4 GDP in the Open Economy

We now analyze the macroeconomic implications of changes in the real exchange rate. Let's focus on an appreciation of the real exchange rate. To understand the consequences of this change, let's return to the national income accounting identity, which was introduced in Chapter 5:

$$Y = C + I + G + X - M.$$

Why Have Chinese Authorities Kept the Yuan Undervalued?

Our discussion of the yuan-dollar nominal exchange rate, which is illustrated in Exhibit 15.5, implies that the yuan has been historically undervalued (and the dollar has been overvalued). To hold down the value of the yuan (and thereby prop up the value of the dollar), the Chinese authorities have sold yuan and purchased dollars (about $2 trillion).

Why would the Chinese authorities try to keep the dollar overvalued? Exhibit 15.10 provides the answer: an overvalued real dollar exchange rate implies greater net exports from China to the United States. Chinese authorities have been supporting an overvalued dollar in order to boost Chinese exports. A consequence of the overvalued yuan-dollar real exchange rate—an exchange rate above the equivalent of E^* in Exhibit 15.10—is the large trade deficit that the United States runs with China.

Exhibit 15.11 shows that this trade deficit was approximately $300 billion in 2013. Export growth has been a key pillar of China's growth strategy since the 1980s.

This strategy might boost the rate of Chinese growth, but it does come with costs for China, not to mention the rest of the world. An undervalued Chinese yuan hurts Chinese workers by lowering their buying power because it makes their imports from the rest of the world more expensive. In addition, an undervalued Chinese yuan creates diplomatic problems with China's trading partners. Higher Chinese exports to the United States distort economic activity in the United States by crowding out industries that compete with Chinese manufacturers. This situation creates considerable friction between the United States and China.

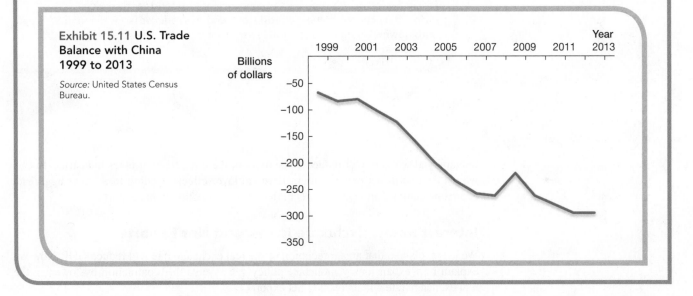

Exhibit 15.11 U.S. Trade Balance with China 1999 to 2013

Source: United States Census Bureau.

Here Y represents GDP, I represents investment (in plants, equipment, and residential construction), C represents consumption, G represents government expenditure, and $X - M$ represents net exports (all for the U.S. economy).

The appreciation of the real exchange rate reduces net exports and causes a decline in GDP—holding all else equal, a decline in $X - M$ on the right-hand side of the national income accounting identity reduces Y or GDP. We can trace out these macroeconomic implications using the labor supply and labor demand diagram introduced in Chapter 9 and used for the analysis of macroeconomic fluctuations in Chapters 12 and 13. Exhibit 15.12 presents the model with downward wage rigidity.

To illustrate how GDP responds to the changes in net exports, suppose that the dollar appreciates and net exports decline. In particular, the foreign demand for certain U.S. products—let's say machine tools—declines because the appreciation of the dollar has made these goods more expensive for foreigners. This decline in demand for machine tools implies that machine-tool producers will shift their labor demand to the left. As shown in Exhibit 15.12, the leftward shift of labor demand induced by the appreciation of the dollar will translate into lower employment and a new pool of unemployed workers.

We also need to consider multiplier effects, which were introduced in Chapter 12. For instance, job losses in an export industry will cause unemployment, and the newly

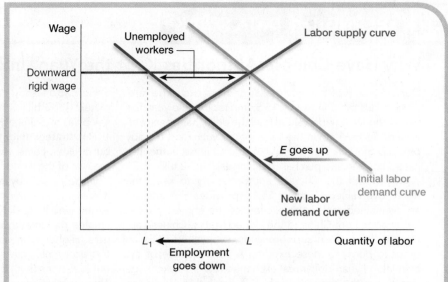

Exhibit 15.12 Employment Falls When the Real Exchange Rate Appreciates

A decline in net exports (such as the move from trade balance to NX_1 in Exhibit 15.10) reduces the demand for the goods and services supplied by certain domestic producers, and this reduces labor demand. With downward rigid wages, the lower labor demand translates into unemployment.

unemployed workers will reduce consumption, thereby affecting other industries. In this way, a decline in net exports might have spillover effects, leading to a larger aggregate economic contraction than the direct effect of the reduction in net exports.

Interest Rates, Exchange Rates, and Net Exports

We just explained that an appreciation of the real exchange rate will reduce GDP. Now we explain how expansionary monetary policy can reverse this contraction by lowering the real exchange rate and increasing net exports.

Imagine that we start from the real exchange rate E_1, as drawn in Exhibit 15.10. Assume that the domestic interest rate falls as the result of expansionary monetary policy. Such a decrease will cause foreigners—say, Europeans—to reduce their holdings of U.S. assets (because with a lower interest rate, the rate of return on U.S. assets relative to foreign assets has declined, making them less attractive). But to do so they need to exchange dollars for euros, and thus there will be a greater supply of dollars from Europeans. The greater supply of U.S. dollars will shift the dollar supply curve to the right in the foreign exchange market. Because the dollar-euro exchange rate is flexible, this greater supply of dollars will lead to a depreciation of the dollar relative to the euro.

In Exhibit 15.10, this depreciation means moving toward a lower real exchange rate, say from E_1 to E^*, which increases net exports from $NX_1 < 0$ to $NX = 0$. In summary, a decrease in U.S. interest rates causes a depreciation of the U.S. dollar, a depreciation in the dollar real exchange rate, and an increase in U.S. net exports.

> **The Fed can increase net exports by lowering domestic interest rates or can lower net exports by raising domestic interest rates.**

On the other hand, contractionary monetary policy will have the opposite impact. When the Fed raises the domestic interest rate, this makes U.S. assets more appealing, which causes foreigners to increase their holdings of U.S. assets. Their increased purchases of U.S. assets cause a rightward shift in the demand curve for dollars, raising the equilibrium nominal exchange rate. This in turn causes the real exchange rate to appreciate, reducing net exports.

Summing up, the Fed can increase net exports by lowering domestic interest rates or can lower net exports by raising domestic interest rates.

Revisiting Black Wednesday

With the help of this discussion, we can revisit the British experience in the early 1990s. As we discussed in the Evidence-Based Economics feature, the British pound came to be overvalued relative to the German mark and this overvaluation eventually led to the sharp depreciation of the pound on Black Wednesday.

The scenario depicted in Exhibits 15.10 and 15.12 reflects the situation of the British economy during 1991 and 1992. The overvalued pound was reducing British GDP. The British economy was effectively at real exchange rate E_1 in Exhibit 15.10 and the corresponding point with employment given by L_1 in Exhibit 15.12.

You might be wondering why the British authorities thought that they could defend the pound despite its overvaluation. The answer is that they believed that the overvaluation was temporary.

The British authorities' optimistic beliefs were not entirely groundless. We have so far explained how a nominal exchange rate depreciation can eliminate overvaluation of a currency. But there is *another* solution that can occur whether or not a country has a flexible exchange rate. Due to the lower net exports shown in Exhibit 15.10, domestic firms might cut their prices to become more competitive, and this would reduce the ratio of domestic prices to foreign prices. Recall that the real exchange rate is

$$E = \frac{(\text{Domestic prices}) \times e}{\text{Foreign prices}}.$$

A falling ratio of domestic to foreign prices (holding e fixed) would correspond to a falling real exchange rate, boosting net exports, raising labor demand, and increasing GDP.

In 1992, the British authorities anticipated that British prices *would* fall relative to the prices of their trading partners and that this would eliminate the overvaluation of the pound because more foreign countries would choose to import goods from the United Kingdom (shifting the demand curve for the pound to the right). However, such domestic price adjustments take a long time to occur, something the British authorities didn't realize at first. By the time they learned this lesson the overvalued pound had already depressed British net exports and caused a severe recession. As the real exchange rate was showing little sign of improvement and British foreign reserves were running out, the stage was set for Black Wednesday and the sharp depreciation of the pound's nominal exchange rate.

Consistent with the models discussed in this chapter, the depreciation of the pound on Black Wednesday led to a decline in the pound's real exchange rate, an expansion of British net exports, and a corresponding increase in the aggregate level of economic activity. In fact, the British economy did so well after Black Wednesday, growing on average at 3.6 percent per year during the next 3 years, that some commentators switched to calling the day that Soros broke the pound "White Wednesday." Pegging the pound to the mark had been damaging the UK economy. Letting market forces determine the price of the pound turned out to be the best policy after all.

The Costs of Fixed Exchange Rates

Both Europe and the United States were plunged into recession during the 2007–2009 financial crisis. The economic contraction and its aftermath have been worse in Europe, as you can see in Exhibit 15.13. In 2013, U.S. real GDP was 7.6 percent *above* its 2007 pre-crisis level. In 2013, eurozone real GDP was still 0.3 percent *below* its 2007 pre-crisis level.

Many economists believe that the greater severity and duration of the economic crisis in Europe has in part been due to the inability of European exchange rates to adjust. Since January 1, 1999, major European economies (excluding the United Kingdom) have been part of the eurozone, which means that they use a single currency, the euro. This is referred to as a *currency union*, a form of fixed exchange rate, in which, by using the same currency, all of these economies are pegging their exchange rates to each other.

As we have seen, when the exchange rate can change, countries can devalue their currencies and thus increase their net exports, stimulating the economy. This is not possible when a country is a member of a currency union (unless the common currency itself is devalued).

Compounding this problem, there is the mismatch between the needs of different European economies. Germany has been doing relatively well compared to the rest of Europe. In 2013, German real GDP was 5.9 percent above its 2007 pre-crisis level. Many other eurozone economies have done much less well. The aggregate real GDP of Greece, Ireland, Italy, Portugal, and Spain, was 7.2 percent *lower* in 2013 than it was in 2007.

If these countries had independent monetary authorities, they might have adopted highly expansionary monetary policies, stimulating their economies and reducing their real exchange rates. This would have increased their net exports and boosted demand for labor. However, the eurozone currency union has necessitated a one-size-fits-all monetary policy, which has ended up being insufficiently expansionary for Greece, Ireland, Italy, Portugal, and Spain.

Exhibit 15.13 Real GDP Set to 100 in 2007

This exhibit plots the path of real GDP in four economic regions: the United States, Germany, the entire eurozone, and a subset of eurozone economies that were particularly hard hit by the financial crisis (Greece, Ireland, Italy, Portugal, and Spain). All of the data is normalized to 100 in 2007 to simplify comparisons. This is done by dividing all of the real GDP observations for a specific country by the value of real GDP for that country in 2007 and then multiplying by 100.

Sources: World Bank Databank and International Monetary Fund World Economic Outlook Database.

Summary

🌑 The nominal exchange rate is the number of units of foreign currency per unit of domestic currency. The real exchange rate, on the other hand, gives the ratio of the dollar price of a basket of goods and services purchased in the United States to the dollar price of the *same* basket purchased in a foreign country.

🌑 The nominal exchange rate is determined by the supply and demand for a currency in the foreign exchange market. When a Chinese producer sells goods to a U.S. firm and receives dollars, the Chinese firm converts the dollars to the

Chinese currency, the yuan, in the foreign exchange market. This is equivalent to demanding yuan and supplying dollars in the foreign exchange market. On the other hand, a Chinese firm that imports from the United States would be doing the opposite in the foreign exchange market: supplying yuan and demanding dollars with which it will pay its U.S. trading partners.

☀ When a country has a flexible exchange rate, changes in the supply and demand for a currency lead to fluctuations in the nominal exchange rate. Many countries, however, manage or fix exchange rates and therefore peg their currencies to another currency, such as the dollar. Under managed or fixed exchange rates, fluctuations in the supply and demand for the currency do not necessarily lead to fluctuations in the exchange rate.

☀ Though managed or fixed exchange rate systems might appear more stable at first, when the exchange rates they generate are out of line with market forces, these systems can lead to sudden changes in the exchange rate. In the process, they create huge profit opportunities, like the one exploited by the financier George Soros when he bet that the British pound would be allowed to depreciate.

☀ The real exchange rate is a key price for the economy in part because it determines net exports. A real exchange rate greater than 1 implies that U.S. goods and services are more expensive than foreign goods and services. Thus a real exchange rate above 1 discourages exports and encourages imports, reducing net exports.

☀ A fall in net exports lowers GDP and shifts the labor demand curve to the left.

☀ Domestic interest rates influence the real exchange rate. A fall in domestic interest rates reduces the appeal of U.S. assets to foreign investors, lowering both the nominal and the real exchange rates. The resulting rise in net exports shifts the labor demand curve to the right and increases GDP.

Key Terms

nominal exchange rate *p. 347*
flexible exchange rate, or floating exchange rate *p. 349*

fixed exchange rate *p. 349*
managed exchange rate *p. 349*

foreign exchange market *p. 349*
real exchange rate *p. 358*

Questions

All questions are available in MyEconLab for practice and instructor assignment.

1. How is the nominal exchange rate between two currencies defined?

2. When is a currency said to appreciate or depreciate?

3. Distinguish among flexible, fixed, and managed exchange rates.

4. What does the demand curve for dollars show? Why does the demand curve for dollars slope downward?

5. What does the supply curve for dollars show? Why does the supply curve for dollars slope upward?

6. What does it mean to say that, at an exchange rate of 1 USD = 60 INR, the U.S. dollar is overvalued and the Indian rupee is undervalued?

7. Why might a country peg its exchange rate at a level that overvalues its own currency?

8. How did George Soros benefit from the overvaluation of the British pound?

9. How is the real exchange rate for the United States calculated?

10. How does a change in a country's real exchange rate affect its net exports?

11. All else being equal, explain how an increase in the real interest rate can affect a country's net exports, labor demand, and level of employment.

12. The economy of Freedonia is currently faced with negative net exports and high unemployment. Explain two measures that the Freedonian central bank could take to increase net exports and lower unemployment.

Problems

All problems are available in MyEconLab for practice and instructor assignment.
Problems marked 🌐 update with real-time data.

1. Suppose that the country Argonia follows a flexible exchange rate regime. The exchange rate between the Argonian dollar (AGD) and the U.S. dollar (USD) is currently 1 AGD = 3 USD.

   a. Use a graph to show the equilibrium in the foreign exchange market with the U.S. dollar-Argonian dollar exchange rate on the vertical axis and the quantity of Argonian dollars on the horizontal axis.

   b. Suppose that the global demand for apricots grown in Argonia increases sharply. Other things being unchanged, how would this affect the value of the Argonian dollar? Use the graph to explain.

2. Recall from Chapter 6 that the Big Mac index is used as a rough measure of purchasing power parity across countries. *The Economist* magazine recently included the Vietnamese dong (VND) in its calculation of the Big Mac index. A Big Mac costs $4.62 in the United States but only 60,000 dong or $2.84 in Vietnam (at the current exchange rate). What does this data suggest about the value of the real exchange rate of the U.S. dollar vs. the Vietnamese dong? Is the real exchange rate likely to be greater than or less than one?

3. As discussed in the chapter, Venezuela has an official exchange rate as well as a black market exchange rate. The following chart shows the official nominal exchange rate between the Venezuelan bolivar (VEF) and the US dollar (USD).

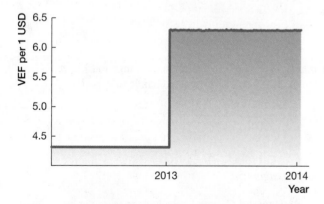

   The Venezuelan authorities increased the value of the VEF/USD nominal exchange rate from 4.3 VEF per dollar to 6.3 VEF per dollar in February 2013. However, in January 2014, buyers and sellers in the black market were exchanging the bolivar for the dollar at a rate of 79 VEF per dollar, leading commentators to believe that the official exchange rate of the VEF is highly overvalued.

   a. Assuming the black market exchange rate reflects what the equilibrium exchange rate would be, use a graph to show the overvalued official exchange rate and the equilibrium exchange rate in the market for VEF. The vertical axis should be expressed as VEF per dollar.

   b. Why might the Venezuelan government choose to maintain an overvalued official exchange rate?

4. The Evidence-Based Economics feature in the chapter discusses how George Soros's hedge fund made money by betting on the devaluation of the British pound. Interestingly, Soros also made money betting against the Thai baht.

   In 1997, the baht had been continually falling against the U.S. dollar. The Bank of Thailand attempted to defend its overvalued exchange rate—the Thai baht (THB) was pegged to the U.S. dollar at a rate of 25 THB per U.S. dollar. Explain how each of the following factors made it difficult for the Thai authorities to continue to defend their exchange rate, leading to a sharp devaluation.

   a. The government's reserves of U.S. dollars fell to a 2-year low in 1997.

   b. A very high level of corporate debt in Thailand was denominated in U.S. dollars.

5. Using the net exports curve and the labor demand and labor supply curve, explain how a fall in the real exchange rate can lead to an increase in employment in a country.

6. Econia trades with its neighbors, the countries of Governmentia and Sociologia. In Econia, the currency is called the econ; in Governmentia, the currency is called the gov; and in Sociologia, the currency is the soc.

   Nominal exchange rates follow:

   200 econ = 1 gov

   1 soc = ¼ gov

   100 econ = 1 soc

   A good that is produced and consumed in all three countries is the Mack Burger. The price of Macks in the three countries is as follows: 1 Mack costs 2 govs in Governmentia, 16 socs in Sociologia, and 600 econ in Econia.

   a. From the perspective of Governmentia, calculate the real exchange rate in Mack Burgers between Governmentia and Sociologia, using the nominal exchange rates and prices listed above. Explain in words what the number you calculated means.

   b. If these three currencies can be freely traded so that their exchange rates are flexible or floating, can the nominal exchange rates listed above persist over time? Why or why not? [Hint: Show that currency traders could make unlimited profits if they could trade at these exchange rates.]

   c. The economy of Econia enters a period of deflation. What will happen as a result of this to the current account in Governmentia, Econia's main trading partner, in the short run? Assume nominal exchange rates are constant in the short run. Explain fully.

7. *Challenge Problem*: The beautiful, mythical country of Coloradial uses the teo as its currency, and the gritty, post-industrial country of Oheo uses the eren. Exactly 1 year ago, you could get 100 teos in exchange for 5 erens in the foreign exchange market. Since then, though, the real interest rate in Coloradial has increased, while staying constant in Oheo.

a. All other things being equal, would you expect the eren to have appreciated or depreciated with respect to the teo? Explain your reasoning.

b. Assume that the change in the value of the eren with respect to the teo (appreciation or depreciation depending on your previous answer) was 50 percent. What is the current nominal exchange rate expressed in teos/eren?

c. One year ago, you borrowed 100,000 teos from a Coloradial bank at a rate of 3 percent per year. You then traded the 100,000 teos for erens at the nominal exchange rate that prevailed at the time (100 teos = 5 erens), and invested those erens in Oheo at 5 percent interest.

   After the year was over, your intention was to exchange the erens back for teos, repay the loan to the Coloradial bank, and keep a tidy profit. (This strategy is called a "carry trade" and at various times has been popular with foreign exchange traders.)

   i. How much would you have made on this strategy if the interest rates did not change *and* if the exchange rate had not changed from 100 teos = 5 erens?

   ii. What will be your profit (or loss) on the trade given the changes in the exchange rate you found in parts (a) and (b)? (Assume the interest rate you paid to the Coloradial bank was fixed in your loan agreement, and so did not change.)

8. The graph below shows the Japanese yen per U.S. dollar exchange rate between 2008 and 2014. The table that follows shows the real interest rates in these two countries during the same period.

Real Interest rate in the United States and Japan

Year	2009	2010	2011	2012	2013
United States	2.5	2	1.3	1.5	1.7
Japan	2.2	3.8	3.4	2.3	1.9

What could explain why the U.S. dollar depreciated vis-à-vis the Japanese yen between 2008 and 2013? Explain your answer with the help of the information given in the table.

9. Over the last 10 years, the dollar has depreciated vis-à-vis the euro.

   a. Suppose that in the short run the Fed wanted both to defend the dollar (that is, stop its decline and/or cause it to appreciate) and stimulate investment. Based on what you have learned in this chapter and in Chapter 13, discuss whether the Fed can achieve both of these goals simultaneously through monetary policy?

   b. Suppose instead that the European Central Bank (ECB) conducts expansionary monetary policy. What is the short-run effect, if any, of this policy on the euro/dollar nominal exchange rate and on the real exchange rate between the United States and the European Monetary Union. In your answer about what happens to the real exchange rate, state any assumptions you are making.

10. Thailand and Taiwan are both rapidly growing economies in East and Southeast Asia that trade actively with other countries.

    a. Suppose rice wine is the only good produced in Thailand and Taiwan. A bottle of wine costs 100 bhat in Thailand and 200 NT (New Taiwan dollars) in Taiwan. The nominal exchange rate is 0.5 bhat per NT. Calculate the real exchange rate from Thailand's perspective (that is, using Thailand as the "domestic" economy). Show your work. Intuitively, what does this number represent?

    b. The Taiwanese trade balance (its current account) with the rest of the world is initially running neither a deficit nor a surplus. Taiwan alone experiences an economic boom and its real interest rate rises at the same time. Thoroughly explain the mechanisms by which the Taiwanese current account is affected by its boom and the increase in its real interest rate.

    c. Assume that the change in the value of the bhat/NT exchange rate was 50 percent, which, depending on your answer in part (b), was either appreciation or depreciation. What is the current nominal exchange rate expressed in bhat/NT? Show your work.

11. Imagine that there are two economies in the world: Bostonia and New Yorkland. Bostonia's currency is the sock and New Yorkland's is the yank. Despite the long-standing rivalry between their citizens, Bostonia and New Yorkland are trading partners.

    The Central Bank of New Yorkland decides to conduct contractionary monetary policy. Explain the short-run effect, if any, on the following:

    a. The yank/sock nominal exchange rate

    b. New Yorkland's net exports

    c. Bostonia's net exports

    d. GDP in New Yorkland recently plummeted. At first, the citizens in Bostonia cheered, happy to see their rivals taken down a notch. But then an economist (always a killjoy) asserts that the fall in New Yorkland's GDP is likely to hurt Bostonia's GDP in the short run. Could the economist be correct? Why or why not?

12. Recall the discussion in "Letting the Data Speak" regarding differences in the recovery of various members of the Eurozone from the recession of 2007–2009. Based on the discussion in this chapter and previous chapters, explain why the adoption of a single currency, like the Euro, would hamper the ability of an individual country to respond to a downturn in its economy.

Endnotes

Chapter 2

1 Philip Oreopoulos, "Estimating Average and Local Treatment Effects of Education when Compulsory Schooling Laws Really Matter," *American Economic Review* 96, no. 1 (2006): 152–175.

2 Sally Sadoff, Steven D. Levitt, and John A. List, "The Effect of Performance-Based Incentives on Educational Achievement: Evidence from a Randomized Experiment," University of Chicago Working Paper (2011).

Chapter 3

1 James Frew and Beth Wilson, "Apartment Rents and Locations in Portland, Oregon: 1992–2002," *Journal of Real Estate Research* 29, no. 2 (2007): 201–217.

Chapter 4

1 Fred Ferretti, "The Way We Were: A Look Back at the Late Great Gas Shortage," *New York Times,* April 15, 1974, p. 386.

2 Stephanie McCrummen and Aymar Jean, "17 Hurt as Computer Sale Turns into Stampede. Source: http://www.washingtonpost .com/wp-dyn/content/article/2005/08/16/AR2005081600738 .htm," *Washington Post*, August 17, 2005.

Chapter 5

1 This is based on a population of 316.4 million in 2013 as reported by the Census Bureau: http://www.census.gov/population/ international/data/countryrank/rank.php

2 Daniel Kahneman and Alan B. Krueger, "Developments in the Measurement of Subjective Well-Being," *The Journal of Economic Perspectives* 20.1 (2006): 3–24.

3 Betsey Stevenson and Justin Wolfers, "Economic Growth and Subjective Well-Being: Reassessing the Easterlin Paradox" Brookings Papers on Economic Activity, Spring 2008.

Chapter 7

1 William D. Nordhaus, "Do Real-Output and Real-Wage Measures Capture Reality? The History of Light Suggests Not," Cowles Foundation Discussion Papers 1078, Cowles Foundation for Research in Economics, 1994.

2 Thomas R. Malthus, *An Essay on the Principle of Population* (1798).

3 Emmanuel Saez and Thomas Piketty, "Income Inequality in the United States, 1913–1998," *Quarterly Journal of Economics* 118, no. 1 (2003): 1–39.

4 Daron Acemoglu and Simon Johnson, "Disease and Development: The Effect of Life Expectancy on Economic Growth," *Journal of Political Economy* 115, no. 6 (2007): 925–985.

5 Robert M. Solow, "A Contribution to the Theory of Economic Growth," *Quarterly Journal of Economics* 70, no. 1 (1956): 65–94; and Trevor W. Swan, "Economic Growth and Capital Accumulation," *Economic Record* 32, no. 2 (1956): 334–361.

Chapter 8

1 Charles-Louis de Secondat Montesquieu, *The Spirit of the Laws, Book XIV*, Chapter 2, 230–235, [1748] 1989.

2 Alfred Marshall, *Principles of Economics, Book IV: The Agents of Production*, Chapter 5 (1890).

3 Jeffrey Sachs, "Tropical Underdevelopment," *NBER Working Paper* 8119 (2001).

4 Max Weber, *The Protestant Ethic and the Spirit of Capitalism* (New York: Routledge, [1905] 2001).

5 Samuel P. Huntington, "The Clash of Civilizations?" *Foreign Affairs* (1993): 22–49.

6 Lawrence E. Harrison and Samuel P. Huntington, *Culture Matters: How Values Shape Human Progress* (New York: Basic Books, 2000).

7 Douglass North, *Institutions, Institutional Change and Economic Performance* (Cambridge: Cambridge University Press, 1990).

8 Tim Culpan, "Taiwan's iPads are Free. The Cases Cost $1,000," *Businessweek Magazine*, October 7, 2010.

9 Adam Smith, *The Wealth of Nations* (1776).

10 Daron Acemoglu and James A. Robinson, *Why Nations Fail: the Origins of Power, Prosperity and Poverty* (New York: Crown Publishers, 2012).

11 Joseph A. Schumpeter, *Capitalism, Socialism, and Democracy* (1942).

12 Joel Mokyr, *The Enlightened Economy: An Economic History of Britain 1700–1850* (New Haven: Yale University Press, 2010).

13 Ritva Reinikka and Jakob Svensson, "Local Capture: Evidence from a Central Government Transfer Program in Uganda," *Quarterly Journal of Economics.* 119, no. 2 (2004): 679–705.

Chapter 9

1 Anna Richey-Allen, "The Pain of Unemployment," *New York Times*, October 31, 2010.

2 Alan Krueger and Andreas Mueller, "Job Search and Job Finding in a Period of Mass Unemployment: Evidence from High-Frequency Longitudinal Data," Princeton University, Industrial Relations Section Working Paper 562 (2011).

3 Nathan Hipsman, "Downward Nominal Wage Rigidity: A Double-Density Model," Harvard University Working Paper (2012).

4 David H. Autor, David Dorn, and Gordon H. Hanson, "The China Syndrome: Local Labor Market Effects of Import Competition in the United States," *American Economic Review* 103, no. 6 (2013).

Chapter 10

1 Irving Fisher, "Appreciation and Interest: A Study of the Influence of Monetary Appreciation and Depreciation on the Rate of Interest with Applications to the Bimetallic Controversy and the Theory of Interest," *Publications of the American Economic Association* 11, no. 4 (1896): 331–442.

2 Eugene F. Fama, "Efficient Capital Markets: A Review of Theory and Empirical Work," *Journal of Finance* 25, no. 2 (1970): 383–417.

3 Robert J. Shiller, *Irrational Exuberance* (Princeton University Press, 2005).

Chapter 12

1 Before 1947, U.S. GDP data are only available on an annual basis. Because the 1945 recession occurred within a single year, we don't know how much real GDP declined, but we can estimate it using the annual data. From 1944 to 1946, real GDP fell by 12.7 percent.

2 Kathryn M. Dominguez, Ray C. Fair, and Matthew D. Shapiro, "Forecasting the Depression: Harvard versus Yale," *American Economic Review* 78, no. 4 (1988): 595–612.

3 Arthur M. Okun, "Potential GNP: Its Measurement and Significance," 1963, reprinted as *Cowles Foundation Paper* 190.

4 Arthur C. Pigou, *Industrial Fluctuations*, New York: Macmillan, 1929.

5 Finn E. Kydland and Edward C. Prescott, "Time to Build and Aggregate Fluctuations" *Econometrica* 50, no. 6 (1982): 1345–1370.

6 John M. Keynes, *The General Theory of Employment, Interest and Money*, Palgrave Macmillan, 1936.

7 Milton Friedman and Anna J. Schwartz, *A Monetary History of the United States*, 1867–1960, Princeton University Press, 1963.

Chapter 13

1 William L. Silber, *Volcker: The Triumph of Persistence*, New York: Bloomsbury Press, 2012.

2 Bank of England, Financial Stability Report, June 2014 Issue no. 35, http://www.bankofengland.co.uk/publications/Documents/fsr/2014/fsrfull1406.pdf.

3 John B. Taylor, "Discretion Versus Policy Rules in Practice," in *Carnegie-Rochester Conference Series on Public Policy* 39 (1993): 195–214.

4 Christina Romer and Jared Bernstein, "The Job Impact of the American Recovery and Reinvestment Act." January 9, 2009.

5 Romer and Bernstein, "Job Impact."

6 Valerie A. Ramey, "Identifying Government Spending Shocks: It's All in the Timing," *Quarterly Journal of Economics* 126, no. 1 (2011): 1–50.

Chapter 14

1 Greg Linden, Kenneth Kraemer, and Jason Dedrick, "Who Captures Value in a Global Innovation Network?: The Case of Apple's iPod," *Communications of the ACM* 52, no. 3 (2009): 140–144.

2 Linden, Kraemer, and Dedrick, "Who Captures Value."

3 Jack Ewing, "The Disassembly Line," *New York Times*, July 15, 2014, B1.

4 Jennifer L. Rich, "U.S. Admits That Politics Was Behind Steel Tariffs," *New York Times*, March 14, 2002, at http://www.nytimes.com/2002/03/14/business/us-admits-that-politics-was-behind-steel-tariffs.html.

5 Dalila Cervantes-Godoy and Joe Dewbre, "Economic Importance of Agriculture for Sustainable Development and Poverty Reduction: The Case Study of Vietnam," OECD: 2010.

6 Ben Bland, "Vietnam's Factories Grapple with Growing Unrest," *Financial Times*, January 19, 2012, For the 2014 minimum wage data, see http://www.amchamvietnam.com/30442612/vietnams-2014-minimum-wage-adjustment-shows-moderation-15-increase-vs-17-5-increase-in-2012/

7 Penn World Tables. Alan Heston, Robert Summers and Bettina Aten, Penn World Table Version 7.1, Center for International Comparisons of Production, Income and Prices at the University of Pennsylvania, Nov 2012.

8 Cervantes-Godoy and Dewbre "Economic Importance."

9 Eric V. Edmonds and Nina Pavcnik, "International Trade and Child Labor: Cross-Country Evidence," *Journal of International Economics* 68, no. 1 (2006): 115–140.

Glossary

Absolute advantage A producer has an absolute advantage in producing a good or service if the producer can produce more units per hour than other producers.

Aggregate production function An aggregate production function describes the relationship between the aggregate output (GDP) of a nation and its factors of production.

Aggregation The process of adding up individual behaviors is referred to as aggregation.

Animal spirits Animal spirits are psychological factors that lead to changes in the mood of consumers or businesses, thereby affecting consumption, investment, and GDP.

Automatic stabilizers Automatic stabilizers are components of the government budget that automatically adjust to smooth out economic fluctuations.

Bank reserves Official bank reserves consist of vault cash and deposits at the Federal Reserve Bank.

Bank run A bank run occurs when a bank experiences an extraordinarily large volume of withdrawals driven by a concern that the bank will run out of liquid assets with which to pay withdrawals.

Bar chart A bar chart uses bars of different heights or lengths to indicate the properties of different groups.

Behavioral economics Behavioral economics jointly analyzes the economic and psychological factors that explain human behavior.

Budget constraint A budget constraint shows the bundles of goods or services that a consumer can choose given her limited budget.

Capital income Capital income is any form of payment that derives from owning physical or financial capital.

Catch-up growth Catch-up growth refers to a growth process whereby relatively poorer nations increase their incomes by taking advantage of knowledge and technologies already invented in other, technologically more advanced countries.

Causation A causation occurs when one thing directly affects another through a cause-and-effect relationship.

Central bank The central bank is the government institution that monitors financial institutions, controls certain key interest rates, and indirectly controls the money supply. These activities constitute monetary policy.

Closed economy A closed economy does not trade with the rest of the world.

Collective bargaining Collective bargaining refers to contract negotiations between firms and labor unions.

Comparative advantage A producer has a comparative advantage in producing a good (or service) when the producer has a lower opportunity cost per unit produced compared to other producers.

Comparative statics Comparative statics is the comparison of economic outcomes before and after some economic variable is changed.

Competitive equilibrium price The competitive equilibrium price equates quantity supplied and quantity demanded.

Competitive equilibrium quantity The competitive equilibrium quantity is the quantity that corresponds to the competitive equilibrium price.

Competitive equilibrium The competitive equilibrium is the crossing point of the supply curve and the demand curve.

Complements Two goods are complements when the fall in the price of one, leads to a right shift in the demand curve for the other.

Consumer Price Index (CPI) The Consumer Price Index is 100 times the ratio of the cost of buying a basket of consumer goods using 2013 prices divided by the cost of buying the same basket of consumer goods using base-year prices.

Consumption Consumption is the market value of consumption goods and consumption services that are bought by domestic households.

Contractionary fiscal policy Contractionary fiscal policy uses lower government expenditure and higher taxes to reduce the growth rate of real GDP.

Contractionary monetary policy Contractionary monetary policy slows down growth in bank reserves, raises interest rates, reduces borrowing, slows down growth in the money supply, and reduces the rate of inflation.

Correlation A correlation means that there is a mutual relationship between two things.

Cost-Benefit analysis Cost-Benefit analysis is a calculation that adds up costs and benefits using a common unit of measurement, like dollars.

Countercyclical fiscal policy Countercyclical fiscal policy, which is passed by the legislative branch and signed into law by the executive branch, aims to reduce economic fluctuations by manipulating government expenditures and taxes.

Countercyclical monetary policy Countercyclical monetary policy, which is conducted by the central bank (in the United States, the Fed), attempts to reduce economic fluctuations by manipulating bank reserves and interest rates.

Countercyclical policies Countercyclical policies attempt to reduce the intensity of economic fluctuations and smooth the growth rates of employment, GDP, and prices.

Creative destruction Creative destruction refers to the process in which new technologies replace old ones, new businesses replace existing businesses, and new skills make old ones redundant.

Credit Credit refers to the loans that the debtor receives.

Credit demand curve The credit demand curve is the schedule that reports the relationship between the quantity of credit demanded and the real interest rate.

Credit market The credit market is where borrowers obtain funds from savers.

Credit supply curve The credit supply curve is the schedule that reports the relationship between the quantity of credit supplied and the real interest rate.

Crowding out Crowding out occurs when rising government expenditure partially or even fully displaces expenditures by households and firms.

Culture hypothesis The culture hypothesis claims that different values and cultural beliefs fundamentally cause the differences in prosperity around the world.

Current account The current account is the sum of net exports, net factor payments from abroad, and net transfers from abroad.

Cyclical unemployment Cyclical unemployment is the deviation of the actual unemployment rate from the natural rate of unemployment.

Data Data are facts, measurements, or statistics that describe the world.

Debtors Debtors, or borrowers, are economic agents who borrow funds.

Deflation The deflation rate is the rate of decrease of a price index.

Demand curve shifts The demand curve shifts when the quantity demanded changes at a given price.

Demand curve The demand curve plots the quantity demanded at different prices. A demand curve plots the demand schedule.

Demand deposits Demand deposits are funds that depositors can access on demand by withdrawing money from the bank, writing checks, or using their debit cards.

Demand schedule A demand schedule is a table that reports the quantity demanded at different prices, holding all else equal.

Demographic transition The demographic transition refers to the decline in fertility and number of children per family that many societies undergo as they transition from agriculture to industry.

Dependent variable A dependent variable is a variable whose value depends on another variable.

Depression Although there is no consensus on the definition, the term depression is typically used to describe a prolonged recession with an unemployment rate of 20 percent or more.

Diminishing marginal benefit As you consume more of a good, your willingness to pay for an additional unit declines.

Downward wage rigidity Downward wage rigidity arises when workers resist a cut in their wage.

Dynamic equilibrium A dynamic equilibrium traces out the behavior of the economy over time.

Economic agent An economic agent is an individual or a group that makes choices.

Economic expansions Economic expansions are the periods between recessions. Accordingly, an economic expansion begins at the end of one recession and continues until the start of the next recession.

Economic fluctuations Short-run changes in the growth of GDP are referred to as economic fluctuations or business cycles.

Economic growth Economic growth, or growth, is the increase in GDP per capita of an economy.

Economic institutions Economic institutions are the aspects of the society's rules that concern economic transactions.

Economics Economics is the study of how agents choose to allocate scarce resources and how those choices affect society.

Efficiency of production Efficiency of production refers to the ability of an economy to produce the maximal amount of output from a given amount of factors of production and knowledge.

Efficiency wages Efficiency wages are above the wage that workers would accept, where the extra pay increases worker productivity and improves the profitability of the firm.

Empirical evidence Empirical evidence is a set of facts established by observation and measurement.

Empiricism Empiricism is analysis that uses data. Economists use data to test theories and to determine what is causing things to happen in the world.

Employed A person holding a full-time or part-time paid job is employed.

Equilibrium Equilibrium is the situation in which everyone is simultaneously optimizing, so nobody would benefit personally by changing his or her own behavior.

Excess demand When the market price is below the competitive equilibrium price, quantity demanded exceeds quantity supplied, creating excess demand.

Excess supply When the market price is above the competitive equilibrium price, quantity supplied exceeds quantity demanded, creating excess supply.

Expansionary fiscal policy Expansionary fiscal policy uses higher government expenditure and lower taxes to increase the growth rate of real GDP.

Expansionary monetary policy Expansionary monetary policy increases the quantity of bank reserves and lowers interest rates.

Expected real interest rate The expected real interest rate is the nominal interest rate minus the expected rate of inflation.

Experiment An experiment is a controlled method of investigating causal relationships among variables.

Exponential growth Exponential growth refers to a situation in which the growth process can be described by an approximately constant growth rate of a variable such as GDP or GDP per capita.

Exports Exports are the market value of all domestically produced goods and services that are purchased by households, firms, and governments in foreign countries.

Extractive economic institutions Extractive economic institutions do not protect private property rights, do not uphold contracts, and interfere with the workings of markets. They also erect significant entry barriers into businesses and occupations.

Factors of production Factors of production are the inputs to the production process.

Federal funds market equilibrium The point where the supply and demand curves cross in the federal funds market is the federal funds market equilibrium.

Federal funds market The federal funds market refers to the market where banks obtain overnight loans of reserves from one another.

Federal funds rate The federal funds rate is the interest rate that banks charge each other for overnight loans in the federal funds market. The funds being lent are reserves at the Federal Reserve Bank.

Federal Reserve Bank The Federal Reserve Bank, or the Fed, is the name of the central bank in the United States.

Fertility Fertility refers to the number of children per adult or per woman of childbearing age.

Fiat money Fiat money refers to something that is used as legal tender by government decree and is not backed by a physical commodity, like gold or silver.

Financial account The financial account is the increase in domestic assets held by foreigners minus the increase in foreign assets held domestically.

Financial intermediaries Financial intermediaries channel funds from suppliers of financial capital to users of financial capital.

Fixed exchange rate If the government sets a long-run value for the exchange rate and intervenes to maintain that value, then the country has a fixed exchange rate.

Flexible exchange rate If the government does not intervene in the foreign exchange market, then the country has a flexible exchange rate, which is also referred to as a floating exchange rate.

Foreign direct investment Foreign direct investment refers to investments by foreign individuals and companies in domestic firms and businesses. To qualify as foreign direct investment, these flows need to generate a large foreign ownership stake in the domestic business.

Foreign exchange market The foreign exchange market is the global financial market in which currencies are traded and nominal exchange rates are determined.

Frictional unemployment Frictional unemployment refers to unemployment that arises because workers have imperfect information about available jobs and need to engage in a time-consuming process of job search.

Fundamental causes of prosperity Fundamental causes of prosperity are factors that are at the root of the differences in the proximate causes of prosperity.

Gains from specialization Gains from specialization are the economic gains that society can obtain by having some individuals, regions, or countries specialize in the production of certain goods and services.

GDP deflator The GDP deflator is 100 times the ratio of nominal GDP to real GDP in the same year. It is a measure of how prices of goods and services produced in a country have risen since the base year.

Geography hypothesis The geography hypothesis claims that differences in geography, climate, and ecology are ultimately responsible for the major differences in prosperity observed across the world.

Government expenditure Government expenditure is the market value of government purchases of goods and services.

Great Depression The Great Depression refers to the severe contraction that started in 1929, reaching a low point for real GDP in 1933. The period of below-trend real GDP did not end until the buildup to World War II in the late 1930s.

Gross domestic product (GDP) Gross domestic product is the market value of the final goods and services produced within the borders of a country during a particular period of time.

Gross national product (GNP) Gross national product is the market value of production generated by the factors of production—both capital and labor—possessed or owned by the residents of a particular nation.

Growth rate The growth rate is the change in a quantity, for example, GDP per capita, between two dates, relative to the baseline (beginning of period) quantity.

Holding all else equal Holding all else equal implies that everything else in the economy is held constant. The Latin phrase *ceteris paribus* means "with other things the same" and is sometimes used in economic writing to mean the same thing as "holding all else equal."

Human capital Human capital is each person's stock of skills to produce output or economic value.

Hypotheses Hypotheses are predictions (typically generated by a model) that can be tested with data.

Identity Two variables are related by an identity when the two variables are defined in a way that makes them mathematically identical.

Imports Imports are the market value of all foreign-produced goods and services that are sold to domestic households, domestic firms, and the domestic government.

Inclusive economic institutions Inclusive economic institutions protect private property, uphold law and order, allow and enforce private contracts, and allow free entry into new lines of business and occupations.

Income (or GDP) per worker Income (or GDP) per worker is defined as GDP divided by the number of people in employment.

Income (or GDP) per capita Income per capita or GDP per capita is GDP divided by total population.

Independent variable An independent variable is a variable whose value does not depend on another variable; in an experiment it is manipulated by the experimenter.

Industrial Revolution Industrial Revolution is the term used for describing the series of innovations and their implementation in the production process that started to take place at the end of the eighteenth century in Britain.

Inferior good For an inferior good, an increase in income causes the demand curve to shift to the left (holding the good's price fixed).

Inflation expectations Economic agents' inflation expectations are their beliefs about future inflation rates.

Inflation rate The rate of increase in prices is the inflation rate. It is calculated as the year-over-year percentage increase in a price index.

Input An input is a good or service used to produce another good or service.

Insolvent A bank becomes insolvent when the value of the bank's assets is less than the value of its liabilities.

Institutions hypothesis The institutions hypothesis claims that differences in institutions—that is, in the way societies have organized themselves and shaped the incentives of individuals and businesses—are at the root of the differences in prosperity across the world.

Institutions Institutions are the formal and informal rules governing the organization of a society, including its laws and regulations.

Interest rate The interest rate (also referred to as the nominal interest rate), i, is the annual cost of a one-dollar loan, so $i \times L$ is the annual cost of an L loan.

Investment Investment is the market value of new physical capital that is bought by domestic households and domestic firms.

Job search Job search refers to the activities that workers undertake to find appropriate jobs.

Labor demand curve The labor demand curve depicts the relationship between the quantity of labor demanded and the wage. The value of the marginal product of labor is also the labor demand curve, because they both show how the quantity of labor demanded varies with the wage.

Labor force participation rate The labor force participation rate is the percentage of potential workers that are in the labor force.

Labor force The labor force is the sum of all employed and unemployed workers.

Labor income Labor income is any form of payment that compensates people for their work.

Labor supply curve The labor supply curve represents the relationship between the quantity of labor supplied and the wage.

Law of demand In almost all cases, the quantity demanded rises when the price falls (holding all else equal).

Law of Diminishing Marginal Product The Law of Diminishing Marginal Product states that the marginal contribution of a factor of production to output diminishes when we increase the quantity used of that factor of production (holding all others constant).

Law of Supply In almost all cases, the quantity supplied rises when the price rises (holding all else equal).

Liquidity Liquidity refers to funds available for immediate payment. To express the same concept a slightly different way, funds are liquid if they are immediately available for payment.

Long-term real interest rate The long-term real interest rate is the long-term nominal interest rate minus the long-term inflation rate.

Macroeconomics Macroeconomics is the study of the economy as a whole. Macroeconomists study economy-wide phenomena, like the growth rate of a country's total economic output, the inflation rate, or the unemployment rate.

Malthusian cycle The Malthusian cycle refers to the preindustrial pattern in which increases in aggregate income lead to an expanding population, which in turn reduces income per capita and puts downward pressure on population.

Managed exchange rate If the government intervenes actively to influence the exchange rate, then the country has a managed exchange rate.

Marginal analysis Marginal analysis is a cost-benefit calculation that studies the difference between a feasible alternative and the next feasible alternative.

Marginal cost Marginal cost is the extra cost generated by moving from one feasible alternative to the next feasible alternative.

Market A market is a group of economic agents who are trading a good or service, and the rules and arrangements for trading.

Market demand curve The market demand curve is the sum of the individual demand curves of all the potential buyers. It plots the relationship between the total quantity demanded and the market price, holding all else equal.

Market price If all sellers and all buyers face the same price, it is referred to as the market price.

Market supply curve The market supply curve is the sum of the individual supply curves of all the potential sellers. It plots the relationship between the total quantity supplied and the market price, holding all else equal.

Market-clearing wage We refer to the competitive equilibrium wage as the market-clearing wage. At this wage, every worker that wants a job can find one: the quantity of labor demanded matches the quantity of labor supplied.

Maturity Maturity refers to the time until debt must be repaid.

Maturity transformation Maturity transformation is the process by which banks take short-maturity liabilities and invest in long-maturity assets (long-term investments).

Mean The Mean or average, is the sum of all the different values divided by the number of values.

Medium of exchange A medium of exchange is an asset that can be traded for goods and services.

Microeconomics Microeconomics is the study of how individuals, households, firms, and governments make choices, and how those choices affect prices, the allocation of resources, and the well-being of other agents.

Model A model is a simplified description, or representation, of the world. Sometimes, economists will refer to a model as a *theory*. These terms are often used interchangeably.

Monetary policy The central bank is the government institution that monitors financial institutions, controls certain key interest rates, and indirectly controls the money supply. These activities constitute monetary policy.

Money Money is the asset that people use to make and receive payments when buying and selling goods and services.

Money supply The money supply adds together currency in circulation, checking accounts, savings accounts, travelers' checks, and money market accounts. This is sometimes referred to as M2.

Movement along the demand curve If a good's own price changes and its demand curve hasn't shifted, the own price change produces a movement along the demand curve.

Movement along the supply curve If a good's own price changes and its supply curve hasn't shifted, the own price change produces a movement along the supply curve.

Multipliers Multipliers refer to economic mechanisms that amplify the initial impact of a shock.

National income accounting identity The national income accounting identity, $Y = C + I + G + X - M$, decomposes GDP into consumption + investment + government expenditure + exports − imports.

National income accounts National income accounts measure the level of aggregate economic activity in a country.

National Income and Product Accounts (NIPA) The National Income and Product Accounts is the system of national income accounts that is used by the U.S. government.

Natural experiment A natural experiment is an empirical study in which some process—out of the control of the experimenter—has assigned subjects to control and treatment groups in a random or nearly random way.

Natural rate of unemployment The natural rate of unemployment is the rate around which the actual rate of unemployment fluctuates.

Negative correlation A negative correlation implies that two variables tend to move in opposite directions. When the variables have movements that are not related, we say that the variables have zero correlation.

Negatively related Two variables are negatively related if the variables move in the opposite direction.

Net exports Net exports are the value of the country's exports minus the value of its imports. Net exports are also known as the trade balance.

Nominal exchange rate The nominal exchange rate is the rate at which one currency can be traded for another.

Nominal GDP Nominal GDP is the total value of production (final goods and services) using current market prices.

Nominal wages Actual wages are also called nominal wages, which distinguishes them from wages adjusted for inflation, or real wages. To calculate real wages, economists divide nominal wages by a measure of overall prices, for example the Consumer Price Index (CPI).

Normal good For a normal good, an increase in income causes the demand curve to shift to the right (holding the good's price fixed).

Normative economics Normative economics is an analysis that prescribes what an individual or society ought to do.

Okun's Law Okun's Law says that the year-to-year change in the rate of unemployment is equal to $-\frac{1}{2} \times (g - 3\%)$, where g represents the annual growth rate of real GDP, in percentage points.

Omitted variable An omitted variable is something that has been left out of a study that, if included, would explain why two variables that are in the study are correlated.

One dollar a day per person poverty line The one dollar a day per person poverty line is a measure of absolute poverty used by economists and other social scientists to compare the extent of poverty across countries.

Open economy An open economy trades freely with the rest of the world.

Open market operations If the Fed wishes to increase the level of reserves that private banks hold, it offers to buy government bonds from the private banks, and in return it gives the private banks more electronic reserves. If the Fed wishes to decrease the level of reserves, it offers to sell government bonds to the private banks and in return the private banks give back some of their reserves. By buying or selling government bonds, the Fed shifts the vertical supply curve in the federal funds market and thereby controls the level of reserves. These transactions are referred to as open market operations.

Opportunity cost Opportunity cost is the best alternative use of a resource.

Optimization in differences Optimization in differences calculates the *change* in net benefits when a person switches from one alternative to another and then uses these marginal comparisons to choose the best alternative.

Optimization in levels Optimization in levels calculates the *total* net benefit of different alternatives and then chooses the best alternative.

Optimization Trying to choose the best feasible option given the available information, is optimization.

Optimum The optimum is the best feasible choice. In other words, the optimum is the optimal choice.

Perfectly competitive market In a perfectly competitive market, (1) sellers all sell an identical good or service, and (2) any individual buyer or any individual seller isn't powerful enough on his or her own to affect the market price of that good or service.

Physical capital Physical capital is any good, including machines and buildings, used for production.

Physical capital stock The physical capital stock of an economy is the value of equipment, structures and other non-labor inputs used in production.

Pie chart A pie chart is a circular chart split into segments, with each showing the percentages of parts relative to the whole.

Political creative destruction Political creative destruction refers to the process in which economic growth destabilizes existing regimes and reduces the political power of rulers.

Political institutions Political institutions are the aspects of the society's rules that concern the allocation of political power and the constraints on the exercise of political power.

Positive correlation A positive correlation implies that two variables tend to move in the same direction.

Positive economics Positive economics is an analysis that generates objective descriptions or predictions about the world that can be verified with data.

Positively related Two variables are positively related if the variables move in the same direction.

Potential workers Potential workers includes everyone in the general population with three exceptions: children under 16 years of age, people on active duty in the military, and institutionalized people, like those in nursing homes or jail.

Price-taker A price-taker is a buyer or seller who accepts the market price—buyers can't bargain for a lower price and sellers can't bargain for a higher price.

Principle of optimization at the margin The principle of optimization at the margin states that an optimal feasible alternative has the property that moving to it makes you better off and moving away from it makes you worse off.

Private property rights Private property rights mean that individuals can own businesses and assets and their ownership is secure.

Productivity Productivity refers to the value of goods and services that a worker generates for each hour of work.

Proximate causes of prosperity Proximate causes of prosperity are high levels of factors such as human capital, physical capital, and technology that result in a high level of GDP per capita.

Purchasing power parity (PPP) The purchasing power parity (PPP) constructs the cost of a representative bundle of commodities in each country and uses these relative costs for comparing income across countries.

Quantity demanded Quantity demanded is the amount of a good that buyers are willing to purchase at a given price.

Quantity supplied Quantity supplied is the amount of a good or service that sellers are willing to sell at a given price.

Quantity theory of money The quantity theory of money assumes a constant ratio of money supply to nominal GDP.

Randomization Randomization is the assignment of subjects by chance, rather than by choice, to a treatment group or control group.

Real business cycle theory Real business cycle theory is the school of thought that emphasizes the role of changes in technology in causing economic fluctuations.

Real exchange rate The real exchange rate is defined as the ratio of the dollar price of a basket of goods and services in the United States, divided by the dollar price of the same basket of goods and services in a foreign country.

Real GDP growth Real GDP growth is the growth rate of real GDP.

Real GDP Real GDP is the total value of production (final goods and services), using market prices from a specific base year to determine the value of each unit that is produced.

Real interest rate The real interest rate is given by the nominal interest rate minus the inflation rate.

Real wage The real wage is the nominal wage divided by a price index, like the consumer price index (CPI).

Realized real interest rate The realized real interest rate is the nominal interest rate minus the realized rate of inflation.

Recessions Recessions are periods (lasting at least two quarters) in which aggregate economic output falls.

Research and development (R&D) Research and development (R&D) refers to the activities directed at improving scientific knowledge, generating new innovations, or implementing existing knowledge in production in order to improve the technology of a firm or an economy.

Reverse causality Reverse causality occurs when we mix up the direction of cause and effect.

Saving rate The saving rate designates the fraction of income that is saved.

Scarce resources Scarce resources are things that people want, where the quantity that people want exceeds the quantity that is available.

Scarcity Scarcity is the situation of having unlimited wants in a world of limited resources.

Scatter plot A scatter plot displays the relationship between two variables as plotted points of data.

Scientific method The scientific method is the name for the ongoing process that economists and other scientists use to (1) develop models of the world and (2) test those models with data.

Securities Securities are financial contracts. For example, securities may allocate ownership rights of a company (stocks), or promise payments to lenders (bonds).

Seignorage Government revenue obtained from printing currency is called seignorage.

Self-fulfilling prophecy A self-fulfilling prophecy is a situation in which the expectations of an event (such as a left shift in labor demand in the future) induce actions that lead to that event.

Sentiments Sentiments include changes in expectations about future economic activity, changes in uncertainty facing firms and households, and fluctuations in animal spirits. Changes in sentiments lead to changes in household consumption and firm investment.

Slope The slope is the change in the value of the variable plotted on the *y*-axis divided by the change in the value of the variable plotted on the *x*-axis.

Solvent A bank is solvent when the value of the bank's assets is greater than the value of its liabilities.

Steady-state equilibrium A steady-state equilibrium is an economic equilibrium in which the physical capital stock remains constant over time.

Stockholders' equity Stockholders' equity is the difference between a bank's total assets and total liabilities.

Store of value A store of value is an asset that enables people to transfer purchasing power into the future.

Structural unemployment Structural unemployment arises when the quantity of labor supplied persistently exceeds the quantity of labor demanded.

Subsistence level The subsistence level is the minimum level of income per person that is generally necessary for the individual to obtain enough calories, shelter, and clothing to survive.

Substitutes Two goods are substitutes when the fall in the price of one leads to a left shift in the demand curve for the other.

Supply curve shifts The supply curve shifts when the quantity supplied changes at a given price.

Supply curve The supply curve plots the quantity supplied at different prices. A supply curve plots the supply schedule.

Supply schedule A supply schedule is a table that reports the quantity supplied at different prices, holding all else equal.

Sustained growth Sustained growth refers to a growth process where GDP per capita grows at a positive and relatively steady rate for long periods of time.

Technological change Technological change is the process of new technologies and new goods and services being invented, introduced, and used in the economy, enabling the economy to achieve a higher level of GDP for given levels of physical capital stock and total efficiency units of labor.

Technology An economy with better technology uses its labor and capital more efficiently and achieves higher productivity.

Time series graph A time series graph displays data at different points in time.

Total efficiency units of labor Total efficiency units of labor is the product of the total number of workers in the economy and the average human capital of each worker.

Trade deficit A trade deficit is an excess of imports over exports and is thus the name given to the trade balance when it is negative.

Trade surplus A trade surplus is an excess of exports over imports and is thus the name given to the trade balance when it is positive.

Trade-off An economic agent faces a trade-off when the agent needs to give up one thing to get something else.

Unemployed A worker is unemployed if she does not have a job, has actively looked for work in the prior four weeks, and is currently available for work.

Unemployment rate The unemployment rate is the fraction of the labor force that is unemployed.

Unit of account A unit of account is a universal yardstick that is used for expressing the worth (price) of different goods and services.

Value added Production-based accounting measures each firm's value added, which is the firm's sales revenue minus the firm's purchases of intermediate products from other firms.

Variable A variable is a factor that is likely to change or vary.

Wage rigidity Wage rigidity refers to the condition in which the market wage is held above the competitive equilibrium level that would clear the labor market.

Willingness to accept Willingness to accept is the lowest price that a seller is willing to get paid to sell an extra unit of a good. Willingness to accept is the same as the marginal cost of production.

Willingness to pay Willingness to pay is the highest price that a buyer is willing to pay for an extra unit of a good.

Zero correlation When the variables have movements that are not related, we say that the variables have zero correlation.

Credits

Key Ideas Icon, TonySoh/Getty; Evidence-Based Economics Icon, Laborant/Shutterstock; Choice and Consequence Icon, Shutterstock; Letting the Data Speak Icon, Siridhata/Shutterstock.

About the Authors: p. viii top: Daron Acemoglu/Peter Tenzer; p. vii bottom: David Laibson/Stu Rosner; p. ix: John A. List.

Chapter 1: p. 2: blue Porsche, F1online digitale Bildagentur GmbH/Alamy; p. 5: roller skater, Chase Jarvis/Ocean/Corbis; p. 6: whooping crane, Critterbiz/Shutterstock; p. 10: re-use blue Porsche: F1online digitale Bildagentur GmbH/Alamy; p. 12 top: cappuccino, By-studio/Fotolia; p. 12 middle left: iPhone, D. Hurst/Alamy; p. 12 middle right: Eiffel Tower, Samott/Fotolia; p. 12 bottom: tropical beach, Wirepec/Fotolia; p. 14: jumping turnstiles, Pedro Armestre/AFP/Getty Images.

Chapter 2: p. 20: mini graduation cap, Zimmytws/Shutterstock; p. 22: New York subway, Martin Shields/Alamy; p. 24: re-use mini graduation cap, Zimmytws/Shutterstock.

Chapter 3: p. 42: globe concept for commute, Photos.com/Thinkstock; pp. 44-45: candy, Courtesy of Mars, Incorporated; p 47: park bench, Vladimirs Koskins/iStock/Thinkstock; p. 53: re-use globe concept for commute, Photos.com/Thinkstock; p. 55: Mount Hood, Vincentlouis/Fotolia.

Chapter 4: p. 60: old gas sign, Richard Decker/Thinkstock; p. 62 top: crates with flowers, DutchScenery/iStock/Thinkstock; p. 62 bottom: competing gas prices, Lynne Sladky/AP Images; p. 63: smart car v. Hummer, David Cooper/ZUMA Press Inc./Newscom; p. 65: crowd at stadium, Monjiro/Fotolia; p. 68: Spam, Helen Sessions/Alamy; p. 69: re-use old gas sign, Richard Decker/Thinkstock; p. 71: offshore drill ship, Paul Andrew Lawrence/Alamy; p. 74: Libyan rebels fight, John Moore/Getty Images; p. 80 top: 1970s gas crisis, ClassicStock/Alamy; p. 80 bottom: No Gas sign, Everett Collection/Newscom.

Chapter 5: p. 86: illustration of factories, Incomible/Fotolia; p. 88 top: Victoria Falls, TanArt/Shutterstock; p. 88 bottom: Depression era sign: Franklin D. Roosevelt Presidential Library and Museum; p. 89: Ford Focus, Mark Scheuern/Alamy; p. 92 left: Mustang production, Bill Pugliano/Getty Images; p. 92 right: Mustang in showroom, Bill Pugliano/Getty Images; p. 92 bottom: We can do it poster, US National Archives/Alamy; p. 93 Exhibit 5.2 logos: Walmart, © PSL Images/Alamy; Staples, © Kristoffer Tripplaar/Alamy; BestBuy, © Q-Images/Alamy; Dell, © PSL Images/Alamy; p. 96: re-use illustration of factories, Incomible/Fotolia; p. 98: money house, OlegDoroshin/Shutterstock; p. 99: weather icon, Pk74/Fotolia; p. 100: sinking ship,

Mark Large/Daily Mail/Rex/Alamy; p. 101: mother and child, WavebreakMediaMicro/Fotolia; p. 102: polluting smoke stacks, Doin Oakenhelm/Fotolia.

Chapter 6: p. 114 left: American classroom, Sergio Azenha/Alamy; p. 114 right: classroom in India, Franck Metois/Getty Images; p. 120: African mother and child, Jake Lyell/Alamy; p. 128: advanced technology glasses, Yanlev/Fotolia; p. 130: re-use American classroom, Sergio Azenha/Alamy.

Chapter 7: p. 138: illustration of graph, Mathagraphics/Shutterstock; p. 142: ball of money, PM Images/Getty Images; p. 143 top: Singapore skyline, Leungchopan/Shutterstock; p. 143 bottom: crowded Nairobi neighborhood, John Warburton-Lee Photography/Nigel Pavitt/Alamy; p. 149: saving rate graphic, Donskarpo/Shutterstock; p. 150: tablet graphic, Violetkaipa/Shutterstock; p. 151: re-use illustration of graph, Mathagraphics/Shutterstock; p. 159: medical syringe, Alexander Raths/Shutterstock.

Chapter 8: p. 172: globe on money, FikMik/Shutterstock; p. 178: North and South Korea satellite, NASA; p. 179: democracy cartoon, Pearson Education, Inc.; p. 184: access denied computer screen, Worker/Shutterstock; p. 185: re-use globe on money, FikMik/Shutterstock; p. 186: mother and child in tropical hut, Tommy Trenchard/Alamy; p. 191 Angelina Jolie in Africa, Boris Heger/Associated Press; p. 186: foreign aid cartoon, Pearson Education, Inc.

Chapter 9: p. 196: Kmart, Jeff Greenberg 4 of 6/Alamy; p. 201: three barbers, Luis Artus/Getty Images; p. 203 top: hair permenant, Topical Press Agency/Getty; p. 203 bottom: woman with curly hair, SvetlanaFedoseyeva/Shutterstock; p. 208: Luddite riots illustration, Associated Press; p. 209: French retirement protest, Thibault Camus/Associated Press; p. 213: re-use Kmart, Jeff Greenberg 4 of 6/Alamy.

Chapter 10: p. 220: bank columns, Pete Spiro/Shutterstock; p. 225: Pirate illustration, Blue Lantern Studio/Corbis; p. 234: Seal of the U.S. Federal Deposit Insurance Corporation, MCT/Newscom; p. 235: Northern Rock Bank, John Giles/Associated Press; p. 236: re-use bank columns, Pete Spiro/Shutterstock.

Chapter 11: p. 242: kite made of 1927 German money, Telesniuk/Shutterstock; p. 244 top: $100 dollar bill, Vladimir Voronin/Fotolia; p. 244 bottom left: old coins, Fullempty/Fotolia; p. 244 bottom right: pile of dollars, Ekostsov/Fotolia; p. 245 top: Bitcoins, Ulchik74/Fotolia; p. 245 middle: demand note, Images courtesy Heritage Auctions, HA.com; p. 245 bottom: fiat money, Images courtesy Heritage Auctions, HA.com; p. 251: one-hundred billion Zimbabwe note, Katherine Welles/Shutterstock; p. 251: re-use kite made of 1927 German money, Telesniuk/Shutterstock;

p. 252: plaque commemorating the 1922–1923 German hyperinflation, Electra Graphics, Inc.;
p. 254: Janet Yellen, Aude Guerrucci/Pool/Pool/Corbis;
p. 258 Exhibit 11.7 left: Federal Reserve, Adamparent/Fotolia; p. 258 Exhibit 11.7 right: Bank of America sign, Jon Hicks/Corbis; p. 262: A380 aircraft, Senohrabek/Fotolia.

Chapter 12: p. 268: house for sale, rSnapshotPhotos/Shutterstock; p. 273: impoverished woman with children, Library of Congress; p. 277: empty warehouse, Alexey Fursov/Shutterstock; p. 289: re-use house for sale, rSnapshotPhotos/Shutterstock.

Chapter 13: p. 298: American recovery highway sign, David R. Frazier Photolibrary, Inc./Alamy; p. 306: William McChesney Martin, Jr., Dennis Brack/Newscom; p. 307: Paul Volcker, AP Photo/Chick Harrity; p. 308: house bubble illustration, Gino Santa Maria/Shutterstock; p. 317 top: Gravina Island, Alaska bridge to nowhere, Hall Anderson/Glow Images; p. 317 bottom: re-use American recovery highway sign, David R. Frazier Photolibrary, Inc./Alamy; p. 318 left: Wreckage of USS Arizona, Pearl Harbor, Courtesy of Library of Congress; p. 318 right: Sputnik, NASA.

Chapter 14: p. 324: sneakers, Sergio Azenha/Alamy; p. 325: Tom Hanks in Castaway, Moviestore collection Ltd./Alamy; p. 328: Steve Jobs, Paul Sakuma/AP Photo; p. 329: iPod assembly line, AP Photo; p. 332: made in Vietnam clothing tag, JohnKwan/Shutterstock; p. 336 Exhibit 14.8 left: laptop computer, Georgejmclittle/Fotolia; p. 336 Exhibit 14.8 right: Treasury note, Images courtesy Heritage Auctions, HA.com; p. 339: Pong, INTERFOTO/Alamy; p. 340 top: re-use sneakers, Sergio Azenha/Alamy; p. 340 bottom: factory workers, SCPhotos/Alamy.

Chapter 15: p. 346 stack of pound notes, ppart/Shutterstock; p. 349: Chinese yuan notes, Dave Newman/Shutterstock; p. 351: Dreamliner 787, Peter Carey/Alamy; p. 356: re-use stack of pound notes, ppart/Shutterstock; p. 356: George Soros, Europa Newswire/Alamy.

Index

Note: Key terms and the page on which they are defined appear in **boldface.** Page numbers with the letter n indicate content appears in a footnote.